A *Complete Course in Canning* consists of Three Books.

This is Book II

The books are designed to be used together. However, the contents are separated in a manner so that they can be used separately. If Book I or III is desired, contact the publisher.

The Contents of Book I include the following Chapters:

Creating A Business Plan
Plant Location And Construction
Food Laws, Regulations And Standards
Kosher And Halal Food Regulations
A Food Labeling Guide; Water
Energy Requirements And Supply
Food Processing Residuals Treatment And Disposal
Canning Operations; Equipment And Sanitary Design
Process Room Operations
Sterilization Systems; Cleaning And Sanitizing
Warehousing Of Canned Foods
Appendix, Glossary of Terms
Figures, Charts, Tables

The Contents of Book III include:

Canning of Vegetables
Canning of Fruits
Canning of Juices and Fruit Drinks & Water
Canning of Dry Pack Products
Canning of Marine Products
Canning of Meat and Poultry Products
Canning of Soups
Preserves (Jams), Jellies and Related Products
Pickles
Mayonnaise and Salad Dressing Products
Manufacture of Canned Baby Foods
Tomato Products
Evaporated Milk
Canned Meat and Vegetable Salads
Appendix, Glossary of Terms
Figures, Charts, Tables

A Complete Course In Canning

And Related Processes

THIRTEENTH EDITION

BOOK II

MICROBIOLOGY, PACKAGING, HACCP & INGREDIENTS

A technical reference book and textbook for students of food technology, food plant managers, product research and development specialists, food brokers, technical salesmen, food equipment manufacturers, and food industry suppliers.

Revised and Enlarged by

DONALD L. DOWNING, PH.D.
Professor of Food Processing
New York State Agricultural Experiment Station
Cornell University
Geneva, New York

A PUBLICATION OF

CTI PUBLICATIONS, INC.

Baltimore, Maryland 21218-4547 USA
410-467-3338 · FAX 410-467-7434

A COMPLETE COURSE IN CANNING

While the recommendations in this publication are based on scientific studies and industry experience, references to basic principles, operating procedures and methods, or types of instruments and equipment, and food formulas are not to be construed as a guarantee that they are sufficient to prevent damage, spoilage, loss, accidents or injuries, resulting from use of this information. Furthermore, the study and use of this publication by any person or company is not to be considered as assurance that that person or company is proficient in the operations and procedures discussed in this publication. The use of the statements, recommendations, or suggestions contained, herein, is not to be considered as creating any responsibility for damage, spoilage, loss, accident or injury, resulting from such use.

ISBN Numbers are as follows:

0-930027-25-6 – A COMPLETE COURSE IN CANNING, (3 Volume set), 13th Edition, 1996 Hardbound
0-930027-26-4 – A COMPLETE COURSE IN CANNING, Volume I, 13th Edition, 1996, Hardbound
0-930027-27-2 – A COMPLETE COURSE IN CANNING, Volume II, 13th Edition, 1996, Hardbound
0-930027-28-0 – A COMPLETE COURSE IN CANNING, Volume III, 13th Edition, 1996, Hardbound

Library of Congress Catalog–In–Publication Data

A Complete Course In Canning and Related Processes – 13th Edition
Revised and Enlarged by Donald L. Downing.
p. cm.
Includes bibliographical references and indexes.
Contents: Book I. Fundamental Information On Canning;
Book II Microbiology, Packaging, HACCP & Ingredients
Book III Processing Procedures for Canned Food Products.
ISBN 0-930027-25-6 (Set); ISBN 0-930027-26-4 (BK I); ISBN 0-930027-27-2 (BK II);
ISBN 0-930027-28-0 (BK III)
Canning and preserving. I. Downing, Donald L., 1931 -
TP371.3.C66 1996
664'.0282--dc20 96-8381
CIP

PREFACE

This book is being presented in three parts: Book I, II and III. Book I includes updated information on canning operations spanning from Business Plan, Plant Location and Construction Through Warehousing, and including, among other subjects, "Food Laws, Regulations and Standards," "Labeling," "Preparing Kosher Foods," "Processing Room Operations," and "Sterilization Systems"; Book II presents the subjects of "Microbiology of Canned Foods,""Packaging," "Quality Control," "HACCP," "Computer Aided Manufacturing," and "Ingredients," as they apply to food processing, and particularly to canning. Book III contains specific procedures for over 210 canned food products, and for salad dressing and pickle products.

This 13th edition of *A Complete Course in Canning* contains chapters not included in previous editions. These are "Creating a Business Plan," "Kosher Food Manufacturing," "Labeling," "HACCP," and "Computer Aided Manufacturing." Further, the 13th edition contains several significantly expanded chapters. These are "Plant Location and Construction," "Food Laws," Regulations and Standards," "Microbiology of Canned Foods," "Metal Containers," "Glass and Plastic Containers," and "Ingredients." The Glossary of Terms has been enlarged to include many technical terms that have come into common usage in the food processing industry. These terms are found in federal and state regulatory literature, and quality control procedures, container specifications, descriptions of new technological methods, and in other food processing publications.

All the material included in this edition has been reviewed and updated.

This work could not have been done without the cooperation of many individuals and firms and the U.S. Food and Drug Administration. National Food Processors Association deserves special recognition, because information from several of its excellent publications was used, and because helpful advice on several topics was received from several of its scientists, as well as many others.

It is hoped that this 13th edition of *A Complete Course in Canning* will be useful to food processors, to other persons associated with the food industry, and to students of food science and technology.

The updating of this 13th Edition would not have been possible without the earlier work of Anthony Lopez, Ph.D., Professor Emeritus, VPI & State University who developed the 9th through 12th Editions. For this earlier work we are extremely grateful. Thank you Dr. Lopez.

Lastly, I would like to thank my wife, Rochelle, Olga Padilla Zakour, and Julia Chia-Day Fu for their help during the preparation of the manuscript.

Donald L. Downing
Geneva, New York
May 1996

This Book Belongs To:

____

TABLE OF CONTENTS

METAL CONTAINERS FOR CANNED FOODS – Continued

METAL CONTAINERS FOR CANNED FOODS – Continued

INGREDIENTS – Continued

INGREDIENTS – Continued

INTRODUCTION

HISTORICAL AND BASIC INFORMATION ON CANNING

The name of this book, *A Complete Course in Canning*, indicates that it is intended as a source of information on canned foods. The reader will find here factual and reliable data on all the important facets of canned foods, such as product formulas, manufacturing procedures, food laws, sanitation, sterilization, spoilage, containers, food plant characteristics, warehousing and others.

At the dawn of this 20th century, when this work first appeared as a serial article in the pages of *The Canning Trade*, the claim "Complete" seemed boastful, if not questionable. Looking back to the years 1902 and 1903, it is easy to see that the Industry, if not then in its infancy, was at best in its kindergarten age and the amount of production was but a fraction of today's. Factory equipment and layout were crude and just commencing to develop; quality and grades of products were as varied and as numerous as the producers, since food laws were then non-existent. Science, as applied to canning and food preservation, was just looming on the horizon. There were no set, definite formulae, except those which experience had taught through dint of heavy cost, and which were accordingly carefully nursed and protected by their possessors, the "expert processors." These "expert processors" lorded over the work and the men who employed them, and refused to divulge their "secrets." Losses from spoilage, as well as from poor quality, were accepted as normal.

Yet, in 1900, in point of numbers, there were as many canners, preservers, picklers, etc., in the business as there are today, and there were no frozen foods. Necessarily their outputs were smaller, but so was the market. Profits were uncertain, and the business mortality heavy, but there was no lack of hope or of optimism, as witnessed by the eagerness of new men or firms to step into the shoes of those who were forced out or gave up. Years before, the late Editor and founder of *The Canning Trade* (now called *Food Production Management*), apparently the first man in the world to have a deep-rooted conviction that canned foods were of real genuine value and held wonderful possibilities, had said: "The day will come when canned foods will be the pantry of the world." There were men in the industry at that time who had little or no faith in the goods they produced, but there were enough to keep the ranks well filled, and the amount of goods produced was on a steady increase.

At the turn of the century, the industry had little or no scientific knowledge or assistance to depend upon. Today, it is soundly based upon scientific principles developed at its own National Food Processors Association laboratories, and at government, industry, and university laboratories. The

National Food Processors Association laboratories are rated foremost among the world food industry research and service laboratories, with major laboratories in Washington, DC, California, and the Northwest. Services are rendered to members of the Association.

Can making companies, glass container manufacturers, and other packaging firms, also, have very well equipped laboratories where, not only container research is done, but where technical services are provided to customers on product quality, processing, formulation, and container usage problems and opportunities.

The U.S. Departments of Agriculture and the Interior, and the Food and Drug Administration have important laboratories in Washington, DC and a number of other laboratories in different regions of the country. These laboratories work on basic food preservation problems, as well as on processing techniques, new product development, food plant sanitation and product adulteration problems, and food analysis methods, all with the objective of helping to place high quality food products in food markets. The States have their own food laboratories, concerned principally with sanitary conditions and quality control of products manufactured and sold within their borders.

Each State also has one or more Agricultural Experiment Stations which study growing conditions in particular areas of that State and do applied research on the processing of the crops grown in the State, as well as on other problems of the food industry. Food processors and producers should realize numerous and significant services are provided by the State Agricultural Experiment Stations and Extension Services. They should especially consult those state agencies in the selection of seed and plants, the use of fertilizer, plant and animal disease and pest control, and food technology problems. Those who are just entering, or intend to enter, the food processing business should consult those agencies on the proper location of the plant, availability of labor and raw materials, applicable federal and state laws and regulations, processing line specifications, markets, and other factors.

WHY THIS BOOK?

Under such conditions as existed in 1902-03, was the publisher not rather presumptuous in publishing a compilation of formulae, and particularly in terming it "complete?" However, having related the subsequent progress, in both production and scientific attainments, the first edition of *A Complete Course in Canning* was published.

The fact that there were no definite formulae obtainable, in printed form or otherwise at that time, brought the canners of that day, and the new men wishing to enter the industry in particular, to *The Canning Trade,* as the sole source of canning information, asking for directions upon the canning of the particular product in which they were interested. Baltimore was then, not only the Mother of the canning industry, but the hub-center of the business, and diligent work among these canners soon afforded formulae for the various products, as then used. Since his earliest association with the industry, in the founding of *The Canning Trade*, first called *The Trade*, in 1878, its first Editor began the accumulation of information on processing and handling, keeping these findings in a big black book – a sort of treasure chest. From this source of information, typewritten formulae were furnished free to inquirers from every section of the country. In fact, the demand was so heavy that it forced consideration of publication of the formulae in the weekly issues of the industry's Journal, *The Canning Trade*, now published monthly as *Food Production Management* magazine.

With that determination in mind came the resolution to offer several thousand dollars in prizes for the best, or most complete, formulae for the canning, preserving or pickling, of all the various products, the stipulation being that all offerings became the publisher's property, whether or not they won prizes. Responses were prompt and plentiful, coming from all manner of "processors," expert chefs, cooks, etc., including the most famous and most experienced. The awards were paid, and then began the compilation of the work. *A Complete Course in Canning* was, accordingly, the expression of the best experience existent, its formulae as dependable as possible. As in previous revisions of this book, this Thirteenth Edition has been brought up-to-date. The aim and desire of these revisions has been to help producers advance the safety and success of food production of this kind, to warn against the dangers and the pitfalls, to keep producers upon safe ground, and to make products safe for public consumption. *A Complete Course in Canning*, as the textbook of this industry, used as it is throughout the entire world, affords the opportunity to put information into the hands of the individuals who need it and can make the best use of it. It is intended to be a compendium of the industry's researches and studies.

This Thirteenth Edition has been thoroughly brought up-to-date on the processing methods used for each product. General Directions include more comprehensive discussions of the factors related to plant facilities, regulations, ingredients, processing, product, plant sanitation and containers that contribute to the quality, sanitation, and keeping characteristics of canned foods. A new chapter on developing a Business Plan, as well as expanded and updated sections on regulations and equipment, have been added.

Mechanical equipment and construction of the factory itself have so advanced and improved that no canner should fail to check carefully with the latest and best sources of information. To that end, they should consult the builders of modern factory buildings, makers of canning and preserving machinery, manufacturers of metal and glass containers, commercial seedsmen, specialists in food labels, etc. Every such firm willingly furnishes detailed information, without obligation, and their recommendations can be relied upon. It is impossible to lay down a uniform factory plan, mechanical equipment or label design. Every man or firm wants to carry out personal ideas or desires and it is well that this is so; but we urge all to call in these experts and have confidence in them, as a surety that the best possible job, under the circumstances, in quality, safety and cost of production, is being done.

Despite the fact that the greatest care has been exercised in the preparation of the formulae, times and directions given in this book, they should, nevertheless, be taken largely as suggestive only, as a reliable working basis, to be altered or changed to fit particular conditions. The formulae given herein are practical and ready to use; they have all been tried and proven, but a change in temperature, altitude, raw material quality or composition, difference in soil or fertilizer used, a wet or dry season, and a hundred and one other causes, may necessitate a change in the process. As was said in the first edition of this book, and repeated here: "there is one reservation that goes with this – "CONSIDERABLE COMMON SENSE MUST BE ADDED TO ALL FORMULAE." As a result, "NO LARGE PACK OF A NEW PRODUCT SHOULD EVER BE PRODUCED UNTIL A TRIAL BATCH HAS BEEN MADE." Keeping careful check upon raw materials received, and on factory operations as they progress, may save heavy losses from spoilage, or a lowering of quality. It is too late to check after the product is in the warehouse.

To quote the last paragraph from the Introduction in the first edition of this work: "If used judiciously, in this manner, these formulae will be found satisfactory, differing possibly with different processors, as is natural, but worthy of the high approval set upon them when they were first published."

One addition to that caveat should be made: Every canner or producer of food products for human consumption is, or should be, a chef unto himself; just as a reputation for fine foods attaches to a restaurant or hotel due to the ability of the chef to take the same foods and produce more delectable dishes, so with the canner or other, who has here the opportunity to display his ability to please. The growth of his business will attest to the degree with which he succeeds in such efforts. There are innumerable ways of preparing foods, some more palatable than others. The opportunities are legion. A solid foundation on which to begin is furnished here; the world is your patron.

A BRIEF HISTORY OF CANNING TECHNOLOGY

Basis of the Canning Process

It is difficult to imagine what life would be in this country without canned foods. Our ancestors got along quite well without them, but spent a lot of time in the kitchen and had little to work with in the winter months. Canned foods changed all this; they were the first convenience food.

Nicholas Appert, a Frenchman, was awarded a prize in 1809 by the French government, known as The Directory, for having developed a new, successful means of preserving foods, a method that eventually became known as "canning." Appert was a confectioner, living in a suburb of Paris in the 1790's, when France was at war with several European nations. The foods available couldn't be transported or stored, except in a dry state. Food was scarce for both the civilian population and the armed forces and, because it was a serious problem for the French Directory, it promoted the award offer. Diseases, now known to be caused by malnutrition, were decimating the men in the French army and navy. In 1810, Appert published the first book on canning, and in 1811, an English translation was published in England. In his work, Appert used wide-mouth glass bottles, which he filled with food, carefully corked, and heated in boiling water. His book described canning methods for more than 50 foods.

Appert found a new and effective way to preserve food, but did not understand why it prevented food spoilage. It took the genius of Louis Pasteur, another Frenchman, to discover, in 1864, the relationship between canning techniques and scientific principle, which laid the foundations for advances in canning methods that eventually revolutionized the industry.

In the 1890's, Prescott and Underwood, who worked in Maine canneries, established the relationship between thermophilic bacteria and the spoilage of canned corn. Working independently during this same time, Russell in Wisconsin, and Barlow in Illinois, discovered the cause of the same type of spoilage in canned peas. In the 1910's and 1920's, the basic biological and toxicological characteristics of *Clostridium botulinum* were first determined by several American investigators. The importance of controlling *C. botulinum* in canned foods became clear and the basis for its control was established. In the early 1920's in the U.S., Bigelow and Esty established the relationship between the pH of foods and the heat resistance of bacterial spores, including those causing spoilage. Their work laid the foundation for the classification of canned foods into acid foods and low-acid foods on the basis of their pH. That classification constitutes a major factor in canned food sterilization methods and in governmental regulations.

In 1918, Weinzirl provided scientific evidence of canned foods safety, from the standpoint of public health, by establishing that commercially canned foods are not sterile, but that food poisoning microorganisms are not found in them.

In the 1920's, Bohart, of the National Canners Association, developed the "C" enamel for tin plate cans to prevent discoloration of canned peas, corn, lima beans, seafood and meat products. This discoloration was caused by the formation within the can of ferrous sulfide resulting from hydrogen sulfide, formed by protein breakdown during thermal processing and iron from the can. By incorporating a small amount of zinc oxide in the enamel covering of the can interior, he averted product discoloration. Since then, other enamels for canned foods have been developed which have contributed in an important manner to achieve the high quality of today's canned foods.

In 1920, Bigelow and Ball developed the first scientifically based method for the calculation of minimum safe sterilization processes for canned food sterilization; it became known as the graphic method. Dr. Ball continued work in the same area at the National Canners Association laboratories and, in 1923, formulated a mathematical method for determination of sterilization processes. In 1939, Olson developed a nomographic method for process determinations. Stumbo and Hicks, in 1948, developed procedures for the calculation of sterilization processes based upon integrating lethality values over the entire volume of the contents of a container with mixed micro-flora. Their work represented an important step toward future application of computer analysis to solve overall mathematical equations, which include consideration of all significant factors contributing to canned food spoilage. In 1957, Ball and Olson published a now classic book on heat processing which combined the research of Stumbo and others with their own. Twenty-five years ago, Hayakawa developed more advanced mathematical methods which eliminated certain relatively small errors inherent to some of the previous mathematical procedures. In the last 25 years, in addition to Ball, Stumbo and Hayakawa, Teixeira, Zahradnik, Flambert, Griffin, Manson, Pflug and others further refined mathematical heat process determination concepts and applications have been developed. This work led to the use of computers for more accurate, rapid, and routine heat process calculations and for monitoring and controlling thermal processes by on-line measurement of accomplished lethality. These developments have made possible the accurate control of thermal processes to achieve commercial sterilization and the development of quality assurance procedures and government regulations to further assure the safety of the processes. It is worthwhile noting that the Graphic Method of Bigelow and Ball, and the original Formula Method of Ball, in spite of some limitations and with modifications, are still the basic procedures used for calculations of sterilization processes in the canned food industry.

Sterilization Systems

Appert's invention included the immersion in boiling water of food contained in stoppered bottles for preservation. There was no change in that method until Solomon, in 1860, added calcium chloride to the water in which cans were processed, producing higher processing temperatures; this reduced the very serious outbreaks of spoilage which occasionally took place when low-acid products, like vegetables and meats, were processed in boiling water. Higher processing temperatures also resulted in better product quality.

In 1851, Chevalier-Appert applied the principle of pressure cooking to canned food processing and thus invented the retort. In 1874, Shriver introduced the autoclave in the U.S.; this made available a more practical method for sterilization of canned foods at higher temperatures. The still retort has been improved significantly since then. In the early 1950's, FMC Corporation introduced continuous agitating cooking and cooling; this advancement, together with the development of higher speed and reliable filling and can closing machines, contributed to a considerable increase in cannery line speeds. In the late 1950's, the Steriflamme process was developed in France by Cheftel, Beauvais, and Thomas. This process consisted of heating rapidly rotating cans by direct contact with gases at temperatures of about 2000°F (1093°C), produced by gas burners.

In 1955, Smith and Ball proposed a process which later, with significant modifications, became known as the "Flash 18" Process. Food at 255°F (124°C) was filled in cans in a pressurized room under 18 psig (124 kPa), the containers closed under the same conditions, and held at that temperature until commercially sterile. With this method, retort processing was eliminated.

Another important milestone in the history of canned foods was the development of aseptic canning processes. Prior to 1948, several attempts were made to sterilize and aseptically can milk using high temperature short-time (HTST) sterilization processes. These attempts were not successful until Martin, working for Dole Engineering Company, developed equipment for the sterilization of cans and lids and the means of aseptic filling of products into cans using superheated steam. Since 1948, the Dole equipment and other systems have been greatly improved. Processor confidence has been gained and justification made for investing in high speed aseptic canning lines, which have rates in excess of 400 8-oz. (225 ml) cans per minute. In the 1960's, an important outgrowth of the aseptic canning system was the development of engineering systems and containers for aseptic filling and closing of 55 gallon (208 l) drums. Some of the best known are the Cherry-Burrell Corporation "No-Bac Fifty-Five Filler," the Hambart sterile filler, and the Fran-Rica drum filler process. Wide use has been made of these systems in the tomato processing industry for sterile filling of concentrated tomato products for shipping and reprocessing. An extension of this principle is the use of specially built tanks holding over one hundred thousand gallons; sterile concentrate is filled in the tanks where it is stored until pumped into specially designed sterile rail tank cars for shipment to reprocessing plants. This system has involved the development of special pumps and valves to transfer product under aseptic conditions. Another similar development is the Purdue-Bishopric process for aseptic storage and shipping of fruits and vegetables under bulk aseptic conditions.

In the early 1960's the Swedish firm Tetra Pak introduced commercially an aseptic processing and packaging system known by the firm's name. The system gained rapid acceptance in European and other countries, first for fluid milk, and then, to a lesser extent, for fruit juices and fruit juice-based drinks. The Tetra Pak system was introduced in the U.S. in the early 1980's, gaining a significant percentage of the market for fruit juices and juice drinks, although the fluid milk product has not gained any significant portion of the U.S. market.

A radically different continuous sterilization process, commonly known as "hydrostatic cookers" was developed in France in the late 1950's and introduced in the U.S. in the 1960's. This system consists basically of a chamber filled with saturated steam through which containers are conveyed. The containers are preheated in a hot water "leg" prior to entering the steam chamber and cooled in a progressively cooler water "leg" after leaving the steam chamber. Water under hydrostatic pressure created by head pressure in the water legs seals the steam in the steam chamber. Containers are carried through the heating leg, into and out of the steam chamber, and through the cooling leg by chain conveyors inside perforated carrier tubes.

The 1960's brought another French invention, the Hydrolock sterilization system. This unit has a chain conveyor which carries containers into a pressurized vessel, through the sterilization and pre-cooling stages, and out to the final cooling, a hydrolock with the function of letting containers in and out of a pressurized vessel, without loss of pressure; and a pressurized vessel in which sterilization takes place in the upper part, with cooling in the lower section. Heating is done by saturated steam for containers that do not require over-pressure. When an over-pressure is required, as with glass containers, aluminum cans or retortable pouches, pressurized air is intimately mixed with saturated steam by means of turbines.

The 1960's also brought the development of two new batch sterilization systems, the Malo Crateless retort, and the FMC Orbitort. The Malo retort is a fully automated autoclave in which cans are mechanically loaded, go through a programmed sterilization cycle, and are mechanically discharged. While the Malo system is a still retort, the Orbitort agitates the cans during sterilization. The mode of agitation utilized by the Orbitort is similar to that of continuous rotary sterilizers. During processing, cans are held in a fixed position with respect to a rotating reel. Loading and unloading of cans is simultaneous, through opposite ends. Sterilization temperature and time, and cooling time are automatically controlled.

In 1972, the Lagarde Company of France patented a process and sterilizing device using forced steam circulation for food products and, in 1973, patented a system for processing and cooling foods with water spraying and water raining in a chamber with steam or steam/air atmosphere. There are similar systems on the market manufactured by ALLPAX, Malo, and FMC in the U.S.

Batch-type water-immersion retorts for end-over-end basket rotation have been used in Europe since the 1950's. Stock Rotomat, manufactured in Germany and distributed by Stock America, Inc., and ALLPAX Inc., manufactured in the U.S., sell these retorts. They consist of a pressurized holding tank the size of the retort mounted above the retort.

Containers for Canned Foods

The two most common containers for canned foods today are basically the same as those used in Appert's day: tinplate cans and glass containers. The containers, however, have changed drastically in design and characteristics, making them vastly superior to their ancestors. The first step was taken in England by Durand, who patented tin-plate metal containers called "cannisters." By 1823, a can with a hole in the top was invented, allowing cans to be heated in boiling water with a loose lid on the hole; the lid was soldered onto the hole after the heat treatment. In 1900, the first open top, "sanitary" style, double seamed, three piece can was used, both plain, and lined with "fruit" enamel. Since 1900, important advances made in the development and use of enamels for canned food cans have resulted in much improved quality and increased shelf-life. By 1921, the sanitary style can was in use for virtually all canned fruits and vegetables in this country. An important development made in 1937 was the electrolytic tinning of tinplate; until then, cans were tinned by a "hot dip" process. This electrolytic method resulted in a thinner coat of tin, higher production rates, closer control of coating weights, and a much more even coating.

The method of fixing the side seam of three-piece metal containers has progressed from soldered to cemented and welded, where essentially no soldered containers are available in the US today.

In the mid-1970's, the "Half Tray," or "Retortable Tray," was introduced by Central States Can Company and by FMC Corporation. It is a two-piece tinplate container, shaped as a half size steam tray, with a double seamed lid.

In 1977, the "retortable" or "sterilizable" pouch was approved for use for low-acid canned foods by both U.S. Food and Drug Administration and the

U.S. Department of Agriculture. Both Reynolds Metals Company and Continental Can Company designs were approved. The retortable pouch is usually made from a laminated flexible material consisting of two plastic films with aluminum foil in between; the seam or seams of the pouch are heat sealed. Research on the retortable pouch started in the late 1950's, done independently by Reynolds Metals Company, Continental Can Company, and the U.S. Army Research and Development Command Laboratories. The pouch was extensively tested in the field by the U.S. Army during the Vietnam war. It was first used commercially in England in 1967, under license from Continental Can Company, and in Japan, under similar circumstances in 1968. Some of the foods carried in the 1969 historic Apollo moon mission were packed in sterilizable pouches. In 1977, ITT Continental Baking Company entered the U.S. market with a line of entrees packed in retortable pouches.

In the 1970's and 1980's, research and development and marketing tests were done on rigid and semi-rigid retortable plastic containers for application to canned products, and to aseptically processed and packaged foods.

The canning industry is constantly improving processing methods, enhancing quality and product safety, and developing better packages and more efficient equipment. Product quality is better and new processing methods heighten retention of nutrients and are designed to use energy more effectively. Examples are the methods for preserving fruits and vegetables for re-processing, new sterilization systems, better quality assurance programs, better metal and glass containers and the new semi-rigid and flexible containers.

Appert would never have guessed what he started!

CHAPTER 1

Microbiology of Canned Foods

Basic Considerations on pH Value

One of the most important properties associated with food chemistry and with microbiological food spoilage is the intensity of the acidity, or the pH of the product. This intensity factor, or pH value, is not to be confused with the amount of acid present in the food, but is attributable only to the ionized acid. In order to state this intensity of the acidity in simple numerical terms, the pH scale, a mathematical notation was developed.

pH of foods depends upon many factors, including maturity of product, variety, and growing conditions. For these reasons, the pH of food is usually within a range of values.

pH is defined as the base-ten logarithm of the reciprocal of H+ (hydrogen-ion) concentration (more correctly, H^+ activity) in moles per liter. The neutral point, pH 7.0, is the mid point of a scale from 0 to 14. A pH of zero indicates an extremely acid condition, and pH 14 extremely alkaline.

TABLE 1.1 - The pH Scale

H^+ concentration (moles/liter)			pH
1.0	10^{0}	[example: 1M HCl]	0
0.1	10^{-1}	[example: 0.1M HCl]	1
0.01	10^{-2}		2
0.001	10^{-3}		3
0.0001	10^{-4}		4
0.00001	10^{-5}		5
0.000001	10^{-6}		6
0.0000001	10^{-7}	[example: pure water]	7

Four points concerning pH follow. The first three are a consequence of the definition of pH, while the fourth is concerned more with the nature of foods.

First, pH is logarithmic. H^+ concentrations progress arithmetically, but each unit increment of pH indicates a tenfold increment in H^+ concentration.

Second, successive increments of pH do not indicate the same increments of H^+ concentration. Therefore, from pH 7 to 6 there is an increase in acidity of ten fold, from 7 to 5 is 100, 7 to 4 is 1000. Simple linear relationships between pH and H^+ concentration can be graphed only by using semilogarithmic graph paper.

Third, the point between whole pH values corresponding to the midpoint of H^+ concentration occurs at pH 0.3, not 0.5. For example, the midpoint of H^+ concentration between pH 4 and 5 corresponds to pH 4.3.

Fourth, most foods have an inherent buffer capacity, i.e., an ability to resist change in pH. This buffer capacity is important in acidification and pH control. Weak acids and their salts in solution establish an equilibrium which resists changes in pH when more acidic or alkaline ingredients are added. The sodium salts of acids, such as acetic, citric, or phosphoric, can be added to buffer foods.

The pH can be measured using colorimetric or electrometric methods. In colorimetric methods, dyes that change color over a limited range of pH values are used; the color change developed after adding indicator solution to a food is then compared to a standard to determine pH. Indicator or pH paper is a type of colorimetric method where dye has been added to strips of paper. Colorimetric methods are used only to obtain approximate pH values and should not be used in foods with pH higher than 4.0. The most common and reliable method to determine the pH of canned foods is an electrometric method using a pH meter. This instrument measures the electrical potential developed between a glass and a reference electrode when imersed in a solution or food; this potential is converted to pH value and read from an analog or digital meter (FPI, 1988).

Influence of pH on Food Microbiology and Spoilage

While different species of microorganisms are characterized by a specific pH value for optimum growth, other chemical and physical characteristics of food are factors that affect the growth rate of bacteria, yeasts, and molds. One important effect of pH is its influence upon resistance of bacteria to heat: the lower the pH value, i.e., the higher the acid intensity, the lower the resistance of bacteria and bacterial spores to heat at a given temperature. When there are several species of bacteria, yeasts, and molds in a food, the pH value of the food is one of the most important factors determining which of those types of microorganisms will multiply faster, and within the types, the species that will prevail. That characteristic of pH is important, both in industrial fermentations and in food spoilage considerations.

TABLE 1.2 - Mean pH Values of Selected Foods

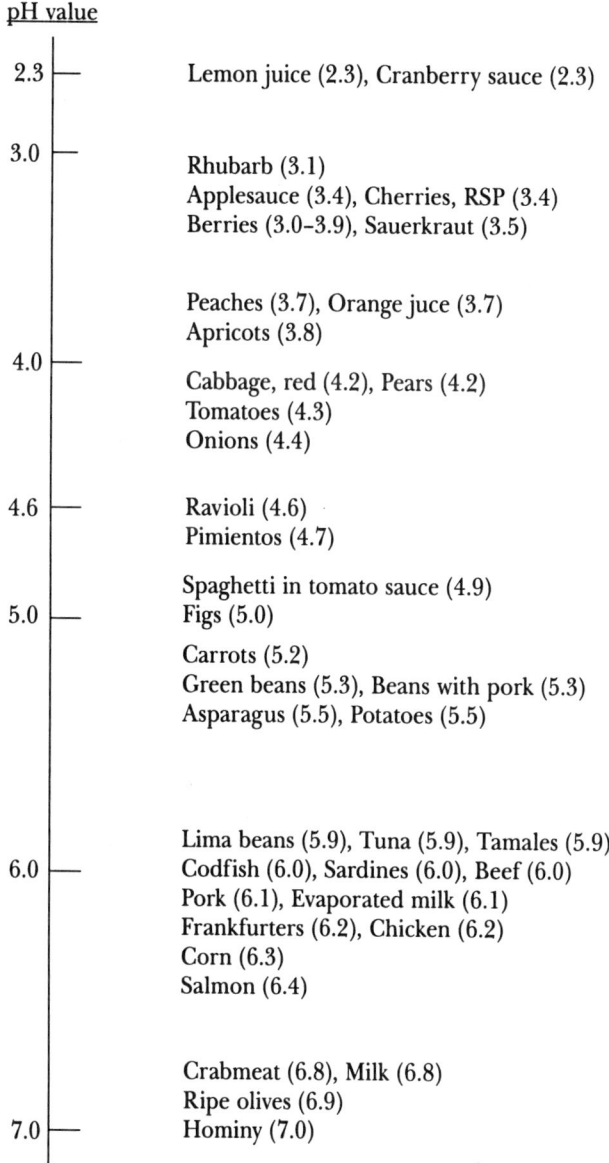

pH value	
2.3	Lemon juice (2.3), Cranberry sauce (2.3)
3.0	
	Rhubarb (3.1)
	Applesauce (3.4), Cherries, RSP (3.4)
	Berries (3.0-3.9), Sauerkraut (3.5)
	Peaches (3.7), Orange juce (3.7)
	Apricots (3.8)
4.0	
	Cabbage, red (4.2), Pears (4.2)
	Tomatoes (4.3)
	Onions (4.4)
4.6	Ravioli (4.6)
	Pimientos (4.7)
	Spaghetti in tomato sauce (4.9)
5.0	Figs (5.0)
	Carrots (5.2)
	Green beans (5.3), Beans with pork (5.3)
	Asparagus (5.5), Potatoes (5.5)
	Lima beans (5.9), Tuna (5.9), Tamales (5.9)
6.0	Codfish (6.0), Sardines (6.0), Beef (6.0)
	Pork (6.1), Evaporated milk (6.1)
	Frankfurters (6.2), Chicken (6.2)
	Corn (6.3)
	Salmon (6.4)
	Crabmeat (6.8), Milk (6.8)
	Ripe olives (6.9)
7.0	Hominy (7.0)

Effect of Temperature on Growth of Microorganisms

In actively growing stages, most microorganisms are readily killed by exposure to temperatures near the boiling point of water; bacterial spores, however, are more heat resistant than their vegetative cells.

Bacteria can be classified according to temperature requirements for growth. Bacteria growing at temperatures between 68–113°F (20–45°C), with optima between 86–104°F (30–40°C), are called *mesophiles*. Other species of bacteria are referred to as *psychrotrophs*, with optimum growth temperatures between 68–86°F (20–30°C) and growing well at or below 45°F (7°C). Those that grow well at and above 113°F (45°C), with optima between 131–149°F (55–65°C), are *thermophiles*. Thermophiles may grow slowly up to 170°F (77°C) (Jay, 1992).

There is an important difference between the optimum temperatures for growth of bacteria and their resistance to heat. Highly heat resistant bacteria are called thermoduric. Mesophilic organisms can be thermoduric due to the high heat resistance of their spores, as can the spores of thermophilic bacteria.

Foods have associated microfloras; certain microorganisms are usually found in certain food groups. These organisms gain entrance into the food during the canning operation, either from the soil, from ingredients, or from equipment. On the basis of acidity classification of foods, it is possible to make general statements relative to the microorganisms which are potentially capable of producing spoilage in canned foods.

pH and Growth of *Clostridium botulinum*

For years, laboratories connected with the canning industry and others have studied *Clostridium botulinum*, its heat-resistance and processing recommendations for low-acid foods. While studying the growth requirements for *Clostridium botulinum*, it was found that the dividing line of acidity between products in which the organism would grow, and those in which it would not grow, was about pH 4.6; below this level, growth of the organism in a favorable medium is inhibited. Under other conditions, such as one in which nutrient value is low, growth may be inhibited, regardless of pH. As a practical matter, this means that products of pH levels higher than pH 4.6 must be processed under steam pressure, at temperatures considerably higher than 212°F (100°C), usually higher than 240°F (116°C), in order to insure destruction of spores, while products at pH 4.6 or lower may be safely processed in an open bath at 212°F (100°C).

Acidity Classification of Canned Foods

Low-Acid Foods. Because *C. botulinum* will not grow at pH levels of 4.6 or below, foods in which it will grow have been categorized as "low-acid foods". Low-acid foods are defined as "any commercially processed food with a finished equilibrium pH value greater than 4.6 and a water activity greater than 0.85, but not including alcoholic beverages, and shall also include any normally low-acid vegetables or vegetable products in which, for the purpose of thermal processing, the pH value is reduced by acidification."

Meat, fish, poultry, dairy products, and vegetables, except tomatoes, generally fall into a pH range of 5.0 to 6.8 (see Table 1.2). While low in acid, they do fall in the acid range of pH values. Figs and pimientos, as well as some manufactured foods such as pasta products, have pH values between 4.6 and 5.0.

High-Acid Foods. Foods with pH values of 4.6 to 3.7 are classified as acid foods; examples include tomatoes, onions and pears. "High-acid foods" have pH values below 3.7 and include fruits, rhubarb, berries, and fermented foods, such as pickles and sauerkraut.

Acidified Foods. U.S. federal regulations define acidified foods as those low-acid foods which have had their pH reduced to 4.6 or lower by the addition of acids or acid foods. Vinegar, or any safe and suitable organic acid or acid food, can be used for this purpose.

Acidification is one means of preserving food products; in addition to preventing bacterial growth, acidification helps maintain a desired product quality. Puddings, cucumbers, artichokes, cauliflower, peppers and fish are examples of low-acid foods which are normally acidified. The addition of an acid or an acid food to such products is a method of preservation designed to prevent bacteria of public health significance from growing. If acidification is not adequately controlled at a pH of 4.6 or below, *Clostridium botulinum*, a toxin-producing micro-organism, can grow in the food.

In the U.S., all operating personnel concerned with the acidification of foods must be supervised by a person who has attended a school approved by the Commissioner of the U.S. Food and Drug Administration. This school presents instructions on pH and the critical factors to be considered in the acidification of foods.

BOTULISM

Botulism is an intoxication caused by a toxin produced in foods by the microorganism called *Clostridium botulinum*. This organism is a rod-shaped, spore forming bacillus. It originates in the soil in all parts of the world. *C. botulinum* is an anaerobic bacterium; it does not grow in the presence of free oxygen, nor on surfaces which support the growth of many other types of bacteria. This bacterium produces an exotoxin which is the most deadly neuro-paralytic toxin known.

Six types of *C. botulinum* have been described and are well known, i.e., Types A, B, C, D, E, and F. Each type produces a specific and somewhat different exotoxin, but each toxin causes similar symptoms. Anti-toxins or serums are specific to the particular type of toxin, but polyvalent vaccines are available. Intoxication is caused by ingestion of the exotoxin produced by the organism *C. botulinum*; it is not caused by the organism itself. The toxins are inactivated by heat in 10 minutes at 212°F (100°C). Types A, C and D are proteolytic, that is, they produce an extremely foul and putrid odor, while Types B and E do not produce this odor. According to Rhodehamel et. al. (1992), Type A was responsible for 60.1% of the confirmed outbreaks in the U.S. since 1978; Type B for 18.5% and Type E for 17.9%

Botulism occurs throughout the world because *C. botulinum* is widely distributed in nature and occurs in both cultivated and forest soils, bottom sediments of streams, lakes, and coastal waters, the intestinal tracts of fish and mammals, and gills and viscera of crabs and other shellfish. Canned vegetables, sausages, meat products and seafood products have been the most frequent vehicle for human botulism.

The types of foods involved in botulism vary according to food preservation and eating habits in different regions. Since any low-acid food can support growth and toxin formation, botulinum toxin has been found in a considerable variety of foods, including canned corn, peppers, green beans, beets, asparagus, mushrooms, ripe olives, spinach, tuna fish, salmon, chicken, chicken livers and liver pate, and in luncheon meats, ham, sausage, lobster, smoked fish, and stuffed eggplant. High acid foods, such as fruits, tomato products, sauerkraut, vinegared foods, etc., are not susceptible unless some form of spoilage has resulted in removal of sufficient acid, thus permiting growth of *C. botulinum.*

Methods of Commercial Control of Botulism

The canning industry employs standardized processes for treating foods insuring that the probability of survival of *C. botulinum* spores is very remote. These processes, which take into account the consistency and chemical nature of the product and the size of the can, are standardized so that the chance of spoilage due to inadequate processing is almost zero; only through recontamination after heating, due to container leakage, is it likely that a significant degree of spoilage could occur. Additional safety is provided by proper sanitary control, specified in U.S. FDA's Good Manufacturing Practice Regulations (21 CFR 110, 113 & 114), which serves to reduce the original bacterial load. The FDA-National Food Processors Association "Better Process Control" schools ensure education of retort operators and seam inspectors.

Whenever there is a question about product safety, cans should be discarded if they show even slightly bulging ends or any other evidence of spoilage, such as souring, gas formation, discoloration, or leaks. These recommendations do not apply to those commercially pressurized canned products, such as canned soft drinks, beer, and coffee; botulism bacteria cannot grow in these products.

Food cans or jars showing bulging lids should be suspected of potential botulism. Under no circumstance should the contents of these containers be tasted; they should be discarded where animals cannot gain access to them.

C. botulinum is a gas producing organism, but it is not a prolific gas former. Cans of food in which there are living organisms do not usually produce a "hard swell"; normally, the type of swell formed is a "soft swell" or a "springer"; in some cases, cans may not swell at all. The optimum growth temperature of the botulism organism for the development of toxin is from 65–85°F (18–29°C). Five to ten percent salt content in products such as salt-cured meats and fish will prevent the growth of *C. botulinum*.

Botulism Outbreaks

Most outbreaks of botulism are dramatic; symptoms appear suddenly within 8 to 72 hours after ingesting the toxin and progress rapidly. Typical symptoms involve the nervous system and result in double vision, difficulty in swallowing, impaired speech, difficulty in breathing, and paralysis of the extremities. Death usually results from paralysis of the respiratory muscles and asphyxia. Some botulism victims show symptoms of nausea, vomiting and constipation.

The illness is difficult to diagnose because at the onset, the symptoms of botulism are often confused with those of other diseases and few physicians are familiar with the diagnostic techniques. By the time the illness is recognized, it is usually too late for therapy; in botulism, the only therapy known is an early administration of anti-toxin serum. Mortality varies with different outbreaks, but the average in the U.S. for the 1971–1989 period was 11% (McClure et. al., 1994), down from about 60% until 1945.

Between 1971 and 1989, home-preserved foods accounted for 92% of the outbreaks of botulism in the United States, while only 8% was attributed to commercial foods. 63 fatal cases were recorded for that period. Of 222 outbreaks studied, 16% were related to meats, 17% to fish, 59% to fruits and vegetables and 9% to other products (McClure et. al., 1994).

Botulism is usually associated with foods that have been given an inadequate or minimal preservation treatment, held for some time non-refrigerated, and consumed without appropriate heating. The growth of *C. botulinum* in foods frequently, but not always, produces a foul, putrid odor that serves as a warning to the consumer. Signs of spoilage, however, have not prevented botulism, because the degree of tolerance to disagreeable odors or off-flavors varies among individuals; in green beans or in foods that are smoked, heavily spiced, or fermented, the off-odor may be difficult to recognize. Because botulinum spores are killed by heat, the culprit in home canning is under-sterilization, either by not using a high enough temperature, or by processing for too short a time, or a combination of these conditions.

From 1926 to 1982, eight deaths were reported from consumption of foods commercially canned in the United States; details appear in Table 1.3. These eight fatalities occurred over a period during which consumers ate the contents of nearly 900 billion containers of canned food. This record supports the fact that properly processed canned foods are safe. The few exceptions, however, were so tragic in their occurrence and consequences that increased effort and diligence by the canner in preventing botulism outbreaks are mandatory. Adherence to the Good Manufacturing Practice regulations and good plant sanitation in processing low-acid canned foods constitute a safeguard against botulism outbreaks.

TABLE 1.3 - Human Botulism Outbreaks Involving U.S. Commercially Canned Foods in Metal Containers, 1940–1982[a]

Year	Product	Out-breaks	Cases[b]	Death[e]	Toxin Type	Cause of Outbreak
1941	Mushroom sauce (single can)	1	3	1	E	Suspected leakage
1963	Tuna fish	1	3	2	E	Alleged leakage[c]
1971	Vichyssoise soup	1	2	1	A	Under-processing[d]
1974	Beef stew (single can)	1	2	1	A	Unknown - can possibly missed retort
1978	Salmon (single can)	1	4	2	E	Leakage - can damaged after processing
1982	Salmon (single can)	1	2	1	E	Leakage - malfunctioning can reformer
1982	Peeled whole tomatoes (single can)	1	1	0	A	Unknown - no evidence of container leakage

[a]No botulism outbreak is recorded from 1926 to 1939 in commercially canned foods in metal containers.

[b]Number of persons afflicted.

[c]21 additional cans recovered by FDA reportedly showed *C. botulinum*; container evaluation was not definitive.

[d]Four additional cans (swollen) of the same code showed type A toxin.

[e]No known deaths in 1981-1985 involving U.S. commercially canned foods.

(Table adapted from: J. M. Dryer, *et al.*, Journal of Food Protection 47(10):801-816, 1984.)

Table 1.4 shows recent cases of reported botulism around the world from commercially prepared foods, including foods from restaurants.

TABLE 1.4 – Worldwide Botulism Outbreaks, 1973–1991

Year	Product	Country	Cases (Type)	Deaths	Cause
1973	Bottled mushrooms	Canada	1 (B)	0	Inadequate acidification
1977	Canned peppers	USA	59 (B)	0	Underprocessing
1978	Canned salmon	UK	4 (E)	2	Post-process leakage
1981	Kapchunka (salt-cured, air-dried uneviscerated whitefish)	USA	1 (B-np)	0	Poorly controlled salting process
1982	Canned salmon	Belgium	2 (E)	1	Post-process leakage
1982	Bologna sauce	Madagascar	60 (E)	30	Inadequate preservation
1982	Beef pot pie	USA	1 (A)	0	–
1983	Sauteed onions	USA	28 (A)	1	Temperature abuse
1984	Karashi-renkon (vacuum packed, deep-fried, lotus root)	Japan	36 (A)	11	Underprocessing/ temperature abuse
1985	Chopped garlic in oil (bottled, no preservatives)	Canada	36 (B)	0	Temperature abuse
1985	Kapchunka	USA	2 (E)	2	Poorly controlled salting process
1986	Bottled peanuts	Taiwan	9 (A)	2	Underprocessing
1987	Kapchunka	USA and Israel	8 (E)	1	Poorly controlled salting process
1987	Kosher airline meal (meat, shelf-stable, from Switzerland)	UK	1 (A)	0	Underprocessing/ temperature abuse
1989	Hazelnut yogurt	UK	27 (B)	1	Inadequately reduced a_w
1989	Chopped garlic in oil (bottled, no preservatives)	USA	3 (A)	0	Temperature abuse
1991	Faseikh (uneviscerated fish)	Egypt	91 (E)	18	Poorly controlled fermentation/salting

Table adapted from McClure et. al. (1994) and Rhodehamel et. al. (1992)

SPOILAGE OF CANNED FOODS – CHARACTERISTICS OF CANNED FOOD SPOILAGE MICROORGANISMS

Low-Acid Canned Foods

Flat sour producing thermophilic bacteria. Aerobic and facultative anaerobic. Spores highly heat resistant. Occur more in canned vegetables and in products high in starch content for which quality considerations necessitate a minimum of heat processing. Produce acid, but not gas. Cans do not swell. Type species: *Bacillus stearothermophilus.*

Thermophilic anaerobic bacteria. Very heat resistant. Obligate anaerobic. Gas and acid producers. Cans swell. Type species: *Clostridium thermosaccharolyticum.*

"Sulfide spoilage" thermophilic bacteria. "Sulfur stinkers." Food turns dark due to production of H_2S and formation of sulfide with iron containers. Cans usually remain flat due to solubility of H_2S in water. Type species: *Desulfotomaculum nigrificans.*

Putrefactive anaerobic bacteria. Mesophilic, spore-formers and gas-formers. Type species: *C. botulinum, C. butiricum,* etc. Destruction of spores of *C. botulinum* is minimum standard for processing low acid foods. Most species of this group are more heat resistant than *C. botulinum.*

Aerobic mesophilic spore-formers. As a group, they are less important than putrefactive anaerobes, due to (a) vacuum in canned foods which inhibits their growth, and to (b) inability to produce marked changes in foods. However, some species of this group have shown considerable heat resistance. Several species of *Bacillus* belong to this group.

Yeasts, molds, and non-spore-forming bacteria. Spoilage by these microorganisms is not common in low acid canned foods. Their presence would indicate: (a) gross understerilization; or (b) contamination due to defective seam. These organisms are readily controlled by relatively short processes at temperatures below 212°F (100°C).

Acid Foods

Spore-forming bacteria. Among the most important are: (a) *Bacillus coagulans,* which is aerobic, not very heat resistant, thermophilic, produces "flat sour;" (b) *C. pasteurianum,* which is spore-former, anaerobic, saccharolytic, gas-producing.

Non-sporing bacteria. Lactic acid producing bacteria: *Lactobacillus* and *Leuconostoc* sp. Some are gas producing and develop best under conditions of reduced oxygen tension.

Yeasts. Due to their very low heat resistance, yeasts cause spoilage in canned foods only in cases of gross under-processing or can leakage.

Molds. Generally molds are of little importance in all canned foods. However, there are exceptions in *Byssochlamys, Neosartorya* and *Talaromyces,* which are molds that produce heat resistant ascospores; they can spoil canned fruit products sometimes with gas production. Heat resistance: 30 minutes at 190°F (88°C), or 16 minutes at 212°F (100°C). These molds are unusually heat resistant in comparison to other molds. For *Byssochlamys fulva,* a D value between one and 12 minutes at 194°F (90°C) with z value of 6–7°C are reported to be practical working values (Jay, 1992).

Autosterilization: This term is used to explain absence of viable bacteria in cultures and plates made from the contents of cans which have evidence of spoilage by microbial action. This condition may result from the death of bacteria which caused the spoilage from accumulation of products of metabolism; it is especially possible in flat sour spoilage of vegetables. When characteristics of bacterial spoilage are evident, plates and cultures remain sterile because of the death of bacteria which caused the spoilage.

TABLE 1.5 - Spoilage Manifestations in Low-Acid Products

Type of Organism	Classification	Manifestations
Flat sour bacteria	Can flat Product	Possible loss of vacuum on storage. Appearance not usually altered. pH markedly lowered, sour. May have slightly abnormal odor. Sometimes cloudy liquor.
Thermophilic anaerobe bacteria	Can swells Product	May burst. Fermented, sour, cheesy or butyric odor.
Sulfide spoilage bacteria	Can flat Product	H_2S gas absorbed by product. Usually blackened. "Rotten egg" odor.
Putrefactive anaerobe bacteria	Can swells Product	May burst. May be partially digested. pH slightly above normal. Typical putrid odor.
Aerobic sporeformers (odd types)	Can flat	Usually no swelling, except in cured meats when nitrate and sugar present. Coagulated evaporated milk, black beets.

TABLE 1.6 - Spoilage Manifestations in Acid Products

Type of Organism	Classification	Manifestations
Bacillus thermoacidurans (flat sour, tomato juice)	Can flat Product	Little change in vacuum. Slight pH change. Off-odor.
Butyric anaerobes (tomatoes, tomato juice)	Can swells Product	May burst. Fermented, butyric odor.
Non-sporeformer bacteria (mostly lactic types)	Can swells Product	Usually burst, but swelling may be arrested. Acid odor.

TABLE 1.7 - Laboratory Diagnosis of Bacterial Spoilage

	Underprocessed	Leakage
Can	Flat or swelled. Seams generally normal.	Swelled; may show defects*.
Product Appearance	Sloppy or fermented.	Frothy fermentation; viscous.
Odor	Normal, sour or putrid, but generally consistent from can to can.	Sour, fecal; generally varying from can to can.
pH	Usually fairly constant.	Wide variation.
Microscopic and Cultural	Cultures show spore-forming rods only. Growth at 98°F and/or 131°F. May be characteristic on special media, e.g., acid agar for tomato juice. If product misses retort completely, rods, cocci, yeast, or molds or any combination of these may be present.	Mixed cultures, generally rods and cocci. Growth only at usual temperatures.
History	Spoilage usually confined to certain portions of pack. In acid products, diagnosis may be less clearly defined; similar organisms may be involved in understerilization and leakage.	Spoilage scattered.

*Leakage may not be due to can defects but to other factors such as contamination of cooling water or rough handling, e.g., can unscramblers, rough conveyor system.

TYPES OF SPOILAGE OF CANNED FOODS

Swells

Swells are caused by gas production by microorganisms, either from lack of sterilization, or by contamination through a leak. When significant numbers of cans swell soon after processing, there is no evidence of leakage, and the general run have a good vacuum, it is very safe to conclude that the cause is under-sterilization. If one organism greatly predominates, grows under anaerobic conditions, and is spore bearing, lack of sterilization is probably confirmed. Cans from the same lot, if placed in a warm temperature, generally develop some swells. Swells caused by under-processing generally develop within two to fourteen days if the warehouse temperature is warm, but may be delayed for some months if held cold. The development of swells may be slow in some heavy products like sweet potatoes, squash, pumpkin, heavy cream-style corn, and tightly packed spinach, so that time must be considered in connection with other factors.

There is an important biological differentiation between spoilage from under-sterilization and from leakage in the case of low-acid foods. When spoilage occurs from under-sterilization, it is usually caused by a single spore-forming type. Where leakage has occured, mixed cultures of non-sporing bacteria which could not have survived the process, but must have entered the can after process, are found. This differentiation does not exist in a clean-cut way in the case of the acid products, because the aciduric organisms which cause spoilage may have been present in the product at the time of canning, or may have entered subsequent to the process. Cause of spoilage may be identified by observations of whether it occurred from one, or a few, or many bacterial types; in the latter instance, leakage is indicated.

Swells may be so mild that the ends of the can are barely destended or so strong that cans burst. The major gas present is carbon dioxide, although it may be mixed with other malodorous gases such as H_2S. The product is most often offensive, sour, and frequently discolored. The term "puffer" has the same significance as "swell" and is used more among meat canners than among canners of fruits or vegetables.

Swells are usually caused by holding the process to minimum time or temperature, and changes in fill or product consistency, all factors requiring consideration

The words "flipper," "springer," "swell," etc., are rather loosely used by the canning trade. The National Food Processors Association's definitions: "Flippers" are cans, the ends of which are flat, but one end of which is forced out when the can is knocked against a hard surface. Such cans have no vacuum and the ends may come out if cases are dropped during loading or shipping. A "springer" is a can, one or both ends of which are slightly bulged, but the interior pressure of which is not sufficient to prevent forcing one or both ends to their normal position by means of pressure with the fingers. A "swell" is a can, both ends of which are bulged and cannot be forced into their normal position with the fingers.

The contents of a can spoiled by micro-organisms passes through various stages. First, enough gas is produced to relieve the vacuum in the can; at this stage the can may be a "flipper". When slightly more gas is produced, the can may become a "springer", and later become a "swell". If the interior pressure is produced by hydrogen developing from the action of acid in the product on container metal, the same thing occurs. Although this rarely occurs, sufficient hydrogen may be produced causing cans to burst. Cans of fruits frequently contain sufficient hydrogen to become hard swells. Hydrogen swells can generally be differentiated from bacterial swells, since bacterial swells develop within about 15 days at warm warehouse temperatures, while hydrogen swells do not become apparent until months after packing.

"Springers" from overfilling occur infrequently. "Springers" caused by insufficient vacuum may occur in foods packed in a cool climate without proper exhaustion and develop when these foods are sent to a warm climate or to a high altitude; they may develop at the same location during the summer of the following season. "Springers" caused by attack of the food material upon the metal are a problem. These usually develop slowly over weeks or months, but may be hastened by storage in a warm place. Those products most apt to cause "springers" are apples, cider, strawberries, sour cherries, loganberries and other seed berries. When a "springer" is punctured, the gas emitted is hydrogen; it will burn if lighted; there is no objectionable odor; the product is generally normal or may be somewhat bleached in appearance. Flavor may be astringent because of iron present; no bacteria are present; the product is sound, but may not sold.

Pinholing

Pinholing is caused by the same conditions that create hydrogen springers, but the effect is localized. Points usually develop where metal has been fractured by the die on a double seamer.

Flat Sours

A "flat sour" is caused by under-processing or under-cooling. The organisms present develop without the production of gas, but some amount of acid is produced, hence the name, flat sours. An exception - hominy - develops a sweetish taste. The "flat sour" condition is caused by heat-resistant, thermophilic, spore-forming bacteria.

Flat sours generally occur when low-acid foods, like vegetables and meats, are warehoused while still hot. If cans are cooled after the sterilization process, thermophilic bacteria that may have survived sterilization do not have enough time to grow and cause spoilage. While there is nothing in the external appearance of the can to indicate that anything is wrong, shaking may disclose a liquid consistency with products like cream-style corn. If the cans are placed in warm water, the ends of those which contain flat sour material will usually be forced out faster than those containing sound food; the reverse will occur on cooling. This fact provides a means by which bad cans may be separated from good ones. Flat sours occur in the interior of stacks of canned food rather than in outer rows. Adequate process, prompt cooling, and good sanitary conditions prevent "flat sour" production. Thorough washing of raw products to eliminate soil and prevention of recontamination of product with soil or other sources of thermophilic bacteria during the canning operations is important.

Stack Burning

Stack burning results if cans are stored while too warm; the contents soften, sometimes to the point of becoming soupy, darken in color, and acquire a disagreeable flavor. The inside of the cans look galvanized or of a dull color. Stack burning probably occurs more often in tomatoes than in any other product, partly because tomatoes will not resist heat as well as most products and because they are packed in large quantities and stored at once without narrow ventilating aisles between double tiers. Stack burn causes peas to become mushy and acquire a scorched taste with the liquor dark and starchy; other fruits and vegetables behave similarly. Stack burning, like "flat sours," occurs on the inside of stacks and not in outer rows.

Food Discoloration

Discoloration may be caused by various metals, by exposure to high or prolonged temperature, or by bacterial action.Discoloration caused by metals may occur from contamination before foods are placed in a can or by reaction between the food material and the container. Discoloration from metals is well illustrated by the blue-gray coloration in corn when the machinery is first started in operation. Contact with copper at any point along the preparation line, particularly at the filling machine, causes darkening of grains and liquor. Blackening of peas is similarly caused; free copper should be eliminated from the equipment by tinning exposed parts or by other means. Blackening of hominy, however, is most often caused by failure to remove the bleaching material rather than by machinery.

The effect of iron upon fruits is such that iron should be minimally used in the preparatory apparatus; fruit juices are so sensitive to metals that their preparation is best carried out in glass lined kettles, stainless steel or aluminum; preparation tables should also be of such material. Tin bleaches fruit juices.

Black Stains

Discoloration caused by food container interaction during processing is a serious problem. The temperature of the processing breaks up sulfur compounds in proteins, which combine with iron, forming black iron sulfide; this is especially objectionable in corn. A black deposit formed in the headspace of the can becomes detached and mixes with the corn; it is avoided by the use of special enamel lined cans which prevent iron exposure. Black stains may occur in canned shrimp, lobsters, crabs, white meats from fish, meats from slaughter houses, pears and light colored fruit. While it produces no harm, except the objectionable appearance, it is eliminated by the use of enamel lined cans known as "C" enamel and developed for this purpose.

The bleaching effect upon foods, especially those which are highly colored, is largely overcome by the use of inside enameled tins. "R" enamel is used with highly colored fruits and other foods that are bleached by the tin.

Heat discoloration usually results in darkening, though in the case of pears, a distinct pink color results. Dark discolorations are caused by leaks. Discoloration from bacterial decomposition is unusual, but occurs in peas, beans, corn, and fish products; it is invariably a blackening.

Glass-Like Deposits in Canned Foods

Canned food consumers occasionally complain of yellow crystals in asparagus, green beans, and onions, of white transparent crystals in grape products, and of crystals resembling particles of glass in canned crab meat, shrimp, and salmon. These crystals are completely harmless and are formed by certain natural components of the food becoming too concentrated in a particular spot and then precipitating out of solution into this form of crystal (struvite).

The addition of substances known as "chelating agents" is recommended to prevent the formation of these glass-like crystals in canned seafood products; laws and regulations that apply to the manufacture of these products must be checked before use of these additives.

Off Flavors

Foreign flavors are most often acquired before foods are placed in cans. While vegetables may acquire an acid taste caused by incipient fermentation, they may also develop a bitterness due to changes in structure. While this is more noticeable in asparagus than in any other product, it is not infrequent in corn and snap beans. Fruits, especially peaches and apricots, acquire a flavor from standing too long in pine lug boxes. It is difficult to describe, but is referred to as piney, a slight suggestion of wood, turpentine, and resin. Fruits which stand in cold storage take on a musty taste, even though there is no evidence of mold. Standing in a closed, unventilated room, they develop a peculiar flavor believed caused by the action of carbon dioxide.

SPOILAGE BY RECONTAMINATION

The assumption that the heat sterilization given canned foods killed all bacteria that might be present, regardless of kind or number, must be modified since certain types of bacteria are very resistant to heat; the presence of any considerable number of such bacteria renders successful processing very difficult. Certain types of equipment, or lack of proper control measures, may permit such bacteria to multiply and become a spoilage hazard. The following statement on spoilage by recontamination is taken from the Appendix to Bulletin 26-L (1982) of the National Food Processors Association.

Precautions For Handling Filled and Sealed Containers

Installation of labor-saving devices for handling filled containers introduces certain hazards. If these are not minimized, some spoilage may result from post process contamination, even with the best possible double seam construction. Before the containers are thoroughly cooled, seams are slightly expanded and the compound lining is somewhat soft or plastic. Rough handling of containers in this condition may result in contamination by spoilage organisms. In addition to these seam considerations, precautions must be taken in handling containers before they are thoroughly cool and dry to prevent dents on or near the double seams. When filled containers are handled automatically at high speeds, seam deformation may be more significant as a spoilage factor than under slow speed, low-impact conditions. The three main factors in spoilage resulting from post-processing container handling operations are:

1. Condition of container double seams,
2. Presence of bacterial contamination in cooling water or on wet container runways, and
3. Container abuse due to poor operation or adjustment of the filled container handling equipment.

The following recommendations will minimize the potential for spoilage by recontamination after processing:

1. Inspect can seams periodically to insure that they are properly formed. Inspection must include both visual and teardown examinations. Observations and any corrective actions must be recorded.

2. Do not allow containers to drop into crates from closing machine discharge tables without cushioning their fall.
3. Do not overfill retort crates. Containers in overfilled crates could be crushed by crate bales or by crates above them in the retort.
4. Prevent sharp impacts between filled crates or against protruding points during transfer by overhead monorail or on dollies.
5. Operate crate dumps smoothly to prevent impact denting.
6. Apply an appropriate and sufficient quantity of germicide to cooling water to assure its sanitary quality. For example, chlorinate or otherwise sanitize all cooling water to a point where there is measurable residual (0.5 ppm free chlorine recommended when chlorine used) at the point of cooling water discharge.
7. In pressure cooling, maintain adequate retort pressure for a sufficient time to prevent permanent distortion of can ends.
8. Inspect the container handling system periodically from the closing machine to the caser. Where rough handling of the container is apparent, smooth out the operation to minimize seam damage.
9. Dry the containers after cooling and before discharge into the container handling system.
10. When containers are handled on belt conveyors, lowerators or belt elevators, construct these units so as to minimize contact by the belt with the double seam. Cans should not be rolled on double seams.
11. Replace all worn and frayed belting, can retarders, and/or cushions with new non-porous material.
12. All tracks and belts, which come into contact with can seams, should be thoroughly scrubbed and sanitized at intervals frequent enough to prevent bacterial buildup.

GENERAL SOURCES AND CONTROL OF SPOILAGE DUE TO CONTAMINATION

Process efficiency depends in large measure upon type and number of microorganisms in the product at the time of processing. All processes for low-acid canned foods recommended in National Food Processors Association Bulletin 26-L, 12th Edition, are designed to provide commercial sterility. These processes are not necessarily adequate in cases of extreme contamination by spoilage bacteria.

Bacterial contamination of product must be minimized by employing comprehensive sanitation and inspection programs, which are an integral part of a plant's operation.

Factory surveys to identify contamination sources, and to develop means for their elimination, have been conducted since 1926. These surveys have shown that major sources of contamination are often located within the processing plant. Heat resistant spoilage organisms are brought to the plant on the raw product. Even though preliminary washing operations are largely sufficient to reduce initial contamination to a level which will not result in spoilage, residual spoilage organisms may become established in processing equipment and increase to a point where they may constitute a spoilage hazard. With some products, such as asparagus and mushrooms, soil-borne contamination of the raw product may be a direct cause of spoilage.

While factory studies have centered chiefly upon asparagus, corn, mushrooms, peas, pumpkin, and spinach processing, facts uncovered in these studies are applicable to other products. Accordingly, adoption of the following information should serve to control contamination to a degree that insures effectiveness of the processes presented in Bulletin 26-L, 12th Ed., 1982.

Wooden Equipment

In general, the use of wood in processing equipment is not recommended. Bacteria may become "seeded" in the pores, and once established, may contaminate food materials to such an extent that spoilage occurs with a process that has been satisfactory for years. Any wooden equipment or other porous material which food materials contact, such as brine and hot water tanks, conveyors, blanchers, inspection or filling tables, and even small items such as paddles and rollers, may be carriers of contamination. For example, wooden tanks used for storage of hot water for general plant purposes may contaminate a whole processing system. At the beginning of a day's run, wooden brine tanks may supply large numbers of organisms to the product; their number decreases markedly during steady operation due to dilution, only to build up again during a shutdown. Since wood is porous, it retains bacteria and protects them from scrubbing and other cleaning processes. "Seeding" may be prevented to a considerable degree by constant cleaning. In spite of all precautions, there is no practical treatment which will rid wood of established organisms.

Pumps, Pipes, Extractors, Cyclones, etc.

Pumps, pipes, extractors, cyclones, etc., should be selected from the standpoint of ease in cleaning. Since such equipment might hold food material, this serves as a medium for bacterial growth, permitting high numbers of organisms to seriously contaminate the first part of the next day's pack. After use, all such equipment should be thoroughly cleaned, cooled with water, and kept cool until its next use; it should be flushed with water again immediately before use.

During cleaning, care should be exercised to force steam through the perforations of steam distribution pipes, which are submerged in food or brine during operation, to insure that all perforations are open.

Pipe systems carrying product should be thoroughly cleaned at least at the end of the day's pack. More frequent cleanings are necessary if transport pipes are normally operated partially full. "Dead ends" should be eliminated; if unavoidable, they should have drains to accommodate flushing at frequent intervals. All cleaning operations should be inspected to insure effectiveness.

Blanchers

Blanching by heat, when required in the preparation of food, should be accomplished by heating food to the required temperature, holding it at this temperature for the required time, and then either rapidly cooling the food, or processing without delay. Thermophilic growth and contamination in blanchers should be minimized by the use of adequate temperatures and by proper cleaning followed by cold water rinsing. If blanched food is washed before filling, potable water should be used.

Fluming

Flumes, such as those used for conveying peas and whole kernel corn, may become sources of bacterial contamination. Water temperatures in the range of 100–180°F (38–82°C) should be avoided, since this may provide a favorable condition for the growth of thermophilic spoilage bacteria. The reuse of hot flume water may aggravate contamination; it is advisable to use only cold water for fluming purposes.

Fillers

Filling machines used with low-acid products may become contaminated with spoilage bacteria, especially when the filler is maintained at temperatures within thermophilic growth range. This might occur during operation from contact with a heated product, or during shutdown periods from leakage of steam supply valves.

Fillers should be dismantled and cleaned as frequently as practicable. After the day's cleanup, fillers should be flushed with cold water with all machinery in motion to chill the equipment. During the overnight shutdown, fillers should be left clean, cold, and empty. If a filler operates at temperatures within the thermophilic range during actual packing operations, it should be emptied of its product every 4 hours and thoroughly flushed with water while all machinery is kept in motion.

Canning Ingredients

Ingredients commonly used in canning, such as sugar, starch, flour, spices and dried milk, may be carriers of spoilage organisms. Before such raw materials and ingredients which are susceptible to microbiological contamination are used, it must be insured that they are suitable for use in processing low-acid foods. A supplier's guarantee of suitability by microbiological examination, or by other acceptable means, serves as a guarantee that standards are met.

SPECIFIC SOURCES OF SPOILAGE DUE TO CONTAMINATION

In addition to the preceding general information on contamination sources, specific information on individual products follows.

Corn

Cream Style

a. Preheating systems, mixing and blending tanks. Increasing use of mixing and blending equipment in which hot corn is handled has demonstrated further need for contamination control. Such equipment, operated at 180°F (82°C) or higher, does not act as a breeding point for spoilage bacteria, but if operated in the range of 100–180°F (38–82°C), there is opportunity for development of thermophilic organisms. This usually occurs overnight and during shutdowns; spores which develop during those times may contaminate the subsequent run. While it is best to hold the tanks empty overnight, they must be held full of cold water to insure that there are no leaky steam valves in the line which might tend to warm the equipment. During cleaning, perforated steam supply pipes should be blown out; they may hold food material that could serve as a bacterial medium. Flushing and cooling may be conveniently accomplished by connecting a cold water line into the steam supply line adjacent to the mixer and blending tank.

b. Circulating systems. Product circulating pipes should be thoroughly cleaned at the end of a day's production. There may be occasions when more frequent cleanings are necessary, for example, if all pipe sections within the system are not completely full during operation.

Whole Kernel

With this product, special care is required to prevent contact with wooden equipment. After cutting, corn should be given an effective wash; failure to wash cut corn properly may result in spoilage. Warm water in flotation washers should be avoided, since such practice may lead to rapid development of spoilage bacteria.

Peas, Beans, etc.

Earlier recommendations are particularly important to control blancher contamination of peas; these recommendations also apply to other products blanched in a conventional pea blancher, such as lima, green and wax beans.

Pumpkin

Procedures in pumpkin canning are not standardized. The following suggestions are based upon a study of systems used by a majority of pumpkin canners. Consideration of contamination sources focuses first on wilting equipment.

(1) Wooden Box or Tower Wilters. Wooden equipment is objectionable, but it may be lined with metal, if this is practicable, and the interior sealed so that product leakage through holes or seams into the wood does not occur.

(2) Continuous Metal or Wooden Box Wilters. Both metal and wooden boxes used as continuous wilters may be sources of contamination; they are difficult to clean and cool.

(3) Continuous Conveyor Presses. There are several variations of this type of equipment; pumpkin from the wilter is dropped into a hopper and carried between two moving belts; the distance between belts gradually decreases toward the outlet end, and pressure exerted squeezes juice from the pumpkin. These presses are mechanically complicated and their parts vary in temperature; where temperature is favorable to thermophilic growth, there may be some bacterial development. Some control may be maintained by spraying the press "aprons" with cold water. For contamination control, a screw type press is preferred; this equipment forces pumpkin through a tapering perforated screen and during operation, the temperature of all parts is so high (180–200°F) (82–93°C) that no bacterial growth is possible. The screw press is readily accessible for cleaning.

(4) Concentration of Pumpkin Juice. The juice from the press is discarded, but, in some cases, it is concentrated and added back to the pumpkin at the finisher. This system is satisfactory, if general packing procedure keeps contamination at a low level, but the contamination level is increased as the volume of juice is reduced by evaporation, and any contamination present is returned to the product.

Spinach

(1) Washers. Spinach washers include "immersion", "spray-rotary" and "spray-belt" types; they are used individually, or in combination; the washer's primary function is to remove grit and adhering soil, along with any soil-borne bacteria. In all types of washers, efficiency is determined, at least in part, by the amount of water used. Since thorough washing is of primary importance, a large volume of water is usually required. Washers should not be overloaded with product, because this limits efficiency. If both immersion and spray types are used in the same

line, better results are achieved if the immersion washer is placed before the spray washer. The first washing should always be done with cold water, since warm water may lead to an increase in bacterial numbers. Equipment could become contaminated. Water from a single washer should not be recirculated.

(2) Blanchers. Blanching equipment may be a thermophilic spoilage bacteria source; to minimize spoilage hazards here, washing and cooling treatments previously discussed should be applied. Occasionally, rotary drum blanchers are used, but since this equipment is difficult to clean, spoilage organisms may develop; their use is not recommended. Makeup water should be added to blanchers at a reasonably rapid rate.

Both rotary drum blanchers and tubular blancher systems may become contaminated with thermophilic spoilage bacteria. Contamination, which occurs during shutdown periods, can be minimized by prompt cooling of the blanchers after use, thorough cleaning, elimination of steam leaks, and flushing of the blancher system before its next use. However, thermophilic contamination may occur during operation of either type of blancher system.

In rotary drum blanchers, contaminating bacteria can grow on inner surfaces above the water line, where temperatures are reduced by cool air drawn into blanchers under loose fitting doors and other openings. Any blancher surface where the temperature ranges between 100–180°F (38–82°C) can serve as a site of bacterial growth. From these surfaces, heat resistant spores are washed by condensate into blanch water and contaminate the product.

To prevent contamination in rotary drum blanchers, inner surface temperatures should be elevated above 180°F (82°C); blancher doors should be closed and fastened at all times during operation; bent doors, or doors similarly in disrepair, should be repaired. Entry of cool air should be prevented; vent stacks should be eliminated from the blancher shell. Since the coldest sections within a drum blancher are at the feed end, a spray or steam jet, inserted at the upper edge of the feed end to deliver steam or hot water (190°F (88°C) or higher) over inside surfaces, is useful in preventing contamination. During operation, blanch water temperature should be as high as practicable (at least 180°F (82°C)); reels should be kept in continuous motion while blanchers are being heated or held at operating temperature; a continuous water overflow from the blancher should be maintained during operation.

In tubular blanching systems, a large percentage of flat sour spore contamination occurs in the de-watering reel into which product is discharged from the blanchers. Thermophilic bacteria grow on the screen mesh and splash board surfaces around the reel and underneath the pan; bacterial spores are added to product as it passes through the reel; they may also be washed into the water and recirculated in the blancher. Such contamination can be reduced if water sprays are installed to wash reel surfaces. This water may be chlorinated; cold water is desirable to lower product temperature before it enters the quality grader.

Sprays should also be provided to wash down inner surfaces of splash boards or canopy surrounding the reel. Tests indicate that cold water sprays are effective in reducing flat sour contamination. Foam accumulating on tanks supplying recovered water to tubular blanchers can be the growth site for thermophilic spoilage bacteria; a large, broad overflow should skim the tank's surface; top sprays delivering streams of water at a flat angle prevent foam formation; they also help to skim the tank.

It is important to wash product thoroughly after blanching; adequate washing removes large numbers of spoilage bacteria, but it cannot remove all bacteria added by heavy contamination. Cold water washing reduces product temperature, which helps to minimize slime growth and prevents undesirable temperature increases further down the processing line.

Blancher water should be dumped as often as practicable, since bacterial spores in the water increase with time and use; drain and water supply pipes should be of sufficient size to permit rapid draining and refilling.

SOURCES OF CONTAMINATION OF VEGETABLES IN GENERAL

Vegetables, as received at the processing factory, usually contain large numbers of viable microorganisms; counts in the millions per gram are not uncommon. While growing field soil is a principal source of contamination, organisms can also originate from the surfaces of harvesters and from the containers used to transport product to the factory.

Actual growth of microorganisms can be responsible for high counts if a vegetable is held for an extended period after harvest, especially when the weather is hot. This cause of high counts can be avoided by proper harvest scheduling.

Usually, the initial wash that is given vegetables only removes a portion of the microorganisms and soil; as a result, microbial populations remain high until a vegetable is blanched. Thus, blanching also serves as a cleaning step, though not usually considered one.

With frozen vegetables, most viable microorganisms in the final product are introduced at processing stages following the blanch. Equipment such as cutters and slicers are often significant sources of contamination, because they are difficult to clean. Belts can be a problem, although many factories prevent growth on them by continuous cleaning with chlorinated water sprays.

Number of Microorganisms

Predominant types. Bacteria greatly outnumber viable yeasts and molds that are present on low-acid vegetables (yeasts outnumber the molds). These data indicate that, if there is a buildup of slime on processing equipment, bacteria would be responsible.

A wide variety of bacteria make up the microflora that are enumerated by aerobic plate counts. The most numerous group is the catalase negative cocci; they increase in numbers as the processing season progresses and may make up 90% or more of the organisms on vegetables, such as corn, which are processed later in the summer.

Fecal indicators. Coliforms and enterococci are present on vegetables as received from the growing field and can be recovered at most stages of processing. It is believed that their presence has no special sanitary significance: they merely make up a part of the processing line microflora, along with lactic acid bacteria and other organisms. *Escherichia coli*, on the other hand, is rarely found and its presence may indicate a problem.

Geotrichum candidum. If this mold is found in processed fruits and vegetables, it is evidence of insanitary processing conditions. While the presence of *Geotrichum* (machinery mold) in certain canned fruits and tomatoes appears to be well explained, the significance of low counts in low-acid vegetables is less well understood. For example, yeast and mold growth on the surfaces of soiled vegetable processing equipment would be expected to parallel that of bacteria, the predominant organism, but no correlation between the incidence of *Geotrichum* and the numbers of bacteria has been found. *Geotrichum*-positive samples did not yield higher viable counts than those that were negative for the mold.

MICROBIOLOGICAL STANDARDS FOR INGREDIENTS

In the analysis of ingredients, a wide variety of thermophilic and mesophilic bacteria are encountered. Relatively few of the mesophilic bacteria, however, are considered significant from the standpoint of food spoilage. In general, yeasts, molds and thermophilic bacteria are the significant spoilage types of organisms.

The types of thermophilic, low-acid, food spoilage, spore-forming bacteria which may be found are characterized into three groups: those which produce flat sour spoilage, i.e., *Bacillus stearothermophilus*; those which produce gas, but not hydrogen sulfide, i.e., the thermophilic anaerobe *Clostridium thermosaccharolyticum;* and the thermophilic anaerobes which produce hydrogen sulfide spoilage, i.e., *Desulfotomaculum nigrificans.*

In general, there are no microbial standards by which the suitability of ingredients for use in canning may be measured. An exception to this are the standards suggested by the National Food Processors Association for thermophilic spore contamination of sugar and starch to be used in low-acid, heat processed canned foods. Those standards follow.

STANDARDS FOR SUGARS AND SYRUPS

Sugars

Granulated sugar, as well as starch, bought under American Bottlers of Carbonated Beverage Association or National Food Processors Association specifications, meets standards for low thermophile count.

1. Standards for thermophilic spore count "for five samples examined, there shall be a maximum of not more than 150 spores per 10 grams of sugar".
2. Flat sour spores "for five samples examined, there shall be a maximum of not more than 75 spores and an average of not more than 50 spores per 10 grams of sugar".
3. Thermophilic anaerobic spores "shall be present in not more than three (60%) of the five samples of starch and in any one sample to the extent of not more than four (65+%) of six tubes inoculated by the standard procedure.
4. Sulfide spoilage spores shall be present in not more than two of the five samples and in any one sample of starch to the extent of not more than two of the five samples and in any one sample of starch to the extent of not more than five colonies per 10 grams. This is equivalent to two colonies in six tubes.

Because NFPA is primarily concerned with canning operations, standards emphasize thermophilic type bacteria; yeast and molds would be killed in the canning process.

Since the process for producing crystalline dextrose at the crystallization step is very similar to that of producing granulated sucrose, the microbiological background is similar. Dextrose producers can routinely meet NFPA and NSDA standards set for sucrose.

Crystalline sugars, in their normal dry state in bags or in other suitable containers, are microbiologically stable if kept dry; low levels of moisture preclude growth of microorganisms.

Syrups

Syrups present a somewhat different microbiological situation than dry sugars; moisture content and wide variety creates a complex situation. The higher the solids content of a syrup, the less tendency there is to microbiological spoilage; conversely, the lower the solids, the greater susceptibility to mold growth. Of course, there are exceptions to these general rules. Osmotic pressure is the explanation for this differential behavior of microbes in syrups.

Corn syrups are produced in a wide range of types; they can vary from a high of 95 dextrose equivalence (D.E.) plus to a low of 20 D.E. Syrups derived from corn below 20 D.E. are designated malto-dextrin syrup. Solids content of all of these corn syrups can vary on a commercial basis from 70–84% solids, depending on handling characteristics and crystallization tendencies. These syrups have a low microbiological profile if handled properly in transit and in plant storage facilities.

Corn syrups are often purchased with a microbiological specification; a typical requirement would be a total plate count of 1,000 per gram maximum and with yeast and molds at 100 per gram maximum for each. Product used by bottlers would require the same NSDA levels as dry sugar and canners would apply NFPA specifications for thermophiles.

Syrups derived from sucrose fall into three general types: liquid sucrose, invert syrups, and molasses. Invert syrup differs from liquid sucrose in that a portion of up to 50% of sucrose is hydrolyzed to dextrose and levulose to allow a higher solids syrup to be produced. This higher solids content gives the syrup better protection against most microorganisms.

Liquid sucrose and invert syrups are produced at low counts and routinely meet requirements for NSDA and NFPA specs. If proper handling facilities are available, these syrups have excellent storage life.

Molasses, a byproduct, can have wide variations in microbiological background. If a good food grade type molasses is purchased, no microbiological problems should be experienced.

Honey is a natural syrup worthy of consideration; even though no particular precautions are taken, honey is generally free of microbiological problems. When a rare fermentation problem is encountered with honey, it is usually attributed to a *Zygosaccharomyces* or *Torula* type yeast.

In the production of table or fountain syrups, classified as mixed syrups, a pasteurization step is usually carried out. This involves heating to 190°F (88°C) and packaging at this temperature. Containers are then inverted to heat the top of the container. Low levels of potassium sorbate or sodium benzoate may be added to protect the syrup after opening.

Some mixed syrups are cold packed; in these instances, the component ingredients must be relatively "clean" and great care exercised to avoid contamination during processing. It is imperative that an inhibitor is used in this type of operation. Even with this protection, these types of syrups can occasionally ferment.

Bulk handling systems for all types of syrups have certain basic requirements. Tanks can be of mild steel with a suitable food grade epoxy coating, stainless steel or fiber glass construction. These tanks should have an air filter-blower system to assure proper air flow over the head space in the tank, or condensation can occur, diluting the syrup at the surface and making it more susceptible to microbial activity, usually yeasts. Once started, a fermentation of this sort will spread throughout the tank.

With syrups at lower solids levels, such as 67–75% solids, it is strongly recommended that incoming air to the tank be passed over an ultraviolet lamp to give further protection. Samples of sugars and syrups should be analyzed occasionally.

References

FPI. 1988. *Canned Foods – Principles of Thermal Process Control, Acidification and Container Closure Evaluation*, 5th Ed. The Food Processors Institute, Washington, DC.

Jay, J. M. 1992. *Modern Food Microbiology*, 4th Ed. AVI Book, Van Nostrand Reinhold, New York.

McClure, P. J., Cole, M. B. and Smelt, J. P. P. M. 1994. "Effects of water activity and pH on growth of *Clostridium botulinum*." *Journal of Applied Bacteriology*, Symposium Supplement 76: 105S-114S.

Rhodehamel, E. J., Reddy, N. R. and Pierson, M. D. 1992. "Botulism: the causative agent and its control in foods." *Food Control* 3(3): 125-143.

CHAPTER 2

Heat Penetration Determinations and Thermal Process Calculations

In 1917, the use of thermocouples in the U.S. was introduced by the National Canners Association, now the National Food Processors Association, to measure temperatures during heating and cooling of foods in sealed containers. This led to graphic mathematical and computerized procedures that are employed to estimate the minimum heat required to produce "commercially sterile" food without excessive damage to their eating quality or nutritional value.

Since that time, progressive scientific, technologic, and engineering improvements have been achieved in canning equipment. Although the conventional still retort remains a widely accepted method for heat processing, it is rapidly losing popularity in favor of more recently developed agitating cookers, hydrostatic cookers, and aseptic processing equipment.

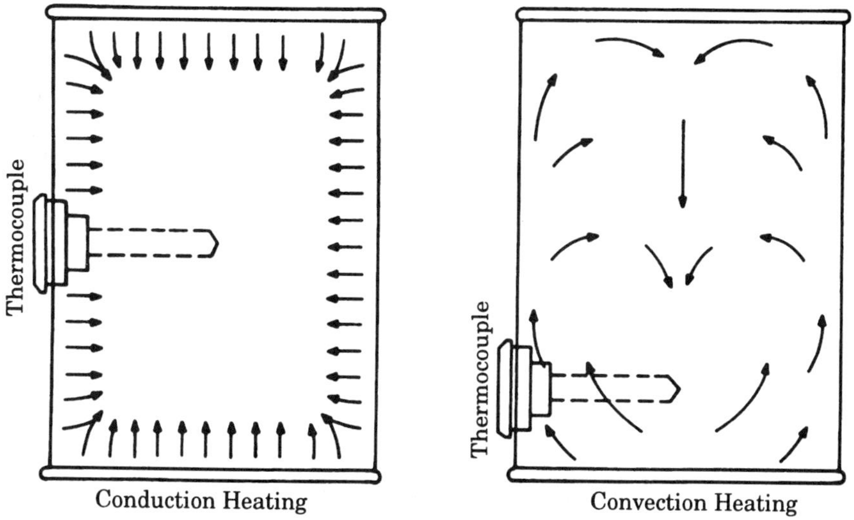

FIGURE 2.1 – Mechanism of Heat Penetration

Except in aseptic canning, the food being processed in a hermetically sealed container must be heated throughout by employing an external source of heat. If the food is a liquid (broth) or contains a liquid of low viscosity (brine peas), the heat is distributed via convection. If it is a solid (meat, fish) or highly viscous (cream style corn), it can be heated only via conduction; as a result, the greater portion of the contents must be severely over-processed in order to sterilize the small volume occupying the geometric center.

Agitation during cooking (axial or end-over-end) may effectively reduce the times and temperatures required for safe processing of some viscous foods as a result of the stirring action and the elimination of conduction as the sole mode of heat transfer. In addition, processing at higher temperatures for shorter periods of time effectively reduces damage to quality while achieving commercial sterility. Hence, increasing interest is being devoted to continuous rotary cookers, discontinuous high-temperature rotary cookers, open-flame processing, and hydrostatic cookers. A pressurized chamber processing method has been introduced that permits the filling of low-acid foods at a high temperature into containers without the danger of flashing. The foods are quickly sterilized by passage through heat exchangers, canned in a pressurized chamber to prevent boiling, held for a prescribed time in the chamber to achieve sterility of can and contents, and cooled as the cans are ejected from the chamber. Aseptic canning, a special application of high-temperature-short time (HTST) processing is now rather commonplace and is particularly useful in processing foods that are easily damaged by heat.

Each of these technological and engineering improvements, in turn, opens up new possibilities in the variety of foods that can be preserved through heat processing. On the other hand, each imposes upon the processor the necessity for more stringent and sophisticated procedures to assure adequate control. Furthermore, the newer heat processing methods are being employed for the production of high quality formulated foods that were not possible to produce using the conventional still retort. Many of these formulated foods are designed to be consumed without further heating, which, in itself, imposes the need for the processor to exercise greater stringency in order to assure product sterility. These processes are discussed in more detail in the section on sterilization systems.

pH Classification of Canned Foods

Canned foods may be classified into two categories based upon pH and acidity, and on the necessary thermal processing required to effect safety as well as microbiological stability:

(a) Low Acid – above 4.6

(b) High Acid – 4.6 or lower

The low-acid category is the only one of importance from the standpoint of the botulinal hazard. No *Clostridium botulinum* spore, regardless of type, has been detected that will germinate, grow, and produce toxin in a food having a pH of 4.7 or lower. Foods in the low-acid range must be fully retorted to assure safety; this is sometimes referred to as a botulinum cook.

The U.S. Food and Drug Administration has promulgated regulations designed to control production of low-acid canned foods. The regulations among other things: (a) provide for the registration of all firms producing low acid canned foods; (b) provide for the filing by each firm of a detailed description of the heat processes used for each low-acid food in each container size (scheduled process); (c) define good manufacturing practices in the processing of low-acid canned foods; (d) require establishments that fail to comply with the regulations to operate under emergency permit control of the Food and Drug Administration. These regulatory controls should serve to further assure the safety of canned foods.

Those foods in the high acid range (pH 4.6 or lower) generally require a considerably lower heat processing to effect preservation, since the processing schedule is primarily designed to kill all vegetative cells. A few spore bearing bacteria, particularly *Clostridium butiricum*, *Bacillus coagulans*, and related species, are able to grow in foods having a pH value as low as 4.1. They have no known public health significance however, and the food processor has learned to prevent spoilages of this nature by employing food sanitation practices to reduce the initial spore load of the food combined with appropriate heat processing schedules.

Foods with a pH lower than 4.0 require only pasteurization or a "hot-fill" to effect stability.

Spores of the fungus *Byssochlamys fulva* are relatively heat resistant and at times spoilage is encountered as the result of survival and growth of these microorganisms even in foods with a pH value lower than 4.0. The fungus can grow extensively at relatively low oxygen tensions. Spoilage of this nature is encountered in some canned fruits and fruit juices, particularly grape juice.

It should be realized that there are no sharp boundaries between these two food classifications. In general, bacterial spores become progressively more sensitive to heat with increasing acidity. For example, it is well known that some foods, such as tomatoes and figs, may be treated as acid foods, even at pH values as high as 4.9, and yet present no botulinal hazard, even though they receive a relatively low heat processing treatment. In addition to the degree of acidity, nutritional adequacy of the food for germination and outgrowth of the *Clostridium botulinum* spores appears to be an important consideration.

High-Temperature Short-Time Processing

New methods for heat processing canned foods (continuous and discontinuous agitating cookers, hydrostatic cookers, open flame cookers), particularly the HTST methods, impose even greater demands for strict controls. Furthermore, the multiplicity of new ingredients on the market for the formulation of new canned foods necessitates more rigid control during production. The canner who wants to take advantage of higher quality products or to formulate new products to be cooked by these processes must have trained supervisors who thoroughly understand the principles underlying these procedures and who appreciate the significance of any change of ingredients or operation. These supervisors must institute adequate control procedures and install suitable instrumentation to assure the manufacture of a safe product. The following are critical points that must be included in an effective quality control program for food processed by one of the HTST methods:

(a) The formula of the product and the character ingredients must be constant since the heat process is designed for a very specific set of conditions. If any of these ingredients is changed, the heating parameters of the product must be changed and a new time and temperature process is required for product safety.

(b) The consistency of each batch of product must be measured, controlled, and recorded. If the consistency changes during heat processing, the change must be taken into consideration in establishing a safe process. A procedure to lower the consistency of a given batch as it is made up or provisions for correcting mistakes in formulation must be available. If variations in ingredients cause the batch to be too thick for appropriate agitation, adding water may be appropriate as a corrective measure.

(c) An experimentally inoculated pack must be made before initial start-up of any processing line to produce a newly formulated product for which there are insufficient processing data. Known members of bacterial spores having a predetermined heat resistance in the specific product are added to the formulated food, and then the product is heat processed through the line at selected times and/or temperatures to yield greater thermal processing values. Attempts are made to select processing values to assure some spoilage by the added spores at the lower processing levels. From the results obtained, combined with heat penetration data, a safe processing schedule can be estimated. The inoculated pack results must confirm the theoretical calculated process derived from the heat penetration data.

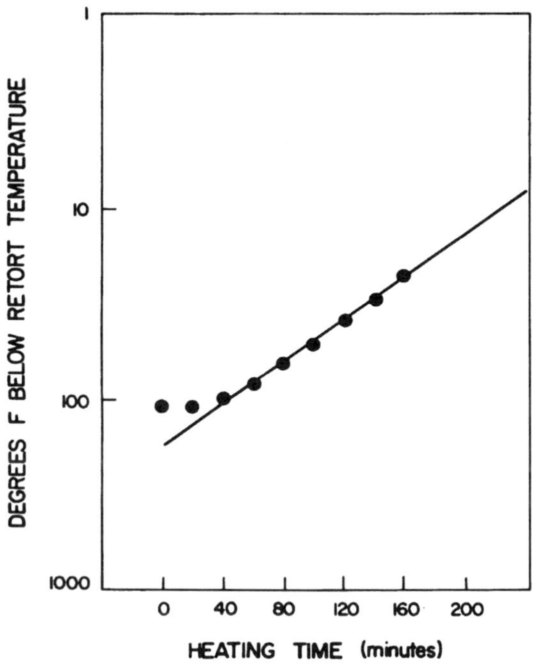

FIGURE 2.2 – Heat penetration curve for pea puree in 603x700 can "still retorted" at 252°F.

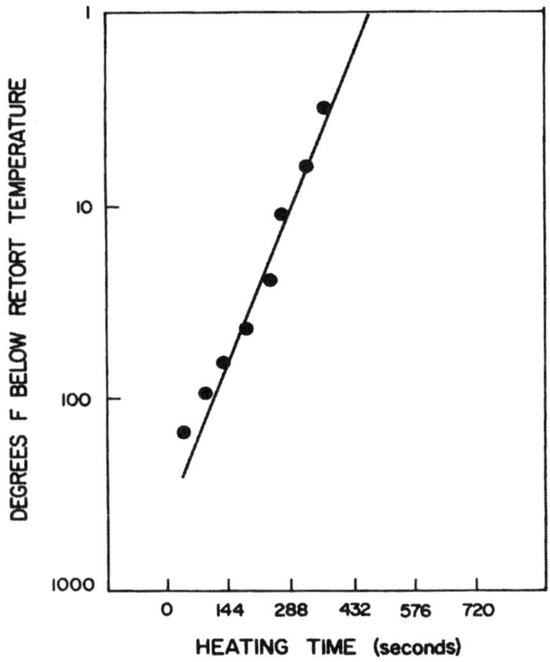

FIGURE 2.3 – Heat penetration curve for peas in brine in 307x409 can "still retorted" at 252°F.

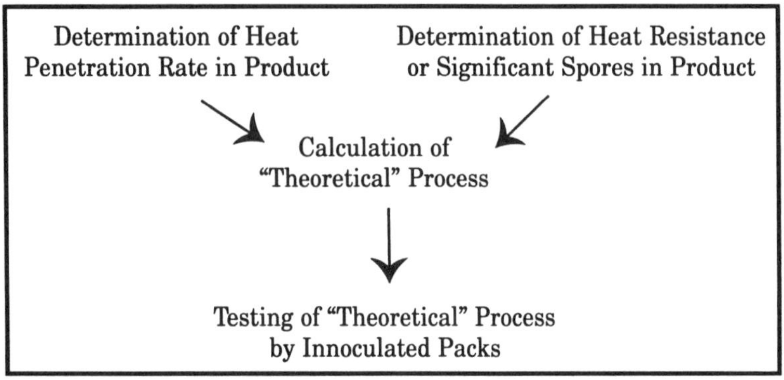

FIGURE 2.4 – Process Determination for Low-Acid Products

The most common spores employed in inoculated pack studies are those obtained from the putrefactive anaerobe, *Clostridium sporogenes*, NFPA strain 3679 (P.A. 3670). This microorganism possesses characteristics quite similar to *Clostridium botulinum* except that it does not produce a toxin. Spores are harvested from a culture grown in a laboratory medium under conditions known to yield spores having a heat resistance slightly greater than the most heat resistant *Clostridium botulinum* spore. To conduct a test on the inoculated pack, a formulated food is generally inoculated with enough of the spore suspension to yield at least 10,000 viable spores per container.

The following considerations must be taken into account:

(a) The inoculated pack studies should be conducted in the actual processing equipment to be used for the commercial production of the food. Data obtained solely from pilot line equipment are inadequate.

(b) If the formulated food contains a dry ingredient (spaghetti, macaroni, noodles, tapioca), spores used for the inoculated pack should be incorporated into the dry ingredient as fabricated. A representative portion of the inoculated dry ingredient is then added to the formula to yield the desired initial spore count. Care should be taken to ensure that the inoculated dry ingredient has rehydration characteristics similar to the ingredient that will be used commercially, and that the individual particle size is as large as, or larger than, any found in the commercially available material.

(c) It is well known that spores are more resistant to dry than to wet heat. Therefore, it is necessary to heat process the product adequately after the dry ingredient has been rehydrated in order to ensure safety. Clumping of spores or product, and other physical barriers to heat penetration, must be avoided. Failure to adequately control the above factors may require a more severe process, thus defeating the main advantage of the HTST system.

(d) The filler bowl temperature for the formulated product should be controlled. In addition, when the cook is started, the initial temperature (IT) of the product must be controlled and recorded. In the event of delays due to line breakdown or other causes resulting in low IT, the ensuing thermal process must be adjusted to compensate.

(e) Container headspace must be positively controlled. In high speed agitating cookers, dependence is placed upon the bubble from the headspace to stir the product, thus simulating a convection heat process. Therefore, constancy of bubble size must be maintained. Controlling headspace by determining container weight is not adequate in most instances because of variations in specific gravity of the product. Precautions must be taken to avoid incorporation of air into the product, since this will affect the headspace needed to achieve the desired weight. In order to assure constancy of agitation, the ratio of solid to liquid must be controlled.

(f) While the product is in an agitating cooker, the time and temperature of the cook, as well as the rotation speed of the cooker, must be controlled and recorded. Specific precautions must be followed to avoid inadvertent changes in time, temperature, or rotational speed of the cooker.

(g) Any canner who installs a new high speed system to produce new products, or to increase production of an existing product, must take into account the capacity of preparation facilities.

The development of new systems, techniques, and formulations for new canned products is inevitable. However, it is necessary that the canner and his research, development, and quality assurance staff devise appropriate control and monitoring procedures and devices for the following factors: formula, consistence, initial temperature, headspace, processing time, processing temperature, and rotation speed of the cooker.

Regardless of the canning technique employed to process low-acid canned foods, failure to achieve commercial sterility in any lot may result from failure to recognize certain product characteristics or operating conditions that effect lethality. Ideally, fail-safe procedures should be devised to assure that commercial sterility is achieved. Although much progress has been made, it is highly unlikely that significant improvements can be made within the foreseeable future, and it will be necessary to continue to rely upon rigid adherence to control procedures.

Thermal Death Time

Safety from botulism in canned low-acid foods stems from the pioneering research done by scientists of the National Food Processors Association in the early 1920s. They determined the thermal resistance of spores harvested from the most heat resistant *Clostridium botulinum* strain known to them. Their studies demonstrated that, by extrapolation from the exponential survival curve, it was necessary to heat a spore suspension in phosphate buffer for 2.78 minutes at 250°F (121°C) to reduce the survival population from about 10^{11} spore/unit to less than one spore/unit; from this study came the 12-D concept (12 decimal reductions in survival population). Later, a correction in come-up time resulted in the amendment of that heating time to 2.45 minutes to achieve the same lethal effect.

Data on thermal death times combined with heat penetration studies can be employed to calculate a safe heat process for any food to be canned. To calculate the process, the graphic method, the nomogram method, or the formula method may be employed; other methods may also may be used; computer programs to calculate processes based on the formula method of Ball are also available. To further substantiate the adequacy of the process, experimental inoculated pack studies can be performed using bacterial spore suspensions of known heat resistance. The manner of performing the inoculated pack studies is prescribed in the Laboratory Manual for Food Canners and Processors, published by the National Canners Association in 1968. Inoculated packs are especially useful in determining the adequacy of the thermal process for any new formulated food, and particularly if one of the HTST processing methods is being employed.

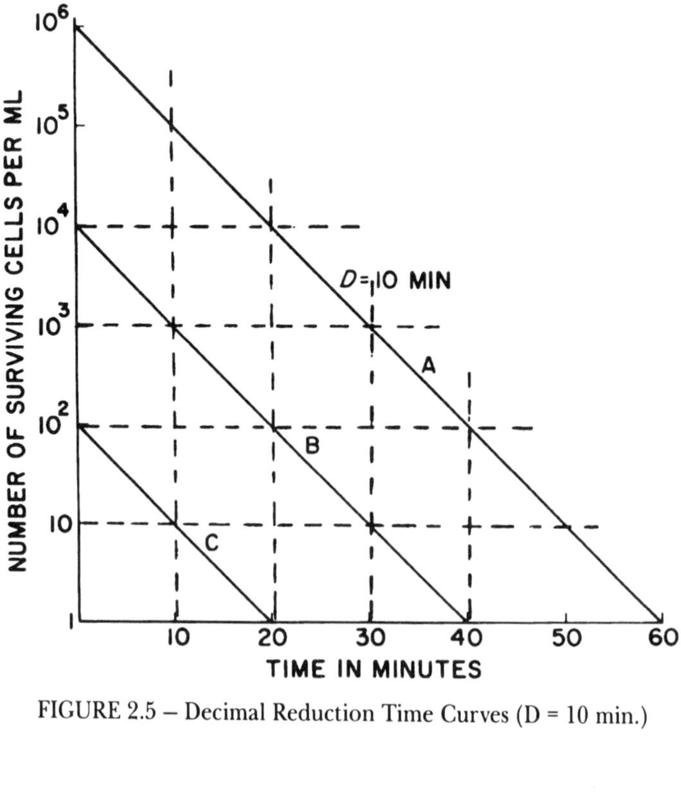

FIGURE 2.5 – Decimal Reduction Time Curves (D = 10 min.)

In conducting thermal death time studies on spore suspensions, the logarithmic survival curve permits determination of decimal reduction values (D values), the time in minutes at constant temperature necessary to destroy 90% of the spores. By plotting determined D values on a logarithmic scale against temperature on a linear scale, a so-called phantom thermal death time curve can be constructed. From this plot, the z value can be obtained which, in essence, is the negative inverse of the slope of the phantom curve and represents the number of degrees Fahrenheit required for the curve to traverse one logarithmic cycle. In other words, the z value denotes the degrees Fahrenheit required to effect a tenfold change in time to achieve the same lethal effect.

The sterilizing value of a process is generally expressed as the F_0 value which is equivalent to the number of minutes required to destroy a specified number of spores at 250°F (121°C) when z equals 18.

The z value for *Clostridium botulinum* spores is generally regarded to be 18 while the time required at 250 °F (121 °C) to reduce the survival population by a factor of 12 decimal values (12 D) in a phosphate buffer is 2.45 minutes (F_0 = 2.45 or F^{18}_{250} = 2.45). The z value indicates, for example, that at 232 °F (250 minus 18), 24.5 minutes heating would be required to achieve the same lethal effect.

FIGURE 2.6 – Mini-Retort System for TDT Determination Using Specially Designed 208 x 006 TDT Cans.
Cans available from American Can Company, Barrington, IL. System designed by National Food Processors Association, and shown in operation at Virginia Polytechic Institute and State University, Blacksburg, VA. (Photo by Anthony Lopez)

FIGURE 2.7 – Close-up View of Two of the Six Mini-Retorts in the Mini-Retort System for TDT Determination (Photo by Anthony Lopez)

Theoretically, spore concentration (numbers per unit volume) does not influence the amount of heat necessary to achieve an equivalent lethal effect on a given spore load. For example, whether 10^{12} spores are distributed among 1,000 containers, or 1 spore residues in each of 10^{12} containers, each container should have to receive the same thermal process to effect an equivalent reduction in the total initial spore population.

While adherence to the 12-D concept for the thermal processing of low-acid foods might appear to be excessively conservative, it has served the canning industry well in minimizing the incidence of botulism. Where accidents have occurred, the 12-D concept had been violated (except in one instance involving a can defect). In actual practice, most thermal processes are calculated to provide additional safety; few recommended processes for canned low-acid foods (other than cured meats) provide for an F_0 value of less than 3.0.

FIGURE 2.8 – Retort Baskets and 208 x 006 TDT Cans Used in Mini-Retort System for TDT Determination (Photo by Anthony Lopez)

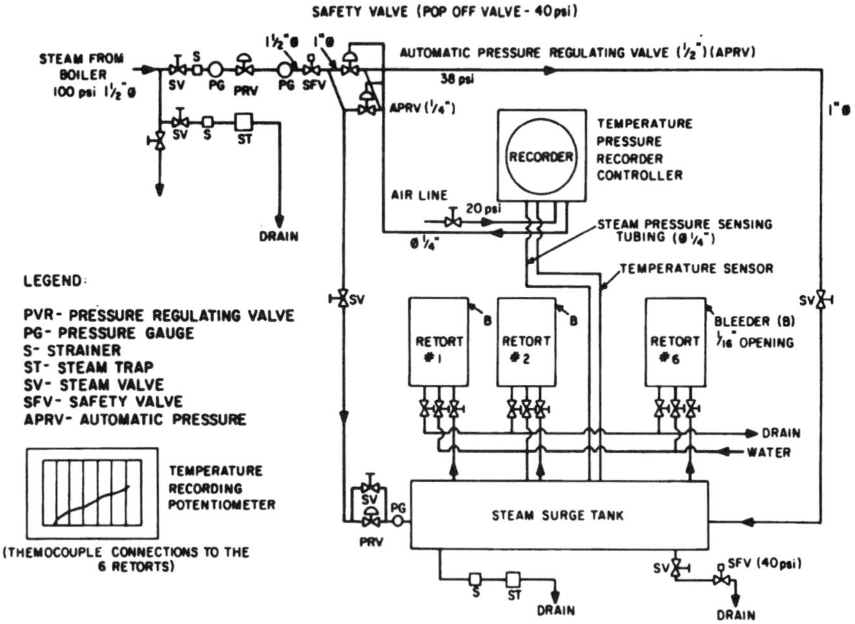

FIGURE 2.9 – Diagram of Mini-Retort System for TDT Determination

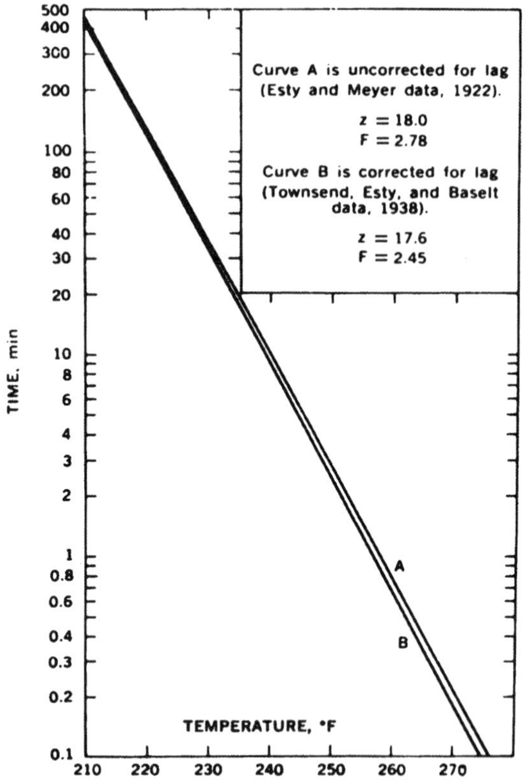

FIGURE 2.10 – Classical Thermal Death Time Curve for *Clostridium botulinum*

Over and above safety considerations, several non-toxin bacterial species are known to occur that produce spores with heat resistances significantly higher than *Clostridium botulinum* spores. To cope with these potential spoilage microorganisms (both mesophyllic and thermophilic) the canner generally chooses to process many low-acid foods at values significantly higher than those required to achieve safety. Other foods may receive even higher processing levels to achieve a desirable texture. In such instances, the 12-D concept is of no consequence except in evaluating safety of a particular lot of such foods that has received an inadvertent under-process.

Most recommended thermal processes for foods subjected to one of the HTST methods (such as in aseptic canning) provide for F_0 values substantially higher than those used for in-can processes. Such high processing schedules are feasible because of the decreased impairment to quality of the foods subjected to high temperatures for a very short time. Because of the importance of a few seconds or minor temperature fluctuations at the high sterilizing temperatures, a reasonable margin above the minimum processing values is required to insure a safe process.

HEAT PENETRATION DETERMINATIONS

Obtaining accurate data regarding the heating and/or cooling of a food in a container is extremely important if an accurate time and temperature for product sterilization is to be determined. The results of a heat penetration test are experimentally derived heating and cooling curves. The type of curve obtained is dependent upon the kind of product involved. Parameters obtained from the data plot are dependent upon the manner in which data are plotted and interpreted.

Factors influencing rate of heat penetration:

1. Processing (retort) temperature (RT)
2. Agitation of containers during sterilization
3. Container orientation in retort
4. Size and shape of container
5. Material of which container is made
6. Headspace
7. Fill-in weight
8. Method of product preparation
9. Ratio of solid to liquid
10. Kind, size, shape, and arrangement of particles
11. Consistency of product
12. Initial product temperature (IT)
13. Heating medium

A discussion of the equipment needed to carry out a heat penetration test, of a procedure for making a heat penetration test, and a description of heat penetration curves follows.

Equipment

Retort: The retort must be capable of simulating the desired type of processing operation – agitating, hydrostatic, or still– for the data obtained to be utilized in designing a process. A properly installed and operated retort is a must for obtaining satisfactory heat penetration results. It must have a sufficient steam supply to enable it to come to retort temperature in a reasonable time. The vents must be large enough to enable air to be removed from the retort during the venting period. The vent required for the retort should be determined, if necessary, from heat distribution tests. The water supply to the retort should be sufficient to allow cooling in a reasonable time. If overriding air pressure is to be used for pressure cooling, processing of glass containers or retort pouches, an adequate air supply should be provided. The retort should be equipped with an accurate mercury-in-glass thermometer the temperature range which does not exceed 17°F per inch (3.5°C/cm) of graduated scale; scale divisions should be no more than 2°F (1°C). The temperature range should adequately encompass the process temperature to be used, and the thermometer should be installed where it can be accurately and easily read.

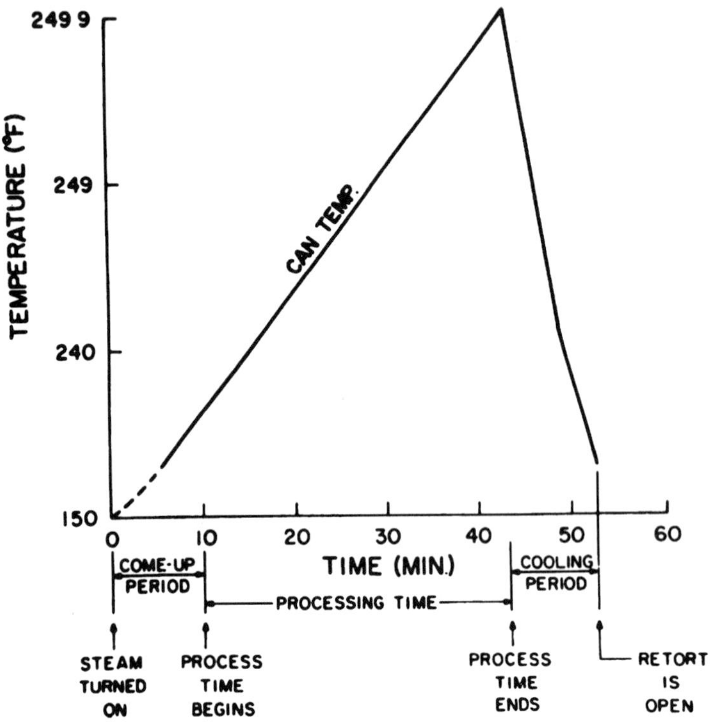

FIGURE 2.11 – Heat Penetration Curve for Can at Cold Point and Retort Temperature (Drawn on semi-log graph paper)

The retort should be equipped with an automatic steam controller to maintain retort temperature. The retort should also have an accurate temperature recording device. The recorder may be combined with a steam controller and be a recording-controlling instrument; it should be adjusted to be in reasonable agreement with a known accurate mercury-in-glass thermometer.

The retort should have a safety valve large enough to prevent excess pressure inside; it should comply with appropriate local, state and national safety codes.

Thermocouples: Scientists of the National Food Processors Association were, in 1917, one of the first to utilize thermocouples for measuring the temperature profile of the canned product. Improvements were made in thermocouple design by a number of individuals until Ecklund, of the American Can Company, designed in 1949 the non-projecting plug-in thermocouple. This type thermocouple is now the most widely used thermocouple in the industry; it is used because the thermocouple can be placed in the container before it is filled with food. Cans can be sealed on commercial seaming equipment with thermocouples in place. Non-projecting type thermocouples and accessories may be obtained from: Ecklund-Harrison Technologies, Inc., 11000/38 Metro Parkway, Fort Myers, FL 33912.

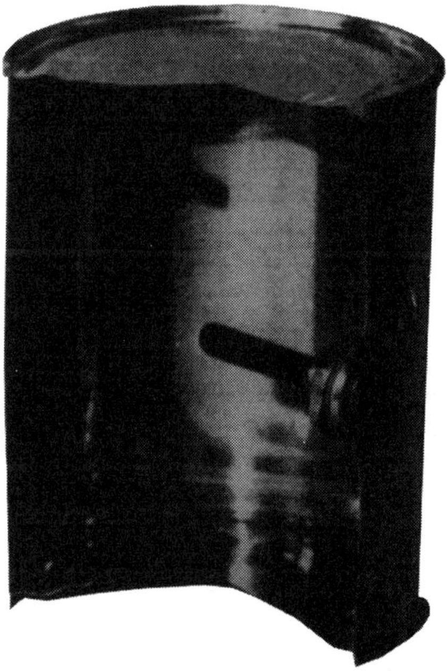

FIGURE 2.12 – Non-Projecting Type Thermocouple (Ecklund)

A thermocouple occurs when wires of two dissimilar metals are joined so that a thermal electromotive force is produced when the junctions are at different temperatures. The resultant electromotive force developed by the thermocouples used by the canning industry is of the order of 5 millivolts or less for a temperature difference between the junctions of 180°F (100°C) or less. In the canning industry, copper-constantan thermocouple systems are the most widely used. If couples are to be fabricated, care should be taken to ensure that the wires are fully cleaned before the junction is formed; the joint may be made by welding the wires together or twisting the wires and soldering them. If wires are twisted, care should be taken to insure that wire contact is short, as a junction is formed at the contact areas; if the twisted area is long, it could contribute to inaccurate temperature measurements. Appropriate tests should be made to determine the effect of errors introduced by conduction of heat along the thermocouple wires and by the fittings required to hold the thermocouple in place. Ecklund, in 1956, published these correction factors for 307 x 409 (87.3 x 115.9 mm) and smaller cans for his thermocouples.

Thermocouples may be bare except for the insulation around the wire found in flexible type thermocouples or they may be enclosed in a stainless steel sheath, Bakelite, or phenolic rod. There are occasions when grounding of the thermocouple is necessary to prevent erroneous data from being gathered; a ground can eliminate stray electrical currents which cause erroneous signal development giving an erroneous data point. Although grounding is not normally necessary when measuring heat penetration in hermetically sealed containers, it is valuable to ground a thermocouple when measuring the heat penetration into flexible retort pouches. The use of isolated junction thermocouples (Ecklund) has been shown to eliminate the need for grounding and to give more accurate readings.

It is important that the potentiometer be properly grounded to prevent interference from power circuits.

Extension wires, connectors – For accurate measurements, wires should be homogeneous, stressed and well insulated from each other, except at junctions. Under ideal conditions, the same wire will extend from the measuring to the reference thermocouple junction. Since this is not practical under most conditions, usually one or more extension wires and connectors are utilized. Extension wires should be similar to those utilized in manufacturing the thermocouples.

Wires may be joined by a variety of means, if they can be joined by welding, care must be taken to ensure that the same wire is utilized throughout. Since low voltage signals are received, care must be given to pick appropriate connectors and switches to ensure that the signal is not disrupted.

Wires may be joined to the thermocouples by welding or, in the case of the plug-in thermocouples male connectors, the connection point crimped after wire insertion. However, crimped connections tend to corrode in time and give erratic results. Soldering the copper connection is not appreciably detrimental. Welding is preferred for constantan connections, but special techniques of soldering (to eliminate temperature differentials in the solder) can be satisfactory. The extension wire may be connected to the potentiometer using jack-type connections or screw type terminals; in making these connections, care should be taken to see that the wires are clean at the connection point.

Fitting wires through the retort shell – Extension wires should lead from the retort in such a manner that steam is not lost during the process. While this can be accomplished by laying wires over the door or gasket of the retort, it is not recommended because of the danger of severing wire, fraying insulation and getting condensate running down the wire to the potentiometer.

A second and more preferable method is to lead the wires through a stuffing box which may be purchased commercially or fabricated in the manner suggested by the NCA Laboratory Manual (1968). The manual suggests a threaded 2-inch (5 cm) opening in the retort shell near the door into which is placed a $2^1/_2$ x 8 x 8" (6.4 x 20 x 20 cm) steel plate with a 2" (5 cm) opening into which is welded a 2" (5 cm) nipple. This plate has half inch (13 mm) steel bolts welded about $1^1/_2$" (38 mm) from the corner. A neoprene backed foam rubber gasket is placed on the inside of the plate, held in place by running the bolts through the gasket. The wires are run through the opening and are spread out singly over the gasket. A cover plate, with the gasket on the inside, is then bolted into place to hold the wires and prevent steam from escaping. Ecklund supplies stuffing boxes with a swivel feature that permits installing the cable in the retort without twisting the cable; these are available in $^3/_4$ and 1-inch (19 and 25 mm) pipe sizes. The purchase of a completely fabricated cable will eliminate many of the problems encountered in a "first-time" installation.

Potentiometers – A manually operated potentiometer may be used for measuring temperature during a heat penetration test. If several thermocouples are to be read, they should be connected to a multi-channel switch which is in turn connected to the potentiometer. The calibration for this potentiometer should be in degrees F, the divisions in 1-2°F (0.5-1°C). The potentiometer should be automatically compensated for temperature.

These potentiometers have the advantage of lower initial cost, lighter weight, and small size making them portable. They have the disadvantage that only a small number of meaningful points can be read per minute. They may require two people for satisfactory operation, one person to operate the switch and the other to operate the potentiometer and record the readings.

Electronic self-balancing potentiometers are also utilized; these are usually multi-channeled strip-chart temperature measuring and recording potentiometers. These instruments are manufactured to mate with a special thermocouple type and usually have automatic reference junction compensation; calibration should be in degrees F and chart division of 1-2°F (0.5-1°C). These potentiometers cost more than manual potentiometers, are larger and heavier, although they can be made portable. The heat penetration test can be carried out by one individual as the instrument automatically records the temperature registered by each thermocouple in the test; a permanent record of the data accumulated is automatically provided.

Data logging systems have a multi-channel temperature measurement combined with digital data output; these instruments are manufactured to mate with specific thermocouple types. A digital data output makes data gathering easier and opens up the possibility of direct analyses of heat penetration data by a computer. This system also enables numerous measurements of many different temperatures within the span of a minute enhancing computer data analysis. This equipment is composed of delicate electronic gear and is the most expensive of the potentiometers described. Although portable, it should be handled with care.

Procedure for Making a Heat Penetration (HP) Test

Heat penetration tests should be conducted on product which is the same in product characteristics and formulation as the final commercial product. If preliminary studies are conducted on prototype product, results should be verified on the final formulated product.

Equipment Check

Prior to starting of a test, the equipment should be checked to be sure it is in proper working order.

(1) The retort selected for the test should vent properly and have the capability of uniformly controlling the processing temperature.
(2) A known accurate mercury-in-glass thermometer should be installed.
(3) An adequate grounding check should be conducted.
(4) Adequate warm up time for electrical components allowed.
(5) The potentiometer located in a dry and steam-free area, if possible.
(6) Water does not reach or wet the panel or switches of the potentiometer.
(7) The timing system should be checked.
(8) All thermocouple and connector plugs cleaned and spread to assure good electrical contact.
(9) Thermocouple wires and connectors should be numbered to enable correlation of potentiometer readings with specific thermocouples in the retort.
(10) The cans used should be numbered and correlated with numbered thermocouple wires.
(11) Location, type, and size of thermocouple used in the test cans recorded.
(12) Retorts should be brought to processing temperature, and
    (a) retort controller operation checked and the desired HP processing temperature set
    (b) thermocouples placed in steam and compared to a known accurate mercury-in-glass thermometer. If they are not in agreement, corrected and rechecked.

Making the Heat Penetration Test

If tests are to be conducted in a commercial canning plant, test cans should first be distinctively marked.

Holes are punched, usually in the side of a can. The thermocouples are inserted into the test can. The cans are then filled with product and seamed. If the product is new and its heating characteristics unknown, a cold (critical) point run should be made to determine the location of its slowest heating zone. This should be done with one or more preliminary runs with thermocouples located in different positions. The data should demonstrate that the cold point has been bracketed between faster heating zones.

For convection heating products, the slowest heating zone in containers processed in a vertical position is about $^3/_4$" (19 mm) above the bottom of the longitudinal axis of small containers, and about $1^1/_2$" (38 mm) above the bottom for large containers, such as size 603 x 700 (157 x 178 mm) cans. For conduction heating products, the slowest heating zone is in the geometric center of the conduction heating product mass. For products which exhibit broken heating curves, the slowest heating zone will usually be between the geometric center of the can and the slowest point for convection heating for the can size tested. For products with unusual characteristics, for example those with large pieces, food in layers, or bundles, care must be taken in establishing the coldest heating zone.

There are a number of variables which may affect the heating rate including fill, product consistency, ratio of solids to liquid, the kind, size and arrangement of particles, method of product preparation, container orientation, size of container, and container headspace. The effect that these variables may have on the heat penetration may depend on the product, container, and type of retort system utilized. Sufficient information should be gathered regarding the critical variables and subsequent tests made in conformance with standardized values.

Once the cold spot has been determined, confirming heat penetration tests should be conducted. Sufficient tests should be run so that satisfactory data can be obtained; this may require several runs for products showing considerable variations.

The test retort should be operated in a manner consistent with good commercial practice. One thermocouple should be placed in the retort to measure the retort temperature outside of the can in the area where the cans are placed in the retort; it should not touch any metallic surface. The temperature from this couple is used as a reference in plotting the heating data.

The closed container, with the thermocouple in place, should be shaken to give a uniform temperature throughout. It has been shown that heating curves may appear distorted if temperatures within test cans are initially non-uniform.

The thermocouples should then be plugged in and cans placed in the retort, all in the same general area and the potentiometer switched on to record the initial temperature of each container. The retort should then be closed and the steam turned on. The chart should be marked at this time at the 0 time; any back-up timing device, if used, should be started. The timing of tests starts when the steam is turned on. The vent time and temperature should be noted as well as the time to reach retort temperature. Theoretically, the temperature indicated on the mercury in glass thermometer should be recorded. Thermocouple readings for each can should be sufficiently frequent to construct an accurate heat penetration curve; this may be as frequent as every minute for rapidly heating products or as infrequent as every 10-20 minutes for extremely slow heating cans. The test should continue until can thermocouples are within 2 degrees of retort temperature; at this point, container cooling may begin. If cooling data are required, it may be necessary to run additional tests using the appropriately calculated process time. If this is not done, accurate cooling data may not be acquired because the product in the can may be at a different temperature. Cooling data should be accumulated until the temperatures are in the logarithmic portion of the cooling curve.

A heat penetration test is not complete until the test cans have been examined for factors which could affect the heating rate such as can vacuum, headspace, syrup strength, thermocouple location, drained weight, fill weight, etc. Measurement of other factors such as pH should also be made.

SOME CAUSES OF UNRELIABLE HEAT PENETRATION DATA

The following is a partial list of some factors that have been associated with unreliable heat penetration data.

1. Thermocouple readings not continued for a sufficient length of time to adequately define heating rate or rates.
2. Heat penetration test conducted in a retort load of commercial production and stopped at the end of the scheduled process for quality determinations, rather than continued long enough to obtain sufficient data.
3. Frequency of readings not sufficient to obtain accurate heating rate or rates.
4. Erroneous temperatures received as a result of inadequate electrical grounding of potentiometer.
5. No initial temperatures taken on the test cans.
6. No notation of retort come-up time, or come-up time significantly different from that used in commercial practice.
7. Multiple thermocouples in small cans of product.
8. No cold spot study, or insufficient number of replicates at the cold spot thermocouple location.

9. No time notation on temperature recorder.
10. No notation of "steam on" for test.
11. No free-lead reference.
12. No mercury thermometer readings.
13. Erratic processing temperature control during test.
14. Critical factors associated with product and processing system not recorded and controlled.
15. Large temperature disagreement between thermocouple free lead and mercury thermometer.
16. Initial temperature of test cans significantly different from that used in commercial production.
17. In agitating retorts, rotation speed incompatible with commercial production.
18. No complete can-position study in rotating-cage retorts.
19. Excessive delay in running test after containers are sealed.
20. Product for tests not prepared according to procedures used commercially for raw product preparation or condition.
21. Large difference in processing temperatures between heat penetration tests and commercial practice.
22. One unexplained abnormally–slow-heating can within a group of cans.
23. Erratic and illogical thermocouple readings.
24. No readings taken until processing temperature in reached.

Plotting Heat Penetration Curve

Heat penetration data are usually plotted on three cycle semilogarithmic paper; temperature represented on the logarithmic scale and time on the linear scale. If the graph paper is inverted, temperatures can be plotted directly as shown in Figure 2.13 for a straight line heating curve and in Figure 2.14 for a broken heating curve.

Temperatures should be numbered from the top down starting with one degree below the retort temperature. The time divisions should be numbered from left to right, starting with 0 and ending with the time at which the test was ended.

Plot the temperatures for corresponding times. Inspect the data plotted. Simple heating curves consist of a lower portion which rises slowly in temperature-time. This is the lag when the container outside is heating rapidly but the product in the cold zone is not receiving heat. When the product in the cold zone begins to receive heat, the temperature rises logarithmically. For straight convection or conduction heating products, a single straight line can be drawn to the data points. This line is known as the heat penetration curve.

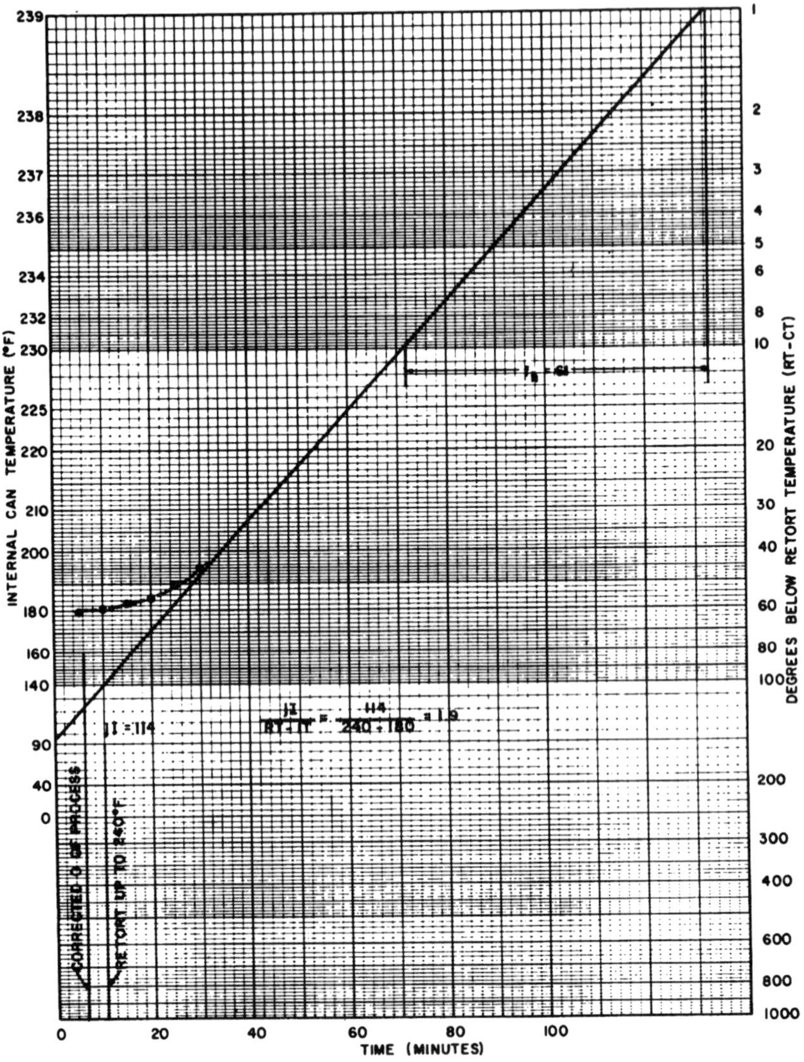

FIGURE 2.13 – Plot of a Simple Heating Curve (Straight Line)

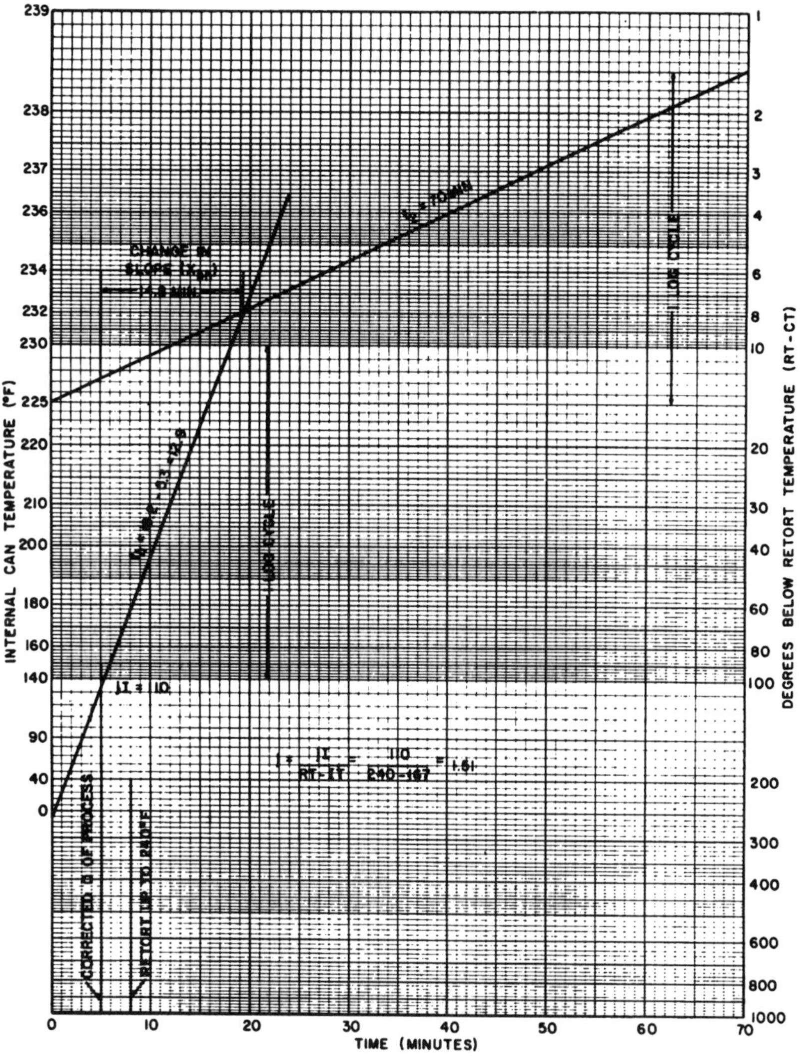

FIGURE 2.14 – Plot of a Broken Heating Curve

PROCESS CALCULATIONS

The symbols used here are consistent with those used in the industry for many years. It is assumed that time and temperature data have been obtained by heat penetration tests or that heat penetration factors for the product involved are available. Values for the parameters m+g and z have been taken as 180°F and 18°F, respectively. All tables and graphs are based on these values. Definition of terms and symbols appear at end of this chapter.

Methods of Analyzing Data

After time and temperature data for a given product in a given can size have been obtained by heat penetration studies, these data may be analyzed by either of two methods:

(1) The "general" or "graphical" method.

(2) The "formula" method.

The two methods of determining process times or levels are based on identical principles but the mechanics or procedures used are different. Each method has its own advantages. The choice of methods may be governed by the following conditions:

The graphical method is used when it is desired to measure the exact sterilizing value of a process when such conditions as come-up time, cooling water temperature, or the holding time after processing but before water cooling are different from normal retorting procedures. This method is also adapted to conditions when the heat penetration curve cannot be represented by one or two straight lines within the lethal temperature range on semi-logarithmic paper. It is not readily adapted to the calculation of processes when the retort temperature and/or initial temperature are different from those under which the heating data were obtained. Time and temperature data during the cooling cycle as well as the heating cycle must be recorded in order to use the graphical method. The graphical method is not applicable to air cooled products.

The formula method is used when the heat penetration curve can be represented by not more than two straight lines on semi-logarithmic paper. The formula permits evaluating processes for retort and initial temperature conditions differing from those under which the heating data were obtained. In the case of heating curves represented by one line only on semi-log paper, the heat penetration factors can be converted to different can sizes. The various methods of calculating processes will be described in detail.

Standards

It is first necessary to set up a standard sterilizing value. Since the greatest interest in processing canned foods is with low-acid products, 250°F (121°C) has been generally established as the reference temperature and the lethal heat expressed in terms of minutes at 250°F (121°C). This reference temperature will be used here.

The Graphical or General Method

As mentioned above, the lethal heat of a process is expressed in minutes at 250°F. One minute at 250°F or an equivalent amount of heat is defined as one unit of sterilizing value; the symbol for sterilizing value is F_o.

Temperatures other than 250°F (121°C) have lethal heat. Under conditions used here, one minute at 250 °F is equivalent to 10 minutes at 232°F (111°C) or 100 minutes at 214°F (101°C). In other words, for each 18 degree drop in temperature, the time necessary to obtain the equivalent bacterial destruction increases ten times.

The lethal ratio (F_o/t) or the sterilizing value effective in one minute at other temperatures (T) is the lethal rate value (often labeled as L), and can be expressed mathematically as:

$L = 10^{(T-Tref)/z}$

For z = 18°F and T_{ref} = 250°F, lethal rate values in the range 200–260°F (0.5 to 1°C) are shown in Table 2.1. The integration of lethal rate values for a given thermal process (including heating and cooling phases) is the accumulated sterilizing value, F_o-value (z = 18°F, T_{ref} = 250°F). Mathematically, this can be expressed as:

$$F^{z}_{Tref} = \int_0^t 10^{(T-Tref)/z}\,dt$$

or

$$F_o = \int_0^t 10^{(T-250)/18}\,dt$$

where t is the time at the end of process, T_{ref} is the reference temperature, z is the z-value of the target organism or spore to be destroyed and T is the slowest heating point product temperature.

At the slowest heating point within the container, there is a gradual rise in the temperature, the rate dependent on the physical characteristics of the product. There will be some lethal effect during each minute of the process; the amount during this interval is dependent upon the temperature at that time. These values are obtained from Table 2.1 and can be added to obtain the total effective lethal heat of the process.

TABLE 2.1 – Lethal Rates For z = 18

Temp.	Tenths of Degrees									
(°F)	0.0	0.1	0.2	0.3	0.4	0.5	0.6	0.7	0.8	0.9
190	0.000	0.000	0.000	0.000	0.000	0.000	0.001	0.001	0.001	0.001
191	0.001	0.001	0.001	0.001	0.001	0.001	0.001	0.001	0.001	0.001
192	0.001	0.001	0.001	0.001	0.001	0.001	0.001	0.001	0.001	0.001
193	0.001	0.001	0.001	0.001	0.001	0.001	0.001	0.001	0.001	0.001
194	0.001	0.001	0.001	0.001	0.001	0.001	0.001	0.001	0.001	0.001
195	0.001	0.001	0.001	0.001	0.001	0.001	0.001	0.001	0.001	0.001
196	0.001	0.001	0.001	0.001	0.001	0.001	0.001	0.001	0.001	0.001
197	0.001	0.001	0.001	0.001	0.001	0.001	0.001	0.001	0.001	0.001
198	0.001	0.001	0.001	0.001	0.001	0.001	0.001	0.001	0.001	0.001
199	0.001	0.001	0.002	0.002	0.002	0.002	0.002	0.002	0.002	0.002
200	0.002	0.002	0.002	0.002	0.002	0.002	0.002	0.002	0.002	0.002
201	0.002	0.002	0.002	0.002	0.002	0.002	0.002	0.002	0.002	0.002
202	0.002	0.002	0.002	0.002	0.002	0.002	0.002	0.002	0.002	0.002
203	0.002	0.002	0.003	0.003	0.003	0.003	0.003	0.003	0.003	0.003
204	0.003	0.003	0.003	0.003	0.003	0.003	0.003	0.003	0.003	0.003
205	0.003	0.003	0.003	0.003	0.003	0.003	0.003	0.003	0.004	0.004
206	0.004	0.004	0.004	0.004	0.004	0.004	0.004	0.004	0.004	0.004
207	0.004	0.004	0.004	0.004	0.004	0.004	0.004	0.004	0.005	0.005
208	0.005	0.005	0.005	0.005	0.005	0.005	0.005	0.005	0.005	0.005
209	0.005	0.005	0.005	0.005	0.006	0.006	0.006	0.006	0.006	0.006

Note: Lethal rate tables for z value other than 18 are also available. Consult a thermal processing authority.

TABLE 2.1 – Lethal Rates For z = 18 - Continued

Temp. (°F)	Tenths of Degrees 0.0	0.1	0.2	0.3	0.4	0.5	0.6	0.7	0.8	0.9
210	0.006	0.006	0.006	0.006	0.006	0.006	0.006	0.007	0.007	0.007
211	0.007	0.007	0.007	0.007	0.007	0.007	0.007	0.007	0.008	0.008
212	0.008	0.008	0.008	0.008	0.008	0.008	0.008	0.008	0.009	0.009
213	0.009	0.009	0.009	0.009	0.009	0.009	0.010	0.010	0.010	0.010
214	0.010	0.010	0.010	0.010	0.011	0.011	0.011	0.011	0.011	0.011
215	0.011	0.012	0.012	0.012	0.012	0.012	0.012	0.012	0.013	0.013
216	0.013	0.013	0.013	0.013	0.014	0.014	0.014	0.014	0.014	0.014
217	0.015	0.015	0.015	0.015	0.015	0.016	0.016	0.016	0.016	0.016
218	0.017	0.017	0.017	0.017	0.018	0.018	0.018	0.018	0.018	0.019
219	0.019	0.019	0.019	0.020	0.020	0.020	0.020	0.021	0.021	0.021
220	0.022	0.022	0.022	0.022	0.023	0.023	0.023	0.024	0.024	0.024
221	0.024	0.025	0.025	0.025	0.026	0.026	0.026	0.027	0.027	0.027
222	0.028	0.028	0.029	0.029	0.029	0.030	0.030	0.030	0.031	0.031
223	0.032	0.032	0.032	0.033	0.033	0.034	0.034	0.035	0.035	0.035
224	0.036	0.036	0.037	0.037	0.038	0.038	0.039	0.039	0.040	0.040
225	0.041	0.041	0.042	0.042	0.043	0.044	0.044	0.045	0.045	0.046
226	0.046	0.047	0.048	0.048	0.049	0.049	0.050	0.051	0.051	0.052
227	0.053	0.053	0.054	0.055	0.056	0.056	0.057	0.058	0.058	0.059
228	0.060	0.061	0.062	0.062	0.063	0.064	0.065	0.066	0.066	0.067
229	0.068	0.069	0.070	0.071	0.072	0.073	0.074	0.075	0.075	0.076

Note: Lethal rate tables for z value other than 18 are also available. Consult a thermal processing authority.

TABLE 2.1 – Lethal Rates For z = 18 - Continued

Temp.	Tenths of Degrees									
(˚F)	0.0	0.1	0.2	0.3	0.4	0.5	0.6	0.7	0.8	0.9
230	0.077	0.078	0.079	0.080	0.081	0.083	0.084	0.085	0.086	0.087
231	0.088	0.089	0.090	0.091	0.093	0.094	0.095	0.096	0.097	0.099
232	0.100	0.101	0.103	0.104	0.105	0.107	0.108	0.109	0.111	0.112
233	0.114	0.115	0.117	0.118	0.120	0.121	0.123	0.124	0.126	0.128
234	0.129	0.131	0.133	0.134	0.136	0.138	0.139	0.141	0.143	0.145
235	0.147	0.149	0.151	0.153	0.154	0.156	0.158	0.161	0.163	0.165
236	0.167	0.169	0.171	0.173	0.176	0.178	0.180	0.182	0.185	0.187
237	0.190	0.192	0.194	0.197	0.200	0.202	0.205	0.207	0.210	0.213
238	0.215	0.218	0.221	0.224	0.227	0.230	0.233	0.236	0.239	0.242
239	0.245	0.248	0.251	0.254	0.258	0.261	0.264	0.268	0.271	0.275
240	0.278	0.282	0.285	0.289	0.293	0.297	0.300	0.304	0.308	0.312
241	0.316	0.320	0.324	0.329	0.333	0.337	0.341	0.346	0.350	0.355
242	0.359	0.364	0.369	0.373	0.378	0.383	0.388	0.393	0.398	0.403
243	0.408	0.414	0.419	0.424	0.430	0.435	0.441	0.447	0.452	0.458
244	0.464	0.470	0.476	0.482	0.489	0.495	0.501	0.508	0.514	0.521
245	0.527	0.534	0.541	0.548	0.555	0.562	0.570	0.577	0.584	0.592
246	0.599	0.607	0.615	0.623	0.631	0.639	0.647	0.656	0.664	0.673
247	0.681	0.690	0.699	0.708	0.717	0.726	0.736	0.745	0.755	0.764
248	0.774	0.784	0.794	0.805	0.815	0.825	0.836	0.847	0.858	0.869
249	0.880	0.891	0.903	0.914	0.926	0.938	0.950	0.962	0.975	0.987

Note: Lethal rate tables for z value other than 18 are also available. Consult a thermal processing authority.

TABLE 2.1 – Lethal Rates For z = 18 - Continued

Temp.	Tenths of Degrees									
(°F)	0.0	0.1	0.2	0.3	0.4	0.5	0.6	0.7	0.8	0.9
250	1.000	1.013	1.026	1.039	1.053	1.066	1.080	1.094	1.108	1.122
251	1.136	1.151	1.166	1.181	1.196	1.212	1.227	1.243	1.259	1.275
252	1.292	1.308	1.325	1.342	1.359	1.377	1.395	1.413	1.431	1.449
253	1.468	1.487	1.506	1.525	1.545	1.565	1.585	1.605	1.626	1.647
254	1.658	1.690	1.711	1.733	1.756	1.778	1.801	1.824	1.848	1.872
255	1.896	1.920	1.945	1.970	1.995	2.021	2.047	2.073	2.100	2.127
256	2.154	2.182	2.210	2.239	2.268	2.297	2.326	2.356	2.387	2.417
257	2.448	2.480	2.512	2.544	2.577	2.610	2.644	2.678	2.712	2.747
258	2.783	2.818	2.855	2.891	2.929	2.966	3.005	3.043	3.082	3.122
259	3.162	3.203	3.244	3.286	3.328	3.371	3.415	3.459	3.503	3.548
260	3.594	3.640	3.687	3.734	3.782	3.831	3.881	3.930	3.981	4.032
261	4.084	4.137	4.190	4.244	4.299	4.354	4.410	4.467	4.524	4.583
262	4.642	4.701	4.762	4.823	4.885	4.948	5.012	5.076	5.142	5.208
263	5.275	5.343	5.412	5.481	5.552	5.623	5.696	5.769	5.843	5.919
264	5.995	6.072	6.150	6.229	6.310	6.391	6.473	6.556	6.641	6.726
265	6.813	6.901	6.989	7.079	7.171	7.263	7.356	7.451	7.547	7.644
266	7.743	7.842	7.943	8.046	8.149	8.254	8.360	8.468	8.577	8.687
267	8.799	8.913	9.027	9.143	9.261	9.380	9.501	9.624	9.747	9.873
268	10.000	10.129	10.259	10.391	10.525	10.661	10.798	10.937	11.078	11.220
269	11.365	11.511	11.659	11.809	11.961	12.115	12.271	12.429	12.589	12.751
270	12.915	13.082	13.250	13.421	13.594	13.769	13.946	14.125	14.307	14.491

Note: Lethal rate tables for z value other than 18 are also available. Consult a thermal processing authority.

(Reprinted from "Calculation of Processes for Canned Foods," American Can Company, Barrington, IL)

Heat penetration time and temperature data are usually recorded at some convenient time interval and can be set up in four columns as shown in Table 2.2. In the third column the sterilizing value effective in one minute (lethal rate) at the temperature indicated is added. The sum of F_0-value of the process could be calculated using either a numerical integration procedure, such as Trapezoidal procedure, Simpson's rule, etc., or the lethal rate graphical method. With the wide application of the computer and calculator, the numerical integration procedure has been widely adopted in the food industry. The fourth column in Table 2.2 is the accumulated F_0-value calculated by using Trapezoidal integration method. For each measured cold spot product temperature, a corresponding lethal rate value can be calculated from the lethal rate equation or obtained from the lethal rate table (Table 2.1) as shown in Table 2.2.

TABLE 2.2 – Heat Penetration Data
Conduction Heating, 211 x 304 Can

Come-up Time: 10 mins. Retort Temperature: 240°F

Heating Time	Temp. °F	Lethal Rate	ΣF_0/min.	Cooling Time	Temp. °F	Lethal Rate	F_0
IT	160.0	.0000	0.00	71	237.8	.2100	5.42
6	164.0	.0000	0.00	72	235.9	.1647	5.61
12	174.0	.0001	0.00	73	232.7	.1094	5.75
18	195.0	.0009	0.00	74	228.7	.0656	5.83
21	210.0	.0019	0.01	75	223.8	.0350	5.88
24	208.0	.0046	0.02	76	218.0	.0167	5.91
27	214.0	.0100	0.04	77	212.0	.0077	5.92
30	218.5	.0178	0.08	78	206.0	.0036	5.93
33	222.5	.0297	0.15	79	199.0	.0015	5.93
36	225.5	.0435	0.26	80	192.0	.0006	5.93
39	228.0	.0599	0.42	85	157.0	.0000	5.93
42	230.0	.0774	0.62	90	132.0	.0000	5.93
45	232.0	.1000	0.89	95	115.0	.0000	5.93
48	233.5	.1212	1.22	100	102.0	.0000	5.93
51	234.6	.1395	1.61	105	94.0	.0000	5.93
54	235.3	.1525	2.05				
57	236.4	.1756	2.54				
60	237.0	.1896	3.09				
63	237.6	.2047	3.68	Heating time F_0 =	5.20 min.		
66	238.0	.2154	4.31	Cooling time F_0 =	0.73 min.		
69	238.4	.2268	4.97	Process F_0 value =	5.93 min.		
70	238.5	.2297	5.20				
70	Steam off						

Plotting lethal rate value versus corresponding process time is the lethal rate curve. Connecting two neighbor lethal rate values by a straight line (dashed line) forms a trapezoidal geometry (shaded area) shown in the following curve:.

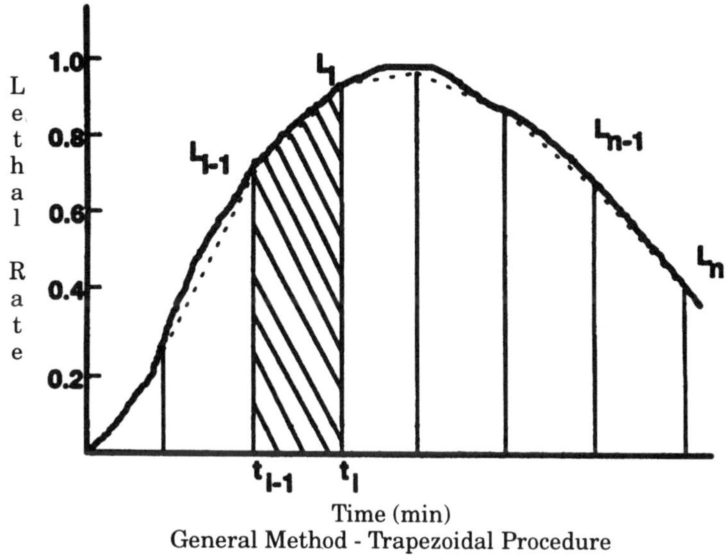

FIGURE 2.15 – Lethal Rate Curve

The lethality contributed from this small trapezoidal area can be calculated as:

$$(F_o)^i = \frac{(L_{i-1} + L_i)}{2} * \Delta t$$

where Δt is the product temperature measurement interval. The sum of all small trapezoidal lethality area is the total accumulated lethality of the process. This type calculation can be easily implemented in a computer program. The same approach may be applied for other numerical integration procedures.

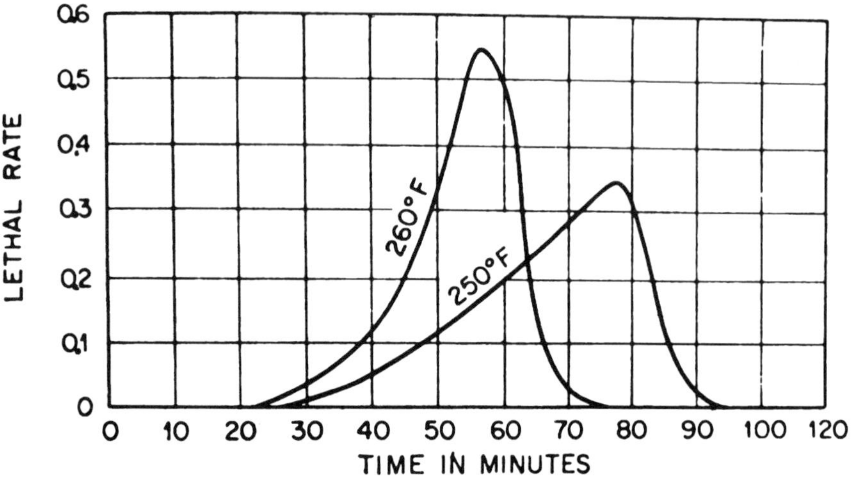

FIGURE 2.16 – Equivalent Lethality Curves with Retort at 260 and 250°F Corn in No. 2 Cans

The procedure for determining the length of a process for a known sterilizing value is quite similar except that instead of measuring area for a known length of process, the process is found to yield a known area under the curve. For example, suppose a process is wanted having a sterilizing value of 10, previous experience having shown that this value gives satisfactory results. It is necessary then to find the time that would yield an equivalent area under the lethality curve. Inspection of the curve leads to the conclusion that this time would not be far from 65 minutes. The cooling curve is estimated from 65 minutes and can be done fairly accurately by drawing it parallel to the actual cooling curve from 78 minutes. Now, the area under this 65 minute curve is measured by one of the methods previously described. Since this process fails to give 10 F_0 units under the curve, 65 minutes is not quite enough. It is almost a certainty that the next higher practical process, i.e., 70 minutes, would yield at least 10 F_0 units; the area under the 70 minute curve yields 11.7 F_0 units. Interpolation between 65 and 70 minutes gives a more exact time, but for practical purposes 70 minutes is selected.

It should be emphasized again that the results obtained by this method are valid only when the initial and retort temperature conditions are the same as those of the heat penetration tests. If the heat penetration curve can be represented by one or two straight lines on semi-log paper, it is possible to make corrections for these factors, but in this case, the graphical method is not the recommended one. Either the formula method or the nomogram method is better suited for such a calculation.

TABLE 2.3 – Effect of 3°F Errors in Retort Temperature on F_0 Value of Heating Phase of Typical Processes for 303 x 406 Cans

Product	Initial Temp. (°F)	Process Time (min.)	Retort Temp. (°F)	F_0 (min.)
Green beans in brine	120	20	237	2.0
			240	3.0
			243	4.7
Cream-style corn	140	95	237	3.2
			240	4.4
			243	6.2

The Formula Method

The first step in calculating processes by the formula method is to plot the time-temperature data on semi-log paper, time plotted as abscissa and temperature as the logarithmic ordinate. Zero time is the time at steam on. The time at which the retort reaches processing temperature is noted as come-up time. Three cycle semi-log paper generally provides a convenient range for plotting the data.

Actually, the temperatures plotted are the retort temperature minus the can temperature. Instead of making these subtractions, it is more practical to turn the semi-log paper upside down and plot can temperatures directly. The temperature on the top line is one degree below retort temperature. At the bottom of the first log cycle, the temperature is 10 degrees below retort temperature, and at the bottom of the second log cycle, 100 degrees below.

Either one straight line (simple heating curve) or not more than two straight lines (broken heating curve) are drawn through the points in the lethal temperature range (above 210°F) (99°C). An attempt should be made to pass the straight lines within 1 degree of all the points rather than fit them by any geometric mean method.

Having drawn the lines on the graph paper, factors must be determined that will describe the positions. Simple and broken heating curves will be discussed separately.

Simple Heating Curve

A plot of a simple heating curve is shown in Figure 2.17. From this plot two factors used in calculating processes may be obtained; j (lag factor) and f_h (slope).

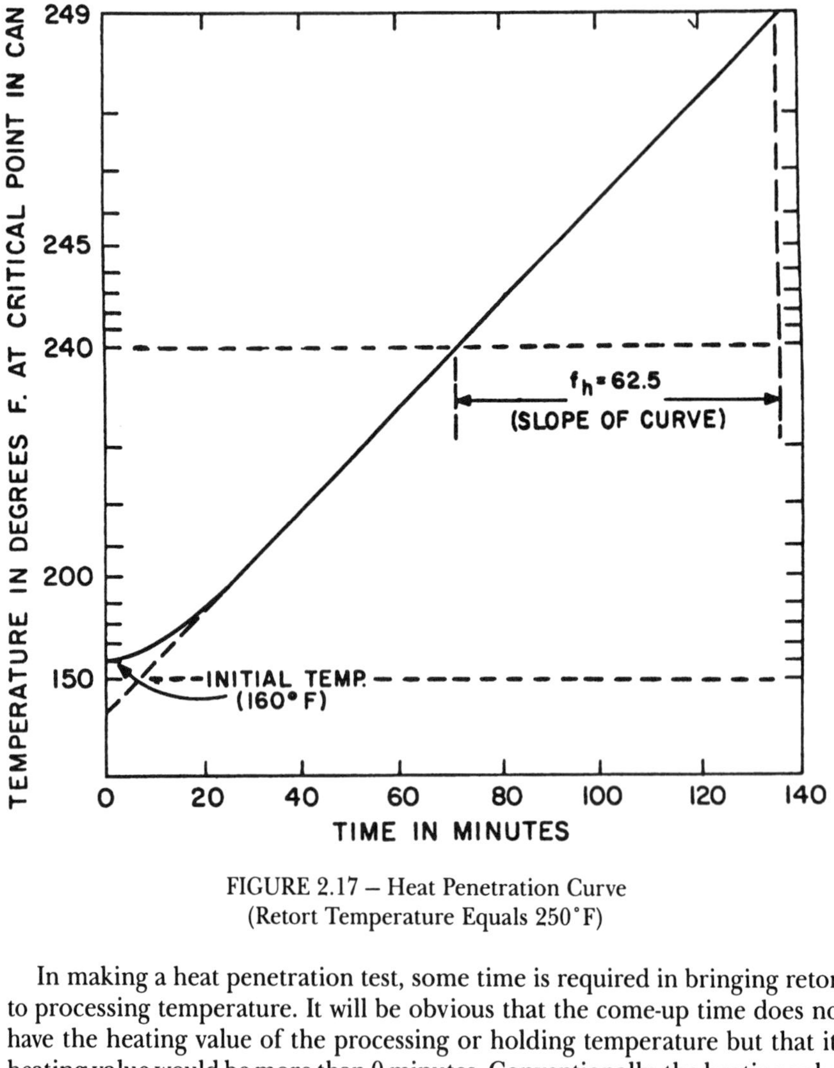

FIGURE 2.17 – Heat Penetration Curve
(Retort Temperature Equals 250°F)

In making a heat penetration test, some time is required in bringing retort to processing temperature. It will be obvious that the come-up time does not have the heating value of the processing or holding temperature but that its heating value would be more than 0 minutes. Conventionally, the heating value of the come-up time is taken as 0.42 of the come-up time. This means the corrected beginning of the process is not when the retort reaches process temperature, but 0.4 of the come-up time before steam-up or 0.6 of the come up time after steam-on. With a 10 minute come-up, the corrected 0 is at 6 minutes on the time scale. It is necessary to make this correction because retort come-up times will vary over comparatively wide limits and, unless means are provided for correcting these to 0, the come-up time will always have to be specified with the heat penetration curve. If because of the long come-up time it is necessary to make allowance for the come-up, 0.4 of the come-up can be subtracted from the calculated process, or if the sterilizing value is the sought unknown, 0.4 of the come-up time is added to the process time.

Having determined the corrected zero time, a vertical line is drawn at this value on the time scale, crossing the extended straight line drawn through the time temperature plotted. The point where these two lines cross will be a certain number of degrees below retort temperature known as "jI." A temperature value can be read on the left side temperature scale corresponding to the point the lines cross and this value subtracted from the retort temperature. If a degree-below-retort-temperature scale is marked on the right hand side of the graph paper, the value of "jI" can be read from this scale directly:

$$(1) \qquad I = RT - IT$$

Retort temperature (RT) is the retort temperature obtained during the heat penetration test, and the initial temperature (IT) is the center temperature of a particular can for which the time-temperature data are plotted, then:

$$(2) \qquad j = \frac{(jI)}{I}$$

This value of j remains constant for the given product; it does not change when converting the heating data to another can size. With smaller cans of conduction heating products, a correction to the j value is advisable to compensate for heat conducted into the product by the thermocouple wires and fittings. These corrections are discussed by Ecklund in his article, "Correction Factors for Heat Penetration Thermocouples." (*Food Technol.* 10:43-44, 1956). The following table gives correction factors for j.

TABLE 2.4 – Correction Factors for "j"

Can Size	Use on Conduction Heating Products Only. Multiple "j" Factor by:
202 x 214	1.36
211 x 400	1.16
300 x 407	1.10
307 x 409	1.06

The second heat penetration factor obtained from the graph of a simple heating curve is f_h. This factor is the time in minutes for the straight line drawn through the time-temperature plots to pass through one logarithmic cycle. A log cycle is the distance between any two points on the logarithmic ordinate in which the number of degrees below retort temperature increases ten times. For example, the distance can be from 1 to 10, 3 to 30, 10 to 100 or 20 to 200 as read on the right hand side of the graph sheet.

With the values of j and f_h obtained from the graph of the heating data, the sterilizing value (F_o) of a process can be determined or the process time in minutes (B_B) can be calculated for a desired F_o value.

To calculate F_o the following equations are used.

$$(3) \qquad \log g = \log jI - \frac{B_B}{f_h}$$

$$(4) \qquad F_o = \frac{f_h}{(f_h/U)\,F_i}$$

In equation (3) the values of j and f_h have already been determined, B_B (process time) is known and I = RT− IT. RT is a retort temperature at which the product will be processed and IT is the initial temperature that will be encountered under commercial canning conditions. These values are substituted into equation (3) and the value of "log g" calculated. The value of "g" is the number of degrees below retort temperature at the slowest heating point in the container at the end of the process. In order to simplify calculations, the log g is used in the equations.

For each value of log g there is a corresponding value of the term f_h/U. This relationship is shown in Table 2.5.

The term "F_i" relates to the retort temperature. It can be calculated by the equation:

$$(5) \qquad F_i = \log^{-1} \frac{(250 - RT)}{18}$$

Values of F_i for various retort temperatures are listed in Table 2.6.

$$(6) \qquad f_h/U = \frac{f_h}{(F_o)\ (F_i)}$$

The proper value of F_i for the retort temperature is selected and substituted in equation (4) along with f_h/U (found from Table 2.7 for the corresponding value of log g) and f_h. The F_o value obtained will be the sterilizing value of the process.

To calculate B_B, the following equations are used:

$$(7) \qquad B_B = f_h (\log jI - \log g)$$

In equation (6), f_h is from the heat penetration curve, F_0 is the desired sterilizing value and F_i is obtained from Table 2.6 for the particular retort temperature involved. With these values, f_h/U is calculated. From the relationship of f_h/U and log g shown in Table 2.5, the value of log g which corresponds to the value of f_h/U calculated in equation (6) can be found.

This value of log g is substituted in equation (7). The values of j and f_h are from the heat penetration curve and I again is RT- IT. The value of B_B calculated would be the process time in minutes.

TABLE 2.5 – LOG G Given FH/U
(m+g = 180°F, z = 18°F)

FH/U	LOG G	FH/U	LOG G	FH/U	LOG G	FH/U	LOG G
0.350	-2.147	0.430	-1.616	0.510	-1.251	0.590	-0.985
0.352	-2.131	0.432	-1.605	0.512	-1.243	0.592	-0.979
0.354	-2.115	0.434	-1.594	0.514	-1.236	0.594	-0.974
0.356	-2.099	0.436	-1.584	0.516	-1.228	0.596	-0.968
0.358	-2.083	0.438	-1.573	0.518	-1.221	0.598	-0.962
0.360	-2.068	0.440	-1.563	0.520	-1.213	0.600	-0.949
0.362	-2.052	0.442	-1.552	0.522	-1.206	0.602	-0.945
0.364	-2.037	0.444	-1.542	0.524	-1.198	0.604	-0.940
0.366	-2.022	0.446	-1.532	0.526	-1.191	0.606	-0.936
0.368	-2.007	0.448	-1.522	0.528	-1.184	0.608	-0.932
0.370	-1.993	0.450	-1.512	0.530	-1.177	0.610	-0.928
0.372	-1.978	0.452	-1.502	0.532	-1.170	0.612	-0.924
0.374	-1.964	0.454	-1.493	0.534	-1.163	0.614	-0.919
0.376	-1.950	0.456	-1.483	0.536	-1.156	0.616	-0.915
0.378	-1.936	0.458	-1.473	0.538	-1.149	0.618	-0.911
0.380	-1.922	0.460	-1.464	0.540	-1.142	0.620	-0.907
0.382	-1.908	0.462	-1.455	0.542	-1.135	0.622	-0.903
0.384	-1.894	0.464	-1.445	0.544	-1.128	0.624	-0.898
0.386	-1.881	0.466	-1.436	0.546	-1.122	0.626	-0.894
0.388	-1.867	0.468	-1.427	0.548	-1.115	0.628	-0.890
0.390	-1.854	0.470	-1.418	0.550	-1.108	0.630	-0.886
0.392	-1.841	0.472	-1.409	0.552	-1.102	0.632	-0.881
0.394	-1.828	0.474	-1.400	0.554	-1.095	0.634	-0.877
0.396	-1.815	0.476	-1.391	0.556	-1.089	0.636	-0.873
0.398	-1.803	0.478	-1.382	0.558	-1.082	0.638	-0.868
0.400	-1.790	0.480	-1.373	0.560	-1.076	0.640	-0.864
0.402	-1.778	0.482	-1.365	0.562	-1.069	0.642	-0.860
0.404	-1.765	0.484	-1.356	0.564	-1.063	0.644	-0.856
0.406	-1.753	0.486	-1.348	0.566	-1.057	0.646	-0.851
0.408	-1.741	0.488	-1.339	0.568	-1.051	0.648	-0.847
0.410	-1.729	0.490	-1.331	0.570	-1.044	0.650	-0.843
0.412	-1.717	0.492	-1.323	0.572	-1.038	0.652	-0.838
0.414	-1.705	0.494	-1.314	0.574	-1.032	0.654	-0.834
0.416	-1.694	0.496	-1.306	0.576	-1.026	0.656	-0.830
0.418	-1.682	0.498	-1.298	0.578	-1.020	0.658	-0.825
0.420	-1.671	0.500	-1.290	0.580	-1.014	0.660	-0.821
0.422	-1.660	0.502	-1.282	0.582	-1.008	0.662	-0.817
0.424	-1.648	0.504	-1.274	0.584	-1.002	0.664	-0.812
0.426	-1.637	0.506	-1.266	0.586	-0.996	0.666	-0.808
0.428	-1.626	0.508	-1.259	0.588	-0.991	0.668	-0.804

TABLE 2.5 – LOG G Given FH/U - Continued
(m+g = 180°F, z = 18°F)

FH/U	LOG G	FH/U	LOG G	FH/U	LOG G	FH/U	LOG G
0.670	-0.800	0.750	-0.635	0.830	-0.494	0.910	-0.379
0.672	-0.795	0.752	-0.631	0.832	-0.491	0.912	-0.376
0.674	-0.791	0.754	-0.627	0.834	-0.488	0.914	-0.373
0.676	-0.787	0.756	-0.624	0.836	-0.485	0.916	-0.371
0.678	-0.782	0.758	-0.620	0.838	-0.482	0.918	-0.368
0.680	-0.778	0.760	-0.616	0.840	-0.479	0.920	-0.366
0.682	-0.774	0.762	-0.612	0.842	-0.476	0.922	-0.363
0.684	-0.770	0.764	-0.609	0.844	-0.473	0.924	-0.361
0.686	-0.765	0.766	-0.605	0.846	-0.469	0.926	-0.358
0.688	-0.761	0.768	-0.601	0.848	-0.466	0.928	-0.355
0.690	-0.757	0.770	-0.597	0.850	-0.463	0.930	-0.353
0.692	-0.753	0.772	-0.594	0.852	-0.460	0.932	-0.350
0.694	-0.748	0.774	-0.590	0.854	-0.457	0.934	-0.348
0.696	-0.744	0.776	-0.586	0.856	-0.454	0.936	-0.345
0.698	-0.740	0.778	-0.583	0.858	-0.451	0.938	-0.343
0.700	-0.736	0.780	-0.579	0.860	-0.448	0.940	-0.341
0.702	-0.732	0.782	-0.576	0.862	-0.445	0.942	-0.338
0.704	-0.727	0.784	-0.572	0.864	-0.443	0.944	-0.336
0.706	-0.723	0.786	-0.568	0.866	-0.440	0.946	-0.333
0.708	-0.719	0.788	-0.565	0.868	-0.437	0.948	-0.331
0.710	-0.715	0.790	-0.561	0.870	-0.434	0.950	-0.328
0.712	-0.711	0.792	-0.558	0.872	-0.431	0.952	-0.326
0.714	-0.707	0.794	-0.554	0.874	-0.428	0.954	-0.324
0.716	-0.703	0.796	-0.551	0.876	-0.425	0.956	-0.321
0.718	-0.699	0.798	-0.548	0.878	-0.422	0.958	-0.319
0.720	-0.694	0.800	-0.544	0.880	-0.420	0.960	-0.317
0.722	-0.690	0.802	-0.541	0.882	-0.417	0.962	-0.314
0.724	-0.686	0.804	-0.537	0.884	-0.414	0.964	-0.312
0.726	-0.682	0.806	-0.534	0.886	-0.411	0.966	-0.309
0.728	-0.678	0.808	-0.530	0.888	-0.408	0.968	-0.307
0.730	-0.674	0.810	-0.527	0.890	-0.406	0.970	-0.305
0.732	-0.670	0.812	-0.524	0.892	-0.403	0.972	-0.303
0.734	-0.666	0.814	-0.520	0.894	-0.400	0.974	-0.300
0.736	-0.662	0.816	-0.517	0.896	-0.397	0.976	-0.298
0.738	-0.658	0.818	-0.514	0.898	-0.395	0.978	-0.296
0.740	-0.654	0.820	-0.511	0.900	-0.392	0.980	-0.293
0.742	-0.651	0.822	-0.507	0.902	-0.389	0.982	-0.291
0.744	-0.647	0.824	-0.504	0.904	-0.387	0.984	-0.289
0.746	-0.643	0.826	-0.501	0.906	-0.384	0.986	-0.287
0.748	-0.639	0.828	-0.498	0.908	-0.381	0.988	-0.285

TABLE 2.5 – LOG G Given FH/U - Continued
(m+g = 180°F, z = 18°F)

FH/U	LOG G	FH/U	LOG G	FH/U	LOG G	FH/U	LOG G
0.990	-0.282	1.175	-0.110	1.375	0.028	1.65	0.168
0.992	-0.280	1.180	-0.106	1.380	0.031	1.66	0.172
0.994	-0.278	1.185	-0.102	1.385	0.034	1.67	0.177
0.996	-0.276	1.190	-0.098	1.390	0.037	1.68	0.181
0.998	-0.274	1.195	-0.094	1.395	0.040	1.69	0.185
1.000	-0.271	1.200	-0.090	1.400	0.042	1.70	0.189
1.005	-0.266	1.205	-0.086	1.405	0.045	1.71	0.194
1.010	-0.261	1.210	-0.083	1.410	0.048	1.72	0.198
1.015	-0.255	1.215	-0.079	1.415	0.051	1.73	0.202
1.020	-0.250	1.220	-0.075	1.420	0.054	1.74	0.206
1.025	-0.245	1.225	-0.072	1.425	0.057	1.75	0.210
1.030	-0.240	1.230	-0.068	1.430	0.059	1.76	0.214
1.035	-0.235	1.235	-0.064	1.435	0.062	1.77	0.218
1.040	-0.230	1.240	-0.061	1.440	0.065	1.78	0.221
1.045	-0.225	1.245	-0.057	1.445	0.068	1.79	0.225
1.050	-0.220	1.250	-0.054	1.450	0.070	1.80	0.229
1.055	-0.215	1.255	-0.050	1.455	0.073	1.81	0.233
1.060	-0.210	1.260	-0.046	1.460	0.076	1.82	0.237
1.065	-0.205	1.265	-0.043	1.465	0.079	1.83	0.240
1.070	-0.201	1.270	-0.040	1.470	0.081	1.84	0.244
1.075	-0.196	1.275	-0.036	1.475	0.084	1.85	0.248
1.080	-0.191	1.280	-0.033	1.480	0.087	1.86	0.251
1.085	-0.187	1.285	-0.029	1.485	0.089	1.87	0.255
1.090	-0.182	1.290	-0.026	1.490	0.092	1.88	0.258
1.095	-0.177	1.295	-0.023	1.495	0.094	1.89	0.262
1.100	-0.173	1.300	-0.019	1.50	0.097	1.90	0.265
1.105	-0.168	1.305	-0.016	1.51	0.102	1.91	0.269
1.110	-0.164	1.310	-0.013	1.52	0.107	1.92	0.272
1.115	-0.160	1.315	-0.010	1.53	0.112	1.93	0.275
1.120	-0.155	1.320	-0.006	1.54	0.117	1.94	0.279
1.125	-0.151	1.325	-0.003	1.55	0.122	1.95	0.282
1.130	-0.147	1.330	-0.000	1.56	0.127	1.96	0.285
1.135	-0.142	1.335	0.003	1.57	0.132	1.97	0.289
1.140	-0.138	1.340	0.006	1.58	0.136	1.98	0.292
1.145	-0.134	1.345	0.009	1.59	0.141	1.99	0.295
1.150	-0.130	1.350	0.013	1.60	0.146	2.00	0.298
1.155	-0.126	1.355	0.016	1.61	0.150	2.01	0.302
1.160	-0.122	1.360	0.019	1.62	0.155	2.02	0.305
1.165	-0.118	1.365	0.022	1.63	0.159	2.03	0.308
1.170	-0.114	1.370	0.025	1.64	0.164	2.04	0.311

TABLE 2.5 – LOG G Given FH/U - Continued
(m+g = 180°F, z = 18°F)

FH/U	LOG G	FH/U	LOG G	FH/U	LOG G	FH/U	LOG G
2.05	0.314	2.45	0.419	2.85	0.500	3.25	0.564
2.06	0.317	2.46	0.421	2.86	0.501	3.26	0.565
2.07	0.320	2.47	0.424	2.87	0.503	3.27	0.567
2.08	0.323	2.48	0.426	2.88	0.505	3.28	0.568
2.09	0.326	2.49	0.428	2.89	0.507	3.29	0.569
2.10	0.329	2.50	0.430	2.90	0.508	3.30	0.571
2.11	0.332	2.51	0.433	2.91	0.510	3.31	0.572
2.12	0.335	2.52	0.435	2.92	0.512	3.32	0.574
2.13	0.338	2.53	0.437	2.93	0.514	3.33	0.575
2.14	0.340	2.54	0.439	2.94	0.515	3.34	0.576
2.15	0.343	2.55	0.441	2.95	0.517	3.35	0.578
2.16	0.346	2.56	0.443	2.96	0.519	3.36	0.579
2.17	0.349	2.57	0.445	2.97	0.520	3.37	0.580
2.18	0.352	2.58	0.448	2.98	0.522	3.38	0.582
2.19	0.354	2.59	0.450	2.99	0.524	3.39	0.583
2.20	0.357	2.60	0.452	3.00	0.525	3.40	0.585
2.21	0.360	2.61	0.454	3.01	0.527	3.41	0.586
2.22	0.362	2.62	0.456	3.02	0.529	3.42	0.587
2.23	0.365	2.63	0.458	3.03	0.530	3.43	0.589
2.24	0.368	2.64	0.460	3.04	0.532	3.44	0.590
2.25	0.370	2.65	0.462	3.05	0.533	3.45	0.591
2.26	0.373	2.66	0.464	3.06	0.535	3.46	0.592
2.27	0.376	2.67	0.466	3.07	0.537	3.47	0.594
2.28	0.378	2.68	0.468	3.08	0.538	3.48	0.595
2.29	0.381	2.69	0.470	3.09	0.540	3.49	0.596
2.30	0.383	2.70	0.472	3.10	0.541	3.50	0.598
2.31	0.386	2.71	0.474	3.11	0.543	3.51	0.599
2.32	0.388	2.72	0.476	3.12	0.544	3.52	0.600
2.33	0.391	2.73	0.478	3.13	0.546	3.53	0.601
2.34	0.393	2.74	0.479	3.14	0.547	3.54	0.603
2.35	0.396	2.75	0.481	3.15	0.549	3.55	0.604
2.36	0.398	2.76	0.483	3.16	0.550	3.56	0.605
2.37	0.400	2.77	0.485	3.17	0.552	3.57	0.606
2.38	0.403	2.78	0.487	3.18	0.553	3.58	0.608
2.39	0.405	2.79	0.489	3.19	0.555	3.59	0.609
2.40	0.408	2.80	0.491	3.20	0.556	3.60	0.610
2.41	0.410	2.81	0.492	3.21	0.558	3.61	0.611
2.42	0.412	2.82	0.494	3.22	0.559	3.62	0.613
2.43	0.415	2.83	0.496	3.23	0.561	3.63	0.614
2.44	0.417	2.84	0.498	3.24	0.562	3.64	0.615

TABLE 2.5 – LOG G Given FH/U - Continued
(m+g = 180°F, z = 18°F)

FH/U	LOG G	FH/U	LOG G	FH/U	LOG G	FH/U	LOG G
3.65	0.616	4.05	0.660	4.45	0.698	4.85	0.731
3.66	0.617	4.06	0.661	4.46	0.699	4.86	0.731
3.67	0.619	4.07	0.662	4.47	0.700	4.87	0.732
3.68	0.620	4.08	0.663	4.48	0.701	4.88	0.733
3.69	0.621	4.09	0.664	4.49	0.701	4.89	0.734
3.70	0.622	4.10	0.665	4.50	0.702	4.90	0.734
3.71	0.623	4.11	0.666	4.51	0.703	4.91	0.735
3.72	0.624	4.12	0.667	4.52	0.704	4.92	0.736
3.73	0.626	4.13	0.668	4.53	0.705	4.93	0.737
3.74	0.627	4.14	0.669	4.54	0.706	4.94	0.737
3.75	0.628	4.15	0.670	4.55	0.707	4.95	0.738
3.76	0.629	4.16	0.671	4.56	0.707	4.96	0.739
3.77	0.630	4.17	0.672	4.57	0.708	4.97	0.740
3.78	0.631	4.18	0.673	4.58	0.709	4.98	0.740
3.79	0.632	4.19	0.674	4.59	0.710	4.99	0.741
3.80	0.634	4.20	0.675	4.60	0.711	5.00	0.742
3.81	0.635	4.21	0.676	4.61	0.712	5.05	0.745
3.82	0.636	4.22	0.677	4.62	0.712	5.10	0.749
3.83	0.637	4.23	0.678	4.63	0.713	5.15	0.753
3.84	0.638	4.24	0.679	4.64	0.714	5.20	0.756
3.85	0.639	4.25	0.680	4.65	0.715	5.25	0.759
3.86	0.640	4.26	0.681	4.66	0.716	5.30	0.763
3.87	0.641	4.27	0.682	4.67	0.716	5.35	0.766
3.88	0.642	4.28	0.683	4.68	0.717	5.40	0.769
3.89	0.643	4.29	0.684	4.69	0.718	5.45	0.773
3.90	0.645	4.30	0.684	4.70	0.719	5.50	0.776
3.91	0.646	4.31	0.685	4.71	0.720	5.55	0.779
3.92	0.647	4.32	0.686	4.72	0.720	5.60	0.782
3.93	0.648	4.33	0.687	4.73	0.721	5.65	0.785
3.94	0.649	4.34	0.688	4.74	0.722	5.70	0.788
3.95	0.650	4.35	0.689	4.75	0.723	5.75	0.791
3.96	0.651	4.36	0.690	4.76	0.724	5.80	0.794
3.97	0.652	4.37	0.691	4.77	0.724	5.85	0.797
3.98	0.653	4.38	0.692	4.78	0.725	5.90	0.800
3.99	0.654	4.39	0.693	4.79	0.726	5.95	0.802
4.00	0.655	4.40	0.694	4.80	0.727	6.00	0.805
4.01	0.656	4.41	0.694	4.81	0.728	6.05	0.808
4.02	0.657	4.42	0.695	4.82	0.728	6.10	0.811
4.03	0.658	4.43	0.696	4.83	0.729	6.15	0.813
4.04	0.659	4.44	0.697	4.84	0.730	6.20	0.816

TABLE 2.5 – LOG G Given FH/U - Continued
(m+g = 180°F, z = 18°F)

FH/U	LOG G	FH/U	LOG G	FH/U	LOG G	FH/U	LOG G
6.25	0.819	8.25	0.903	11.0	0.979	19.0	1.102
6.30	0.821	8.30	0.905	11.2	0.984	19.2	1.104
6.35	0.824	8.35	0.906	11.4	0.988	19.4	1.106
6.40	0.826	8.40	0.908	11.6	9.992	19.6	1.108
6.45	0.829	8.45	0.910	11.8	0.997	20.0	1.112
6.50	0.831	8.50	0.911	12.0	1.001	20.5	1.117
6.55	0.834	8.55	0.913	12.2	1.005	21.0	1.122
6.60	0.836	8.60	0.914	12.4	1.008	21.5	1.126
6.65	0.838	8.65	0.916	12.6	1.012	22.0	1.131
6.70	0.841	8.70	0.918	12.8	1.016	22.5	1.135
6.75	0.843	8.75	0.919	13.0	1.020	23.0	1.139
6.80	0.845	8.80	0.921	13.2	1.023	23.5	1.143
6.85	0.848	8.85	0.922	13.4	1.027	24.0	1.147
6.90	0.850	8.90	0.924	13.6	1.030	24.5	1.151
6.95	0.852	8.95	0.925	13.8	1.033	25.0	1.155
7.00	0.854	9.00	0.927	14.0	1.037	25.5	1.158
7.05	0.857	9.05	0.929	14.2	1.040	26.0	1.162
7.10	0.859	9.10	0.930	14.4	1.043	26.5	1.165
7.15	0.861	9.15	0.931	14.6	1.046	27.0	1.169
7.20	0.863	9.20	0.933	14.8	1.049	27.5	1.172
7.25	0.865	9.25	0.934	15.0	1.052	28.0	1.175
7.30	0.867	9.30	0.936	15.2	1.055	28.5	1.178
7.35	0.869	9.35	0.937	15.4	1.058	29.0	1.181
7.40	0.871	9.40	0.939	15.6	1.061	29.5	1.184
7.45	0.873	9.45	0.940	15.8	1.063	30.0	1.187
7.50	0.875	9.50	0.942	16.0	1.066	31.0	1.193
7.55	0.877	9.55	0.943	16.2	1.069	32.0	1.198
7.60	0.879	9.60	0.944	16.4	1.071	33.0	1.204
7.65	0.881	9.65	0.946	16.6	1.074	34.0	1.209
7.70	0.883	9.70	0.947	16.8	1.076	35.0	1.214
7.75	0.885	9.75	0.948	17.0	1.079	36.0	1.218
7.80	0.887	9.80	0.950	17.2	1.081	37.0	1.223
7.85	0.889	9.85	0.951	17.4	1.084	38.0	1.227
7.90	0.890	9.90	0.952	17.6	1.086	39.0	1.231
7.95	0.892	9.95	0.954	17.8	1.089	40.0	1.235
8.00	0.894	10.0	0.955	18.0	1.091	41.0	1.239
8.05	0.896	10.2	0.960	18.2	1.093	42.0	1.243
8.10	0.898	10.4	0.965	18.4	1.095	43.0	1.247
8.15	0.899	10.6	0.970	18.6	1.098	44.0	1.250
8.20	0.901	10.8	0.975	18.8	1.100	45.0	1.254

TABLE 2.5 – LOG G Given FH/U - Continued
(m+g = 180°F, z = 18°F)

FH/U	LOG G	FH/U	LOG G	FH/U	LOG G	FH/U	LOG G
46.0	1.257	82.0	1.339	122.0	1.390	162.0	1.423
47.0	1.260	84.0	1.343	124.0	1.392	164.0	1.425
48.0	1.264	86.0	1.346	126.0	1.394	166.0	1.426
49.0	1.267	88.0	1.349	128.0	1.396	168.0	1.427
50.0	1.270	90.0	1.352	130.0	1.397	170.0	1.429
52.0	1.276	92.0	1.355	132.0	1.399	172.0	1.430
54.0	1.281	94.0	1.357	134.0	1.401	174.0	1.431
56.0	1.287	96.0	1.360	136.0	1.403	176.0	1.433
58.0	1.292	98.0	1.363	138.0	1.405	178.0	1.434
60.0	1.296	100.0	1.365	140.0	1.406	180.0	1.435
62.0	1.301	102.0	1.368	142.0	1.408	182.0	1.436
64.0	1.306	104.0	1.370	144.0	1.410	184.0	1.438
66.0	1.310	106.0	1.373	146.0	1.411	186.0	1.439
68.0	1.314	108.0	1.375	148.0	1.413	188.0	1.440
70.0	1.318	110.0	1.377	150.0	1.414	190.0	1.441
72.0	1.322	112.0	1.379	152.0	1.416	192.0	1.442
74.0	1.326	114.0	1.382	154.0	1.417	194.0	1.443
76.0	1.329	116.0	1.384	156.0	1.419	196.0	1.445
78.0	1.333	118.0	1.386	158.0	1.420	198.0	1.446
80.0	1.336	120.0	1.388	160.0	1.422	200.0	1.447

TABLE 2.6 – Fi Values for Various Retort Temperatures (°F)
($z = 18°F$, $T_{ref} = 250°F$)

RT	Fi	RT	Fi	RT	Fi
214	100.00	233	8.799	252	0.7743
215	87.99	234	7.743	253	0.6813
216	77.43	235	6.813	254	0.5995
217	68.13	236	5.995	255	0.5275
218	59.92	237	5.275	256	0.4642
219	52.75	238	4.642	257	0.4085
220	46.42	239	4.085	258	0.3594
221	40.85	240	3.594	259	0.3163
222	35.94	241	3.163	260	0.2783
223	31.63	242	2.783	261	0.2449
224	27.83	243	2.449	262	0.2154
225	24.48	244	2.154	263	0.1896
226	21.54	245	1.896	264	0.1668
227	18.96	246	1.668	265	0.1468
228	16.68	247	1.468	266	0.1292
229	14.68	248	1.292	267	0.1136
230	12.92	249	1.136	268	0.1000
231	11.36	250	1.000	269	0.0880
232	10.000	251	0.8799	270	0.0774

Reprinted from "Calculation of Processes for Canned Foods,"
Former American Can Company, Barrington, IL.

TABLE 2.7 – FH/U for Given LOG G
(m + g = 180°F, z = 18°F)

LOG G	.000	.002	.004	.006	.008
-1.990	0.3704	0.3701	0.3698	0.3695	0.3693
-1.980	0.3717	0.3715	0.3712	0.3709	0.3706
-1.970	0.3731	0.3729	0.3726	0.3723	0.3720
-1.960	0.3745	0.3743	0.3740	0.3737	0.3734
-1.950	0.3759	0.3757	0.3754	0.3751	0.3748
-1.940	0.3774	0.3771	0.3768	0.3765	0.3762
-1.930	0.3788	0.3785	0.3782	0.3779	0.3776
-1.920	0.3802	0.3799	0.3797	0.3794	0.3791
-1.910	0.3817	0.3814	0.3811	0.3808	0.3805
-1.900	0.3831	0.3828	0.3826	0.3823	0.3820
-1.890	0.3846	0.3843	0.3840	0.3837	0.3834
-1.880	0.3861	0.3858	0.3855	0.3852	0.3849
-1.870	0.3876	0.3873	0.3870	0.3867	0.3864
-1.860	0.3891	0.3888	0.3885	0.3882	0.3879
-1.850	0.3906	0.3903	0.3900	0.3897	0.3894
-1.840	0.3922	0.3918	0.3915	0.3912	0.3909
-1.830	0.3937	0.3934	0.3931	0.3928	0.3925
-1.820	0.3953	0.3949	0.3946	0.3943	0.3940
-1.810	0.3968	0.3965	0.3962	0.3959	0.3956
-1.800	0.3984	0.3981	0.3978	0.3975	0.3971
-1.790	0.4000	0.3997	0.3994	0.3990	0.3987
-1.780	0.4016	0.4013	0.4010	0.4006	0.4003
-1.770	0.4032	0.4029	0.4026	0.4023	0.4019
-1.760	0.4049	0.4045	0.4042	0.4039	0.4036
-1.750	0.4065	0.4062	0.4058	0.4055	0.4052
-1.740	0.4082	0.4078	0.4075	0.4072	0.4068
-1.730	0.4098	0.4095	0.4092	0.4088	0.4085
-1.720	0.4115	0.4112	0.4108	0.4105	0.4102
-1.710	0.4132	0.4129	0.4125	0.4122	0.4119
-1.700	0.4149	0.4146	0.4143	0.4139	0.4136
-1.690	0.4167	0.4163	0.4160	0.4156	0.4153
-1.680	0.4184	0.4181	0.4177	0.4174	0.4170
-1.670	0.4202	0.4198	0.4195	0.4191	0.4188
-1.660	0.4219	0.4216	0.4212	0.4209	0.4205
-1.650	0.4237	0.4234	0.4230	0.4227	0.4223
-1.640	0.4255	0.4252	0.4248	0.4244	0.4241
-1.630	0.4274	0.4270	0.4266	0.4263	0.4259
-1.620	0.4292	0.4288	0.4284	0.4281	0.4277
-1.610	0.4310	0.4307	0.4303	0.4299	0.4296
-1.600	0.4329	0.4325	0.4322	0.4318	0.4314

TABLE 2.7 – FH/U for Given LOG G - Continued
(m + g = 180°F, z = 18°F)

LOG G	.000	.002	.004	.006	.008
-1.590	0.4348	0.4344	0.4340	0.4337	0.4333
-1.580	0.4367	0.4363	0.4359	0.4355	0.4352
-1.570	0.4386	0.4382	0.4378	0.4374	0.4371
-1.560	0.4405	0.4401	0.4398	0.4394	0.4390
-1.550	0.4425	0.4421	0.4417	0.4413	0.4409
-1.540	0.4444	0.4440	0.4437	0.4433	0.4429
-1.530	0.4464	0.4460	0.4456	0.4452	0.4448
-1.520	0.4484	0.4480	0.4476	0.4472	0.4468
-1.510	0.4505	0.4500	0.4496	0.4492	0.4488
-1.500	0.4525	0.4521	0.4517	0.4513	0.4509
-1.490	0.4545	0.4541	0.4537	0.4533	0.4529
-1.480	0.4566	0.4562	0.4558	0.4554	0.4550
-1.470	0.4587	0.4583	0.4579	0.4575	0.4570
-1.460	0.4608	0.4604	0.4600	0.4596	0.4591
-1.450	0.4630	0.4625	0.4621	0.4617	0.4613
-1.440	0.4651	0.4647	0.4643	0.4638	0.4634
-1.430	0.4673	0.4669	0.4664	0.4660	0.4655
-1.420	0.4695	0.4690	0.4686	0.4682	0.4677
-1.410	0.4717	0.4713	0.4708	0.4704	0.4699
-1.400	0.4739	0.4735	0.4730	0.4726	0.4721
-1.390	0.4762	0.4757	0.4573	0.4548	0.4744
-1.380	0.4785	0.4780	0.4776	0.4771	0.4766
-1.370	0.4808	0.4803	0.4798	0.4794	0.4789
-1.360	0.4831	0.4826	0.4822	0.4817	0.4812
-1.350	0.4854	0.4850	0.4845	0.4840	0.4836
-1.340	0.4878	0.4873	0.4869	0.4864	0.4859
-1.330	0.4902	0.4897	0.4892	0.4888	0.4883
-1.320	0.4926	0.4921	0.4916	0.4912	0.4907
-1.310	0.4950	0.4946	0.4941	0.4936	0.4931
-1.300	0.4975	0.4970	0.4965	0.4960	0.4955
-1.290	0.5000	0.4995	0.4990	0.4985	0.4980
-1.280	0.5025	0.5020	0.5015	0.5010	0.5005
-1.270	0.5051	0.5045	0.5040	0.5035	0.5030
-1.260	0.5076	0.5071	0.5066	0.5061	0.5056
-1.250	0.5102	0.5097	0.5092	0.5086	0.5081
-1.240	0.5128	0.5123	0.5118	0.5112	0.5107
-1.230	0.5155	0.5149	0.5144	0.5139	0.5133
-1.220	0.5181	0.5176	0.5171	0.5165	0.5160
-1.210	0.5208	0.5203	0.5198	0.5192	0.5187
-1.200	0.5236	0.5230	0.5225	0.5219	0.5214

TABLE 2.7 – FH/U for Given LOG G - Continued
(m + g = 180°F, z = 18°F)

LOG G	.000	.002	.004	.006	.008
-1.190	0.5263	0.5258	0.5252	0.5247	0.5241
-1.180	0.5291	0.5285	0.5280	0.5274	0.5269
-1.170	0.5319	0.5313	0.5308	0.5302	0.5297
-1.160	0.5348	0.5342	0.5336	0.5330	0.5325
-1.150	0.5376	0.5371	0.5365	0.5359	0.5353
-1.140	0.5405	0.5400	0.5394	0.5388	0.5382
-1.130	0.5435	0.5429	0.5423	0.5417	0.5411
-1.120	0.5464	0.5459	0.5453	0.5447	0.5441
-1.110	0.5495	0.5488	0.5482	0.5476	0.5470
-1.100	0.5525	0.5519	0.5513	0.5507	0.5501
-1.090	0.5556	0.5549	0.5543	0.5537	0.5531
-1.080	0.5587	0.5580	0.5574	0.5568	0.5562
-1.070	0.5618	0.5612	0.5605	0.5599	0.5593
-1.060	0.5650	0.5643	0.5637	0.5631	0.5624
-1.050	0.5682	0.5675	0.5669	0.5663	0.5656
-1.040	0.5714	0.5708	0.5701	0.5695	0.5688
-1.030	0.5747	0.5741	0.5734	0.5727	0.5721
-1.020	0.5780	0.5774	0.5767	0.5760	0.5754
-1.010	0.5814	0.5807	0.5800	0.5794	0.5787
-1.000	0.5848	0.5841	0.5834	0.5828	0.5821
-0.990	0.5882	0.5875	0.5869	0.5862	0.5855
-0.980	0.5917	0.5910	0.5903	0.5896	0.5889
-0.970	0.5952	0.5945	0.5938	0.5931	0.5924
-0.960	0.5988	0.5981	0.5974	0.5967	0.5959
-0.950	0.5994	0.5984	0.5974	0.6002	0.5995
-0.940	0.6042	0.6032	0.6023	0.6013	0.6003
-0.930	0.6090	0.6080	0.6071	0.6061	0.6051
-0.920	0.6137	0.6128	0.6118	0.6109	0.6099
-0.910	0.6185	0.6175	0.6166	0.6156	0.6147
-0.900	0.6232	0.6223	0.6213	0.6204	0.6194
-0.890	0.6279	0.6270	0.6260	0.6251	0.6241
-0.880	0.6326	0.6316	0.6307	0.6298	0.6288
-0.870	0.6373	0.6363	0.6354	0.6345	0.6335
-0.860	0.6419	0.6410	0.6400	0.6391	0.6382
-0.850	0.6466	0.6456	0.6447	0.6438	0.6428
-0.840	0.6512	0.6503	0.6493	0.6484	0.6475
-0.830	0.6558	0.6549	0.6540	0.6531	0.6521
-0.820	0.6605	0.6596	0.6586	0.6577	0.6568
-0.810	0.6651	0.6642	0.6633	0.6623	0.6614
-0.800	0.6698	0.6689	0.6679	0.6670	0.6661

TABLE 2.7 – FH/U for Given LOG G - Continued
(m + g = 180°F, z = 18°F)

LOG G	.000	.002	.004	.006	.008
-0.790	0.6744	0.6735	0.6726	0.6716	0.6707
-0.780	0.6791	0.6782	0.6772	0.6763	0.6754
-0.770	0.6838	0.6829	0.6819	0.6810	0.6801
-0.760	0.6885	0.6876	0.6866	0.6857	0.6847
-0.750	0.6932	0.6923	0.6913	0.6904	0.6895
-0.740	0.6980	0.6970	0.6961	0.6951	0.6942
-0.730	0.7028	0.7018	0.7009	0.6999	0.6989
-0.720	0.7076	0.7066	0.7056	0..7047	0.7037
-0.710	0.7124	0.7114	0.7105	0.7095	0.7085
-0.700	0.7173	0.7163	0.7152	0.7144	0.7134
-0.690	0.7222	0.7212	0.7202	0.7192	0.7183
-0.680	0.7272	0.7262	0.7252	0.7242	0.7232
-0.670	0.7321	0.7311	0.7301	0.7291	0.7281
-0.660	0.7372	0.7362	0.7352	0.7342	0.7332
-0.650	0.7423	0.7413	0.7402	0.7392	0.7382
-0.640	0.7474	0.7464	0.7454	0.7443	0.7433
-0.630	0.7526	0.7516	0.7505	0.7495	0.7485
-0.620	0.7579	0.7568	0.7558	0.7547	0.7537
-0.610	0.7632	0.7621	0.7611	0.7600	0.7589
-0.600	0.7686	0.7675	0.7664	0.7654	0.7643
-0.590	0.7740	0.7729	0.7719	0.7708	0.7697
-0.580	0.7796	0.7784	0.7773	0.7762	0.7751
-0.570	0.7851	0.7840	0.7829	0.7818	0.7807
-0.560	0.7908	0.7897	0.7885	0.7874	0.7863
-0.550	0.7966	0.7954	0.7943	0.7931	0.7920
-0.540	0.8024	0.8012	0.8000	0.7989	0.7977
-0.530	0.8083	0.8071	0.8059	0.8047	0.8036
-0.520	0.8143	0.8131	0.8119	0.8107	0.8095
-0.510	0.8204	0.8191	0.8179	0.8167	0.8155
-0.500	0.8266	0.8253	0.8241	0.8228	0.8216
-0.490	0.8328	0.8316	0.8303	0.8290	0.8278
-0.480	0.8392	0.8379	0.8366	0.8354	0.8341
-0.470	0.8457	0.8444	0.8431	0.8418	0.8405
-0.460	0.8522	0.8509	0.8496	0.8483	0.8470
-0.450	0.8589	0.8576	0.8562	0.8549	0.8536
-0.440	0.8657	0.8644	0.8630	0.8616	0.8603
-0.430	0.8726	0.8712	0.8699	0.8685	0.8671
-0.420	0.8797	0.8782	0.8768	0.8754	0.8740
-0.410	0.8868	0.8854	0.8839	0.8825	0.8811
-0.400	0.8941	0.8926	0.8911	0.8897	0.8882

TABLE 2.7 – FH/U for Given LOG G - Continued
(m + g = 180°F, z = 18°F)

LOG G	.000	.002	.004	.006	.008
-0.390	0.9015	0.9000	0.8985	0.8970	0.8955
-0.380	0.9090	0.9075	0.9060	0.9045	0.9030
-0.370	0.9166	0.9151	0.9136	0.9120	0.9105
-0.360	0.9244	0.9229	0.9213	0.9197	0.9182
-0.350	0.9324	0.9308	0.9292	0.9276	0.9260
-0.340	0.9404	0.9388	0.9372	0.9356	0.9340
-0.330	0.9487	0.9470	0.9454	0.9437	0.9421
-0.320	0.9570	0.9554	0.9537	0.9520	0.9503
-0.310	0.9656	0.9638	0.9621	0.9604	0.9587
-0.300	0.9742	0.9725	0.9708	0.9690	0.9673
-0.290	0.9831	0.9813	0.9795	0.9778	0.9760
-0.280	0.9921	0.9903	0.9885	0.9867	0.9849
-0.270	1.0013	0.9994	0.9976	0.9957	0.9939
-0.260	1.0106	1.0087	1.0069	1.0050	1.0031
-0.250	1.0201	1.0182	1.0163	1.0144	1.0125
-0.240	1.0299	1.0279	1.0259	1.0240	1.0221
-0.230	1.0397	1.0378	1.0358	0.1338	1.0318
-0.220	1.0498	1.0478	1.0458	1.0438	1.0417
-0.210	1.0601	1.0580	1.0560	1.0539	1.0519
-0.200	1.0706	1.0685	1.0664	1.0643	1.0622
-0.190	1.0813	1.0791	1.0770	1.0748	1.0727
-0.180	1.0921	1.0899	1.0878	1.0856	1.0834
-0.170	1.1032	1.1010	1.0988	1.0966	1.0943
-0.160	1.1146	1.1123	1.1100	1.1077	1.1055
-0.150	1.1261	1.1238	1.1214	1.1191	1.1168
-0.140	1.1379	1.1355	1.1331	1.1308	1.1284
-0.130	1.1499	1.1474	1.1450	1.1426	1.1402
-0.120	1.1621	1.1596	1.1572	1.1547	1.1523
-0.110	1.1746	1.1721	1.1696	1.1671	1.1646
-0.100	1.1873	1.1848	1.1822	1.1796	1.1771
-0.090	1.2003	1.1977	1.1951	1.1925	1.1899
-0.080	1.2136	1.2109	1.2082	1.2056	1.2029
-0.070	1.2271	1.2244	1.2217	1.2190	1.2163
-0.060	1.2409	1.2381	1.2354	1.2326	1.2298
-0.050	1.2550	1.2522	1.2493	1.2465	1.2437
-0.040	1.2694	1.2665	1.2636	1.2607	1.2579
-0.030	1.2841	1.2811	1.2781	1.2752	1.2723
-0.020	1.2990	1.2960	1.2930	1.2900	1.2870
-0.010	1.3143	1.3113	1.3082	1.3051	1.3021
-0.000	–	1.3268	1.3237	1.3206	1.3174

TABLE 2.7 – FH/U for Given LOG G - Continued
(m + g = 180°F, z = 18°F)

LOG G	.000	.002	.004	.006	.008
0.000	1.3300	1.3331	1.3363	1.3395	1.3427
0.010	1.3459	1.3491	1.3524	1.3557	1.3589
0.020	1.3622	1.3655	1.3688	1.3722	1.3755
0.030	1.3789	1.3822	1.3856	1.3890	1.3924
0.040	1.3958	1.3993	1.4028	1.4062	1.4097
0.050	1.4132	1.4167	1.4203	1.4238	1.4274
0.060	1.4310	1.4346	1.4382	1.4418	1.4454
0.070	1.4491	1.4528	1.4565	1.4602	1.4639
0.080	1.4676	1.4714	1.4572	1.4789	1.4828
0.090	1.4866	1.4904	1.4943	1.4981	1.5020
0.100	1.5059	1.5099	1.5138	1.5178	1.5218
0.110	1.5257	1.5298	1.5338	1.5378	1.5419
0.120	1.5460	1.5501	1.5542	1.5584	1.5625
0.130	1.5667	1.5709	1.5751	1.5794	1.5836
0.140	1.5879	1.5922	1.5965	1.6008	1.6052
0.150	1.6096	1.6140	1.6184	1.6228	1.6273
0.160	1.6317	1.6362	1.6408	1.6453	1.6499
0.170	1.6544	1.6591	1.6637	1.6683	1.6730
0.180	1.6777	1.6824	1.6871	1.6919	1.6967
0.190	1.7015	1.7063	1.7111	1.7160	1.7209
0.200	1.7258	1.7308	1.7357	1.7407	1.7457
0.210	1.7508	1.7558	1.7609	1.7660	1.7712
0.220	1.7763	1.7815	1.7867	1.7920	1.7972
0.230	1.8025	1.8078	1.8132	1.8185	1.8239
0.240	1.8293	1.8348	1.8403	1.8458	1.8513
0.250	1.8568	1.8624	1.8680	1.8737	1.8793
0.260	1.8850	1.8908	1.8965	1.9023	1.9081
0.270	1.9139	1.9198	1.9257	1.9316	1.9376
0.280	1.9436	1.9496	1.9557	1.9617	1.9679
0.290	1.9740	1.9802	1.9864	1.9926	1.9989
0.300	2.0052	2.0116	2.0179	2.0243	2.0308
0.310	2.0373	2.0438	2.0503	2.0569	2.0635
0.320	2.0701	2.0768	2.0835	2.0903	2.0971
0.330	2.1039	2.1108	2.1177	2.1246	2.1316
0.340	2.1386	2.1456	2.1527	2.1599	2.1670
0.350	2.1742	2.1815	2.1888	2.1961	2.2034
0.360	2.2109	2.2183	2.2258	2.2333	2.2409
0.370	2.2485	2.2561	2.2638	2.2716	2.2794
0.380	2.2872	2.2951	2.3030	2.3110	2.3190
0.390	2.3270	2.3351	2.3433	2.3514	2.3597

TABLE 2.7 – FH/U for Given LOG G - Continued
(m + g = 180°F, z = 18°F)

LOG G	.000	.002	.004	.006	.008
0.400	2.3680	2.3763	2.3847	2.3931	2.4016
0.410	2.4101	2.4187	2.4273	2.4360	2.4447
0.420	2.4535	2.4623	2.4712	2.4802	2.4891
0.430	2.4982	2.5073	2.5164	2.5256	2.5349
0.440	2.5442	2.5536	2.5630	2.5725	2.5820
0.450	2.5916	2.6013	2.6110	2.6208	2.6306
0.460	2.6405	2.6504	2.6605	2.6705	2.6807
0.470	2.6909	2.7011	2.7115	2.7219	2.7323
0.480	2.7429	2.7534	2.7641	2.7748	2.7856
0.490	2.7965	2.8074	2.8184	2.8295	2.8406
0.500	2.8518	2.8631	2.8744	2.8859	2.8974
0.510	2.9089	2.9206	2.9323	2.9441	2.9560
0.520	2.9680	2.9800	2.9921	3.0043	3.0166
0.530	3.0289	3.0414	3.0539	3.0665	3.0792
0.540	3.0919	3.1048	3.1177	3.1308	3.1439
0.550	3.1571	3.1704	3.1838	3.1973	3.2108
0.560	3.2245	3.2382	3.2521	3.2660	3.2801
0.570	3.2942	3.3085	3.3228	3.3372	3.3518
0.580	3.3664	3.3812	3.3960	3.4109	3.4260
0.590	3.4412	3.4564	3.4718	3.4873	3.5029
0.600	3.5186	3.5344	3.5504	3.5664	3.5826
0.610	3.5989	3.6153	3.6318	3.6484	3.6652
0.620	3.6821	3.6991	3.7162	3.7335	3.7509
0.630	3.7684	3.7861	3.8039	3.8218	3.8398
0.640	3.8580	3.8763	3.8948	3.9134	3.9321
0.650	3.9510	3.9700	3.9892	4.0085	4.0280
0.660	4.0476	4.0674	4.0873	4.1074	4.1276
0.670	4.1480	4.1686	4.1893	4.2101	4.2312
0.680	4.2524	4.2737	4.2953	4.3170	4.3389
0.690	4.3609	4.3831	4.4055	4.4281	4.4509
0.700	4.4739	4.4970	4.5203	4.5438	4.5675
0.710	4.5914	4.6155	4.6398	4.6643	4.6890
0.720	4.7139	4.7390	4.7643	4.7899	4.8156
0.730	4.8415	4.8677	4.8941	4.9207	4.9476
0.740	4.9746	5.0019	5.0294	5.0572	5.0852
0.750	5.1134	5.1419	5.1706	5.1996	5.2288
0.760	5.2583	5.2881	5.3180	5.3483	5.3788
0.770	5.4096	5.4407	5.4720	5.5036	5.5355
0.780	5.5677	5.6001	5.6329	5.6659	5.6993
0.790	5.7329	5.7669	5.8011	5.8357	5.8706

TABLE 2.7 – FH/U for Given LOG G - Continued
(m + g = 180°F, z = 18°F)

LOG G	.000	.002	.004	.006	.008
0.800	5.9057	5.9413	5.9771	6.0133	6.0498
0.810	6.0866	6.1238	6.1613	6.1992	6.2374
0.820	6.2760	6.3149	6.3543	6.3939	6.4340
0.830	6.4744	6.5152	6.5564	6.5980	6.6400
0.840	6.6824	6.7252	6.7684	6.8121	6.8561
0.850	6.9006	6.9455	6.9909	7.0367	7.0829
0.860	7.1296	7.1768	7.2244	7.2725	7.3211
0.870	7.3701	7.4197	7.4697	7.5202	7.5713
0.880	7.6228	7.6749	7.7275	7.7807	7.8344
0.890	7.8886	7.9434	7.9987	8.0546	8.1111
0.900	8.1682	8.2259	8.2841	8.3430	8.4025
0.910	8.4626	8.5233	8.5847	8.6467	8.7094
0.920	8.7728	8.8368	8.9015	8.9669	9.0329
0.930	9.0997	9.1673	9.2355	9.3045	9.3742
0.940	9.4447	9.5160	9.5880	9.6608	9.7344
0.950	9.809	9.884	9.960	10.037	10.115
0.960	10.194	10.273	10.354	10.435	10.517
0.970	10.600	10.684	10.770	10.856	10.943
0.980	11.031	11.120	11.210	11.301	11.393
0.990	11.486	11.581	11.676	11.772	11.870
1.000	11.969	12.069	12.170	12.272	12.376
1.010	12.481	12.587	12.694	12.803	12.913
1.020	13.024	13.136	13.250	13.366	13.482
1.030	13.601	13.720	13.841	13.964	14.088
1.040	14.213	14.341	14.469	14.600	14.732
1.050	14.865	15.001	15.138	15.277	15.417
1.060	15.560	15.704	15.850	15.998	16.147
1.070	16.299	16.453	16.608	16.766	16.926
1.080	17.088	17.251	17.418	17.586	17.756
1.090	17.929	18.104	18.281	18.461	18.643
1.100	18.828	19.015	19.205	19.397	19.592
1.110	19.789	19.989	20.192	20.398	20.606
1.120	20.817	21.032	21.249	21.469	21.693
1.130	21.919	22.149	22.382	22.618	22.857
1.140	23.100	23.346	23.596	23.850	24.107
1.150	24.367	24.632	24.900	25.172	25.448
1.160	25.729	26.013	26.301	26.594	26.891
1.170	27.192	27.498	27.808	28.123	28.443
1.180	28.767	29.097	29.431	29.770	30.115
1.190	30.465	30.820	31.180	31.546	31.918

TABLE 2.7 – FH/U for Given LOG G - Continued
(m + g = 180°F, z = 18°F)

LOG G	.000	.002	.004	.006	.008
1.200	32.295	32.678	33.067	33.462	33.864
1.210	34.271	34.685	35.105	35.532	35.966
1.220	36.407	36.855	37.309	37.771	38.241
1.230	38.718	39.202	39.695	40.195	40.704
1.240	41.221	41.746	42.280	42.822	43.374
1.250	43.935	44.505	45.084	45.673	46.272
1.260	46.881	47.500	48.130	48.770	49.421
1.270	50.083	50.757	51.442	52.138	52.847
1.280	53.568	54.301	55.047	55.806	56.579
1.290	57.364	58.164	58.977	59.805	60.648
1.300	61.505	62.378	63.266	64.171	65.091
1.310	66.028	66.982	67.953	68.942	69.948
1.320	70.974	72.017	73.080	74.163	75.266
1.330	76.389	77.533	78.698	79.885	81.094
1.340	82.326	83.581	84.859	86.162	87.490
1.350	88.843	90.222	91.627	93.060	94.520
1.360	96.01	97.52	99.07	100.65	102.26
1.370	103.89	105.57	107.27	109.01	110.78
1.380	112.59	114.43	116.31	118.23	120.19
1.390	122.19	124.22	126.30	128.42	130.59
1.400	132.80	135.05	137.35	139.70	142.10
1.410	144.54	147.04	149.59	152.20	154.85
1.420	157.57	160.34	163.17	166.06	169.01
1.430	172.03	175.11	178.26	181.47	184.76
1.440	188.12	191.55	195.05	198.63	202.29
1.450	206.03	209.86	213.77	217.76	221.85
1.460	226.02	230.29	234.66	239.12	243.69
1.470	248.36	253.14	258.02	263.02	268.13
1.480	273.36	278.72	284.19	289.79	295.53
1.490	301.40	307.40	313.55	319.84	326.29

Broken Heating Curve

Some products heat quite rapidly during the first part of the cook, and then heat more slowly as the process progresses. For such products, it is usually necessary to draw two straight lines in order to stay as nearly as possible within 1 degree of all points in the lethal range. A broken heating curve is shown in Figure 2.14.

From the graph of a broken heating curve 4 factors are needed:

j (lag factor)
f_h (slope of first heating curve)
f_2 (slope of second heating curve)
x_{bh} (time to junction of the two curves, from corrected 0 of process)

The values of j and f_h are determined in the same manner as described for the simple curve procedure.

f_2 is the time required for the second portion of the heating curve to pass through one log cycle previously discussed.

The fourth factor, x_{bh}, is the time from the corrected 0 to the point where the two straight lines (f_h and f_2) cross.

With these four factors the sterilizing value (F_o) or the process time (B_B) can be calculated.

SUMMARY

1. A process is the application of heat to food for a scientifically-determined specified time and temperature.
2. A process which has been scientifically determined is specific for the given product, its formulation, methods of preparation, container size and type of retort system.
3. The determination of a process depends upon reliable heating information and the heat resistance of microorganisms in the product.
4. The heat resistance of microorganisms depends upon the microorganism used, the food in which it is heated, and the food in which the organisms grow.
5. The determination of heating data (time/temperature) should be conducted on a product which simulates commercial preparation.
6. The data obtained from thermal resistance and heat penetration tests are used to calculate a process.
7. It is sometimes desirable to check the calculated process by means of an inoculated test pack.

TABLE 2.8 – r_{bh} For Given LOG G (In Hundreths) (m + g = 180°F, z = 18°F)

LOG G	.00	.01	.02	.03	.04	.05	.06	.07	.08	.09
-1.00	0.9471	0.9474	0.9477	0.9480	0.9483	0.9486	0.9490	0.9493	0.9496	0.9499
-0.90	0.9440	0.9443	0.9446	0.9449	0.9452	0.9456	0.9459	0.9462	0.9465	0.9468
-0.80	0.9409	0.9412	0.9415	0.9418	0.9422	0.9425	0.9428	0.9431	0.9434	0.9437
-0.70	0.9376	0.9379	0.9383	0.9386	0.9389	0.9393	0.9396	0.9399	0.9402	0.9406
-0.60	0.9340	0.9344	0.9347	0.9351	0.9355	0.9358	0.9362	0.9365	0.9369	0.9372
-0.50	0.9300	0.9305	0.9309	0.9313	0.9317	0.9321	0.9325	0.9329	0.9332	0.9336
-0.40	0.9256	0.9261	0.9265	0.9270	0.9274	0.9279	0.9283	0.9288	0.9292	0.9296
-0.30	0.9206	0.9211	0.9216	0.9222	0.9227	0.9232	0.9237	0.9242	0.9247	0.9251
-0.20	0.9148	0.9155	0.9161	0.9166	0.9172	0.9178	0.9184	0.9189	0.9195	0.9200
-0.10	0.9083	0.9090	0.9097	0.9103	0.9110	0.9117	0.9123	0.9130	0.9136	0.9142
-0.00		0.9016	0.9023	0.9031	0.9039	0.9046	0.9054	0.9061	0.9069	0.9076
0.00	0.9009	0.9000	0.8992	0.8984	0.8975	0.8967	0.8958	0.8949	0.8940	0.8931
0.10	0.8922	0.8913	0.8903	0.8894	0.8884	0.8874	0.8864	0.8854	0.8844	0.8834
0.20	0.8823	0.8812	0.8801	0.8790	0.8779	0.8768	0.8757	0.8745	0.8733	0.8721
0.30	0.8709	0.8697	0.8684	0.8672	0.8659	0.8646	0.8633	0.8620	0.8606	0.8593
0.40	0.8579	0.8565	0.8550	0.8536	0.8521	0.8506	0.8491	0.8476	0.8461	0.8445
0.50	0.8429	0.8413	0.8397	0.8380	0.8363	0.8346	0.8329	0.8312	0.8294	0.8276
0.60	0.8258	0.8239	0.8221	0.8202	0.8183	0.8163	0.8144	0.8124	0.8103	0.8083
0.70	0.8062	0.8041	0.8020	0.7998	0.7976	0.7954	0.7931	0.7909	0.7886	0.7862
0.80	0.7838	0.7814	0.7790	0.7765	0.7740	0.7715	0.7689	0.7663	0.7637	0.7610
0.90	0.7583	0.7556	0.7528	0.7500	0.7471	0.7442	0.7413	0.7384	0.7354	0.7323
1.00	0.7292	0.7261	0.7230	0.7198	0.7165	0.7132	0.7099	0.7065	0.7031	0.6997
1.10	0.6962	0.6926	0.6890	0.6854	0.6817	0.6780	0.6742	0.6704	0.6665	0.6626
1.20	0.6586	0.6546	0.6505	0.6464	0.6422	0.6380	0.6337	0.6294	0.6250	0.6205
1.30	0.6160	0.6115	0.6068	0.6022	0.5974	0.5927	0.5878	0.5829	0.5779	0.5729
1.40	0.5678	0.5627	0.5574	0.5522	0.5468	0.5414	0.5359	0.5304	0.5248	0.5191
1.50	0.5134	0.5075	0.5017	0.4957	0.4897	0.4836	0.4774	0.4711	0.4648	0.4584

(Reprinted from "Calculation of Processes for Canned Foods," American Can Company, Barrington, IL)

To determine F_o, the following equations are used:

$$\text{(8)} \qquad \log g_{bh} = \log jI - \frac{x_{bh}}{f_h}$$

$$\text{(9)} \qquad \log g_{h2} = \frac{f_h \log jI + (f_2 - f_h) \log g_{bh} - B_B}{f_2}$$

$$\text{(10)} \qquad F_o = \frac{f_2}{\left(\frac{f_h}{U_{h2}}\right) F_i} - \frac{r_{bh}(f_2 - f_h)}{F_i \left(\frac{f_h}{U_{bh}}\right)} \quad \text{(when fc equals f2)}$$

Using j, f_h and x_{bh} obtained from the heating curves and I = RT IT, the log g_{bh} is calculated. g_{bh} is the number of degrees below retort temperature at the break in the curve and is related to f_h/U_{bh} in the same way that g is related to f_h/U, discussed under simple heating curves. The value of f_h/U_{bh} is obtained from Table 2.5 for the corresponding value of log g_{bh}. This value will be used in equation 10.

The value of log g_{h2} is calculated using equation 9. All factors in this equation are known. g_{h2} is the number of degrees below retort temperature in the container at the end of the process. Log g_{h2} is related to f_h/U_{h2} as given in Table 2.6. The value of f_h/U_{h2} is used in equation 10.

The last unknown factor in equation 10 is r_{bh}, a factor which is related to log g_{bh} according to Table 2.8. F_i in equation 10 is found from Table 2.6 corresponding to the retort temperature. All factors for equation 10 are now known and can be solved for F_o.

To determine B_B when the heating curve is broken, the following equations are used:

$$\text{(11)} \qquad \log g_{bh} = \log jI - \frac{x_{bh}}{f_h}$$

(12)
$$\frac{f_h}{U_{h2}} = \frac{f_2}{F_o F_i + \dfrac{r_{bh}(f_2 - f_h)}{\dfrac{f_h}{U_{bh}}}}$$

(13)
$$B_B = f_h \log jI + (f_2 - f_h) \log g_{bh} - f_2 \log g_{h2} \quad (\text{when } f_c = f_2)$$

The value of log g_{bh} is readily calculated since j, f_h, and x_{bh} are known from the heat penetration curve and I = RT–IT.

With this value of log g_{bh}, the value of f_h/U_{bh} can be found from Table 2.5 and the r_{bh} value found from Table 2.8. These values are substituted in equation 12.

In equation 12, F_o, the desired sterilizing value, is known, f_i is determined from Table 2.6 for the retort temperature used, and f_2 and f_h are from the heat penetration curve. f_h/U_{h2} can now be calculated.

f_h/U_{h2}, as determined by equation 12, is related to log g_{h2} according to Table 2.7. The value of log g_{h2} thus found is used in equation 13.

All factors in equation 13 are now known and the process time (B_B) can be calculated.

TABLE 2.9 – Calculated Sterilizing Values (F_o) for Some Current Commercial Processes

Product	Can Sizes	Approx. F_o
Asparagus	All	2-4
Green beans, brine packed	No. 2	3.5
Green beans, brine packed	No. 10	6
Chicken, boned	All	6-8
Corn, whole kernel, brine packed	No. 2	9
Corn, whole kernel, brine packed	No. 10	15
Corn, cream-style	No. 2	5-6
Corn, cream-style	No. 10	2.3
Dog food	No. 2	12
Dog food	No. 10	6
Mackerel in brine	301 x 411	2.9-3.6
Meat loaf	No. 2	6
Peas, brine packed	No. 2	7
Peas, brine packed	No. 10	11
Sausage, Vienna, in brine	Various	5
Chili con carne	Various	6

(Courtesy of American Can Company, Inc.)

HTST Process Calculation:
Calculation of Holding Tube Length

HTST processing is limited to fluid foods, i.e., foods containing particulates that may have shorter residence times than the fluid portions should not be processed in HTST units. Current thermal processing regulations assume that entire sterility is achieved in the holding tube. Therefore, the holding time must be sufficiently long to achieve the desired sterility. The safe design criterion for calculating the length of a holding tube (HTL) is based on sterilizing the fluid elements with the shortest residence time, i.e., on the maximum velocity (V_{max}) of a fluid food in the holding tube, e.g.,

$$HTL = F_T \times V_{max} ,$$

where F value is at the holding temperature (T). The calculation of V_{max} is described next.

The maximum velocity (V_{max}) in a holding tube depends on the volumetric flow rate (VOL, ft^3/minute or m^3/s) and the rheological characteristic of the fluid food. If necessary, the volumetric flow rate can be estimated by dividing the mass flow rate (W, lbs./minute or kg/s) with the density (ρ, lbs./ft.3 or kg/m^3) of the fluid food;

$$VOL = W/\rho.$$

For a fixed pumping rate, one can obtain the average velocity (V_{avg}) of the fluid food in the holding tube by dividing the volumetric flow rate (VOL, ft.^{3}/ minute or m^3/s) by the area of cross-section (A) of the holding tube:

$$A = \frac{\pi D^2}{4}$$

where D = diameter of the holding tube (feet or meters).

$$V_{avg} = VOL/A.$$

As a safe criterion, V_{max} is assumed to be equal to twice the average velocity:

$$V_{max} = 2.0 \times V_{avg}.$$

This last criterion, $V_{max} = 2.0 \times V_{avg}$, is based on laminar and turbulent flow velocity profiles, in tubes of circular cross section, of fluids with rheological characteristics of foods that are commonly encountered, Newtonian and pseudoplastic (shear thinning); it is not applicable to dilatant (shear thickening) foods because the maximum velocity would be greater than twice the average velocity. Although, thus far, dilatant (shear thickening) rheological behavior has not been reported for many foods, one should be aware of the assumptions made in calculating the required length of a holding tube.

Symbols Used

A – area of cross-section of holding tube (ft.^{2} or m^2)
D – diameter of holding tube (ft. or m)
FT – F value at holding temperature (T)
HTL – holding tube length (ft. or m)
V_{avg} – average velocity in holding tube (ft./min. or m/s)
V_{max} – maximum velocity in holding tube (ft./min. or m/s)
VOL – volumetric flow rate (ft.^{3}/min. or m^3/s)
W – mass flow rate (lbs./min. or kg/s)
r – density of food at process temperature (lbs./ft.^{3} or kg/m^3)

Computerized Data Acquisition and Evaluation of Thermally Processed Foods

Accurate determination of the time/temperature history at the slowest heating point in the container is vitally important in the calculation of a thermal process. The heat penetration test is used for documenting this time/temperature history under a set of controlled retort processing conditions. The measurement of this time/temperature history is generally accomplished by inserting a thermocouple through the container body or end such that the thermocouple "hot junction" is located in the geometric center of the container or other predetermined cold spot location. Other tests and temperature distribution, are performed to measure the quality of the heating-cooling medium surrounding containers in the retort during critical phases of the sterilization cycle. The food industry normally uses a type "T" copper-constantan thermocouple. In North America, "T" type copper-constantan non-projecting, plug-in thermocouples manufactured by Ecklund-Harrison Technologies, Inc. (11000/38 Metro Parkway - Fort Myers, FL 33912) are widely used, whereas in Europe, "T" type thermocouples manufactured by Ellab (Krondalvej 9, DK-2610 Roedovre, Denmark) are commonly used.

The thermocouple "lead" is connected to a copper-constantan temperature indicating or temperature recording datalogger, which is an analog to digital conversion instrument. There are a number of widely used datalogger systems available. In the food industry, dataloggers such as "CALPlex" manufactured by TechniCAL, Inc., now owned by FMC; "Data Acquisition System" manufactured by Ellab (in U.S.: PhF Specialists, Inc., 1299 Del Mar Ave., 3rd fl., San Jose, CA 95128; in Europe: Krondalvej 9, DK-2610 Roedovre, Denmark); and "Digistrip" from Kaye Instruments, Inc. (15 De Angelo Dr., Bedford, MA 01730) are commonly utilized for logging time/temperature data.

There are also a number of software packages available for logging thermal process data and, subsequently, for thermal process evaluation. "CALSoft" developed by TechniCAL Inc., "PC SOFT92" developed by Ellab, and "T-Pro" developed by the University of Wisconsin (Dr. John P Norback, Food Science Dept., 1605 Linden Drive, Madison WI 53706) are software programs that are, in part, used to collect time/temperature data during a heat penetration or temperature distribution test. The General Method and Ball Formula Method are also implemented in CALSoft and PC SOFT92 for the purpose of thermal process calculation. These software packages provide complete routines for data acquisition and data analysis for the thermal processing of canned foods.

Numerical modeling (finite difference) methods have been used to establish thermal processes and evaluate process deviations since the 1970s. Since 1988, NumeriCAL and NumeriCAL derivative software packages (FMC Corporation, Food Processing Systems Division, 2300 Industrial Ave., Box A, Madera, CA 93639), have been used to perform these offline calculations by using a finite difference method to solve the partial differential equation of unsteady state heat transfer. This new generation process modeling software eliminates the inaccuracies inherent in the Ball Formula Method, Stumbo Method and other scientific methods currently utilized in the establishment and evaluation of thermal processes used to sterilize or pasteurize foods. This unique tool provides a universal application to thermal processing for all types of foods packaged in all styles of containers.

The greatest advantages of NumeriCAL are its accuracy and flexibility. NumeriCAL can be used to simulate Slowest Heating Zone (SHZ) product temperatures inside a container under a condition of variable retort temperatures and boundary layers outside of the container tested. Thus, this method can more accurately determine true lethality in the process than can the Ball Formula Method. NumeriCAL is convenient in that the method utilizes heating and cooling factors (j_h, f_h, j_c, f_c, etc.) and can be used to extrapolate equivalent process times or sterilizing (F) values as in the Ball Formula Method. Because any of the factors related to the product heating and cooling parameters can be altered, a precise simulation and temperature comparison to a set of directly-measured time/temperature thermocouple data can be made.

As in the General method, the NumeriCAL simulated SHZ product temperatures relate directly to the accumulated lethality and, are thus, highly accurate. However, unlike the General method, the model can, in an off-line or on-line, real-time mode, simulate the product temperature at the SHZ without a direct, thermocouple measurement at the SHZ inside the container. Once the heating and cooling factors (j_h, f_h, j_c, f_c, etc.) are established from data obtained by direct thermocouple measurement, there is no further requirement to directly measure process variations within reasonable extrapolated limits.

NumeriCAL works well for convection, broken-heating and conduction-heating products as they pass through various stages of sterilization or pasteurization, and requires the use of heating-cooling factors which are widely recognized by process specialists who are familiar with the Ball Formula Method. This model is a useful tool for thermal process evaluation, process development and process deviation analysis for foods processed in all types of batch retort and continuous container handling retort such as Hydrostatic sterilizers and FMC Rotary Pressure Sterilizers. The NumeriCAL calculation results are accepted by both USFDA and USDA.

TABLE 2.10 – Definition of Terms and Symbols

Term	Symbol	Definition
Retort Temperature	RT	The temperature in °F of the medium in which the containers are processed.
Can Temperature	CT	The temperature of the can contents at the slowest heating point.
Initial Temperature	IT	The value of CT at the beginning of the process.
	I	A factor representing the difference between the retcrt temperature and the initial temperature, i.e., I = RT - IT.
	jI	The number of degrees below RT where the extended straight line of the heating curve crosses the corrected 0 of the process.
Lag Factor	j	A number representing the time lag before RT-CT assumes straight line characteristics on semi-log paper with time, $j = \frac{jI}{I}$
Process Time	B_B	The time in minutes from the beginning of the process to the end of the heating period.
Heat Penetration Curve Slope or Heating Curve Slope	f_h	The number of minutes required for the straight line portion of the heating curve, plotted on semi-logarithmic paper, to pass through one log cycle, i.e., the points (RT-n) and (RT-10n), where n can have any convenient value.
Sterilizing Value	F_o	The equivalent value of the process in terms of minutes at 250°F when no time is involved in heating to 250°F or cooling to sub-lethal temperatures.
	(f_h/U)	Factor related to g value in accordance with Table 2.5.
	F_i	Factor related to RT. Mathematically, $\log F_i = \frac{250-RT}{18}$ (see Table 2.4).
	g_{bh}	The number of degrees below retort temperature at which the heating curve exhibits a change of slope.
	x_{bh}	The number of minutes from the corrected beginning of the process to the point of break in the heating curve.
	g_{h2}	The number of degrees below retort temperature on a broken heating curve at the end of the heating period.

TABLE 2.10 – Definition of Terms and Symbols - Continued

Term	Symbol	Definition
Second Slope of Heating Curve	f_2	When the heating curve is expressed as a broken curve (two straight lines of different slope), this term represents the number of minutes required for the second portion of the curve to pass through the points (RT-n) and (RT-10n), where n can have any convenient value.
	f_h/U_{bh}	Factor related to g_{bh} value in accordance with Table 2.5.
	r_{bh}	Factor related to g_{bh} value in accordance with Table 2.6.
	f_h/U_{h2}	Factor related to g_{h2} value in accordance with Table 2.5.
Cooling Water Temp.	CW	The temperature of the cooling water in °F.
Cooling Curve Slope	f_c	The number of minutes required for the cooling curve, plotted on semi-logarithmic paper, to pass through the points (CW + n) and (CW + 10n), where n can have any convenient value.
	U or U_o	Sterilizing value in terms of minutes at retort temperature.
	U_3	Difference in sterilizing value between that which is obtained when heat penetration curve has slope of f_h, and when it has slope of f_2, for a g value equal to g_{bh} without considering the lethal value under the cooling portion of the curve.
	U_4	Sterilizing value if heat penetration curve has single slope equal to f_2.
	g	The number of degrees below retort temperature on a simple heating curve at the end of the heating period.
	m	CW - product temperature (critical point temperature) at end of process.
	m + g	RT - CW

Courtesy of American Can Company, "Calculation of Processes for Canned Foods," 1967 and Institute of Food Technologists, "Introduction to the Fundamentals of Food Processing," 1978.

ACKNOWLEDGEMENTS

The author thanks American Can Company for permitting the use of material from the memorandum entitled "Calculation of Processes for Canned Foods" (1967), the Institute of Food Technologists for allowing the use of material from its publication "Introduction to the Fundamentals of Food Processing" (1978), M.A. Rao, Cornell University, and Z. Weng, TechniCAL, Inc. for reviewing the material.

CHAPTER 3

Metal Containers for Canned Foods

Canners of low-acid foods should comply with the requirements of Part 113, Good Manufacturing Practices, promulgated by U.S. Food and Drug Administration. Under the regulations, the definition of an "hermetically sealed container" is as follows: "Hermetically sealed container means a container which is designed and intended to be secure against the entry of microorganisms and to maintain the commercial sterility of its contents after processing."

The container is an essential factor in the preservation of foods by canning. After canned foods are sterilized, it is the container that protects the canned food from spoilage by recontamination with microorganisms. It is then most important for the success of the canning operation to use good quality, reliable containers and properly adjusted closing machines. Thus, the seams and closures produced will be within the guidelines necessary to prevent access of microorganisms into the container during the cooling operation and during the shelf life of the product.

The food processor must adhere closely to can manufacturers guidelines for can seam dimensions. He must also carefully control the finish and closure dimensions of the glass containers used, to make sure that they agree with the measurements that have been found to produce tight and safe glass containers. Container manufacturers assist food processors in the selection of the most efficient container for specific food products, and in the selection, operation, and maintenance of closing machines.

Can manufacturers warranty the performance of the cans, covers and sealing compounds for each product application. They also sell and lease closing machines for the cans and provide technical services to their customers. In addition, can manufacturers have machinery service men who make regular visits to canneries during their season to assist with general maintenance of closing machinery and to instruct the canners' personnel in proper procedures for checking seams, replacing parts, etc. It is important to note here, however, that the can maker does not take responsibility for the top seam. It is a general practice to offer a one year warranty on cans for standard type products although the anticipated shelf-life on most canned items is considerably longer.

When sold by the can maker, closing machines carry a one year warranty on performance and parts except on those parts which normally wear and must be replaced by the canner.

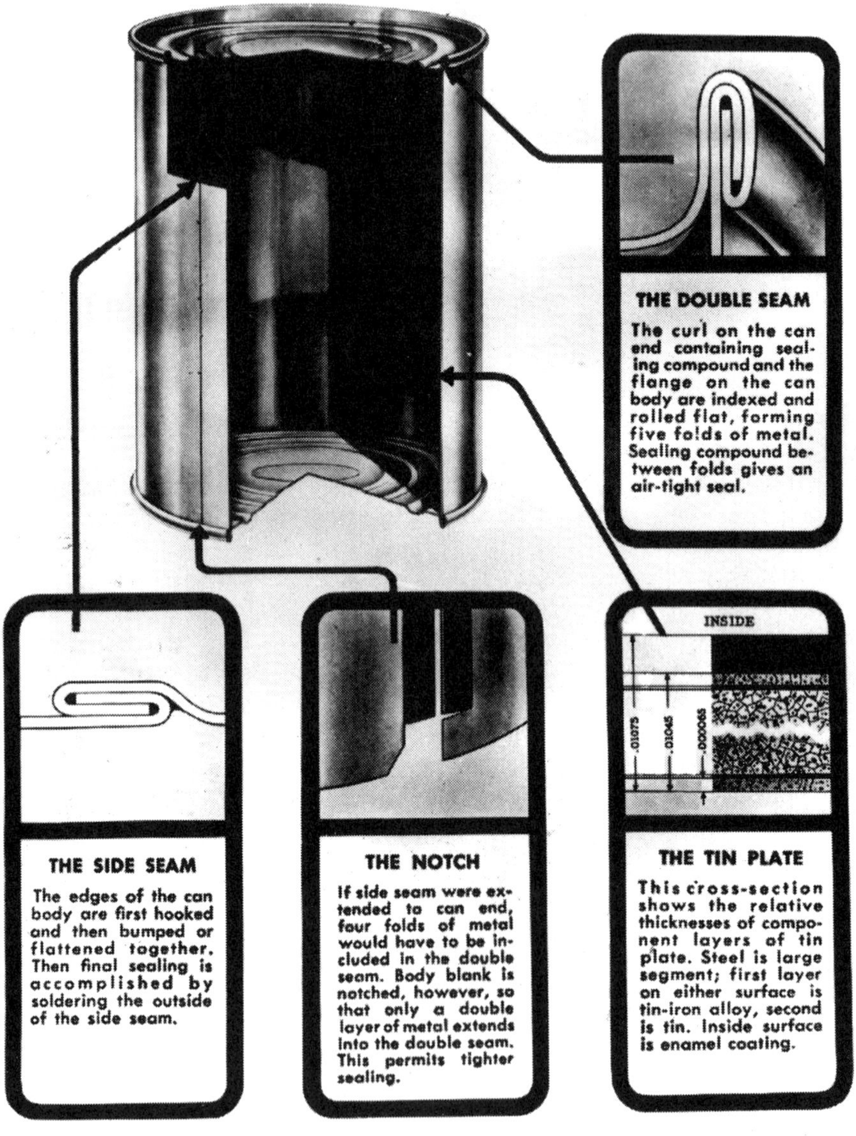
THE DOUBLE SEAM
The curl on the can end containing sealing compound and the flange on the can body are indexed and rolled flat, forming five folds of metal. Sealing compound between folds gives an air-tight seal.
INSIDE
.01075
.01045
.00065
THE SIDE SEAM
The edges of the can body are first hooked and then bumped or flattened together. Then final sealing is accomplished by soldering the outside of the side seam.
THE NOTCH
If side seam were extended to can end, four folds of metal would have to be included in the double seam. Body blank is notched, however, so that only a double layer of metal extends into the double seam. This permits tighter sealing.
THE TIN PLATE
This cross-section shows the relative thicknesses of component layers of tin plate. Steel is large segment; first layer on either surface is tin-iron alloy, second is tin. Inside surface is enamel coating.

FIGURE 3.1 – Architecture of the Enameled Sanitary Tin Can
(Courtesy American Can Company)

The basic soldered side seam can used successfully for many years has been replaced to a great extent by the welded and two-piece container. By 1987, less than 5% of all food cans were soldered, and in 1991 soldered cans with lead added solder were barred for food products in the U.S. A few cans with tin soldered side seams are manufactured for products like asparagus, but their total is very small.

In the 1970s, the U.S. Food and Drug Administration expressed concern about the lead exposure of young children. The metal container industry took steps to reduce the lead in cans. As a result of improved manufacturing operations of soldered cans and the conversion to lead free containers, the amount of lead in canned foods decreased from 0.31 ppm in 1980 to 0.19 ppm in 1983, according to retail market surveys conducted by the National Food Processors Association and the Can Manufacturers Institute. This voluntary conversion to lead-free containers was accomplished in a short time and with considerable investment by the metal container industry. As of 1996 there are virtually no lead soldered, seamed food cans used in the United States.

TIN PLATE CANS

Three-Piece Cans

The basic soldered side seam can and its descendants, the cemented side seam and welded side seam cans, constitute the bulk of cans produced. Two-piece cans are becoming popular for some applications, but three piece cans remain one of the most economical, reliable, and acceptable packages ever conceived. In 1975, 14% of the nation's food and beverage output of 47 billion pounds was packed in three-piece cans.

TABLE 3.1 – Percent Composition of Grade A Tin Used for Food Cans

Tin, minimum	99.80
Antimony, maximum*	0.04
Arsenic, maximum*	0.05
Bismuth, maximum*	0.015
Cadmium, maximum*	0.001
Copper, maximum*	0.04
Iron, maximum*	0.015
Lead, maximum*	0.05
Nickel + Cobalt, maximum*	0.01
Sulfur, maximum*	0.01
Zinc, maximum*	0.005

*These impurities represent no more than 0.20% and, when applying tin coatings electrolytically, some refining is inherent in the process and the coating becomes almost pure tin. (Courtesy Reynolds Metals Company)

Types of Steel Plate

Type L plate: Used for strongly corrosive products, this steel carries the most rigorous restrictions on composition.

Type MR plate: Furnishes benefits of low phosphorus steel for uses where small amounts of non-ferrous metals are of no consequence. Used for mildly corrosive foods.

Type MC steel plate: Contains added phosphorous for strength. Used for applications where neither this nor other residual elements matter. Used for food producing little corrosion.

Soldered Side Seam

Manufacture of the three-piece soldered side seam can starts with receipt of plate from supplier mills. This is usually in coil form that gets cut into sheets and fed into a slitter to produce individual can-body blanks. The blanks are then fed to a bodymaker where they are notched (i.e., removal of metal at juncture of crossover of side seam and end), rolled, and hooks are formed on both edges. Flux, as well as serrations and vents, promotes wetting and flow of solder into the seam.

After the body cylinder has been formed from the blank, it passes automatically over a burner followed by a solder roll which introduces molten solder into the side seam folds. Excess solder is removed by wiping. Finally, a stripe of lacquer may be applied to interior and exterior surfaces of the soldered side seam for product compatibility. Subsequent steps include flanging and beading the bodies, double-seaming one end onto the bodies, and testing for integrity.

TABLE 3.2 – Chemical Composition of Four Types of Base Steel

(Percentage Permitted According to Base Steel Type)

Element	Type L	Type MS	Type MR	Type MC
Manganese	.25-.60	.25-.60	.25-.60	.25-.60
Carbon	.12 max.	.12 max.	.12 max.	.12 max.
Phosphorus	.015	.015	.02	.07-.11
Sulfur	.05	.05	.05	.05 max.
Silicon	.01	.01	.01	.01
Copper	.06	.10-.20	.20	.20
Nickel	.04	.04 max.	*	*
Chromium	.06	.06	*	*
Molybdenum	.05	.05	*	*
Arsenic	.02	.02	*	*

*No limitations specified. (Courtesy Reynolds Metals Company)

Three-piece soldered constructions formed the bulk of general line, food, and beverage cans for many years. Welded cans have replaced soldered cans for nearly all food products. Benefits of using three-piece cans include no size limitations, wide range of plate thicknesses and tempers for body and ends, abuse resistance strong end profiles; long shelf-life, and compatibility with filling, retorting, casing and labeling equipment in common use by the nation's packers.

1. Notching 2. Folding 3. Hooking 4. Bumping
5. Soldering, Welding or Cementing 6. Flanging

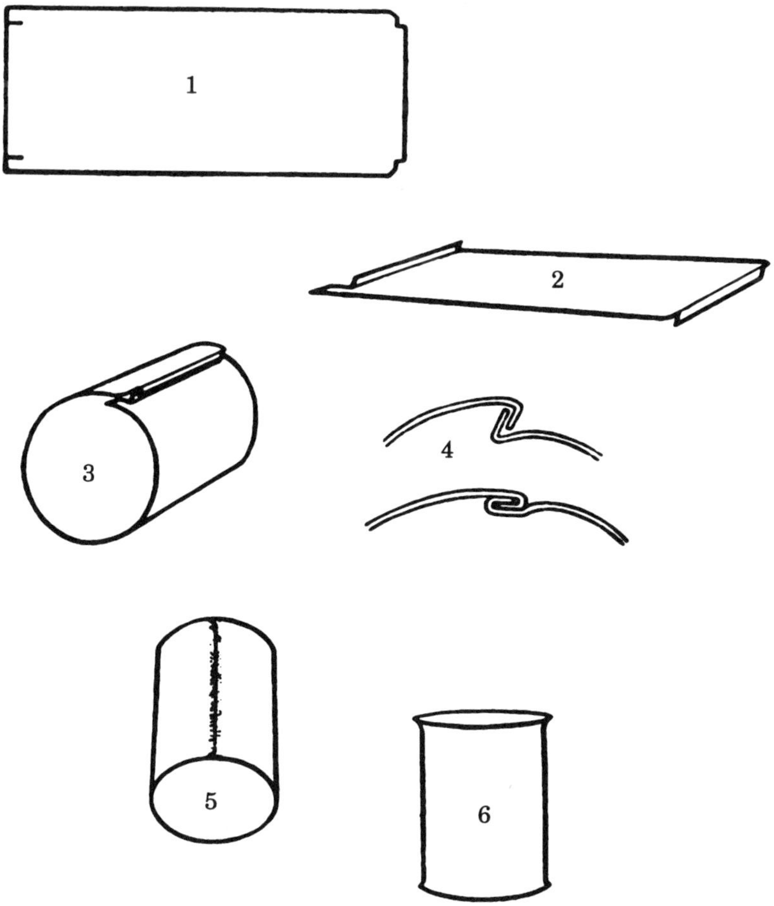

FIGURE 3.2 – Steps in Soldered Can Manufacturing

Cemented Side Seam

Oblong aluminum cans with lap seams sealed with polyamide adhesive for processed luncheon meats are the only cemented side seam cans manufactured today. Cylindrical drawn two piece cans and three piece cans with welded side seams are more versatile and economical than cemented side seam cans.

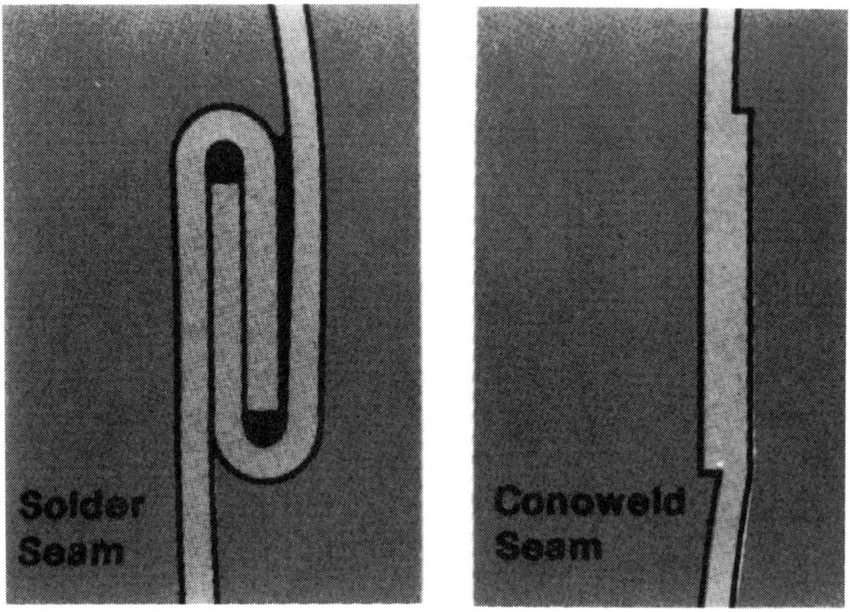

FIGURE 3.3 – Profiles of Soldered Side Seam and of Welded Side Seam (Courtesy former Continental Can Company)

Welded Side Seam

Welded side seam cans have been the dominant construction for three piece food cans in the U.S. for over ten years. Two types of welding machines are available. The first for welding tinplate, uses flattened copper wire for the welding electrode. Tin contaminates the copper wire during the welding, but is reclained. This is the most commonly used type of welder for three piece food cans used in the U.S. The second type welder for welding black plate and tin free steel, uses a rotary copper base electrode. The material to be welded must first be skived to provide a clean surface.

Figure 3.4 – Tinplate Can with Welded Side Seam
(Courtesy former Continental Can Company)

The welded can is made by forming a flat rectangular metal body blank into a cylinder and overlapping the edges at the side seam. The cylindrical body then traverses to the welding station where electrodes apply pressure and simultaneously send pulses of electric current through the overlap. By proper control of pressure, current and interface resistance, consistent high quality welds can be produced. After welding, the overlap area may be side seam striped to prevent the reaction of the product with the base metal.

The welded can has a number of advantages over the soldered can. The welded can does not use conventional lead solder and eliminates container contributed lead. The thin side seam of the welded can is much narrower than the wide soldered seam which allows more of the can to be decorated when a lithographed can is required. Double seaming of these cans is more reliable since there are only two metal thicknesses at the overlap. The welded side seam is more durable than a soldered side seam. The ability to weld blackplate or tin-free steel makes the process attractive since cheaper materials can be used.

TWO-PIECE CANS

In 1963, a radically different method for making cans was introduced: "drawn-redrawn" cans and the "drawn-and-ironed" cans.

Draw and Redraw

These cans are punched from flat sheet stock. For shallow bodies (i.e., height less than one-half of diameter), a single operation suffices. For deeper bodies, multi-stage drawing (i.e., redrawing) is required. The method has much to recommend it, as perhaps the simplest way to make a can, requiring the fewest operations, and equally adapted to tin-free steel, tinplate or aluminum. Elimination of the side seam and one seamed end obviously improves structure and eliminates leakage problems that occasionally occur in three-piece cans.

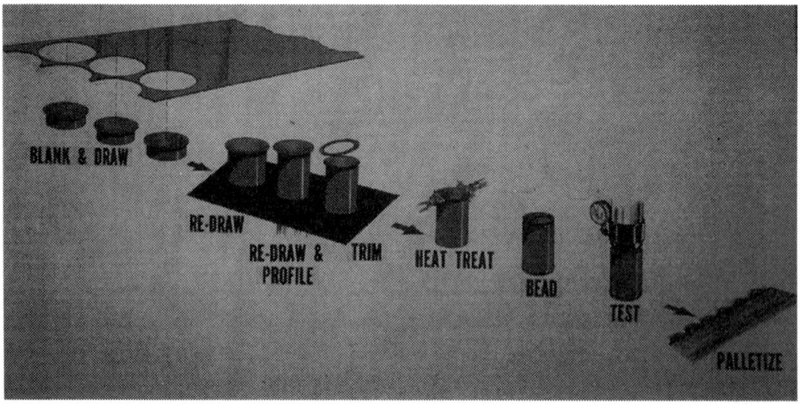

FIGURE 3.5 – Flow Chart of Drawn Can Manufacturing
(Courtesy former American Can Company)

Production of a drawn can starts with formation of a flanged 'cup' from coated coil stock. At a second press it is redrawn to proper size, flanged, trimmed and bottom-profiled. Multiple dies are used, permitting formation of more than one can at each stroke of the press. The final operation is performed on a beader which beads and necks-in the bottom to provide an integral stacking feature for food cans.

Two-piece drawn-redrawn cans, unlike their three-piece counterparts, nest top-to-bottom in stacks, giving greater stack stability and lower shelf profiles for an equal number of cans.

Drawn and Ironed

"D & I" cans are made by feeding sheet or coil stock into presses, where progressive dies form an integral can body and one end in a single piece. Such bodies are then trimmed, cleaned, printed, coated, necked, flanged and palletized for shipment. Both aluminum and low-carbon steel are used.

At time of filling, an end, usually one of the convenience closure types, is seamed on; this is the derivation of the name "two-piece," i.e., integral body-and-end plus one end.

As with draw-redraw, the process starts with formation of a cup in the press. This is then fed to an ironing press where the first die forms the cup around the ironing punch. The punch continues its downward thrust, pushing the cup through progressively smaller die rings. This procedure thins the sidewalls and forces metal upward to give the can the desired height. Carefully metered coolants and lubricants are required during this forming cycle.

Can bodies are then trimmed and sidewalls beaded to increase strength. Next, bodies are washed to remove lubricant residues. Finally, exteriors are varnished and interiors coated and baked. Flanging completes the cycle.

Positive aspects of draw-redraw and draw-and-iron include superior integrity (over three-piece), no solder or cement, only one seamed end, use all can-making metals, stackability, full-circle lithography-reducing carton, overwrap and labeling costs.

FIGURE 3.6 – Two-piece Draw/Redraw Sanitary Can
(Courtesy former Continental Can Company)

TIN FREE STEEL (TFS)

Steel companies introduced TFS in 1965. This material is the same as tinplate with no tin, but instead a much thinner ($^1/_{30}$th as thick) layer of chromium-chromium oxide designed to protect the steel from rusting in transit and in storage before it is made into cans. Once the can has been fabricated, the coatings on the inside and outside give it the necessary extra corrosion resistance which had previously been supplied by the tin.

TFS was first used for can ends. Can body use was limited to welded cans because can bodies could not be efficiently soldered without tin plating.

The current method of TFS body fabrication is welding. Electric resistance heating is used in the welded can because of the necessity to keep the heat effect of the weld to as narrow a strip of the can as possible. In this process the can body is then formed into a cylinder and the diameter is fixed by four tack welds spaced about $1^1/_2$ in. (3.8 cm) apart along the length of the can. The can body is then continuously seam welded by passing a high current through the overlap can edges as it passes between two rotating copper electrode wheels. In both of the above methods the resultant body is compatible with existing line equipment with minor modifications.

Recommended Can Sizes

In earlier years a large assortment of cans were used for fruit and vegetables. This was confusing to consumers and burdensome to canners. Through its Committee on Simplification of Containers, the then National Canners Association (now National Food Processors Association) worked toward a reasonably small list of cans. In 1934, the first simplified practice recommendation was promulgated by the National Bureau of Standards (NBS). The list was revised in 1937 and the latest one was promulgated in 1949. This last list recommends a total of 32 can sizes, but for each product, only a few sizes are permitted.

The following recommended can sizes, names dimensions and designated use were presented to and accepted by canners, can manufacturers, wholesale and retail grocers, consumer groups and other interested parties in late Summer 1948. On June 1, 1949, the list was promulgated as Simplified Practice Recommendations R155-49 by the Commodity Standards Division, National Bureau of Standards, (now "Office of Technical Services") U.S. Department of Commerce.

For each product, there is a particular kind of can that is best suited and cheapest. Specifications include the weight and type of the steel base plate, the amount of tin coating and the manner of application (electrolytic and differential coating), and the kind of enamel (if any).

TABLE 3.3 – Recommended Can Sizes

Can Name	Dimensions*	Products
	202 x 204	Mushrooms
	202 x 214	Baby Foods
	202 x 308	Juices (except Pineapple), Mushrooms, Tomato Paste
	202 x 314	Citrus and Grape Juice
	211 x 200	Olives, Pimientos
	211 x 212	Mushrooms
8 oz.	211 x 300	Dry Beans, Tomato Sauce
10 oz.	211 x 304	Fruits, Juices, Olives, Soups, Spaghetti, Vegetables
	211 x 400	Dry Beans, Tomato Sauce, Meat Products (Vending), Vegetables
	211 x 414	Juices, Pinapple, Prunes (dried)
	211 x 600	Olives
	300 x 206	Pimientos
	300 x 308	Dry Beans
	300 x 400	Mushrooms
300	300 x 407	Asparagus, Citrus Segments, Cranberries, Dry Beans, Juices (except Pineapple), Pimientos, Spaghetti
	301 x 411	Fruits (except Pineapple), Vegetables, Olives
303	303 x 406	Dry Beans, Fruits (except Pineapple), Hominy, Soups, Vegetables
	303 x 509	Soups
	307 x 113	Seafoods
	307 x 203	Pineapple
	307 x 214	Dry Beans
	307 x 306	Vegetables (vacuum packed), Meat
	307 x 400	Dry Beans, Snap Beans (asparagus style)
	307 x 409	Dry Beans, Fruits, Hominy, Juices, Vegetables
	307 x 510	Asparagus, Dry Beans, Mushrooms
	307 x 512	Juices (except Pineapple), Soups
	307 x 704	Olives
	401 x 207.5	Pineapple
	401 x 411	Dry Beans, Fruits, Hominy, Kraut Juice, Olives, Pimientos, Soups, Vegetables
	404 x 307	Sweet Potatoes, Meat Products
	404 x 700	All Products (except Pineapple)
No. 10	603 x 700	All Products

*In the statement of each dimension, the first digit gives the number of whole inches, and the second and third digit gives the fraction expressed in sixteenths of an inch. Thus, 211 x 400 means that the can is $2^{11}/_{16}$ in. in diameter and 4 in. high. These dimensions apply only to regular-type sanitary or open-top cans.

In 1970, the National Canners (now NFPA) submitted a package proposal to the National Bureau of Standards seeking the establishment of 16 separate Voluntary Products Standards for certain commodity and commodity groups.

In 1972, because of various policy decisions, the National Bureau of Standards decided to discontinue the program. At that time, the NBS noted there was no undue proliferation of can sizes in the industry. Even though work with the NBS ended, the 16 Recommended Product Standards remain a voluntary industry effort.

Table 3.4, gives the main characteristics of cans and the can sizes used for some of the more important canned foods. The table was compiled by American Can Co., and updated to 1986. The cooperation of Mr. Dwight E. Reed, Manager, Metal Container Research, American Can Co., in updating the table is gratefully acknowledged.

Truck Trailer Shipping of Empty Cans

In the past, cans were shipped from the can manufacturing plant to the packer in various ways such as bulk cans in trailers, in cartons, or in bags. Today, nearly all canners are receive empty cans bulk palletized.

Bulk palletization was a method developed to economically and efficiently handle vertically stacked tiers of empty cans on wooden pallets which measure 5"x44"x56" (12.7x112x192 cm). Cans are mechanically loaded onto pallets in the can manufacturing plants. The number of tiers per pallet can be decreased or increased depending upon conditions, i.e., truck size, customer door heights, etc. The average finished pallet measures approximately 53" high x 44" wide x 56" long (135x112x142 cm) for a single high pallet, and 106" high x 44" wide x 56" long (270x112x142 cm) for a double high pallet.

A sheet of tough fiberboard separate each tier of cans and acts as a floor for each tier above. In some instances, the loaded pallet is completely wrapped with plastic shrink wrap or corrugated board which protects cans from dust and dirt and further braces the cans for warehouse stacking. Pallet shrouds are then taped, strung or strapped prior to shipping. If the pallet is not wrapped, the method of shipping is to place a wooden frame over the top separator sheet and apply strapping.

Loaded pallets are picked up in the warehouse by fork trucks and delivered to trailers at the loading platform. Here the pallets are loaded into a trailer by means of fork trucks or are lowered onto roller conveyors installed on the floor of the trailer. At the packers plant, the pallet can be unloaded from trailers by two methods:

1. Fork truck to warehouse storage, or
2. Conveyed directly to the can depalletizer by means of an automatic conveyor system.

TABLE 3.4 – Characteristics of Cans Used for Canned Food Products

Product	Common Can Sizes	Tin Coating Body	Tin Coating Ends	Inside Enamel Coating Body	Inside Enamel Coating Ends	Type Steel L	Type Steel MR
Apple Slices	603 x 700	50-25KI	25	PL	E		X
	307 x 409						
	303 x 406						
Apple Butter	603 x 700	75-25	75-25	E*	E	X	
	401 x 411						
	303 x 406						
Apple Juice	404 x 700	50-25KI	25	EE*	EE	X	
	202 x 308						
	202 x 314						
Applesauce	303 x 406	50-25	25	PL	E		X
	603 x 700						
	211 x 304						
Apricots	401 x 411	50-25KI	25	PL	E		X
	303 x 406						
	603 x 700						
Asparagus	303 x 406	135-25	25	PL	EE		X
HTF Side Seam	211 x 400	25	25	E	EE		X
	603 x 700						
Beans, Green	303 x 406	100-25	25	PL	E		X
HTF Side Seam	603 x 700	50-25	50-25	E*	E		X
	211 x 304	25	25	E	E		X
Beans, Lima	303 x 406	25	25	E	E		X
	603 x 700						
	211 x 304						
Beets	303 x 406	50-25	50-25	E*	E		X
	603 x 700	75-25	75-25	E*	E	X	
	211 x 304	25	25	E*	E		X
Blackberries & Similar Berries	303 x 406	75-25	75-25	E*	E	X	
	603 x 700						
	211 x 304						
Blueberries	300 x 407	100-25	25	E*	EE	X	
	300 x 108						
	603 x 700						

For symbols, see footnotes following table.

TABLE 3.4 – Characteristics of Cans Used for Canned Food Products - Cont.

Product	Common Can Sizes	Tin Coating Body	Tin Coating Ends	Inside Enamel Coating Body	Inside Enamel Coating Ends	Type Steel L	Type Steel MR
Carrots	303 x 406	50-25	50-25	E*	E		X
HTF Side Seam	603 x 700	75-25	25	PL	E		X
	211 x 304	25	25	E	E		X
Cherries, RSP	303 x 406	75-25	75-25	E*	E	X	
	603 x 700						
	307 x 409						
Cherries, Sweet	303 x 406	75-25	75-25	E*	E	X	
Dark & Light	603 x 700						
Color	211 x 304						
Light Color only		100-25K	25	PL	E		X
Corn	303 x 406	25	25	E	E		X
	307 x 306						
	603 x 700						
Fruit Cocktail	303 x 406	50-25KI	25	PL	E		X
	401 x 411						
	603 x 700						
Fruit Jellies	603 x 700	75-25	75-25	E*	E	X	
Colored Fruit	401 x 411						
(incl. Apple)	303 x 406						
Light Colored Fruit (except Apple)		75-25K	25	PL	E		X
Fruit Salad	303 x 406	50-25KI	25	PL	E		X
	603 x 700						
	401 x 411						
Grape Juice	404 x 700	75-25	25	EE*	EE	X	
	202 x 314						
	202 x 308						
Grapefruit Juice	404 x 700	75-25K	75-25K	PL	PL		X
	307 x 409						
	202 x 314						
Mushrooms	211 x 212	50-25	25	PL	E		X
	202 x 204						
	211 x 300						
Mushrooms, acidified		25	25	E*	E		X

For symbols, see footnotes following table.

TABLE 3.4 – Characteristics of Cans Used for Canned Food Products - Cont.

Product	Common Can Sizes	Tin Coating		Inside Enamel Coating		Type Steel	
		Body	Ends	Body	Ends	L	MR
Okra	303 x 406 603 x 700 211 x 304	100-25	25	PL	E	X	
Olives, Ripe or Green Ripe	301 x 411 300 x 407 211 x 200	25	25	E*	E		X
Onions	211 x 304 603 x 700 303 x 406	50-25	50-25	E*	EE		X
Orange Juice	404 x 700 211 x 212 307 x 409	75-25K	75-25K	PL	PL		X
Peaches	401 x 411 303 x 406 603 x 700	50-25KI	25	PL	E		X
Pears	303 x 406 401 x 411 603 x 700	75-25KI	25	PL	E		X
Peas	303 x 406 603 x 700 211 x 304	25	25	E	E		X
Peas, Field	300 x 407 303 x 406 603 x 700	25	25	E	E		X
Pickles	603 x 700 303 x 406 211 x 304	100-25	100-25	EE*	EE	X	
Pimientos	300 x 206 211 x 200 401 x 411	50-25K	25	PL	E		X
Pineapple	307 x 409 603 x 700 211 x 414	75-25K	75-25K	PL	PL		X

For symbols, see footnotes following table.

TABLE 3.4 – Characteristics of Cans Used for Canned Food Products - Cont.

Product	Common Can Sizes	Tin Coating		Inside Enamel Coating		Type Steel	
		Body	Ends	Body	Ends	L	MR
Pineapple Juice	404 x 700 211 x 414 307 x 409	75-25K	75-25K	PL	PL		X
Plums, Dark	401 x 411 603 x 700 303 x 406	75-25	75-25	E*	E	X	
Potatoes, White	303 x 406 603 x 700 300 x 407	25	25	E	E		X
Pumpkin (Squash)	303 x 406 401 x 411 603 x 700	25	25	E*	E		X
Raspberries	303 x 406 603 x 700 211 x 304	75-25	75-25	E*	E	X	
Sauerkraut	303 x 406 401 x 411 603 x 700	100-25K	25	PL	E	X	
Sauerkraut		25	25	E*	E	X	
Spinach	303 x 406 603 x 700 401 x 411	25	25	E	E		X
Sweet Potatoes	404 x 307 603 x 700 303 x 406	50-25	50-25	E*	E		X
Tomatoes	303 x 406	75-25	75-25	E*	E		X
HTF Side Seam	603 x 700 401 x 411	25	25	E	E		X
Tomato Catsup	603 x 700	75-25	75-25	E*	E		X
HTF Side Seam		25	25	E	E		X
Tomato Juice	404 x 700	50-25	25	EE*	EE		X
HTF Side Seam	202 x 308 303 x 406	25		E	E		X

For symbols, see footnotes following table.

TABLE 3.4 – Characteristics of Cans Used for Canned Food Products - Cont.

Product	Common Can Sizes	Tin Coating		Inside Enamel Coating		Type Steel	
		Body	Ends	Body	Ends	L	MR
Tomato Paste HTF Side Seam	603 x 700	75-25	75-25	E*	E		X
	401 x 411	25	25	E	E		X
	303 x 406						
Tomato Puree HTF Side Seam	603 x 700	75-25	75-25	E*	E		X
	401 x 411	25	25	E	E		X
	303 x 406						
Hominy	300 x 407	25	25	E	E		X
	401 x 411						
	303 x 406						
Spaghetti in Tomato Sauce	401 x 602	25	25	E*	E		X
	211 x 410						
	404 x 309						
Beans with Pork in Tomato Sauce	300 x 407	25	25	E	E		X
	307 x 214						
	307 x 510						
Meat Stews	404 x 309	25	25	E	E		X
	300 x 407						
	211 x 300						
	404 x 307	(Drawn, TFS)		E	E		
	300 x 405	(Drawn, TFS)		E	E		
Chili con Carne	300 x 407	25	25	E	E		X
	211 x 300						
	404 x 309						
Corned Beef Hash	404 x 307	(Drawn, TFS)		E	E		
	300 x 405	(Drawn, TFS)		E	E		
Potted Meat	208 x 108	Al.	Al.	E	E		
Drawn bodies for aluminum	208 x 207	25	25	E	E		X
	208 x 201						
Pork and Gravy	404 x 200	25	25	E	E		X
	401 x 211						
	404 x 700						
Chicken, Boned	307 x 109	25	25	EE	EE		X
	404 x 700						
	303 x 109						

For symbols, see footnotes following table.

TABLE 3.4 – Characteristics of Cans Used for Canned Food Products - Cont.

Product	Common Can Sizes	Tin Coating Body	Tin Coating Ends	Inside Enamel Coating Body	Inside Enamel Coating Ends	Type Steel L	Type Steel MR
Ham, refrigerated	710x506x300 K.O.	25	25	E*	E		X
Alum. anode one end	904x606x308 K.O.						
	512x400x211 K.O.						
Meat, Luncheon	314x202x304 K.O.	25	25	E*	E		X
Normal storage temp.	314x202x201 K.O.						
Refrigerated	400x400x1100 K.O.	25	25	E	E		X
Alum. anode one end							
Mackerel	607x406x108#1Oval	25	25	E	E		X
	211 x 300						
	202 x 308						
Herring	607x406x108#1Oval	25	25	E	E		X
	300 x 407						
Salmon	301 x 411	25	25	E	E		X
	307 x 200						
	301 x 106						
Sardines in Oil	405x301x014.5	Al.	Al.	E	E		X
Drawn bodies both		25	25	E	E		X
aluminum & tin plate							
Sardines in Tomato	405x301x014.5	Al.	Al.	E	E		X
or Mustard Sauce		50-25	25	E	E		X
Drawn bodies both							
aluminum & tin plate							
Tuna	307 x 113	25	25	E	E		X
	211 x 109						
	401 x 205						
Clams	307 x 202	25	25	EE*	EE		X
	404 x 700						
	211 x 400						
Oysters	211 x 400	25	25	E	E		X
	211 x 300						
	211 x 304						
Fish Roe	211 x 400	25	25	E	E		X
	211 x 203						
	208 x 314						

For symbols, see footnotes following table.

TABLE 3.4 – Characteristics of Cans Used for Canned Food Products – Cont.

Product	Common Can Sizes	Tin Coating		Inside Enamel Coating		Type Steel	
		Body	Ends	Body	Ends	L	MR
Crab Meat	307 x 200 307 x 113 401 x 211	100-25	100-25	EE*	EE		X
Lobster	211 x 400 211 x 203 208 x 314	25	25	EE	EE		X
Shrimp	307 x 113 211 x 300 301 x 106	100-25	100-25	EE*	EE		X

*Inside side stripe of enamel

PL - Plain
E - Single-coat enamel
EE - Double-coat enamel

Al. - Aluminum can
HTF - High Tin Fillet
TFS - Tin Free Steel

- All welded, enameled bodies require a side seam stripe.
- K-plate Ingot cast (KI) used for plain bodies for fruits.
- If two-piece containers are used, plate and enamel specifications may differ from those in table.

In warehouse storage, palletized cans will increase storage capacity by approximately 18%. (Compared to receiving cans in reshippers). In storage, palletized cans are more economically and efficiently handled. Loaded pallets can be stacked one atop the other to full ceiling height. Transit in and out of the storage warehouse by fork truck is fast.

Some can makers and canners chose to reduce the numbers of cans per layer to confine the cans totally within the area of the pallet. This substantially reduces empty can damage during handling and transporting and lessens scrap disposal. Table 3.5 (following page) shows the reduced numbers of cans per layer used to attain this for several can sizes. A comparison with the numbers on Table 3.5 shows the losses per pallet or truckload with reduced layers.

TABLE 3.5 – Palletized Cans in Trailers

Can Size	Cans/ Pallet	Cans/ Layer	Layers	O.A.H.* in Trailer Inches	Cans/ Trailer**
211 x 304	11,160	360	31	107 1/4	200,880
	10,440	360	29	100 3/4	187,920
	5,400	360	15	107 3/4	194,400
	5,040	360	14	101 1/4	181,440
211 x 400	9,000	360	25	106 3/8	162,000
	8,280	360	23	98 3/8	149,040
	4,320	360	12	106	155,520
	3,960	360	11	98	142,560
300 x 407	6,732	306	22	104	121,176
	6,426	306	21	99 1/2	115,668
	3,366	306	11	107 1/2	121,176
	3,060	306	10	98 3/4	110,160
303 x 406	6,256	272	23	107	112,608
	5,712	272	21	98 1/4	102,816
	2,992	272	11	107 1/8	107,712
	2,720	272	10	98 1/4	97,920
307 x 306	6,496	224	29	104 3/8	116,928
	6,272	224	28	101	112,896
	3,136	224	14	104 3/4	112,896
401 x 411	3,402	162	21	104 3/4	61,236
	1,620	162	10	103 3/4	58,320
404 x 700	2,100	150	14	104 1/8	37,800
	1,950	150	13	97 1/8	35,100
	1,050	150	7	107 3/4	37,800
	900	150	6	93 3/4	32,400
603 x 700	952	68	14	104 1/8	17,136
	884	68	13	97 1/8	15,912
	476	68	7	107 3/4	17,136
	408	68	6	93 3/4	14,688

*O.A.H. indicates overall height of the pallet(s) in trailer.
**Cans/trailer based on 45' trailer, 110" high (door openings).

<u>Note</u>: Sufficient clearance (difference in trailer height and overall height of the pallets) should be allowed on the trailer so that the pallets can readily be unloaded without damage.

TABLE 3.6 – Palletized Cans in Trailers

Can Size	Cans/Pallet	Cans/Layer	Layers	Cans/Trailer
300 x 407	5,184	288	18	93,312
	5,472	288	19	98,496
	5,760	288	20	103,680
303 x 406	4,845	255	19	87,210
	5,100	255	20	91,800
401 x 411	1,248	156	8	44,928
	2,652	156	17	47,736
	2,808	156	18	50,544
404 x 700	1,584	132	12	28,512
603 x 700	384	64	6	13,824
	704	64	11	12,672
	768	64	12	13,824
	832	64	13	14,976

Carload Shipping of Empty Cans

The following are the maximum capacities of standard, 40-ft. (12 m) box cars for the can sizes shown, when loaded as indicated. This information was supplied by the Association of American Railroads and by American Can Company.

1) Bulk loading, with load extending to doorposts and bulkheads at that point, with can lids loaded in doorway between bulkheads:

   No. 303 ....140,000 cans
   No. $2^1/_2$ .... 60,000 cans
   No. 10 .... 15,000 cans
   46 oz. .... 50,000 cans

2) When cans are shipped in paper carrier bags, load extending from end to end of car:

   No. 303 ....160,000 cans
   No. $2^1/_2$ .... 80,000 cans
   No. 10 .... 20,000 cans
   46 oz. .... 60,000 cans

3) When loaded on pallets 44x56 in. (112x142 cm) size, load extending 50 to 54 in. (127–137 cm) high; 38 pallets are loaded in a 40-ft. (12 m) car and 48 pallets in a 50-ft. (15 m) car, with the following number of cans per pallet:

   No. 303 ....2,720 cans/pallet
   No. $2^1/_2$ ....1,620 cans/pallet
   No. 10 .... 408 cans/pallet
   46 oz. .... 966 cans/pallet

The empty fiberboard container for the can sizes mentioned have the following dimensions:

	Length (in/cm)	Width (in/cm)	Depth (in/cm)
No. 303 (12 cans)	12.75/32.4	9.56/24.3	4.38/11.1
No. 303 (24 cans)	12.75/32.4	9.56/24.3	8.75/22.2
No. 2-1/2 (24 cans)	16.25/41.3	12.19/31.0	9.38/23.8
No. 10 (6 cans)	18.56/47.1	12.38/31.4	7.00/17.8
46 oz (12 cans)	17.00/43.2	12.75/32.4	7.00/17.8

Can Corrosion

Much progress has been made in the technical aspects of packaging since the early years of canning, yet the criterion for successful packaging is essentially the same today, namely, that the canned product must remain in a wholesome condition for the normal expected shelf life of the particular product. Since there are no objective standards for most of the details, normal shelf life expectancy is established collaboratively by can supplier and packer through research pack tests and commercial experience. As progress is made in packaging a particular product, the performance factor, which limits the shelf life, very often changes. For example, the limiting performance factor for soft drink product shelf life changed from perforation failure in the early stages of development of a tinplate package to iron pickup tolerance in today's package.

It has been estimated that in excess of three thousand products are successfully packaged in metal containers. Containers for this wide variety of products must satisfy a number of internal and external corrosion requirements. The effective corrosivity of any particular product may vary due to both natural or formulation causes and those related to the canning operation.

External corrosion is governed in general by the same factors which are responsible for the atmospheric corrosion of metals. The internal corrosion of cans, however, differs because practically no air or at least only limited air is present. How these factors and others influence corrosion problems can best be understood by successively examining problem areas, controlling factors, and means of control.

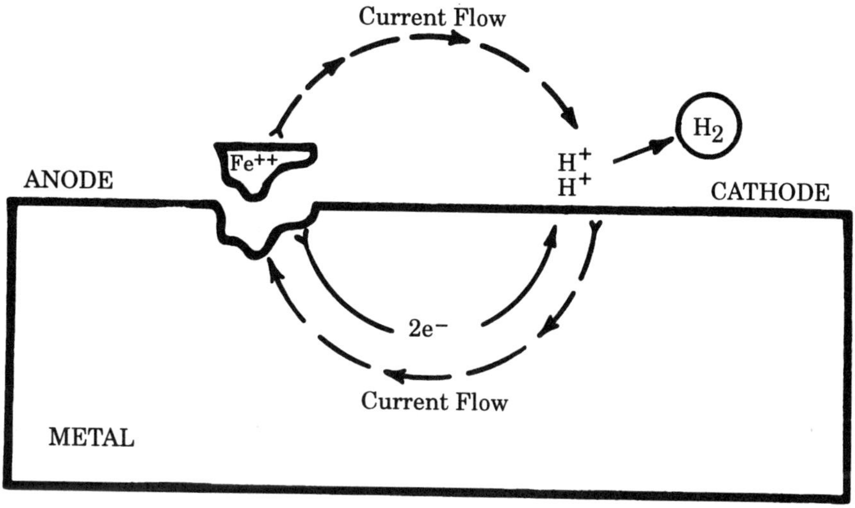

FIGURE 3.7 – Schematic Corrosion of Cell of Iron in Acid Environment

Fundamental Electrochemical Basis of Can Corrosion

Basic Principle: Electron gain or acceptance results in reduction. Electron loss results in oxidation.

Basic Principle: When an electrochemical cell discharges spontaneously, electrons flow through the external circuit from anode (–) (oxidation) to cathode (+) (reduction).

1. Dissimilar metals in an electrolyte (food) establish a voltage or potential difference (E_o).
2. Upon dissolution at the anode, metals lose electrons which are taken up by H+ at the cathode site. H_2 gas is produced.
3. Reaction continues until conditions change which result in (a) a reduction of E_o differential, (b) one of the reactants is exhausted, or (c) the cell is polarized.
4. In the diagram presented here, Fe is oxidized to Fe^{++} while $2H^+$ are reduced to H_2 (gas).
5. In most canned foods there is a reversal of polarity. This reversal results in Sn being more anodic than Fe, while according to their standard electrode potentials, Fe is more anodic than Sn; therefore when both are available to form electrochemical cells, Fe should dissolve first. Because of the reversal of polarity, Sn dissolves preferentially and protects the tinplate steel. It is then said that Sn is sacrificial to Fe.

Internal Corrosion

Perforations are pinholes through the container metal caused by localized corrosion of iron. These type failures should be avoided because not only is the individual can lost, but secondary spoilage of other cans is possible through exterior corrosion caused by the spilled product.

Springers or swells. Springers or hydrogen swells are evidenced by a bulging of the can ends caused by hydrogen gas formation. Although the product may be satisfactory, springers are unacceptable because product spoilage is usually associated with the same external appearance. Hydrogen swells maybe accompanied by excessive detinning in a plain can and certainly by high iron solution in a plain or organic-coated can.

Detinning is dissolution of tin from the tinplate surface, and although usually associated with plain tinplate, may take place through enamel films. A reaction resulting in general overall etching of the tinned surface is expected with some products and is acceptable; however, localized detinned areas where black-appearing base metal is exposed may not be acceptable. Product bleaching or color loss usually accompanies detinning; certain flavor changes may also occur. These changes are desirable for some products but not for others.

Rusting is the formation of loosely adhering, reddish-brown ferric oxide corrosion product on the corrosion site. Rust formation requires an excess of oxygen and thus when present in a can is usually found in the headspace area. Corrosion will continue under the rust layer; if sufficient corrosion capacity is available, perforation will result. Rust in itself is unsightly and may drop into and contaminate the product.

Enamel lifting is detachment of the organic film from the plate surface. Bubbles or loose flaps of film may be formed; film detachment is usually accompanied by mild corrosion at the area of detachment; base metal may be exposed resulting in increased corrosion. The possibility that particles or organic coating may drop into and contaminate the product is always present when lifting occurs.

Staining is adherent gray-black stannous tin sulfide formation on the plate surface and occurs under organic films as well as on plain tinplate. Dark tin sulfide deposits appear about the same as base metal exposed through detinning and are just as objectionable.

Discoloration or formation of loose black iron sulfide, which occurs in the headspace, is the reaction product of exposed iron and hydrogen sulfide. When it forms on an organic-coated surface, it forms on the surface of the organic coating, not at the plate surface. Formation of large quantities of iron sulfide usually result in black deposits on the product since the deposits are very loose.

Factors Influencing Internal Corrosion

1. Food pH.
2. Food composition: (a) corrosion accelerators-red and purple pigments (anthocyanins), sulfur compounds, copper ions (Cu^{2+}), certain amino acids, oxygen (gaseous or dissolved). (b) corrosion inhibitors: lecithin, betain.
3. Temperature and length of storage of canned food.
4. Can vacuum. Oxygen is a depolarizer in the electrochemical corrosion reaction.
5. Headspace in can. This factor is related to amount of oxygen available in the headspace.
6. Rate of cooling of canned product after sterilization.
7. Type and characteristics of container. Factors include whether can is made of tin plate, chromed steel, or aluminum, the type of inside can enamel, the type of steel plate and the tin coating weight. Size of can may also be a factor.

External Corrosion

Rusting is the formation of loosely adhering reddish-brown ferric oxide (Fe_2O_3) at pores in the tin coating. Rusting may occur during processing because of corrosive water conditions, during storage because of poor warehouse conditions, or during shipment because of poor transportation facilities. Perforations due to exterior corrosion are unlikely even with the thinnest tin coated plates, but rusty appearance of cans, especially rust spotting through paper labels, is very objectionable.

Detinning, dissolution of tin from the tinplate surface, may result in localized base steel exposure in a general overall surface etching, depending on severity of the reaction and cause of attack. Detinning can be caused by alkaline retort water or alkaline rinse water and can also be caused by rusty equipment in electrochemical contact with cans. Appearance of the can may be readily degraded further because corroded areas are more susceptible to subsequent attack.

Staining is formation of any surface change other than detinning or rusting which interferes with normal bright appearance of the tin surface.

CORROSION ATTRIBUTABLE TO CANNING PRACTICES

Fill and Vacuum

Maintenance of proper fill of the container is of great importance in controlling corrosive influences. A well balanced fill must be attained. The headspace should be large enough to provide an adequate reservoir for hydrogen formation, but it should not be so large that excessive air is left in the can to promote corrosion. As a rule of thumb, a 5% headspace is considered optimum.

For many products, control of headspace, in itself, is not enough. To obtain high initial vacuum, headspace control must be supplemented by removal of gases contained in the product and in the headspace. Adequate thermal exhausting, maintenance of high closing temperatures, effective vacuum syruping, or efficient vacuum or steam closure lead to the production of internal vacuum and thereby improve the life of the container and the quality of the product. Excessive air trapped within the can, as the result of inadequate exhausting or ineffective syruping or closure, may result in rapid corrosion of the can, product discoloration and peeling of inside enamels.

Thermal Exhausting

When cans must be exhausted in steam, it is imperative that the exhaust box temperature be held above 205°F (96°C). When exhausting temperatures are below 205°F (96°C), considerable air is mixed with the steam, and under such conditions, some rusting is apt to occur.

In hot water exhaust boxes, the temperature should be as near the boiling point as possible. In addition, care must be taken to avoid aeration of the water and accumulation of corrosive agents due to product spillage and concentration through evaporation. Thermal exhausting equipment must be kept clean and free from rust.

Code Marking

Can covers are usually coded mechanically by an embossing device driven by the closing machine. Excessive depth of impression, worn or damaged type, too sharp a profile in the marking dies or misalignment of the type used in the marking device will produce sharp imprints which permit external rusting or rapid corrosion on the inside of the can due to fracture of the tin or enamel coating. Closing machine operators should be instructed to secure type without excessively sharp edges, to determine that they are held in exact alignment in the marking device and to maintain the marking pressure as light as possible to avoid fracture of the inside enamel and still obtain legible imprint.

The use of ink marking devices avoids such difficulties; this method of coding is recommended for cans packed with acid products. Ink marking is also used for aluminum cans with easy-opening ends since it is impractical to emboss the special ends. Ink with a phenolic base should be avoided to preclude the possibility of product off-flavors.

Faulty Closures

Improperly formed top double seams may permit leakage and spoilage. Product leakage will result in external corrosion on cans in contact with the leaking product. Accelerated internal corrosion can result if a can leaks, permitting air to enter the can.

Washing the Sealed Can

Even with well controlled filling and syruping operations, some spillage of salt brine or acid sugar syrup is to be expected. Allowed to remain on the can, the residues resulting from spillage will induce corrosion and rust formation.

To avoid trouble from this source, sealed cans should be washed with water sprays delivered under good pressure as they leave the closing machine. Spray washers can be set in the line in the closing machine discharge. Hot water spray is preferable for effective cleaning. It is essential with those products where a hot fill alone is depended upon for sterilization or where a high initial temperature at the start of the process is a requirement of the heat treatment.

Some canners of products which require only a boiling water process depend upon the processing water to wash the outside of the cans. This is not good practice because continuous delivery of unwashed cans to the processing water builds up a concentration of acid, sugar or salt in the water to the point where residues remain on the surfaces of the cans after they are taken from the processing bath. Even after thorough drying, such residues have a tendency to absorb moisture from the air and thereby promote rusting. Whether the cans are processed in steam or boiling water, exterior surfaces should be thoroughly washed before retorting.

Meat and fish canneries wash cans after closing to remove residues of grease which accumulate on the outside of cans during filling and closing operations. Hot alkaline detergent solutions are generally used for this purpose. It is most important to use a minimum concentration of detergent and control it carefully lest it attack the tin coating or outside enamel. If, in spite of these precautions, signs of attack appear, the supplier should be consulted for alternative materials. Cans should always be rinsed with fresh water following an alkaline detergent wash. Highly alkaline detergents should not be used for cleaning aluminum cans since alkalies react readily with aluminum.

Open Water Bath Operation

Temperature is the principal factor determining the rusting tendency in water bath processing. The oxygen of the air is soluble in water; increasing temperatures reduce rusting by lowering oxygen solubility. On the other hand, for the same oxygen content, higher temperatures will produce more rust. The net effect of these two conflicting tendencies is to produce the greatest rust hazard at about 175°F (80°C); from here to the boiling point, the rusting tendency gradually decreases.

Rusting in boiling water processing can be minimized by being sure that the water is actually boiling at the time the cans are introduced and not "rolling." "Rolling" can be caused by the injection of steam into the water and, while it resembles boiling, occurs at temperatures considerably below the boiling point. The oxygen content of "rolling" water may be comparatively high.

Chemical treatment of the water may be necessary when using water processes, particularly when the processing temperature is below the boiling point. Air agitation of water cooks at temperatures below the boiling point should not be used because the water becomes saturated with oxygen and aggravate rust formation.

Steam Retort Operation

In processing cans, strict attention must be given to the details of correct retort operation. "Retort rusting" is promoted by the following improper practices in steam retort operations:

1. Inadequate venting and bleeding of retorts.
2. A low-pressure steam supply.
3. Excessively long come-up time.

Conditions established by any of these practices tend to expose the cans to a combination of air, moisture, and high temperature conducive to corrosion and rust formation.

Corrosion caused by improper retort operation is generally characterized by rust development at points of greatest draw or mechanical strain in the plate. Dark red rust usually appears first on the top and bottom double seams. In more severe cases it will form on the can end profiles and embossed code marks.

In general, suggestions for retort operation provided by the latest edition of National Food Processors Association Bulletin 26-L, should be observed.

To remove air rapidly from the retort at the beginning of the process, retort vents should be left wide open for the temperature and time prescribed by the Bulletin for the particular type of equipment. Automatic controllers may be bypassed if necessary to prevent an excessive come-up time. In accordance with FDA Good Manufacturing Practice regulations (21 CFR-Part 113) the bleeders must be open during the entire process to assist in eliminating small residues of air that may be trapped in the retort. Venting of automatic loading systems should be closely checked. Occasionally, steam may contain excessive amounts of oxygen or carbon dioxide which will attack the can under the conditions of heat and moisture in the steam retort. This can be avoided by the installation of suitable deaerators and preheaters for the boiler feed water.

Special precautions are required in processing aluminum cans. Separator sheets should be placed between layers in the retort basket. These separators should not be made of a dissimilar metal since galvanic reactions between the metals could cause corrosion of the aluminum cans, particularly at the scored area of an easy-opening end. Aluminum cans with easy-open ends should always be pressure cooled after processing to avoid undue strain on the scored ends.

Contact with Rusty Iron

A condition somewhat related to rust is sometimes caused during sterilization by contact with rusted retort crates or trays. The discolored condition is termed "steam burning" and is evidenced by a typical multi-colored iridescent film on the can found only at points where it contacts the rusty iron. No discoloration occurs where the iron is clean and unrusted. If this problem is encountered, rusted areas of the retort crates or trays should be covered with an inert material. Avoid closing any of the openings in the crates or trays as this could retard steam circulation in the retort.

Contact with Alkaline Water

Alkaline water may produce unsightly etching and spangling of the can. Prolonged exposure results in an attack on the tin coating or outside enamel, leaving the cans readily subject to rusting. Alkaline water may also cause severe corrosion of aluminum containers, particularly at score lines.

Alkalinity of water may result from alkaline detergents carried to the retort on cans, from carry-over of alkaline salts from the boiler, or from the concentration of naturally alkaline water in the retort. Corrective treatment may be applied to each condition and if corrosion of this nature occurs, advice should be sought from a competent laboratory. In any event, it is good practice to not allow condensate to build up in the bottom of retorts.

Improper Cooling

When water cooling is employed, the contents of cans should be cooled to 95–105°F (35-41°C) average temperature, that temperature obtained after thoroughly mixing the contents of the cans by shaking. If the cans are cooled to an average temperature appreciably below 95°F (35°C), heat retained in the cans is insufficient to evaporate the residual moisture on can surfaces and rusting may occur. On the other hand, if the average temperature after water cooling is greater than 105°F (41°C), there is danger of flat sour spoilage, early hydrogen springer formation, or quality degradation, depending upon the nature of the product.

Elimination of residual water by evaporation must be supplemented by mechanical removal. This may be accomplished by tipping retort crates after they come from the cooling tank or by use of one of several types of can drying systems.

The practice of taking cooled cans from retort crates without draining, or with only superficial draining, and packing directly into cases should be avoided.

Corrosive Water Supplies

The chemical composition of water used in processing and cooling may be a factor in the production of rust. The danger of accumulation of alkaline residues or the carry-over of alkaline substances from the boiler into processing water has been referred to above. Waters of high natural alkalinity attack metal surfaces during boiling water processing or pressure processing carried on under water. The action of these waters will etch or spangle cans, and, in addition to this undesirable discoloration, will leave them more easily subject to rusting during storage. If the offending water contains appreciable concentrations of chlorides, sulfides, or sulfates, the can may be attached with formation of rust and discoloration during the process.

In a similar manner, alkaline water, excessively chlorinated water, water high in chlorides or sulfates, or slightly acid water may induce corrosion when used for cooling purposes. Factors which influence the degree of this type of attack, other than the condition of the water itself, are the time of cooling and water temperature. Following the general rule for chemical reactions, the attack by corrosive waters is accentuated as the temperature rises. If the cooling water is warm, cans must be exposed to the water for longer periods of time to effect the necessary cooling.

In general, the problems associated with the use of alkaline or corrosive waters require specific remedial treatments for each water supply. Accordingly, if there is any indication that the water supply may be involved in a rusting problem, a laboratory associated with the industry should be consulted.

Scratches and Abrasions

Scratching or abrasion of the tin coating on cans exposes the steel base metal, with consequent danger of rusting; the coating of the can may be marred or scratched by rough handling of either empty or filled cans. Operators must be cautioned to exercise care in loading cans onto runways, in transferring them to retort trays or baskets, and in the casing operation. Runways, gravity drops, elevators, exhaust boxes and can dividers must be carefully inspected to eliminate points where scratching, abrasion, or denting can occur.

Particular care is required in handling aluminum cans with easy-opening ends. The easy-opening feature which provides easy access to the contents for the consumer also reduces resistance to abusive handling. Modifications of equipment may be necessary to avoid all rough handling. Filled cans should be cased with a separator sheet between layers to avoid damage to the easy-open end by flexing action on the opening tab.

CORROSION ATTRIBUTABLE TO STORAGE CONDITIONS

High Storage Temperature

Perhaps the greatest enemy of long service in metal cans is high storage temperatures. Prolonged exposure to temperatures above 75°F (24°C) will result in early development of hydrogen swells and perforations, regardless of the weight of tin coating on the cans. Under abnormally severe conditions, losses may occur even in foods usually considered non-corrosive.

It is imperative that adequate attention be given to the maintenance of reasonable warehouse temperatures. Special emphasis must be given to the temperature of the cans at the time of casing and also to the method of stacking cases in the warehouse. Palletized storage or stacking in narrow blocks permits ventilation, quickly reducing can temperature to that of the warehouse.

Sweating

Moisture on the surface of the can will lead to rust formation during storage. One of the most frequent causes of external rusting during storage or shipment is the process of sweating.

Sweating will not occur if the temperature of cans is equal to or greater than that of the surrounding atmosphere. If the temperature of the cans is less than that of the atmosphere, sweating may occur, depending upon the magnitude of the temperature difference, and also upon the relative humidity. These conditions most likely to cause sweating are high relative humidity and a can temperature well below that of the air.

Theoretically, the best storage condition from the standpoint of rust prevention would prevail if cans were always maintained at a temperature somewhat higher than that of the surrounding atmosphere. This is not practicable, of course, and from commercial standpoint the best conditions are established when cans are maintained at the same temperature as the surrounding atmosphere. This may be accomplished by proper heating and ventilating of the storage quarters; warehouse temperatures and relative humidities should be measured frequently.

Most sweating develops when sudden increases in temperature and humidity of the atmosphere occur. In most areas this condition is met in the Spring when warehouses are likely to be cool. If a cool warehouse is opened to the outside air on a warm, humid day following a cool period, some sweating is almost certain to occur, particularly on uncased cans near the outside of the stack. When such atmospheric conditions occur, warehouse doors should be kept tightly closed until the temperature of the cans is brought up to that of the outside air, or slightly higher. Any planned change in warehouse temperature should be made gradually. Sweating may also occur during shipment of cold cans into warmer areas.

The introduction of steam into the warehouse from brine tanks, boiling water baths, retorts, or other sources will increase the relative humidity and may also effect atmospheric temperature. For these reasons, warehouses should be so located and so protected as to prevent the access of steam.

Other Causes of Rusting

Cans stored in warehouses located near seacoasts or transported by ship are particularly subject to external rusting because of the corrosive action of salt spray. To protect cans from salt and high humidity, it is advisable to store them in tight cases. Coastal warehouses should be so constructed and ventilated that a minimum of air currents from the ocean enters storage areas.

Rust may occur in fibre cases if the fiberboard is damp. Green lumber with comparatively high moisture content may produce rust when used for cases or pallets. Special care must be taken to avoid casing wet cans in moisture-resistant cartons from which evaporation is very slow. Rusting has occurred with fiberboard having a high salt content. An unsuitable carton adhesive can also lead to rust formation.

Some instances of staining and rusting have been attributed to the hygroscopic nature, i.e., moisture-absorbing property, or certain label pastes. Packers should receive assurance from the manufacturer that the paste and glues used in labeling operations are satisfactory from this standpoint. It is possible for label papers to accelerate rusting; some are more hygroscopic than others and may contain rust producing substances.

Rusting of cans may also result from exposure to such corrosive atmospheres as vinegar fumes in pickle plants. Sulfur dioxide in the atmosphere, which can result from the storage of brined cherries and similar products in the same warehouse as canned goods, may also produce rusting.

CAN ENAMELS (LININGS, COATINGS)

Organic coatings are useful on cans for canned foods to prevent chemical interactions between the food and the container when these reactions may adversely affect canned food quality. Although many attempts have been made to develop an all-purpose protective coating, they have not been successful. Some 20 different enamels are needed to meet the requirements of the many products now packed in cans. Plain (uncoated) cans are used when the can-food interactions are not significant, or when the quality of the food is better in a plain can. The plain tin causes a bleaching action and improves the color of some products which normally would darken in a fully enameled can.

Types of Enamels

Epoxy and Epoxy-Phenolic

Epoxy coatings were first characterized for their high heat stability as shown by their lack of discoloration from soldering the side seam of a can. It was noted that they also had excellent fabrication resistance (body bead formation, end profile rings, and drawn aerosol tops). They give excellent performance with cans for aseptically canned products. Epoxy-phenolic coatings have been available for many years, but took a back seat to oleoresinous coatings for economic reasons. In 1985 coating manufacturers brought the price of epoxy-phenolic coatings close enough to that of oleoresinous materials that the can manufacturers making only food cans could use a single base material for all their cans and ends. Epoxy-phenolic coatings can be used as a transparent gold coating both as single or double coat, a C-enamel by adding zinc oxide paste, or an aluminum pigmented material for meat products, spaghetti sauce, or sauerkraut.

Oleoresinous and phenolic coatings are more economical than epoxy-phenolic coatings, but are more limited in the variety of products they can satisfactorily protect. Phenolic coatings can cause flavor problems with some products.

Water base and powdered coatings: environmental problems leading to legislation controlling the disposition of organic coatings and solvents have caused the canmakers and their coating suppliers to seek coatings that are environment-friendly. Water base coatings and powdered coatings are two developments in this direction.

Water base coatings will protect cans from many products, but are not as universal as epoxy-phenolic coatings. They can be run on the same roller coater equipment as organic solvent reduced coatings. There are water base vinyl spray coat materials that have been used on cans for beer, carbonated beverages, and fruit drinks for many years. However, coater equipment cleanup to change from solvent base coating to water base coating and vise-versa is difficult and very time consuming. Water based coatings are presently used commercially by can manufacturers who have long production runs and few changeovers.

Powdered coatings are environmentally friendly because they are one hundred percent solid and do not pollute the atmosphere. Their application is currently limited to spray coating and electrostatic coating. This precludes their use from the coil coating and sheet coating methods used by food can manufacturers. They form films by the fusion of the thermoplastic particles with heat. These films are resistant to all food products.

Powdered coatings have been used as inside side seam stripes, coatings covering the inside of side seams of three piece cans for many years. These coatings have excellent resistance to most food products. Adhesion to uncoated tin plate can be a problem and a check for proper adhesion should be incorporated into the quality control program for the manufacture of welded cans where powdered inside side seam stripes are used.

Some products such as blueberries tend to undercut the powdered side seam stripe at double seam crossovers and lift the stripe from the can. This condition can be discovered within two or three months of test packing and storage at room temperature. It is caused by loss of side seam stripe adhesion at the lap areas of the bodies and occurs during double seam fabrication.

Vinyl. These enamels are usually used as a double coating in combination with an oleoresinous or a phenolic enamel. They are commonly used for more highly corrosive foods. A typical example is a system having a basic coat of "R" enamel and a top coat of vinyl with side seam striping used for apple juice. Side seam striping consists of an additional coating striped on the inside of the can side seam. Vinyl enamels are tough and free from flavor. They have poor resistance to steam but are well suited for products sterilized at 200°F (93°C) or less.

Other enamels are the epoxy-modified vinyl used for highly colored fruits over a phenolic-modified epoxy the modified phenolic, which when aluminum pigmented, is used for meats' the epoxy-ureaformaldehyde; and the alkyds.

Application of Enamels

Application of enamels to tin plate: (a) applied to flat sheets by roller coaters and baked at 400–450°F (204–232°C) in continuous ovens before being made into cans, or (b) sprayed into cans or on their component parts.

Desired Qualities of Enamels

Enamels for food cans should have the following characteristics: (a) lack of toxicity, (b) should not affect the flavor or color of food, (c) should be an effective barrier between food and container, (d) should be easy to apply on tin plate; (e) should not peel-off or blister during canned foods sterilization and storage, (f) should have mechanical resistance to can manufacturing operations, and (g) should be economical.

Trends

There is a trend to decrease the thickness of the tin coating on the steel plate for economic and strategic reasons. Better enamels, improvements in steel metallurgy, and the development and improvement of electrolytic tin plating have resulted in continually improved performance of tin plate cans for canned foods.

Evaluation of Enamels

In the development and evaluation of an inside enamel for cans, flavor testing justifiably received great attention. The flavor of every product is affected to some extent by the container whether it be made of glass, metal, or flexible packaging material. After a time, consumers become more or less accustomed to the flavor which may be associated with a specific type of container and may reject as unsatisfactory many other containers. As an illustration, enamel linings have been accused of imparting an "enamel flavor" to some products normally packed in plain tin cans. Generally, tomato juice packed in plain cans is preferred from the standpoint of flavor to the same juice packed in enamel cans. By coincidence, it appears that this preference of the tomato juice from the plain can is related to the presence of small amounts of tin dissolved from the container, or perhaps to the reducing action of the plain tin surface on the tomato juice.

When tin is exposed to some food products, a bleaching action occurs. Although this is very objectionable with many products such as the red fruits, and is avoided by the use of a suitable can lining, there are instances when this bleaching action is desirable. This is particularly true with lighter colored products such as grapefruit juice, grapefruit segments and sauerkraut. This slight bleaching action keeps the color light and compensates for the normal darkening effect which may result from processing or sterilization. Peaches and pears packed in cans completely enameled inside will be somewhat darker in color and slightly different in flavor than if packed in cans lined with plain tin. Although some individuals may prefer peaches packed in all enameled cans, it is doubtful if such cans will be produced under present conditions because the presence of an appreciable area of plain tin greatly increases the shelf life of this canned product.

Under current manufacturing conditions an all-enameled can will have all but a few very small areas covered with the enamel. Corrosion attended by the formation of sufficient hydrogen to displace the vacuum normally found in packed food cans and actually causing the ends to "swell," may occur in much less time in enameled cans than in "plain" or partly plain cans. In some cases the corrosion may be so confined to localized areas that the can may become perforated by one or more "pinholes." Not all corrosion problems can be eliminated by the use of can linings presently available.

There are instruments available to determine the continuity of the enamel coating on the steel plate, i.e., to detect the number and area of the points on the tin plate where the steel plate is not covered with enamel. These points are usually microscopic in size. One such instrument, the Waco Enamel Rater, operates on a principle which relates coating integrity to the amount of current flowing in a conductivity cell. Under normal test conditions, the electrode acts as the cathode and the can as the anode. An electrolyte solution added to the can is the medium for current flow. The enamel coating on the interior of the can inhibits flow of current by acting as an insulator. The amount of current flow, therefore, is related to the amount of metal exposure due to incomplete enamel coverage.

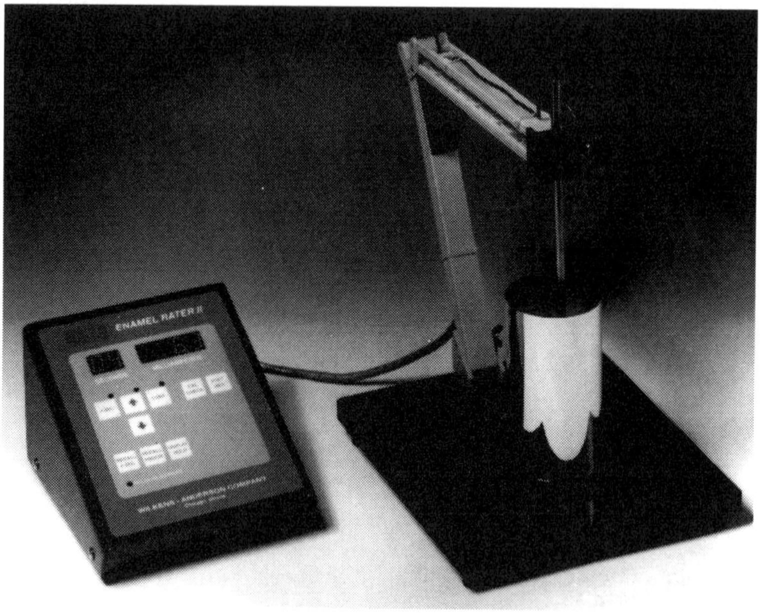

FIGURE 3.8 – Can Enamel Rater
(Courtesy Wilkens-Anderson Company)

CAN SEAM INSPECTION

Good can double seams are absolutely essential to prevent losses due to spoilage. The food processor is responsible for the quality of double seams produced in his plant. He must provide adequately trained personnel to perform double seam evaluations and make closing machine adjustments. Making consistently good double seams requires careful closing machine maintenance, frequent regularly scheduled double seam evaluations, the keeping of complete and accurate double seam records, and immediate correction of double seam conditions that are outside established tolerances. Minimum schedules for visual and teardown examinations are stated in 21 CFR Part 113.60 along with a required list of evaluations. All evaluations must be recorded.

The quality of double seams cannot be judged by measurements alone. The evaluator should keep two things in mind:

(1) The double seam is completely formed in the first operation. The second operation only irons the double seam out and determines its tightness.
(2) The goal, a properly formed seam is reached by attaining satisfactory body hook/cover hook overlap and minimum cover hook wrinkle. The other measurements and evaluations help attain these characteristics.

Expert visual examination of the double seam is very important. In this aspect of double seam evaluation there is no substitute for training and experience.

Ideal dimensions produce the best seams; however, over-adjustment to try to maintain ideal measurements is undesirable. There are normal variations in plate weight, can and end dimensions, and machine capability which must be recognized. Variations are permissible within the recommended adjustment limits.

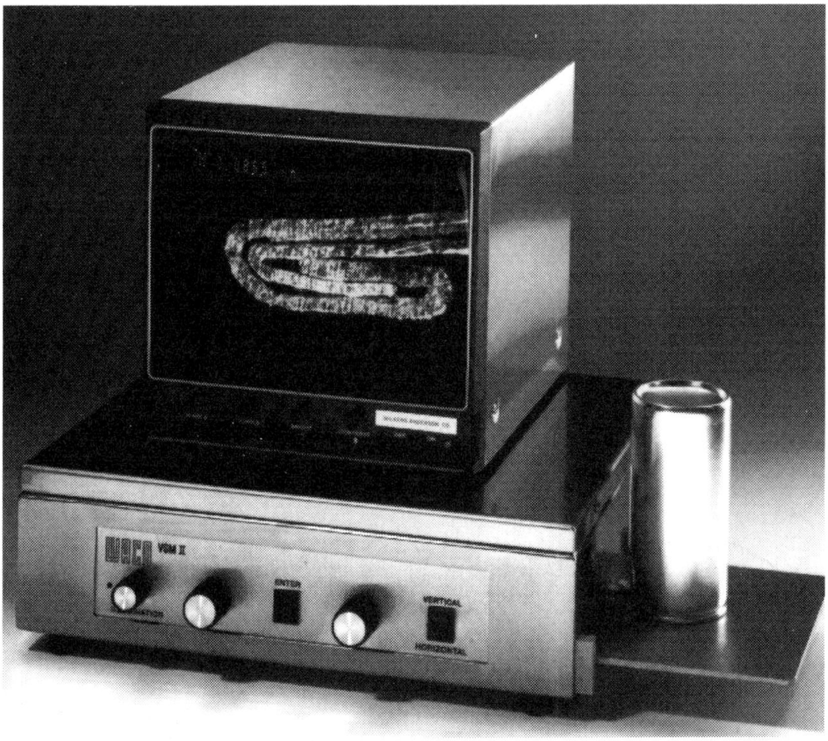

FIGURE 3.9 – Video Seam Monitor
(Courtesy Wilkens-Anderson Company)

The importance of keeping good double seam inspection records cannot be overemphasized. Good records help maintenance and quality control personnel spot trends and provide the data needed to make sound judgements. Records should be examined regularly by supervisory people.

In the final analysis, the judgement of seam quality depends upon the competence and experience of the people on the job.

Can manufacturing companies usually give advice and help set up can seam inspection programs in canning plants. Can manufacturers also have available excellent bulletins describing the can seam inspection procedure with the aid of illustrations. A discussion of the main factors related to can seam inspection follows. For more detail, consult a can seam inspection manual published by one of the can making companies.

TABLE 3.7 – Inspection Frequencies

EXTERNAL SEAM MEASUREMENTS		
FIRST OPERATION		
Inspection Items	Frequency	Sample Size
1. Thickness 2. Width	At set-up and at least after every 40 hours of operation.	One can from each seaming spindle.
SECOND OPERATION		
1. Width 2. Thickness 3. Countersink	At set-up. After adjustments, jams and change-overs. Minimum–every 4 hours.	One can from each seaming spindle.

VISUAL INSPECTION AFTER TEAR DOWN		
Inspection Items	Frequency	Sample Size
1. Cover Hook Tightness 2. Jumped Seam 3. Cover Hook Droop 4. Pressure Ridge	At set-up. After adjustments, jams and change-overs. Minimum–every 4 hours.	One can from each seaming spindle.

INTERNAL SEAM MEASUREMENTS		
Inspection Items	Frequency	Sample Size
1. Overlap (check on Seam Projector 2. Body Hook Length 3. Cover Hook Length	At set-up. After adjustments, jams and change-overs. Minimum–every 4 hours.	One can from each seaming spindle.

Visual Examination of Double Seams

During regular production runs, it is essential that a constant watch be maintained in order to catch gross maladjustments such as deadheads, cutovers, droops, lips, false seams, spinners (skids) or any other similar double seam defects. Maintaining this constant check may be accomplished in several ways, depending on the type of machine, line speeds, and general equipment layout. It may best be performed by the closing machine operator trained to recognize irregularities by visual examination. However, an equally adequate check program can be maintained through use of other trained personnel.

The operator or can closure supervisor should visually examine, at intervals of not more than 30 minutes, the top seam of a randomly selected can from each seaming station, and should record his observations. Rotating the seam between the thumb and forefinger is very helpful in detecting certain types of seam defects. Additional visual seam inspections should be made immediately after a can jam in a closing machine, or after start-up of a machine following a prolonged shut-down. All pertinent observations should be recorded. If irregularities are found, the action taken should be noted. See tables on Inspection Frequencies, Record and Visual External Seam Examinations, and on Recording Double Seam Measurements.

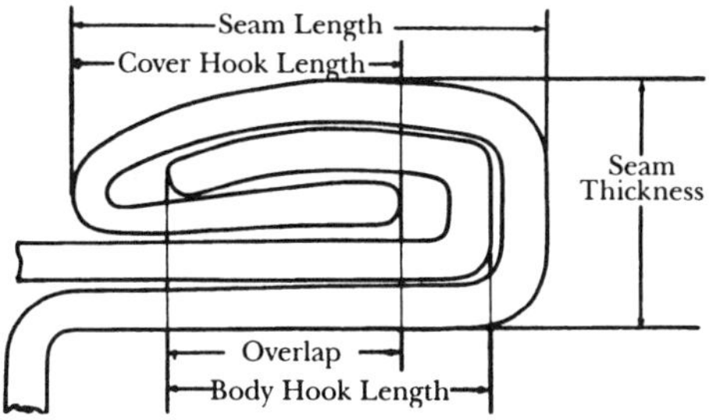

Exact measurement of hook lengths is of real importance. Most companies have established minimum limits. Hook lengths, therefore, are measured in 1,000ths of an inch, without guessing.

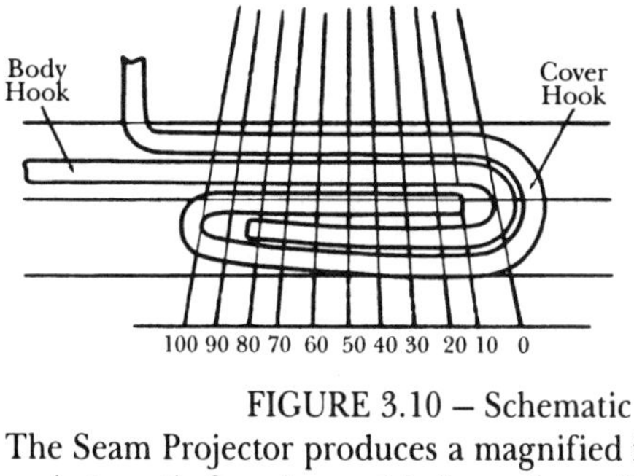

Butting and exact overlap percentages are read directly without computations on the Nomograph Card.

FIGURE 3.10 – Schematic of Can Seam Projector
The Seam Projector produces a magnified image of the cross-section of can seams. Automatic focusing and independence from factory lighting conditions make it an accurate and practical production control tool for the plant.
(Courtesy Wilkens-Anderson Company)

TABLE 3.8 – Record of Visual External Seam Examination

DATE __________ LINE NO.__________ CAN SIZE __________ CAN CODE ________

Time	Spindle No.	Decision on Seams		Remarks
		Accept	Reject	

TABLE 3.9 – Recording Double Seam Measurements

PLANT __________ DATE __________ LINE NO. __________ CAN SIZE __________ CAN CODE __________

Time	Spindle	Width	Thickness	Countersink Depth	Body Hook Length		Cover Hook Length	Overlap Optical	Tightness Rating	Pressure Ridge	Remarks
	No.	Max.		Max.	Min.	Max.				[See Legend]	[See Note]
Recommended →											

LEGEND: N - No G - Good S - Severe [Record forms may also be obtained from can suppliers.]

Note: Under remarks, indicate all abnormal seam conditions which are observed, such as Jumped Seams, Cut Overs, Cut Seams, Droops, Lips, etc. When adjustments are made, duplicate measurements should be shown in a color different from the original recording. Indicate under remarks when measurements are recorded after an adjustment has been made to the seaming station.

Tear-Down Examination of Can Seams

The minimum frequency recommended for making tear-down examinations is one can per seaming station taken at intervals not to exceed 4 hours. It should be made as soon as possible after starting up following a shut-down, waiting only long enough for the machine to "warm up." Cans for visual inspection should be taken during this warm up period. The results of the tear-down examinations should be recorded, and corrective actions, if any, should be noted.

Essential and Optional Seam Measurements

Optical System (use of seam scope or projector)

Essential – Body hook, Overlap, Tightness (observation for wrinkle).

Optional – Width (length, height), Cover hook, Countersink and Thickness.

Micrometer Measurement System

Essential – Cover hook, Body hook, Width (length, height), Tightness (observation of wrinkle thickness).

Optional – Overlap (by calculation) and Countersink.

Regardless of whether or not a seam scope or seam projector is used, the double seam should be torn down for examination.

It is standard procedure to make two measurements for each double seam characteristic if a seam scope or seam projector is used. If a micrometer is used, three measurements are made at points approximately 120 degrees apart excluding the side seam. The high and low measurements must fall within limits considered to be normal for the conditions, and should be recorded.

With regard to measurement limits, the canner should follow the working limits recommended by the can supplier.

The following diagram of a double seam shows the characteristics and the terminology for the measurements. A diagram such as this one should be displayed in the plant area where seams are to be examined. An expanded diagram may be obtained from a can supplier.

FIGURE 3.11 – Double Seam Terminology

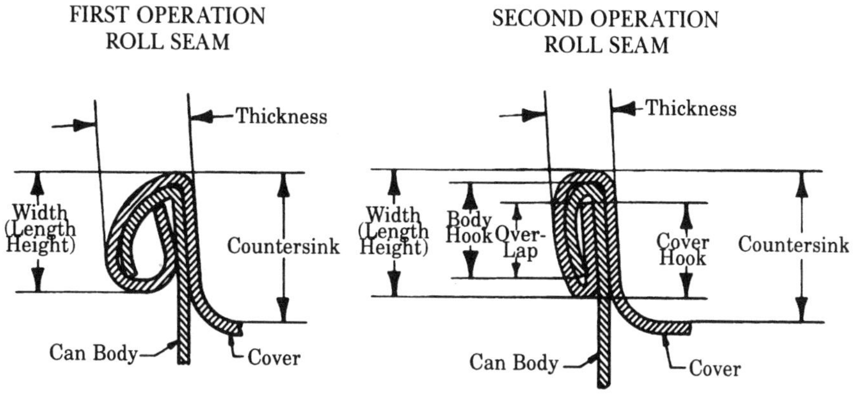

Minimum Measurements

Width* (not essential, if overlap measured optically)
Thickness*
Countersink (desirable, but not essential)
Body Hook*
Cover Hook* (required, if micrometer used)
Overlap* (essential, if optical system used)
Tightness* or Wrinkle

*Essential requirements.

Calculation of Overlap Length

Overlap length = CH+BH+T−W,
where CH = cover hook
BH = body hook
T** = cover thickness
W = seam width.

**In general practice, 0.010 may be used for the tin plate thickness.

TEARING DOWN THE DOUBLE SEAM FOR INSPECTION

The method preferred by most is to separate the body and cover hook of the finished seam in the following manner, illustrated in Figures 3-12 through 3-29. Use special can opener to cut out center section of cover approximately $^3/_8$ in. (1 cm) from double seam. Use nippers to remove remainder of center of cover. Cut through double seam about one inch (2.5 cm) from lap. Remove stripped part of cover by gently tapping with nippers, taking care not to distort can body hook. Proceed to make internal seam measurements.

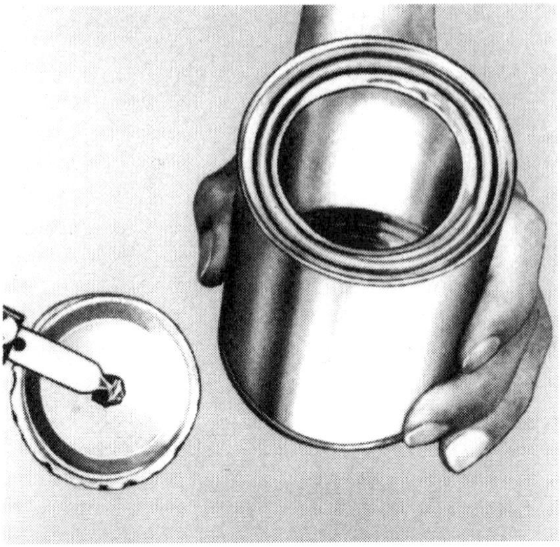

FIGURE 3.12 – Use special can opener to cut out center section of cover approximately $^3/_8$ in. from double shown, as shown. (Courtesy former American Can Company)

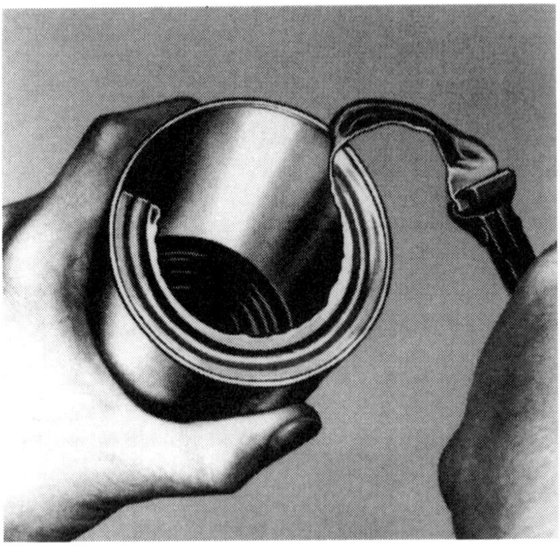

FIGURE 3.13 – Use nippers and remove remainder of center of cover. (Courtesy former American Can Company)

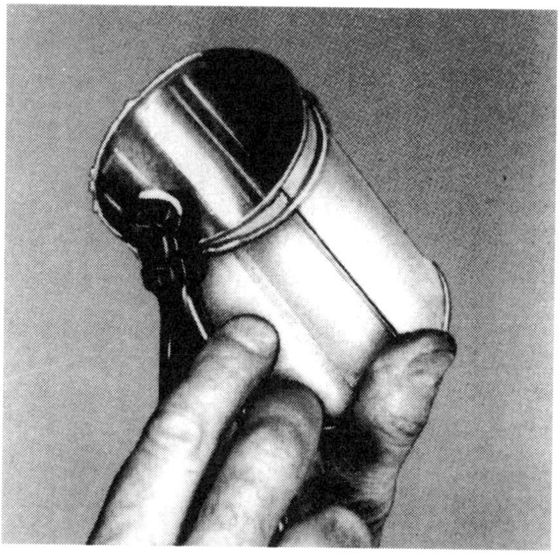

FIGURE 3.14 – Using nippers, cut through double seam about one inch from lap and remove stripped part of cover by gently tapping with nippers, taking care not to distort can body hook. (Courtesy former American Can Company)

FIGURE 3.15 – Double seam micrometer.
(Courtesy former American Can Company)

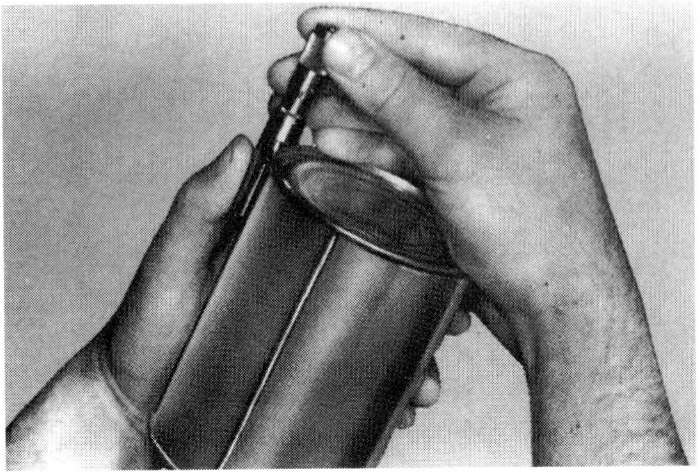

FIGURE 3.16 – Measuring seam width (height, length).
(Courtesy former American Can Company)

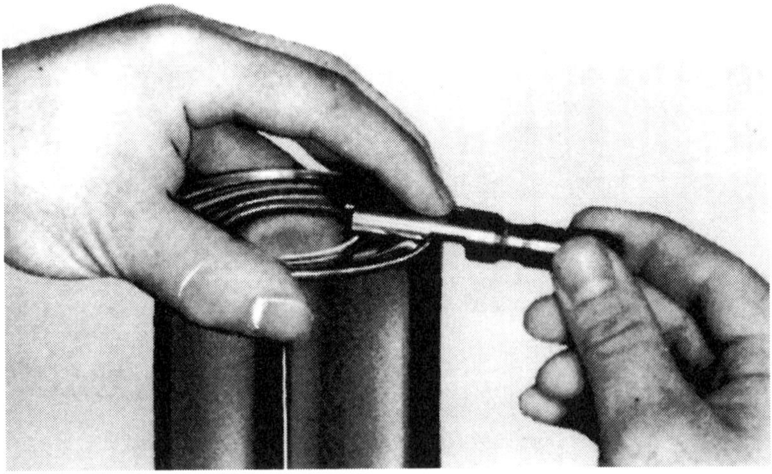

FIGURE 3.17 – Measuring seam thickness.
(Courtesy former American Can Company)

FIGURE 3.18 – Measuring countersink depth using a special depth gage. (Courtesy former American Can Company)

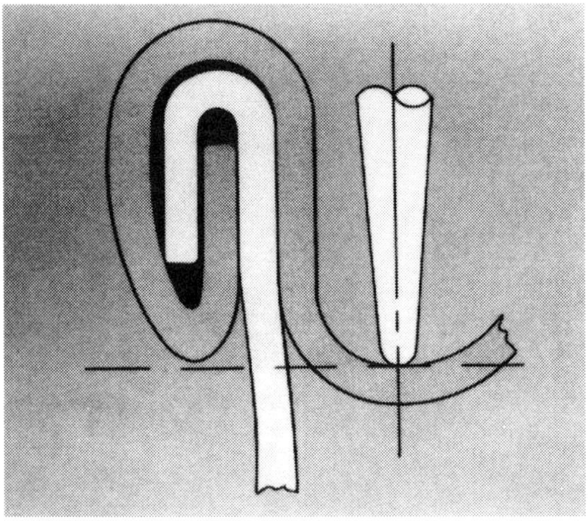

FIGURE 3.19 – The point of the countersink depth gage pin should be positioned at the lowest point adjacent to the countersink wall, away from the crossover. (Courtesy former American Can Company)

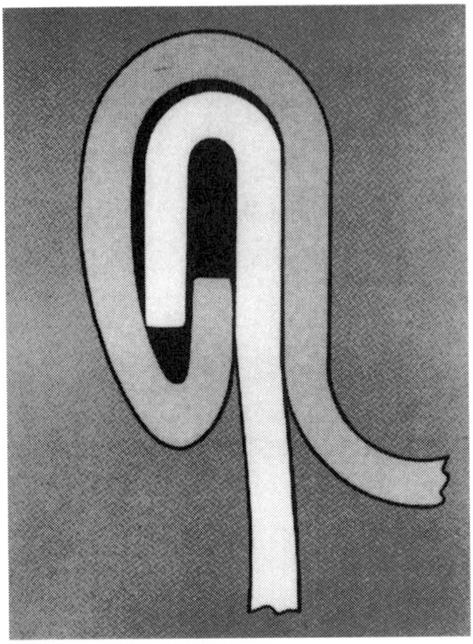

FIGURE 3.20 - Long body hooks. (Courtesy former American Can Company)

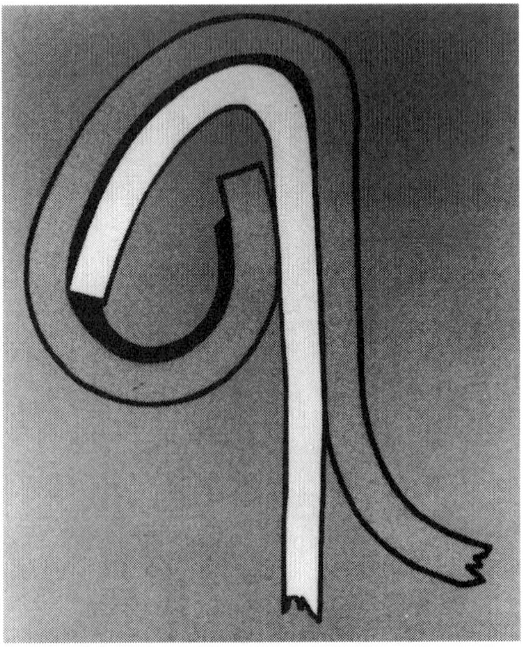

FIGURE 3.21- Correct first operation. (Courtesy former American Can Company)

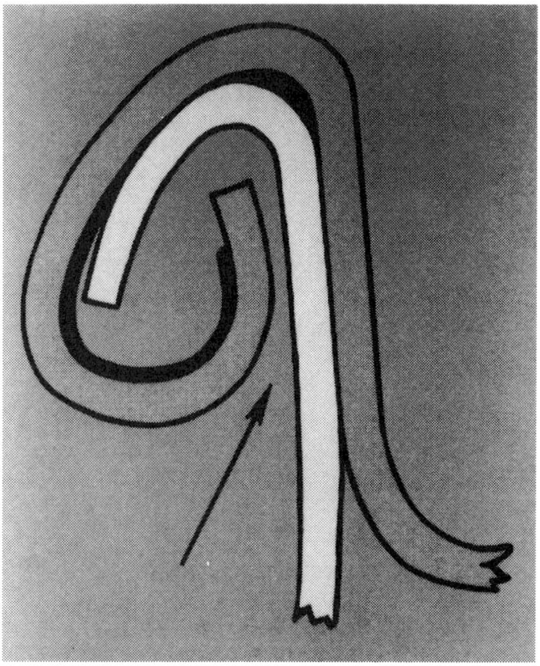

FIGURE 3.22 - Loose first operation. (Courtesy former American Can Company)

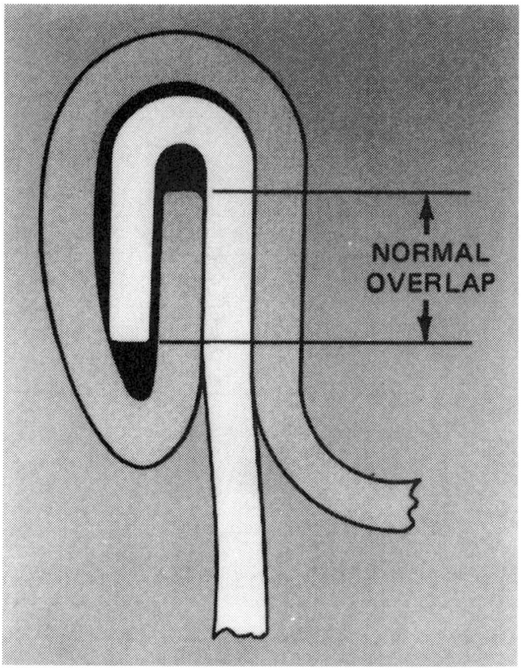

FIGURE 3.23 - Normal double seam. (Courtesy former American Can Company)

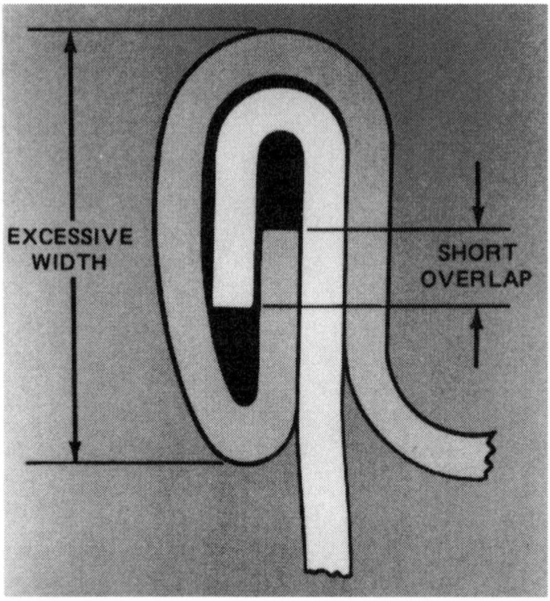

FIGURE 3.24 – Wide double seam.
(Courtesy former American Can Company)

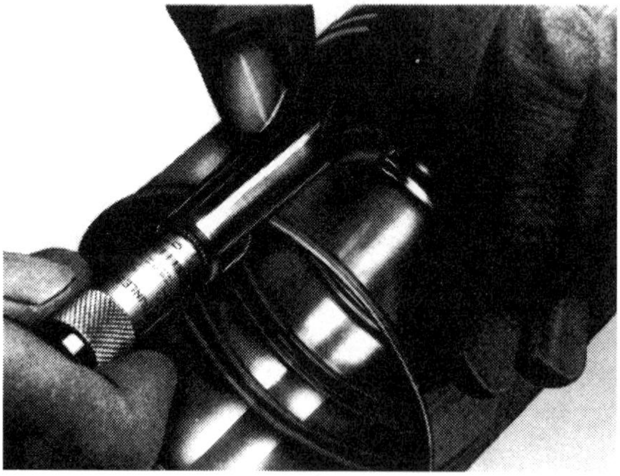

FIGURE 3.25 – Measuring body hook length using double seam micrometer.
(Courtesy former American Can Company)

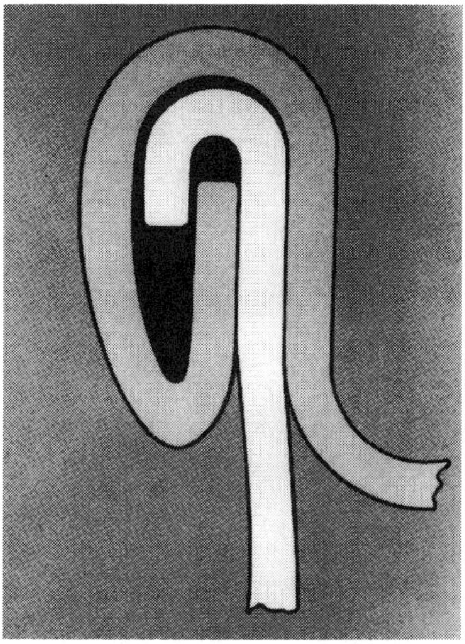

FIGURE 3.26 – Short body hooks. (Courtesy former American Can Company)

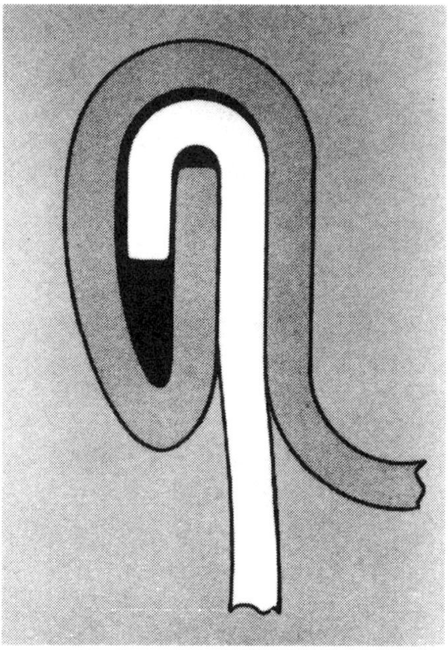

FIGURE 3.27 – Long cover hooks. (Courtesy former American Can Company)

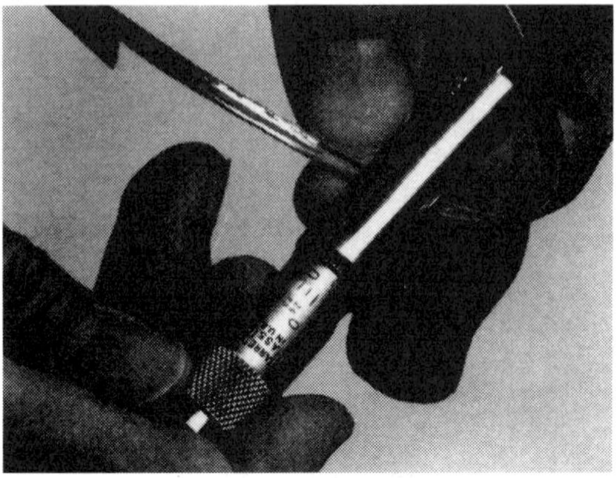

FIGURE 3.28 – Measuring cover hook length using double seam micrometer. (Courtesy former American Can Company)

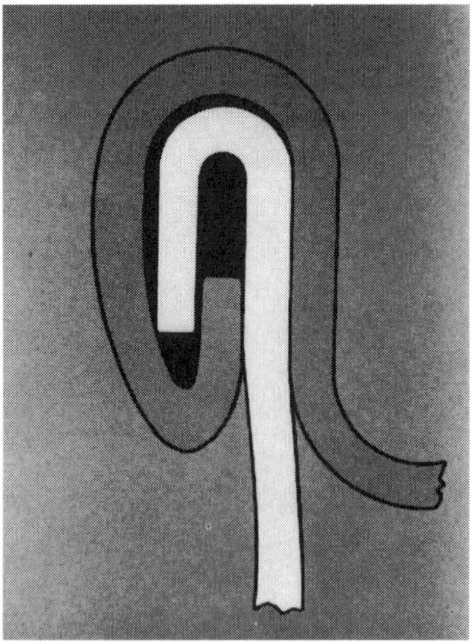

FIGURE 3.29 – Short cover hooks. (Courtesy former American Can Company)

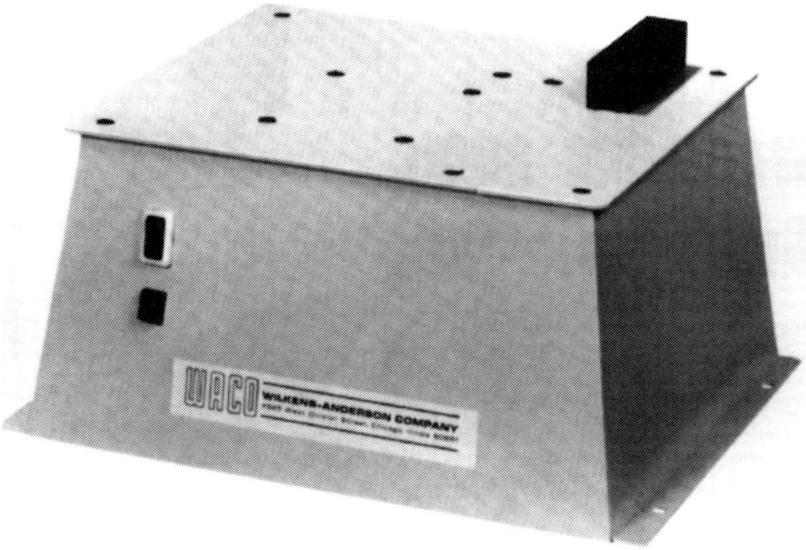

FIGURE 3.30 – Can seam saw. (Courtesy Wilkens-Anderson Company)

Adequacy of Double Seams and Recognition of Defects

There are mechanical differences in various manufacturer's closing machines. While closing machines all produce good sound double seams when properly set up and adjusted, how one manufacturer's double seam construction may vary slightly from another. It is very difficult, if not impossible, to give one set of double seam specifications that would apply in all cases and for all sizes of cans. For that reason, it is recommended that each processor's closing machine operators and other interested personnel obtain detailed double seam information and specifications from their container supplier.

There are, however, the following fundamental characteristics of a double seam that, if followed, will result in good quality seam on any standard closing machine.

A – There should be no "cut overs" which may cause cans to leak. (Caused by metal being rolled over the chuck.)

B – Double seams should not be rolled so tightly that they become distorted and stretched or result in an excessively deep pressure ridge. An otherwise good double seam can easily be ruined by rolling it too tightly.

C – A good seam is one in which the first operation has been rolled just tightly enough to produce the desired length of cover hooks and the second operation tightly enough to iron out the wrinkles in the cover hook without stretching the metal.

Looseness (or tightness) wrinkles are generally classified by one of two methods. The first method is a measure of smoothness of the coverhook measured in percentage. For example, if looseness wrinkles are found extending 20% down the coverhook, the double seam is considered 80% tight. The second method measures the wrinkles on a zero to ten scale. A completely ironed out cover hook gets a rating of 0 by this method, and a cover hook with wrinkles extending 30% its depth is rated 3.

D – Can and cover hooks should each be about the same length and kept within a tolerance range of from .074–.084 in. (1.88–2.13 cm) in length. The best results will be obtained by maintaining a hook length halfway between these limits. (These dimensions refer to cans with diameters ranging from 301 to 404 inclusive.)

E – Countersink depth from the top of the seam to the cover should be approximately .125 or $^1/_8$ in. (0.32 cm), depending in some cases on size ranges of cans. A good seam has good overlap or "butting" of the end or cover hook and body hook.

The general appearance of the cans should also be noted, especially if there is anything abnormal. Canners become so familiar with normal cans of food that any abnormal feature will be quickly noticed. A complete description of the abnormal cans should be recorded so that the cause of the trouble may be determined and steps taken to overcome it.

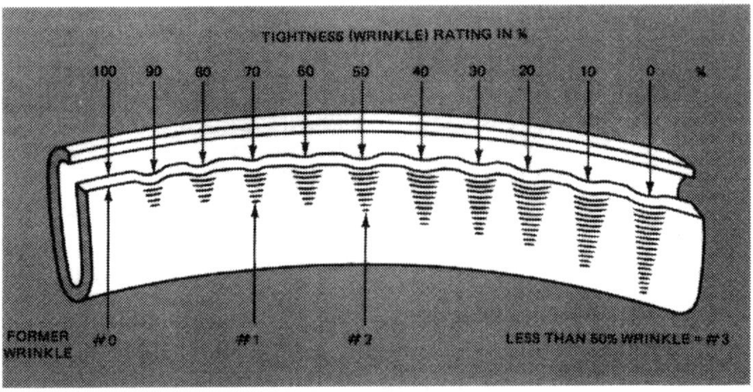

FIGURE 3.31 – Tightness (Wrinkle) Rating in Percentage

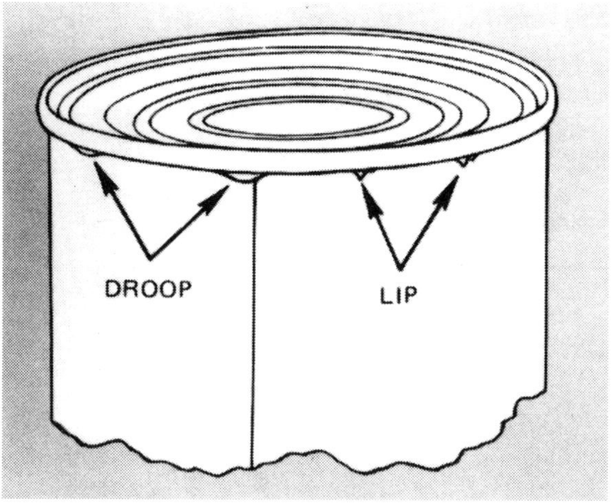

FIGURE 3.32 – An irregularity in a double seam, showing as a sharp "V" projection below the normal seam, is illustrated here. It is called a "lip" and sometimes a "droop." If lips or droops are observed, the cause should be determined and corrections made.

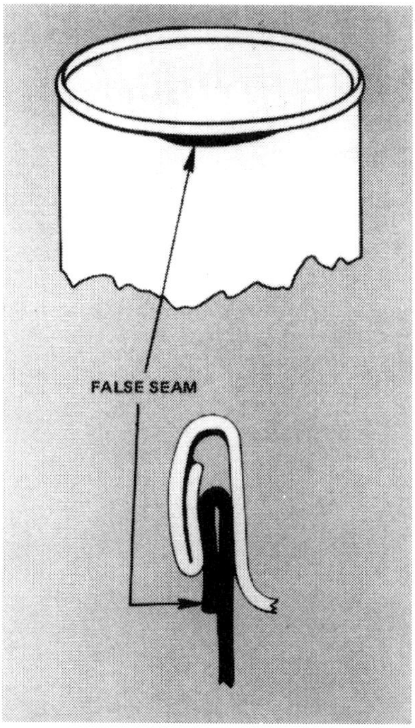

FIGURE 3.33 – A false seam, illustrated here, is a seam or portion of a seam which is entirely unhooked and in which the folded cover hook is compressed against the folded body hook. Sometimes, the folded body hook does not project below the seam and the false seam can be detected only by very close inspection.

MISCELLANEOUS INFORMATION ON CANS

Following are two tables that are useful for calculating data related to can handling and shipping. Since the last edition of this book 300x407 size cans have replaced 303x406 size cans as the standard shelf size can for fruits and vegetables. The following tables are altered to reflect this change.

TABLE 3.10 – Equivalent, in Cases of 24/300's of the More Commonly Used Cans

Case of 48 8Z short (211x300)	= 1.04 cases 24 No.300's
Case of 48 8Z tall (211x304)	= 1.14 cases 24 No.300's
Case of 48 8Z No. 1 (picnic) (211x400)	= 1.43 cases 24 No.300's
Case of 24 No. 300 (300x407)	= 1.00 cases 24 No.300's
Case of 24 No. 303 (303x406)	= 1.11 cases 24 No.300's
Case of 24 No. $2^1/_2$ (401x411)	= 1.96 cases 24 No.300's
Case of 6 No. 10 (603x700)	= 1.80 cases 24 No.300's

The capacity of a 16 oz. glass container is approximately the same as the No. 303 can. The capacity of a No. $2^1/_2$ glass container is approximately the same as the No. $2^1/_2$ can.

TABLE 3.11 – Capacity and Conversion Factors of Cans Most Commonly Used in Canning Fruits and Vegetables

Name	Dimensions	Total Capacity Water@68°F/20°C Avoir. oz. / g	No. 2 Can Equiv.	No. 303 Equiv.	No. 300 Equiv.
6Z	202x308	6.00 / 170	0.2927	0.3561	0.3947
8Z Short	211x300	7.90 / 224	0.3854	0.4688	0.5197
8Z Tall	211x304	8.65 / 245	0.4220	0.5134	0.5691
No. 1 (Picnic)	211x400	10.90 / 309	0.5317	0.6469	0.7171
No. 211 Cylinder	211x414	13.55 / 384	0.6610	0.8042	0.8914
No.300	300x407	15.20 / 431	0.7415	0.9021	1.0000
No. 300 Cylinder	300x509	19.40 / 550	0.9463	1.1513	1.2763
No. 1 Tall	301x411	16.60 / 471	0.8098	0.9852	1.0921
No. 303	303x406	16.85 / 478	0.8220	1.0000	1.1085
No. 303 Cylinder	303x509	21.85 / 619	1.0659	1.2967	1.4375
No. 2 Vacuum	307x306	14.70 / 417	0.7171	0.8724	0.9671
No. 2	307x409	20.50 / 581	1.0000	1.2166	1.3487
Jumbo	307x510	25.70 / 729	1.2537	1.5252	1.6908
No. 2 Cylinder	307x512	26.35 / 747	1.2824	1.5638	1.7335
No. $2^1/_2$	401x411	29.75 / 843	1.4512	1.7656	1.9572
No. 3 Vacuum	404x307	23.85 / 676	1.1634	1.4154	1.5691
No. 3 Cylinder	404x700	51.70 / 1466	2.5220	3.0682	3.4013
No. 5	502x510	59.10 / 1675	3.3244	4.0445	3.8881
No. 10	603x700	109.45 / 3103	5.3390	6.4955	7.2006

In the preceeding table, the "No. 2 Can Equivalent" indicates the number of No. 2 cans equal to each of the cans designated in column 1. The No. 2 case equivalent may be obtained by dividing the number of cans per case of the can to be converted by 24, except for No. 10 Cans where the factor is 6, and multiplying the result by the "No. 2 Can Equivalent." The same applies to "No. 303 and No. 300 Equivalent."

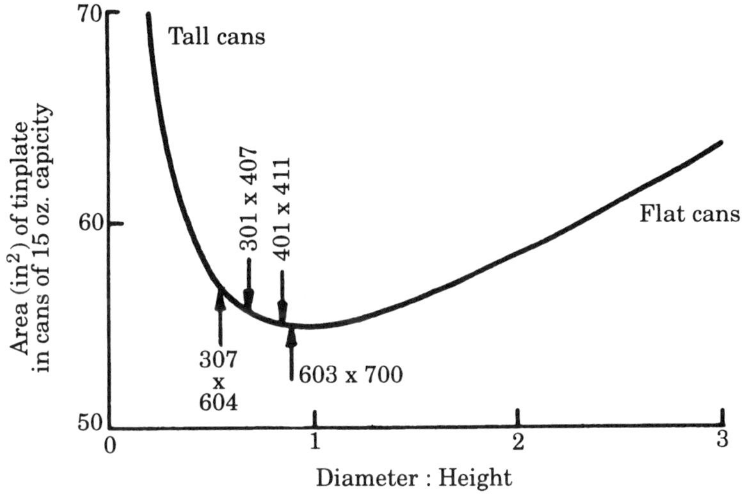

FIGURE 3.34 – Area of tin plate required for cans having the same capacity but different dimensions. The curve is specific for 15 oz. cans, but the same curve having different values on the vertical axis would apply to cans of different capacity.

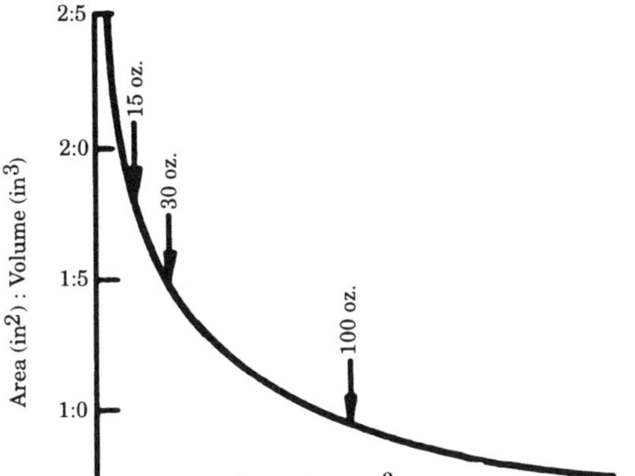

FIGURE 3.35 – Area of tin plate required to contain unit volume of product decreases as the capacity of the can increases. Curve calculated for can in which the diameter is equal to the height.

TABLE 3.12 – Tin Plate Basis Weights

The base box is the unit of area of 112 sheets, 14"x30", or 31,360 sq. in. (217.78 sq. ft.). Basis weights, which determine the approximate thickness of the plates, are customarily expressed in pounds per base box.

Weight			Weight		
Lbs./Base Box (Basis Weight)	Lbs./Sq. Ft.	Thickness Inches	Lbs./Base Box (Basis Weight)	Lbs./Sq. Ft.	Thickness Inches
45	0.2066	0.0050	148	0.6796	0.0163
50	0.2296	0.0055	155	0.7117	0.0171
55	0.2525	0.0061	168	0.7714	0.0185
60	0.2755	0.0066	175	0.8036	0.0193
65	0.2985	0.0072	180	0.8265	0.0198
70	0.3214	0.0077	188	0.8633	0.0207
75	0.3444	0.0083	195	0.8954	0.0215
80	0.3673	0.0088	208	0.9551	0.0229
85	0.3903	0.0094	210	0.9643	0.0231
90	0.4133	0.0099	215	0.9872	0.0237
95	0.4362	0.0105	228	1.0469	0.0251
100	0.4592	0.0110	235	1.0791	0.0259
107	0.4913	0.0118	240	1.1020	0.0264
112	0.5143	0.0123	248	1.1388	0.0273
118	0.5418	0.0130	255	1.1709	0.0281
128	0.5877	0.0141	268	1.2306	0.0295
135	0.6199	0.0149	270	1.2398	0.0297
139	0.6383	0.0153	275	1.2627	0.0303

Tin plate is also produced for special uses in weight other than those shown in the above table.

Warehousing of Empty Cans

The warehouse must be protected from dampness and steam. Cans stored in bulk in bins should lay on their sides in even and regular tiers. When stored in shipping cases, the bottom layer should be placed end up. Bulk pallets should be stored so that there is space between stacked pallets and exterior walls.

Empty can storage areas should be free of smoke and any chemical odors which may originate with tires, household, or industrial products, etc., stored in adjacent areas. These odors may be picked up in the can enamel resulting in associated off-flavors. If warehouses are exposed to fumes such as those found in sauerkraut or pickle plants, external can corrosion may also take place.

See Chapter on Warehousing in Book I.

THE HALF-SIZE STEAM TABLE TRAY

The half-size steam table tray was introduced by Central States Can Company, of Massillon, Ohio. It is a low-profile, two-piece, retortable institutional-size container that is formed from "M" or "L" chromed steel plate, pre-enameled with modified vinyl inside and out. Bodies are made of 90 or 95 #/BB and tops 85 #/BB steel plate. The container dimensions are approximately 10"x12"x2$^{1}/_{8}$" high (25.4x30.5x5.4 cm). It has a capacity of approximately 105 oz. (3.1 l), or about the same as a No. 10 can (603x700). The lid is double seamed like a standard 3-piece cylindrical can. Especially modified double seaming machines are used.

FIGURE 3.36 – A vacuum seamer to automatically vacuumize and double seam the half-size, 105 fl. oz., institutional tray and other similar containers. (Courtesy Callahan AMS Machine Co.)

Advantages of the steam table tray over the No. 10 cans are said to include: reduction in sterilization time by as much as 60% because heat reaches the center of the product in the container and achieves sterility much faster, packing of canned foods previously available only as frozen, tray serves the purposes of shipping container, heating container, and serving container, elimination of cleaning and washing of pan at the food service outlet, and lead side seams have been eliminated. Advantages over frozen foods include: shelf-stability, no energy usage during transportation and storage, and no need to defrost.

Disadvantages of the tray are slower line speeds; handling the trays is considerably more labor intensive than round, cylindrical cans.

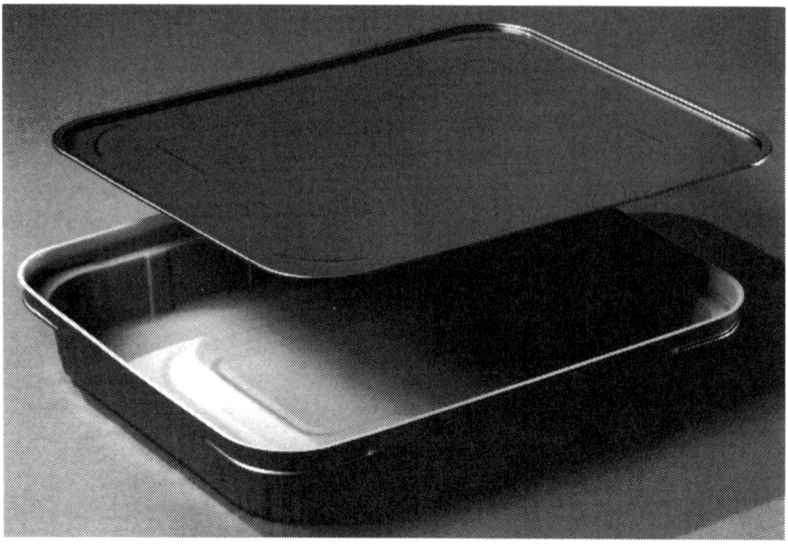

FIGURE 3.37 – The half-size institutional tray can has a capacity of 105 ounces. (Courtesy Central States Can Co.)

Thermal Processing

The tray can be successfully processed in a water cook similar to that used for products packed in glass or pouches. Special attention must be given to filling, closing and processing because of the low pressure resistance (1-2 psi or 7-14 kPa) of the end unit. Deformation of cans at the bottom corners and/ or the step shoulder may occur if excessive mechanical vacuum is used for cans with a large headspace. Cans should be closed so that a vacuum is achieved after processing. Depending on its characteristics, the product can be packed "hot," i.e., 180°F (82°C) and closed atmospherically. If the product lends itself to cooler closing temperatures; for example, 140°F (60°C), vacuum closing can be used.

The seamed units should be loaded inverted into the retort baskets. The conventional plastic or metal perforated divider sheets are not satisfactory for separating the layers of cans in order to provide adequate heat distribution. Acceptable heat distribution has been achieved using custom fabricated racks to insure separation between layers. Galvanized steel has been found to be satisfactory as would be plastic racks. Plain aluminum separators have been found to cause galvanic corrosion on the exterior of the containers.

The water can be preheated in the retort or held at 240–260°F (115–127°C) in a separate pressure vessel. After the retort is closed, air is introduced at a level 3 psi (62 kPa) greater than the process pressure. Water is then pumped into the retort to a level about six inches above the top-most cans. The air is closed off and steam introduced. In order to achieve adequate heat distribution, agitation of the water is achieved by mechanical pumping or by bubbling air. Processing and cooling are completed as for a glass cook (NCA Bulletin 30-L). Acceptable heat distribution and process control have been documented for sterilizing the tray in agitating retorts such as the Stock Rotomat.

Under laboratory conditions, some success has been achieved with steam atmosphere cooks. The pressure differential between cans and retort must be precise to prevent buckling. Minimum headspace and adequate vacuum are also critical in this manner of processing, in effect, making it impractical for commercial operation.

With the exception of buckle resistance limitations, the tray should be considered a "conventional" can.

FIGURE 3.38 – Retort baskets loaded with half-size tray cans
(Courtesy Central States Can Co.)

Vacuum Determination

The conventional puncture vacuum gauge method of vacuum determination cannot be used on the half-size tray because the headspace is distributed over a relatively large area so that the puncturing needle penetrates into the product and no vacuum is "measured." Some success has been achieved using the neutral buoyancy test (Natick Labs Technical Report, AD 798 046, "Study of a Non-destructive Test for Determining the Volume of Air in a Flexible Food Package"). This method is only valid for air volumes exceeding 30 ml.

The best method of determining vacuum in the half-size tray is visual inspection as described in 18.11 (e) Regulations Governing Meat Inspection "Canned products shall not be passed unless after cooling to atmospheric temperature, they show the external characteristics of sound cans; the cans shall not be overfilled; they shall have concave sides, and all ends shall be concave; there shall be no bulging; the sides and ends shall conform to the product; there shall be no slack or loose tin."

Double Seam Evaluation

The half-size tray double seam is evaluated in the conventional manner. Manufacturers specifications should be followed.

Figure 3.39 - Half-size steam table tray.
(Courtesy Central States Can Co.)

ALUMINUM CANS

In 1993, the amount of aluminum used for fabricating containers reached 3.98 billion pounds. Ninety-eight and seven-tenths percent were used by the beverage and food industries.

Increasingly greater attention is being given to aluminum for fabricating cans and other containers for processed foods. Its use to date has been mainly in applications where there is some inherent advantage over the use of tinplate such as flavor sensitive products, lower shipping expense, freedom from food and can black sulfide discoloration or rust, easier puncture opening, and where special easy opening features are desirable.

Steel cans are so well established in the canning industry that exceptionally good reasons are required before a change of material is contemplated. The present and future use of aluminum for cans, particularly in the large market for processed food use, is to a great extent dependent on the price at which it may be sold to the users, relative to that of an equivalent steel can.

On the other hand, while aluminum might appear to be more costly per unit area than steel, it would be wrong to draw the conclusion that aluminum cans are in no position to compete with tinplate cans. The materials are sufficiently different in their properties for steel to do well under conditions that are not conducive to the use of aluminum, and for aluminum to replace tinplate when aluminum shows advantage. When all applicable factors are considered, there are instances where aluminum cans offer advantages of product quality, economy, and national strategic value for the canning of certain food products. The use of easy-open lids is also a significant point which has a strong appeal. Aluminum cans do not rust. Their appearance, always bright, can be an important sales argument. An important advantage of aluminum cans is that they are lead-free.

Two-piece aluminum cans have been available for more than 30 years. Two-piece metal containers offer several advantages over their three-piece counterparts. Leakage possibilities are greatly reduced as a result of eliminating two seams; instead of three seams–top and bottom double seams and side seam–there is only one, the top double seam. Production problems appear to be, likewise, reduced in making the two-piece can and the equipment manufacturers claim that less experienced personnel can operate the two-piece line. Two-piece cans use less metal as there is no overlap for the side seam and bottom double seam. This not only reduces cost but permits making a greater number of cans from a given quantity of metal. Bottom configurations can be designed for improved stackability on grocery shelves. And most of all, aluminum cans are recyclable, which conserves valuable natural resources and helps out with litter and solid waste disposal problems.

Production of the two-piece can is either by a drawn and ironed or a draw and re-draw operation. With either method, the first steps are the same. A disc is stamped from a sheet or ribbon of metal. The disc is then drawn into a cup by use of a hydraulic ram and die. After the can body is formed, the top is trimmed, a flange is produced on the top, and finished treatment applied. Some cans are available with a necked-in configuration. The two methods differ in how the can body is formed from the cup. With the drawn and ironed method, the cup is forced by a ram through a series of dies, each slightly smaller than the preceding one, which elongates the side of the body by stretching out "ironing" the side and in the process, reducing the thickness of the metal. With the draw and re-draw method, the cup is likewise forced through dies by hydraulic ram, but in the process, the circumference of the container is reduced with the excess metal being used to elongate the side wall and with only a slight thickening of the side wall. All drawn and ironed cans are necked and flanged as the last operation prior to light and/or computer video inspection. Many drawn and redrawn cans are not necked and have straight side walls. Aluminum for can ends and bodies is, without exception, coated with enamel on both sides.

TABLE 3.13 – Recycling of Aluminum Cans

Year	Number Recycled	Percentage Recycled
1990	51.0 billion	63.6%
1991	57.5 billion	62.4%
1992	62.7 billion	67.8%
1993	60.0 billion	63.1%

Source: Reynolds Metals Company

Plant Handling of Aluminum Cans

Outside enameled ends are required to facilitate handling in the cannery and to reduce the buildup of aluminum fines in the canning lines. To effect smooth transfer of aluminum cans, many pieces of equipment must be hard chrome plated. In some instances, the installation of Teflon-covered conveying systems is advantageous. All equipment parts using a magnetic principle must, of course, be replaced with a vacuum system for handling aluminum cans.

In the more general application of aluminum to processed vegetables, fruits, fish, and meats, consideration must be given to providing a can strong enough

FIGURE 3.40 – How All-Aluminum Beverage Cans Are Made
(Courtesy Reynolds Metals Company, Can Division)

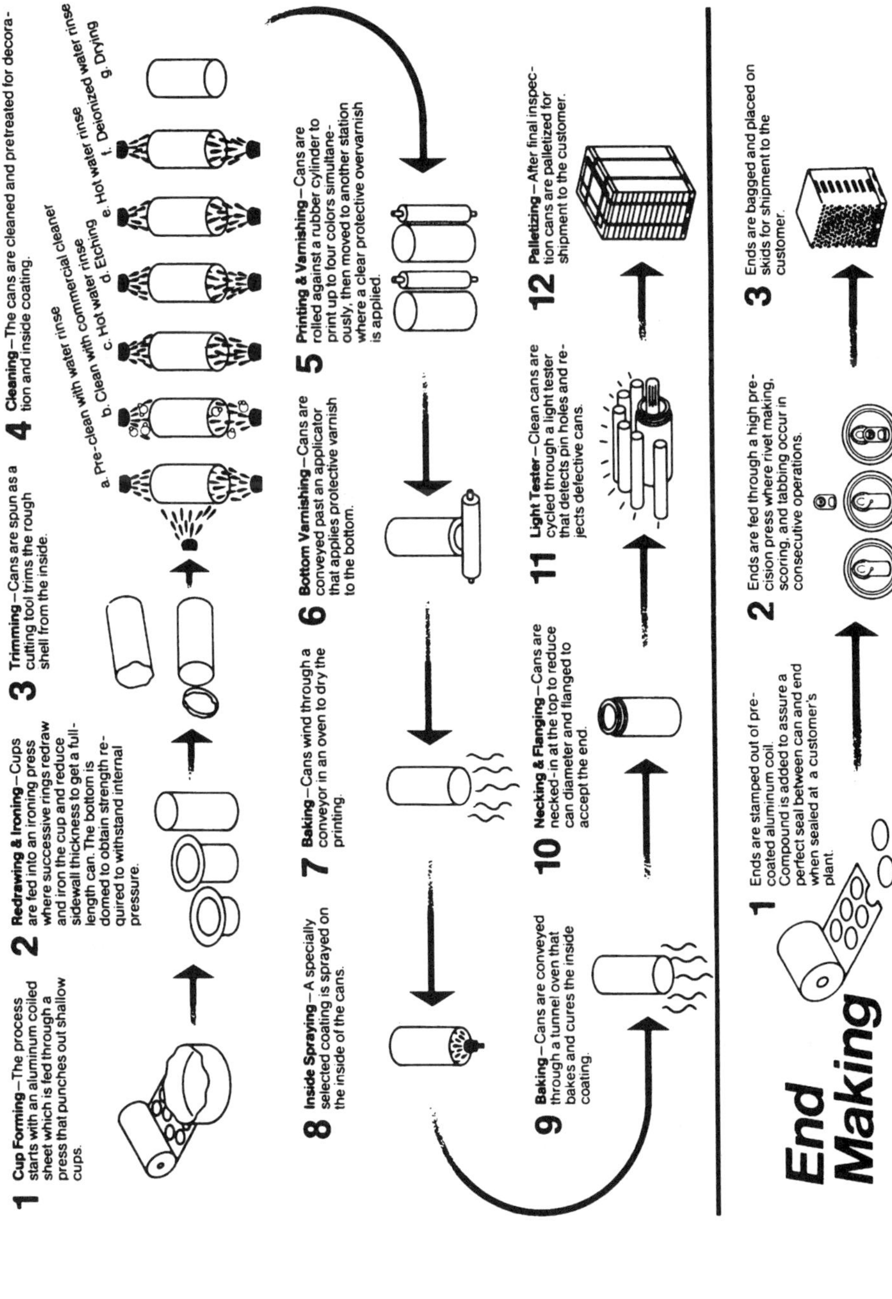

to withstand the handling and mechanical stresses imposed during processing and distribution. Aluminum producers are striving to formulate an alloy with physical properties such that it can be substituted for tinplate on a gauge for gauge basis. However, the higher strength alloys employed still require an increase of about 35% in the gauge of aluminum to provide equivalent buckling resistance to conventional tinplate in 303 diameter cans. An increase in gauge of approximately 50% over that of nitrogenized double cold reduced tinplate is required.

For some foods in smaller can sizes, modifications of the canning procedure have permitted the use of less rugged cans than are currently employed. As an example, to avoid the buckling or straining of the ends, pressure cooling could be used after sterilizing in autoclave. However, there must be a delicate balance between the pressure required to maintain flat ends and that which would cause paneling of bodies as the cans are cooled. For some products superimposed pressure during the entire sterilizing process may be required.

In addition to considering the practicability of aluminum cans in terms of their initial cost and to forecast what would need to be changed in a packer's operation to accommodate aluminum cans, it is necessary to know what the shelf-life of the products will be in aluminum containers. This revolves around the inherent corrosion resistance of the container and the chemical activity of the product, matters which cannot always be altered by engineering nor accomplished at tolerable increases in costs, even though the economics and engineering pictures of aluminum cans are changing rapidly and making aluminum more competitive as a food packaging material.

Corrosion Resistance

As a household metal and in food processing operations, aluminum is considered a corrosion-resistant metal. Experimental and practical experience in food canning has shown that most beverages and foods in uncoated aluminum cans react with the metal quite readily. The addition of alloying elements to pure aluminum influences its corrosion resistance properties, imparts strength and improves formability characteristics. In general, these alloys have good corrosion resistance with most foods and beverages. However, processed foods, as well as juices, soft drinks and alcoholic beverages, require containers with inside enamels to maintain an acceptable shelf life. Table shows various types of organic coatings (enamels) used in the interior of aluminum cans and ends.

TABLE 3.14 – Internal Coatings Used on Aluminum Cans and Ends

Product	Can Body	Can End
Beer	Water-borne, modified Epoxy	Solvent-borne Vinyl
Soft Drinks	Water-borne, modified Epoxy	Solvent-borne Vinyl
Sardines	Epoxy Phenolic	Epoxy Phenolic
Potted Meat	Vinyl Phenolic	Vinyl Phenolic
Puddings	Vinyl Phenolic	Vinyl Phenolic

Liquid Nitrogen Injector System

Several innovations in can making technology have reduced the weight of seamed aluminum cans to 33 pounds (15 kg) per thousand. At this weight the can design uses the internal pressure created naturally by carbonated products to enhance sidewall rigidity and strength. Some products, especially those with low or no carbonation, benefit from the introduction of additional pressure to the can. Pressurizing cans of these products insures that the can's sidewall rigidity will be equivalent to that of carbonated products.

Previously, gaseous nitrogen was used to pressurize cans, but this technique has had limited success. The Reynolds Liquid Nitrogen Injector System makes it possible to create internal can pressures which are consistently equivalent to those found in cans of carbonated beverages. This process does not slow the operation of the can line.

The nitrogen injector injects a controlled amount of pressurizing agent - liquid nitrogen - into the can immediately after filling and prior to the seaming operation. Once injected the liquid nitrogen warms up and changes to a gas creating the internal pressure required to obtain sidewall rigidity equivalent to that of carbonated products.

The nitrogen injector is installed directly on the filling line, slightly above the tops of the cans. After initial setup and adjustment procedure is complete, very little operator attention is required to insure optimum accuracy and reliability. The control system is engineered to allow for easy adaptation to a wide range of operating speeds and applications.

Fruit and Vegetable Canning

Fruit and vegetables may be packed in aluminum cans provided that an appropriate inside enamel is used. In general, the shelf-life of vegetables packed in aluminum cans is longer than that of fruits.

Meats and Seafoods

Aluminum cans properly protected against interior corrosion are especially satisfactory for canned meats and seafood products. The problem of black iron-sulfide staining of the container or of the product does not exist with aluminum. However, the tendency of aluminum to bleach some pigments is what causes the pinkish color of shrimp to turn muddy gray and produce hydrogen sulfide-like odor. The use of citric acid or lemon juice to lower the pH of the product to 6.0–6.4 reduces these problems significantly. The development of organic coating systems exceptionally effective in blocking the direct contact of aluminum with the product may solve this problem.

Shallow drawn aluminum cans are being used for canned tuna, sardines, crab meat, lobster, and oysters. When crab or lobster is packed in aluminum cans, there is no need to line the cans with parchment paper to avoid discoloration of the product. Sardines prepared in tomato sauce and mustard sauce should not exceed 3% total acidity, expressed as acetic acid. Tomato sauce and mustard sauce are corrosive products that can attack enameled metal containers.

Other processed foods marketed in shallow drawn cans include potted meats, luncheon meats, corned beef hash, boned chicken, chili con carne, chili with beans, and dehydrated soups. These products, as well as Vienna sausages and pet foods, are also sold in drawn and redrawn cans with or without easy-open lids.

Carbonated Beverages and Beer

Aluminum cans fabricated by the impact extrusion or the drawing and ironing method are extensively used for pressurized beverages such as beer and soft drinks.

Non-Carbonated Beverages

New applications for thin walled two piece draw and iron aluminum cans have been made possible by the development of the Reynolds Metals Liquid Nitrogen Injector System.

This system is used on commercial filling lines for hot filled (180–200°F) (82–93°C) juice drinks, single strength juices and isotonic drinks. It is also used for packing retort processed chocolate drinks and cold filled beverages such as wine, club cocktails and iced tea where liquid nitrogen pressurization is more efficient than the older method using nitrogen gas.

Collapsible Tubes

Aluminum may also be used in the form of collapsible tubes for packaging processed food products. Although aluminum tubes have been used for some non-processed foods, the development of a tube suitable for a sterilized product presented several problems. Industry and federal government laboratories working in cooperation have solved those problems and developed sterilized foods packaged in collapsible tubes for the feeding of astronauts and high altitude aviators.

The aluminum tube, fitted with a hollow-handled plastic spoon which can be attached to the neck of the tube, should make a desirable and convenient package for feeding infants or bed-ridden patients.

Flexible Packages and Semi-Rigid Containers

Aluminum is widely used in flexible specifications and semi-rigid containers for the protective packaging of a very large number of food products. As a result of extensive development and testing by thermoprocessing and aseptic techniques, the use of flexible, laminated pouches and formed aluminum containers for shelf-stable foods is nearing commercial reality. The increased use of aluminum for food packaging has been made possible by successfully combining it with specialized plastics, papers, adhesives and coatings. In many applications, aesthetic as well as protective characteristics are also provided.

The retortable pouch as a package for heat preserved foods offers potential improvements in convenience and quality by virtue of its shape and composition. The pouch is a thin rectangular package. During heat processing, this configuration allows for rapid heat transfer to destroy microorganisms at the innermost part of the package without excessively overheating the product near the pouch wall. At the end of the process, the contents are likewise more rapidly cooled. On average, there is less exposure to heat which adversely affects certain foods. Consequently, when those foods are processed in the pouch, their inherent properties are less severely degraded and a quality improvement is always observed. Foods processed in pouches are easy to store without refrigeration, and are quickly heated to serving temperatures in 3–5 minutes as a boil-in-bag.

SHIPPING CASES

There are standard specifications for corrugated and for solid fiberboard cases. Cases for metal containers should provide a close fit; they should be the exact height of the can or tiers of cans, and only enough wider and longer to permit easy filling. An excess of $^1/_8$" (3 mm) in width and $^1/_4$" (6 mm) in length is ample, although when casing is done directly from the labeling machine, the custom has been to allow more dimension. The advantage of close packing, both in the lessening of damage to cases and contents as well as in conserving of shipping space, has been conclusively demonstrated.

In the packing of glass containers, requirements for the outer container are the same as those for metal containers; however, glass, being relatively fragile to impact from a non-resident substance, requires that the container be provided with interior partitions where the usual arrangements of bottles or jars are followed. Shipping specifications for products packed in glass provide for the minimum quality and thickness of material which may be used for these purposes. Fiber board has displaced almost all other kinds due to its economy, efficiency, and cleanliness. Non-partion packaging in corrugated trays is gaining in popularity, but should be used only after proper evaluation.

Casing

Small volume packers still take cans from retort crates by hand and place them into cases direct. Other canners take cans from the crate by hand but roll them to a boxing machine. More often the entire crate is lifted and turned over by a special machine and the cans are straightened out by what is called an "unscrambler." They then roll to the labeling machine and boxer. Cans may otherwise be lifted from still retort crates one layer at a time by means of a magnet.

The most common method in use today consists of casing cans by means of case packers at the end of the canning line. Cans may be cased labeled or unlabeled and then taken to the warehouse. In some instances, cans are warehoused uncased and unlabeled. Glass containers may be handled in the same manner.

The new case packers are constructed so the operator does not lift the filled case. It falls from the caser onto a conveyor, which takes the cases through the mechanical case sealing unit where both top and bottom flaps are sealed in place.

ACKNOWLEDGMENTS

The contributions of the following persons and organizations are gratefully acknowledged:

Tin Plate Cans: Dwight E. Reed, (retired) Manager, Metal Container Research American Can Company for earlier additions and John A. Bennett II (retired) Vice President, Finger Lakes Packaging Co., Inc.

Aluminum Cans: David J. Scheuerman, Field Research Service and New Products Can Division, Reynolds Metals Company. Tel-804-743-5168.

CHAPTER 4

Glass and Plastic Containers

GLASS CONTAINERS

Glass containers are ideally suited for the packaging of many foods and are widely used for the canning of fruits, vegetables and juices. Meat and poultry products may also be packed in glass containers. When combined with the appropriate closure, the glass jar or bottle provides an inert, hermetic, durable packaging medium for a wide variety of foods. The transparency of glass makes it the ideal choice for many products displayed for the consumer on the retail shelf. In addition, the resealability and storage characteristics of glass containers give them added consumer appeal.

Some of the commonly used glass containers and the appropriate finishes are listed in the tables on the following pages. Listings of current container drawings and finish drawings are available free from the Glass Packaging Institute, 6845 Elm St., Suite 209, McLean, VA 22101.

Glass containers are presently handled at line speeds in excess of 1200 containers per minute. With the proper attention to the design and fabrication of glass handling, conveying and processing equipment, the glass container can be utilized with a minimum of breakage and an overall defective package percentage unrivaled by other packaging materials. Glass containers supplied for foods and beverages are available with a number of different surface treatments designed to protect the container from abrasion and to increase lubricity which facilitates automatic, high speed handling. Container suppliers can advise customers on the surface treatment best suited to their needs. The closure supplier should also be consulted as the glass surface treatment can affect closure application and removal.

VACUUM CLOSURES – GENERAL CHARACTERISTICS

Currently, there are primarily two types of vacuum hermetic closures used for low-acid food products. These are the lug-type twist cap and the PT (Press-on Twist-off) closure, although the pry-off (side seal) cap may still be in use outside of the U.S.

Each of these closures are primarily held in place on the glass finish by vacuum. Even though some mechanical principles are used in the closure design to hold the closure, the vacuum is the most important.

The lug-type twist cap and the PT cap are referred to as "convenience" or utility closure, because they can be removed without a tool and form a good reseal for storage.

Factors Affecting Vacuum Formation

Factors affecting vacuum formation are primarily the following:

1. Headspace.

Headspace is important in the efficient sealing of glass packages, particularly with steam-flow cappers. There must be sufficient headspace or void at the top of the container at the time of sealing to allow adequate steam to be trapped for forming a vacuum and to accommodate product expansion during heating and/or retorting. The proper amount of headspace varies with the specific product, process and package design, but a rule of thumb indicator for low-acid foods is that it should be not less than six percent of the container volume when measured at the capping temperature. Closure displacement or deformation can be the result of inadequate headspace.

2. Product sealing temperature.

The product sealing temperature affects the final package vacuum due to the effect of the product contraction upon cooling. With other factors being constant, the higher the product temperature at the time of sealing, the higher the final package vacuum. The product temperature may also affect the final vacuum by its interaction with the amount of air remaining in the product. As a rule, the higher the fill temperature, the less the amount of air entrapped in the product.

3. Air in the product.

Air in the product can have a direct effect on the final package vacuum and should be held to a minimum for good sealing, product quality, and product appearance. The more air that is entrapped in the product prior to sealing, the lower the vacuum.

4. Capper vacuum efficiency.

The capper vacuum efficiency is the ability of the capper to produce a vacuum in sealed containers. The most convenient, routine check that should be used to evaluate the vacuum efficiency of a steam-flow capper is the "cold water vacuum check." The measurements are made with a vacuum gauge. This check is used at the startup of the actual filling operation or after extended breaks, at changes of container sizes, after major container jams or whenever there is an unexplained significant change in vacuum level on line samples.

Method of Cold Water Vacuum Check

Jars are filled with cold tap water to the approximate headspace maintained when the product is run. These are sealed in the capper after the capper has warmed up to operating temperature and the normal capper steam setting has been attained. These jars are then opened and re-run through the capper, and at this point, the vacuums are checked. The first sealing passing through the capper serves to deaerate the water and provides a truer vacuum reading when the vacuum is checked. The vacuum is measured by use of a standard vacuum gauge. The vacuum readings obtained with a closed gauge should be 22 in. (56 cm) or more or as recommended by the closure supplier.

Vacuum Closure Application for Glass Containers

Two different type cappers used to apply closures while forming a vacuum in the package are the mechanical vacuum capper and the steam-flow capper. The mechanical vacuum capper applies the closure to the jar in an evacuated chamber, primarily on dry products, and is rarely used on low-acid processed food products. The steam-flow type capper may be either a straight line or a rotary unit. The container is subjected to a controlled steam atmosphere which displaces headspace gases from the jar by a flushing action. The steam atmosphere is trapped in the headspace at the time the closure is applied, then the steam condenses to form a vacuum which helps hold the closure. The gasket in plastisol lined closures is softened by steam during application to assist in good seal formation.

Auxiliary Equipment

The use of auxiliary equipment such as headspacers, cocked-cap detectors and ejectors, and dud detectors either directly or indirectly affect the sealing of glass containers. Their proper use is important.

Headspacer

Headspace is of critical importance on products requiring additional heating or retorting and important is obtaining good seals with certain closure types and is of significant importance with all vacuum closures. Product over the sealing surface can sometimes result from the headspacing operation, which may be detrimental to good sealing.

Cocked-Cap Detector and Ejectors

These devices installed downstream from the capper, serve to eliminate problem packages that would otherwise become mixed with the flow of normal packages. Their efficient operation also serves to signal both the capper operator and quality assurance personnel when a problem exists or is developing.

Dud Detectors

When properly maintained and checked, a dud detector can monitor the quality of the seals being formed on all packages. They are a particularly useful tool when the defective seals are constantly analyzed to determine the specific package failure problem.

Closures for Glass Containers–Applications

Hermetic closures are required for any food products subject to microbiological spoilage such as baby foods, prepared infant formulas, fruits, vegetables, meat products, juices, jams, jellies, preserves, tomato sauce (such as catsup and spaghetti sauce), chicken products, processed pet foods, pasteurized pickles and many other products where preservation by the use of heat is required. Functionally speaking, hermetic closures consist of a metal shell made of either tin plate, tin-free steel or aluminum, an inside coating, and an impervious sealing material. This material may be rubber, either natural or synthetic, a plastisol or sheet polyvinyl chloride material, or other suitable plastics.

Hermetic seals may be applied to packages in many different ways under many different conditions. They can be applied with a wide variety of capping equipment and be achieved by being pushed on, crimped on, rolled on, screwed on, or turned on as in the case of lug caps. They may be crowns, side seal closures, rolled on closures, screw caps or lug caps.

Vacuum Sealing

Closures of the type shown in Fig. 4.5 and 4.6 are widely used on dry products where a hermetic seal is required to retain product freshness, usually in conjunction with a vacuum. Inert gas, such as nitrogen, can also be used to partially replace the oxygen in the container. Packages on which this type of cap may be found contain product such as nuts, grated cheese, trail mix, etc. Due to the nature of the products which have a low tolerance for moisture, this type of package is normally sealed in a mechanical vacuum capper such as the one shown in the accompanying illustration Figure 4.7. These cappers employ a collar which seals on the shoulder of the jar and a vacuum pump system which evacuates the air from the container prior to the application of the cap. Some of these units also incorporate a provision for breaking back the vacuum with an inert gas such as nitrogen. Mechanical vacuum cappers usually are multiple head rotary units with the number of heads determining the rate of speed at which containers can be sealed. The volume of the container, as well as the nature of the product and the desired vacuum level, also serve to govern the rate at which packages can be sealed.

Figure 4.1 – Plain Round Jar

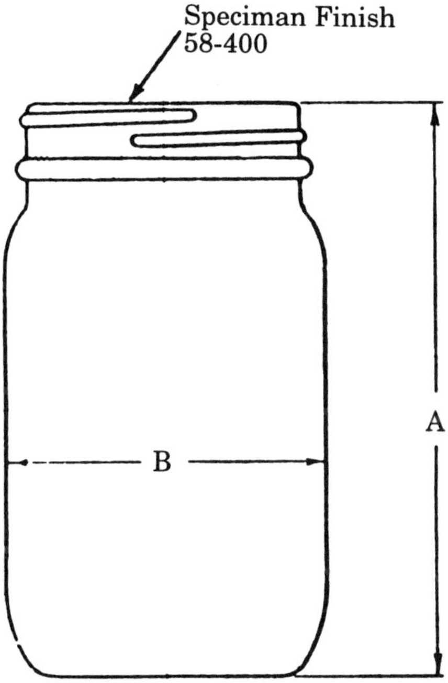

Capacity of Flow (fl. oz.)	Weight (max. oz.)	A	B	Specimen Finish
$4^1/_4$	$3^3/_4$	$3^{25}/_{64}$	$2^1/_{16}$	48-400
$6^1/_4$	$4^1/_4$	$3^{55}/_{64}$	$2^9/_{32}$	53-400
$8^3/_8$	$4^3/_4$	$4^9/_{32}$	$2^{29}/_{64}$	58-400
$11^1/_2$	6	$4^{25}/_{32}$	$2^3/_4$	58-400
$12^1/_2$	$6^1/_4$	$4^{27}/_{32}$	$2^{53}/_{64}$	58-400
$15^1/_2$	7	$5^1/_8$	$3^1/_{32}$	63-400
$16^1/_2$	$7^1/_2$	$5^7/_{32}$	$3^1/_8$	63-400
$22^3/_4$	$9^1/_2$	$5^7/_8$	$3^{29}/_{64}$	63-400
$24^1/_2$	$10^1/_2$	$5^{61}/_{64}$	$3^9/_{16}$	63-400

NOTES:

1. When other finishes are used, capacity, weight and height specifications are adjustable within the requirements of the finish used.
2. The dimensioned contour shown, except the dimensions locating and defining the label space, may be moderately varied to accord with individual manufacturer's practice.
3. When lower glass weights are used, adjustment to make correct capacity should be made in the 'B' dimension.

Figure 4.2 – High Shoulder Jar

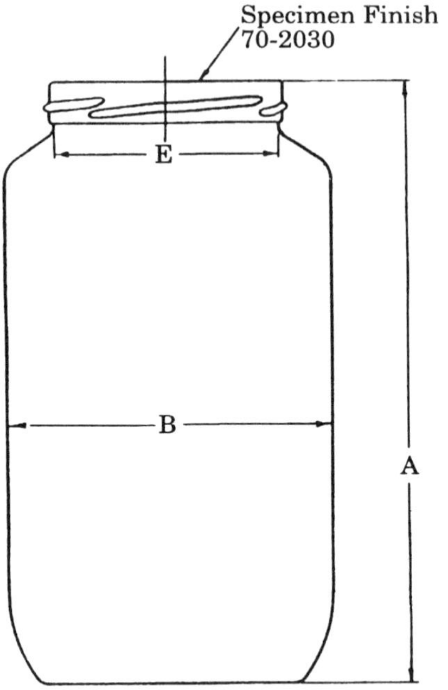

Capacity of Flow (fl. oz.)	Weight (max. oz.)	A	B max.	E	Specimen Finish
$8^1/_4$	5	$4^{17}/_{32}$	$2^3/_8$	$1^{59}/_{64}$	53-2020
17	$7^1/_2$	$5^1/_2$	$2^{63}/_{64}$	$2^7/_{32}$	63-2030
$23^1/_8$	$9^1/_2$	6	$3^{15}/_{16}$	$2^1/_2$	70-2030
$33^1/_8$	12	7	$3^{21}/_{32}$	$2^1/_2$	70-2030
$33^1/_2$	12	7	$3^{11}/_{16}$	$2^1/_2$	70-2030
$66^1/_2$	23	$8^7/_{16}$	$4^{49}/_{64}$	$2^{61}/_{64}$	82-2040

NOTES:

1. When other finishes are used, capacity, weight and height specifications are adjustable within the requirements of the finish used.
2. The dimensioned contour shown, except the dimensions locating and defining the label space, may be moderately varied to accord with individual manufacturer's practice.
3. When lower glass weights are used, adjustment to make correct capacity should be made in the 'B' dimension.

Figure 4.3 – Round Food Line Bottle (Short Neck)

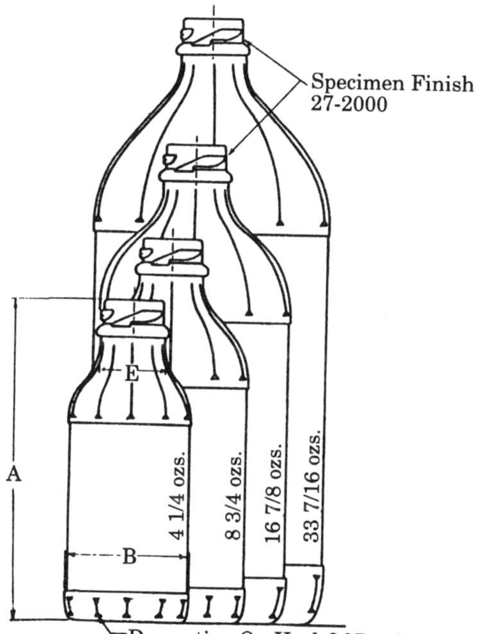

Capacity of Flow (fl. oz.)	Weight (max. oz.)	A	B max.	E	Specimen Finish
$4^1/_4$	$4^3/_8$	$4^7/_8$	$1^{29}/_{32}$	1	27–2000
$8^3/_4$	$6^1/_2$	$5^{27}/_{32}$	$2^{13}/_{32}$	1	27–2000
$16^7/_8$	10	$7^1/_4$	$2^{59}/_{64}$	1	27–2000
$17^3/_8$	10	$7^1/_4$	$2^{61}/_{64}$	1	27–2000
$33^7/_{16}$	16	$9^3/_{16}$	$3^{37}/_{64}$	1	27–2000

NOTES:

1. When other finishes are used, capacity, weight and height specifications are adjustable within the requirements of the finish used.
2. The dimensioned contour shown, except the dimensions locating and defining the label space, may be moderately varied to accord with individual manufacturer's practice.
3. When lower glass weights are used, adjustment to make correct capacity should be made in the 'B' dimension.

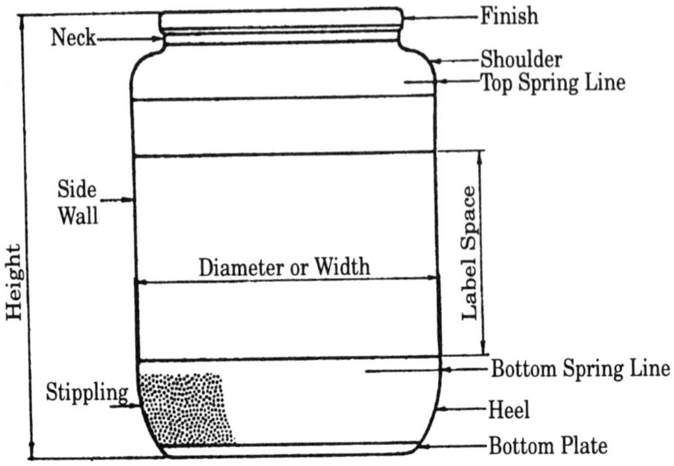

Figure 4. 4. – Nomenclature of Glass Containers for Foods

It should be noted that while all vacuum sealed packages must have hermetic seals, not all packages with hermetic seals necessarily contain vacuum. For example, hermetic continuous thread (CT) closures are moving forward in areas where a vacuum seal is not required and the small amount of residual oxygen in the headspace is of little consequence.

The simplest procedure to produce vacuum in the finished package using a hermetic seal is to fill the product at an elevated temperature. As the product cools and shrinks, a vacuum is produced in the container. Fruit juices and fruit drinks sealed with crown caps achieve a vacuum in this manner.

While the crown is not widely used on food products in the U.S. today, it is, along with similar types of crimped-on closures, widely used in other countries around the world.

Steam-vacuum applied closures are the most widely used vacuum seals in the U.S. food industry. With steam-vacuum application, air in the headspace of the package is replaced with steam and the closure is applied. As the steam condenses, a vacuum is formed in the package. This is true whether the closure is a roll-on, a side seal closure, a lug closure, or a push-on turn-off closure.

Automatic cappers which seal jars and bottles by the steam vacuum method are available through closure suppliers. Most are adjustable to handle a range of cap and glass sizes. A capper of this type is pictured in Figure 4.8.

Figure 4.5 – The "Guard-Seal" Cap

The "Guard-Seal" cap is a metal and plastic, tamper-indicating closure, which provides a vacuum and/or hermetc seal. It can be applied by machine or by hand, and is suitable for non-vacuum items. It affords a simple one-step, press-on application, is easy to open, and reseals by simply pressing on the cap. The metal disc, with its plastisol gasket, is held in a plastic collar which includes a built-in pull ring. The pull ring is held to the face of the cap by tiny plastic bridges that are broken when the ring is lifted to remove the cap. The broken bridges indicate an attempt to open package. (Courtesy White Cap Div., Continental Group)

Figure 4.6 – The "Tamper-Seal" Cap

The "Tamper-Seal" cap is a metal and plastic, tamper-indicating closure, which provides a vacuum and/or hermetic seal. It affords a simple one-step, press-on application, is easy to open, and reseals by simply pressing on the cap. The metal disc, with its plastisol gasket, is held in a plastic collar which includes a built-in, tamper-indicating tear band. This tear band is held to the cap by tiny plastic bridges that are broken when the end is torn to allow removal of the closure. A broken or missing tear band indicates an attempt to open the package. (Courtesy White Cap Div., Continental Group)

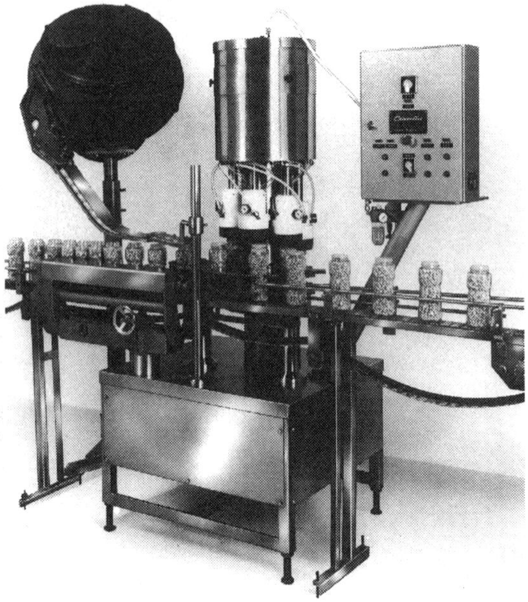

Figure 4.7 – Six-Station, Rotary Glass Container Capper
The "Calumatic" capper operates at moderate speeds and is particularly suited to packing dry, powdered or loose products. Vacuum is produced with a patented sealing head which forms a seal on the jar shoulder, mechanically evacuates air to the desired vacuum level, and seals the closure on the glass finish. Line speeds are governed by container volume/vacuum ration, up to a maximum of 240 jars per minute.
(Courtesy White Cap Division, The former Continental Group, Inc.)

The rubber-lined side seal closure, applied with steam-vacuum, gave the greatest single impetus to packing processed foods in glass containers. A cut rubber gasket forms the seal against the glass finish. In the U.S., its use has given way to newer types of closures designed to provide a reseal factor. The majority of these closures contain sealing gaskets composed of plastisol-type materials.

Hermetic lug caps (Figures 4.9 and 4.10) are used on a wide variety of products including fruits and vegetables, pickles, jams, jellies and preserves, fruit and vegetable juices, tomato products and, many, many others. This closure is normally applied using steam vacuum and because of extremely high production speeds and efficiencies, it is replacing many CT closures, even where the complete protection of the hermetic seal may not be required.

One of its major advantages is that it is easier to remove than the CT closure, especially under conditions of high vacuum. Also, if there is a possibility of the food product spilling over the finish of the container and onto the glass threads or lugs, it is easier to wash out the product from this area, a procedure which is virtually impossible with a CT cap, and again would make for easier cap removal.

Figure 4.8 – Glass Container Steam-Vacuum Capping Machine in Operation (Courtesy White Cap Division, The former Continental Group, Inc.)

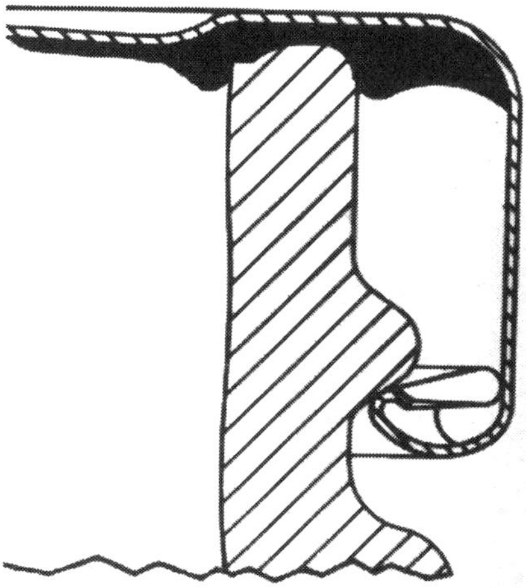

Figure 4.9 – Schematic of "Twist-Off Cap on Glass Container Finish

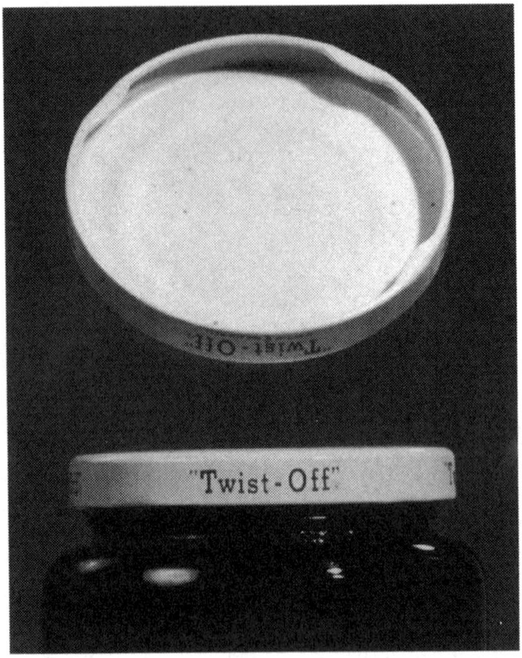

Figure 4.10 – "Twist-Off" or Lug Cap
(Courtesy White Cap Division, The Continental Group, Inc.)

Figure 4.11 – Press-On, Twist-Off Finish Glass Jar
(Courtesy White Cap Division, The Continental Group, Inc.)

The PT closure is plastisol lined and designed to be pressed onto the glass finish. It can be turned off and also resealed. Developed originally for baby food, its use has spread to a number of other heat processed products. This closure is illustrated in Figures 4.11, 4.12 and 4.13.

Figure 4.12 – Press-On, Twist-Off Cap
(Courtesy White Cap Division, The Continental Group, Inc.)

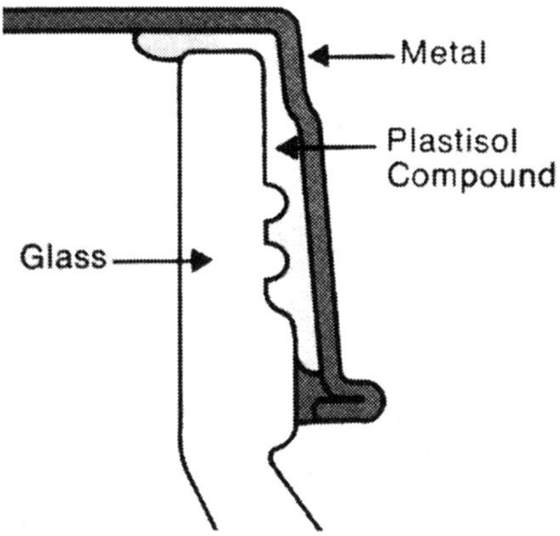

Figure 4.13 – Schematic of "Press-Twist" Cap on Glass Finish
(Courtesy White Cap Division, The Continental Group, Inc.)

Vacuum-sealed jars can be 100% inspected by the use of automatic, electronic dud detectors (Figure 4.14) which are available for on-line installation and operate efficiently at all line speeds. Such units are a great adjunct to quality control and container inspection programs.

Figure 4.14 – Electronic Dud Detector to Automatically Reject Low-Vacuum Jars (Courtesy CARE Controls)

Figure 4.15 – Tumbler Cap–DSR (Courtesy White Cap Div., The Continental Group, Inc.)

The Good Manufacturing Practice Regulations for Low-Acid Foods require the coding of individual containers to show place, date and shift at which the product was packed. Automatic coders of the type illustrated in Figure 4.16, which imprint the cap with an inked code, are available for in-line use. Other coders, which ink code the bottom of jars, as well as label coders, are also used. Embossed codes should not be used on jar caps due to the potential for corrosion and fracture.

Figure 4.16 – Glass Container Coder
(Courtesy White Cap Division, The Continental Group, Inc.)

Shipping Containers and Casing

Check under metal containers for this information.

COMMERCIAL PACKAGING OF FOOD PRODUCTS IN PLASTIC CONTAINERS

Introduction

The following list of items should be considered when thinking about packaging a food product in a plastic container. A small discussion of possible selection criteria for each item can be found below.

- Consumer Acceptance
- Container Design/Structure
- Shelf Life Required/Product Compatibility
- Decorating Techniques
- Filling Line Requirements
- Sealing Techniques/Tamper Indication
- Warehousing/Transportation
- Plastic Package Recycle Potential

Consumer Acceptance

It is obvious that if consumers do not buy a package, it is unacceptable even if it is a great technical success. A unique feature of many plastics, compared to other packaging materials, is that they can be molded in shapes that contain useful features for the consumer in addition to inherent physical properties of the plastic itself. Plastics vary widely in price so care must be taken to use something that is viable economically. The following list contains some of the items that should be considered in consumer acceptance. Consumers have different points of view in deciding the total package value of the sum of these items:

Package Cost

Package Safety

- External tamper indication
- Resistance to abuse
  - Shatter resistance
  - Elasticity
- Handling features
- No sharp edges

Graphics

- Retention of graphics: labels, inks, shrink wraps, etc.
- Product identification: unique shape, logos, color
- Adequate directions for safety, use, storage, product removal and preparation, etc.
- Embossing, debossing, recycling logo

Product Quality

- Taste
- Color
- Texture
- Viscosity

Ease of Product Removal

- Ease of removal of external tamper-indicating features
- Ease of removal of internal seals (usually foil)
- Dispensing features, if any
- Container flexibility
- Size of neck and finish
- Product adhesion to internal container surface

Reclosing Capability

Package Storage

- Height
- Ease of removal from and return to storage
- Temperature considerations
- Product permeation
  - Contamination of other products with odor, etc.

- Unacceptable buildup of product on external surfaces and in package clarity

Package Clarity
- Some want to see everything
- Some like the appeal of frostness
- Some like contents hidden because of poor eye appeal
- Some want a view strip to tell fill level

Package Cleanliness
- Over-wraps
- Anti-static surface for cleaning and staying cleaner

Container Design/Structure

Plastic containers can be made by many different forming techniques. The forming techniques used and the exact machine variations used are dependent on the melting and forming properties of the specific plastic used and the container design needed. Some of the design features will have been considered above, based on consumer preferences. Some designs are also based on characteristics of the filling line. Whatever design and plastic is considered, it must be makable on a forming process at acceptable economics, be able to meet filling line and shelf life needs; and be able to be stored and/or transported without damage. This is a functional package. Therefore it is imperative to get forming people and filling line people into the loop of determining the final container design as soon as possible to help determine the functionality of the desired design. Contrary to some beliefs that still exist, plastics are not indestructible when subjected to an impact force. All plastics can be made to fracture when subjected to the wrong type of stress. Some plastics are more temperature sensitive than others, so designs should take this into consideration. There are methods of improving impact failure resistance versus temperature which depend on the type of plastic used. The following items need to be considered:

Forming Features
- Plastic-type and limitations of molding machines that can mold that type of plastic
- Container wall thickness distribution capability of the molding process, both peripherally and axially
- Special finish features
  - Support ledges and/or grooves to facilitate handling, closing and use in tamper-indicating systems
  - Insert molding
  - Temperature resistance: thicker finishes, crystallization levels, design masking, special layering

  - Sterility seal to be faced off at filling lines
- Handles: hollow/solid
- Container surface effects
  - Roughness/smoothness
  - Raised or sunken lettering and/or logos
- Additions of additives to achieve color, reduce cost, static reduction, increases in strength and/or clarity, reduction of permeation, etc.
- Melt bonded multiple layers to achieve special properties
- Incorporating graphics application features consumer accpetance features
- Shape: round, oval, square, pinch waste, tapered, etc.
- Handling: ledges in finish, grip indentations, handles, etc.
- Finishing of containers: no sharp edges, reclosing system fills well, dispensing features work well, no unexpected leakage from planned and unplanned openings

Filling Line Handling Features

- Easy draining for pre-washed containers
- Bottle alignment features to reduce or eliminate shingling
- Minimizing hot fill distortion both vertically and peripherally
- Storage and transportation features

Shelf Life Requirements/Product Compatibility

The consumer has the right to expect that a product that is available for purchase from the store shelf should be acceptable for consumption. There are large variances in acceptance of a taste because people are all chemically different resulting in different responses to chemical reactions with their systems. Most of the chemicals that are present are due to the selection of product ingredients and the product preparation process. However, there are a few things that can change due to interaction of the product with the package or because of chemicals leaving the product or coming into the product by permeation (passing through the package walls or neck sealing system: closure, closure liner, foil or plastic seals, etc.). It should be remembered that in some cases, controlled interactions and permeation are actually preferred as opposed to total elimination. Chemicals such as oxygen or product components that pass through open passages, whether the openings are intended or unintended, is not considered permeation. Graphics should also stay on the package in legible form.

When properly matched, many food products can be packaged with more than adequate shelf life. There are many plastics and additives packages that can be put together to make suitable containers that meet FDA regulations for packaging foods at various temperatures. Components of the plastic walls that might migrate, a topic covered below, fall under the FDA section on indirect additives. Chemical changes and migration rates can be slowed significantly by refrigeration.

Some of the interactions that can occur are listed below:

Permeation of Oxygen into the Product

- There is a specific rate inherent for each virgin plastic
- Some additives put into the plastic can reduce permeation
- Barrier plastics can be melt-bonded in thinner layers with thicker layers of more permeable plastics to achieve permeation reductions while minimizing cost effects (called 'multi-layering')
- Barrier coatings can be applied to the outside
- Barrier labeling can be added to the outside

Permeation of Product Ingredients to the Outside

- There is a specific rate inherent for each virgin plastic with respect to flavorants, odorants, gases, water, etc.
- Multi-layering for reduction
- Addition of additives to the plastics for reduction product component absorption
- The chemical components of the product that are absorbed are specific to the chemical structure of the plastic; for instance, polyolefins absorb several essential oils that are flavorants and odorants
- Multi-layering with barrier layer on inside
- Increase initial level of absorbed chemicals to make up for equilibrium absorption losses

Migration of Plastics Components into the Product (Check FDA Regulations for Indirect Additives to Determine Acceptable Levels)

- Monomers
- Low molecular weight components
- Catalyst residues
- Additives: plasticizers, antioxidants, slip agents, antistatic modifiers, etc.

Organic Destablizers Present: Enzymes, Molds, Yeasts, Bacteria

- Inadequate temperature and total heat transfer to total product
  - Heat transfer coefficient of plastics is lower than that of metal or glass
  - Plastic container walls are almost always thinner than glass, but heat transfer per unit of time is still normally lower
- Contamination of filling equipment
- Inadequate pre-treatment of containers, closings systems, and/or washing equipment with washing solutions such as chlorine or bromine solutions, hydrogen peroxide solution, hot water
- Inadequate pre-treatment of equipment with stem
- Contamination through premature opening of package by non-buyers (one reason for using external tamper indication)

Poor Graphics Retention

- Surface tension of container surface too low for types of inks and adhesives used due to inadequate preparation of surface or migration of additives
- Inadequate bonding if using in-mold labeling
- Inadequate volume of glue on label before application when using hot melt or cold glues
- Incorrect heating if using heat transfer labeling
- Loss of shrink or stretch labeling
  - Inadequate label retention features
  - Stretch or orientation recovery too slow or low
  - Lack of heat/time
  - Tension too high, causing fracture

Decorating Technique

There are several methods of decorating plastic containers. The procedures below dwell on graphics added to the surface of the outside of the container as opposed to items such as colorants, special effects multi-layering, embossing and debossing, stretch wraps, shrink wraps, and like items. All the techniques of adding graphics are not equally applicable because of the type of plastic used, the type of surface preparation needed, or the shape. The best retention for hot melt and cold glues and inks occurs when the surface tension of the surface on which a graphic is applied is higher than the dried form of the graphic applied. Retention is still possible if the application surface is lower in surface tension, but retention of the graphic is less secure. If the differential in surface tension is high, the application surface is low in surface tension compared to the dry form of the applied graphic, the graphic can be removed with only minor abuse.

IML (in mold labeling) is a special form of graphic application because the label is stuck to the container surface while the container is being made. When properly applied, the back of the label melt bonds to the bottle surface.

Generic Bonding Materials

- Hot melt glue
- Cold glue
- Pressure-sensitive glue
- IR-sensitive inks
- Heat-sensitive glue
- Polymer layers (IML)
- Hot leaf stamping

Generic Label Materials

- Paper
- Plastic laminates
- Plastic foam laminates

Filling Line Requirements

Out of the various filling techniques of gravity, pressure gravity, vacuum, fill level sensing, weight sensing, timed, piston, and volumetric, only vacuum tends to be severe. Plastic containers, being relatively flexible, tend to distort so that the vacuum is minimized. Gravity and pressure gravity require top loading to achieve seals during filling which can cause distortion if the product is hot. Distortion can be used to an advantage to make up for the decreased density of the product and still minimize head space.

Commercial packages are run on several different types of filling lines, with regard to actual fill temperature. The combination of the type of plastic chosen, the product to be packaged, and the type and level of residual organic destabilizers that are tolerable to maintain expected shelf life plus maintain an absence of toxins at the time of the first opening for consumption, determine the actual fill temperature and/or the preparation of the line before filling.

Based on fill temperature and post treatment, the types of filling lines used might be generically classified as:

Retort
Hot Fill
Warm Fill
Cool Fill/Aseptic
Commercially Acceptable.

The types of plastics currently used are called thermo-plastics. They do not maintain a rigid profile when squeezed, even though some are less flexible than others. As the temperature of the plastic is increased it becomes more flexible.

Plastics have what is known as a heat distortion temperature. In theory, this is the temperature at which a certain amount of force will create a specific amount of deflection when the wall is a standard thickness. Although there is a heat distortion temperature that is representative of each generic type of plastic, there are variances within the generic type, when tested under standardized conditions, due to the way in which the specific type was made. The purpose of obtaining a heat distortion temperature (or range) is to know when there is a possibility of obtaining an unacceptable handling of the package on the filling line or result in such permanent deformation that the package becomes unacceptable aesthetically or functionally. By knowing the representative heat distortion temperature of the generic types, it is possible to know something about the type of filling line to use if a specific plastic is desired. The heat distortion temperature of plastics that might be used to package foods range from less than 100°F/38°C to about 200°F/93°C. Since the heat distortion temperature measured is the result of the characteristics of the basic plastic, the force applied, the geometry of the test sample, and wall thickness, the actual distortion seen in a container is a composite of the same factors. A low force filling and capping system combined with containers that have geometry that resists distortion and/or heavier walls can hold products at temperatures somewhat higher than typically accepted heat distortion temperatures. It is also possible to increase distortion through multi-layering a small amount of high heat distortion resin (which is usually more expensive) with a larger amount of less expensive carrier resin. Plastic containers are relatively low in weight so the filling line should be designed to minimize any concepts that require gravity alone to move containers. Plastic containers are also somewhat compressible, so it is a good idea not to have long straight run lines going into feed screws or star wheels. Plastic containers can usually take a higher level of abuse than other packaging materials without producing cracks, open seams, or retaining permanent dents.

Retort: There are many types of retorts which supply heat, over-pressure, and cooling in different ways. There are some common factors which are known. All products expand with heat, as does the container. All products need to be brought to some minimum standard of temperature and transfer of heat to the product to eliminate or reduce to an acceptable minimum, the organic destabilizers that can affect the product. This has to be done while preserving acceptable product integrity and quality. To adequately use a plastic container it is necessary to consider the effects of temperature on possible container distortion due to gravitation forces of the product, distortion due to low over pressure, and the effect on seal maintenance. Heat transfer rates will determine heating and cooling rates in conjunction with over pressure. For nearly all retorted foods there is a desire to condition the atmosphere inside the container before passing it into the retort. Conditioning is usually done to make the head space as free of reactive gasses as possible and also to create a vacuum. What ever vacuum exists at the beginning, using rigid sided containers, is close to the same when the container exits the retort. For most sealing systems, this vacuum creates a usable distortion in the sealing unit, rather than the container, so the distortion can be used to determine if the container is truly sealed. Because of the flexibility of plastic containers, especially under high temperatures, sealing of retorted plastic containers is not easy using conventional sealing systems. Plastic container finishes do not retain good dimensions under the forces used to retain the sealing system.

On the other hand, plastics can be sealed using fusion bonded plastic or foil laminates which maintain excellent seal integrity. A re-seal type closure or overcap can be added after the retort process. A nitrogen flush can be used to make a more inert head space.

Since the heat distortion temperature of typical plastics used is lower than the 250–270°F (121–132°C) temperatures used, it is advisable to use some method of holding the shape of the container. This can be done through use of physical restraints or having a good tight packing design. Over pressure is needed very early in the heating process in order to minimize distortion. Although it is obvious that overpressure must be maintained during high temperatures, as it is for other packaging materials, it is very important to hold high over pressures during the cooling process because the lower heat transfer of the plastic allows higher vapor pressure inside the container for a longer period. Minimizing distortion is necessary to be able to efficiently run containers through capping and labeling systems that come after the retort process.

Retort systems generate as close to a sterile product condition as is possible.

Hot fill: Hot fill for purposes of this discussion, is defined as a line filling a product above 180°F/82°C but not in excess of 205°F/96°C. Hot fill temperatures are generally at the upper end of the temperature range that typical plastics can withstand, in a free standing form, and remain functional. Two such plastics that fall into this range are polypropylene and heat set PET. Copolymers of polypropylene and polyethylene can be used for temperatures just below this range but can be extended just into the range through multi-layering and careful container design. Multi-layering may also be needed to achieve an adequate permeation barrier.

Since the heat transfer of plastics is relatively low, it is possible to take advantage of this during filling by minimizing the time it takes to fill and apply the primary seal to the container. By minimizing fill time, the distribution of temperature though the sidewall shows that the average temperature can be kept below a major distortion temperature by the time the container moves on the sealing unit. Once the seal is applied, distortion remains minimized because the volume of the container is essentially fixed. Since heat moves into the container more slowly than for other packaging materials, and since the volume of plastic is small, the temperature of the product does not drop as fast, so the product, head space area, and closing system are more easily brought up to the temperature to achieve good kill rates for organic destabilizers before cooling is started. Vapor pressure at these temperatures will not significantly distort a closed container. The container will have a tendency to round out, if it is not round already, and if it is round, it may take on a slight circular bulge similar to a donut shaped bulge. In some respects this is beneficial because the product will take up more space when it is hot and the expanded container will be able to hold the larger hot volume of the filled product. This effect determines whether or not the container should be measured for volume when it is filled with cold or hot product or liquids. It is a good idea to minimize top load force on containers before closing to minimize compression distortion. During cooling, usually a shower tunnels, while the head space gases and product are contracting, as well as the container, a vacuum tries to form. However, since plastic containers do not easily resist a vacuum, the container begins to pull in while at the same time it is shrinking slightly. By proper application of shape design, the aesthetic effects and functional effects of the change can be minimized. The net result is that the final head space will be small. Whereas with some packaging materials, that are more rigid, one of the principles might be to use larger head spaces to maximize vacuum, the objective with plastic containers is to minimize head space to reduce distortion.

Hot fill systems are usually used to package acidic or acidified products because the combination of adequate heat plus an acid nature can kill off or adequately control the organic destabilizers that can shorten shelf life or render the product unsuitable for use when purchased.

Warm fill: Warm fill, for purposes of definition, includes products that are filled from 120°F/49°C to 180°F/82°C. Except at the upper end of the temperature range, from 165°F/74°C to 180°F/82°C, the plastics mentioned under hot fill can usually be used without tunnel cooling as long as product integrity does not suffer due to the prolonged heat. Heat not removed before case packing and storage can remain in containers at relatively high temperatures for days. Since warm fill, except at the upper temperature, does not have much killing power for organic destabilizers, the product must have considerable resistance, or not be naturally susceptible to destabilizers, or contain additives. Warm fill is sometimes used just to change product viscosity to make transporting and filling possible with less pressure.

Cool fill/aseptic: Aseptic filling is not the same as sterile filling, although its objective would be to approach such a level. There are products that can not be aseptically filled because it is not possible to maintain perfectly "clean" lines and a perfectly "clean" atmosphere around the line. The lines have to be scrupulously cleaned and separated from the surrounding atmosphere, unless the line is in a maintained clean room. In these types of lines, products that have to undergo high temperature treatment are properly treated in one section of the line and are then cooled down, before filling, to temperatures that are compatible with the type of plastic or shape desired while minimizing distortion. For these lines, after proper conditioning of the filling system, the entire container must be pre-treated before coming into the filler and the closing system must be pretreated before application. Once the container is sealed, it can be handled in a normal manner.

Sealing Techniques/Tamper Indication

Terminology revolving around tamper features does not seem to be well defined. From a cursory point of view, three terms are considered and defined as follows:

Tamper proof–Not to be used: Can't guarantee there is absolutely no way to add something to the package through entry ports or using something to penetrate the sealing system, package shell, or through spaces left such as between the sealing system and the container.

Tamper evident: Implies that some noticeable distortion of the package or sealing system takes place, while securing entry into the package, which is very difficult to repair or hide. It is evident that something has happened. In order to achieve this level, it is common that packaging features be included to make it very difficult to get into the package through normal entry ports without seeing damage to the container, sealing system, or tamper features.

Tamper indicating: Implies that when someone tries to gain entry into the package through the sealing system, damage occurs so that the damage could usually be detected either obviously or by close examination.

Tamper features can be either external, so they are quite visible, or sheltered, which means they are protected by some other feature and not easily visible.

Plastic containers can incorporate features to work in conjunction with various tamper features to complete their function. The most widely used external systems are shrink wraps, with and without tear strips, and closures with breakaway bands. The most widely used sheltered system is heat seals. More will be said on heat seals later because they can also protect the quality of the product packaged.

It is doubtful that any one person or even any single organization can supply information on all the current sealing techniques that are available. It is not possible to use all the techniques that are used to seal non-food containers. It is also not possible, at this time, on plastic containers, to efficiently use all the techniques used on other food packaging mediums. However, there are many systems under study that appear capable of expanding current technology soon. There is a sealing method that is applicable to plastics which can not be easily used on other packaging materials.

The type of seal most widely used for plastics, excluding beverages, is a heat seal laminate applied to the seal surface of the finish. Although plastic laminates, especially plastic barrier laminates, can be used, the preference goes to foil laminates. It is best to talk to the heat seal suppliers to get details on the combinations of time, temperature, pressure and chemical resistance that are available, as well as suggestions as to what laminates apply best to what generic plastics in containers. Foiless seals can be glued to the surface by heat conduction. Foil seals can be glued to the surface by heat conduction or heat induction. For either type, there must be sufficient pressure applied by some method to maintain intimate contact between the seal material and the container finish. There must also be sufficient heat transferred to that interface to obtain a bond between the two surfaces. There is not sufficient room here to discuss all the types of equipment available but some note needs to be made that if the seal is to be placed in a closure and bonded through induction sealing, it is best to have a seal or liner retention bead and to apply more torque than normal to hold sufficient compression when the bonding surface begins to distort.

The type of bond can be adhesive, which allows pealability, or fusion, which means the seal can not be separated without significant distortion to the seal. Fusion bonded seals might be necessary because of filling line stresses or the perceived need for a sheltered tamper evident seal. Adhesive bonded seals are more "user friendly" and could be used as a tamper indicating seal if the bonding temperature approaches fusion temperatures. In either case, when properly applied, the seals primary function is to preserve the product.

Solids, oils, or similar materials left on the finish seal surface can cause an interference with bonding. It is best to see that these parts of the product do not get on the surface or are removed form the surface before seal application.

Various closures can be used for sealing, many of which can include tamper features. It is difficult to obtain seals with closures that do not have inserted liners due to the flexibility of the finish and the forces needed to assure a seal. This is one of the greatest areas of testing in the lab and commercially. Fill temperature has a great deal to do with selection of the closure and liner style where conduction heat sealing is not used. When using conduction heat sealing, the closure is not a primary seal, it is for reseal or a safety cover. Therefore, a hot filled product can be cooled before closure application, a hermetic seal between the closure and package is not required, so the choice of thread pattern as well as closure strength can be adjusted to suit the consumer need.

Warehousing and Transportation

Warehousing and transportation have two segments: unfilled ware, as delivered and stored prior to use, and filled ware. Since plastic containers are relatively light, their weight does not normally contribute much to bulk weight being transported either empty or filled. Trucks can almost always be sent out with the maximum load that pallet stacking patterns will allow to be put into the cubage of the truck.

Manufacturers of plastic containers pack containers in the method that matches the filler's unloading and line integration methods. Containers can be packed in reshippers, in disposable shippers, layer packed in bulk with trays and stretch wrap or in cartons, random packed in bulk cartons, etc. If containers are packed in other than re shippers, care must be taken to see that containers are not unduly compressed either peripherally or vertically or the containers might retain a permanent distortion due to cold flow. This could result in changes in aesthetics, volume, or line handling characteristics. It is entirely possible to overcome difficulties with proper planning.

Although each packager of products has to decide the best value of the shipping retainer used versus warehousing and transportation circumstances, it is best, at the outset, not to expect the plastic container to assume a major portion of the vertical stacking load. Cold flow can occur over time, which would reduce support strength.

Because of the flexibility of the plastic container, abuse from fork lifts and other collisions which might damage more rigid packaging would be either greatly reduced or not take place, thus saving product and cleanup problems.

Plastic package recycle potential: All thermoplastic materials used to make food containers can be recycled, but all recycled plastics do not command the same value. "Recycled plastics," to plastics processors means post consumer resin (PCR). PCR is material reclaimed from containers returned by consumers through various collection systems. Collection, separation, cleaning, and distribution to processors add costs to plastics which are to be reused. The type of plastic (resin identification) a container is made from is quite frequently noted on the container in the form of a numbered logo molded into the base. Resin identification is currently required in 39 states.

There is resistance to using PCR back into the food contact layer of food containers because of concern about possible contamination due to the retention of products stored in the containers other than a food product. Methods are being developed to test for the acceptability of using PCR for food container. As cleaning and testing become more refined and common place and use of PCR grows, it is expected that confidence and acceptance of PCR in food containers will grow. Meanwhile, these plastics can be used in making other non-food containers which are relatively high value articles.

The value of reclaimed resin is determined by a number of items, some of which are listed below:

1. Value of the part that can contain PCR
2. Cost of virgin plastic that may be displaced
3. Physical properties of the PCR
4. Purity of the PCR
   - Presence of colorants and additives
   - Presence of mixed plastics
   - Presence of foreign objects

Value judgments are changing as technology for separation and cleaning is changing and competition for available PCR grows.

ACKNOWLEDGEMENTS

The author acknowledges with thanks the contribution of Rolf C. Myers, Senior Fellow, Owens-Brockway Plastics Products, Owens-Illinois, Inc., One Sea Gate, Toledo, OH 43666, Tel. 419/247-5000 and Roger Ritzert, Ph.D. (retired), Manager, Packaging and Processing Services, Glass Container Division, Owens-Illinois.

CHAPTER 5

Retortable Flexible Containers

Retort Pouch and Semi-Rigid Containers

Note: In the text of this chapter, reference is made to several firms using abbreviated names. Following is a list of the full company names:

Gasti-Jagenberg Gruppe
Mahaffy & Harder Engineering Company
Metal Box p.l.c.
Rampart Packaging, Inc.
Reynolds Metals Company
Rychiger (represented in the U.S. by Paxall Circle Machinery)

Introduction

Retortable flexible containers are laminate structures that are thermally processed like a can, are shelf-stable, and have the convenience of frozen boil-in-the-bag products. The materials for flexible containers must provide superior barrier properties for a long shelf-life, seal integrity, toughness and puncture resistance, and must also withstand the rigors of thermal processing. Retortable flexible containers may be retort pouches or semi-rigid containers.

Development of the retort pouch concept began in the United States in the early 1950s. Much of the work done by the U.S. Army Natick Development Center was to use retort pouches to replace the can components in military combat rations. Material development was pioneered by Reynolds Metals Co. and Continental Group, Inc.

During the 1960s, test runs were made using the retort pouch. The results of these tests are encouraging. Japanese and European firms obtained U.S. methods and technology through licensing arrangements which allowed them to start production of foods packed in retort pouches in the late 1960s. In 1968 the U.S. Army Natick Development Center undertook a reliability study of the pouch; in comparing seal integrity, sterility, and overall defects, it was found that retort pouches could be produced that were equal to metal cans.

In 1974, the U.S. Department of Agriculture gave approval for use of retort pouches with all meat products, but in 1975, the U.S. Food and Drug

FIGURE 5.1 – Retort Pouch and Overwrap Carton
(Courtesy U.S. Army Natick Development Center)

Administration asked the USDA to withdraw this approval because FDA was concerned that the polyester and epoxy components of the laminating adhesive used in the pouch could migrate into the food. In 1977, the FDA issued a regulation for high temperature laminates which specified the materials acceptable for manufacture of the pouch and set extraction limits for these materials. The USDA concurred with this regulation but limited pouch fill to 16 oz. (0.45 kg) for meat and poultry products.

A variety of low-acid foods thermally sterilized in the retort pouch have been successfully marketed in Japan for more than 20 years. Retort pouch products for the retail market were expected to compete with frozen foods such as single serve entrees and side dishes. To date, these packages have been established only in niche products such as smoked salmon and camping rations.

Commodity foods such as canned corn, green beans, peaches and pears in #10 cans are candidates for replacement by institutional size retort pouches, as well as foods now being marketed in half size steam table trays. Products such as fruits and other acid foods which do not come under the low-acid food regulations and require sterilization temperatures not higher than 212°F (100°C) have already been test marketed, although to date, penetration of these markets has met with limited success. Today, by far the most important market for flexible retortable pouches in the U.S. is the military combat rations program, Meals Ready to Eat (MRE).

FIGURE 5.2 – Semi-Rigid Aluminum Containers
(Courtesy Reynolds Metals Co.)

During the 1970s, some companies began investigating the potential for semi-rigid containers. These containers were manufactured from aluminum with interiors of polypropylene film or coating or standard can coatings. Like standard cans, the containers achieved a hermetic seal through double-seaming; these containers were significantly lighter than cans and generally shaped to be shallow. In Europe, some containers were commercialized using membrane lids with heat seal coatings. The primary drawback to the aluminum semi-rigid container was its susceptibility to denting.

In the early 1980s, the first high barrier plastic containers were developed. These containers were laminates of polypropylene/EVOH or PVDC/polypropylene. They were capable of withstanding thermal processing temperatures and conditions while maintaining their shape and barrier properties. In 1984, the first market test for an entree was conducted in Europe and in San Francisco, California. These containers could be reheated in microwave ovens or in boiling water like the retort pouch. The materials used in manufacture comply with FDA regulations for high temperature laminates and meet the stringent USDA standards for shipping and distribution.

A package which falls roughly between the flexible retortable pouch and the high barrier plastic container is the formed retortable pouch. The bottom of the pouch is formed in a horizontal configuration which allows easy in-line filling of placeable items such as meat patties, sausage and lasagna, as opposed to the vertically filled non-formed pouch which is better with pumpable foods such as stews. This package has found some acceptance in Europe, where it is promoted as offering taste quality approaching frozen food in shelf stable form, for a market without extensive home freezer capacity.

Products Packed in Retortable Flexible Containers

The following types of foods may be packed in the retort pouch: meats, sauces with or without particulates, soups; fruits and vegetables, specialty items like potato salad, bakery products, pet foods, and other products. Some entrees that have been packed are meatballs and gravy or tomato sauce, chicken a la King, chicken stew, beef stew, ravioli, spaghetti and meat, Hungarian goulash, beef Stroganoff, barbecue chicken, sukiyaki, and others. Generally, any product currently packaged in cans or glass may be packaged in flexible containers. Some products which now appear only in frozen form can transfer to the semi-rigid container or formed pouch where product can be layered.

Structure of Flexible Containers

The structure of the retortable pouch in general use today is a three-ply laminate composed of 0.00048 in. (0.012 mm) polyester film, adhesive laminated to 0.00035 or 0.0007 in. (0.0089 or 0.018 mm) aluminum foil, which is laminated to a 0.003 in. (0.076 mm) polypropylene film. The polyester film is used for high temperature resistance, toughness and printability; the polyester may be reverse printed, that is, the ink is embedded between the film and the foil. The aluminum foil can be laminated with either the matte or shiny side exposed to view; normally the matte side is to the outside. Aluminum foil provides a barrier to light and gas for extended shelf life. The polypropylene provides the critical heat-seal integrity, flexibility, strength and taste and odor compatibility with a variety of food products. The inherent characteristics of polyester and polypropylene enable the pouches to be processed at up to 275°F (135°C).

The formed bottom of the formable pouch is composed of 0.0012 in. (0.030 mm) oriented polypropylene film adhesive laminated to 0.00175 in. (0.044 mm) aluminum foil which is adhesive laminated to 0.003 in. (0.076 mm) polypropylene film. The unformed top is the standard retortable pouch structure described above. The oriented polypropylene has sufficient extensibility to allow forming but is tough enough to help protect against puncture and abrasion.

Although most work with the retort pouch relates to individual serving size, there is interest in using flexible retortable materials for larger institutional packages. Some changes in laminate structure may be involved for these larger sizes; heavier gauge components may be needed, or an additional ply in the overall structure might be utilized. Customization of structures for specific needs can be anticipated. Generically, however, they must all be flexible, retortable, heat sealable and conform with regulatory stipulations.

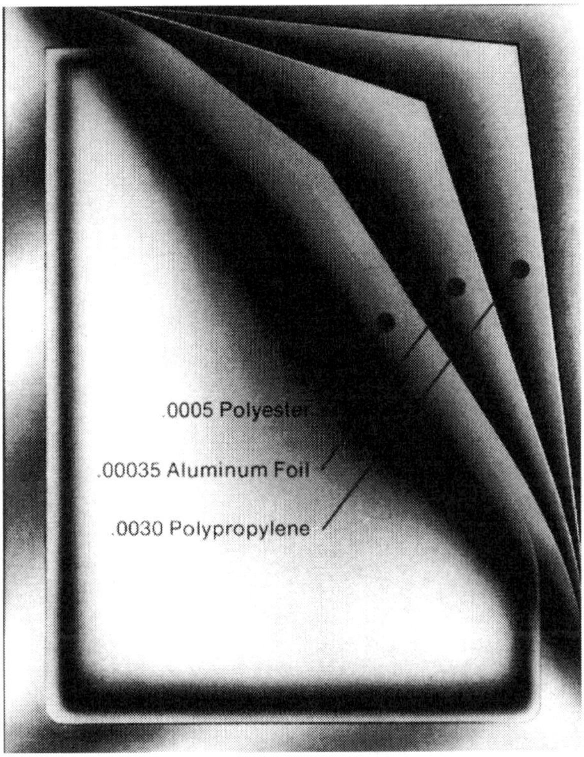

FIGURE 5.3 – Structure of the Retort Pouch
(Courtesy Reynolds Metals Co.)

Packages for thermally processed, commercially sterile foods must remain impenetrable to bacteria. A number of studies have been conducted on the permeability of plain films and laminated materials to a variety of bacteria. The result of these studies demonstrates that retortable laminates do not allow bacterial penetration unless an actual fracture in the laminate exists. Where actual fractures exist, they can be readily detected by dye stain techniques which penetrate the defect. Consequently, aluminum foil flex cracks in the structure represent no microbiological hazard unless the crack is accompanied by cracks in the plastic components of the laminate which would allow for dye stain penetration completely through the laminate.

With the availability of high oxygen barrier films, such as EVOH and PVDC, a great deal of research has been done to develop a non-foil retortable pouch with extended shelf life. The first known commercial product was a polyester/ polyurethane adhesive/modified high density polyethylene structure. It was used for retort packaging of items requiring shelf life of three months or less or for products held under refrigeration. A nitrogen gas flush between the pouch and an overwrap helped to extend shelf life. Current research is concentrating on co-extrusions of polyolefins with either EVOH or PVDC as the core. The core materials significantly reduce the oxygen transmission rate of polyolefin films and therefore extend the stability of the food product. In turn, co-extruded films may be laminated to polyester to give the material strength, scuff resistance and a printable surface.

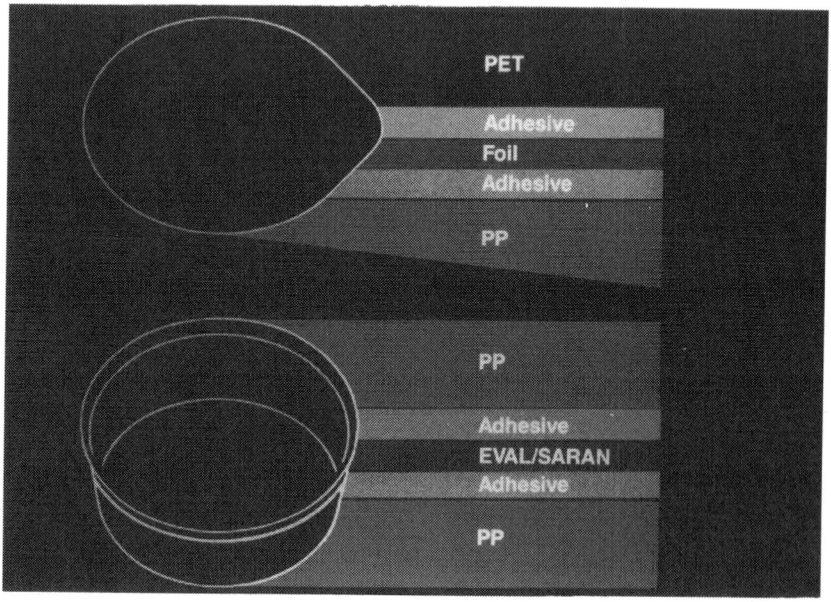

FIGURE 5.4 – Section View of Lid and Body of High Barrier Multi-Layer, Plastic Retortable Container (Courtesy Reynolds Metals Co.)

Although the original semi-rigid containers were aluminum, high barrier plastic retortable containers were produced in the 1980's. The primary structure of these containers is a polypropylene/EVOH or PVDC/polypropylene sandwich with appropriate tie layers and filler. Structures may contain 2 to 8 layers in thicknesses from 6–80 mils (0.006–0.080 in. (0.15–2.0 mm)). Alternate materials under investigation include high impact polystyrene, crystallized polyester and polycarbonates. Container manufacturers claim 12-month shelf life, although acknowledge that the actual life may vary with food product.

In addition to providing the barrier properties required, these containers survive the high temperature required for filling and processing, whether aseptic, hot fill or retort up to 275°F (135°C). Structural integrity is such that dimensional stability is maintained throughout the retort process. The design of the container and rigidity of its flange affect ability to easily remove a fusion sealed membrane from the container.

FIGURE 5.5 – Semi-Rigid, Retortable Containers with
High Barrier Lidding Materials and Lids
(Courtesy Reynolds Metals Co.)

High barrier containers require lidding materials whose barrier properties are equal to or better than the container itself. The lidding system must be abuse resistant, printable, sealable (preferably by heat) and easy to open. Lidding materials currently available are extensions of retort pouch technology; the exterior is polyester for printability, scuff and tear resistance, heavy gauge aluminum foil is used for stiffness and to provide light, moisture and oxygen barrier, and polypropylene film or proprietary coatings provide the interior heat seal component. While some of these lid structures can be removed without the use of a scissors or knife, early testing indicates they provide a completely hermetic high integrity seal and will be able to survive the abuse of shipping and handling. Non-foil barrier lidding is currently being introduced, providing increased ease of microwave heating.

Retort Pouch Forming, Filling and Sealing

The first step in the manufacture of laminate for pouches involves printing the polyester film. Excellent print quality, multiple color registration, repeat length and long run economy are associated with gravure printing which is usually employed. The printed polyester film can be adhesive laminated to the aluminum foil and then laminated to the polypropylene, or the printed polyester film can be laminated to a pre-mounted, foil-polypropylene, base laminate. In either case the adhesive is applied to a substrate and then passed through an oven which sets the adhesive; the combining of the two webs is done on a heated roll by employing pressure.

Pouches are pre-formed, or formed as an in-line operation with filling and sealing. In either event, they are formed from roll stock by folding a single roll along its center line or by bringing two separate rolls together heat sealed side to heat sealed side. A testing procedure is necessary to ensure adequacy of pouches, regardless of the forming technique used. In addition to dimensional and aesthetic properties, pouches should be tested for seal strength and for internal burst resistance.

Production filling machines now generally operate in the 30-60 pouch per minute range. However, it is expected that higher speeds will be achieved as commercial applications expand. Filling machines are either of the pre-formed pouch type or of the roll fed form-fill-seal type.

It is advantageous to remove all possible headspace air to prevent expansion in the retort and ballooning of pouch when placed in boiling water for heat and serve. Several methods are available for removing air from the pouch prior to sealing. The most elementary method involves mechanically squeezing the pouch. This is effective mainly with liquid products which conform nicely to mechanical pressure. Elevating the product temperature is also effective for air removal pressure; when sealed and cooled, a reduction in headspace gas volume would take place.

Vacuum sealing can be accomplished either by applying a vacuum to the inside of the pouch or by placing the entire unsealed pouch into a vacuum chamber prior to sealing. Vacuumizing the pouch may also be accomplished by use of a snorkel tube or by pulling the vacuum through an orifice in a plate which seals off the top of the pouch.

Steam flush air removal is an extension of the hot fill principle. Here, saturated or superheated steam is injected into the filled pouch just prior to making the final top seal. Condensation of water vapor minimizes the amount of headspace gas when cooled. Superheated steam is less effective than saturated steam, but superheated steam is often used because it causes less moisture condensation in the seal area.

All retort pouches are heat-sealed. The most common methods used for this are hot bar and impulse seals. Visual examination of seals is required on 100% of the pouches. The U.S. Army Natick Development Center and the National Food Processors Association have published visual standards for acceptable and rejectable top seal defects. Random samples are also evaluated for internal burst strength.

There are several retort pouch filling and sealing systems commercially available. Manufacturers include Rexham, FMC, Mitsubishi, Acme and Bosch. Descriptions of three systems follow.

Bartelt IMR Packagers are form, fill and seal machines or fill and seal machines used to produce flexible pouches in an intermittent motion (stop-start) flow pattern. The Bartelt form, fill and seal packager folds flexible pouch material into a "V" shape with the open end up. Two-sided heat seals and the bottom seal of the pouch are made while the web of packaging material is in a vertical flat folded state. This forming step provides that when the critical top seal is made, both sides of the pouch are of precisely equal length.

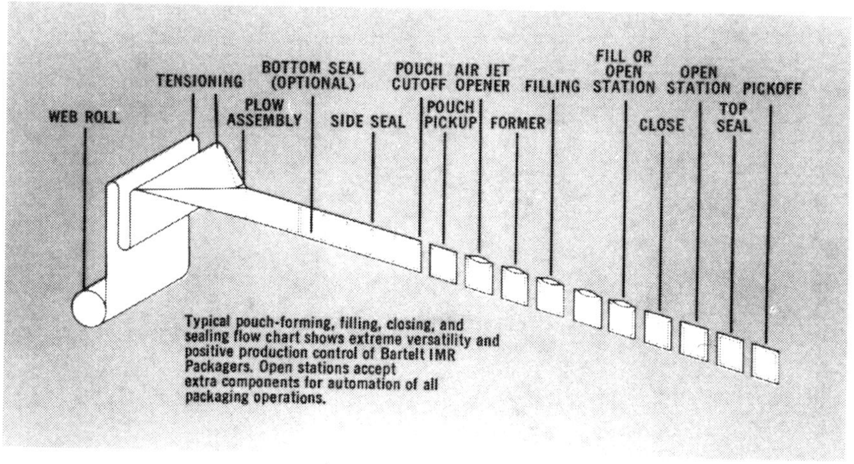

FIGURE 5.6 – Flow Chart of Bartelt Intermittent Motion Pouch Packager (Courtesy Rexham Corp., Packaging Machinery Div.)

Individual pouches are served from the folded web by cutting through the middle of the side seals. The pouch is opened prior to product filling by the action of mechanisms. Five stations following pouch opening supply adequate space to fill most solid food pieces in chunks, small pieces and liquid sauces. Pieces and particles can be automatically or manually deposited into pockets of in-line or carousel conveying devices and placed into the pouch by duckbill type depositors. It is desirable to remove a maximum amount of air from the filled pouch prior to final top heat sealing.

Top heat sealing of the pouch done on the packager in a four-step process:

1. Initial seal to make the pouch air tight;
2. Prime heat seal which utilizes an impulse seal method and provides hermetic tightness and strength to insure package integrity;
3. Final top heat seal to extend the seal to the top extremity of the pouch (eliminate channel where contaminates may become lodged);
4. Chill seal area.

A production rate of up to 60 pouches per minute can be attained; the fillers can dispense quantities as large as 15 oz. (0.42 kg).

The FMC Corporation has designed a different in-line steam flow filler and sealer for pre-formed retort pouches. The rotary filler from FMC uses twin clips that grasp the bag on both side seams near the top to move the pouch from the pouch former or from the pre-formed pouch loading station to the filling and sealing stations. As the pouch moves from the loading station, it is opened using low pressure steam, and then filled with measured amounts from an overhead hopper. After the filling process, high pressure steam shoots into the pouch to condense and form a vacuum. Next comes the sealer, where

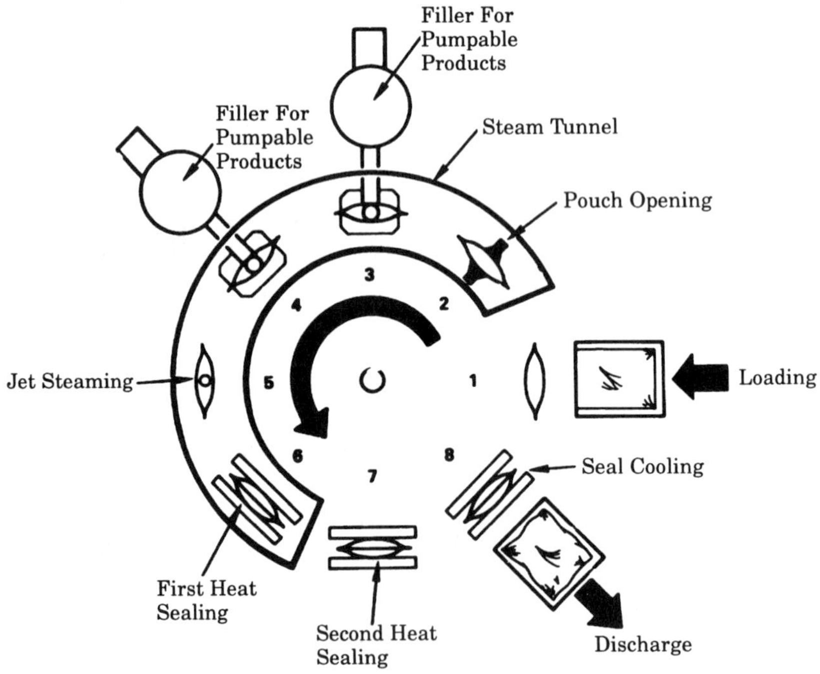

FIGURE 5.7 – Steam Flow Pouch Filler/Sealer
(Courtesy FMC Corp., Food Processing Machinery Div.)

impulse sealing bars seal the pouch. The output is 30 filled and sealed pouches per minute. FMC uses the steam flush principle of creating a vacuum because it allows for product filling at higher initial temperatures than mechanical vacuum producing procedures. This method was favored also because of its effects on contaminates in the seal area as the steam dilutes the contaminate.

The Mitsubishi equipment is an intermittent motion fill and seal machine which operates at 50 to 60 pouches per minute utilizing pre-made pouches. Air removal is usually by steam injection, but may be done by drawing a vacuum. Pouches travel perpendicular to the machine which provides the operator with a clear view of the top seal to spot contamination. The equipment offers several stations for dispensing individual components of a food product.

In the early 1980s, Bartelt Machinery (now a part of Klochner-Bartelt, Inc.) developed the first high speed form/fill/seal packager for the retort pouch. This machine is capable of filling pouches in continuous motion at speeds of 250 packages/minute, a speed which is competitive with some can lines. Some units were sold commercially but use has been limited by the lack of successful development of the consumer retort pouch market.

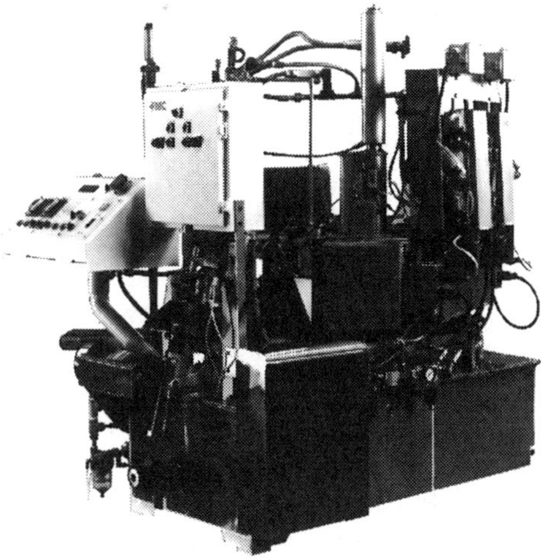

FIGURE 5.8 – Pouch Filler/Sealer
(Courtesy FMC Corp., Food Processing Machinery Div.)

The total cost of a filled package depends not only on material cost, but on the total of the processor's variable and fixed costs as well. Here, filling speeds and capital investment in suitable machinery become very important. Presently, pouch filling speeds of 60 per minute can be expected; this should be projected to 120 per minute with two 60 per minute pouch forming, filling and sealing machines plus suitable continuous retorting and automatic handling equipment. Non-automated pouch filling and sealing and static retorting can be used for the pouch with significantly lower equipment costs; however, operational costs would likely be higher. For any desired rate of production, a cost study of each equipment option should indicate the preferable equipment installation.

Semi-Rigid Containers–Filling and Sealing

While the technology of high barrier plastic materials has been evolving, so have the adaptations or design of equipment for filling and sealing. Like aseptic filling and sealing lines, it is necessary to minimize residual headspace and provide a hermetic seal. Unlike aseptic containers, semi-rigid retortable containers use heavier materials which require higher temperatures and pressures for sealing, may or may not be filled hot to assist in vacuumizing and must go on to survive retort processing at elevated temperatures.

Laboratory testing has been conducted on one-up heat sealing units. They are available from Reynolds Metals Co. (PC-based Reycon 203), Rychiger (Jenny Press) and Rampart Packaging. Each of these units seals in a vacuum chamber. The Reycon 203 and Jenny Press also have gas flush capabilities. The heat sealing unit is easily converted to accept a variety of container shapes. Sealing speeds are 1-2 containers per minute depending upon product handling.

For semi-production, such as pilot plant operations, equipment is available from Mahaffy & Harder, Metal Box and Rychiger. These are intermittent motion fill and seal machines operating between 15 and 25 units per minute depending upon the food product. In each of these systems, the lidding material is roll fed and die-cut in the sealing station. Sealing and air removal take place in a vacuum chamber in both the Mahaffy & Harder system and the Metal Box system. The Mahaffy & Harder vacuum chamber can be adapted for gas flushing. The Metal Box machine can partially form the lids in line. The Rychiger equipment utilizes vacuum based on the Venturi Principle for air removal.

Production equipment is available from Gasti and is being developed by other manufacturers of filling and sealing equipment. Unlike semi-production equipment, the Gasti line is continuous motion and operates at speeds of 250 units per minute. This system stack feeds pre-cut lids to the filled containers prior to entry into a vacuum chamber; air removal and sealing take place in the vacuum chamber.

Formed Pouches–Forming, Filling and Sealing

Bottom formed pouches are processed on a Tetra Laval Food Tiromat VA and Multivac (Koch) rollstock horizontal form fill and seal machines. These units also thermo form plastic materials giving them the versatility to package a wide variety of meat, cheese and prepared foods. Roll fed bottom stock is formed in a mold with a combination of compressed air, vacuum and stamping in a horizontal position. This permits easy filling of placeable items. Both units permit vacuum evacuation and gas flushing prior to sealing with roll fed lid stock. Sealing heat is applied to the top only, hence the heat resistant polyester exterior of the top stock and not the heat sensitive oriented polypropylene film exterior of the formed bottom is exposed to high temperature contact.

Formable pouches are currently being evaluated for military combat rations. The U.S. Army has determined that meals based on placeable items such as ham slices, roast beef and the like are more popular with personnel in the field than pumpable meals such as stews and chili. These formed pouch horizontal machines are more widely available than the vertically oriented machines, providing a much broader manufacturing base for faster production ramp-up in times of military emergency.

A recent joint development of Reynolds Metals Co., The Valspar Corp. and Rutgers University's Center for Advanced Food Technology (CAFT) is the use of colored adhesives for the exterior lamination of the bottom structure. This feature can add eye appeal to consumer pouches and is a firm requirement for military combat rations which are always olive drab in color. Prior to this advance, a colored, formed, retortable bottom structure was not feasible because available printing inks on polypropylene film could not survive the severe stresses of forming and retorting.

Equipment for Thermal Sterilization of Retortable Flexible Containers

Under proper conditions, retortable flexible containers can be processed in batch retorts or in continuous retorts, static or agitating. The heating medium may be saturated steam, steam air mixtures, or water with air pressure cooling. Retorts especially designed or modified for use with the retort pouch are available in the U.S., Europe and Japan. Some of the better known systems for continuous sterilization of retort pouches are the Stock "Rotomat," ALLPAX, and the FMC "ABR System with FMC/SUDRY Retort." This equipment is described in the chapter on "Sterilization Systems" in Book I.

Dr. I. J. Pflug of the University of Minnesota, established overall heat transfer coefficients of various heating media. He found that saturated steam has the highest coefficient, hot water rates next, and steam/air mixtures had the lowest heat transfer coefficients. The coefficient drops significantly as the percentage of air in the mixture goes up. With 100% hot air, the coefficient drops to 3.

Hot water with overriding air pressure was selected as the processing medium because it has a higher heat transfer coefficient, and because it is easier to control than a steam/air mixture.

TABLE 5.1 – Overall Heat Transfer Coefficient (u) of Various Heating Media*

	Btu/(hr.°F ft.^{2}) of heating surface	W/(K m^2)
Steam	170	965
Water	105	596
Steam/Air Mixture (75% Steam/25% Air)	87.5	497
Air (100%)	2.96	16.8

*Theoretical calculations based on work done by Dr. I. J. Pflug for U.S. Army Natick Development Center.

Uniform heat distribution within the sterilizer during processing is most important. It takes only 30 seconds to fill the car with hot water and in another four minutes, the coldest water in the retort car is up to retort temperature. This process can be started in about 4.5 minutes versus 12 to 14 minutes required by more conventional type static retorts. Within several minutes after the process has started, process temperature levels off to about 1°F (0.5°C) maximum spread from target temperature. At the end of the process, cold water is introduced and hot water is flushed back into a hot water storage tank; this requires approximately 1.5 minutes compared to 8 to 10 minutes for a conventional retort.

Heat-sealed containers, such as pouches and semi-rigid trays, can be agitated during processing as long as adequate precautions are taken to confine the pouch or tray to prevent leakers due to seal integrity failure, puncture or flexing. Similar to can processing, times can be further reduced using agitation, especially in trays and institutional size pouches. Seal strength decreases dramatically as retort temperature is increased. At 75°F (24°C), burst pressure in a pouch may be greater than 30 psi (207 kPa), but at 250°F (121°C), the pressure drops to about 7 psi (48 kPa). It should be noted that after a pouch has been cooled back to room temperature, the seal regains 90 percent of its original strength.

Hydrostatic systems can also be used for the commercial sterilization of retort pouches or semi-rigid containers. (See chapter on "Sterilization Systems.") The hydrostatic sterilizer has an automated high-speed handling system for pouches and only one operator is needed for the unit, thus minimizing labor costs. In addition, this sterilizer offers economical use of utilities. The manufacturer, Stork Food Machinery, reports that steam, water and air consumption can be reduced by 70% compared with batch systems. In addition, the vertical construction of the hydrostatic sterilizer takes very little floor space.

The hydrostatic sterilizer for flexible containers is similar in operating principle to units used for glass containers and cans. That is, the pressure of saturated steam in the sterilizing section is in equilibrium with two water columns; the temperature in the sterilization section depends on the height adjustment of the water columns. The unit is equipped with two endless chains, between which are fitted holders for the pouches. An automatic infeed mechanism transfers pouches into the holders and the holders containing the pouches pass through the various sections of the hydrostatic unit: preheating, sterilization, and cooling. After completion of the process cycle, the pouches are removed from the holders by an automatic discharge system.

For rapid, even heat penetration and careful handling of the retortable flexible container, it is essential that the right type of transport holder be designed. The holder must permit uniform distribution of product in the container, uniform distribution of the heating media around the container, uniform support for the container and it should not scratch or damage the container in any way. Holders should be specifically adapted to the pouch or container dimensions at each individual installation.

The infeed of pouches into a hydrostatic sterilizer takes place automatically and the unit may be connected to as many as 16 pouch lines. Pouches are admitted in rows and each row is synchronized with the main conveyor. In other words, the rows are faced with the traveling speed of the holders. A safety system precludes improper loading. Once pouches have been loaded into the holders, they are automatically closed; each pouch is thereby locked in its own pocket.

The sterilizer is also equipped with an automatic discharge system; this system unloads the holders one by one via a slide plate that transfers the pouches to a discharge conveyor. As with the infeed system, careful pouch handling has been designed into the discharge system to prevent damage to pouch seams as well as to prevent scratches on the laminate material.

Heating Mediums for Sterilization

It has been clearly shown that heat sealed flexible containers respond to pressure-volume relationships according to theory. Since the most critical container differential pressure occurs at the start of the cooling cycle, superimposed air pressure adequately controls pouch expansion and prevents bursting. It is possible to calculate the required total process pressure and consequently the amount of override pressure beyond that of saturated steam. It is also possible to process pouches in saturated steam alone, bringing in an over pressure during cooling as long as there are good controls of container headspace and of pressure variations during processing.

Three heating mediums are advocated for processing flexible containers: (a) steam/air, (b) water with overriding air pressure, and (c) saturated steam.

Japanese and European systems tend to favor steam/air or saturated steam, although some water systems are in use in those markets too. The U.S. Food and Drug Administration approved the proposed systems when thermal processes were established to compensate for the slowest heat transfer container.

Water systems are already in wide use in the U.S. The system for retortable flexible containers is essentially the same as for glass containers. Familiarity with the system, plus accessibility, seem to be the key reasons for selecting water as the heating medium in this country.

Whatever the heating medium, both heat distribution and heat penetration profiles are critically important for each product line. For this reason, racking configuration is important in container processing and should be designed for the specific container and retort system. Horizontal racks are preferred to vertical, although both orientations have been successfully used. Even with screen-type trays, the container should not completely cover the tray; some middle area should be left empty to create a chimney effect for circulation purposes. Containers should be secured in position to prevent shifting and overlapping due to water flow pressure. However, if the tray duct around each container is too tight, the configuration will transmit pressure to the sealed area; it can also lead to underprocessing the product. Racks must keep containers from touching each other during processing. They should provide for adequate circulation of the heating medium. Perforated stainless steel or aluminum racks are commonly used.

Critical Factors in Thermal Processing of Flexible Containers

Title 21 of the Code of Federal Regulations, Parts 108, 113 and 114, outline how scheduled processes are to be established for low acid and acidified foods. The National Food Processors Association has published *Guidelines for Thermal Process Development for Foods Packaged in Flexible Containers*. This booklet provides information on conducting heat penetration and temperature distribution tests for products processed in flexible containers.

The U.S. Food and Drug Administration states: "Critical factors that may affect the schedule process, shall be specified in the scheduled process." Critical factor is defined as "Any property, characteristic, condition, aspect or other parameter, variation of which may affect the scheduled process and attainment of commercial sterility." The major critical factors that affect thermal processing of retort containers are the following: minimum headspace, product consistency, maximum filling or drained weight, initial temperature (IT), processing temperature (RT), processing time (t), temperature distribution, container orientation, residual gas in headspace and in food, processing and racking systems, processing medium (saturated steam, water with air pressure for cooling; steam/air,

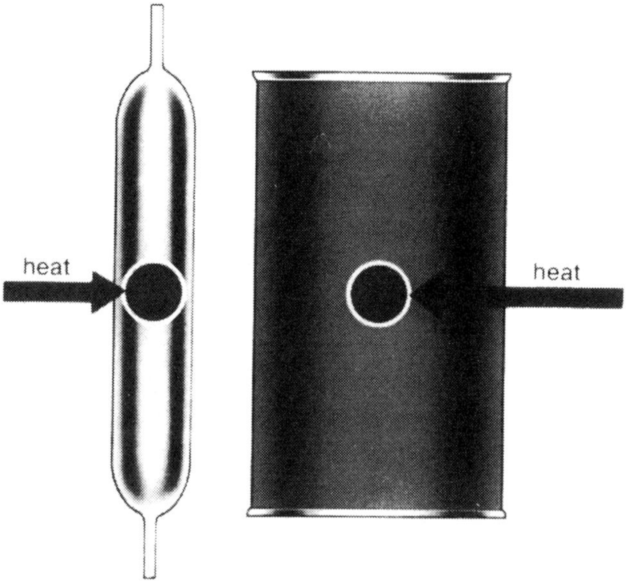

FIGURE 5.9 – Conduction Heating in the Retort Pouch and in a Cylindrical Can (Courtesy Reynolds Metals Co.)

overriding air pressure), product heating rates, materials from which pouch rack is constructed, divider sheet hole sizes and spacing, and possibly other factors.

Cylindrical containers have two characteristics that are significant in thermal processing: they have a relatively large cross-sectional diameter and a relatively small surface area when compared to their volume. Both characteristics are responsible for a relatively low rate of heat transfer to the critical point; this can cause over-processing for some of the product before an adequate process is obtained, even with agitating retorts.

Studies show that flexible films offer little resistance to heat conductivity into the packages and that variances among tested materials, 1.25-3 mils (0.032-0.076 mm) in thickness, were nil. Heating times are more nearly a function of the conductivity of the food and the shape of the container.

The pouch, because of its characteristic thinner profile, transfers heat faster to its critical point. In processing, this permits the required amount of heat for sterilization to reach the critical point with minimal overcooking of the product near the peripheral container areas. Therefore, for food products subject to quality loss from excessive heating during processing, the flexible container offers the attainment of higher quality together with better retention of heat sensitive nutrients.

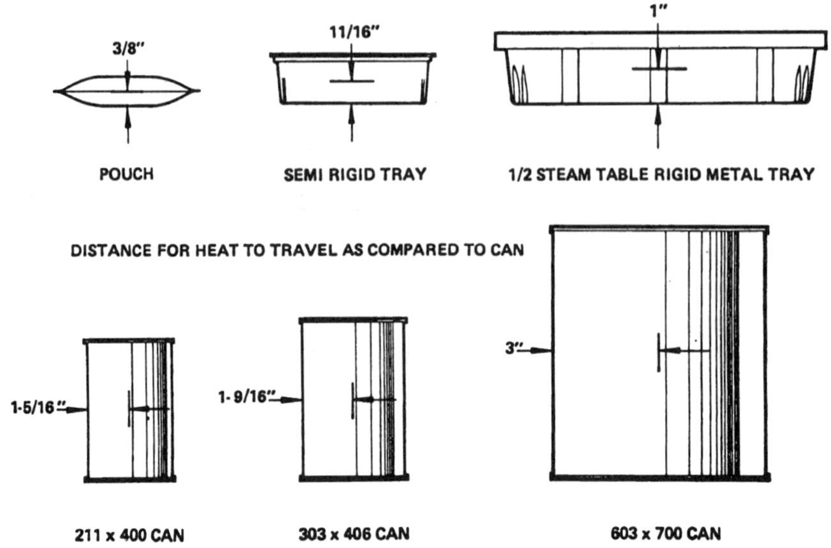

FIGURE 5.10 – Heating Characteristics of New Containers Compared to Standard Cylindrical Cans

Quality Control Tests For Pouch Laminate, Pouch and Semi-Rigid Container

Control of laminate quality begins with quality control of all of the component materials. Close control of each raw material must be insured by establishing specifications and by an effective monitoring program. The important properties of laminates and control tests to monitor conformity to specifications follow.

The basis weight of the laminate is determined by use of a laboratory balance. A sample cutter is used to cut the material into a side that allows for direct conversion of grams into pounds/ream when weighed.

The basis weight of the laminate is largely a dependent variable, but it is important to monitor it to insure adequate uniformity of product. The laminate gauge or thickness is measured by use of a standard paper and paperboard micrometer.

Laminate tensile strength is measured using an Instron or similar tensile tester. Bond levels of polyester film to foil and polypropylene film to foil are also measured by tensile tester. Flat sheet burst resistance is measured using a standard Mullen bursting strength tester for paper and paperboard. Sealability tests can be made using seals produced on a laboratory bench sealer such as a Sentinel sealer. Generally, hot bar seals are employed, but impulse seals may also be made and tested. After making the hot bar or impulse seal, its strength is measured on a tensile tester.

FIGURE 5.11 – Seal Strength of the Retort Pouch
(Courtesy former Continental Group, Inc.)

Another test for the quality of the laminate is the internal burst test. Here, a fixture is used to confine the pouch to a maximum thickness while pressurizing from within. For pouches whose maximum thickness is less than $^1/_2$ in. (13 mm), the confining space will be no greater than $^1/_2$ in. (13 mm). For all other pouches and semi-rigid containers, the confining space will be 10% greater than the thickness of the container (i.e., if the container is 2 in. (51 mm) thick, the plates will be 2.2 in. (55 mm) apart). Fixtures can be designed to test either 3-side sealed empty pouches or 4-side filled and sealed pouches. Internal pressure testing can be very informative, since the entire sealed area of a pouch is examined on a single test.

It is important that pouch material impart no objectionable odor to food packaged in it. Laminate odor is tested using the standard jar odor technique by conditioning a sample at 180°F (82°C) for 16 hours, allowing it to cool and then by smelling the headspace of the sample jar. An intermediate control of odor is established during manufacture by measuring the amount of retained solvent using gas chromatography. Confirming tests are conducted by using the jar odor technique.

In addition to the control tests just described, new structures are subjected to qualification tests. One of the most important is the compatibility test. Ultimate suitability of new laminate with a food product must be determined by testing with a specific product. Nonetheless, important information bearing on the likelihood of the ultimate acceptance can be obtained with accelerated storage testing at 120°F (49°C). Thirty days or longer storage data are obtained using a variety of foods and food-simulating substances. After the selected periods of storage, evaluations are made of the bond value of the interior film to foil.

Abuse testing begins with the slide drop test. Individual containers with or without board carton are subjected to two impacts of 40 in.-lb. (46 cm-kg), one for each container end. A 15 degree inclined slide drop tester is used. Candidate materials surviving this test are then subjected to a simulated shipping test; these tests consist of case vibration and case drop exposures, the total abuse intended to develop failures so that materials can be rated on a relative basis. Materials acceptable to this point then undergo actual shipping tests.

Whenever changes are involved which might affect heat sealability of the laminate, detailed studies are made for this property by using a gradient heat sealer. The bar temperature is recorded by several thermocouples secured into the sealed bar near each heater element in the bar. Sealability profiles are then established by testing seal strength across the width of the seal sample. Each sample represents a range of seal temperatures at a selected pressure and time condition.

Two methods may be used to measure the volume of air in a sealed container. A non-destructive method involves the principle of natural buoyancy where the volume of gas is found by entering certain measured values into an equation derived from Archimedes' principle, Boyle's law, and the combined gas law. Actual measurement of gas volume can be made by piercing a submerged pouch and capturing the escaping gas in an inverted graduated cylinder which is also submerged and filled with water prior to the test. A glass funnel is helpful in directing the escaping gas into the inverted cylinder.

The U.S. Army Natick Development Center supported a reliability program that documented a 0.017% failure rate in tests including six different food formulations. In Japan, a 0.2% defect rate was reported after filling, but when the tested containers were correctly sealed, the defect level dropped to 0.02% after retorting. Since the 3-piece can has been the standard in this country, a comparative test was performed by the Natick Development Center with the retort pouch and the tin plate can. Each container in a case lot was subjected, in sequence, to vibrations at 1 G for one hour, 10 drops from 18 in. (46 cm) and incubation for 20 days at 100°F (38°C), followed by standard bio-testing of both containers. Rail and truck transportation were used to check over the road failures. In Alaska, products were carried both by man and sled. The failure rate was found to be 0.011% which included manufacturing defects as well as transportation related failures. Results showed no significant difference between 3-piece tin plate cans and retort pouches.

The U.S. Department of Agriculture criteria for evaluating pouches are covered in the Food Safety Inspection Service publication MPI Bulletin 75-4. In that bulletin, USDA gives some very specific descriptions of critical defects outlined in Table 5.2.

TABLE 5.2 – Critical Defects in Pouches

Types of Critical Defects	Description
Improper Seal	a. Wrinkle over half of the width of seal. b. Fold over material on seal area.
Severely Deformed Distorted Container	Due to mechanical malfunction.
Leakers	Broken or loose seal, or container damage.
Disintegrated Container after retort	Evidence of delamination or degradation.
Overstuffed area, or detrimental to package.	Overfilled, thus contaminating the seal. performance.
Blown or Hard Swell (not caused by underprocessing)	Greatly distended or ruptured due to internal gas formation.
Major Defects	
Punctures or Cuts	Due to mechanical action.
Dirty	Smeared with product trapped in top edges.
Others	Must be specified; missing label, etc.

Advantages and Disadvantages of Retortable Flexible Containers

Retort pouches combine the advantages of the metal can with the frozen boil-in-the-bag. The attributes of flexible containers offer benefits for the consumer, retailers, and manufacturer alike:

(A) The thin profile of the pouch or container provides rapid heat transfer for both preparation and for sterilization during processing. A 30–40% reduction in processing time is possible, with energy savings.

(B) Reduced heat exposure results in improvements in taste, color and flavor; there are also less nutrient losses.

(C) Preparation of products which need to be heated to serving temperature can be accomplished in 3–5 minutes by immersing the pouch in boiling water, or placing the plastic container in a microwave oven; there are no pans to clean up in the kitchen.

(D) Food can be consumed directly from semi-rigid container.

(E) Storage space of the retort pouch or container in a paperboard carton is no larger than that for cans; disposal space is less.

(F) Shelf life of retort pouch products is at least equal to that of foods in metal cans; refrigeration or freezing is not required by packers, retailers, or consumers. Shelf life of products in higher barrier plastic containers is one year.

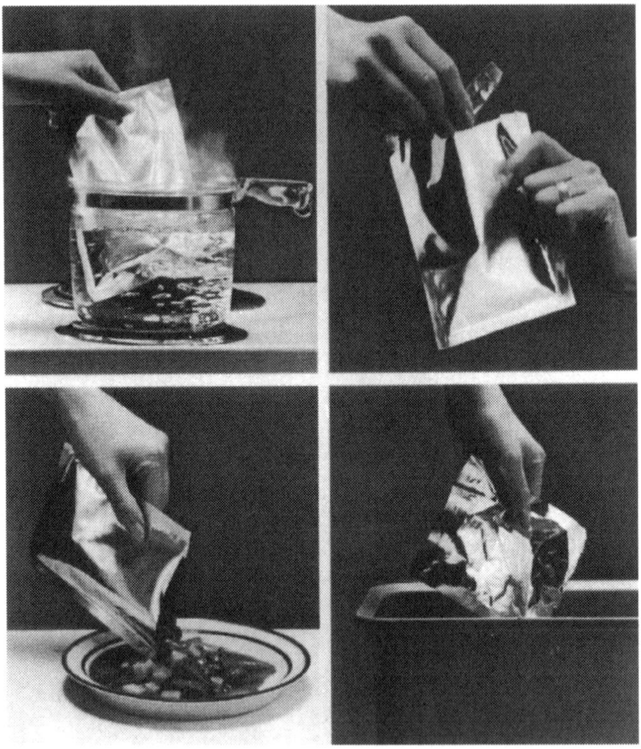

FIGURE 5.12 – Retort Pouch: Heating, Opening, Serving and Disposing (Courtesy Reynolds Metals Co.)

(G) Pouches and containers do not corrode externally and there is a minimum of product-container interaction.
(H) Opening the pouch requires only tearing the pouch across the top at the notch in the side seam, or by using scissors. The container lid may be peeled open or cut with a knife.
(I) The flexible container is safer in that a consumer would not be cut as on a metal can or be faced with broken glass as with glass jars.
(J) The flexible container lends itself to portion control and thus has a marketing advantage for single people and the elderly.
(K) Package size flexibility is another advantage. It is difficult for a canner to switch from a 6-oz. to an 8- or 9-oz. (170–227 or 255 g) rigid package; with the pouch system, size changes are comparatively easy. Many products such as sliced meats, meat loaf, etc., fit the pouch more logically than a can.

(L) Empty retort pouches and nesting containers offer processors a reduction in storage space and lighter weight. Compared with empty cans, an equal number of retort pouches use 85% less space; one thousand 4.5 x 7 in. (11.4 x 17.8 cm) pouches weigh 9.4 lbs. (4.09 kg) compared with one thousand 211 x 304 (68.3 x 82.6 mm) metal cans weighing 112.5 lbs. (51.14 kg); a 45 ft. (13.7 m) trailer holds less than 200,000 light-ounce (227 g) empty metal cans, whereas on the same trailer over 2.3 million empty pre-formed pouches can be shipped.

(M) Dented cans, according to the U.S. Department of Agriculture market service reports, are the single largest spoilage factor in supermarkets today, representing 49% of the total. Adoption of flexible containers could potentially eliminate or at least greatly reduce this problem for both the retailer and the manufacturer.

(N) Advantages for the retailer include savings in shelf space. For example, a carton carrying two 8-oz. (227 g) pouches provides a 10% savings in shelf space when compared to two 8-oz. metal cans. Also, the carton shape makes it easier for the retailer to handle and display the product.

(O) The use of a flat carton as an overwrap to hold one or two pouches provides for better product identification on the shelf than do cans. The pouch also offers the opportunity to market multipacks, e.g., entree in one pouch and accompaniment such as rice in another.

(P) Individual container cost to the canner likely will be less than the conventional rigid type containers presently in use. However, with the protective overwrap costs could be about the same as that of metal cans.

(Q) Energy requirements for container construction are less than that for cans.

The disadvantages of flexible containers follows:

(1) Major capital investment would have to be made in new filling and closing equipment for the particular container and modifications made in some thermal processing systems.

(2) Filling is slower and more complex. Retort pouch filling lines currently run from 30 to 60 pouches a minute, compared with some 400 per minute for canned and frozen foods and up to 1,200 per minute for glass containers. Semi-rigid container lines may run at 120 per minute.

(3) Thermal processing of flexible containers is more complex and processes have to be established for each product in the particular type and size of container.

(4) There are limitations in the size of containers which can be reasonably handled and processed.

(5) Retort pouches at present require overwrapping such as a carton and may be required for semi-rigid containers.
(6) Since the pouch is a flexible container, the detection of leakage is more difficult than with a conventional type container.
(7) Pouches and semi-rigid containers may be punctured.
(8) Marketing studies indicate very positive acceptance of foods packed in retort pouches. Nevertheless, considerable advertising expenditures may be needed to educate the retail consumer, although the institutional market may allow easier entry into the marketplace.

ACKNOWLEDGEMENTS

Sincere appreciation is expressed for the valuable contributions of materials on "Retortable Flexible Containers" by the following organizations:

American National Can Company, Chicago, IL.
FMC Corporation–Food Processing Machinery Division, Madera, CA.
National Food Processors Association, Washington, D.C.
Reynolds Metals Company–Flexible Packaging Division, Richmond, VA.
Klochner Bartelt, Inc., Sarasota, FL.
Stork Food Machinery, Inc., Somerville, NJ.
U. S. Army Natick Development Center, Natick, MA.

Special recognition is given to James H. Guida, Flexible Packaging Division, Reynolds Metals Company, Richmond, VA, for his contributions to the updating of the chapter "Retortable Flexible Containers."

CHAPTER 6

Packages for Aseptic Packaging

A package suitable for aseptic packaging must be able to be sterilized, must be capable of aseptic filling and of application and maintenance of a hermetic seal, and must maintain commercial sterility of product under severe handling conditions.

The functions that packages for aseptically processed foods must fulfill are similar to those of packages used for other commercially sterile products that require a potentially long shelf-life, in the range of one to two years or longer. To fulfill the first function of a package, i.e., containing the product, the package must be able to withstand a large compression force when packaging process factors and factors related to warehousing are considered. Ideally this function must be fulfilled by the primary package (shipping case) in order to reduce the cost of the secondary package (aseptic package).

To protect the food product, the package also must be opaque and have low water vapor, odor and oxygen transmission characteristics. Finally, package shape and decorations must be such that the container will be appealing to consumers.

Classification of Aseptic Packages

Packages used for aseptic packaging may be classified into three types: rigid, semi-rigid, and flexible. The following definitions have been proposed by the Canadian Health Protection Department, Ottawa, Canada:

> Rigid means that the shape or contours of a filled and sealed container are neither affected by the enclosed product nor deformed by an external mechanical pressure of up to 70 kPa.
>
> Semi-rigid means that the shape of contours of a filled, sealed container are not affected by the enclosed product under normal atmospheric temperature and pressure, but can be deformed by an external pressure of less than 70 kPa (10.2 psi).
>
> Flexible means that the shape and contours of a filled, sealed container are affected by the enclosed product.

Rigid containers include metal cans, glass containers and rigid cups. Among them are the cans used in the Dole Canning System, the metal drums used by the Fran-Rica Aseptic drum filling systems, the glass containers used by the Dole and other systems for aseptic packaging of fruit juices in consumer sizes, and pre-fabricated and form-fill-seal cups.

Among the semi-rigid containers are those made of laminations of paper/plastic film/aluminum foil mainly used by the Tetra Pak, Ex-Cell-O and Pure Pak processes, the thermally formed packages used in the International Paper Company system and in the Conoffast system of Continental Can Company, and aseptic plastic bottles.

The flexible packages are bags or pouches with or without exterior support. Among these are the aseptic pouches in consumer sizes, the Scholle bag-in-box system and the Fran-Rica bag in metal drum or wood bin.

Basic Characteristics of Packaging Materials for Aseptic Packaging

Materials used in the package for aseptically packaged foods must be such that the package fulfill the functions necessary for effective aseptic packaging and required product shelf-life.

The degree of permeability of packaging materials to gases, such as oxygen, and to light is important because of the detrimental effects that oxygen and light have upon product flavor, color, nutritive value and shelf-life. Further, the packaging materials must be an effective barrier against penetration by volatile substances and water vapor which would also affect product quality and shelf-life. These materials must also be chemically inert to avoid food contamination with chemical constituents of the package. The package to be formed with the packaging materials must be hermetically sealable to prevent product adulteration by external factors, to prevent product recontamination with microorganisms, and to prevent entry of liquids and of any other foreign substances that would cause adulteration and, potentially, spoilage.

Another critical characteristic that packaging materials must have is that of being sterilizable. Thermal sterilization is the most common method. Several other sterilization procedures use a combination of heat and hydrogen peroxide or UV-irradiation and hydrogen peroxide. Another method for sterilizing packaging materials is irradiation with gamma rays or with accelerated electron beams. These latter technologies are mainly applied to laminate bags for the so-called "bag-in-box" or "bag-in-bin" systems, and for the Scholle process. The sterilization method must not affect permeability characteristics, chemical inertness, hermetic sealability, or lack of toxicity of packaging materials.

Packaging materials must also be durable, i.e., they must be able to withstand the physical and chemical stresses that they will be subject to during package forming, filling and sealing, and during package and product warehousing and distribution.

INTRINSIC PROPERTIES OF PACKAGING MATERIALS
AND PACKAGES FOR ASEPTIC PROCESSING

1. Very low permeability to water, gases (O_2) volatile compounds, and light.
2. Inertness of packaging material.
3. Sealability of packaging material.
4. Package must be sterilizable.
5. Package must be durable.
6. Package must be an effective barrier against microbial contamination.
7. Package must be appealing to consumer.

Materials Used in the Manufacture of Packages for Aseptic Packaging

The basic materials are plastics and plastic films, paper, metal foils and sheets, and less commonly, glass. Plastic films are generally used in laminations of two or more films with aluminum foil or paper. Metal containers have been used from the beginning of the commercial development of aseptic sterilization, specifically by the Dole Aseptic Canning Process. Metal containers are very well suited because they are easily sterilizable, because they are very effective barriers against liquids, gases, and microorganisms, and because of their physical characteristics and efficient and effective hermetic sealing. The most important disadvantages are their relatively high cost and the limitations with relation to the package geometry. Glass characteristics as a material for containers for aseptically packaged foods are very similar to those of metals, with the additional disadvantages of fragility and density of glass.

Presently there does not exist any plastic material that by itself alone has all the characteristics that are desirable or necessary for packages for aseptically processed foods. Therefore laminations or extrusions of two or more plastic materials having complementary characteristics are used. The large variety of plastic materials and combinations thereof offer many options to design packages for aseptic packaging that have different needed characteristics and cost. Aluminum foil is used in laminations with plastic films to improve the barrier characteristics of the package and with paper to improve the barrier characteristics and physical resistance of the package.

The first material used in the manufacture of semi-rigid containers for aseptic packaging was a thin paper board laminated to aluminum foil. Packaging materials technology has made considerable progress. An example of a packaging material presently used in Tetra Pak and in Pure-Pak packages is made up as follows:

Outside – Polyethylene
Printing ink / Paper / Polyethylene /
Aluminum foil / Surlyn
Inside – Polyethylene

Obviously this is a complex packaging material. It has to a high degree the characteristics that are desirable for aseptic packaging.

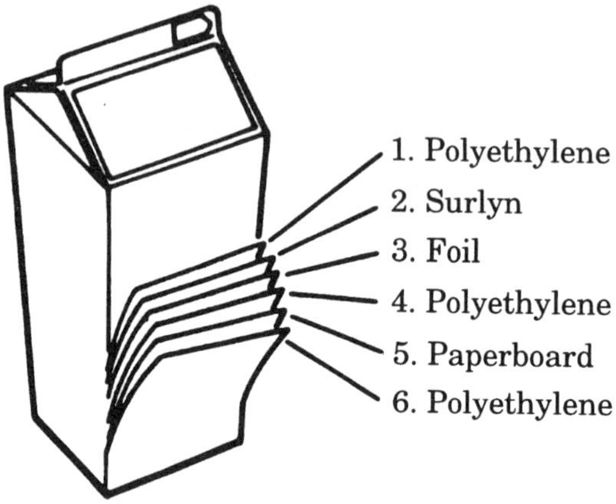

FIGURE 6.1 – 6-ply Construction of Shelf-stable Pure-Pak Package

Another example of progress in the technology of packaging materials is that made by Cobelplast with a material made up of Saran as a water vapor barrier, and by ethyl vinyl alcohol (EVOH) in combination with up to eight laminations with polyethylene, polystyrene, and polypropylene. This material may also be used for thermally sterilizable (retortable) flexible packages at temperatures of up to 250°F (121°C) and somewhat higher. It is the same material used by the Conoffast system of Continental Can Company. This material is characterized as the only one available today that does not require chemical sterilization, such as with hydrogen peroxide.

Still another example of laminated structures is the use of metallized polyester in the manufacture of bags for lining metal drums and bins for aseptic packaging of tomatoes and fruits for reprocessing. Metallized polyester improves physical resistance and barrier characteristics. An inside lining of vinyl ethyl acetate is used because of its heat sealing characteristics. Nylon, because of its physical resistance, is used in the exterior of another laminated structure, with aluminum foil in the middle for its barrier characteristics, and polyethylene on the interior because of its heat sealing characteristics and its chemical inertness as a food contact surface.

Co-extruded, high-barrier materials can be designed to combine economy and thermoformability with special packaging requirements from a wide variety of oxygen and moisture barriers, light and ultraviolet light inhibitors, resistance to high and low temperatures, sealing and contact surfaces and colors, and anti-static coatings, including sheets with PVdC or EVOH barrier materials.

STERILIZATION OF PACKAGING MATERIALS AND PACKAGES

The most common sterilization methods are based on the use of (a) superheated system, (b) hot, dry air, (c) combination of hydrogen peroxide and ultraviolet light, (d) combination of hydrogen peroxide and heat, (e) heat of the co-extrusion process, and (f) irradiation by gamma rays.

Superheated steam is used for the sterilization of metal containers because it makes it possible to use high temperatures at atmospheric pressure. However, bacteria are more heat resistant under the conditions characteristic of superheated steam than under those of saturated steam. Hot, dry air has advantages and disadvantages that are similar to those of superheated steam.

Hydrogen peroxide in relatively low concentration is a good bactericidal agent. Its activity is enhanced when combined with high temperatures as well as in combination with ultraviolet light. The mechanism of action of hydrogen peroxide is still not fully understood but is attributed to the formation of a nascent oxygen atoms by the effect of heat and to the formation of hydroxyl radicals by ultraviolet irradiation. No harmful residues are left.

In the U.S., hydrogen peroxide is used in concentrations that are limited by FDA regulations to 35% by weight. The amount of residual hydrogen peroxide that may be left in treated food product is limited by law to 0.1 ppm. Hydrogen peroxide is applied to the packaging material either before or after the package is formed. The application may be made either by spray systems or immersion of material in H_2O_2.

The system that uses heat of co-extrusion process is based on the fact that the high temperatures reached by thermoplastic resins during co-extrusion produce sterile packaging materials. During package forming in the aseptic packaging line, a superficial film is delaminated under aseptic conditions from the thermoplastic multi-laminated material. This operation exposes the sterile container surface that will contact the food product. The material is then thermoformed into bowl-shaped containers. The material to form the lids is also a thermoplastic laminated film from which a superficial film is aseptically delaminated and then the exposed sterile surface is sealed over the bowls after these are aseptically filled with the food.

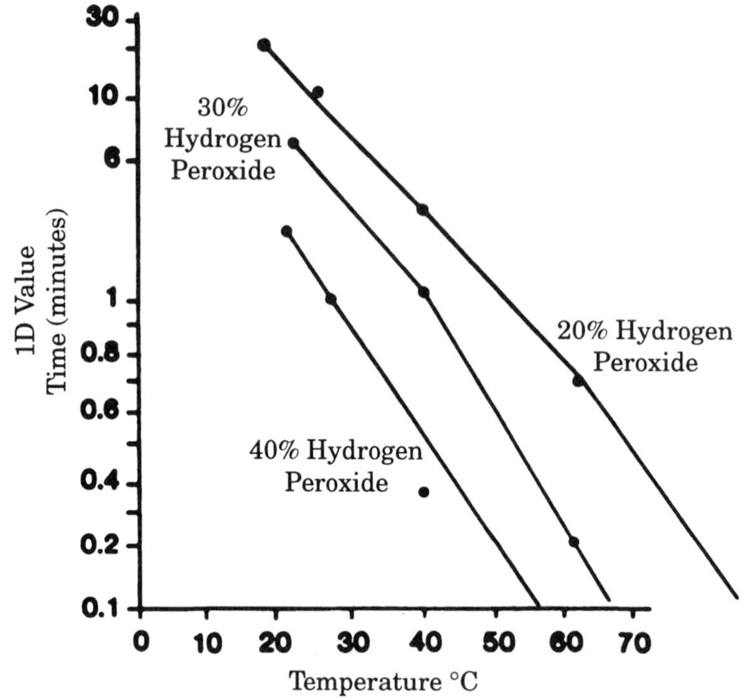

FIGURE 6.2 – Sterilization as a Function of Hydrogen Peroxide Concentration, Time and Temperature
(Courtesy Dr. Cerny, University of Munich, Germany)

The use of gamma rays is a very effective sterilization method, but the relatively long exposure times required limits its applicability. At present, this method is being commercially used to pre-sterilize a nylon/aluminum foil/polyethylene laminate as well as other materials used to make up the structure for containers of the "bag-in-a-box" type.

ASEPTIC PACKAGING SYSTEMS

The principal aseptic packaging systems used in the U.S. are Achilles, Asepak, Bosch Hypa, Tetra Pak, Cherry-Burrell, Combibloc, Dogatherm, Dole (canning), Gasti, FranRica, Fresh Seal, International Paper, LiquiPak, Metal Box, Scholle, Servac-78, and Enerfab (metal tanks for aseptic storage in bulk).

Companies such as Combibloc, Dole, International Paper and LiquiPak offer aseptic packaging equipment for paper composite flexible packages. Others like Bosch and Metal Box have aseptic systems for plastic composite containers. Dole also offers a system that uses metal cans.

Considering all the above mentioned systems, it is possible to aseptically package foods in containers of a capacity ranging from approximately 200 ml to several gallons, 55-gal. (208 l) drums and metal tanks of up to several thousand gallons, the latter intended for foods for reprocessing.

A summarized description of some of the aseptic packaging systems mentioned above, beginning with those designed to package in small, consumer-size containers, and then those systems that use containers of large capacity to preserve foods to be commercially reprocessed follows.

The Tetra Pak System

The Tetra Pak equipment, developed and manufactured by the Swedish firm of the same name, aseptically forms, fills and seals packages. Consumer size packages of fluid foods are aseptically formed, filled and sealed in the model AB-9 and other Tetra-Pak units. The packaging material is received in 100-lb. (45.4 kg) rolls, enough to produce approximately 4,500 250-ml Brik-Pak packages, which is the hourly production rate of the machine. The packaging material is a 6-layer lamination of polyethylene/printing ink/polyethylene/aluminum foil/Surlyn/polyethylene. The packaging material ascends up the back of the unit while a thin strip of a plastic material is applied first on one edge and then on the other edge of the material that later forms the longitudinal package seal. Prior to the formation of that seal the packaging material is immersed in a 30% hydrogen peroxide bath and is then run between rolls which dry the packaging material surface and eliminate the excess H_2O_2. In the upper section of the unit, which is 18 ft. (5.5 m) high, the material passes over a roll to begin its descent to the machine areas where package forming, filling and sealing take place in the front section of the unit. The first package forming step consists of running the packaging material over horizontal rolls which begin to fold the material and give it the shape of a tube. After leaving this area, the material is already folded as a cylinder around a stainless steel product filling tube which extends down through the center of the packaging material cylinder. The cylinder of packaging material continues descending through the pre-heating section and then through a ring which joins and seals the longitudinal edges of the material. After leaving the package forming ring, the tube shaped material passes around an electric heating element which sterilizes the material by radiant heat, raising the web temperature to 230°F (110°C). It must be noted that both the H_2O_2 bath and the radiant heat contribute to sterilizing the packaging material.

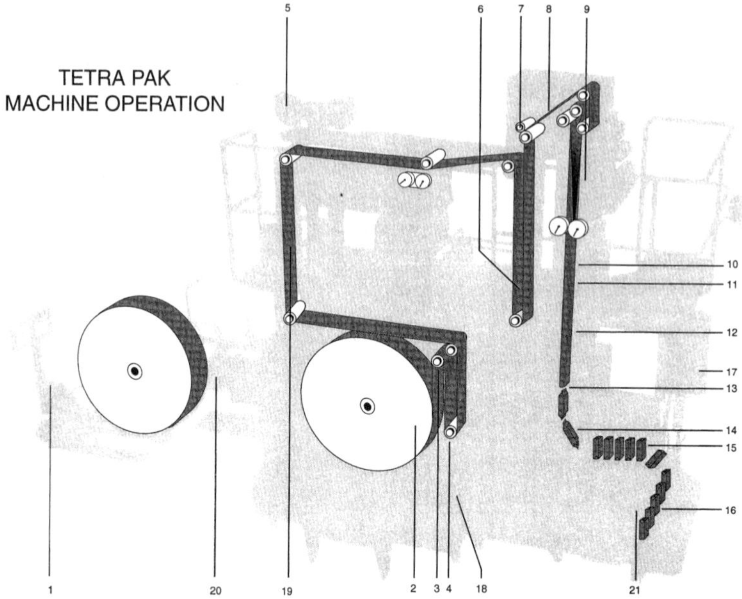

FIGURE 6.3 –Tetra Pak Machine Operation
(Courtesy Tetra Pak, Inc.)

1. Special trolley with hydraulic lift for handling packaging material.
2. Packaging material.
3. Motor-driven roller for smooth, even feed of the packaging material.
4. Idler. Its action starts and stops the motor-driven roller.
5. Strip applicator which applies a plastic strip to one edge of the packaging material. Later, at the longitudinal sealing stage, this is welded to the opposite edge. The result is a tight and durable seal.
6. Deep bath of heated hydrogen peroxide.
7. Rollers which remove the hydrogen peroxide from the packaging material.
8. Nozzle through which hot, sterile air is blown to dry the packaging material.
9. Product filling pipe.
10. Element for the longitudinal seam which welds together the two edges of the packaging material.
11. "Short-stop element" which completes the longitudinal seam when the machine restarts after any brief halt in production.
12. Photocells which control the machine's automatic design correction system.
13. Transverse sealing is performed by two pairs of sealing jaws, operating continuously.
14. When the filled packages have been cut from the paper tube they fall down into the final folder.
15. In the final folding unit the top and bottom flaps are folded over and sealed onto the package.
16. The finished product is conveyed out of the machine.

17. Pivoting control panel.
18. Easy-access compartment for topping up the oil in the central lubrication and hydraulic systems and the detergent for the automatic cleaning system.
19. Date-stamping unit.
20. Splicing table for packaging material.
21. Bath which fills with water and detergent automatically for external cleaning of the machine.

FIGURE 6.4 – The Tetra Brik Model AB-9 Machine
This macine is designed for aseptic packaging of liquid food products. Any solids in the liquid interfere with the sealing operation. The AB-9 model fills 100 ml, 125 ml and 250 ml brick-type packages at speeds up to 5,000 packages/hour. The entire pre-sterilization, production operations and cleaning-in-place sequence can be programed into the programable logic controller and initiated at the push of a button. (Courtesy Tetra Pak, Inc.)

The fluid food is brought by a filling tube to the longitudinally sealed and sterilized, cylindrically shaped packaging material. Fluid food level is automatically regulated by a floating valve which keeps fluid level higher than the outlet of the filling tube. The packages are heat sealed below the liquid level within the packaging material cylinder. This procedure totally eliminates a headspace in the Brik-Pak container. Equipment operates at 60–75 packages/min. depending on size which ranges from 200 to 1,000 ml and is non-adjustable. Use of system is limited to liquids.

FIGURE 6.5 – Tetra Brik Packages

The Combibloc System

In the Combibloc System laminations of paperboard and extruded polyethylene are produced printed, dye cut and flame sealed to produce carton sleeves. On the packaging machinery, the carton sleeves are formed into open containers, chemo-thermally sterilized and, under aseptic conditions, filled with sterile product, top sealed, and ejected ready for packing and shipping.

The Combibloc Process

The Combibloc System uses pre-formed cartons sleeves made from gravure-printed paperboard/aluminum foil and multiple extrusions of polyethylene and adhesive polymer. Unlike other roll-fed systems, the pre-formed carton sleeves are fed into the Combibloc filling equipment in a flat state.

The cartons are removed by vacuum from the carton magazines one by one, opened into a rectangular shape and pushed downwards onto a mandrel wheel which carries the cartons through the bottom sealing process.

The bottom formed cartons are transferred from the mandrel wheel into the cellular transport chain. The carton is then pre-folded at the top creases before entering the aseptic zone, enabling the equipment to carry out final folding more precisely. In the enclosed aseptic zone, the carton is sterilized, filled and sealed. Cold sterile air is used to maintain a slight overpressure in the aseptic zone, preventing the penetration of non-sterile air from the outside. The sterile air is supplied from a separate high efficiency particulate air (HEPA) filtration unit.

Within the aseptic zone, each carton is first preheated and then passed under a binary nozzle which introduces hot hydrogen peroxide to the entire inside of the carton. The amount of hydrogen peroxide sprayed into each carton is computer controlled and visually displayed in digital form to ensure accuracy.

The carton is then passed through a drying zone, where the sterilization of the internal surface is achieved by evaporating the hydrogen peroxide by means of sterile hot air at 392°F (200°C) blown into the carton over several consecutive drying stations.

Individually controlled electric heaters provide the sterile hot air emanating from the sterile cold air filtration unit. The vapor formed during the sterilization process is discharged through an exhaust ventilator.

At this stage, the sterilized cartons are filled with pre-sterilized products, such as milk, milk drinks, cream, fruit juices, wine, soups, etc.

Sterile cold air is fed into the sealed pre-run tank from the aseptic zone to prevent the formation of a vacuum. Precise quantity metering by fine adjustment of the volume can be done during operation. Should a product develop foam, a defoaming unit assures that the sealing zones of the package are clean and product-free.

The headspace in the package is then injected with steam and the top fin seal effected by the use of the ultra-sonic energy. The resulting vacuum enhances the shape and stability of the package as it cools. After the cartons leave the aseptic zone and the top fin is folded flat, the ears of the fin are hot-air-activated and folded flat against the sides of the carton.

The finished cartons are then ejected from the cellular transport chain onto a rotary cross unit and discharged onto a single lane exit conveyor.

The finished product receives a date code on the top fin utilizing ink jet technology.

The International Paper System

The International Paper System uses roll-stock material to produce rectangular-shaped packages. The roll-stock material is first passed through a solution of hydrogen peroxide then travels over a stainless steel drum which is heated to 194°F (90°C). After the packaging material is sterilized, it is formed into a core around sterile air and a side seam is made via induction sealing. The filling section consists of two stainless steel pipes, one for sterile air, the other for product. After product is introduced into the core of packaging material, the web is cut and sealed below the product line to eliminate headspace in the package.

The final package has a fin seal around three sides of it to provide good structural integrity. There is no gusset on top of the package, so the top is free to contain graphics and promotional material.

The Gasti System–American Can Company

The Gasti System operates with pre-formed cups which can be plastic or aluminum. In operation, the Gasti system dispenses pre-formed cups from a magazine and sterilizes them with hydrogen peroxide vapor after which the cups pass under sterile hot air dryers which convert the residual hydrogen peroxide into water vapor and oxygen. The machines can also be supplied with ultraviolet irradiators for package sterilization.

Product is filled into the sterile cups under aseptic conditions in a pressurized sterile air chamber. Then the cups are sealed with lids pre-sterilized with hydrogen peroxide. Packaging speeds range from 5,000-12,000 cups per hour.

The Liqui-Pak System

This is an aseptic system that uses standard Pure-Pak cartons and a combination of sterilizing agents to obtain aseptic packages. The agents used are hydrogen peroxide and ultraviolet light. These agents have a synergistic effect which results in a bactericidal action many times more effective than high concentrations of hydrogen peroxide or ultraviolet light alone.

The Liqui-Pak System uses plastic bellows instead of pistons to dispense product into cartons. In addition, a stainless steel flexible diaphragm rises and falls with the liquid level in the filler bowl to eliminate headspace.

The Metal Box "FreshFill" System

The Metal Box "FreshFill" system is characterized by the use of pre-formed, rigid plastic, bowl-shaped containers. The bowl-shaped containers are fed to the equipment to be first sterilized with a 30-35% hydrogen peroxide fog, followed by heating with hot air; the material used to make the lids is sterilized in the same manner. All the filling and closing operations take place in a chamber under sterile conditions and positive pressure of hot, sterile air. A hot, sterile gas such as steam, nitrogen or carbon dioxide is used to exhaust air from the container headspace. The sterile lids are applied under sterile conditions on the bowls, heat sealed and then cut to separate one container from another.

The Dole Corporation Hot Air Aseptic Packaging System for Fruit Juices

This system by the Dole Division of Graham Engineering Corporation is characterized by low operation and package costs when using composite laminated aluminum foil/paperboard cylindrical containers instead of metal cans. The system is specially suited for 46-oz. containers.

Basically, four separate components make up the aseptic system: the container sterilizing unit, the filling section, the cover sterilizing unit, and the container closing section. A general idea of the setup is shown in the diagram below. Not shown is the plate-type or tubular heat exchanger for sterilizing the product.

Linking and coordinating the functions of the various aseptic units is an integrated network of instrumentation, controls and alarms which permit the process to perform properly at high speed. It is imperative from a microbiological standpoint that accurate temperature be maintained at critical points in the process. Thermocouples in these critical areas transmit continuous temperature readings which are detailed on a strip chart recorder to become a permanent record of the operation.

Visual temperature devices are also included as a support system. Should the temperature in any part of the system fall below a pre-determined critical level, both visual and audible alarms are activated.

The Container Sterilizing Unit

The Container Sterilizing Unit is an enclosed hot-air chamber. It contains a spiral conveyor that moves the cans through the unit while hot air is directed around and into the containers. In approximately 45 seconds of passage the temperature of the containers reaches 240°F (116°C), which is the temperature required to be reached for the destruction of bacteria when acid foods, such as fruit juices, are used.

These container temperatures are a departure from the conventional aseptic can sterilizer used with metal cans for low-acid foods where super-heated steam at temperatures around 550°F (288°C) are used to sterilize the cans; the temperature of the cans themselves reaches 420°F (216°C).

The Filling Section

The hot, sterile containers move into the filling section where pre-sterilized product is introduced into the containers by one of several specially-designed filling mechanisms. Filling speed for the 46-oz. cans of juice is around 300 cans/min. For smaller size cans, speeds of 500 cans/min. are feasible.

The Cover Sterilizing Unit

The third basic component of the aseptic canning system, the cover sterilizing unit, is arranged as part of the closing machine. Covers are fed in stacks into the unit through one of several mechanical devices, and are completely enveloped in hot air for approximately 75 to 90 seconds until they are sterile. They are then conveyed into the closing machine.

The Container Closing Section

The fourth and last component of the system, the closing machine, is usually a standard machine modified to operate in an aseptic canning system. To accommodate the sterile containers filled with cold sterile product and the seaming of the pre-sterilized containers, the closing machine is completely shrouded. This shrouding permits initial sterilizing of the equipment and maintains a completely sterile atmosphere in the area where the sterile container, cover and product are exposed.

The aseptic system for composite cans is very similar to that for metal cans. The big difference is that composite cans are used only for high-acid foods and hot-air can be used as the sterilizing agent. With low-acid foods in metal containers, superheated steam is used.

STERILIZATION OF EQUIPMENT FOR ASEPTIC PACKAGING

It is essential to sterilize and maintain the sterility of equipment for aseptic packaging, including the areas where containers are formed, filled and sealed. Likewise, all the lines that transport and provide sterile air, as well as lines which transport already sterilized product to the filling area, must be sterilized and maintained sterile. This includes surge tanks, valves and pumps. The sterilization procedure must be designed so that it will produce a condition of commercial sterility in the equipment. Equipment sterilization is done by circulating steam or hot water at a temperature and for a time sufficient to create a condition of commercial sterility in the equipment. The lines that transport sterile air and the pipes that receive the product in the filling area are sterilized using hot air.

Testing and Start-Up of an Aseptic Processing and Packaging Facility

Safety concerns should be considered even before a machine is purchased; a pre-purchase review of processing as well as filling and packaging equipment is recommended. Applicable government regulations should be considered at this time to ensure compliance. The ability to maintain a sterile environment is mandatory for aseptic operations and must be ensured before operations are set up.

After installation is complete, a series of tests should be conducted to assure that processing, filling and packaging equipment are functioning properly before beginning commercial operation. Critical control factors must be identified which can be used as a basis for conducting biological sterility testing and establishing operational guidelines for production equipment.

After the sterilization processes for product and equipment have been established, inoculated packs of product should be conducted for confirmation of proper system operation. A procedure for testing a new aseptic facility consists of four short commercial production runs, approximately one-half hour each preceded by a sterilization cycle and followed by a clean-in-place cycle. The intent of this procedure is to simulate four separate days of production.

Plant start-up is conducted once the processing plant and the product piping to and from the fillers are completely and thoroughly cleaned. If an aseptic tank is to be used, that too must be cleaned.

Personnel selection and training are especially important. The aseptic packaging equipment is more complex than most other food processing equipment. Thus, the technical training of production supervisors, machine operators, mechanics, and quality control technicians requires a formal planned program.

ASEPTIC PACKAGING LOW-ACID FOODS WITH PARTICULATES

A proposed aseptic system for low-acid foods containing particulates may consist basically of the following components:

1. A twin-piston positive displacement pump.
2. A product heater (scraped-surface heat exchanger).
3. A holding tube.
4. A product cooler (scraped-surface heat exchanger).
5. A control panel.
6. A surge tank or pump for back pressure.

Product could be packaged by a bag-in-box filler.

It is recommended that food processors interested in aseptically packaging low-acid foods with particulates contact the National Food Processors Association. Because NFPA has vast experience and expertise in low-acid canned foods, in inoculated pack studies, and in food sterilization in general, that organization can assist in establishing the process, evaluating process deviations, and preparing the appropriate forms for filing with regulatory agencies. The

NFPA address is:

National Food Processors Association
1401 New York Ave., N.W.
Washington, DC 20005

Prospective packers of aseptically packaged, low-acid foods with particulates must take into consideration the processing and packaging parameters they must establish. These are related to product formulation, time-temperature profiles, packaging equipment and materials, and other variables. When filing with regulatory agencies for commercial production of aseptic low-acid particulates, processors must submit data on product flow rates, product sterilization and cooling, control instrumentation, alarms, monitors, recorders, measuring devices, diversionary systems, packaging materials and containers, sensors, lot control, pre-sterilization of the processing and packaging equipment, product formulation, instrument calibration, handling of process deviations, chemical sterilants, system pre-testing and in-process testing, quality control programs of both the processing and packaging operations, shelf-life studies, documentation/record keeping, shipping conditions, and other parameters.

The requirements outlined above and stated in detail in 21 CFR 113.40(g) indicate that aseptic processing and packaging of low-acid foods with particulates requires a large capital investment and many months or years of research and development work.

ASEPTIC CANNING SYSTEMS

Aseptic canning systems have been developed to minimize quality changes that may occur in slow-heating foods processed in conventional retorting systems. Heat exchangers are used in aseptic canning systems to rapidly sterilize and cool food products before they are filled aseptically into sterile cans. Cream sauces, soups, and products containing rice, cheese or high tomato content are particularly improved by the high temperature-short time (HTST) processing used in the aseptic canning techniques. Both low-acid and high-acid products may be processed and packaged aseptically.

With the Dole Aseptic Canning System, it is possible to carry out simultaneous canning operations in a closed, interconnected system as a continuous process. The several component operations are synchronized mechanically so that the product, containers, covers and finished canned product move through the system without interruption. Various temperature controllers and alarm systems are included in the design of the equipment.

In the heat exchange systems used in conjunction with the Dole System, the liquid or semi-liquid food product is pumped continuously under pressure through the heating section of the sterilizer, in which it is quickly brought up to sterilization temperature (275–300°F or 135–149°C), then through a holding section for the determined length of time to ensure commercial sterilization, and finally through a cooling section to the Dole Aseptic Canning System. The process temperature and process time are both automatically controlled by a

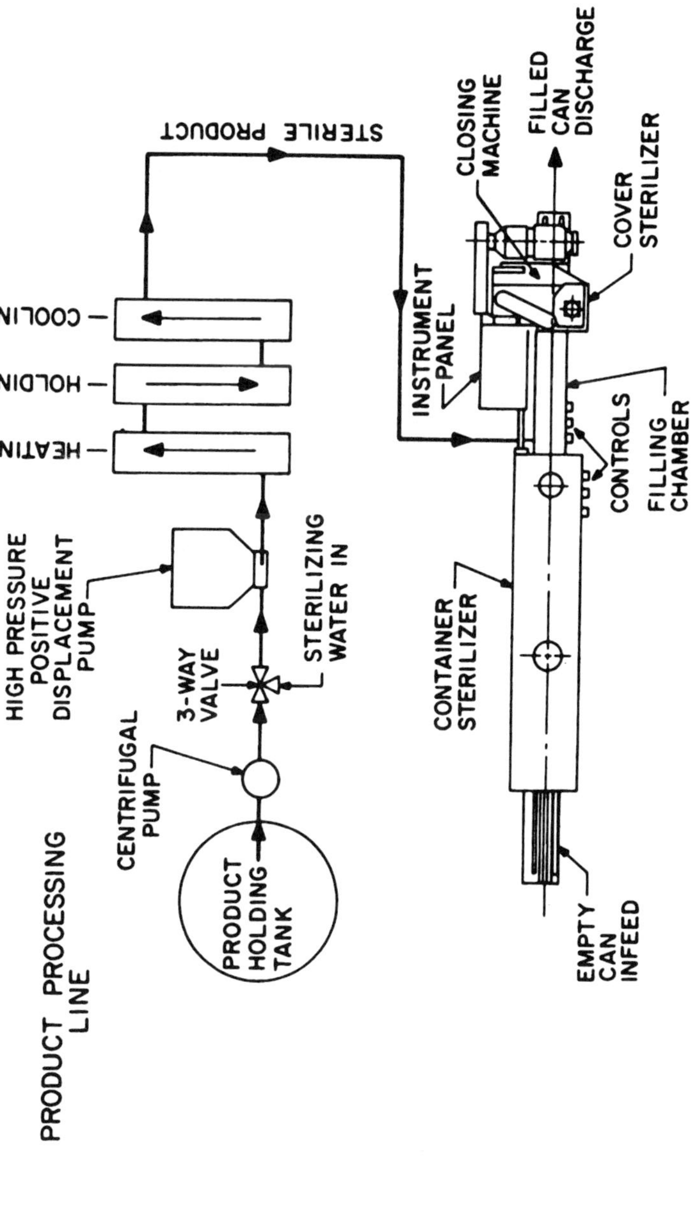

FIGURE 6.6 — Schematic Diagram of an Aseptic Canning Line

controller-recorder type instrument. The process time is controlled by the rate of flow of the product through the system, which is maintained uniform by a product pump operating at constant speed.

The heat exchange system, in which the product is heated and held under pressure for the time necessary to complete sterilization, constitutes in effect a continuous-flow pressure cooker. Four general types of heat exchange equipment are presently used in conjunction with the Dole Aseptic Canning System. The steam injection type, the swept surface or scraper type, the tubular type, and the plate type. The type of exchanger utilized is in part determined by the nature of the product to be sterilized; some exchanger types have inherent characteristics which limit their use to some extent.

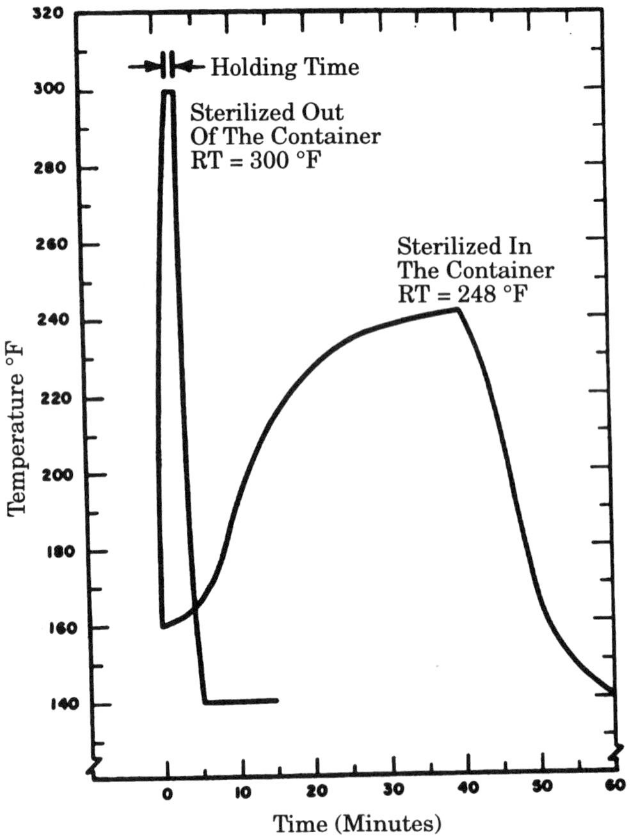

FIGURE 6.7 – Comparison of Product Heating Curves for Thermal Processes of Equivalent Lethality in an Aseptic System, etc.

For instance, the standard tubular exchanger requires cleaning at regular intervals to remove product which tends to build up on the tubing walls, but techniques are in use for cleaning in place with only brief interruption of the operation. In the past the plate type exchanger has possessed pressure limitations, but new designs on the market seem to have corrected this limitation. The scraper or swept surface type depends on a rotor equipped with scraper blades to prevent the accumulation of product on the heat exchange surface and because of its basic design features has proved unusually effective, especially with products of higher viscosity. The steam injection type of heat exchanger depends on the direct impingement of the steam into the product. The condensate may later be removed in a flash chamber which also serves as the cooling operation. This almost instantaneous heating method, either with evaporative cooling or when used in conjunction with one of the other types of exchangers performing as a cooling element, is in increasing use.

The heat exchanger does not differ in principle from the conventional "in-the-can" pressure cookers or retorts insofar as the lethal effect of time and temperature in the destruction of bacterial spores are concerned, but merely provides for the use of extremely short process times at high temperatures which cannot be realized by standard retort methods. The capability of the system to actually measure and control the process temperature and time eliminates the problem of any variations or fluctuations due to the heat-transfer properties of the product. This ensures uniform product quality.

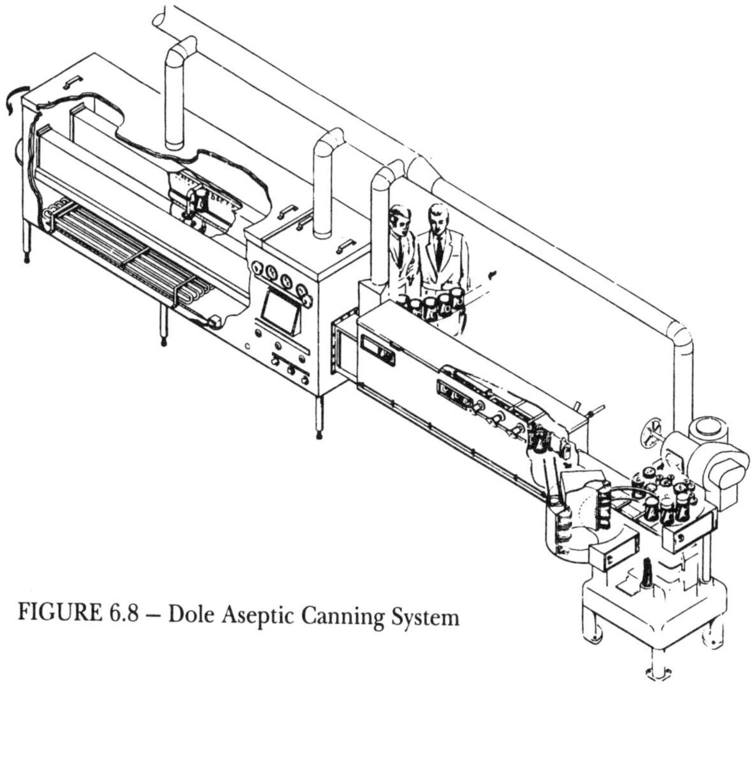

FIGURE 6.8 – Dole Aseptic Canning System

Sterilization of Containers

The containers are sterilized with super-heated steam or hot air as they are conveyed continuously through the container sterilizer to the filler. Superheated steam or hot air temperatures in the range of 500°F (260°C) are used to raise container temperatures up to the neighborhood of 435°F (224°C) in the sterilization period, a temperature safely below the melting point of low tin solder.

The temperature of the superheated steam or hot air is thermostatically controlled. At the same time the exposure of the containers to the steam or hot air is regulated by the speed at which they are conveyed through the sterilizer. The machine's unitized design means that multiple-section can sterilizers can be utilized to increase the speed of the system.

Sterilization of Covers

The covers are sterilized with superheated steam or hot air in a manner similar to that used to sterilize the containers. The cover sterilizer is attached to and operated as an accessory portion of the closing machine, mechanically separating the covers and transporting the covers through the sterilizer in order to expose all surfaces to superheated steam or hot air. Here again the temperature of the steam or hot air and the time of exposure of the covers are positively controlled and adjusted so as to provide a wide margin of safety against under-sterilization.

Aseptic Filling and Sealing Operations

Two types of filling devices, simple in principle and construction, are used primarily in the Dole Aseptic Canning System. One, a slit filler, has no moving parts. Empty cans pass under the slit opening of the filler with their flanges overlapped and a thin, continuous film of cold, sterile product from the heat exchanger feed line fills the containers. The other type of filling device can be a positive displacement rotary filler that is commercially available from a choice of manufacturers, depending on the specific application. The slit filler type depends on a positive pumping rate of product for accuracy of fill. The cold sterile product, flowing continuously from the heat-exchanger, is filled into the sterile cans as they are conveyed from the can sterilizer through the filler.

An atmosphere of super-heated steam or sterile air or gas is maintained in the filling section, closing machine, and interconnecting conveyor system to maintain sterility and to prevent the entry of airborne bacteria into the system. The continuous outward flow of super-heated steam through joints and any other apertures in the equipment is a simple and effective safeguard against atmospheric contamination. The canning operations are carried out at substantial atmospheric pressure, thereby eliminating the use of complicated and expensive pressurized equipment.

The Dole Model 540 unit is capable of operating at speeds of 450 (202 x 314) cans per minute. The new Model 2500 uses hot air as the sterilizing medium (rather than superheated steam mentioned above). This new machine consists of a spiral container sterilizing unit, a filler, an automatic lid de-stacker and a closing machine. The unit has been designed to aseptically package both high and low-acid foods into a variety of containers to include but not limited to metal, glass and plastic.

Summary of Products Packed by the Dole Aseptic Canning System

The Dole Aseptic Canning System is being used in an increasingly wide range of commercial operations. Although milk processors were among the first to recognize the merits of the system for canning milk and milk products, packers of other products–especially baby foods, soups, dessert puddings, custards, sour cream, dips and other heat-sensitive products–have turned to the system in increasing numbers.

Dairy products successfully packed with the Dole System include whole milk, evaporated and concentrated milks, flavored milks and other dairy drinks, milk-based baby food formula, cream, butter and some types of cheese. Whole milk and concentrated milks processed by aseptic fill methods are capable of being stored for extended periods of time and shipped without seriously affecting flavor or nutritive value. Progress made in recent years indicates that milk in more convenient form, such as sterile milk concentrate with fresh-tasting flavor and long shelf-life without refrigeration, will take on new significance in the dairy market in the future. The delicate flavor structure of milk products is much more faithfully preserved by the Dole System than by conventional canning methods which subject the product in the container to an extended heating period.

With the substantial number of Dole installations in the field and the wide application of the system, an increasing number of other food products are being commercially packed successfully. Heat sensitive products such as white sauce and Hollandaise sauce, a broad range of soups, tomato paste, pear, peach and banana purees, baby foods and non-milk formula, meat purees, puddings, and pet food, and many other standard and specialty items–all are packed advantageously by the Dole Aseptic Canning System. In fact, practically any product capable of being pumped through heat exchange equipment will possess quality improvement not afforded by conventional methods.

FIGURE 6.9 – Aseptic Canning Line
(Courtesy Dole Division, Graham Engineering Corp.)

ASEPTIC PACKAGING FOR REPROCESSING

A description of aseptic packaging systems that are used to preserve foods in bulk for storage, transportation and reprocessing follows. These systems are characterized by using one of the following as aseptic containers:

1. Aseptic 55 gallon (208 liters) tin-plated steel drums.
2. Aseptic flexible bags in sizes to 60 gallons (230 liters) in steel or fiber drums, or fiber boxes.
3. Aseptic flexible bags in wooden, fiber, or metal bins in sizes to 300 gallons (1,140 liters).
4. Aseptic bulk storage tanks ranging in sizes to 750,000 gallons (2,810 kiloliters).
5. Aseptic stainless steel "tote" type containers in sizes to 1,000 gallons (3,785 liters).
6. Railroad tank cars.
7. Tank trucks.

ASEPTIC DRUM FILLERS

"Tote" Type Containers

These are stainless steel containers, as manufactured by Spartenburg Steel Products, Inc., in sizes up to 520 gallons (2000 liters). Procedures virtually identical to those used for drums are applied for the sterilization and filling of the "tote" type containers. The primary exception is the design of the opening cap which has been developed to provide not only an hermetic seal, but also an integral pressure safety relief.

FIGURE 6.10 – Spartenburg Aseptic Containers

FranRica "Quadraseptic" Drum and Tank Aseptic Filling System

The basic operation of any aseptic fill sterilization system can be considered as follows:

Initially, product is heated to a minimum sterilizing temperature, held for a period of time at that temperature to cause sterilization, cooled to ambient temperature to minimize product damage resulting from heat treatment, and then held, handled and filled aseptically to eliminate any possibility of bacterial recontamination. Although this procedure is easily understood, there are precise techniques involved which must be followed to insure that the product is processed correctly and at all times handled in a manner to insure proper quality and sterilization.

To properly complete the operating conditions outlined above, the "Quadraseptic" drum and tank filling system can be provided. The system is composed of four key elements:

1. The agitated surge tank
2. The "Quadraseptic"
3. The aseptic drum filler
4. Aseptic bulk storage tanks

The primary processing portion of this system is centered within the "Quadraseptic" itself. This unit is an assembly of processing equipment mounted within a common support structure. The main components of the "Quadraseptic" include the FranRica Model 24 scraped surface heat exchanger (heating), an aseptic hot product holding tank and aseptic removal pump, a FranRica Model 50 scraped surface heat exchanger (cooling) and an aseptic cold product surge tank and aseptic removal pump. All components are factory mounted and aligned on the support structure prior to shipment and interconnected with necessary product and utility piping, valves, fittings and controls.

Single-point utility connections are provided to facilitate the system installation. The system control panel, provided separately, mounts immediately adjacent to the base unit.

FIGURE 6.11 – FranRica "Quadraseptic" Drum and Tank Filling System (Courtesy FR Manufacturing, Division FMC)

The basic system operating sequence can be described as follows:

Product being discharged from the plant evaporator or process surge tank is pumped into the 800 gal. (3,028 l) agitated surge tank. This tank is required so that the "Quadraseptic" system receives a continuous and uniform flow of product necessary to maintain stable operation characteristics.

The product removal pump transfers the product to the "Quadraseptic" where it enters the FranRica Model 24 scraped surface heat exchanger. In the initial phase, the product is being heated and returned to the surge tank while the remainder of the system is being steam sterilized prior to beginning aseptic operation. The "Quadraseptic" is designed to be presterilized using 15 psig (101.3 kPa) saturated steam. During the pre-sterilization cycle, all product contact surfaces are to be sterilized to a minimum temperature of 240°F (116°C) for a period of one hour.

Following completion of the pre-sterilization cycle, the product low temperature divert is closed to begin the flow of hot, sterile product discharged from the scraped surface heat exchanger (heater) at the required sterilization temperature. Product flows from this heat exchanger into the hot product holding tank wherein the product is held for the required period of time to insure complete sterilization. Product in the hot product holding tank is maintained under positive steam pressure at all times.

This hot product holding tank is designed to allow fill product control and maintenance of the necessary retention time for the product. The product flow rate and the maintained level within the tank are the methods used for controlling the determined residence time.

The head space above the product within the tank is constantly maintained at 3 psig (20.64 kPa) steam pressure at all times. This allows low temperature diversion at the sterilizer without the possibility of any of the remaining portion of the system going to a negative pressure condition, thus maintaining the system's aseptic integrity. Excessive steam pressure which may develop within the tank is vented to the atmosphere via a 3-psig (20.64 kPa) pressure relief valve.

Excessive product level within the tank is sensed by a high level probe which places the sterilizer divert valve into a bypass condition, returning additional product back to the agitated surge tank.

The scraped surface heat exchanger (cooling) and the aseptic cold surge tank are also designed to be presterilized using steam at 15 psig (101.3 kPa) as described above. Upon completion of the pre-sterilization cycle, hot, sterile nitrogen, maintained at a minimum temperature of 450°F (232°C) at 7.5 psig (51.6 kPa), is purged into the aseptic cold surge tank and scraped surface heat exchanger. This prevents the formation of a vacuum during product transfer. Stabilization of the pressure within these vessels is attained with the nitrogen media before product flow begins.

Once the proper product level has been attained in the product holding tank, the hot, sterile product is fed to the scraped surface heat exchanger by means of the hot holding tank product removal pump. The heat exchanger rotor is started and the flow of cooling water is begun.

Initially, 150 to 200 gallons (3 to 4 drums) of hot product is passed through the aseptic cold surge tank. This flow condition is due to the time required to reach proper cooling conditions within the cooling scraped surface heat exchanger. As the product flows into the tank, it displaces the nitrogen within the tank and product transfer line from the aseptic cold surge tank to the drum filler. This back pressure of nitrogen gas thus maintains positive product pressure at the first fill. The product pressure within the line subsequently maintains the positive pressure conditions on following fills.

As the aseptic cold surge tank fills, the nitrogen pressure is increased due to the decreasing head space volume.

As the nitrogen pressure reaches 15 psig (101.3 kPa), an automatic relief valve vents the excess nitrogen. Excessive product level within the aseptic cold surge tank is sensed by the high level probe which places the hot holding tank product removal pump into a bypass condition.

Once the desired product level is reached within the aseptic cold surge tank, the aseptic drum filler feed pump (cold tank product removal pump) is started, allowing product to circulate in the bypass loop at a low speed.

Upon demand for product from the drum filler, the pump is changed to high speed by means of an air operated speed control on the pump variable speed drive. At the same time, the bypass valve at the pump closes, allowing full flow of product to the drum filler. Upon completion of the drum filling cycle, the pump once again reverts to the low speed, bypass mode.

Automated Aseptic Filling of Drum Containers

Aseptic filling of drum containers is accomplished by the FranRica Model PBF-18 drum filling system. This system, as with all other equipment, is designed to be presterilized with 15 psig (1 atm) steam.

Previously, we have described the operation of the sterilizing portion of this system, resulting in the flow of product to the drum filler. The following, therefore, is the description of the drum filler operation.

The FranRica Model PBF-18 drum filler is designed to receive a Rheem or Van Leer standard aseptic 55 gal. (208 l) drum. The container, manually placed at the infeed of the drum filler, will be automatically positioned and indexed for filling. Once the container and the cap are positioned, the operator manually depresses the sequence start button which automatically raises the container toward the fixed sterilizing and filling chamber.

FIGURE 6.12 – 55-gallon Sterile Pack Drum
Clingage and rinsing problems are simplified by the sterile pack drum. Exposing the semi-finished food product to less than one-quarter of container surface, in comparison to the same quantity product in traditionally used smaller containers, waste through clingage is further eliminated through efficient rinsing. Product shown here is apricot concentrate. (Courtesy Rheem Manufacturing Co.)

The chamber, which houses the sterilizing, filling and sealing equipment, is designed to seal against the top double seam of the container. The operation from this point on is completely automatic and requires no further control by the operator.

Once the container has been sealed against the sterilizing chamber, the sealing head (swedging tool) removes the bung cap and the sterilization cycle begins through the introduction of steam into the container and sterilizing chamber. The system vents to the atmosphere for 1 minute and 20 seconds to ensure removal of all air from the interior of the container and sterilizing chamber. Following the venting cycle, the vent closes automatically and the container is pressurized to 15 psig (101.3 kPa) and maintained at that pressure for 40 seconds. Following the sterilizing cycle, the chamber is then vented once again, reducing the internal pressure to 1.5 psig (10.1 kPa) and maintained at that pressure throughout the filling cycle.

The first step of the filling cycle is the automatic insertion of the fill tube. Once the fill tube has reached full penetration, approximately $2^1/_2$ in. from the bottom of the drum, the product fill valve is automatically opened starting the product fill cycle. At this time, the aseptic cold surge tank product removal pump shifts to the high speed mode, delivering product to the container at a rate of approximately 75 gpm (284 l).

The filling timer is automatically started when the product valve is opened, timing the flow of the product for a period of approximately 40 seconds. During the period of filling, the fill tube raises at a uniform rate to insure a level product fill within the drum container.

After 40 seconds, the aseptic cold surge tank product removal pump is returned to its normal recirculating speed. At this lower speed, the container is then filled to a level allowing approximately $^1/_2$ in. (1.3 cm) of head space within the container. After closing the product valve, the fill tube is retracted into the fill tube housing and rinsed with sterile condensate in preparation for filling the next container.

The swedging tool (sealing head) automatically moves to position and replaces the cap in the bung for sealing. The drum cap is then sealed and the container is ready to be released from the sterilizing chamber.

Removal of Filled Drum Container

The filled, sealed container is then released, indicating the completion of the cycle. The drum is automatically removed by a pair of mechanically actuated hinge clamps, advancing the drum to the weigh station. Here the drum is weighed and the final weight is recorded by the operator.

To allow for the removal of the full drum from the drum filler, as well as the placement of the empty drum at the filler prior to the sterilization and filling cycle, a non-powered roller conveyor system is provided. This system is designed to allow the manual transfer of empty drums from pallets to the drum filler infeed section and the transfer of full drums from the drum filler following completion of filling and weighing.

After weighing and labeling of the filled drum, the drum is upended prior to palletizing and storage. The purpose for upending the drum is to eliminate product dehydration in the head space and cap area and to minimize accumulation of dirt, etc. on the top head at the bung seal area.

The operator then guides the upended drum to the palletizer. The palletizer power hoist lifts one drum at a time onto the pallet. When four drums have been placed on a pallet, the full pallet is manually moved on the roller conveyor to a point where it can be removed by a forklift truck.

The system described here has been designed to allow continuous operation for seven days or more without shutdown for cleaning and resterilization.

Filling of Flexible Plastic Bags

The FranRica Model PBF-18 drum filler may be modified to allow for the filling of flexible "plastic" bags in open top steel or fiber drums. The basic operation of the sterilizing and drum filling system remains unchanged except for the following modifications:

1. The closing tool on the drum filler is revised from a swedging type to a heat sealing element with heating coil, vacuum cap holder and revised positioning device.
2. Provision of six adaptor rings for the top of the steel or fiber drums to retain the filling spout of the "plastic" bag and also provide the seal for the drum filler sterilizing chamber.
3. Modification of the product fill sequence to permit the "inflation" of the bag with air or nitrogen prior to the start of the drum sterilization cycle.

FIGURE 6.13 – ABF-1200 Aseptic Bag Filler
(Courtesy FR Manufacturing)

SCHOLLE ASEPTIC FILLING SYSTEM FOR BAG-IN-BOX/DRUM PACKAGING

Scholle Corporation has developed a system for aseptically filling pre-sterilized food products into aseptic, flexible bags which are then placed into corrugated boxes, barrels or tote bins. The "Auto Fill" 10-2 series aseptic bag filler can handle a wide range of container sizes and products. It is capable of filling containers from 1 to 330 gal. (3.8 to 1,249 l) at speeds up to 600 containers per hour. The system is ideal for aseptically packing tomato pastes and sauces, fruit purees and other foods such as crushed pineapple and concentrates. Single-strength juices, particulates and other sensitive foods can also be handled effectively.

The Auto Fill 10-2 is designed for a continuous filling operation. Before use, both filling chambers, piping and all steam seals are sterilized with steam. Sterility during filling is maintained in the chamber by steam and the positive pressure of a constant automized chlorine spray.

FIGURE 6.14 – The Scholle Aseptic Filling System for Bag-in-Box and Drum Filling (Courtesy Scholle Corporation)

In use, the capped spout of a pre-sterilized bag is inserted into one of the chambers which are completely air tight before spout insertion, as well as during filling. The filler automatically removes the cap, inserts a filling valve into the spout, fills the bag to a pre-set volume of product, recaps the spout and finally, drops it out of the chamber for loading into a waiting box, drum or tote. With twin filling chambers, product can flow continuously as it is instantly diverted from the filled bag to the pre-set empty bag.

This filling system uses bags that have been sterilized by gamma radiation prior to filling. These bags are composed of an inner ply of polyethylene and an outer ply of a metallized polyester laminate which improves the bag's flex-crack resistance and provides a superior gas barrier.

ASEPTIC BULK STORAGE AND TRANSPORTATION

Bulk Storage Processing of Tomato Products

The tomato industry has made tremendous advances in the past 50 years. New cultivars and cultural practices, improved and enlarged processing equipment and facilities, and streamlined warehousing and marketing practices have kept the industry constantly growing. However, the industry is still faced with a number of serious problems even with past innovations. Some of the more serious problems include processing bottlenecks, over-production of certain products, large equipment investment, large warehousing costs, and raw product scheduling. Until the problem of seasonality is diminished, the tomato industry cannot be freed to become more efficient and orderly in its processing and marketing functions. One solution is to enhance the holdability of partially processed fruit at some step of processing. By extending the storage life of partially processed fruit to allow year-round plant operations, the problems of seasonality are sharply reduced; the development of bulk storage processing assists in this problem.

Factors that are important to consider in bulk storage processing include: 1) rapid pectic enzyme inactivation to maintain high viscosity, 2) high temperature treatment to destroy spore-forming bacteria, and 3) protection of the sterile product to prevent microbial recontamination and exposure to oxygen.

The Process

Bulk storage as the name implies is holding a large unit of food under storage conditions that prevent spoilage. The stored product is held for later distribution and/or remanufacture. The concept is simple, but the technology required to assure product protection under bulk storage conditions is considerably more demanding. An industry/university (Purdue University/ Bishopric Products Co., now Enerfab) research project resulted in an aseptic processing-bulk aseptic storage process designed to store products from single strength juices to highly concentrated material.

The Purdue/Bishopric process can be broken down into two areas, tank sterilization and product sterilization.

Tank Construction and Sterilization

The large, non-refrigerated tanks are fabricated from carbon steel, lined with Bishopric "Lastiglas-Munkadur" Lining. The tanks are either shop or field constructed depending upon size. There are two openings in the tank. A top manway permits the introduction of a sprayball for CIP washing, a N_2 gas inlet equipped with a microbial filter, two sight glasses and a positive pressure vacuum safety device. A 4-in. (10 cm) opening placed in the conical bottom of the tank allows for filling and emptying.

Valves that come in contact with the sterile product must be aseptic. In the system designed by the Bishopric Products Co. special patented valves are used to prevent microbial recontamination of the product. Special chambers that encompass the valve stems allow the circulation of a chemical sterilant, such as a halogen. By using this technique, the problem of requiring culinary steam and localized overheating of the product is overcome. When closed, the valve seats are also protected by the chemical solution. Once thoroughly cleaned, the tanks are sterilized by contact with a halogen solution at a concentration of approximately 20 ppm. The tanks are then purged with sterile N_2 gas or air, sealed and ready to accept sterile product. This cleaning and sterilizing procedure may be accomplished well ahead of the processing season.

Product Sterilization and Transfer

Conventional sterilization practices can be used to sterilize tomato products. With product below 16% solids, a process equivalent of 250°F (121°C) for 0.7 min. is required. At 18% solids or higher, heating to 190°F (88°C) should be adequate. In all instances the sterile product is cooled to below 90°F (32°C) before introduction into the tanks. All transfer lines are presterilized with hot water or steam prior to operations with positive pressure maintained on the sterile product at all times. It is important that the system be designed so that only properly sterilized product be allowed to enter the tanks. This requires a control system and recycle or bypass lines.

The system should be designed to permit partial filling of the tanks during one operation with complete filling at a later date. Likewise, partial emptying of the tanks can be accomplished by replacing the removed product volume with sterile N_2 gas. Periodic microbial and quality monitoring should be carried out.

Other products such as apple sauce, cranberry sauce, grape juice, and single strength orange not from concentrate have also been successfully bulk-stored. While each product has its own specific processing requirement, the basic bulk storage technology can be adapted for each product.

FIGURE 6.15 – Tomato Storage
At Purdue University, research to develop a better method of storing semi-processed tomatoes led to the construction of 40,000-gal. aseptic food storage tanks by the Bishopric Products Co., Cincinnati, OH. During harvest season, the tanks are filled with tomatoes to await further processing or transporting. The Bishopric/Purdue system is currently provided worldwide by FR Manufacturing, Inc., Stockton, CA. (Courtesy Agricultural Information Dept., Purdue University, West Lafayette, IN)

Bulk storage innovations have also allowed the shipment of preprocessed product in bulk. These sterile products are shipped in non-refrigerated tanks by truck and rail for final processing at distant processing facilities. This makes it possible to produce the raw solids in optimum growing areas and final-process them in distant consumption areas. Avoiding the shipment of ingredients, bottles, cans and cartons greatly reduces transportation costs.

Bulk storage technology is expected to continue to have a significant impact on the fruit and vegetable processing industries.

Bulk Tomato Paste Available in Rail Cars

A specially designed 20,000-gal. (75,706 l) rail car delivers tomato paste in bulk from California to eastern markets. A modified hopper car, it features an enclosed, aseptic system that minimizes chances of product spoilage by maintaining positive nitrogen pressure in the car's headspace. Specially designed valves allow aseptic loading and unloading of the car. The car is built in a 3-hopper configuration, with slope sheets angled at 51° to funnel the paste to the individual discharge valves.

FIGURE 6.16 – The "Asepticar"
A unique railcar for aseptic bulk transfer of food products with a 20,000-gal. capacity. (Courtesy Bishopric Products Co.)

A brief outline of the car's operation follows.

(1) After thorough cleaning with detergents, the interior is sterilized with chemical solution. Unloading lines are also sterilized.
(2) As the car is drained of solution, nitrogen is pumped into the headspace.
(3) After the car is filled with nitrogen, tomato paste is pumped through sterile loading lines with the use of the car's aseptic valves.
(4) When loading is complete and the loading line is disengaged, valves are repositioned for transit.
(5) On arrival to destination, the car is unloaded by connecting a hose to the unloading valve on one hopper section at a time, and pumping the paste through a positive displacement pump.

TANKS FOR ASEPTIC STORAGE FOR REPROCESSING

Reinforced concrete tanks of several hundred thousand gallon capacity are used, as well as lined steel tanks of 40,000-gal. (151,412 l) capacity, described earlier in this chapter. The concrete tanks are inside lined with a synthetic resin, like epoxy. These tanks are used to store large quantities of semi-prepared products for remanufacturing. These tanks have been used mainly for cut-up tomatoes, concentrated tomato juice and fruits. The product may be shipped large distances under aseptic conditions in a specially designed railroad car, previously described.

In practice, for using the concrete tanks for aseptic storage, the product is first sterilized for a time and at a temperature sufficient to obtain a commercially sterile product. The sterile product is aseptically pumped into the concrete tank which has previously been sterilized with hydrogen peroxide. Once it is sterile, the tank is filled with sterile nitrogen gas and hermetically sealed until it is filled with the product. All the pipes and valves used to transfer products are presterilized with hot water or saturated steam.

The product for reprocessing that has been in storage under aseptic conditions in concrete or steel tanks may be also aseptically shipped long distances using a specially designed railroad car. The product is aseptically transferred into the railroad car, and then aseptically transported and delivered at its destination by aseptically transferring the product into a sterile holding tank.

The railroad car is used as a giant package of 20,000 gal (75,706 L) capacity. This aseptic transportation and delivery system makes it feasible to ship a product for manufacturing in a region far removed from where the raw material was produced, and to do so during any season of the year.

REGULATIONS THAT APPLY TO ASEPTIC PROCESSING AND PACKAGING SYSTEMS

Aseptic packages and processing systems must meet appropriate regulatory requirements for products packed under the jurisdiction of the U.S. Department of Agriculture. The USDA published *Guidelines for Aseptic Processing and Packaging Systems in Meat and Poultry Plants* in June 1984, which delineates review and acceptance procedures by the USDA.

Products which are packed under the jurisdiction of the U.S.

Food and Drug Administration must comply with 21 CFR 108 - Emergency Permit Control and 21 CFR 113 - Thermally Processed Low-Acid Foods Packaged in Hermetically Sealed Containers. Specific requirements for aseptic processing and packaging systems are delineated under 21 CFR part 113 Subject C 113.40(g). FDA has recently published a new section of its *Inspection Operations Manual on Aseptic Packaging*. This gives FDA inspectors background on operation of equipment and instructions for inspection.

Adherence to these requirements is in addition to adherence to the other appropriate regulations concerning sanitation, use of appropriate materials, etc.

The primary regulatory concern is the assurance that the packaging system will be commercially sterile; packages will be free from inadvertent contaminants and will produce products which are commercially sterile. In addition, since new packaging procedures are used there is concern about the ability of these packages to form and retain a hermetic seal.

ACKNOWLEDGEMENTS

The author thanks Philip E. Nelson,Ph.D, Purdue University, for reviewing this chapter and the following firms for their contributions of information and/or graphic materials to the chapter on Aseptic Processing and Packaging.

APV CREPACO, Inc.
Enerfab, Inc.
Cherry-Burrell Corp.
Combibloc, Inc.
Continental Can Co., Inc.
Cryovac Div., W. R. Grace & Co.
Dole Division, Graham Engineering
FR Manufacturing, Inc.
National Food Processors Association
Purdue University
Rheem Manufacturing Co.
Scholle Corporation
Spartenburg Steel Products, Inc.
Tetra Pak, Inc.

CHAPTER 7

In-Plant Quality Control

Organization of Quality Control

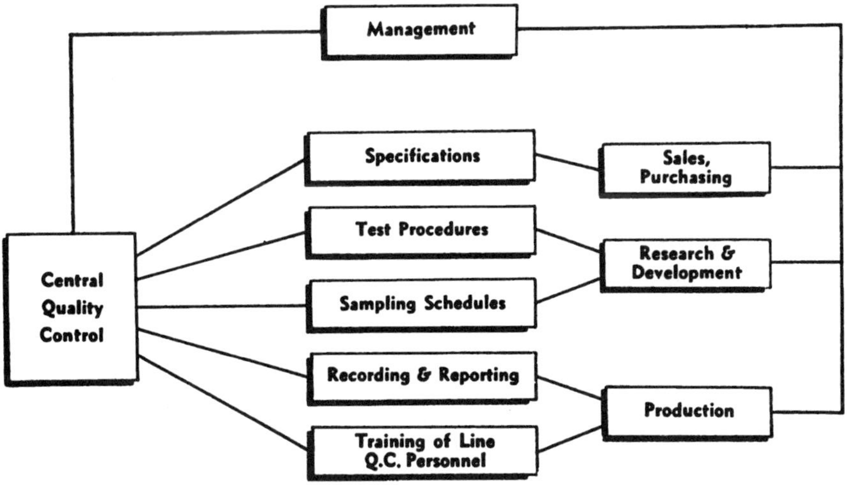

FIGURE 7.1 – Organization and Function of a Quality Control (QC) Department. The QC department should be directly responsible to management and not to sales and purchasing, research and development, or production.

Quality control in the food processing plant is generally assumed to have three basic aims:

1. To assure compliance with government regulations.
2. To maintain or improve the quality grade, thereby enhancing product value in the market place.
3. To reduce the probability of spoilage and resultant hazards to consumers and economic loss.

A wide range of attitudes toward the accomplishment of these aims exists in the industry. It is extremely difficult to estimate the value of a quality control department until an avoidable loss has been encountered due to a lack of such control. It is practically impossible to estimate the gains that might be realized by slight improvements in quality that would increase product value or saleability. Thus, there are plants in which little effort is expended on quality control measures and no definite program of any kind is followed.

Most certainly this condition exists, not because the processor would not like a quality control system, but rather that he does not realize how small the cost might be when compared to the risks involved. Too often, thoughts of quality control bring visions of spacious, gleaming laboratories full of complicated expensive equipment and even more expensive, apparently non-productive, highly trained scientists. There is no denying that such laboratories do exist in the industry, but it is also true that they usually justify their existence and that generally they are no larger or more expensive than they need be.

The promulgation of the U.S. Food and Drug Administration Good Manufacturing Practices Regulations for low-acid foods (CFR 21, Parts 113 and 108), and for acidified foods (CFR 21, Part 114) makes it even more important to organize and maintain an efficient quality control program. Even though those regulations legally apply only to acidified and low-acid foods, processors of high-acid foods would be well advised to voluntarily apply pertinent portions of those regulations, that would contribute to improved finished product quality and to reducing incidence of canned food spoilage.

A quality control program can be started with a minimum of expenditure and expanded as the need arises. As a matter of hard fact, the laboratory is only one facet of quality control, being in essence a place where the results of quality control in the plant are checked. Much of the actual work should take place in the plant and should include an inspection of each phase of the operation to determine whether performance is satisfactory or where improvement can be made.

The first requirement for quality control is the designation of a quality control supervisor. If at all possible, this person should have no other duties, but if other functions must be performed they should be subordinate to quality control. Also, while it is important that the QC person cooperate in every way possible with the operating personnel, he/she should be directly responsible to top management.

The organization and operation of a quality control department may be discussed under three headings: first, qualifications required in the individual to be selected; second, laboratory requirements; and third, general operations.

Personnel Requirements

The degree of technical training required for quality control work is largely dependent on the size of the operation and the complexity of the foods being processed. The college-trained food technologist is, of course, ideally suited for this type of work providing the plant production justifies employing such an individual. For smaller plants, or those operating only on seasonal products, it has been found that the work can be carried on without formally trained personnel, by selecting an individual who is experienced in the details of the plant operation and trained specifically for the work required. A person with real interest in the type of work is essential and, of course, some technical background is highly desirable. A process which allows for continuing education is necessary for Quality Control Management (QCM) to build on existing skills, and to track advances in technology.

If the plant operations justify only a part-time employee, a college student or high school or college science teacher may be the most practical type of person for quality control work. If at all possible, however, the quality control work should be assigned to a year-round employee, as the full benefit of such a program can only be obtained when continued on a year to year basis.

Aside from the quality control aspects, a more highly trained individual might be able to use some of his off-season time in developing new products that fit present operations or assist is devising new methods of preparing old products.

Additional personnel should be employed when the nature of the product requires constant routine laboratory work–for example mold and insect fragment counts for tomato products or moisture tests for corn. Summer help is entirely satisfactory for such duties.

Laboratory Facilities

The QC laboratory need not be elaborate nor large. A square room, approximately 18 ft. x 18 ft. (approx. 5.5 m x 5.5 m) will provide ample working space, as well as storage areas for retaining samples and an incubator which may be added later. The room should be well lighted and apart from, but with easy access to, the processing floor. A minimum of 20 linear feet (approx. 6 m) of bench space is highly desirable. The room should be supplied with electric power and running water at a sink. Provision should be made for the collection and disposal of refuse.

A desk for the preparation of records and reports, as well as a file cabinet to store them, are necessary. The value of the control program increases with the years and is dependent on the availability of data.

Equipment requirements will vary considerably with the products packed, but basic items include a hot plate, a heavy duty can opener, vacuum gauges, headspace gauges, a scale, a set of drained weight screens, size grading screens, grading trays, and a can center temperature device if fruits or acidified products are packed. A hydrometer calibrated in percent salt will be found useful, and where syrup packs are made, a set of syrup hydrometers or a refractometer is necessary. Tomato products make a microscope a must. A line operated pH meter is a must and a simple chlorine test kit is a worthy addition.

General Operations

In general, the operations of the quality control department may be divided into three areas: inspection and grading of raw products and of other ingredients, control of processing operations and of packages and packaging materials, and examination of finished products. Before any of these functions can be carried out, it should be clearly understood in detail, what is wanted at each step of the manufacturing procedure, and what specifications or standards are expected in the finished product.

Towards this end, it is suggested that the first function of quality control be the preparation of a plant operating manual. This manual should be prepared in cooperation with management and the key production personnel and should represent the combined company know-how for each canning operation. All steps in the operation, or operations labeled and critical control points identified on detail flow charts of the lines. Control specifications must be established for all pertinent points in the process, such as segregation of raw product for the various quality grades (for example, Tenderometer grades for peas or moisture content for corn), blanching schedules for various products

FIGURE 7.2 - The Succulometer
By a compression test measures maturity of sweet corn,
storage quality of apples, and oil and water content of canned tuna.

or grades, fill-in weights, syrup or brine concentrations, closing temperatures, and sterilizing processes. Production capacities should be set up so that proper supplies of raw materials will be available to prevent starving operations with resultant costly production interruptions, or causing an over-supply of perishable product that spoils or is downgraded on the plant dock.

Product specifications should also be set up in written form to include net or drained weights, headspace, and where applicable such data as a unit count, consistency, syrup cut-out concentration and other pertinent information. This manual should be reviewed annually and brought up to date as additional experience is acquired. By the use of the manual as a guide, the operation of quality control resolves itself into the periodic inspection of the raw product and each step of the processing procedure to determine whether the prescribed methods are being followed, and daily examination of packaged samples to determine whether the finished product conforms to the standard desired.

Cooperation with the field department is an important feature of the quality control program. It is necessary that each group understands the problems and goals of the other. No finished product can be any better than the raw material supplied nor should impractical quality levels be set that would reduce yields to an uneconomic level. Wherever possible, objective test methods should be used or sought to minimize misunderstandings, since such tests, when used on individual lots or loads, may speed handling in the cannery.

An overall visual appraisal of raw material when it arrives and a periodic check as it awaits processing should not be forgotten. It is important to foresee deterioration due to delay in transportation, handling, weather conditions or maturity and to recommend steps to forestall the effects of such deterioration. For example, rapid handling of a particular lot may prevent the need for extra inspection, additional trimming or production loss.

CONTROL OF FACTORY OPERATIONS

At the time of instituting the quality control program, an initial inspection should be made of the plant equipment for conditions which are not compatible with good canning practices. If possible, this should be done before the start of the canning season. One purpose of such inspection should be to check equipment for possible sources of metal contamination. Copper is a particular offender in this regard; it causes discoloration in products such as peas and corn, and may act as a corrosion accelerator when present in apple juice and other fruit products.

This metal may be contributed by equipment made from copper or copper-bearing alloys such as brass, bronze, or Monel metal. Such metals should not be used for kettles, brine tanks, brine lines, valves, fillers or other equipment contacting the product during preparation. A program must exist to replace all rigid, food contact surfaces with stainless steel. For maintenance and clean-up efficiency, all rigid, non-food contact surfaces should also be made on stainless steel.

Filler parts or certain other equipment made from these metals may be plated with a non-corrosive metal if replacement is not economically feasible. Iron may also cause discoloration in some products, although no problems are ordinarily encountered if the equipment is kept free of loose rust. Product contact parts should be made of #304 or #316 stainless steel, glass, or approved plastics. #316 stainless steel is more corrosion resistant to food acids than #304.

Another objective of the initial plant inspection should be to check for obvious spoilage hazards such as wooden equipment and worn or porous conveyor belts. Such porous materials in contact with the product during preparation become seeded with spoilage organisms and, being practically impossible to clean, act as a source of infection to contaminate the product subsequently run through the line. Contact of product with wood should be avoided.

Wooden equipment should be replaced with metal, and worn belting should be replaced. Other spoilage hazards such as "dead ends" in brine or product lines may also be noted during such an inspection. As previously mentioned, this equipment inspection should be made well in advance of the actual canning season in order that necessary changes or replacements may be carried out.

Attention may also be given to the condition of retort and other sterilization equipment during this pre-season inspection. Steps should be taken to see that automatic pressure controls and recorders are in proper working order, and thermometers and pressure gauges should also be checked for accuracy. Sterilization equipment piping in general should also be examined to make certain that hook-up, pipe sizes, safety valves, and venting provisions are in accordance with latest recommendations. For acidified foods and low-acid foods pay special attention to the FDA Good Manufacturing Practices regulations.

Daily Sanitation Survey

Before the start of each day's operations, an inspection should be made to check the sanitary condition of the equipment in the canning line. This should be in addition to any inspection made by the foreman in each department; any evidence of poor clean-up of the equipment should be reported so that the condition may be corrected before canning operations begin. Particular attention should be given to all products where bio-films may harbor spoilage organisms on surfaces that appear clean.

Observation should also be made for other potential spoilage hazards such as leaky steam valves permitting blanchers, blending tanks, or similar equipment to be heated within the thermophilic growth range during non-operating periods, holdover of syrup at temperatures favorable to bacterial growth, or inadequately drained syrup or brine lines.

The quality control technologist should at all times be on alert for operating practices which may represent possible spoilage hazards since such conditions may frequently be overlooked by production personnel, particularly during periods of heavy production.

Daily Plant Inspection

At the beginning of each day's pack and, if possible, at two hour intervals during the day, the various steps in the canning procedure should be checked by the quality control management. These inspections should be made according to a definite plan, and the points checked should be recorded on a form appropriate to the particular product. Forms should be prepared in duplicate, one copy for the plant manager, and the other to be kept on file in the laboratory. In addition to the written report, any deviations in operating procedure should be reported immediately to the department involved.

As mentioned earlier, periodic inspections of the plant operations should begin with the raw product, noting the quality, condition, and if applicable, the quality grade of product on hand. Proceeding along the canning line, the efficiency of washing, sorting, and trimming operations should be noted. In washing operations making use of recirculated water, condition of the wash water, and quantity of fresh make-up water should be observed.

In such preliminary cleaning operations the rate at which product is being fed into equipment is also closely related to cleaning efficiency.

Sorting and trimming efficiency, likewise may be hampered if the line is being overloaded. The latter operations should also be observed for evidence of excessive waste from over-trimming, particularly at the beginning of the season or where inexperienced help are involved.

At the blanchers, observations should include time and temperature of the blanch, amount of make-up water being added, and concentration of salt or other blanching supplements, if used. If tubular blanchers are employed, water recovery tanks should be observed for excessive foam accumulation as such conditions have been found conducive to a build-up of thermophilic spoilage organisms. The temperature of recirculated water should also be checked to insure that the entire system is maintained at a temperature above the thermophilic growth range.

Details of daily inspections of the intermediate operations in the canning line will, of course, depend upon the type of product being packed. Tomato juice and related products require particular emphasis at the sorting and trimming belts to reduce mold content, and microscopic examination of each batch of product is essential in this regard.

Operations on fruits or vegetables, such as peeling, coring, slicing, dicing, or comminuting should also be observed at each plant inspection and appropriate notes made a part of the daily record.

The filling operation should receive special attention. The filler operator should make frequent weight checks to make certain that the fills are within the desired limits for the product, size, and grade being run. Quality control management, in turn, should check this running record at each inspection interval, as well as actually observing the appearance of the containers leaving the filler.

When weight checks are made, consecutive containers should be sampled from each filler pocket to insure that all pockets are operating properly. Statistical methods are available to evaluate the operation of fillers and to determine whether the desired fill-in weights are being obtained.

If the range between minimum and maximum fills cannot be held within reasonable limits, the filler should be checked for mechanical defects or improper adjustment. Brine or syrup temperature and fill should also be noted at the filler, and concentration of these media should be checked in the syrup or brine preparation room.

Terminal exhausts, if used, should also be checked for exhaust box temperature and average product temperature after exhausting.

Operation of the closing machine should also be given careful attention. Actual adjustment of the machine and maintenance of good seams are the responsibility of the closing machine operator, and this individual should examine and measure seams at the start of each run and at intervals of one to two hours during the pack.

The operator should also make a note of any machine changes or adjustments and this information, together with the closing machine count at the time such change is made, should be part of the permanent record. Quality control management should be responsible for checking the record of hourly seam measurements and should collect the operator's report for filing at the end of each day.

Visual observation of the cans at the discharge of the closing machine may also prove helpful in detecting certain types of machine failure, such as broken chuck or seaming roll, which might occur between periodic seam inspections by the closing machine operator. Quality control management should also note the vacuum (if vacuum closure is used) or, if steam flow closure is employed, the efficiency of this operation should be checked periodically. Average product temperature at the time of closure should also be recorded.

Proper retort operation, as well as that of other sterilization equipment, is one of the most critical steps in the entire canning procedure and should receive careful attention in the periodic quality control checks. Any abnormal delay between closure and processing of the containers should be noted, as well as the actual operation of the sterilization equipment. Venting during the come-up period in retorts is particularly important, as entrapped air in the retort may cause "cold spots" and result in under-processed portions of the retort load.

Recommended venting schedules are available for various sizes and types of sterilization equipment and the proper venting procedure, once determined for the particular plant conditions, should be checked both as to time and indicated temperature before the vents are closed.

The time and temperature of processing for each container size should be checked, and where temperature recorders are used, charts should be collected each day. Before filing, charts should be checked carefully and any irregularity in come-up or processing time should be reported immediately. Proceed in accordance with CFR 21, Part 113.

When pressure cooling is employed, this procedure should be checked periodically, and containers removed from the retort should also be observed for evidence of buckling or paneling. The temperature of the containers at the completion of the cooling cycle should also be determined and recorded.

If chlorination of the cooling water is employed, the residual chlorine content should be checked at each inspection.

If whole tomatoes or fruit products are packed, container-center temperatures should be determined at the end of the process in addition to recording the time and temperature of processing. Adjustment of the processing time may be necessary since the maturity or condition of the fruit changes during the season.

Plant inspection should also include periodic examination of the warehouse. Evidence of spoilage should be looked for and the incidence of any rusted containers noted. The technologist should also be on the alert for indications of can damage due to rough handling, maladjusted runways, or damage in unscramblers, labelers, or casing machines. A record of warehouse temperatures may also prove useful for future reference.

Examination of Line Samples

In addition to observations of the canning procedure to determine compliance with operating instructions and federal and state regulations, the quality control laboratory should conduct a daily examination and grading of line samples to check the finished product against the desired specifications set up by management. Samples for laboratory examination may conveniently be obtained during the plant inspection. Samples should be taken at sufficient frequency to ensure control of the processing function. Retained samples should be collected at the prescribed intervals. A minimum of two containers from each line should be collected every two hours, or from each lot change if this occurs more frequently. One container, properly identified, should be retained for possible future reference and the other container from each sampling should be examined immediately.

The examination to be made will vary somewhat with the product. In general, data should include net weight, vacuum, headspace, drained weight (if applicable), and general observations for unit size, color, flavor, texture, defects, extraneous material, and compliance with any other specifications under which the canner is operating. Syrup packed fruits should also be checked for cut-out syrup concentration. Where needed, special instruments may be utilized to assist in grading the product for additional factors such as color, maturity, viscosity, specific gravity, pH, or total acidity. Control of the pH is very important where acidification of the product is employed.

Data obtained in the examination of canned samples should, of course, be recorded on a form prepared for the particular product. Identifying information such as can size, embossed code, date and time of packing should also be a part of the record.

Quality control management, through daily plant inspections, may be of invaluable assistance in pinpointing the responsibility for any operational deviations noted.

Control should also be exercised over certain critical ingredients such as sugar, starch, salt, and spices. Laboratory examination of these materials at the canning plant may not be feasible, particularly where bacteriological tests are involved, but the quality control technologist should set up purchasing specifications and, if necessary, samples may be submitted to outside laboratories for examination.

Examination of Water

Water may also be considered an important ingredient in canned food products. The texture of certain vegetables, such as peas and dried beans, may be adversely affected by excessive water hardness, particularly calcium and magnesium salts, and if this problem exists, water softening may be necessary. Checking the operation of the water softener would then become a responsibility of quality control.

The bacteriological condition of water in the plant is also important from the standpoint of spoilage prevention. Where in-plant chlorination of the water supply or treatment of the cooling water is employed, effectiveness of chlorination should be checked periodically by quality control to make certain that desired results are obtained.

Some form of boiler water treatment is also necessary in many plants, and quality control may serve as a check on certain abnormal boiler practices. Inadequate treatment of the boiler water, or improper boiler operation may adversely affect the processed cans by causing external detinning, removal of outside enamel or lithography, form an unsightly white deposit on the cans, or even contaminate the product during preparation..

In examining cans after processing and cooling, the quality control technologist should be alert for conditions of this type in order that an immediate check of the boiler operation may be made to determine the source of the difficulty.

TESTING CANNED FOODS

Following are descriptions of some of the laboratory procedures used more generally to ascertain quality of canned foods for determination of compliance with grade and standards. For a more comprehensive explanation of these tests, the National Food Processors Association publication, *Laboratory Manual for Food Canners and Processors*, or *Total Quality Assurance for the Food Industry*, by Gould and Gould, may be consulted. That publication also includes other laboratory procedures used by the canning industry.

Vacuum

For taking the vacuum, the can or jar lid is punctured with a vacuum gauge. The lid should be punctured near the edge to minimize deformation of the lid by the pressure required to penetrate it. Cans should be read at room temperature, because a warm can will have a lower vacuum and a cold can a higher vacuum than they would have at room temperature. Readings on severely dented cans are lower than readings on normal cans. A reading on a can that is completely full or which contains too small a headspace is not always accurate, because the gauge tip may penetrate the product and fail to register, or air in the gauge itself may produce a large error causing the reading to be much too low.

Also available (Benthos, Inc.) is a portable electronic device for checking the condition of cans and glass containers inside sealed cases. The instrument taps on cans electronically. Frequency of tone heard indicates degree of vacuum or pressure in container. The instrument may also be used for in-line inspection for vacuum in cans and glass containers.

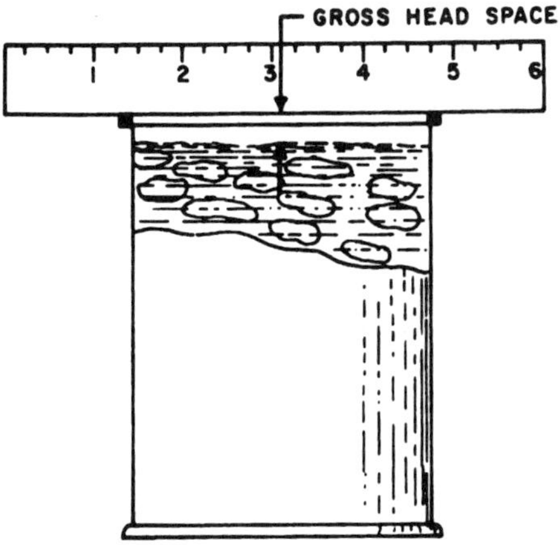

FIGURE 7.3 – Measuring Gross Headspace

Headspace

Gross headspace is the vertical distance from the top of the double seam of a can or the top edge of a glass jar to the level of product in the container. In determining the distance the headspace gauge or ruler is placed in such a position that the measuring rod can descend in a vertical position to the approximate center of the can. The rod is slowly pushed down until its end just penetrates the surface of the liquid. The point of intersection of the rule with the horizontal bar is then read; headspace is customarily read in $^1/_{32}$ inches.

In some instances, the solid portion of the product may extend above the liquid, and must be pushed below the liquid level before headspace is measured. In case the product will not remain below the liquid while the headspace measurement is being taken, it must be held down with a depressor. If a depressor is used, a correction equivalent to its liquid displacement should be added to the measured headspace.

The net headspace of a container having a double seam, such as a can, is the distance from the liquid level to the inside surface of the lid. This may be estimated by subtracting from the gross headspace $^6/_{32}$ of an inch (5 mm), the average height of the double seam.

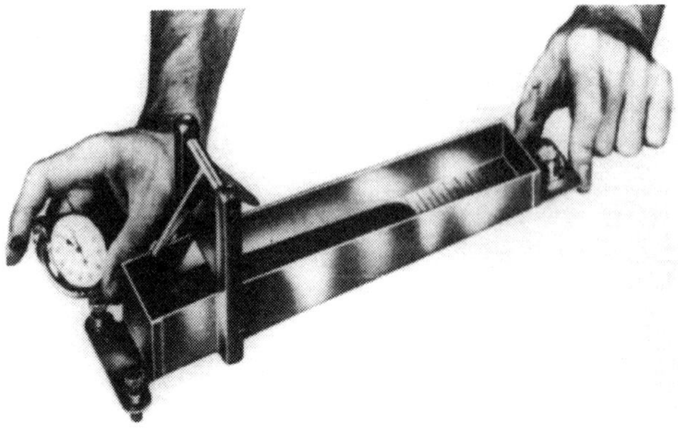

FIGURE 7.4 - Bostwick Consistometer
Measures the consistency of foods by measurement of the distance over which the material flows on a level surface under its own weight during a given time interval. (Courtesy Central Scientific Company)

Fill of Container – Cans

It is generally assumed in the canning industry that a container must be filled to not less than 90% of its total capacity. This is the standard of fill of container promulgated under the U.S. Food and Drug Law for canned tomatoes, cream-style corn, and pineapple juice. It is also included as a general requirement by the USDA Agricultural Marketing Service for establishing product grades for which no standard of fill of container has been promulgated. This requirement can be taken to mean that the net headspace of the container should not be greater than 10% of its internal height. It is possible, therefore, to compute the maximum gross headspace which is permissible in each size container.

The following formula may be used to calculate percent fill:

$$\text{Percent Fill} = 100 - (\text{Net Headspace}) \times C$$

where C = Percent Can Capacity per $^1/_{32}$ inch (per mm) Headspace.

If a table of capacity of can per $^1/_{32}$ inch (per mm) headspace is not available, calculate the inside height of the can by subtracting $^{12}/_{32}$inch (10 mm) from the total height of the can measured to the nearest $^1/_{32}$ inch (mm) and determine the net headspace of the contents by subtracting $^6/_{32}$inch (5 mm) from the gross headspace. The percent fill is obtained by subtracting the net headspace from the calculated inside height of the can, dividing this difference by the inside height of the can, and multiplying by 100.

$$\text{Percent Fill} = \frac{\text{Inside Height of Can} - \text{Net Headspace}}{\text{Inside Height of Can} \times 100}$$

FIGURE 7.5 – LabScan II Spectrocolorimeter combines a 0°/45° sensor linked to an IBM personal computer (Courtesy HunterLab)

Fill of Container - Glass Jars

In determining the fill of container of products packed in glass jars, the weight of water required to fill the jar level with the top (overflow capacity) is used in place of the "water capacity" as determined for cans. Because the diameters of glass jars usually are not exactly the same from top to bottom, the simplified method of obtaining percent fill cannot be used, but measurements of the weight of water required to fill the container to the actual headspace must be made.

The percent fill may be calculated as follows:

$$\text{Percent Fill (Jars)} = \frac{\text{Weight of Water to Actual Headspace}}{\text{Overflow Capacity} \times 100}$$

Fill of Container - Juice Products

In addition to determining if the product meets the general requirement of 90% fill described in the previous section, it is frequently necessary to know the volume fill in fluid ounces or cubic centimeters. This may be calculated from the weight of water at 68°F (20°C) required to fill the container to the actual headspace of the product. The following factors may be helpful in converting from avoirdupois ounces of water at 68°F (20°C) to fluid ounces and cubic centimeters.

Capacity in fluid ounces = Avoirdupois ounces of water at 20°C x 0.9603

Capacity in cubic centimeters = Avoirdupois ounces of water at 20°C x 28.40

Fluid ounces = Cubic Centimeters/0.03382

Fill/Drained Weight

Some of the USDA Standards for Grades of Canned Foods specify minimum drained weights for the product covered by the Standards. On the other hand, some thermal processes specify a maximum fill weight. It is important not to exceed specified maximum fill weights. A larger than specified fill weight would have the effect of lowering the Fo value of the thermal process given the product.

The maximum fill weight is the amount of solid component (i.e. - product such as cut green beans) filled into the can prior to the addition of packing medium (i.e. - brine, water, syrup, etc.). Containers tested for maximum fill weight should be drained of any product juices that may enter with the product.

Drained weight is determined by emptying the contents of a container upon the meshes of a circular screen. For all products except tomatoes, an 8-mesh screen (0.097 in. (2.5 mm) square openings) and for tomatoes a 2-mesh screen (0.446 in. (11 mm) openings with the wire 0.054 in. (1.4 mm) in diameter) is used. For cans containing less than 48 oz. (1.36 kg), an 8 in. screen is required, while for cans containing more than 48 oz. (1.36 kg) the screen should be 12 in. (30 cm) in diameter. All products except spinach are distributed evenly over the meshes of the sieve. Cut fruit is turned by hand to the cup down position so that the liquid can drain out of the cups. Except in the case of spinach, the screen is tilted so that one side is approximately two inches higher than the other. This may be accomplished by placing the sieve in a pan with one edge resting on the raised edge of the pan. Spinach is drained by removing the lid and inverting the can on the draining screen, after which the can is gently raised, leaving the spinach in a mound. The spinach is not disturbed during the draining period and the screen is not tilted, but the meshes of the screen should be raised above the bottom of the pan sufficiently to permit free drainage of liquid.

Exactly two minutes after the product is placed on the screen, the drained solids are weighed by one of the following procedures:

A) The screen containing the drained solids is placed directly on the balance and weighed; the weight of the draining screen is then subtracted. When several drained weights are to be determined, the additional weight of liquid which has seeped into cracks in the screen and cannot be wiped out during cleaning should be included in the tare (this is usually 0.05-0.10 oz. (1-3 g)). The liquid which continues to drain from the screen is held by the balance pan, or a separate pan must be tared with the screen to catch the drainings. For the most accurate work, the screen should be clean and dried between each sample. Sample should be weighed to 0.1 oz. or nearest gram.

B) The solids are transferred from the draining screen to a tared pan or dish and weighed to 0.1 oz. or nearest gram. In this method, the liquid which clings to the meshes of the draining screen is not weighed and the resulting drained weights are slightly lower than those obtained in Method A. The difference is less in samples containing non-viscous syrup or brine than in samples with viscous syrup.

Method A is specified in U.S. Food and Drug standards for fruit cocktail, tomatoes, corn and green beans for separating solid and liquid portions. It is also specified by the USDA for U.S. grades.

Method B is used for determining the drained weights of peas and pineapple, and, in California, for determining the drained weight of spinach.

Control of the filling operation is best achieved by analyzing data from a shift or period using statistical methods. The data collected should be evaluated using average, range, and standard deviation. Of these, standard deviation is the best measure of filling line efficiency. Since most food product filling operations fit a normal distribution pattern the following formula can be used to calculate standard deviation:

$s = (x-x)/(n-1)$

s = the standard deviation
x = the value of an item in the sample
x = the average of the sample
n = the number of items in the sample.

In-line equipment, such as check weighers, are helpful in increasing filling operation efficiency by rejecting containers that fall outside pre-set limits. Some models also do a statistical review of the containers monitored.

Cut-Out-Brix

This shows the amount of soluble solids in the liquid portion of canned fruits in terms of percent by weight of sugar. (Almost all of these solids are sugar and for practical purposes may be regarded as sugar.) The sugar in the liquid is a mixture of the sugar added to the container in the syrup used as a packing medium and the sugar dissolved out of the fruit in the container. The final concentration or cut-out Brix therefore depends on four factors:

1. The weight of fruit in the container
2. The percent of sugar in the fruit
3. The weight of syrup added to the container
4. The percent of sugar in the syrup (Brix).

With small units, such as cherries, the weight of fruit and of added syrup in each can is quite uniform and the cut-out Brix of successive containers will be similarly close to each other. But with large units, such as large half-pears, the weight of fruit that can be put in each container varies greatly. The amount of syrup that can be added varies similarly and the cut-out Brix of successive containers will show large variations.

The cut-out Brix may be determined with a Brix hydrometer (or Saccharometer). Two hydrometers should be provided, one reading from 10–20% and the other from 20–30%. A glass or metal cylinder of about 200 milliliters (ml) capacity should also be available. The hydrometers should be graduated at 68°F (20°C) rather than any lower temperature. When the hydrometer has come to rest in the syrup in the cylinder, the reading should be taken at the level of the liquid rather than where the liquid rises around the stem of the hydrometer.

The cut-out Brix may also be determined with a refractometer. Only one drop of the liquid is needed. Some refractometers have a sugar scale which will also show the Brix direct. When only the refractive index is given, it is necessary to use a conversion table to show the cut-out Brix.

TABLE 7.1 – Relation Between the Refractive Index at 68°F (20°C) and the Percent by Weight of Sugar (Brix)

Percent Sugar (Brix)	Refractive Index (68°F)	Percent Sugar (Brix)	Refractive Index (68°F)
10	1.3478	41	1.4016
11	1.3494	42	1.4036
12	1.3505	43	1.4056
13	1.3525	44	1.4076
14	1.3541	45	1.4096
15	1.3557	46	1.4117
16	1.3573	47	1.4137
17	1.3589	48	1.4158
18	1.3605	49	1.4179
19	1.3622	50	1.4200
20	1.3638	51	1.4221
21	1.3655	52	1.4242
22	1.3672	53	1.4264
23	1.3689	54	1.4285
24	1.3708	55	1.4307
25	1.3723	56	1.4329
26	1.3740	57	1.4351
27	1.3758	58	1.4373
28	1.3775	59	1.4396
29	1.3793	60	1.4418
30	1.3811	61	1.4441
31	1.3829	62	1.4464
32	1.3847	63	1.4486
33	1.3865	64	1.4509
34	1.3883	65	1.4532
35	1.3902	66	1.4555
36	1.3920	67	1.4579
37	1.3939	68	1.4603
38	1.3958	69	1.4627
39	1.3978	70	1.4651
40	1.3997		

For strict accuracy, it is necessary to take the temperature of the syrup at the time the Brix is determined–by either the spindle or the refractometer, or make a correction. If the determination is made at ordinary room temperature, the correction is small. Prior to making Brix readings, the refractometer should be adjusted to read a refractive index of 1.3330 for distilled water at 68°F(20°C).

Flavor

It is advisable to include flavor evaluation as a responsibility of the quality control department. The quality control supervisor should select the flavor evaluation test that he deems adequate for the product under consideration.

Net Weight

This is determined by subtracting the weight of the dried empty container from the weight of the full container. It is usually reported to the nearest 0.1 oz.or gram.

pH Measurement

pH measurements are made almost exclusively with line operated meters with a variety of electrode(s). The determination is usually made on a small amount of syrup or brine poured from the can into a beaker, but in some instances the electrode(s) may be inserted directly into the can. In the latter case, the can should be placed on some non-conducting surface to avoid current fluctuations. However, where pH is a factor of a filed, acidified process, the test must be performed on a blended sample as prescribed in 21 CFR 114.9.

Total Acidity

For routine work, acidity usually is determined on a 10 ml sample of syrup or brine, but for greater accuracy, a 10 gram sample of the entire can contents, after blending, should be used. pH meters or electrometric titrimeters are being used more and more in place of visual indicators to detect titration end points. Samples should be titrated to an end point of 8.1, which corresponds approximately to the phenolphthalein end point. Results are expressed as percent of anhydrous citric acid with the following exceptions: grapes and grape juice as tartaric acid, apples and apple juice as malic acid, catsup and various hot sauces as acetic acid, and sauerkraut and other fermented products as lactic acid.

PURCHASING RAW PRODUCTS FOR CANNING

Most products are bought on the basis of some specifications. Much progress has been made in developing more precise descriptions of the kinds of materials the processor must have in order to produce the types of canned product desired. Instruments, such as the Tenderometer for testing raw peas, the shear-press for determining food texture and firmness, and color and color difference instruments have been devised to assist in the accurate appraisal of many products.

Certain of the specifications are in the form of Official Government Grades. Some state marketing bureaus have their special standards. Canners groups, such as the California League of Food Processors, have assisted their members in purchasing fruits. Any processor may obtain any or all of this information to aid in formulating a buying policy to fit individual circumstances.

Each lot of produce should be examined at the factory and paid for on the basis of its quality for canning and yield of processed product. Usually the processor enters into a contract with each grower for the purchase of all of produce from a stated number of acres on the basis of suitability for canning of each load as it is delivered to the factory. The processor pays more for carefully selected produce than for the field-run delivery.

It is possible for the processor to employ official graders to test each load. This is usually done through an agreement with the State Department of Agriculture or other appropriate agency. Many processors do their own testing. Carefully worded specifications that are thoroughly understood by both the grower and the processor help preserve friendly relations that are so essential to a continuing and expanding industry.

Many canners employ one or more "fieldmen" to keep track of the produce that is to be canned. They are in frequent touch with each grower all through the season. Usually, the processor furnishes seed so to obtain the desired particular variety. The more desirable varieties of fruits and vegetables usually bring higher prices to the growers. The time of planting is regulated to try to spread the canning season over as long a period as possible. The fieldman says when each plot is to be harvested. Only by such far-sighted planning can an operator be sure of enough tonnage of the right produce to keep his factory running efficiently.

The Past and Future of Quality Control

The strive for quality in the food industry has been evolutionary. Historically, production was monitored during operation for fill of container, brine and syrup composition and closing machine operations and the like, doing the best with the material available; then after the work was completed at the end of the day, a review of records might have been conducted. The following day an opening of samples of the previous day's production or "cutting" was performed and occasionally compared with a competitor's samples. This was and is called Quality Control.

As standards were developed so were more precise methods of evaluating and producing products; these methods were called Statistical Quality Control and Statistical Process Control or SQC and SPC, respectively. During the 1950s another method of optimizing a process to accommodate changing conditions called evolutionary operations or EVOP came into existence.

In the 1960s the term Quality Assurance became popular and continues to be so. According to Gould and Gould (1988) "Quality assurance is the modern term for describing the control, evaluation and audit of a food processing system. Its primary function is to provide confidence for management and the ultimate customer." A quality assurance program is built around a quality control program.

The food industry, like other industries, continued to improve quality and production operations to improve profitability. During the 1970s a management tool called Quality Circles, the concept of which originated in the U.S. but was developed in Japan, came back into practice in the U.S. (Bregande,1982). The Quality Circle principle is the involvement of workers who have shared areas of responsibility. These workers attend classes in group communication processes, quality strategies, and measurement and problem-solving techniques. This training encourages the workers to discuss and evaluate quality problems, recommend solutions and take corrective action.

Because of continued pressure from international companies, another management tool, called Total Quality Management (TQM), became popular in the 1980. Fulks (1991) states that the utilization of TQM would greatly improve a company's ability to survive global competition during the 1990s, and defines quality management as "a systematic way of guaranteeing that organized activities happen the way they are planned; it is a management discipline concerned with preventing problems from occurring by creating the attitudes and controls that make prevention possible."

Fulks (1991) identifies some of the steps which management can follow in implementing a TQM program as:

- Making a total quality management a priority starting with top management;
- Eliminating barriers to effective communication in both directions between the worker and the supervisor;
- Drafting a mission statement identifying the company's goals in terms that are understandable to all;
- Creating an environment that encourages total quality, such as improving the production facility to make the workplace easy to function in;
- Practicing sound management principles by relieving tension, where possible;
- Maintaining an ongoing awareness of plant problems;
- Instituting a system to measure results; and
- Providing an employee training program.

Although the European Community (EC) began in 1957, it was December 1992 that an internal European market was finalized. This market consists of 12 member states with a goal to encourage trade and to increase confidence in the safety and reliability of products marketed within. Concurrently, there was a movement for the International Organization for Standardization (ISO) based in Geneva, Switzerland to develop a unified set of standards to control the flow of goods between nations. In 1987, the ISO published the ISO 9000 series of international standards which have become an internationally recognized common language for quality, encouraging global trade and helping to improve the economies of the world. These standards have been adopted by 74 countries through out the world (Peach, 1994). The standards were modeled after British Standards (BS) 5750 with considerable input from the U.S. and Canada. The American National Standards Institute (ANSI) represents the U.S. at ISO.

In the U.S., the standards are published as the ANSI/ASQC Q9000, (previously known as Q90); the EC publishes the standards as the European Norm (EN) 2900 series.

According to Peach (1994), the two main roles of the ISO 9000 Series are to provide guidance for suppliers of all types of products who want to implement effective quality systems in their organizations or to improve their existing quality systems and provide generic requirements against which a customer can evaluate the adequacy of a supplier's quality system. This is done by establishing consistent quality practices that cross international borders, providing a common language or set of terms, minimizing the need for on-site customer visits or audits and to harmonize international trade by supplying a set of standards with worldwide credibility and acceptance.

The ISO 9000 Series is composed of five standards: ISO 9000-1 and 9004-1 are guidance standards providing guidance to "all organizations for quality management purposes," while ISO 9001, 9002 and 9003 are conformance standards used for external quality assurance to provide confidence to the customer that the company's quality system will provide a satisfactory product or service (Peach, 1994). ISO 9001 covers specifications for the design/development, production, installation and services industries. ISO 9002 covers specifications for production and installation operations, while ISO 9003 covers specifications for final inspection and test procedures. ISO 9001 and 9002 are the most applicable for the food industry (Anonymous, 1992). To become registered, an organization undergoes an audit by a third-party called a registrar; the registrar is a private and independent organization competent in the audit process and the applicant's field of activity. A successful audit results in a registration certificate which states that the applicant is within compliance to a quality standard.

ISO 9001 is the most comprehensive standard requiring a company to develop a system that meets 20 basic requirements. ISO 9002 permits registration of a quality system when design control and after servicing are not required by agreements. ISO 9003 is a model for quality assurance in final inspection and test and is the least comprehensive standard composed of only 12 standards.

To begin the process of obtaining registration, a company first determines the desired standard. As mentioned earlier most food companies should consider registering to either ISO 9001 or 9002 standard. The company then defines the products, services, and corporate locations that will be covered by the registered quality system and then registers the system which covers just the production of specific goods which are produced at specific locations.

Surak (1992) outlines the following steps in obtaining registration to an ISO standard:

1. A commitment by top management that will be actively involved in the implementation process.
2. The formation of an ISO Steering Team which will be responsible for the development and implementation of the plan which will lead to registration.
3. Supply the necessary training in ISO standard, registration process, and audit procedures to all employees who can affect the quality of the products.
4. Develop a Quality Manual which describes the quality management system, procedures and work instructions.
5. Begin internal audits to determine the effectiveness of the quality management system.
6. Select a Registrar.
7. Conduct a pre-assessment to determine if major problems in the quality system exist.
8. Correct any pre-assessment problems.
9. Make arrangements for the formal assessment by the Registrar.
10. Correct deficiencies.
11. Obtain registration from Registrar.
12. Maintain proper surveillance to maintain registration.

What is the Difference between TQM and ISO 9000? According to Peach (1994), ISO 9000 series requirements are clearly defined, but how the requirements are to be met is left largely to the organization. Clear documentation of all work processes affecting quality is required, but how that documentation is written is not defined.

TQM systems have no firm requirements other than to meet and/or exceed customer needs through an understanding of the organization and effects of current management practices and by the use of applied statistics.

ISO 9000 series has clear requirements that may or may not be significant in TQM. ISO 9000 requirements dictate that contract review be addressed in specific terms while TQM leaves the details entirely up to the organization

Although TQM, ISO 9000 and HACCP are compatible, one does not replace the other. Surak (1992) offers a good review of ISO 9000 while Peach's Handbook offers significantly more detailed information.

References

Anonymous. October 1992. "Eurowatch-ISO 9000." *Prepared Foods*, p. 58.

Bregande, Michael D. "Statistics in Quality Control–An Overview in Basic Statistics." Symposium Special Report No. 44, p. 1-8. New York State Agriculture Experiment Station.

Fulks, Fred T. July 1991. "Total Quality Management." *Journal of Food Technology*, p. 96-101.

Gould, Wilbur A. and Ronald W. Gould. 1993. *Total Quality Assurance for the Food Industries*. CTI Publications, Inc., Baltimore, MD.

Kramer, Amihud and Bernard A. Twigg. 1970. *Quality Control for the Food Industry*. 3rd Ed., Vol. 1&2. The AVI Publishing Company, Inc., Westport, CT.

National Canners Association. 1968. *Laboratory Manual for Food Canners and Processors*, 3rd Ed., Vol. 1&2. The AVI Publishing Company, Inc., Westport, CT.

Peach, Robert W. 1994. *The ISO 9000 Handbook*. 2nd Ed. CEEM Information Services, Fairfax, VA.

Surak, John G. November 1992. "The ISO 9000 Standards–Establishing a Foundation for Quality." *Journal of Food Technology* , p. 74-80.

ACKNOWLEDGEMENT

The author wishes to acknowledge the contribution of Donald E. Hawbecker, Comstock Michigan Fruit Div., Curtice Burns Foods, Inc. in revising this chapter.

CHAPTER 8

Hazard Analysis and Critical Control Point Inspection (HACCP)

HACCP is a voluntary program administered in the U.S. by the FDA, Food Safety and Inspection Service (FSIS) of USDA and the National Marine Fisheries Service (NMFS) of the U.S. Department of Commerce. It is a systems approach that eliminates risk in producing a food product by attempting to anticipate all possible hazards, specify procedures for eliminating avoidable risks and set acceptable limits for unavoidable ones.

The HACCP concept had its beginning in the 1960s at the Pillsbury Co., the U.S. Army Natick Research and Development Laboratories, and the National Aeronautics and Space Administration in their joint effort to develop foods for the U.S. space program (Sperber, 1991). According to Bauman (1990) "The most difficult part of the program was to come as close as possible to 100% assurance that the food products we were producing for space use would not be contaminated with pathogens, either bacterial or viral, that could cause an illness that might result in a failed or even catastrophic mission."

The Pillsbury Co. presented the HACCP concept publicly at the first Conference for Food Protection in 1971 and in the following year conducted a three-week workshop for FDA inspectors, which culminated in the use of HACCP principles in the Thermally Processed Low Acid Canned Foods in Hermetically Sealed Containers regulations, which became effective in 1973. Since that time many food companies and government agencies around the world have initiated HACCP principles.

The Hazard Analysis and Critical Control Point inspection approach compliments traditional inspection methods. It determines which points in a process are critical to the safety and sanitary quality of a product and how well a firm controls these points. This new FDA inspection approach is preventive in nature, attempting to bring potential dangers to the attention of management for before-the-fact corrective action. The continued development of this trouble-preventing approach to plant inspections is an important objective in regulatory programs. Ultimately, it should insure that the consumer is not exposed to substandard, potentially unsanitary or hazardous foods resulting from improper plant practices.

In 1980, the FSIS, FDA, NMFS, and the U.S. Army Natick Research entered into an agreement with the National Academy of Sciences where by the Academy was to provide guidance on the best manner to develop uniform approaches to be used to establish microbiological criteria for foods (Shank, 1991). This agreement led to the establishment of the National Advisory Committee on Microbiological Criteria for Foods.

After many meetings and reviewing, a report prepared by the HACCP Working Group of the Codex Committee on Food Hygiene, a final document, "Hazard Analysis and Critical Control Point System," to guide the industry in the implementation of HACCP systems, was submitted.

After reviewing available literature on the subject of HACCP, The International Life Science Institute (ILSI) Scientific Committee on Microbiology concluded that "the description and definitions used in various texts lack consistency, there is no simple 'how-to-do-it' guide for users, and, there is no explanatory summary text which can be used by decision-makers in industry and government who wish to learn about the concept." With this in mind, the ILSI Committee developed "A Simple Guide to Understanding and Applying the HACCP Concept." In their guide, the ILSI Committee states that the ideal time to implement HACCP is when a product or process is being developed to permit potential hazards to be "designed out" at the earliest stage. For existing products, a HACCP study should be carried out according to their plan. The guide further states that a HACCP study should be carried out before making any significant changes in, "for example, raw and packaging materials, production line layout, product formulation or product use."

The Microbiology & Food Safety Committee of the National Food Processors Association (NFPA) stated in conclusion of a document, "Implementation of HACCP in A Food Processing Plant," that "the HACCP concept, which focuses on food safety, is a systematic approach to hazard identification, assessment, and control. The system offers a rational approach to the control of biological, chemical, and physical hazards in foods; it avoids many weaknesses inherent in the traditional, end-product inspection approach. The focus of the system is to direct attention to the control of key factors that affect the safety of the food. HACCP is applicable to all parts of the food chain from production, through processing, to use in the home."

In July 1993, the Codex Alimentarius Commission adopted the basic principles of HACCP and published "Guidelines for the Application of the HACCP System," which stated that "the application of HACCP is compatible with the implementation of quality management systems, such as the ISO 9000 series, and is the system of choice in the management of food safety within such systems. (Gruspaardt-Vink, 1995) By December 14, 1995, all food companies in the European Union (EU) will be required to have in place an effective HACCP system. This is the result of the directive concerning food product hygiene (EEC directive 93/43) which was passed June 14, 1993 by the Council of Europe.

"In concrete terms, this means that by the end of this year every food company in the EU will be required to apply HACCP principles: not only the international food product concerns and medium-size companies, but also the baker around the corner and other small businesses, including catering establishments."

In the August 4, 1994, *Federal Register,* the FDA published "Advance Notice of Proposed Rulemaking," asking for public comment about whether and how the agency should develop regulations that would establish requirements for a new comprehensive food safety assurance program for both domestically produced and imported foods. Such regulations, if promulgated, would enhance FDA's ability to ensure the safety of the U.S. food supply. In their request, the FDA proposed that the program be based upon the principles of HACCP.

In the August 4 publication, FDA makes reference to the fact that "HACCP is becoming the worldwide standard to ensure the safety of food and will thus serve as basis for harmonizing U.S. food safety regulations with those of other nations." Predictably, with an issue of this magnitude, it will take time to get agreement among all interested parties as illustrated by the January 9, 1995 report in *The Food Chemical News* that the European Union "has objected to the FDA's blueprint for a mandatory HACCP System for the food industry, saying such a concept is too bureaucratic and places unnecessary restrictions on the application of HACCP principles."

Since the concept of the HACCP System was initiated in the U.S. and formalized by the National Advisory Committee on Microbiological Criteria for Foods (NACMCF), the document has been reprinted here in its entirety.

HAZARD ANALYSIS AND CRITICAL CONTROL POINT SYSTEM

National Advisory Committee on Microbiological Criteria for Foods

(Adopted March 20, 1992)

CONTENTS

1. EXECUTIVE SUMMARY

The National Advisory Committee on Microbiological Criteria for Foods (Committee) reconvened a Hazard Analysis and Critical Control Point (HACCP) Working Group in July 1991. The primary purpose was to review the Committee's November 1989, HACCP document, comparing it with a draft report prepared by a HACCP Working Group of the Codex Committee on Food Hygiene. Based upon its review, the Committee has determined to expand upon its initial report by emphasizing the concept of prevention, incorporating a decision tree intended to facilitate the identification of Critical Control Points (CCPs), and providing a more detailed explanation of the application of HACCP principles.

The Committee again endorses HACCP as an effective and rational means of assuring food safety from harvest to consumption. Preventing problems from occurring is the paramount goal underlying any HACCP system. Seven basic principles are employed in the development of HACCP plans that meet the stated goal. These principles include hazard assessment, CCP identification, establishing critical limits, monitoring procedures, corrective actions, documentation, and verification procedures. Under such systems, if a deviation occurs indicating that control has been lost, the deviation is detected and appropriate steps are taken to reestablish control in a timely manner to assure that potentially hazardous products do not reach the consumer.

In the application of HACCP, the use of microbiological testing is seldom an effective means of monitoring critical control points (CCPs) because of the time required to obtain results. In most instances, monitoring of CCPs can best be accomplished through the use of physical and chemical tests, and through visual observations. Microbiological criteria do, however, play a role in verifying that the overall HACCP system is working.

The Committee believes that the HACCP principles should be standardized to create uniformity in its work, and in training and applying the HACCP system by industry and regulatory authorities. In accordance with the National Academy of Sciences recommendation, the HACCP system must be developed by each food establishment and tailored to its individual products, processing and distribution conditions.

In keeping with its charge of providing recommendations to its sponsoring agencies regarding microbiological food safety issues, this document focuses on this area. The Committee recognizes that in order to assure food safety, properly designed HACCP systems must also consider chemical and physical hazards, in addition to other biological hazards.

In order for a successful HACCP program to be implemented, management must be committed to a HACCP approach. A commitment by management will indicate an awareness of the benefits and costs of HACCP, and include education and training of employees. Benefits, in addition to food safety, are a better use of resources and a timely response to problems.

The Committee designed this document to guide the food industry in the implementation of HACCP systems. The Committee recommends that future documents address the role of regulatory agencies in the HACCP system.

2. DEFINITIONS

2.1 CCP Decision Tree: A sequence of questions to determine whether a control point is a CCP.

2.2 Continuous Monitoring: Uninterrupted collection and recording of data, such as temperature on a strip chart.

2.3 Control: (a) To manage the conditions of an operation to maintain compliance with established criteria. (b) The state wherein correct procedures are being followed and criteria are being met.

2.4 Control Point: Any point, step, or procedure at which biological, physical, or chemical factors can be controlled.

2.5 Corrective Action: Procedures to be followed when a deviation occurs.

2.6 Criterion: A requirement on which a judgment or decision can be based.

2.7 Critical Control Point (CCP): A point, step, or procedure at which control can be applied and a food safety hazard can be prevented, eliminated, or reduced to acceptable levels.

2.8 Critical Defect: A deviation at a CCP which may result in a hazard.

2.9 Critical Limit: A criterion that must be met for each preventive measure associated with a critical control point.

2.10 Deviation: Failure to meet a critical limit.

2.11 HACCP Plan: The written document which is based upon the principles of HACCP and which delineates the procedures to be followed to assure the control of a specific process or procedure.

2.12 HACCP System: The result of the implementation of the HACCP plan.

2.13 HACCP Team: The group of people who are responsible for developing a HACCP plan.

2.14 HACCP Plan Revalidation: One aspect of verification in which a documented periodic review of the HACCP plan is done by the HACCP team with the purpose of modifying the HACCP plan as necessary.

2.15 HACCP Plan Validation: The initial review by the HACCP team to ensure that all elements of the HACCP plan are accurate.

2.16 Hazard: A biological, chemical, or physical property that may cause a food to be unsafe for consumption.

2.17 Monitor: To conduct a planned sequence of observations or measurements to assess whether a CCP is under control and to produce an accurate record for future use in verification.

2.18 Preventive Measure: Physical, chemical, or other factors that can be used to control an identified health hazard.

2.19 Random Checks: Observations or measurements which are performed to supplement the scheduled evaluations required by the HACCP plan.

2.20 Risk: An estimate of the likely occurrence of a hazard.

2.21 Sensitive Ingredient: An ingredient known to have been associated with a hazard and for which there is reason for concern.

2.22 Severity: The seriousness of a hazard.

2.23 Target Levels: Criteria which are more stringent than critical limits and which are used by an operator to reduce the risk of a deviation.

2.24 Verification: The use of methods, procedures, or tests in addition to those used in monitoring to determine if the HACCP system is in compliance with the HACCP plan and/or whether the HACCP plan needs modification and revalidation.

3. PURPOSE AND PRINCIPLES

HACCP is a systematic approach to food safety consisting of seven principles:

3.1 Conduct a hazard analysis. Prepare a list of steps in the process where significant hazards occur and describe the preventive measures.

3.2 Identify the CCPs in the process.

3.3 Establish critical limits for preventive measures associated with each identified CCP.

3.4 Establish CCP monitoring requirements. Establish procedures for using the results of monitoring to adjust the process and maintain control.

3.5 Establish corrective actions to be taken when monitoring indicates that there is a deviation from an established critical limit.

3.6 Establish effective record-keeping procedures that document the HACCP system.

3.7 Establish procedures for verification that the HACCP system is working correctly.

4. EXPLANATION AND APPLICATION OF PRINCIPLES

The HACCP concept is relevant to all stages throughout the food chain from growing, harvesting, processing, manufacturing, distributing, and merchandising, to preparing food for consumption. Certain points in the food chain are better suited to the application of the HACCP principles. For example, food manufacturing facilities are very well suited to the adoption of the HACCP concept. The Committee recommends the adoption of HACCP to the fullest extent possible and reasonable throughout the food chain.

The Committee recognizes that education and training is an important element of the HACCP concept. Employees who will be responsible for the HACCP program must be adequately trained in the principles of HACCP, its application and implementation. However, education and training programs do not have to be limited to those directly involved with HACCP and its implementation. Educational and training programs should be designed to address the needs of industry, government and academic personnel, as well as consumers. Educating home food handlers in the recognition and application of critical control points will improve the safety of foods prepared in the home. It is recommended that educational materials be provided to home food handlers that address the safe acquisition and proper handling of foods.

The following figure lists steps used in the application of Principle 1.

FIGURE 8.1 – First Six Steps for the Development of a HACCP Plan

1. Assemble the HACCP Team

↓

2. Describe the Food and its Distribution

↓

3. Identify Intended Use and Consumers of the Food

↓

4. Develop Flow Diagram

↓

5. Verify Flow Diagram

↓

6. Conduct Hazard Analysis

(a) Identify and List Steps in the Process Where the Hazards of Potential Significance Occur

(b) List All Identified Hazards Associated with Each Step

(c) List Preventive Measures to Control Hazards

(a) Step	(b) Identified Hazard	(c) Preventive Measures

4.1 Assemble the HACCP team.

The first step in developing a HACCP plan is to assemble a HACCP team consisting of individuals who have specific knowledge and expertise appropriate to the product and process. It is the team's responsibility to develop each step of the HACCP plan. The team should be multi-disciplinary (e.g., engineering, production, sanitation, quality assurance, food microbiology). The team should include local personnel who are directly involved in the daily processing activities, as they are more familiar with the variability and limitations of the operation. In addition, this fosters a sense of ownership among those who must implement the plan. The HACCP team might require outside experts who are knowledgeable in the potential microbiological and other public health risks associated with the product and the process. However, a plan which is developed totally by outside sources will likely be erroneous, incomplete, and lacking in support at the local level.

Due to the technical nature of the information required for a hazard analysis, it is recommended that experts who are knowledgeable about the food and process should either participate in or verify the completeness of the hazard analysis and the HACCP plan. These individuals should have the knowledge and experience to correctly (a) identify potential hazards; (b) assign levels of severity and risk; (c) recommend controls, criteria, and procedures for monitoring and verification; (d) recommend appropriate corrective actions when a deviation occurs; (e) recommend research related to the HACCP plan, if important information is not known; and (f) predict the success of the HACCP plan.

4.2 Describe the food and the method of its distribution.

A separate HACCP plan must be developed for each food product that is being processed in the establishment. The HACCP team must first fully describe the food. This consists of a full description of the food, including the recipe or formulation. The method of distribution should be described, along with information on whether the food is to be distributed frozen, refrigerated, or shelf stable. Consideration should also be given to the potential for abuse in the distribution channel and by consumers.

4.3 Identify the intended use and consumers of the food.

The intended use of the food should be based upon the normal use of the food by end users or consumers. The intended consumers may be the general public or a particular segment of the population, such as infants, the elderly, etc.

4.4 Develop a flow diagram which describes the process.

The purpose of the diagram is to provide a clear, simple description of the steps involved in the process. The diagram will be helpful to the HACCP team in its subsequent work. The diagram can also serve as a future guide for others (e.g., regulatory officials and customers) who must understand the process for their verification activities.

The scope of the flow diagram must cover all the steps in the process which are directly under the control of the establishment. In addition, the flow diagram can include steps in the food chain which are before and after the processing that occurs in the establishment. For the sake of simplicity, the flow diagram should consist solely of words, not engineering drawings.

4.5 Verify flow diagram.

The HACCP team should inspect the operation to verify the accuracy and completeness of the flow diagram. The diagram should be modified as necessary.

4.6 **Principle No. 1.** Conduct a hazard analysis. Prepare a list of steps in the process where significant hazards occur and describe the preventive measures.

The HACCP team next conducts a hazard analysis and identifies the steps in the process where hazards of potential significance can occur. For inclusion in the list, the hazards must be of such a nature that their prevention, elimination or reduction to acceptable levels is essential to the production of a safe food. Hazards which are of a low risk and not likely to occur would not require further consideration. The team must then consider what preventive measures, if any, exist which can be applied for each hazard. Preventive measures are physical, chemical, or other factors that can be used to control an identified health hazard. More than one preventive measure may be required to control a specific hazard. More than one hazard may be controlled by a specified preventive measure.

The hazard analysis and identification of associated preventive measures accomplishes three purposes: First, those hazards of significance and associated preventive measures are identified. Second, the analysis can be used to modify a process or product to further assure or improve safety. Third, the analysis provides a basis for determining CCPs in Principle 2 (Section 4.7).

The hazard analysis procedure differs from the Committee's original HACCP document. This does not negate the validity of current HACCP plans, based on the earlier method of hazard analysis. The procedures outlined in this document are recommended for future use. The hazard analysis consists of asking a series of questions which are appropriate to the specific food process and establishment. It is not possible in these recommendations to provide a list of all the questions which may be pertinent to a specific food or process. The hazard analysis should question the effect of a variety of factors upon the safety of the food. Appendix A lists examples of questions that may be considered during the hazard analysis. The original hazard analysis format is included as Appendix B for comparison.

The hazard analysis must consider factors which may be beyond the immediate control of the processor. For example, product distribution may be beyond the immediate control of the processor, but information on how the food will be distributed could influence, for example, how the food will be processed.

During the hazard analysis, the potential significance of each hazard should be assessed by considering its risk and severity. Risk is an estimate of the likely occurrence of a hazard. The estimate of risk is usually based upon a combination of experience, epidemiological data, and information in the technical literature. Severity is the seriousness of a hazard.

The HACCP team has the initial responsibility to decide which hazards are significant and must be addressed in the HACCP plan. This decision can be debatable. There may be differences of opinion, even among experts, as to the risk of a hazard. The HACCP team must rely upon the opinion of the experts who assist in the development of the HACCP plan.

During the hazard analysis, safety concerns must be differentiated from quality concerns. Hazard is defined as a biological, chemical or physical property that may cause a food to be unsafe for consumption. The term, 'hazard,' as used in this document, is limited to safety. The HACCP team must make the determination whether a potential problem is a safety concern, and of its likelihood of occurrence.

Upon completion of the hazard analysis, the significant hazards associated with each step in the flow diagram should be listed along with any preventive measures to control the hazards (step 6 of Figure 8.1). This tabulation will be used in Principle 2 to determine CCPs.

For example, if a HACCP team were to conduct a hazard analysis for the production of frozen cooked beef patties (Appendix C), enteric pathogens in the raw meat would be identified as a potential hazard. Cooking is a preventive measure which can be used to eliminate this hazard. Thus, cooking would be listed along with the hazard (i.e., enteric pathogens) and the preventive measure as follows:

Step	Identified Hazard	Preventive Measures
5. Cooking	Enteric pathogens	Cooking sufficiently to kill enteric pathogens

4.7 **Principle No. 2.** Identify the CCPs in the process.

A critical control point is defined as a point, step or procedure at which control can be applied and a food safety hazard can be prevented, eliminated, or reduced to acceptable levels. All significant hazards identified by the HACCP team during the hazard analysis must be addressed.

The information developed during the hazard analysis in section 4.6 should enable the HACCP team to identify which steps in the process are CCPs.

Identification of each CCP can be facilitated by the use of a CCP decision tree (Figure 8.2). All hazards which reasonably could be expected to occur should be considered. Application of the CCP decision tree can help determine if a particular step is a CCP for a previously identified hazard.

Critical control points are located at any point where hazards need to be either prevented, eliminated, or reduced to acceptable levels. For example, a specified heat process, at a given time and temperature to destroy a specified microbiological pathogen, is a CCP. Likewise, refrigeration required to prevent hazardous microorganisms from multiplying, or the adjustment of a food to a pH necessary to prevent toxin formation, are also CCPs.

Examples of CCPs may include, but are not limited to: cooking, chilling, specific sanitation procedures, product formulation control, prevention of cross contamination, and certain aspects of employee and environmental hygiene.

CCPs must be carefully developed and documented. In addition, they must be used only for purposes of product safety.

Different facilities preparing the same food can differ in the risks of hazards and the points, steps, or procedures which are CCPs. This can be due to differences in each facility such as layout, equipment, selection of ingredients, or the process that is employed. Generic HACCP plans can serve as useful guides; however, it is essential that the unique conditions within each facility be considered during the development of a HACCP plan.

In addition to CCPs, nonfood safety concerns may be addressed at control points. These control points will not be further discussed in this document, because they do not relate to food safety and are not included in the HACCP plan.

4.8 **Principle No. 3.** Establish critical limits for preventive measures associated with each identified CCP.

4.8.1 A critical limit is defined as a criterion that must be met for each preventive measure associated with a CCP. Each CCP will have one or more preventive measures that must be properly controlled to assure prevention, elimination or reduction of hazards to acceptable levels. Each preventive measure has associated with it, critical limits that serve as boundaries of safety for each CCP. Critical limits may be set for preventive measures, such as temperature, time, physical dimensions, humidity, moisture level, water activity (a_w), pH, titratable acidity, salt concentration, available chlorine, viscosity, preservatives, or sensory information such as texture, aroma, and visual appearance. Critical limits may be derived from sources such as regulatory standards and guidelines, literature surveys, experimental studies, and experts. The food industry is responsible for engaging competent authorities to validate that the critical limits will control the identified hazard.

FIGURE 8.2 - Critical Control Point Decision Tree
(Apply at each step of process with an identified hazard.)

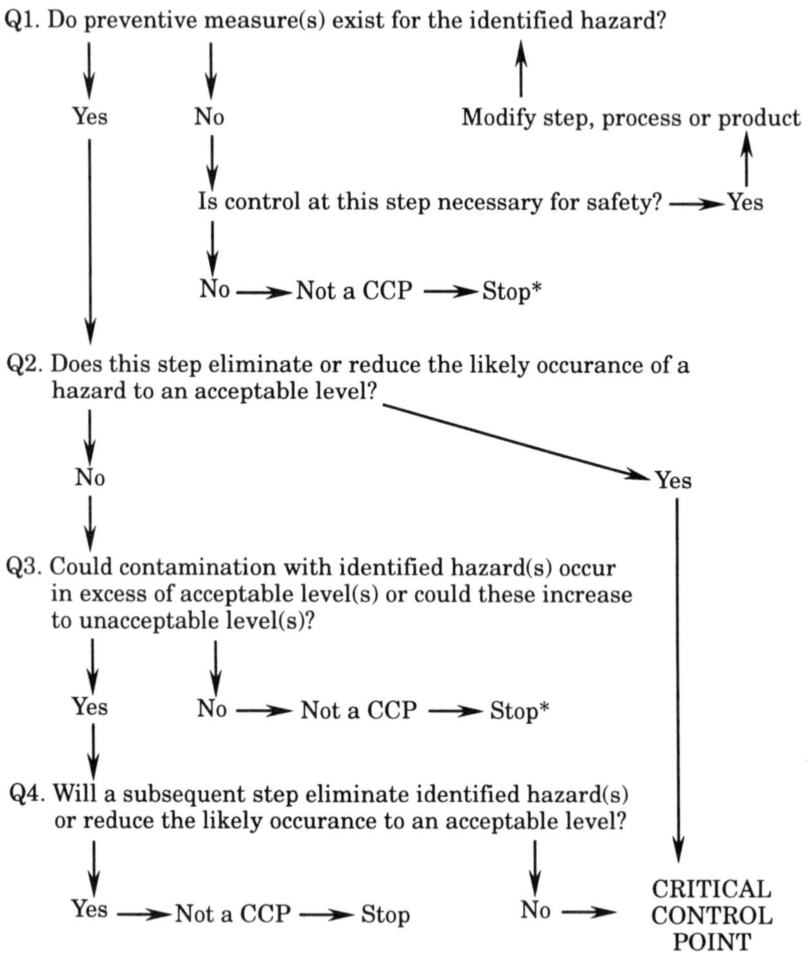
Q1. Do preventive measure(s) exist for the identified hazard?
Yes
No
Modify step, process or product
Is control at this step necessary for safety?
Yes
No
Not a CCP
Stop*
Q2. Does this step eliminate or reduce the likely occurance of a hazard to an acceptable level?
No
Yes
Q3. Could contamination with identified hazard(s) occur in excess of acceptable level(s) or could these increase to unacceptable level(s)?
Yes
No
Not a CCP
Stop*
Q4. Will a subsequent step eliminate identified hazard(s) or reduce the likely occurance to an acceptable level?
Yes
Not a CCP
Stop
No
CRITICAL CONTROL POINT

* Proceed to next step in the described process

For example, an acidified beverage that requires only hot fill and hold as a thermal process may have acid addition as a CCP. If insufficient acid is added, the product would be under-processed and allow the growth of pathogenic spore forming bacteria. One preventive measure for this CCP may be pH with a critical limit of pH 4.6. The critical limit for controlling a potential health hazard may be different from criteria associated with quality factors. For example, the product may be of unacceptable quality when the pH exceeds 3.8; however, a health hazard is avoided when the critical limit of pH 4.6 is not exceeded.

In some cases, processing variations may require certain target levels to assure that critical limits are attained. For example, a preventive measure and critical limit may be an internal product temperature of 160°F (71.1°C) during one stage of a process. The oven temperature, however, may be +5°F (2.8°C) at 160°F; thus an oven target temperature would have to be greater than 165°F (73.9°C) so that no product receives a cook of less than 160°F.

An example for Principle 3 is the cooking of beef patties (Appendix C). The process should be designed to eliminate the most heat-resistant vegetative pathogen which could reasonably be expected to be in the product. Criteria may be required for factors such as temperature, time and meat patty thickness. Technical development of the appropriate critical limits requires accurate information on the probable maximum numbers of these microorganisms in the meat and their heat resistance. The relationship between the CCP and its critical limits for the meat patty example is shown below:

Process/Step	CCP	Critical Limits
5. Cooking	Yes	Minimum internal temperature of patty: 145°F Oven temperature: _____°F Time; rate of heating and cooling (belt speed in rpm): _____rpm Patty thickness: _____in. Patty composition: e.g., all beef Oven humidity: _____% RH

4.9 <u>**Principle No. 4.** Establish CCP monitoring requirements. Establish procedures for using the results of monitoring to adjust the process and maintain control.</u>

4.9.1 Monitoring is a planned sequence of observations or measurements to assess whether a CCP is under control and produce an accurate record (Appendix D) for future use in verification. Monitoring serves three main purposes. First, monitoring is essential to food safety management in that it tracks the system's operation. If monitoring indicates that there is a trend towards loss of control, i.e., exceeding a target level, then action can be taken to bring the process back into control before a deviation occurs. Second, monitoring is used to determine when there is loss of control and a deviation occurs at a CCP, i.e., exceeding the critical limit. Corrective action must then be taken. Third, it provides written documentation for use in verification of the HACCP plan.

An unsafe food may result if a process is not properly controlled and a deviation occurs. Because of the potentially serious consequences of a critical defect, monitoring procedures must be effective. Ideally, monitoring should be at the 100% level. Continuous monitoring is possible with many types of physical and chemical methods. For example, the temperature and time for the scheduled thermal process of low-acid canned foods is recorded continuously on temperature recording charts. If the temperature falls below the scheduled temperature or the time is insufficient, as recorded on the chart, the retort load is retained as a process deviation. Likewise, pH measurement may be performed continually in fluids or by testing of a batch before processing. There are many ways to monitor CCP limits on a continuous or batch basis and record the data on charts. Continuous monitoring is always preferred when feasible. Equipment must be carefully calibrated for accuracy.

Assignment of the responsibility for monitoring is an important consideration for each CCP. Specific assignments will depend on the number of CCPs and preventive measures and the complexity of monitoring. Such individuals are often associated with production (e.g., line supervisors, selected line workers and maintenance personnel) and, as required, quality control personnel. Those individuals monitoring CCPs must be trained in the technique used to monitor each preventive measure; fully understand the purpose and importance of monitoring; have ready access to the monitoring activity; be unbiased in monitoring and reporting; and accurately report the monitoring activity. Personnel assigned the monitoring activity must report the results. Unusual occurrences must be reported immediately so that adjustments can be made in a timely manner to assure that the process remains under control. The person responsible for monitoring must also report a process or product that does not meet critical limits so that immediate corrective action can be taken.

When it is not possible to monitor a critical limit on a continuous basis, it is necessary to establish that the monitoring interval will be reliable enough to indicate that the hazard is under control. Statistically designed data collection or sampling systems lend themselves to this purpose. When using statistical process control, it is important to recognize that critical limits must not be exceeded. For example, when a pH of 4.6 or less is required for product safety, the maximum pH of the product may be set at a target that is below pH 4.6 to compensate for variation.

Most monitoring procedures for CCPs will need to be done rapidly, because they relate to on-line processes and there will not be time for lengthy analytical testing. Microbiological testing is seldom effective for monitoring CCPs due to their time-consuming nature. Therefore, physical and chemical measurements are preferred because they may be done rapidly and can indicate the conditions of microbiological control in the process.

Examples of measurements for monitoring include: Visual observations; Temperature; Time; pH; Moisture level.

Random checks may be useful for supplementing the monitoring of certain CCPs. They may be used to check incoming pre-certified ingredients, assess equipment and environmental sanitation, airborne contamination, cleaning and sanitizing of gloves and any place where follow-up is needed. Random checks may consist of physical and chemical testing and, as appropriate, microbiological tests.

With certain foods, such as microbiologically sensitive ingredients or imports, there may be no alternative to microbiological testing. However, it is important to recognize that a sampling frequency that is adequate for reliable detection of low levels of pathogens is seldom possible because of the large number of samples needed. For this reason, microbiological testing has limitations in a HACCP system, but is valuable as a means of establishing and randomly verifying the effectiveness of control at CCPs (challenge tests, random testing or for troubleshooting).

All records and documents associated with CCP monitoring must be signed or initialed by the person doing the monitoring.

4.10 **Principle No. 5.** Establish corrective action to be taken when monitoring indicates that there is a deviation from an established critical limit.

4.10.1 The HACCP system for food safety management is designed to identify potential health hazards and to establish strategies to prevent their occurrence. However, ideal circumstances do not always prevail and deviations from established processes may occur. For instance, where there is a deviation from established critical limits, corrective action plans must be in place to (a) determine the disposition of non-compliance product, (b) fix or correct the cause of non-compliance to assure that the CCP is under control, and (c) maintain records of the corrective actions that have been taken where there has been a deviation from critical limits. Because of the variations in CCPs for different foods and the diversity of possible deviations, specific corrective action plans must be developed for each CCP. The actions must demonstrate the CCP has been brought under control. Individuals who have a thorough understanding of the process, product and HACCP plan are to be assigned responsibility for taking corrective action. Corrective action procedures must be documented in the HACCP plan.

Should a deviation occur, the plant will place the product on hold pending completion of appropriate corrective actions and analyses. As appropriate, scientific experts and regulatory agencies are to be consulted to determine additional testing and disposition of the product.

Identification of deviant lots and corrective actions taken to assure safety of these lots must be noted in the HACCP record and remain on file for a reasonable period after the expiration date or expected shelf life of the product.

4.11 **Principle No. 6.** Establish effective record keeping procedures that document the HACCP system.

4.11.1 The approved HACCP plan and associated records must be on file at the food establishment. Generally, the records utilized in the total HACCP system will include the following:

1. The HACCP Plan
    - Listing of the HACCP team and assigned responsibilities.
    - Description of the product and its intended use.
    - Flow diagram for the entire manufacturing process indicating CCPs.
    - Hazards associated with each CCP and preventive measures.
    - Critical limits.
    - Monitoring system.
    - Corrective action plans for deviations from critical limits.
    - Record-keeping procedures.
    - Procedures for verification of HACCP system.

Process Step	CCP	Chem. phys. biolog. hazards	Critical Limits	Monitoring procedures/ frequency/ person(s) responsible	Corrective action(s)/ person(s)/ responsible	HACCP records	Verification procedure/ person(s) responsible
1.	Yes or no	1. 2. 3. etc.					

In addition to listing the HACCP team, product description and uses, and providing a flow diagram, other information in the HACCP plan can be tabulated as follows:

2. Records obtained during the operation of the plan (Appendix D).

4.12 **Principle No. 7.** Establish procedures for verification that the HACCP system is working correctly.

The National Academy of Science (*An Evaluation of the Role of Microbiological Criteria for Foods and Food Ingredients,* 1995, National Academy Press, Washington, DC) pointed out that the major infusion of science in a HACCP system centers on proper identification of the hazards, critical control points, critical limits, and instituting proper verification procedures. These processes should take place during the development of the HACCP plan. There are four processes involved in verification.

4.12.1 The first is the scientific or technical process to verify that critical limits at CCPs are satisfactory. This process is complex and requires intensive involvement of highly skilled professionals from a variety of disciplines capable of doing focused studies and analyses. The process consists of a review of the critical limits to verify that the limits are adequate to control the hazards that are likely to occur.

4.12.2 The second process of verification ensures that the facility's HACCP plan is functioning effectively. A functioning HACCP system requires little end-product sampling, since appropriate safeguards are built in early in the process. Therefore, rather than relying on end-product sampling, firms must rely on frequent reviews of their HACCP plan, verification that the HACCP plan is being correctly followed, review of CCP records, and determinations that appropriate risk management decisions and product dispositions are made when process deviations occur.

4.12.3 The third process consists of documented periodic revalidations, independent of audits or other verification procedures, that must be performed to ensure the accuracy of the HACCP plan. Revalidations are performed by a HACCP team on a regular basis and/or whenever significant product, process or packaging changes require modification of the HACCP plan. The revalidation includes a documented on-site review and verification of all flow diagrams and CCPs in the HACCP plan. The HACCP team modifies the HACCP plan as necessary.

4.12.4 The fourth process of verification deals with the government's regulatory responsibility and actions to ensure that the establishment's HACCP system is functioning satisfactorily. Examples of verification activities are included as Appendix E.

APPENDIX A. Examples of Questions to be Considered in a Hazard Analysis

The hazard analysis consists of asking a series of questions which are appropriate to each step in a HACCP plan. It is not possible in these recommendations to provide a list of all the questions which may be pertinent to a specific food or process. The hazard analysis should question the effect of a variety of factors upon the safety of the food.

A. Ingredients

1. Does the food contain any sensitive ingredients that may present microbiological hazards (e.g., *Salmonella, Staphylococcus aureus*); chemical hazards (e.g., aflatoxin, antibiotic or pesticide residues); or physical hazards (stones, glass, metal)?

2. Is potable water used in formulating or in handling the food?

B. Intrinsic Factors

Physical characteristics and composition (e.g., pH, type of acidulants, fermentable carbohydrate, water activity, preservatives) of the food during and after processing.

1. Which intrinsic factors of the food must be controlled in order to assure food safety?
2. Does the food permit survival or multiplication of pathogens and/or toxin formation in the food during processing?
3. Will the food permit survival or multiplication of pathogens and/or toxin formation during subsequent steps in the food chain?
4. Are there other similar products in the market place? What has been the safety record for these products?

C. Procedures used for processing

1. Does the process include a controllable processing step that destroys pathogens? Consider both vegetative cells and spores.
2. Is the product subject to recontamination between processing (e.g., cooking, pasteurizing) and packaging?

D. Microbial content of the food

1. Is the food commercially sterile (e.g., low acid canned food)?
2. Is it likely that the food will contain viable spore forming or nonspore forming pathogens?
3. What is the normal microbial content of the food?
4. Does the microbial population change during the normal time the food is stored prior to consumption?
5. Does the subsequent change in microbial population alter the safety of the food, pro or con?

E. Facility design

1. Does the layout of the facility provide an adequate separation of raw materials from ready-to-eat foods if this is important to food safety?
2. Is positive air pressure maintained in product packaging areas? Is this essential for product safety?
3. Is the traffic pattern for people and moving equipment a significant source of contamination?

F. Equipment design

1. Will the equipment provide the time-temperature control that is necessary for safe food?
2. Is the equipment properly sized for the volume of food that will be processed?
3. Can the equipment be sufficiently controlled so that the variation in performance will be within the tolerances required to produce a safe food?

4. Is the equipment reliable or is it prone to frequent breakdowns?
5. Is the equipment designed so that it can be cleaned and sanitized?
6. Is there a chance for product contamination with hazardous substances; e.g., glass?
7. What product safety devices are used to enhance consumer safety?
   - metal detectors
   - magnets
   - sifters
   - filters
   - screens
   - thermometers
   - deboners
   - dud detectors

G. Packaging

1. Does the method of packaging affect the multiplication of microbial pathogens and/or the formation of toxins?
2. Is the package clearly labeled "Keep Refrigerated," if this is required for safety?
3. Does the package include instructions for the safe handling and preparation of the food by the end user?
4. Is the packaging material resistant to damage, thereby preventing the entrance of microbial contamination?
5. Are tamper-evident packaging features used?
6. Is each package and case legibly and accurately coded?
7. Does each package contain the proper label?

H. Sanitation

1. Can sanitation impact upon the safety of the food that is being processed?
2. Can the facility and equipment be cleaned and sanitized to permit the safe handling of food?
3. Is it possible to provide sanitary conditions consistently and adequately to assure safe foods?

I. Employee health, hygiene and education

1. Can employee health or personal hygiene practices impact upon the safety of the food being processed?
2. Do the employees understand the process and the factors they must control to assure the preparation of safe foods?
3. Will the employees inform management of a problem which could impact upon safety of the food?

J. Conditions of storage between packaging and the end user
   1. What is the likelihood that the food will be improperly stored at the wrong temperature?
   2. Would an error in improper storage lead to a microbiologically unsafe food?

K. Intended use
   1. Will the food be heated by the consumer?
   2. Will there likely be leftovers?

L. Intended consumer
   1. Is the food intended for the general public?
   2. Is the food intended for consumption by a population with increased susceptibility to illness (e.g., infants, the aged, the infirm, immuno-compromised individuals)?

APPENDIX B

4.1.2 Hazard Analysis and Assignment of Risk Categories

4.1.2.1 Rank the food according to hazard characteristics A through F, using a plus (+) to indicate a potential hazard. The number of pluses will determine the risk category. A model diagram outlining this concept is given under section 4.1.3. As indicated, if the product falls under Hazard Class A, it should automatically be considered Risk Category VI.

Hazard A: A special class that applies to non-sterile products designated and intended for consumption by at-risk populations, e.g., infants, the aged, the infirm, or immuno-compromised individuals.

Hazard B: The product contains "sensitive ingredients" in terms of microbiological hazards.

Hazard C: The process does not contain a controlled processing step that effectively destroys harmful microorganisms.

Hazard D: The product is subject to recontamination after processing before packaging.

Hazard E: There is substantial potential for abusive handling in distribution or in consumer handling that could render the product harmful when consumed.

Hazard F: There is no terminal heat process after packaging or when cooked in the home.

Note: Hazards can also be stated for chemical or physical hazards, particularly if a food is subject to them.

4.1.2.2 Assignment of risk category (based on ranking by hazard characteristics):

Category VI. A special category that applies to non-sterile products designated and intended for consumption by at risk populations, e.g., infants, the aged, the infirm, or immuno-compromised individuals. All six hazard characteristics must be considered.

Category V. Food products subject to all five general hazard characteristics. Hazard Class B, C, D, E, F

Category IV. Food products subject to four general hazard characteristics.

Category III. Food products subject to three of the general hazard characteristics.

Category II. Food products subject to two of the general hazard characteristics.

Category I. Food products subject to one of the general hazard characteristics.

Category 0. Hazard Class–No hazard.

Note: Ingredients are treated in the same manner in respect to how they are received at the plant, before processing. This permits determination of how to reduce risk in the food system.

4.1.3 It is recommended that a chart be utilized that provides assessment of a food by hazard characteristic and risk category. A format for this chart is given as follows:

Food Ingredient or Product	Hazard Characteristics (A,B,C,D,E,F)	Risk Category (VI,V,IV,III,II,I,O)
T	A+ (Special Category)*	VI
U	Five +'s (B through F)	V
V	Four +'s (B through F)	IV
W	Three +'s (B through F)	III
X	Two +'s (B through F)	II
Y	One + (B through F)	I
Z	No +'s	O

*Hazard characteristic A automatically is Risk Category VI, but any combination of B through F may also be present.

[Appendix B was extracted from Committee's November 1989 HACCP document.]

APPENDIX C. Examples of a Flow Diagram for the Production of Frozen Cooked Beef Patties

1. Receiving (Beef)

↓

2. Grinding

↓

3. Mixing

↓

4. Forming

↓

5. Cooking

↓

6. Freezing

↓

7. Boxing

↓

8. Distributing

↓

9. Reheating

↓

10. Serving

APPENDIX D. Examples of HACCP Records

A. Ingredients
   1. Supplier certification documenting compliance with processor's specifications.
   2. Processor audit records verifying supplier compliance.
   3. Storage temperature record for temperature sensitive ingredients.
   4. Storage time records of limited shelf life ingredients.

B. Records relating to product safety
   1. Sufficient data and records to establish the efficacy of barriers in maintaining product safety.
   2. Sufficient data and records establishing the safe shelf life of the product, if age of product can affect safety.
   3. Documentation of the adequacy of the processing procedures from a knowledgeable process authority.

C. Processing
   1. Records from all monitored CCPs.
   2. Records verifying the continued adequacy of the processes.
D. Packaging
   1. Records indicating compliance with specifications of packaging materials.
   2. Records indicating compliance with sealing specifications.
E. Storage and distribution
   1. Temperature records.
   2. Records showing no product shipped after shelf life date on temperature sensitive products.
F. Deviation and corrective action records
G. Validation records and modification to the HACCP plan indicating approved revisions and changes in ingredients, formulations, processing, packaging and distribution control, as needed.
H. Employee training records

APPENDIX E. Examples of Verification Activities

A. Verification procedures may include:
   1. Establishment of appropriate verification inspection schedules.
   2. Review of the HACCP plan.
   3. Review of CCP records.
   4. Review of deviations and dispositions.
   5. Visual inspections of operations to observe if CCPs are under control.
   6. Random sample collection and analysis.
   7. Review of critical limits to verify that they are adequate to control hazards.
   8. Review of written record of verification inspections which certifies compliance with the HACCP plan or deviations from the plan and the corrective actions taken.
   9. Validation of HACCP plan, including on-site review and verification of flow diagrams and CCPs.
   10. Review of modifications of the HACCP plan.
B. Verification inspections should be conducted:
   1. Routinely, or on an unannounced basis, to assure selected CCP are under control.
   2. When it is determined that intensive coverage of a specific commodity is needed because of new information concerning food safety.
   3. When foods produced have been implicated as a vehicle of food-bome disease.
   4. When requested on a consultative basis or established criteria have not been met.

5. To verify that changes have been implemented correctly after a HACCP plan has been modified.

C. Verification reports should include information about:
1. Existence of a HACCP plan and the person(s) responsible for administering and updating the HACCP plan.
2. The status of records associated with CCP monitoring.
3. Direct monitoring data of the CCP while in operation.
4. Certification that monitoring equipment is properly calibrated and in working order.
5. Deviations and corrective actions.
6. Any samples analyzed to verify that CCP are under control. Analyses may involve physical, chemical, microbiological or organoleptic methods.
7. Modifications to the HACCP plan.
8. Training and knowledge of individuals responsible for monitoring CCPs.

References

Bauman, Howard. 1990. "HACCP: Concept, Development, and Application." In: "Symposia–Hazard Analysis and Critical Control Point (HACCP) System and Food Safety." *Journal of Food Technology*, May 1990, p. 156-159.

Committee on Food Hygiene of the Codex Alimentarius Commission. 1993. "Guidlines for the Application of the HACCP System." *Alinorm* 93/13A, Appendix II, p. 26-32.

Food Chemical News. January 9, 1995. "EU Calls FDA HACCP Plan Too Restrictive, Bureauratic," p. 15-16.

Gruspaaardt-Vink, Carina. 1995. "HACCP in the EU." *Journal of Food Technology*, March 1995, p. 36.

ILSI Europe Scientific Committee on Microbiology. 1993. "A Simple Guide to Understanding and Applying the HACCP Concept." International Life Sciences Institute, 13 pgs.

Microbiological and Food Safety Committee of the National Food Processors Association. 1993. "Implementation of HACCP in a Food Processing Plant," p. 548-554.

Shank, Fred R. 1991. "The National Advisory Committee on Microbiological Criteria for Foods: An Introduction." In: "Symposia–National Advisory Committee on Microbiological Criteria for Foods." *Journal of Food Technology*, April 1991, p. 142-144.

Sperber, William H. 1991. "The Modern HACCP System." In: "Symposia–When Traditional HACCP is not Enough." *Journal of Food Technology*, June 1991, p. 116-119.

U.S. Food and Drug Administration. 1994. "Development of Hazard Analysis Critical Control Points for the Food Industry; Request for Comments." *Federal Register*, Vol. 59, No. 149, p. 39888-39896.

CHAPTER 9

Consumer Complaints and Market Recall

Consumer complaints come in many forms and the manner in which they are handled may be either a valuable promotional tool for a company or a very costly claim. The individual whose responsibility it is to respond to complaints becomes a very important person because the consumer may interpret that individual's attitude as the attitude of the company.

Organization

If a company does not have a written policy for handling consumer complaints, then it is highly recommended that such a document be prepared and issued to everyone in the company who may become involved in complaint handling. Complaint handling may be done by one person or a committee, or there may be different people/committees for the different types of complaints. Complaints may be of an esthetic quality nature, a public health or illness concern, or a packaging problem, and may originate from a consumer, retailer or wholesaler. Complaints of a public health nature should be given priority and will be discussed in detail later in this chapter under Recalls. If a company is small and/or produces a limited number of simple products, such as canned fruit or vegetables, then the question of who handles the complaints may be much simpler than in a larger company or one producing complex formulated products.

The National Food Processors Association, Washington, DC (NFPA) (1988), list a number of questions that might be asked in establishing a consumer complaint program.

1. What standards will you set to respond to complaints? Response to complaints should be made as quickly, but as reasonably, as possible.
2. How will you rate priority of complaints? A public health problem, such as food poisoning, would take precedence over a product quality issue.
3. What consumer information will you want to record? Standardized forms should be developed.
4. How will you obtain as many relevant facts about complaints as possible?

5. What will be the telephone reporting procedure for complaints that may be received at times other than working hours?
6. Who in the company should be notified if critical complaints are reported? This refers to situations involving reports of illness, injury or bizarre foreign objects.
7. What specific guidelines will you use for handling illness, injury, bizarre foreign object complaints, and for abusive, extremely hostile or threatening consumers?
8. What will be your company's procedures for collecting, shipping, sorting and handling food samples and exhibits involved in complaints of illness or injury?
9. Should you consider using an independent laboratory to analyze food samples when a consumer alleges illness?
10. How will you handle complaints in which an attorney is involved?
11. Will your system guarantee that all promises are kept to persons who may become involved in the resolution of a complaint?
12. How will a consumer know how to contact you?
13. When do consumer complaints become a market withdrawal or a product recall?

Trade organizations in other countries, such as the Campden Food & Drink Research Association (CFDRA), Chipping, Campden, Gloucestershire, England, may also be a source of information on this subject.

Recording Complaints

When complaints arrive at the company, whether by telephone, letter or in person, certain information should be recorded. This process will improve with time depending upon the type and nature of complaint. At the very least, record the consumer's name, address, telephone number, product involved and in what size and type of container, nature of complaint, the date complaint was received, how it was handled and by whom and the plant code or location should be recorded. There are very detailed reporting forms suggested for the record keeping of consumer complaints in the NFPA publication, "A Manual for Successful Resolution of Consumer Complaints in the Food Industry."

Responding to Complaints

Unless complaints are of a serious nature, they probably would be handled on a first-come-first-served basis. If it is anticipated that there will be a delay in resolving a complaint, then an interim response should be given to the customer to assure them they are not being ignored.

Several choices exist for companies to use in responding to consumers' letters, telephone calls, personal visits, or a consultant or third-party response.

Correspondence might be considered the most efficient method to handle complaints regarding product quality or damaged or difficult packaging. With the newer methods of word processing, it appears as though one is receiving personalized attention instead of older types of form letters or cards. If it is the intent of the company to replace the product, refunds or coupons might be included, or the customer might be informed that a gift package is on the way. It is very important for the written response not to give the perception of a "form" letter, for this may disappoint or even anger the customer. A personal tone is set by thanking the person for their inquiry, identifying the product, and stating how the issue will be handled by the company.

Responding by telephone might be reserved for emergency situations where additional information is wanted and the consumer needs to be assured that the company is giving the situation its immediate attention. If the situation is an emergency, then a written version of the conversation would be desired to have a permanent record.

If the company makes available a toll-free number(s) for consumers, then probably many complaints are resolved at that time. These numbers may be part of the label information. If this method is employed, then forms should be used by company employee(s) to insure conformity of the information obtained.

Responding by personal contact is an option that could be used to follow-up on a consumer complaint, but would probably be reserved for situations of a serious personal nature where it may be necessary to obtain additional information. If this method is employed, it is extremely important that the individual be well trained in personnel relations to present a positive attitude and concern, but yet not make any commitments for the company unless instructed to do so. Some companies may choose to employ a third party, such as a trade association or independent laboratory that specializes in resolving complaints, to handle the matter.

Whatever avenue a company chooses to work with the consumer, there are several ways to reimburse the individual to their satisfaction. A refund for cost of the product and inconvenience to the consumer might be the best method to resolve the situation, particularly if it is the only option acceptable. This approach is a necessity, if promotional material states that it will be done.

Coupons for or direct product replacement is a very common practice companies use in many situations that are not of a serious nature. While mailing coupons is the cheapest and most efficient approach, mailing replacement product might add a greater sense of sincerity. Product replacement also allows the customer to try a good representation of the company's product quality and encourage continued purchases.

Resolving a consumer complaint with a cash settlement greater than the value of a normal refund mentioned above would be reserved for special cases where obvious injury did or might have occurred. In such situations, this approach would only be used after thorough investigation and advice from legal council.

There are situations where multiple complaints are received from the same individual over a period of time. It is these incidences that make thorough record keeping very important. Even though the second or more complaint from the same individual may seem questionable, it is very important to respond in a prompt and thorough manner so as not to ignore a valid one.

In responding to second complaints, you might remind the individual of the situation and ask for more details (as well as the product). The National Food Processors Association (NFPA) suggests including the following paragraph in correspondence:

> If you should ever have reason to be dissatisfied with our product again, please return the product in its container, cover or wrap well, and refrigerate or freeze before contacting us. It is possible that we may wish to have a company representative call on you to examine the product and discuss the problem.

After satisfactory investigation of multiple complaints, the company can decide upon the policy and course of action to take.

Product Tampering

Product tampering threats are very serious situations and are a federal offense in the United States. They not only affect the company involved, but other companies, as well as the general public. Many companies have organized a Crisis Management Team to handle these situations. Having a Team is only part of the job; the other part is to have a Crisis Plan that is detailed and well rehearsed. As is true with handling consumer complaints, detailed record keeping and getting the involvement of the proper regulatory and law enforcement agency is crucial to resolving such situations.

PRODUCT RECALLS

Introduction

The United States Food and Drug Administration, under 21 CFR 108.35(f), and the United States Department of Agriculture's Food Safety Inspection Service (FSIS), 9 CFR 318.311 and 9 CFR 381.311, require processors of low-acid foods to have in the files a current procedure for withdrawing products from the marketplace, if necessary.

The recall of a food product from the market is extremely difficult and costly. It may even involve litigation. A recall must be conducted quickly and effectively when a product is a potential health risk. In addition, accurate information must be provided to the public. Food processors and all members of the food distribution chain (including retailers and distributors) are responsible to assist with the removal of a defective product that is being recalled. Obviously, the manner in which corporate officials handle, or bungle, a product recall will effect their company's future.

Consider these vital questions:

- How would your company handle a product recall situation?
- Who in your company would coordinate the recall?
- What information would be included in press releases? (Regulatory agencies require press releases for some recall classes.)
- Would needless costs occur because of infrequent product code changes?
- How would your company assure that the recall has adequately recovered the packages of defective product without having to recall every single package of the product?

Documented procedures and decisions to answer these questions need to be established before a recall situation ever becomes a reality.

A recall is a major crisis which severely disrupts a corporation. It is imperative that a company prepare for this type of disaster before it occurs. This can best be done in the following manner:

1. Take measures to produce food which is not in violation of federal or state regulations.
2. Develop a recall plan.
3. Practice implementation of the recall plan.
4. Periodically update the recall plan.

Recalls are started by the food processor. In the US, the FDA or the USDA may request a food processor to start a recall when the agency suspects that an adulterated, unwholesome, unsafe, or mislabeled product has been shipped. By strict legal definition, recalls are "voluntary" in nature, whereby neither the FDA nor the USDA have legal authority to conduct a food product recall. If a recall request is ignored, the FDA and USDA can utilize other legal options. These options include obtaining a court order to either seize a product or condemn a product manufactured or held under conditions in violation of federal regulations. In addition, both FDA and USDA have authority to issue substantial public warnings about defective products. Because of the power of the regulatory agencies and the need to remove unsafe, adulterated or mislabeled products from the marketplace, food processors should work closely with all regulatory agencies on recall matters.

The FDA or the USDA will request a recall under the following conditions:

1. The product presents a risk of illness, injury or gross consumer deception.
2. The firm has not initiated a recall.
3. Any action necessary to protect the consumer's health and welfare.

A government agency-initiated recall request is reserved for urgent situations. It should be noted that the FDA or USDA requests a recall only after the agency feels it has sufficient evidence to pursue legal action if the company decides not to cooperate.

It should be noted that the term "recall" has legal significance, with respect to insurance and product liability claims. Therefore, the term "recall" should be used only when a marketed product is deemed to be in violation of the food regulations.

All recalls under FDA jurisdiction are published in the "FDA Enforcement Record." This publication has a wide distribution, including the news media. USDA does not have a formal method for disclosing recall information, however, details regarding a USDA recall may be obtained under the Freedom of Information Act.

The following are two situations by which food processors may remove product from the marketplace which are not classified as a recall: 1. Market Withdrawal 2. Stock Recovery.

Market Withdrawal is a situation in which the removal or correction of a distributed product involves a minor violation which would not be subject to legal action by the agency, or which involves no violation, e.g., normal stock rotation practices, routine equipment adjustment and repairs, etc.

Stock Recoveries occur when the firm removes or corrects a product that has not been marketed, nor left the direct control of that firm, i.e., the product is still located on the premises owned or under the control of the firm and no portion of the lot has been released for sale or use.

Since stock recoveries and market withdrawals are not recalls, these actions will not be listed in the FDA Enforcement Record, covered in a press release, nor will there be a requirement to conduct effectiveness checks to account for the amount of marketed product recovered. However, market withdrawals cannot be used by a firm to recover product in which the defect represents a form of consumer deception, or if there is a safety risk.

To help a company in their decision making, the FDA has identified classifications of recalls as follows:

Class I. This is a situation in which there is a reasonable probability that the use of, or exposure to, a violative product will cause serious adverse health consequences or death and probably necessitates:

1. Notification of FDA
2. Recall to consumer or user level
3. Product placed on FDA's public recall list
4. Public warning be issued via news media
5. 100% removal from all direct accounts and sub-accounts and, if necessary, from the possession of consumers (Level A "effectiveness check").

Class II. This is a situation in which use of, or exposure to, a violative product may cause temporary or medically reversible adverse health consequences, or where the probability of serious adverse health consequences is remote and probably necessitates:

1. Notification of FDA
2. Recall product to retail or dispensing level
3. Product placed on FDA's public recall list
4. Press release announcing the recall, when public interest requires
5. "Effectiveness check" varies according to the degree of consumer hazard associated with the product

Class III: This is a situation in which use of, or exposure to, a violative product is not likely to cause adverse health consequences and probably necessitates:

1. Notification of FDA
2. Recall product to wholesale level
3. Product mentioned on FDA's public recall list
4. Ordinarily, no press release; company may be contacted by news media because of FDA's public recall list mentioning
5. "Effectiveness check" varies according to degree of consumer hazard associated with the product

PREPARING FOR A RECALL

The Recall Team is the basic unit which a company can use to manage a recall situation. The number of team members is a function of corporate size. In smaller corporations, an individual may have multiple responsibilities, thus the person will be responsible for more than one recall team function.

The Recall Team

The Recall Team is responsible for collecting and analyzing a large amount of information. The company president and the chief executive officer (CEO) should not be members of the team, even though they will closely interact with the team. This will allow them to be free to evaluate the information and to make appropriate decisions. The president and the CEO are legally responsible for all actions taken by the team.

A Recall Team, along with individual responsibilities, provides the following functions:

1. Immediately develops a plan of action to minimize the risk of any public health hazard.
2. Assesses whether a problem actually exists.
3. Determines an appropriate corrective plan.
4. Develops a specific recall plan.

5. Communicates information to the corporate president, CEO, employees, customers, and news media.
6. Coordinates actions with regulatory agencies.

A Recall Team consists of the following personnel and information:

Recall Coordinator: Responsible for preparing a product recall strategy and direction of all activities/personnel to satisfactorily carry out the recall procedures; direct liaison with regulatory agencies involved.

Name:
Office Phone:
Home Phone:
Position/Title:
Address:

Alternate Recall Coordinator: Requires the same information.

Recall Team Members: Key company personnel that the Recall Coordinator needs to adequately evaluate, initiate and expedite the recall procedures/activities. The same personnel information is required as for the coordinator.

1. Purchasing. Provide information on raw products and ingredients used, involving suppliers, if necessary.
2. Production. Provide information on possible manufacturing deficiencies.
3. Quality Assurance. Provide quality control record information and various samples that may be necessary to determine what went wrong.
4. Marketing/Sales. Provide information to trace shipments and follow up on any complaints about the product received through distribution channels.
5. Corporate Headquarters. Make final policy decisions as necessary.
6. Public Relations. Provide all public and press release information.
7. Legal Counsel (optional). Must be kept informed; may be needed to become involved in instances of potential litigation. Assesses legal implications of the recall. Insures that the decisions and actions are made in accordance with the applicable regulations. Coordinates legal activities with the regulatory agency.
8. Technical Services or Research & Development. Evaluates the extent of the problem. Evaluates the health hazard of the problem. Provides technical assistance in determining the cause and procedure to prevent reoccurrence of the problem.

Information Required

Blueprints and Flow Diagrams

Current facility blueprints and process flow diagrams for all processes should be available to the Team. This material should identify all pieces of equipment, storage areas for food and non-food items, designated areas in which to store quarantined products, etc. This information will assist in identifying the cause of the problem and implementation of the recall plan.

Ingredient Identification

Only marketed products deemed to be in violation of the regulations must be recalled. Very often, an excessive amount of product is recalled because of the impossibility of accurately identifying the specific defective lot or the defective portion of a lot. Furthermore, the amount of the product recalled may be significantly reduced if appropriate records are available to track quantity by locations of a product lot throughout the distribution chain and to determine which source lots of raw material were used in the manufacture and packaging of the product. To do this effectively, the following records are required:

<u>Supplier, Vendor and Raw Material Records</u>

1. Supplier List. a. Maintain a current list of all suppliers and vendors and type of raw materials received. b. Identify the recall contact person for each supplier and vendor.
2. Ingredient Handling and Utilization Records. a. Forms to trace each lot of raw material going into each finished product lot. b. Retain receiving records, e.g., invoices and bills of lading.

<u>Production and Distribution Records</u>

1. Records should identify the actual production lot number and lot size.
2. Records should be able to trace the destination of all cases of a lot.
3. Retain copies of the distribution records, e.g., invoices and bills of lading. The records should be able to identify item, size, brand, date of manufacture, plant, amount shipped, and destination.

<u>Distribution List</u>

1. Maintain a list of all warehouses, distributors, brokers, wholesalers and retailers who receive direct shipments.
2. Identify a recall contact person for each warehouser, distributor, broker, wholesaler and retailer who receives direct shipments (Form 1).

<u>Product Coding Program</u>

1. Production codes should be legible for the shelf-life of the product.
2. All shipping cases should be identified with the production code. In addition, all of the cases in a production lot should be sequentially numbered.
3. Production codes should be changed frequently enough to keep the lots small.
4. A code explanation occurs later in the chapter (Form 2). The code should identify the item, batch, line, time, period, day, month, year, and plant.

<u>Other Aspects</u>

1. Develop and implement a product inventory rotation procedure.
2. Establish and implement adequate quality control procedures.
3. Establish and implement appropriate processing control procedures.
4. Insure that the corporation has adequate insurance coverage.
5. Update the recall plan annually.

Description of Recall Strategy Elements

I. Depth of Recall:

Depending on the product's degree of hazard and extent of distribution, the recall strategy should specify the level in the distribution chain to which the recall is to extend.

Recall depth is defined as:

A. Consumer or user level, product in consumer's hands or home shelves may vary with product. The levels below are included in this level.

B. Retail level, product in possession of retailer, in immediate retailer warehouse or storage. The level below is included in this level.

C. Wholesale level, product in possession of wholesaler and not in direct control of manufacturer.

II. Public Warning:

The purpose of a public warning is to alert the public that a product being recalled presents a serious hazard to health, or where other means for preventing use of the product appear inadequate. The decision on the type and style of public warning is generally a joint decision of FDA officials and the manufacturer.

The two types of warnings issued are:

A. General public warning through the general news media, either national or local, as appropriate (Form 3).

B. Public warning through specialized news media, e.g., professional/trade press, or through specific segments of the population, e.g., physicians, hospitals.

III. Effectiveness Checks:

The purpose of effectiveness checks is to assure that all receivers, purchasers or users of the product at the recall depth specified by the strategy have received notification of the recall and have taken appropriate action. Individuals should be contacted by personnel visits, telephone calls, letters, or any combination thereof. The recall strategy will specify the method(s) to be used and the level of effectiveness check as follows:

A. Level A – 100 percent of the total number of users, etc., contacted.

B. Level B – a percentage of users contacted to be determined in each recall, less than 100 percent but greater than 10 percent.

C. Level C – 10 percent of total number of users contacted.

D. Level D – 2 percent of total number of users, etc., contacted.

E. Level E – no effectiveness check.

THE RECALL PROCEDURE

Identification of a Potential Recall Situation

All customer complaints, threats of sabotage, notifications from a distribution channel and/or co-packer, communications from a regulatory agency or a company discovery in its own records (indicating a product that should be withdrawn from distribution), shall be directed to the Recall Coordinator.

All complaints and threats of sabotage should be taken seriously and thoroughly investigated. The Recall Coordinator should be informed of the resolution of all complaints.

Assessment of a Potential Recall Situation

1. The Recall Committee shall substantiate that a problem exists by observing relevant facts via:
   a. A Problem Information Report (Form 4), should be used to document public or regulatory agency contacts which reveal potential problems. Each report should be prepared by a Recall Committee Member or designated employee. Completion of a report may require the preparer to travel to the problem site when obtaining crucial decision-making information. Samples of the suspected lot should be obtained and properly shipped to a designated site (home, office, laboratory, etc.) for further evaluation. Samples from the suspected lot and other lots manufactured in the same time frame should be obtained from retailers, wholesalers or distributors for further evaluation.
   b. Examination and analysis of laboratory results on the suspected lot.
   c. Examination and laboratory results on other product packages of the same code as the suspected material.
   d. Examination of other lots, shipments and records to make sure no other lots or brands are involved.
2. If the Recall Committee determines that a potential recall situation exists, they should immediately:
   a. Inform the appropriate regulatory agency (FDA or USDA) that a recall problem may exist.
   b. Place under quarantine all remaining inventory of the suspected lot(s).
   c. Determine the source of the problem by examination of raw materials, processing records, quality control records; or determine if there was transportation or handling abuse in the warehousing distribution chain.
3. If a problem is verified, the Committee needs to determine whether or not to recall the product. A decision to recall the product is triggered by either of the following situations:
   a. A health hazard (serious or acute) exists to humans or animals, and/or
   b. A person can be grossly deceived by the product.

The Recall Team often makes the hazard evaluation determination with help from outside consultants.

4. When the Committee decides to proceed with a recall, the Committee must establish a recall strategy consisting of the following elements:
   a. Recall class.
   b. Depth of the recall.
   c. The type of recall notification to members of the distribution system.
   d. Methods used to recover the recalled product.
   e. Type of public warning (if necessary).
   f. Methods and appropriate level of effectiveness checks.

   The following factors will need to be considered when determining a specific strategy:
   a. Results of the health hazard evaluation.
   b. Ease in identifying the lot(s) being recalled.
   c. Degree to which the product's deficiency is obvious to the consumer.
   d. Degree to which the lot(s) remains unused in the market.
   e. Amount of product involved.
   f. Continued availability of essential products (for FDA-administered recalls).

Steps to Conduct a Recall

The prime objective of a recall is to protect the public against a health hazard. For this reason, the order of actions taken to conduct a product recall are prioritized as:

1. Notify the appropriate FDA district office or the Food Safety Inspection Service (FSIS) regional director in the area in which a product recall is being initiated. USDA requires notification within 24 hours after starting a recall. Regulations do not require notification of FDA that a recall has been started, however, it is advisable to work with the FDA on all recalls. Provide the following information as detailed as possible, but do not delay notifying either FDA or USDA if all of the information is not immediately available. (Remember, the first concern is to remove hazardous product.)
   a. Identify the product and the amount of defective product which is involved.
   b. Provide the reason for the recall and provide the date and circumstances under which the product deficiency, or possible deficiency, were discovered.
   c. Provide evaluation of the risk associated with the deficiency or possible deficiency.
   d. Provide the total amount of defective product produced and/or the time span of the production.
   e. Provide the total amount of defective product estimated to be in distribution channels.

f. Provide distribution information, including the number of direct accounts and, when necessary, the identity of the direct accounts.
g. Attach a copy of the firm's recall communications, if issued. If a communication has not been issued, provide a copy of proposed communication.
h. Provide a copy of the proposed strategy for conducting the recall.
i. Provide the name and telephone number of the firm's official designated to be contacted concerning the recall.

Note: After the FDA or the USDA receives notification of a recall, the agency assigns a recall number. Next, the agency reviews the recall strategy submitted by the company. The agency may independently develop a strategy plan that may or may not coincide with the company's determination for the following:

- Recall classification;
- Recall level;
- Recall communications;
- Public notice (if needed);
- Effectiveness checks;
- Necessary audit checks and inspections (FDA);
- Disposition or potential reconditioning of the recalled product.

It is important for the company to submit as complete a recall strategies plan as possible, and to clearly state their recommendations to the regulatory agency. The FDA and USDA tend to request that more product be recalled than what may be involved, to best assure protection of the consumer.

2. Notify appropriate state regulatory agencies, i.e., health departments, state agriculture departments, etc.
3. Notify by phone or in person the appropriate local health and medical authorities.
4. Issue press, radio, and TV releases; coordinate with the FDA statement (if issued), using the press guidelines at the end of the chapter. All contacts with the media should be documented using the Media/Public Inquiry Form.
5. Notify all distribution points, using the recall communication procedure.
6. Contact appropriate trade association(s) and professional societies for assistance, as necessary, with:
   a. Removal of product from retail shelves.
   b. Help in verifying effectiveness of product removal from retail shelves.
7. Maintain a cumulative record of the recalled units that have been recovered and quarantined. Maintain a check on the effectiveness of the removal of recalled product from the distribution chain. Compare the cumulative recalled tally to the total number of defective units manufactured that was determined in the Problem Information Report.
8. Conduct effectiveness checks.

9. Provide periodic effectiveness reports to the appropriate regulatory agency, FDA or USDA, on the status of the recall.
10. Obtain approval for the disposition method(s) of all recalled product from the appropriate regulatory agency.
11. Termination of the recall can be requested from the appropriate regulatory agency after all aspects of the recall plan have been completed.

Suggestions

1. Steps 5 and 6 should be practiced initially and periodically to:
   a. Determine that the product code information is adequate for everyone to locate the product quickly, and
   b. Keep the distribution point lists up to date.
2. Encourage your distributors and brokers to develop and maintain their own complete lists of all accounts to whom your product may be distributed.
3. Maintain adequate records that track each production lot released. This can be done by including the product lot code(s) on each shipping order, invoice, and bill of lading. Taking a few moments to include lot information on each shipping ticket can become the "salvation-factor" for a company during a product recall situation.

References

Chadwick, All Collins. 1988. *A Manual for Successful Resolution of Consumer Complaints in the Food Industry*. National Food Processors Association, Washington, DC.

21 *CFR* 108.35. 1994. U.S. Government Printing Office, Superintendent of Documents, Mail Stop: SSOP, Washington, DC 20402-9328.

Khan, Paul, et al. 1972. "Symposium: Recall of Food Products." *Food Technology*, Vol. 26, 10:22 .

Morrison, Margaret. 1974. "How Defective Products Are Recalled." *FDA Consumer*, Vol. 8, 2:15 .

"Successfully Managing Product Recalls and Withdrawls," Bulletin 34-L, 1988. National Canners Association, Washington, DC.

Federal Register, Vol. 43, No. 117, June 16, 1978, p. 26202-26221.

Titus, Terry C. and John G. Surak. 1990. "Product Recall Guidelines for Food Processors Under FDA or USDA Regulations." *Food Science*, Miscellaneous Series 10. Clemson University, Clemson, SC.

Form 1

Company Warehouses

Company Name:____________________________

<u>Location/Address</u> <u>Manager Name</u> <u>Phone Number</u>

1.

2. Continue as may be necessary.

Distributors

Company Name:____________________________

<u>Distributor Co.</u> <u>Name & Address</u> <u>Manager Name</u> <u>Phone Number</u>

1.

2. Continue as may be necessary.

Brokers

Company Name____________________________

<u>Broker Co.</u> <u>Name & Address</u> <u>Manager Name</u> <u>Phone Number</u>

1.

2. Continue as may be necessary.

Wholesalers

Company Name____________________________

<u>Wholesaler Co.</u> <u>Name & Address</u> <u>Manager Name</u> <u>Phone Number</u>

1.

2. Continue as may be necessary.

Retailers

Company Name____________________________

1.

2. Continue as may be necessary.

Form 2 - Coding

A. PRODUCT CODE EXPLANATION:

1. Code Symbol Position (reading left to right):

Information	Code Symbol Product	Code Symbol Package	Position Shipping Case
a. Day manufactured			
b. Manufacturing line used			
c. Period (of day or shift)			
d. Plant designation			
e. Product identification			
f. Year manufactured			
g. Month manufactured			

2. Designed Code Symbols for:

a. Day Manufactured

Day of Month	Code Symbol Package	Code Symbol Case	Day of Month	Code Symbol Package	Code Symbol Case
1			17		
2			18		
3			19		
4			20		
5			21		
6			22		
7			23		
8			24		
9			25		
10			26		
11			27		
12			28		
13			29		
14			30		
15			31		
16					

b. Month Manufactured

Month	Code Symbol Package	Code Symbol Case
January		
February		
March		
April		
May		
June		
July		
August		
September		
October		
November		
December		

(Form 2 cont'd)

Form 2 - Coding (cont'd)

c. Manufacturing Line Used

Line number:	1	2	3	4	5
Code symbol:					

d. Period: (i.e., the increments of processing time: hours, AM or PM, shift, etc., represented by the code symbol)

Time Increment	Code Symbol Product	Package	Case

e. Plant Designation

Plant Location	Code Symbol Product	Package	Case
(1)			
(2) Continue as needed.			

f. Product Identification

Product Name & Package Size	Code Symbol Product	Package	Case
(1)			
(2)			
(3)			
(4)			
(5)			
(6)			
(7)			
(8)			
(9)			
(10)			

g. Year Manufactured

Year	Symbol Code Package	Case
1995		
1996		
1997		
1998		
1999		
2000		
2001		
2002		
2003		

Form 3 – Press Release Guideline

A. EXAMPLE FOR COMPANY RELEASE:

DATE RELEASED:

THE (COMPANY) AND FDA HAVE ASKED (HOUSEWIVES, SUPERMARKETS, ETC.) TO CHECK THEIR SHELVES FOR (CANS, PACKAGES, ETC.) OF (BRAND) LABELED (STYLE) (PRODUCT). (COMPANY SPOKESMAN'S NAME AND TITLE) ANNOUNCED THAT CERTAIN CODES OF (BRAND) (PRODUCT) ARE BEING RECALLED BECAUSE OF (DESCRIPTION OF PROBLEM) DISCOVERED IN (A FEW, NUMBER OF UNITS, ETC.) OF THE PRODUCT. (SPOKESMAN'S NAME) STATED THAT THE RECALL WAS "BEING CONDUCTED IN THE PUBLIC'S BEST INTEREST AND THAT NO OTHER CODES HAVE BEEN FOUND DEFECTIVE. PRODUCT BEING RECALLED WAS DISTRIBUTED IN (LIST STATES, CITIES, ETC.) WITH CODE(S) (LIST CODE) AND (CODE LOCATION). FDA HAS ASSISTED (COMPANY NAME) TO LOCATE (NUMBER OF UNITS LOCATED) OF THE (NUMBER OF UNITS MANUFACTURED) RECALLED. THE SPOKESMAN SAID CONSUMERS HAVING ANY OF THE (8 OZ., 1 LB., ETC.) SIZE (PACKAGES, CANS, ETC.) IN THEIR POSSESSION SHOULD RETURN THEM TO THE PLACE OF PURCHASE (OR HEALTH AGENCY, FDA OFFICE, ETC.) UNOPENED AND UNTASTED.

Form 4 – Problem Information Report

Company Name: ______________________________

Instruction: The following information must be immediately submitted to the Company Recall Coordinator, who is:

Name: __________________ Position: __________________

Phone: (__)_______________ Address: __________________

A. SITUATION:

1. Person(s) affected (if any): __________________ Age: _____

   Phone: (__)_____________ Address: __________________

2. Description of complaint/product defect: __________________

   Symptoms (if any): ______________________________
   (Attach correspondence if available)

3. Doctor and/or hospital report attached: _____ yes _____ no

4. Health agency report attached: _____ yes _____ no

5. Regulatory agency report attached: _____ yes _____ no

B. SUSPECT PRODUCT DATA:

Code(s): _______________ Product: __________________

Package Size: _______________ Quantity Purchased: ____________

Product Style: _______________ Product Style: _______________
(cut, whole, etc,) (can, box, etc.)

Label Brand: _______________ Date Purchased: _______________

1. Manner product was handled/stored/prepared after purchase:

   ____

2. Is a sample of the suspect product available? ___ yes ___ no

3. Where can a portion of suspect sample be obtained? _____________

4. Is the sample of suspect product stored? ___ yes ___ no

5. Is the suspect product's package/container available? ___ yes ___ no

6. Where can the suspect product's package/container be obtained?

   ____

7. Did review of all ingredients/packaging materials (and their storage history) used to manufacture the suspect product indicate possible abnormalities? (If yes, attach explanation) ___ yes ___ no

8. Did review of all processing/quality assurance records for the suspect product indicate possible abnormalities? ___ yes ___ no
   (If yes, attach explanation)

Form 4 – Problem Information Report (Cont'd)

C. EFFECTIVENESS CHECK FORM:

1. Business purchased from: ______________________________

   Address: ______________________________ Zip: ________

   Manager: ____________________ Phone: ( ) ____________

   a. Has the manager been notified? Date: ______ no ___

   b. Has all suspect product/codes been removed from shelves, segregated, and plainly marked? Date: ______ no ___

   c. Has all suspect product/codes stored on the premise been located and measures taken to prevent distribution? Date: ______ no ___

   d. Instruction given to the manager for disposition of material on hold:

   ____

   e. Number of suspect containers on hold: __________

2. Name and address of the distributor/broker from which retailer's suspect product/codes were obtained:

   ____

   Phone: ________________

D. Status report to FDA District Office (determine for each suspect code)

1. Total number of suspect units manufactured: ____________

2. Number of suspect units located and accounted for at:

   a. company warehouse ______________

   b. distributors ______________

   c. brokers ______________

   d. wholesalers ______________

   e. retailers ______________

   f. other ______________

E. Other comments: ______________________________

____

Report prepared by: ____________________ Date: __________

Title: ____________________ Phone: (___)____________

F. Additional recall measures taken if recall found not effective:

____

CHAPTER 10

Computer-Integrated Manufacturing

COMPUTER TECHNOLOGY

There are few businesses in the world today which do not utilize computers in their daily transactions. Increased power, decreased cost, and general usefulness account for their popularity. The comfort level of non-expert users of computers has increased greatly over the last decade. Computers are better suited than humans for many activities. Tasks which are complicated and slow for the human mind are done much more quickly and accurately with a computer. The rapidly expanding and changing field of computer technology allows only a brief mention of several concepts. Some are very well known and others perhaps less familiar.

Hardware

Hardware is the machinery or equipment. It consists of items such as the central processing unit (CPU), disk drives, circuit boards, memory chips, monitors, and printers. In recent years CPU's have become very powerful and fast. Memory capacity has expanded greatly. Work that could previously be done only on large mainframe computers can now be accomplished with a small personal computer.

Software

Software refers to sets of codes or computer instructions used to accomplish certain purposes. They are usually referred to as programs. Common programs include word processors, spreadsheets, and databases. A wide variety of these is available depending upon the amount and size of the work to be accomplished and the size and type of computer.

Networks

With the large increase in numbers of personal computers in the workplace, systems to connect them so that information can be shared have become widespread. These are referred to as networks. Networks provide many advantages within a company and even between companies. Information exchange can be made quickly and economically. One copy of software can be installed on a system called a server. By paying a licensing fee to the software provider, other computers can more economically share this single copy.

Vision Systems

Specialized devices have been developed which can visually input images without having to enter the information indirectly through a keyboard or some file transfer mechanism. These include scanners, bar code readers, and image analyzers. Bar code readers are the simplest devices, and have found widespread use in inventory control.

Scanners and image analyzers must convert an essentially analog image to a digital format. The computer is then able to store, analyze, and manipulate the data. There has been a great deal of interest in using image analyzers for on-line inspection purposes. Hardware improvements in recent years have made this approach more practical. High speed image analysis systems have been developed for vegetable grading and sorting. Systems can grade produce at a rate of 40 objects/sec. (Onyango and Marchant, 1994).

INTELLIGENT SYSTEMS

One of the most significant developments in computer applications over the last decade has been intelligent or knowledge-based systems. Although this deals mainly with software, powerful computers are usually required to efficiently operate this software. Intelligent systems allow the computer more freedom to find relationships and solve problems than traditional programs. Terms for this software include neural networks, fuzzy logic, and expert systems.

Expert systems are rule-based systems in which sets of rules are assembled to find logical conclusions from various input data. These have often been used to capture the knowledge of an expert in the form of these rules. Although it can be an arduous task to assemble expert systems, once established they can serve as advisors solving problems such as tracing defects in product quality to their source, scheduling routes, or giving advice on equipment repair.

Fuzzy logic allows computer analysis of incomplete or noisy data. Neural networks are programs which create patterns between input and output data. To develop these patterns the programs proceed through a "learning" process using previous data. Sometimes referred to as Artificial Neural Networks (ANN) these programs are very useful at discriminating essential from redundant data (Hourigan, 1994). Fuzzy logic and neural networks used for modeling and control of food processes ranging from fermentations and extrusion cooking to drying cereal grains (Eerikainen, 1993).

USE IN FOOD INDUSTRY

In many areas of the food industry competitiveness has required cost cutting measures resulting in reductions in employees and physical resources. As savings in these areas have been maximized, automation and the intelligent use of information play a key role in continued competitiveness. Various industry terms have been used to refer to computer incorporation. These include Computer-Aided Management and Computer-Integrated Management. Another more recent term is Manufacturing Execution Systems (MES) (Hollingsworth, 1994). They all generally refer to computer based control over the production process and demonstrate the interest and intent of the industry to optimize computer use. Two basic categories of computer usage in manufacturing are information management and process control. However, these categories are becoming less distinct with increased integration within the plant and between the plant, suppliers, and customers. An ultimate objective for a company wanting to take advantage of computer resources is to integrate decision making across the supply chain from supplier to consumer (Schutt, 1993).

Information Systems

Information was initially a front office function. Data such as inventories, billings, payrolls and production records were some of the first subjects of computerization. Improved methods of data collection in the processing area, receiving, warehouse and storage area, and laboratory have both allowed and required better integration of increasing amounts of data. Automated data collection, using bar code scanners and data logging devices in many formats, has contributed to the data proliferation.

Computerized maintenance management systems (CMMS) have proved to be cost-effective in food industries. They handle the paperwork associated with maintenance including work order preparation and tracking, labor scheduling and allocation, spare parts inventories and purchasing, report generation and preventive maintenance scheduling. A large US processor reported $2.5 million reduction in maintenance parts inventory over 18 months by using CMMS. The system detected inactive and/or obsolete parts, defined adequate stocking levels for required parts and helped perform physical inventory regularly. In general, the use of CMMS could cut inventory costs by 10 to 30%, improve equipment productivity by 20 to 30% and workforce productivity 10 to 20%, due to reduced machine breakdowns and maintenance costs (Mans, 1994).

Purchasing, Sales and Distribution

With computerized storage, supplier files can contain a great deal of information on product specifications and costs (Blythe, 1994). This is valuable in formulation and costing work. Computer systems can even monitor farm production costs, climatic parameters, and predict potential attack by pathogens and probable pesticide residues.

Sales and marketing can maintain information on customer activities with much greater accuracy. Consumer trends can be tracked using information obtained immediately from sales outlets. This is the basis for Efficient Consumer Response (ECR) in which a plant's production schedule is tied directly to the customer's purchasing pattern. Computers are an integral part of this process.

A major US processor is using electronic data interchange (EDI) through a wide area network to carry information between the company and its customers. About 70% of the purchase orders and 50% of the invoices are transmitted through EDI. The company analyzes the sales volume, inventory information, local market intelligence and any other information provided by the buyer and initiates purchase orders on its own, resulting in a continuous replenishment program. A 12-month pilot program produced a 50% reduction in inventory, 50% fresher on-shelf product and 40% drop in unsalable product (Demetrakakes, 1994).

Hand-held units for distributors can print bills and receipts on-site. They can also display instructions and give geographical directions. Upon returning to the distribution outlet, the handheld computer is downloaded and a report printed.

Packaging material waste can be saved by using programs which maximize use of package size and product arrangement, space on pallets, space in trucks, design of containers and overwraps.

Product recalls are greatly assisted with proper product information storage and retrieval systems.

Production Control

Supervisory control and data acquisition (SCADA) systems are becoming well established. These involve communication with control systems, communication with various databases, formulation controls, and various reporting and program interfaces. Computerized production control depends upon the type of food processing operation. Typically, a process with a high degree of automation has been a more likely candidate for computer interfaces. Processes requiring more flexibility have tended to be more manual in nature. Processes with little automation can still take advantage of computer technology using specific formulation programs and data logging devices.

Automation and computer control can be seen along most of the manufacturing chain, from raw materials to finished product. Automatic computer-based fruit and vegetable sorters and graders are gaining in speed and accuracy while the costs are decreasing (Demetrakakes, 1995). Computerized control of basic processing steps such as weighing can be performed using machines equipped with programmable logic controllers that weigh and record different ingredients.

Computer control in thermal processing of canned foods provides for greater accuracy. Control operations such as venting, cooking and cooling, are sequenced automatically. Predictions of the extent of heat treatment can be made. Methods have been developed using optimization techniques to predict temperature changes in a can during sterilization. The model determines a lethality value which is used in the heating turn-off decision (Ryniecki and Jayas, 1993). Boiler efficiency can also improve with the use of microprocessor controls to optimize the air and fuel ratios. Large hydrostatic retorts' processors can benefit from expert systems developed to determine and correct problems inherent to these sterilization systems.

Vision systems have been developed to check cans on-line (Robe, 1992). Capabilities of digital cameras to capture images of food products during the process, and to evaluate and store essential parts of the digitized image is a rapidly developing and expanding field. High speed video motion analysis can be used to solve production problems caused by can making and food processing machines (Larson 1989). In the food industry, image processing has been applied to detection of slicing defects, color of baked goods, dough thickness, surface texture and size, missing or damaged labels, faulty closures, defective pieces, and extraneous matter such as glass or bone fragments (Mans, 1988).

In the packaging area, computer controlled printers can help meet legal requirements for date and production detail. Programs can stores variable text, logos, designs or bar codes.

Warehouse automation offers reduced product cost and improved customer service through either the use of minor software automation or multi-million dollar renovation/construction depending on production volume and physical restrictions. The simplest approach is to implement a warehouse management system (WMS) involving forklift operators interfacing with a remote computer. Reported improvements by WMS included 20% in daily throughput and 40% in lift-truck productivity (Berne, 1994).

Another area in automation is the use of robotics. Today, robots are smarter, faster, capable of operating at speeds similar or better than human operators in some applications. The main advantage is that they do not suffer from fatigue or develop repetitive motion illnesses. A small meat products producer is using a USDA-approved two-robot system to pack up to 160 frozen patties per minute into cases. The robots are equipped with machine vision and interchangeable grippers to handle various patties shapes and different layer patterns in the cases. The investment on the system will be recovered in about 2 years, running two shifts per day (Swientek, 1993).

Quality Assurance

Statistical Process Control (SPC) and Hazard Analysis Critical Control Points (HACCP) programs are commonly monitored using computer systems. The large amounts of data generated can more easily be manipulated and schedules maintained using electronic media. A promising area of development in this area is the use of neural networks to correlate processing or raw material information with final product analysis and quality. Feedback can be rapid with high accuracy.

Product Development

Least cost formulations using linear regression are facilitated and in many cases made possible by the use of computer programs. Software is available to assist with experimental design.

Computer modelling can help to formulate beverages. Models consider potential ingredients which may contribute to a typical type of beverage. Rather than one-variable-at-a-time experimentation, computed multidimensional modelling and optimization combined with experimental test design can identify essential variables. A trained sensory panel is essential in this case (Bomio, 1994).

Nutritional Labeling

Well developed nutritional databases are in use. Camera-ready labels can be prepared in formats that conform to new Nutritional Labeling and Education Act (NLEA) regulations.- Credibility of the database is critical.

APPLICATION CONSIDERATIONS

Review Current Process

Before any efforts to computerize a process or information flow, the state of the current business must be examined. This is particularly important anticipating the need for most companies to network computers for data and information exchange. Computers cannot efficiently help a poorly organized business. However, if a company is suffering from disjointed activities, computerization is an opportunity to take an integrated approach to the product/process design cycle (Bruin 1992). Regarding computers, consider that the more natural tasks that humans do almost without thinking tend to be very difficult for a computer. Highly analytical jobs involving complex number manipulations are much better handled by computers.

Assignment

An individual or committee needs to be responsible for assessing the needs of the company. Input should be obtained from all individuals involved. Once needs have been established internally, a vendor can be contacted. These responsibilities would belong to the Information Systems department in most medium and large companies. It is still valuable to involve as many interested parties as possible. Features to consider include conversations and reports from other users, interfaces, vendor support and upgrades.

Implementation and Evaluation

Once a system is selected and installed, training is essential for a smooth transition. Effective education helps to teach basic principles and helps the user to have confidence in the system. The full range of tasks for which the computer upgrade is designed should be evaluated.

ACKNOWLEDGEMENTS

The author wishes to thank Robert L. Olsen, Schreiber Foods, Inc., Green Bay, WI and Olga Padilla-Zakour, Cornell University/NYSAES, Geneva, NY for their contributions to this chapter.

REFERENCES

Berne, S. 1994. The ins and outs of automated warehousing. *Prepared Foods* (4):81-85.

Blythe, K. 1994. Computerized monitoring of suppliers ans supplies. *Food Technology International Europe*, 155-157.

Bomio, M. 1994. Magic ingredients. *International Food Ingredients* (3):37-42.

Bruin, S. 1992. Integrated process design: issues and opportunities. *Food and Bioproducts Processing* 70(C3):126-130.

Demetrakakes, P. 1995. Graders appeal to fruit, vegetable market. *Food Processing* 56(2):49-51.

Demetrakakes, P. 1994. Casting a wide net. *Food Processing* 55(10):69-70.

Eerikainen, T., Linko, P., Linko, S., Siimes, T. and Zhu, Y. H. 1993. *Trends in Food Science & Technology* 4(8):237-242.

Hollingsworth, P. 1994. Computerized manufacturing trims production costs. *Food Technology* 48(12):43-45.

Hourigan, J. A. 1994. Artificial neural networks in the dairy industry. *Australian Journal of Dairy Technology* 49(Nov):110-133.

Larsen, M. 1989. Slow down motion to speed up line. *Packaging* (Newton) 34(16):89.

REFERENCES - Continued

Mans, J. 1994. Software for the toolbox. *Prepared Foods* (6):95-96.

Mans, J. 1988. Sensors: windows into the process. *Prepared Foods* 157(3):81.

Onyango, C. M. and Marchant, J. A. 1994. Transputers for high speed grading. *Food Control* 5(1):29-32.

Robe, K. 1992. On-the-fly can line checking. *Food Processing* (Chicago) 53(8):128, 130.

Ryniecki, A. and Jayas, D. S. 1993. Automatic determination of model parameters for computer control of canned food sterilization. *Journal of Food Engineering* 19(1):75-94.

Schutt, J. H. 1993. Integrated planning makes inroads at food companies. *Food Processing* 54(11):112-114.

Swientek, B. 1993. Ergonomics: applying science to job design. *Prepared Foods* (4):52-55.

CHAPTER 11

Ingredients

This chapter presents a discussion of basic properties, applications, and regulations pertaining to some of the main groups of ingredients used in the preparation of canned and other processed foods.

FOOD ADDITIVES

Foods are made up of a mixture of chemicals put together by nature, but not all foods produced by nature are harmless, some contain toxic substances; examples are the presence of oxalic acid in spinach and rhubarb and other toxic substances in certain species of mushrooms and berries are other examples. Even the most innocent substances, salt for example, can be harmful when used to excess. Then, again there are strychnine and arsenic compounds which are extremely toxic substances, but that in very small amounts are used for medicinal purposes. The criterion used as a guide is not whether a food is or is not of natural origin, but whether the particular food or ingredient has or does not have toxic characteristics in the amounts used. The burden of the proof today is on food processing firms or on additive manufacturers.

To scientists and food technologists and, practically speaking, to the general public, a food additive is "a substance or a mixture of substances, other than a basic foodstuff, which is present in a food as a result of any aspect of production, processing, storage or packaging." These substances are frequently divided into two classes, (1) **intentional additives,** added on purpose to perform specific functions, and (2) **incidental additives** which, though they have no function in the finished food, become part of a food through some phase of agricultural production, or processing, packaging or storage. According to this definition, chemicals such as sodium bicarbonate, citric acid, ascorbic acid (Vitamin C), thiamine, gelatin, and even common spices are considered additives, along with many other formidable sounding chemicals.

On the other hand, a lawyer must view a food additive as defined in the Food Additives Amendment to the Federal Food, Drug and Cosmetic Act: "Any substance the intended use of which results, or may reasonably be expected to result, directly or indirectly in its becoming a component or otherwise affecting the characteristics of any food (including any substance intended for use in producing, manufacturing, packing, processing, preparing, treating, packaging, transporting, or holding food; and including any source of radiation intended for any such use), if such substance is not generally recognized, (GRAS substances) among experts qualified by scientific training and experience to evaluate its safety, as having been adequately shown through scientific procedures to be safe under the conditions of its intended use (or, in the case of a substance used in food prior to January 1, 1958, through either scientific procedures or experience based on common use in food)."

In other words, the legal definition of food additives excludes most additives in common use because they are "generally recognized as safe" (GRAS) or because they have been previously approved for use. Other substances, such as pesticides and colors, are excluded because they are covered under other sections of the law. Thus, a food additive (to scientists and laymen) is not a food additive (to lawyers and legislators) when its use in a food has been approved according to the specifications of the Food Additives Amendment. For the purposes of this section the laymen's definition will be used.

Some additives are employed to perform specific functions in food products: such as to improve nutritive value, preserve the quality of the food, or to flavor or color the food. Other additives become part of the food product through some phase of fresh food production, processing, storage, or packaging. For example, an agricultural chemical applied to crops might be carried over into some processed foods, or a substance present in the food package might migrate into the food contained in that package. An example of the latter instance is calcium propionate used to control mold in bread or cheese by its activity in the bread wrapper. Additives such as agricultural chemicals, or substances that migrate from food packages may be present in foods, although usually only in minute amounts. Farmers and food processors, as well as federal and state public health authorities should all cooperate to make sure that these additives do not exceed safe limits. Food additives should be used in scientifically controlled amounts, no more than the amount necessary to perform the needed function, assuming that the amount has been found and declared safe by U.S. Food and Drug Administration.

Functions of Additives

Additives perform nine distinct functions:

1. **As Nutrition Supplements.** Vitamins, minerals, and amino acids used to improve general nutrition. Rickets has been practically eliminated in this country through the widespread availability of vitamin D-fortified milk. Incidence of goiter has been reduced by the use of iodized salt. A general improvement in health standards can be traced to the supplementation of cereal products with thiamin, riboflavin, niacin, iron, and in some

cases, with calcium and vitamin D. It has been estimated, for example, that enrichment of cereal foods alone provides 12% to 23% of the daily supply of thiamine, niacin, and iron, and 10% of our riboflavin. Breakfast cereals combined with milk are, according to nutrition experts, nutritionally good foods.

2. **As Coloring Agents.** The natural coloring materials in foods may be intensified, modified, or stabilized by the addition of neutral coloring materials or certified food dyes. While these chemicals alter only the appearance of food, they are important for the esthetic value they add and the psychological effect they have on food consumption habits.
3. **As Preservatives.** Chemicals may be used to help prevent or retard microbiological spoilage and chemical deterioration. However, they must not disguise spoilage, deceive the consumer, or permit unsanitary food handling.
4. **As Flavoring Agents.** In number, flavor additives probably exceed all other intentional chemical food additives combined; in volume, their use is small. All natural as well as synthetic flavors used in foods must first be approved as safe for health. The similarity of synthetic flavors to those produced in nature permits both types to be used freely in combination, with results not different from either used alone. Flavor enhancers, which do not add flavors, but instead intensify those already present, also require approval for use. Chemical enhancers were developed originally for commercial food processing, however one such chemical, monosodium glutamate (MSG), has since found a market as a consumer product. The safety of MSG was reaffirmed by the National Academy of Sciences National Research Council, but, since it was not found to benefit infants, NCA/NRC recommended that it not be used in infant foods.
5. **As Agents to Improve Functional Properties.** Chemicals in this classification act as thickening, firming, and maturing agents, or affect the colloidal properties of foods, such as in gelling, emulsifying, foaming, and suspending. Calcium salts, for example, help firm the texture of canned tomatoes.
6. **As Processing Aids.** Sanitizing agents, metal binding compounds, anti-foaming agents, chemicals that prevent fermentation and chemicals that remove extraneous materials are grouped in this classification. Examples are silicones to prevent foam formation in wine fermentation, and citric acid to combine with metals and prevent oxidative rancidity.
7. **As Moisture-Content Controls.** Chemicals are sometimes used to increase or decrease the moisture content in food products, for instance, glycerine is approved for use in marshmallows as a humectant to retain soft texture. Calcium silicate is frequently added to table salt to prevent caking caused by moisture in the air.

8. **As Acid-Alkaline Controls.** Various acids, alkalis and salts may be added to food to establish a desired pH. Phosphoric acid in soft drinks and citrate salts in fruit jellies are examples of this chemical control of acid-alkaline balance.
9. **As Physiologic Activity Controls.** The additives in this group are usually added to fresh foods to serve as ripeners or anti-metabolic agents. Examples of application for this purpose are ethylene, used to hasten the ripening of bananas, and malic hydrazide, used to prevent potatoes from sprouting.

Safety of Additives

The safety of additives is tested through animal feeding experiments. These studies sometimes require two years or more and may involve such experimental animals as rats, guinea pigs, and monkeys.

When all studies are completed and proposers of a new additive are convinced the additive will perform the needed function in food and that it is safe for its intended use, research data are submitted to the U.S. Food and Drug Administration. Government scientists make a thorough examination of the research data with regard to its proposed use and safety of the additive. They then approve or disapprove use of the additive for the application requested, or added information may be requested.

The concept of safety involves the question of whether a substance is hazardous to the health of man or animal and requires proof of reasonable certainty that no harm will result from the proposed use of an additive; it does not and cannot require proof beyond any possible doubt that no harm will result under any conceivable circumstances. In determining safety, the following must be considered: (1) the quantity consumed of the additive; (2) any substances formed in the food because of the presence of the additive; (3) the cumulative effect of such additive in the diet of man or animals, taking into account any chemically or pharmacologically related substances in the diet; and (4) safety factors which, in the opinion of experts qualified by scientific training and experience to evaluate the safety of food additives, are generally recognized as appropriate for the use of animal experimentation data.

When Additives Should Not Be Used

The use of additives is not in the best interest of consumers and should not be permitted in the following situations:

1. To disguise the use of faulty processing and handling techniques, e.g., to reduce bacterial counts or conceal off-odors.
2. To deceive the consumer, e.g., addition of color when its use has not been legally approved.
3. When the use of a food additive results in a substantial reduction in the nutritive value of a food.

4. When the desired effect can be obtained by good manufacturing practices which are economically feasible.

SALT, SALT TABLETS, AND COMBINATION TABLETS IN CANNING

Sodium chloride, or common salt, incorporated directly into canned foods, should be of the highest purity with stringent tolerances on trace heavy metal and hardness impurities. Even minute traces of iron, copper and chromium contributed by salt can cause a spotty discoloration in canned vegetables by reverting green chlorophyll to brown pheophytin and forming brownish complexes with tannins and anthocyanins in the liquor. With the conversion from tinplate to enamel-coated containers, iron has become a particularly serious problem with so-called "sulfide-stainer" vegetables–asparagus, beans, potatoes and carrots–requiring supplemental addition of calcium salts to ensure adequate firmness, drained weights or consistency. Calcium and magnesium impurities can cause a cloudy brine in pickled vegetables by precipitating tannins, oxalate and gums.

Recommended hardness in canning for various vegetables are shown on the following page.

Generally, an adequate salt purity for salting canned foods can be assured by the use of granulated salt produced by vacuum pan crystallization; such salt should be of 99.6% minimum sodium chloride purity. For vegetables sensitive to heavy metal discoloration or hardness impurities, a high purity salt with a minimum of 99.9% sodium chloride and maximum tolerances of 100 ppm for calcium and magnesium calculated as calcium, 1.5 ppm for iron, and 1.0 ppm for copper should be used. Most salt used today for canned foods is 99.9+% NaCl.

TABLE 11.1 – Recommended Hardness of Can Brine for Various Vegetables

	Optimum Range as Calcium (ppm)
Asparagus	45–80
Green Beans	45–80
Dry Kidney & Lima Beans	30–65
Beets	30–65
Carrots	100–200
Corn	50–100
Peas	20–65
Potatoes (less than 1.075 sp. gravity)	30–65
Spinach	25–50
Tomatoes (net contents)	250–500

Brine

Most canned vegetable brines are prepared with one to two percent salt; for some products, like peas and corn, a sweetener is also added. For reasons cited previously, a soft, iron and sulfide-free water supply should be used to prepare brine. Saturated salt brine (26.4% sodium chloride) can be prepared in automatic brine making equipment and pumped to the use point. To avoid serious corrosion problems, such equipment and in-plant brine pipes should be constructed of fiberglass or plastic material, or fabricated of 316 stainless steel construction or its equivalent. Automatic brine makers charged with bagged salt are available in small sizes capable of continuously producing 10 gpm (38 l/min) of brine. Large bulk storage tanks filled by pneumatic bulk trucks, can produce in excess of 40 gpm (150 l/min) saturated brine.

Brine Dispensing

Saturated brine or mixtures of brine with hot, concentrated sugar syrup can be pumped directly to automatic liquid dispensers which accurately dispense

FIGURE 11.1 – Salt Storage Tank with 72-Ton Capacity (Courtesy Scienco)

5-80 milliliters "shots" to individual cans. Dispensers must be mounted on the in-feed to the product filler where empty containers can be indexed to dispenser controls. Liquid dispensers are limited to line speeds of less than 250 cans per minute due to an increased frequency of misses at higher line speeds and splashing of corrosive brine.

Other water soluble additives in trace amounts may be incorporated and dispensed with brine, but this usually requires some dilution with water. For example, addition of more than 2% calcium chloride to a saturated brine will result in some precipitation of sodium chloride. Certain unstable additives such as ascorbic acid (Vitamin C) and ethylendiamine tetra-acetate salts (EDTA) should not be dispensed in combination with salt brine.

Saturated brine may be diluted with water to single strength brine and dispensed by valve filler (syruper) or by sanitary overflow briners. Since single strength brine must be heated to 180–190°F (82–88°C) to ensure an adequate vacuum, such equipment must be fabricated from highly corrosion resistant 316 stainless steel or monel. Since EPA regulations severely restrict the amount of salt permitted in plant sewage discharges, brine must be recycled when overflow briners are employed which, in turn, requires that containers be washed prior to filling as a minimal sanitary precaution.

FIGURE 11.2 – Liquid Dispensing System (Courtesy Scienco).

Potassium Chloride

The only generally recognized salt substitute is potassium chloride which exhibits an unpleasant bitter aftertaste; this bitterness is essentially masked in 50 percent mixtures with sodium chloride. Such 50/50 mixtures can substitute on a nearly equivalent basis for regular salt and yet provide a similar degree of flavor enhancement in canned vegetables, thus reducing sodium contribution by 50 percent and restoring potassium lost in processing.

Federal regulations require label declaration of sodium and potassium content. Accordingly, the method for adding potassium chloride or mixtures with sodium chloride should be extremely accurate.

Measuring Salt Content

Several methods are employed for measuring the salt content of can and pickling brines. The simplest and most rapid procedure is specific gravity measurement using a graduated hydrometer or salometer. However, the accuracy of salometer method is inadequate for weak solutions of less than about 2.5% sodium chloride (10°S) limiting applications to concentrated canning and pickling brines. Refractometers have some practical application in relatively pure solutions, but are useless for sweet brines and juices. Electrical conductivity meters are practical for relatively pure brines and sweet brines which do not contain significant levels of other electrolytes such as calcium chloride or various organic acids.

The official methods (AOAC) for determining salt content in canned foods are based on titration of chloride ion by silver nitrate against a potassium dichromate indicator. Titration is by far the most accurate procedure, but has the disadvantages of being time consuming and requiring somewhat skilled technicians. Various quick test titration devices are available which provide faster results at the sacrifice of precision. Chloride ion titration will always yield a higher salt content value than the theoretical amount added due to a natural content in vegetables and will not, or course, distinguish sodium chloride from other chloride salt ingredients such as calcium chloride. Atomic absorption or flame photometry methods should be employed if sodium and potassium label declarations are required.

Tablets and Tablet Depositors

Preformed, ball-shaped tablets containing salt or other micro-ingredients can be dispensed into individual containers by mechanical depositors. Standard can or gear driven depositors service a range of line speeds up to 400 cans per minute. Special computer-controlled equipment is available to service faster lines up to 1000 cpm. One or two tablets can be dispensed per container. Depositors are designed to service all sizes of cylindrical containers up to 603 x 700 (157 x 178 mm).

Standard plain salt tablets are available for various applications, ranging in size from 10-400 grains (0.65-25.76 grams). Combination tablets incorporate salt with one or more other additives or ingredients such as acidulants, calcium chloride or calcium sulfate for firming, ascorbic acid and other vitamins and minerals, EDTA salts for color preservation, potassium chloride, sugar and other sweeteners, spice and flavor compounds. Accuracy is ±5%.

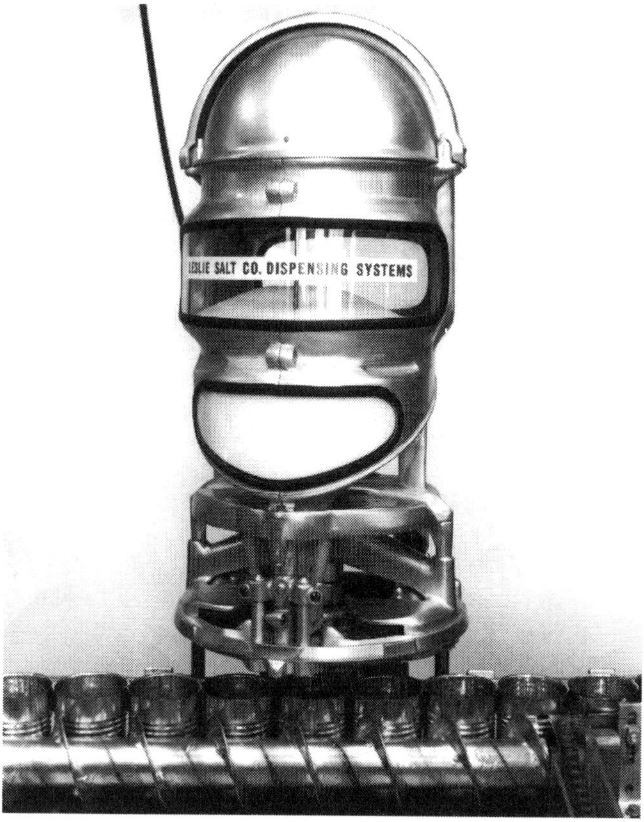

FIGURE 11.3 – Dry Bulk Dispenser for Salt

Dry Bulk Dispensing

Container driven and line powered bulk dispensers are widely employed in food processing for depositing dry, free-flowing ingredients. New, improved models are successfully used for depositing fine granular ingredients, i.e., vacuum processed sodium chloride, granular citric acid, calcium chloride and ascorbic acid. Dehydrated bulk vegetable dispensers are available for depositing aromatic vegetables such as cut bell pepper, flake and diced onion, various seasoning seeds and chopped nuts.

These mechanically operated bulk dispensers are easily adaptable to cylindrical containers and unusual shapes such as pear shaped, semi-rigid containers, glass barrel, shoulder and short line types with range of container sizes from 202/214 ounce glass to 603/812.

Deposit portions are controlled by a flat, revolving disc manufactured to required "charge" specifications at tested, actual line speeds. The disc is container rotated through use of a can turret which revolves as a container travels past. Timing of the "charge" drop is controlled by relating the position of the can setting in the turret with the portion control opening in the disc. Deposit speeds range widely depending on a deposit amount, container opening, and container size.

Multiple bulk dispensers can be mounted in line, dispensing partial charges or separate ingredients. Interchangeable metering discs simplify the change of deposit amounts or container size.

CARBOHYDRATES IN CANNING AND PRESERVING

Carbohydrates are used by the food industry principally for sweetening or thickening processed foods; they are also used to provide bulk and nutritive solids. Table 11.2 lists several foods that use carbohydrates for these principal functions. Wide use over a long period of time has revealed a host of additional reasons for the addition of carbohydrates; some of the more important reasons are listed in Table 11.3. Selection of appropriate carbohydrate ingredients involves more than simply deciding upon desired properties and then selecting carbohydrates that provide those properties; with regard to economics, availability, world markets, distribution advantages, and applicable federal and state regulations must also be considered.

These other factors notwithstanding, it is extremely important to the modern food processor to take advantage of specific characteristics of each carbohydrate available in order to gain the greatest quality advantage for products. No single carbohydrate could be expected to provide all the characteristics listed in Table 11.3; practically any processed food requires two or more carbohydrates to provide these properties.

As noted, all carbohydrates used in foods can be placed in one of two categories based on their principal function. Those carbohydrates used for sweetening are known technically as saccharides, and commonly as sugars. Those used for thickening are, technically, polysaccharides, and commonly, starches and gums.

TABLE 11.2 – Canned Foods That Usually Contain Added Carbohydrates

Fruits	Canned Puddings
Fruit Juices	Jams, Jellies, Preserves
Tomato Products	Table Syrups
(Catsup)	Peanut Butter
(Chili Sauce)	Pie Fillings
(Tomato Sauce)	Condiments
(Tomatoes)	(Salad Dressings)
Vegetables	(Mayonnaise)
(Pork and Beans)	Meat Products
(Harvard Beets)	(Chili)
(Sweet Potatoes)	(Stews)
Pickles-Relishes	(Sausages)
	Soups

This division, relative to function, is artificial, and some sweeteners may also provide thickening to some degree, and thickeners may be used to provide or modify the perception of sweetness. The division is, however, convenient in terms of principal use and will be retained here for purposes of discussion.

TABLE 11.3 – Carbohydrate Functions

Nutrition	Body
Sweetness	Surface Tension
Flavor Control	Osmotic Pressure
Color	Crystallization
Sheen	Cohesiveness
Viscosity	Texture

SWEETENERS

Introduction

When over one billion pounds of high fructose corn syrup was produced by the corn refining industry in 1974, the event was noted as an acknowledged change in the identity of an industry from "sugar" to "sweetener." The designation "sweetener industry" emphasizes the change in the U.S. food system that began after World War II with a major shift in food preparation from the home kitchen to the food processing plant. This shift was accompanied by an expansion in the use of corn-derived sweeteners and helped stimulate technological advances in the corn refining industry which culminated in the introduction of high fructose corn syrup.

The full impact of high fructose corn syrup on the U.S. sweetener system is yet to be felt in all segments of the system. New products introduced into a free market must display advantages to the consumer before their acceptability and continuity are assured. In the case of high fructose corn syrup, the worldwide shortage of sugar (sucrose) in 1974 hastened this acceptance. Acceptance by industrial consumers is widespread and, without question, insures expanding usage. As familiarity with high fructose corn syrup increases, and as continuing research and development by the corn refining industry produces new high fructose products, the added flexibility that these materials offer to the sweetener user will help to clarify the concepts of "sweetener industry" and "sweetener system."

Corn-derived sweeteners, particularly syrups, became well established in the United States as acceptable commercial products in the late 19th century, but were classified as substitutes because of their lesser sweetness. For the most part their use was restricted to the food industry. A long series of quantitative limitations were imposed on the use of corn syrup in standardized foods such as canned fruits and jams and jellies. Through the years new syrups with improved functional properties were developed by corn refiners, but they remained less sweet than sucrose. In the 1980s, however, this barrier has been broken by the introduction of high fructose corn syrup, a product equivalent in sweetness to invert (sugar) syrup.

Achievement of sweetness equality by enzymatic isomerization of glucose (which gives rise to a mixture of glucose and fructose, the two constituents of sucrose) was a notable event. Originally a limitation was imposed on the use of corn sweeteners in a number of standardized foods. High fructose corn syrup is no longer limited in either standardized or any food formulations other than by its intrinsic physical and chemical properties. This same limitation, of course, applies to all nutritive sweeteners.

As anticipated, further research and development has produced new high fructose corn syrups-particularly variations containing larger amounts of fructose. Advanced sugar technology allows glucose and fructose to be separated so that the fructose content of high fructose corn syrup can be increased virtually at will. Such products promise to increase the sweetness of food products, notably beverages, without increasing the caloric load, and will also help control crystallization in jam and jelly formulations, among other possibilities.

Dextrose (d-Glucose)

Dextrose is a monosaccharide (simple sugar) and occurs naturally in all plant and animal systems, either in its free or bound form, e.g., example in corn starch. It is the primary sugar in fruits. Dextrose is commercially available as a white crystalline material, usually as a monohydrate crystal. The U.S.

Food and Drug Administration defines dextrose monohydrate as: "Purified and crystallized d-glucose containing one molecule of water of crystallization with each molecule of d-glucose. The name of the food is 'dextrose monohydrate' or dextrose."

In the United States, commercial dextrose is manufactured almost exclusively from corn starch. Dextrose is used extensively in all types of fruit and vegetable canning where sweeteners are permitted. It is usually present as a component of other corn sweeteners, as corn syrup and high fructose corn syrup. The reasons for its current mode of use are partly economics and partly the functional properties of dextrose.

The properties of dextrose depend on its structure; it is a simple sugar of relatively low molecular weight (180.16) and contains a chemically reactive center called an aldehyde group. Sugars with this chemical structure are known collectively as aldoses. All possess the characteristic property of reducing salts of heavy metals in alkaline solution; thus aldoses (including dextrose) are commonly called reducing sugars.

Because of its low molecular weight, dextrose solutions provide high osmotic pressure causing rapid penetration of the sugar into fruits and vegetables when it is used. This high osmotic pressure also provides excellent preservation properties by causing dehydration of microbial cells with subsequent inhibition of growth or actual death of microorganisms.

The aldehyde structure in dextrose is responsible for its reactivity with nitrogenous compounds such as amino acids and proteins. When dextrose is mixed with these materials and heated, it undergoes a complex series of changes called collectively "non enzymatic browning" which results in the production of brown pigments of varying degrees of color intensity. This property makes dextrose a desirable sugar in products such as pork and beans or canned sweet potatoes.

Dextrose is freely soluble in water; at ambient temperatures (70–80°F) (21–27°C), saturated dextrose solutions hold about 50–53% of dextrose. At 110–120°F (43–49°C), saturated solutions hold about 65–69% dextrose; these solutions typically are low viscosity (10–100 centipoise).

Dextrose, at most use levels, is about 0.7 to 0.8 times as sweet as sucrose, i.e., it is less sweet than sucrose. For this reason dextrose is often considered the sweetener of choice where sucrose produces an overly sweet taste. When used in about a 30/70 ratio with sucrose, however, there is no reduction in sweetness due to a synergistic effect of the two sugars.

Pure dextrose is distributed in dry or liquid form. Dextrose is also a component of other sweeteners which may be available in either dry or liquid form.

Levulose (d-Fructose)

Levulose, like dextrose, is a monosaccharide that occurs naturally in virtually all plant and animal systems, either in its free or bound form.

Unlike dextrose, fructose is commercially available mostly in liquid form, and rarely as a pure solution. Since it is extremely soluble (79% w/w at 68°F) (20°C) and can be crystallized only from very pure solutions, the crystalline product is 3 to 10 times more expensive than conventional products such as high fructose corn syrups.

Fructose possesses essentially the same functional properties as dextrose with two notable exceptions. Where the chemically active center of dextrose is an aldehyde, in fructose it is a ketone; fructose is a member of the class of sugars called "ketoses" which, like the aldoses, are reducing sugars.

Ketoses (including fructose) also react with nitrogenous compounds to produce brown pigments. They are characteristically more reactive than aldoses and produce more intense color in a shorter time. Thus fructose may be undesirable when it is necessary to have good control over color development in a food.

Probably the most significant difference in functional property is sweetness. Pure crystalline fructose is nearly 1.8 times sweeter than sucrose and 2.3 times sweeter than dextrose. Pure fructose solutions are 1.3 to 1.5 times sweeter than sucrose and 1.6 times sweeter than dextrose.

Since most fructose is sold as a component in a syrup, uses of fructose will be covered under high fructose corn syrup and invert sugar syrup.

Sucrose

Sucrose, common table sugar, is a disaccharide. It is composed of one molecule each of dextrose and levulose which are chemically bound so that the respective aldehyde and ketone groups are no longer chemically reactive; sucrose is not a reducing sugar.

Sucrose is obtained commercially from both sugar beets and sugar cane. Pure sucrose from either source is indistinguishable. It is the most traditional sweetener, commonly used in almost all canning processes which require sweeteners. Because of the historical acceptance of sucrose as a sweetener, it is the one sugar allowed in all foods which permit addition of sweeteners. This same historical acceptance has led to sucrose's being considered the reference standard for comparing sweetening power i.e., relative sweetness is traditionally measured in terms of iso-sweet sucrose solutions.

The primary functions of sucrose are to provide sweetness and nutritive solids. Other functions are due to its chemical and physical properties. Since it is a disaccharide (dextrose plus levulose), its molecular weight (342) is nearly twice that of either of the simple sugars; it provides lower rates of penetration in fruits and vegetables and has less of a preservation effect than either of the monosaccharides.

It is more soluble at ordinary temperatures than is dextrose, but is less soluble then fructose. Since sucrose is not a reducing sugar, it does not participate in browning reactions.

Because it is a disaccharide, it is susceptible to being broken down into its component simple sugars. This breakdown process is called hydrolysis and can be accomplished by either heat and acid, or enzymatically by an enzyme called invertase. The decomposition product is called invert sugar syrup and is usually a mixture of sucrose, dextrose and fructose. This decomposition process is known to occur commonly in processed foods, especially in high acid foods. When it occurs, functionality is no longer due only to sucrose, but to the combined functionality of the simple sugars, dextrose and levulose, and the remaining sucrose.

The fact that sucrose decomposition is such a common occurrence in foods has led to the ready acceptance of high fructose corn syrup as a total replacement for sucrose in those foods. Acceptance of high fructose corn syrup has been enhanced by more favorable economics while preserving functionality.

Invert Sugar

Invert, or invert sugar (syrup), is the common name applied to a variety of products prepared commercially by the decomposition of sucrose. The most common invert sugar is a mixture of approximately 50% sucrose and 25% each dextrose and levulose. Total invert is a mixture of about 6% sucrose and about 47% each dextrose and levulose.

The sweetness of invert sugar syrups varies depending on their composition. Generally they are 1.05 to 1.2 times as sweet as sucrose. Functional properties such as osmotic pressure and browning reactions vary, depending upon the composition of the syrup.

Invert syrups are used principally for sweetening. Because of their slight to greater sweetness, invert syrups may provide some modest economic advantage, especially when sucrose would not be expected to decompose into an invert type of sweetener.

Invert sugar syrups, like sucrose, are rapidly being replaced by high fructose corn syrups in many foods where invert syrup has been the traditional sweetener; the reason again is because of economic advantage while functionality is retained.

Corn Syrup (Glucose Syrup)

The U.S. Food and Drug Administration identifies corn syrup as a purified and concentrated mixture of saccharides obtained by hydrolysis of corn starch.

When the type of starch used is not specified, the more general name, glucose syrup, is applied to the product. The Standard of Identity specifies in part that corn (glucose) syrup contain not less than 70% by weight total solids, and a reducing sugar content (D.E.) expressed as d-glucose (dextrose) of not less than 20% by weight calculated on a dry basis. The hydrolytic process which results in corn syrup can be accomplished by either heat and acid, or by the action of enzymes, or by a combination of the two. The type and extent of hydrolysis will determine the composition of the saccharide mixture and dextrose equivalent. Corn syrup is, consequently, a generic name for a whole spectrum of nutritive sweeteners prepared from corn starch. Mild hydrolysis results in a saccharide mixture possessing a low D.E. and a high molecular weight, while extensive hydrolysis results in a saccharide mixture with a high D.E. and a low molecular weight.

The corn wet milling industry has, for classification purposes, identified four specific types of corn syrup as shown in Table 11.4; the variable used for classification is the dextrose equivalent. This particular attribute is important since it relates to the composition of the mixture of saccharides and some of the relevant functional properties. Because of its importance, it is essential to understand exactly what the term D.E. means.

TABLE 11.4 – Corn Syrup Classification

Corn Syrup	D.E. Range
Type I - Low Conversion	20–38
Type II - Regular Conversion	39–58
Type III - High Conversion	59–73
Type IV - Extra High Conversion	74–99 (approx.)

The saccharides in corn syrup are all aldoses and, hence, all are reducing sugars. Table 11.5 shows the typical composition of several corn syrups. Note that all contain saccharides, dextrose, maltose, maltotriose, and higher saccharides. The dextrose equivalent measures the aggregate reducing power of these saccharides (reducing sugar content), and compares it to d-glucose calculated on a dry basis. For example, if two parts by dry weight of corn syrup have a reducing power equivalent to one part by dry weight of dextrose, the corn syrup would have a dextrose equivalent of 50.

The functional properties of any particular corn syrup, as well as its D.E., are determined by the composition of the saccharide mixture. In Table 11.6, the qualitative effect of D.E. (or composition) on some functional properties is indicated. It is the interrelationships between composition, D.E., and functionality that have resulted in corn syrup's traditionally being selected for functionality based on its dextrose equivalent.

TABLE 11.5 – Corn Syrup, Typical Composition (Carbohydrate Basis)

Saccharide	~ 29 D.E.	~ 49 D.E.	~ 65 D.E.	~ 95 D.E.
Dextrose	9	20	35	93
Maltose	10	31	35	1
Maltotriose	12	18	10	2
Higher Saccharides	69	31	20	4
TOTAL	100	100	100	100

Low D.E. syrups may be used in products containing milk or other proteins where it is desirable to control consistency and color development and where high sweetness levels are not required. Low D.E. syrups are also used as a binder in semi-solid or highly concentrated foods such as some meat products where it is permitted by standards.

TABLE 11.6 – Corn Syrup Properties vs. Dextrose Equivalent

	Low (25 D.E.)	High (65 D.E.)
Browning	Low	High
Crystal Inhibitor	High	Low
Fermentables	Low	High
Osmotic Pressure	Low	High
Viscosity	High	Low
Reducing Sugars	Low	High
Molecular Weight	High	Low
Body (Mouthfeel)	High	Low

Regular D.E. corn syrups are commonly used in table syrups and in some jam, jelly and preserve recipes in conjunction with either sucrose or high fructose corn syrup. In table syrups, regular D.E. corn syrup provides body and mouthfeel and acts as a crystal inhibitor for either sucrose or dextrose. In jams, jellies and preserves, regular D.E. corn syrup is used to limit the amount of dextrose added to these foods and to serve as a crystal inhibitor for the dextrose already present in the fruit and from the high fructose corn syrup or invert syrup formed from sucrose. In this application, regular D.E. corn syrup is usually 20-40% of sweetener solids. Table syrups are generally made of 65 D.E. corn syrup blended with high fructose corn syrup.

High D.E. corn syrups (58–70 D.E.) are most widely used in canned fruit, fruit juice, and vegetables. They are frequently used in blends with sucrose and/or high fructose corn syrup, either of which provides the requisite level of sweetness. Corn syrup is used for its contribution to body and mouthfeel, the sheen it produces on the surface of fruit, and the desirable amount of browning, for example, in canned sweet potatoes.

In addition to these widely used corn syrups, there is a specialty syrup commonly called high maltose corn syrup. It is made by an enzymatic process that produces a saccharide mixture low in dextrose and high in maltose; it is nearly the functional equivalent of regular D.E. corn syrup. It differs in that it provides less browning tendency and presumably less chance of dextrose crystallization, especially in foods like jams, jellies and preserves, which are concentrated and normally contain high dextrose levels. Similar to regular syrups, it is mostly used in blends with either sucrose and/or high fructose corn syrup.

High Fructose Corn Syrup

This relatively new kind of corn syrup is made from extra high conversion (95 D.E.) corn syrup by an enzymatic process called isomerization. This process produces a syrup containing about 43% fructose, 52% dextrose, and 5% higher sugars. More recently, new technology has permitted manufacturers to prepare, by physical separation processes, new syrups containing up to 90% fructose. This whole body of technology has led to the commercial availability of three basic types of high fructose corn syrup, as shown in Table 11.7. These syrups contain mostly the monosaccharides fructose and dextrose; because of their composition, these syrups possess the functional properties associated with these monosaccharide sugars, that is, the syrups possess high osmotic pressures, are highly fermentable, readily participate in browning reactions, and may match or exceed the sweetness of sucrose.

The commercialization of high fructose corn syrup has thus made available a series of nutritive sweeteners equal to or surpassing sucrose and invert syrup in sweetness, and in many cases, providing the equivalent functionality. Because of its nearly functional equivalence and favorable cost, regular (42) high fructose corn syrup has found wide acceptance in many food products. In some foods it has entirely replaced sucrose, and in other foods, a partial replacement has been made. In either case, regular high fructose corn syrup is most widely used in conjunction with regular or high D.E. corn syrups that are in current use.

Fruit canners have replaced the traditional 75/25 sucrose/corn syrup cover syrup with 20/40/40 sucrose/high fructose corn syrup/corn syrup blends with the possibility of total replacement of sucrose when the 55% or 90% high fructose corn syrup is used.

Preservers are using approximately the same three way blend in jams, jellies and preserves. In fact, many preservers have successfully removed all of the sucrose and their products are sweetened with 100% corn sweetener, usually a 60/40 or 50/50 blend of high fructose corn syrup and regular corn syrup.

TABLE 11.7 – Typical Composition and Properties
High Fructose Corn Syrup (HFCS)

Saccharide	42% HFCS	55% HFCS	90% HFCS
Fructose	43	55	90
Dextrose	52	42	7
Higher Sugars	5	3	3
Total Solids	71	77	80
Relative Sweetness	90–100	100–110	110–130
Storage Temperature, °F Min.	85°	80°	
Storage Temperature, °C Min.	30°	27°	

Salad dressing, catsup, table syrup and pickle manufacturers have been able to totally replace sucrose with the 42% high fructose corn syrup in their product while retaining, or even increasing, the amount of regular corn syrup in formulations.

Because of the slight to moderate increase in sweetness in the 55% to 90% high fructose corn syrup, it is possible to slightly decrease total sweetener solids and maintain desirable sweetness levels. A further benefit of these syrups is their availability at higher total solids (6-9% greater than 42% high fructose corn syrup) which, in certain processes such as jelly making, means that less cooking is required to achieve finished solids.

The most recently available syrup, 90% high fructose corn syrup, has been tested extensively in low calorie or reduced calorie foods. Since its sweetness level is greater than sucrose, this affords the opportunity for the reduction of the carbohydrate level in formulation without sacrifice of sweetness.

Since these newer syrups (55% to 90% high fructose corn syrup) provide increased sweetness due to the higher fructose content, they are also less expensive to use than the 42% high fructose corn syrup in most canning applications. Because this economic advantage, most canners and preservers have accepted 42% high fructose corn syrup as a standard sweetener in canning and preserving processes.

Maltodextrins

The maltodextrins represent a special class of starch hydrolysates differentiated from corn syrups because they are less than 20 D.E. Like the corn syrups, they are prepared by acid and/or enzyme hydrolysis of starch. The maltodextrins are usually supplied as white, free flowing powders possessing a very bland taste.

Characteristically, maltodextrins have relatively high molecular weights and a low reducing power. The high molecular weights of maltodextrins cause their solutions to exhibit low osmotic pressures, high viscosities, and little or no sweetness. The low reducing power means that maltodextrins participate only slightly in browning reactions.

As with the carbohydrates, the characteristics and properties of maltodextrins suggest their utility in processed foods. High solution viscosity indicates their use to provide body and mouthfeel to fruit and vegetable drinks without adding to sweetness. For example, maltodextrin can be used in tomato cocktails to help suspend tomato solids and to improve the mouthfeel. Likewise, maltodextrins have been used in fruit juice based beverages to improve flavor and provide mouthfeel.

STARCH

Starch is widely distributed in nature and is the principal reserve carbohydrate in plants. Starches used by the food industry are usually obtained from grains such as corn and wheat or tubers such as tapioca and potato. Starch occurs in the form of small, white granules that vary in size from 3 to 100 microns. Starch granules from grains are usually 3 to 30 microns in size, while those from tubers are usually 10 to 100 microns.

Starch is a homopolymer of alpha-glucopyranose; the repeating unit of the polymer is called anhydroglucose (Figure 11.4, Part A). The chemical and physical properties of starch are largely due to the hydroxyl groups present in this structure; carbons 2, 3 and 6 each possess a primary hydroxyl.

The anhydroglucose units are chemically linked through alpha-1-4 glucosidic bonds (Figure 11.4, Part B) or secondarily through alpha-1-6 glucosidic bonds (Figure 11.4, Part C). The ability to polymerize at either of two linking sites gives rise to two different types of starch molecules.

PART A.

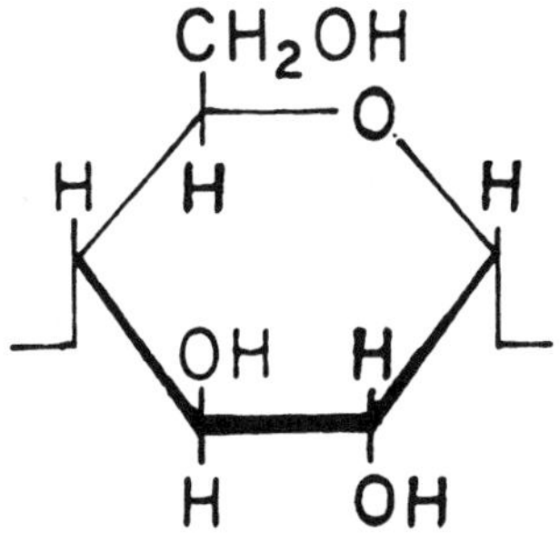

PART B.

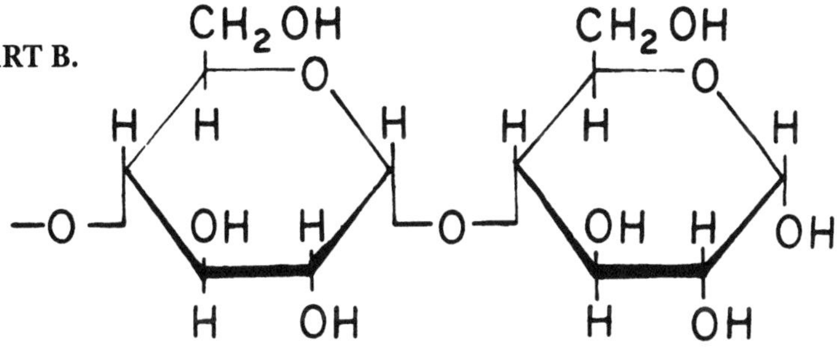

PART C.

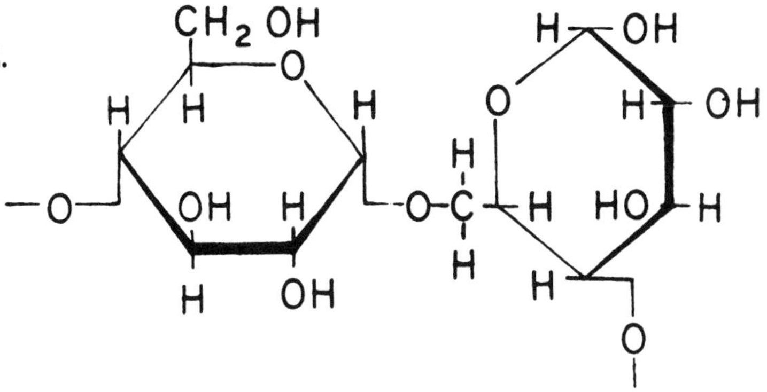

FIGURE 11.4 –
Part A. Repeating Units of Anhydroglucose
Parts B&C. Linking of Anhydroglucose Units

The primary alpha-1, 4 link causes formation of a linear polymer with one terminus having a hemiacetal reducing group (Figure 11.5). These linear polymers may form a branched molecule via the alpha-1, 6 glucosidic bond. These branched molecule consists of three types of polymer subunits. Type A consists of unbranched polymer linked via the alpha-1, 6 bond to type B subunits. The latter are branched polymers linked via the alpha-1, 6 bond to other type B subunits or to a Type C subunit. This last is a branched polymer possessing the hemiacetal reducing group. This branched structure is illustrated in Figure 11.6.

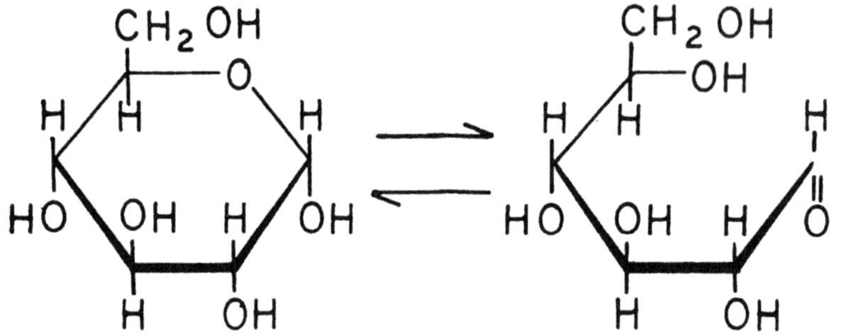

FIGURE 11.5 – Formation of Linear Polymer

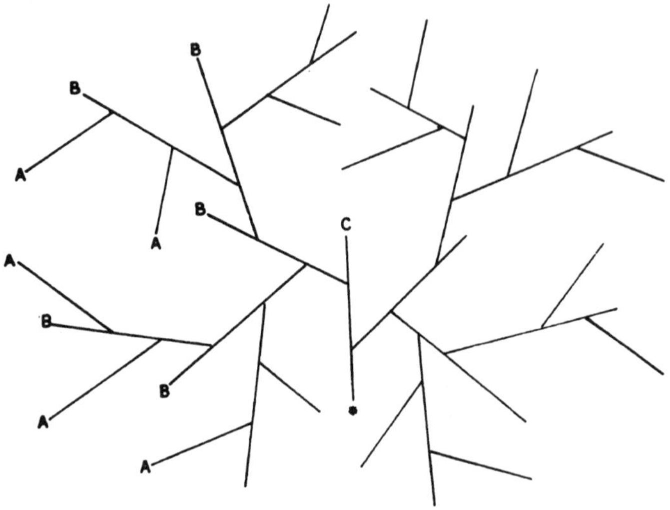

FIGURE 11.6 – Branched Polymeric Structure

The simple linear polymer is called amylose; it possesses 400-1200 anhydroglucose units. The more complex branched molecule is called amylopectin; it possesses 2000-5500 anhydroglucose units.

Most starches contain 15-30% amylose and 70-85% amylopectin; these starches are generally called "regular starch." Starches that contain nearly 100% amylopectin are called "waxy starch," while starches with 50-85% amylose are called "high amylose starch."

Whatever the structure, each molecule contains thousands of reactive hydroxyl groups. In native starch granules, these molecules are associated through intermolecular hydrogen bonding between hydroxyl groups. The large number of such bonds is responsible for the fact that native starch granules are insoluble in cold water. Chemical and physical modifications of starch are directed to interference with the formation of intermolecular hydrogen bonding via alteration of the hydrogen bonding between hydroxyl groups.

Simple cooking of starch in water is no more than an effort to break intermolecular hydrogen bond; this allows hydroxyl groups to form new hydrogen bonds with water molecules or with different hydroxyl groups on other starch molecules.

The difference in the structure of amylose and amylopectin accounts for the difference in properties and behaviors of cooked corn starch.

When a water slurry of starch is heated, the granules imbibe water and begin to swell due to loss of intermolecular hydrogen bonds. As the granules become swollen, they occupy a greater volume and consequently, are crowded together. This causes an increase in the viscosity of the slurry. At this stage, the slurry is nearly a sol, and it possesses a salve-like texture considered desirable. This step is short-lived; as heating continues, the swollen granules begin to disintegrate, viscosity decreases, and the salve-like texture disappears. Starch molecules and aggregates of starch molecules (still with intact intermolecular hydrogen bonds) are dispersed to form a typical starch sol. At this stage, the starch is said to be "cooked out" or "pasted."

When hot paste cools, it forms a rubbery gel caused by the formation of intermolecular hydrogen bonds between adjacent dispersed starch molecules; this is particularly evident in starch pastes containing amylose. Reassociation of molecules occurs to such an extent that water is exuded, a condition known as syneresis. If the sol is dilute, starch molecules may reassociate through hydrogen bonding to the extent that precipitation of starch occurs; this is called retrogradation.

Pastes of waxy starch containing only the highly branched amylopectin exhibit a somewhat different behavior. Because of a highly branched structure, amylopectin molecules are hindered from forming the highly associated molecular aggregates found in amylose; hence, waxy starch pastes, on cooling, do not form rigid gels nor do they retrograde. A weak gel usually forms due to reassociation of the outer unbranched chains of the molecules; these weak gels possess a highly cohesive texture.

Starch Modifications

Modern processing techniques require starch products which possess optimum thickening power, are non-gelling, are resistant to heat, acid, and shearing forces, and which exhibit stability at low temperatures. Starches must also be bland, possess good mouthfeel, and give good clarity and sheen.

Regular corn starches yield cooked pastes which are opaque, gel on storage, lack cohesiveness, have poor mouthfeel and poor temperature stability. Waxy starches possess much the same properties, except they are non-gelling and too cohesive, rather than lacking cohesiveness.

The result of the poor match between what canners might require of a starch and what native corn starches can provide is that many food starches are chemically modified to provide the properties required by canners.

There is a large body of literature on the preparation and use of modified starches for foods. The following descriptions for preparation and use of modified starches are intended to be merely illustrative of these techniques.

Bleaching

Starches in slurry form are treated with low levels of oxidizing agents such as hydrogen peroxide or chlorine bleaches as sodium hypochlorite; these oxidants lighten the color of starch by destroying natural pigments such as xanthophyll. These oxidants also help sterilize starch so that it will meet the rigid microbiological requirements of canners.

Parenthetically, most food grade starches do meet the NFPA microbiological specifications; it is probably more than coincidence that starch manufacturers are concerned about the same kinds of microorganisms as are canners. Microorganisms present in a starch processing operation can result in sour, foul-smelling, poor quality starch if not controlled. Simple economics dictate that starch processes be run in such a way as to minimize levels of microorganisms responsible for quality problems.

When bleaching of modified starches is completed, excess bleaching agent may be removed by addition of sodium bisulfite. The starch is then washed and dried. Aside from lightening the color of the starch and further reducing the level of microorganisms, bleaching produces no effect on the properties of cooked starch.

Viscosity Reduction

The viscosity of starch pastes is a consequence of the way in which long chain polymers react to shearing forces. A reduction in viscosity of polymer systems can be effected by simply reducing the length of the polymer molecules. In starch, this is accomplished by breaking glucosidic bonds using a simple reaction called acid catalyzed hydrolysis; this reaction is carried out on intact starch granules under controlled conditions to achieve a predetermined viscosity reduction; the reaction is shown in Figure 11.7. When the reaction is complete, the acid is neutralized and the starch granules are washed and dried.

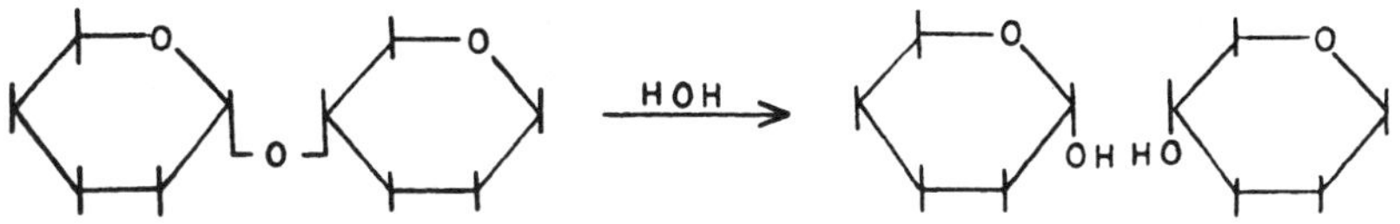

FIGURE 11.7 – Hydrolysis of the Bond

Viscosity reduction can also be accomplished by oxidation of hydroxyl groups present in the starch molecule. A starch slurry is treated with sodium hypochlorite; during the reaction, temperature and pH are carefully controlled to achieve the desired viscosity reduction. When the reaction is complete, the oxidant is removed by addition of sodium bisulfite. This oxidation process is much more complex than the simple hydrolytic reaction; hydroxyl groups are randomly oxidized to produce carboxyl or carbonyl groups with concomitant breaking of glucosidic bonds. Conversion of hydroxyl groups to carboxyl groups effectively reduces the ability of amylose to retrograde. Thus, oxidized starches, in addition to producing low viscosity pastes, also have much less tendency to gel on cooling.

Acid modified and oxidized starches typically do not satisfy many of the requirements for starch that canners need. These modified starches have no resistance to the effects of processing conditions such as heat, acidity, and shearing forces. In order to satisfy these special requirements, starch is modified by forming chemical derivatives.

Crossbonding

Textures produced by heating a water dispersion of native starch granules until swollen is generally considered desirable. Unfortunately, the swollen granules lack stability during processing and this desirable texture is readily lost. The swollen granule exists only as long as there are a sufficient number of intermolecular hydrogen bonds present in solution to keep the starch molecules in the granule associated.

In crossbonding, adjacent molecules are linked with chemical bonds that are resistant to heat and shearing forces. These bonds make the swollen granules more resistant to disintegration.

If crossbonding is not carefully controlled, a sufficient number of crossbonds might be introduced such that the starch becomes less digestible. Crossbonding is generally controlled so that less than one crossbond per 1,000 anhydroglucose units is produced; this level, crossbonding results in markedly improved granule resistance to disintegration while the nutritive value of the starch is preserved. Crossbonded starches intended for use in highly acid foods are somewhat more crossbonded than those starches intended for neutral or slightly acidic foods.

Crossbonding reactions are carried out in mild alkaline slurries of starch. The agents used for crossbonding are either inorganic phosphates or organic acid anhydrides; crossbonds are formed at random hydroxyl sites on adjacent starch molecules. Reaction products are crossbonded starch and harmless inorganic salts or organic acids commonly found in foods. When this reaction is completed, the slurry is neutralized; the starch is washed to remove soluble material and then dried.

The effects of crossbonding on the properties of starch pastes are dramatic. Crossbonding inhibits swelling of the granules as well as making them more resistant to disintegration. Hence, the cooked pastes are not as thick or viscous as unmodified starch. However, when the paste achieves its peak viscosity, heat, shearing forces, and pH cause little or no decrease from the peak value.

By contrast, unmodified starch, after reaching its peak viscosity, shows a marked decrease in viscosity. Consequently, when unmodified starches are used, higher levels are required in order to obtain an adequate final viscosity; the higher initial starch levels required cause much higher initial viscosities to develop during early processing stages. This excessive viscosity may interfere with heat penetration and produce an adverse effect on finished product quality. When crossbonded starches are used, the amount of starch required may be reduced by as much as 40% and still provide the desired texture and thickening yielding much better quality in the finished food.

While crossbonding affords a means of stabilizing starch to the rigors of the canning process, it does little to correct another problem encountered with starch used as a thickener; crossbonded starches, like unmodified starch, may still retrograde. This tendency is particularly evident in foods that are refrigerated or frozen since low temperatures favor reassociation of starch molecules. Hence, foods containing starch may exhibit undesirable textural changes when exposed to cyclic temperature variation; the ability to resist these changes is called freeze-thaw stability.

Stabilization

While starch oxidation produces changes in the molecule that effectively inhibits retrogradation, oxidation also reduces the paste viscosity to an undesirable level. Starch may be stabilized by forming esters or ethers at hydroxyl groups; formation of these derivatives is performed on water suspensions of starch under the required conditions of pH and temperature. When the reaction is completed, the slurry is neutralized, washed, and dried. Introduction of these substituent groups to the starch molecule effectively hinders reassociation of starch molecules in starch paste. These derivatized starches exhibit little or no tendency to form gels. These derivatives, however, exhibit no resistance to the rigors of processing; the final textural characteristics may not be those desired.

Summary

Modification of starch is seen as a means of overcoming deficiencies inherent in native starch. Since no single type of modification results necessarily in a desired product, it is fairly common for a starch to be modified by two different procedures, e.g. crossbonding and formation of esters, to produce a product with the desired characteristics.

Use of Modified Starches

Crossbonded starches are the most widely used starch derivatives where starch is used for thickening and modifying texture. Lightly crossbonded starches are used in neutral or slightly acidic foods; high acid foods require more highly crossbonded starches.

Where clarity and resistance to gelling are not required, for example in gravies, sauces, cream soups and puddings, crossbonded regular corn starch is used. When good thickening ability, low gel strength, and high clarity are required, as for example in pie fillings or baby foods, crossbonded waxy starches are used.

When the finished product is to be frozen or stored for long periods, for example in frozen dinners and/or specialty foods, double derivatized starches are required. Crossbonding provides stability during processing and the ester or ether linkage provides storage stability.

Both modified and unmodified starches are available as cold or hot water soluble products. The cold water soluble starches are called pregelatinized starches; the manufacturer takes either the modified or unmodified starch and cooks it to a paste before drying. After drying, the pregelled starch will reconstitute to a cooked paste on addition of water with little or no heating. Pregelled starches are used as components in instant food products such as pudding mixes.

SORBITOL AND MANNITOL

Sorbitol and mannitol are carbohydrates which are classified as polyols; they contain more than one hydroxyl group, and no carbonyl groups. In addition to sorbitol and mannitol, this class includes glycerine and propylene glycol as well as many other alcohols. Both sorbitol and mannitol occur naturally in fruits such as apples, cherries, and apricots; commercially available material is produced by the hydrogenation of sugars. Both exist as white, solid, crystals. In addition to the solid state, sorbitol is also sold commercially as a 70% (w/w) aqueous solution.

The Food and Drug Administration allows the use of sorbitol and mannitol in foods in an amount reasonably required to accomplish the intended physical or technical effect. Sorbitol, as a carbohydrate, has a nutritional value of approximately 4 calories/gram. Mannitol, also is a carbohydrate; because of incomplete absorption and metabolism its nutritional value is approximately 2 calories/gram. Relatively slow absorption from the gastrointestinal tract is responsible for the laxative properties of both polyols; the laxative threshold for sorbitol is about 40 grams/day and for mannitol about 10–20 grams/day.

Sorbitol has a relative sweetness of about 55% and mannitol about 50% as compared to sucrose; both have negative heats of solution which resulting in a cool sweet taste.

Since sorbitol and mannitol are higher alcohols rather than sugars, they are relatively resistant to fermentation and resulting acid formation caused by microorganisms found in the mouth. For this reason they are used for sweetening and bodying of "non-cariogenic" foods and soft drinks.

In soft drinks, sorbitol solution is typically used 1–2% to provide body and mouthfeel, enhance flavor, and impart sweetness. Sorbitol may also be effective in masking the characteristic bitter taste of saccharin in beverages containing that sweetener. A small amount of sorbitol (0.5–3.0%) in wine has been shown to chelate low levels of iron and copper and smooth out bitterness in lower quality wine. Bodying and flavor smoothing make sorbitol useful in prepared cocktail bases and in foamers. Its chelating or sequestering property has also been observed in fruit drinks.

Sorbitol is used to provide body and sweetness in products other than beverages. Sorbitol may be used as a replacement for cane and corn sugars in maple flavored pancake and waffle syrup; It is used at 10–15% of the syrup in combination with a small amount of sodium carboxymethylcellulose. In so-called "dietetic" imitation jellies and jams, sorbitol is used in combination with saccharin for sweetness and body. 15% sorbitol in jelly results in a 25°Brix value; pectin is used to provide the additional necessary thickening. For ease in handling, as well as economy, the sorbitol in these products is added as the 70% solution rather than as a solid.

One of the chief differences between sorbitol and mannitol is in their humectance. Sorbitol is highly soluble in water and is an excellent humectant. When added as a 70% solution, sorbitol protects the soft, moist texture of shredded coconut. Mannitol is considerably less soluble and is non-hygroscopic. Consequently, it is used as a solid agent to encapsulate flavors used in canned, powdered beverage bases.

The USDA permits the use of up to 2% sorbitol as a replacement for corn syrup solids in cooked sausage labeled frankfurter, furter, wiener, or knockwurst. In these sausages, sorbitol improves flavor, facilitates the removal of casings, and helps maintain a desirable color by minimizing caramelization and charring.

SPICES, ESSENTIAL OILS AND OLEORESINS, AND SOLUBLE AND DRUG EXTRACTIVES

Spices

The American Spice Trade Association (ASTA) has evolved a broad new marketing definition for Spice: Products of plant origin which are used primarily for the purpose of seasoning food.

Several forms of spices are available to the food manufacturer, ranging from whole and ground natural spices to a variety of extractives, all originating, however, in natural plant products.

Ground spices are the standard by which flavor quality is measured in seasoning materials. Grinding spices reduce them to a form which is easily added to and dispersed throughout a food. Since some protective cell structure is broken down and a gradual release of flavor is begun, ground spices act faster in a food product, flavoring it much more quickly.

Normally, ground spices are processed to allow them to pass through U.S. Standard sieves ranging from No. 20 to No. 60 mesh. These degrees of fineness do not completely break up the natural cell structure and as a result, the ground product will retain an adequate amount of flavor through normal storage, handling and processing. It will also survive re-heating at home, and in some cases, still more spice flavor is released as the food is chewed. Different particle sizes of ground spice are recommended for different end uses.

Some processors grind spices to microscopic fineness, pulverized as fine as 50 microns in diameter; this is done to aid in uniform dispersion, to reduce the possibility of color flecks in the product, and to produce a more complete breakdown of cell structure.

Low temperature grinding is a relatively recent type of spice processing technique; the whole spices are processed through pre-chilled or water-cooled mills, designed to reduce volatilization due to heat generated during processing. Mills which operate at slower speeds present an alternative approach.

Quality in ground spices can depend on many factors: the type of spice, its grade, its country of origin, how it was processed, and where, how, and how long it has been stored. Spices are natural plant products that vary according to type and grade. A modern, well equipped spice grinding firm analyzes each lot of raw material it receives and then is able to deliver specified levels of quality in the ground product by its methods of processing. If necessary, lots which test at varying strengths are blended until desired specifications are met. In this way, the grinder can assure his consumer of consistent quality in every shipment. The normal practice for grinders is to retain a sample of every shipment so that it can be compared with the next order.

Quality Evaluation of Spices

The only publicly circulated specifications for quality in spices are contained in Federal Specification EES-631J, which is available from the Naval Publications and Forms Center, 5801 Tabor Ave., Philadelphia, PA 19120. The research committee of the American Spice Trade Association assisted in developing these specs. The spice association offers ASTA Analytical Methods, 3rd Edition, a 65 page unbound book containing 28 different procedures for running chemical analyses on spices.

Additionally, a microbiological laboratory manual is available from the American Spice Trade Association, which contains all the necessary microbiological test methods used for evaluation of spices. It is an 83-page unbound book containing 22 methods. Both of these texts may be purchased from the Association's executive office, P. O. Box 1267, Englewood Cliffs, NJ 07632.

Microbiology of Spices

Spices are grown and harvested in many different areas of the world; most of these areas have sanitation standards less stringent than those in the United States and other developed countries. It is not unexpected, therefore, to find high levels of microorganisms on spice materials and, on some occasions, low levels of organisms of sanitary significance can also be found. Spices, however, are not usually cited among food materials that are vehicles of foodborne disease.

Usual indices of microbial quality include standard plate count values which may range from a few hundred, in the case of cloves, to many millions, in the case of black and white pepper. The majority of plate count bacteria are represented by genus *Bacillus* and, as might be expected, a great many organisms representing the plate count are as spores rather than as vegetative cells. Molds and yeasts vary from low levels to 30,000 per gram in black and white pepper. Sanitary indicator organisms, namely coliforms, are present in varying levels, but are usually less than several hundred per gram and *E. coli*, the specific fecal indicator organism, is usually absent or present at extremely low levels. *Staphylococcus aureus* is seldom found in spice materials, but other pathogens such as *Salmonella* may occasionally be isolated from some spices. Pathogenic spore forming bacteria, such as *Clostridium perfringens, Bacillus cereus,* and the anaerobe, *Clostridium botulinum*, may be isolated in spice materials but are usually present at very low levels, namely less than 100 per gram. An ongoing surveillance program to assure that organisms of sanitary and public health significance are absent from spice materials offered for sale is necessary.

Spice grinders offer microbial control in spices through the use of ethylene oxide in dry sterilization procedures or ionizing radiation; methyl bromide is also used as a fumigant. Spices are first inspected and analyzed at port of entry and must meet the standards of the Food and Drug Administration before they leave the port. Under a program initiated a few years ago by ASTA, every lot of incoming spices is now inspected by an independent laboratory.

Lots which do not meet FDA requirements must be reconditioned at the port or returned to the shipper overseas. At this point, all spices, except paprika, are in the whole form and represent the raw materials of seasoning. Before sale to a food manufacturer or the public, they go next to spice grinding plants where they are further analyzed, cleaned and processed.

Essential Oils and Oleoresins

Essential oils and oleoresins are the most basic extractive of spices. The volatile oils of raw spices are removed by various methods appropriate to the character of the particular spice. Extractive methods include steam distillation, pressing, absorption on a neutral fat, and enzymatic action, followed by steam distillation. Concentrated terpeneless and sesquiterpeneless essential oils which are derived through chromatographic separation or by countercurrent extraction with polar and non-polar solvents are also available. The aim of these latter products is improved stability, since terpene and sequiterpene components of essential oils tend to oxidize easily when exposed to air or light.

In some spices (notably black pepper), an oleoresin, rather than an essential oil, is the preferred extractive. An oleoresin is a viscous resinous material, the essence of a solvent extraction after the solvent is removed; This essence contains both volatile and non-volatile fractions.

While it is possible to use essential oils and oleoresins as is, it is more common in food manufacturing applications to add these materials to some type of carrier; this makes them less concentrated and therefore more manageable; the carrier may be chosen for solubility or some other desirable characteristic.

Soluble Extractives

Soluble extractives may be liquid or dry, depending on the carrier. Liquid ones are either water or oil dispersible. Water soluble essential oils and oleoresins are prepared with solubilizing agents such as the polysorbates; pickle packers and condiment manufacturers use these water soluble flavors.

Extractives are also added to dry carriers, such as salt, or dextrose; individual crystals are coated with the essential oils or oleoresins; this product is often called a "dry soluble"; these are free flowing and easily handled. The carriers dissolve during the processing of the product, leaving the extractives well dispersed.

Spray-Dried Extractives

These are another form of seasoning material. Here the essential oils or oleoresins are dispersed in an edible, water soluble gum, often arabic, and then spray dried and blended with a dry carrier. When the water evaporates from the spray particles, the extractives are trapped in a protective coating of the gum. In a sense, the spray drying is designed to reconstruct the protective qualities of the original spice materials, giving the product more stability and longer storage life.

Buying

There is still no substitute for buying top quality in all types of seasoning materials. The rule of thumb in spices is that prime grades are characterized by higher oil content and therefore are more intensely flavored. Such spices will be more economical in the long run because their flavor will go farther in the final products in which they are used. However, in all respects, the first step in spice buying is to make sure to deal with the most reputable firms; this is an area of purchasing where supplier advice can mean a great deal. There is such an array of products and grades coming from so many constantly changing sources, that it is next to impossible for a food company buyer to keep up with the market.

A general practice followed by manufacturers of seasonings is to work out formulas for specific seasonings in cooperation with suppliers of raw materials.

Storage

Spices should be kept in a cool, dry, well ventilated place; excessive heat robs them of flavor, and dampness will cake them. Since Paprika and other capsicums are sensitive to strong light, the spice storeroom should not be subject to direct sunlight. All spices should be stored on skids and shelves and kept away from contact with outside walls, techniques that avoid dampness. It is good procedure to mark all spice containers with their date of arrival, so that first in is first used. All employees handling spices should be instructed to re-seal containers immediately after each use and to make sure they are tight. The drums in which spices are typically shipped today have closures which make re-sealing easy, but they only work if those persons handling them are well trained.

TEXTURED VEGETABLE PROTEINS

Textured vegetable proteins are products which have been transformed from a flour type material into one which has a meat-like texture. The resulting textured vegetable protein product provides chewiness and fibrous character. In 1971 the USDA defined textured vegetable proteins as "food products made from edible protein sources and characterized by having structural integrity and identifiable texture such that each unit will withstand hydration in cooking and other procedures used in preparing the food for consumption."

Soy proteins are the most commonly used base materials for textured vegetable proteins. However, cottonseed, corn, wheat, peanut and similar proteins can be texturized.

Two common methods for texturizing proteins are thermoplastic extrusion and fiber spinning. The extrusion process uses either soy flour (50% protein) or soy protein concentrate (70% protein) as the starting material; this process has a cost advantage since the spinning process uses isolated proteins (90% protein) as a starting material.

In the extrusion process, soy flour is mixed with water, sodium chloride and other ingredients. The mixture is passed under pressure through a cooker extruder. The product expands as it leaves the extruder die and forms a textured vegetable protein product. The size and shape of extruded material is controlled by the size and speed of the cutting knife on the extruder. The sized textured protein product is then dried and packaged for shipment. Ingredients such as colors, flavors, seasonings and nutritional additives may be added to textured proteins used in the canning industry.

Spun soy protein products are made by spinning isolated soy protein into fibers much like spinning nylon. The spun fibers are produced by solubilizing isolated soy protein in an alkaline medium. The protein solution is passed through a spinneret to form fibers which are coagulated in an acidic bath. The coagulated fibers are then stretched by a series of rolls moving at increasingly faster rates. Binders such as egg albumin are added to hold bundles of fibers together. Colors, flavors and other ingredients similar to those used in textured soy flour may be added to make the finished product. The spun fiber based products are more expensive than extruded products because of the more expensive process and starting material. For this reason, they are generally sold as meat analogs to completely replace meat in specialized markets. Spun soy protein analogs are usually sold frozen as ham, chicken, beef, fish or bacon slices, cubes, bits or granules. The extruded soy flour products and soy protein concentrate products are the ones most generally used to extend meat in canned meat products. they are also used to totally replace meat in meatless entrees.

TABLE 11.8 – Typical Chemical Analysis of Thermoplastic Extruded Soy Products

Component	Soy Flour	Soy Protein Concentrate
Protein (Nx6.25)	50	67–70
Moisture	7	7
Ash	7	6.5
Fat	1	0.8
Carbohydrates (by difference)	32	16–18
Fiber	3	3.7

Textured vegetable proteins have a PER (Protein Efficiency Ratio) of at least 80% of casein. Soy protein contains all the essential amino acids. The amino acid lysine is present in substantial levels and methionine is the first limiting amino acid. Methionine may be added to soy protein products to give a PER value equal to casein. The processes involved in fabricating textured vegetable proteins provide an opportunity to incorporate essential nutrients into food products.

The wide variety of textured vegetable proteins available in the market allows the food processor to use these products in many applications. The primary area of usage is in ground meat-containing products. Textured vegetable proteins may be used to extend or completely replace ground meat in canned meat products such as chili, Sloppy Joes, spaghetti sauces, meat stews and meat sauces. It can extend ground meat in canned products such as patties and meatballs.

USDA permits the use of textured vegetable proteins in canned meat products; however, USDA specifies maximum levels of addition and requires a specified amount of meat. Products, such as meatless chili, that use textured vegetable proteins to completely replace meat would not fall under USDA jurisdiction. However, FDA labeling requirements would have to be met.

USDA has conducted studies with chili, meat stews, meat sauces and barbecue sauces to develop a labeling policy for the use of textured vegetable proteins based on the ratio of fresh meat to dry soy analog in the product formula. For products in which the fresh meat to dry soy protein is greater than 13 to 1 (13 parts fresh meat to 1 part dry soy protein), the label only need reflect soy protein in its proper position in the ingredient list. For products with ratios between 13:1 and 10:1, the label should have a qualifying phrase that reads "textured vegetable protein added" or similar wording. For products with formulas having ratios of less than 10:1, e.g., $6^1/_2$ parts beef to 1 part dry textured soy protein, the label should bear wording that equates the textured vegetable protein with meat ("beef and textured vegetable protein stew" or "textured vegetable protein and beef chili sauce"). Since USDA and FDA regulations are changing to reflect new technology, it is important to consult with USDA and FDA in conjunction with private legal counsel for the latest regulations.

Textured vegetable protein can be used to prepare meatless canned foods such as meatless chili, meat-like sauces, etc. Textured vegetable protein is generally used at a level of 10-15% in meatless chili. Formulas for meat-like products using textured vegetable protein are usually made up to provide the same protein content in the textured vegetable protein containing product as the level found in the meat based formulation.

Granular or flake-like textured vegetable protein products can be used in canned foods. Particle size of the textured vegetable protein is selected to match the size of meat particles normally found in the product. Large textured vegetable protein chunks are available for meat stews as well as granules to simulate ground meat particles.

Textured vegetable protein can be hydrated in water before adding to the remaining ingredients or it can be added dry and allowed to hydrate in the liquid present in the formulation. Most textured vegetable protein products will absorb 2-3 times their weight in water or other liquids. Textured vegetable protein will absorb some fat, thereby reducing free fat in the canned product. It is important to provide enough liquid for hydration so that the finished retorted product will have an acceptable consistency.

Extruded textured vegetable protein products offer an attractive economic advantage in partial replacement or extension of meat products. An example is the use of hydrated (3:1) textured soy protein concentrate into ground beef at a 25% replacement level. This results in savings based on the ingredient costs.

Other advantages of textured vegetable proteins use in canned food products include:

1. The extruded products are dried to less than 8% moisture and under normal storage conditions have a shelf life of about one year. Freezers or cold storage are not required.
2. Textured vegetable proteins can be fortified with vitamins, minerals and other supplements to provide balanced nutrition in the final canned product.
3. Textured vegetable proteins maintain their structure upon hydration and provide a meat-like texture.

4. They normally absorb 2-3 times their weight in water and have good fat absorption properties.
5. They have low bacteria counts in comparison to meats.
6. The products can be colored, flavored and sized to resemble a wide variety of food products.
7. They allow canners a means of making meat-like canned products in the off-season, thereby allowing year-around utilization of equipment.

As the price of meat increases, the use of textured vegetable proteins in canned meats and related products should continue to expand.

MONOSODIUM GLUTAMATE

Glutamic acid, one of the most common amino acids, is a constituent of almost all proteins. Although a non-essential amino acid, it is an important source of nitrogen and may act to conserve essential amino acids against depletion.

Although a number of salts of glutamic acid may be used in food preparation, the sodium salt of glutamic acid–monosodium glutamate (MSG) is commonly used for enhancing, balancing, blending and generally rounding out flavors–all without its presence being obvious. Therefore, MSG is widely used as a flavor enhancer in both family food preparation and in commercial food processing. Other cations such as the K^+ and NH_4^+ salts are also available and are used in salt substitute formulations.

Glutamate occurs naturally in varying amounts in many foods including milk, meat, fish, poultry and vegetables. There tends to be a high free glutamate content in foods that have a relatively strong flavor. Mushrooms and soup stocks are cited as those exceptionally high in free glutamate. It is suggested that high free glutamate content may be one of the reasons mushrooms enhance the flavor of foods to which they are added. The superior flavor of young, freshly harvested vegetables as compared to older samples may be due to higher glutamate content. Although the mechanism(s) by which glutamate acts as a flavor enhancer is unknown, it is believed it may be associated with foods losing a considerable amount of their free glutamate content during the first 24 hours after harvesting, causing a concomitant loss of flavor.

Similarly, it has been observed that numerous food processing procedures (washing, blanching, cooling, exhausting and cooking) cause loss of some soluble natural components, including water soluble proteins, vitamins, minerals and amino acids including glutamate leading to a marked loss of flavor in foods. It has been suggested that addition of glutamate in processing or at the table is merely a replacement of depleted naturally occurring glutamate. Glutamate is also effective in a variety of products such as meat and poultry where the natural glutamate content is not low.

Monosodium glutamate (MSG) is made from natural food substances. A fermentation process beginning with molasses derived from sugar cane or beets is generally used. The 6-carbon carbohydrate is transformed into the appropriate 5-carbon amino acid microbiologically. The end product, a fine, white, crystalline salt, is sold in the U.S. according to Food Chemicals Codex specifications, and in other countries, according to other national and international standards.

Although foods that are basically protein in origin are likely to be improved in flavor by the addition of monosodium glutamate, flavor enhancement is also observed in low protein those vegetable-based recipes. Effective application ranges from meats, and poultry, to seafoods, soups and vegetables. Conversely, addition of MSG to foods such as fruits, fruit juices, candy and cereal products does not indicate improvement in flavor. Degree of acidity of the food also effects the amount of flavor contributed by MSG generally speaking, the higher the acidity of foods, the lower the effectiveness of MSG as a flavor enhancer.

MSG is effective in maintaining the flavor of foods from the time of processing to consumption. Widely used for three decades in the U.S., and longer in the Orient, MSG has long been recognized as an effective flavor enhancer by food processors, and has been used in such canned foods as meats, soups, soup bases, gravy, etc., in addition to frozen, and dehydrated formulations. Glutamate does not require a special technique for its use; it is generally added at the same point in the process that salt, spices and sugar are normally added.

Use levels vary widely, depending on the product. Concentrations of 0.2–0.8% ($3^1/_4$–13 oz. per 100 lb. of food) on an as consumed basis are usually employed in most canned liquid products such as soups and stews. For more concentrated formulations, such as dried soups, actual glutamate concentrations would, of course, be higher, but are correspondingly diluted on serving in the home. In other specialty products not common to food markets in the U.S., glutamate levels on an as consumed basis of 2–3% or more may be found.

A major area of application of monosodium glutamate is in the commercial production of canned, dehydrated, condensed, or frozen soups. The addition of MSG to soups and stews gives them a more full-bodied, blended flavor.

Monosodium glutamate, popular in a variety of cuisines, is a common commodity in international trade and enjoys particular popularity in the Orient, Europe and the Americas. Consequently, standards on the food use of MSG have been established by both national and international regulatory agencies.

MSG is on the list of Substances Generally Recognized as Safe (GRAS) (21 CFR 182.1) which, along with regulated food additives, governs the use of most food ingredients, components and additives used in the United States. Thus, MSG is regulated into the same category as salt, pepper, sugar, vinegar and baking powder.

Various standards of identity govern the use of glutamate in numerous foods listed below:

TABLE 11.9 – Standards of Identity:
Monosodium Glutamate Use in Canned Foods
"Code of Federal Regulations," Title 21

Food	Section
Canned Vegetables	
Green & Waxed Beans	155.120
Corn	155.130
Peas	155.170
Certain Other Vegetables	155.200
Mushrooms	155.201
Fish	
Tuna	161.190
Mayonnaise & Salad Dressings	
French Dressing	169.115
Mayonnaise	169.140
Salad Dressing	169.150
Non-Specified Approvals/Non-Standardized Foods	
Field Corn	155.131
Dry Peas	155.172
Omnibus	182.1

In addition to the various meat uses listed in the Table described in 9 CFR, MSG may be used in pumping and cover pickles, curing agents, meat soups, bouillon cubes, fluid extract of beef, imitation sausages, cubed or comminuted types of steak.

Government regulatory policy, in general, permits use of MSG in any food product in which it has utility and in which its presence is indicated by suitable label declaration of "monosodium glutamate" in the appropriate position of the ingredients statement.

Internationally, the Food and Agriculture Organization/World Health Organization (FAO/WHO) has established an Acceptable Daily Intake (ADI) for monosodium glutamate of up to 153 mg/kg body weight for humans over the age of 12 weeks.

TABLE 11.10 – Standards of Identity:
Monosodium Glutamate Use in Meats and Poultry
"Code of Federal Regulations," Title 9

Food	Section
Specific Listings	
Chopped Ham	319.105
Bockwurst	319.281
Corned Beef Hash	319.303
Omnibus – Meats	318.7
Omnibus – Poultry	381.147
Use of MSG Permitted/Non-Specific Approval	
Beef – Chopped, Ground Hamburger, Beef Patties, Fabricated Steak	319.15
Sausages – Fresh, Pork, Beef, Breakfast, Hog, Italian	319.140-145
Smoked Pork Sausage	319.160
Frankfurters, Franks, Furters, Hotdogs, Wieners, Vienna, Bologna, Garlic Bologna, Knockwurst and similar products	319.180
Cheesefurter	319.181
Luncheon Meat, Meat Loaf	319.260 & 261
Hash, Meat Stews	319.302 & 304
Meat Pies	319.500

WATER SOLUBLE GUMS (HYDROCOLLOIDS)

The range of ingredients and products made more useful in their various applications through the use of gums or hydrocolloids would be startling to the average consumer, but should not come as a surprise to the food technologist who is interested in improving his products.

Vegetable gums, or natural plant hydrocolloids, have served for centuries as foodstuffs, as well as thickeners and extenders of other foods. The chemical components of gums are present in almost every natural food and are largely responsible for the structure and textural properties of plants.

All food processes, by their very nature, involve some modification or denaturation of the characteristic food texture which results from a change in the moisture content or the physical state of water. Either moisture is partially or wholly removed, as in dehydrated foods, or it is changed physically to the gaseous state in cooking and blanching operations, or to the solid state as in freezing processes. It is evident that a change in the amount of water or in its physical states is largely responsible for alterations in the texture of processed food products.

Plant hydrocolloids, by definition, are hydrophilic materials which can influence the processing conditions and behavior of a food product in several ways.

The most important functions performed by gums in processed food product formulations are: (a) Retention of water; (b) Reduction in moisture evaporation rates; (c) Alteration of freezing rates; (d) Modification of ice crystal formation; and (e) Regulation of rheological properties or viscosity.

Table 11.11 lists the many functions of plant hydrocolloids in foods and provides an example of each. Many factors need to be considered when a hydrocolloid is selected: (a) Viscosity required; (b) Gel characteristics, if any; (c) Emulsification required; (d) Rate of hydration; (e) Dispersion problems; (f) Mouth feel; (g) Processing conditions, including temperature; (h) Particle size requirements; (i) Availability and cost at the required use level.

TABLE 11.11 – Summary of Functions of Plant Hydrocolloids in Foods

Function	Example
Adhesive	Bakery Glaze
Binding Agent	Sausages
Calorie Control Agent	Dietetic Foods
Crystallization Inhibitor	Ice Cream, Sugar Syrups
Clarifying Agent (Fining)	Beer, Wine
Cloud Agent	Fruit Juice
Coating Agent	Confectionery
Emulsifier	Salad Dressing
Encapsulating Agent	Powdered Flavors
Film Former	Sausage Casings, Protective Coatings
Flocculating Agent	Wine
Form Stabilizer	Whipped Toppings, Beer
Gelling Agent	Puddings, Desserts, Aspics
Molding	Gum Drops, Jelly Candies
Protective Colloid	Flavor Emulsions
Stabilizer	Beer, Mayonnaise
Suspending Agent	Chocolate Milk
Swelling Agent	Processed Meats
Syneresis Inhibitor	Cheese, Frozen Foods
Thickening Agent	Jams, Pie Fillings, Sauces
Whipping Agent	Toppings, Icings

Table 11.12 summarizes natural plant hydrocolloids and describes typical characteristics of each hydrocolloid. Major food applications for which they are currently used are also listed.

TABLE 11.12 – Summary of Characteristics of Plant Hydrocolloids

Hydrocolloid	Major Applications	Typical Characteristics
Agar	Icings, Glazes	Forms firm gels at 1% concentration.
Alginates	Desserts, Ice Cream and Ices, Beverage Emulsions	Low viscosity emulsifier.
Arabic	Bulking Agent, Beverage Emulsions, Protective Colloid, and Beverages	Good emulsifier, low viscosity, up to 50% concentration.
Carrageenan	Milk Reactivity, Ice Cream Desserts	Milk reactivity.
Furcelleran	Desserts, Flans	Firm gels without refrigeration.
Ghatti	Heavy Emulsions	Moderate viscosity, good emulsifier.
Guar	Ice Cream, Pet Foods, Sauces, Processed Cheese	Viscous solutions, suspending agent.
Karaya	Ices and Ice Cream	Acid resistant, good adhesive.
Locust Bean Gum	Ice Cream, Sauces, Bakery Products, Processed Cheese	Solutions must be cooked to develop full viscosity.
Tamarinds	Confectionery, Jujubes, Ice Cream Stabilizer	Low viscosity.
Tragacanth	Pourable Dressings, Bakery Emulsions, Sauces	Emulsifier, acid resistant.

Natural plant hydrocolloids can be classified into three major categories: plant exudates, seaweed extracts and seed gums, as summarized in Table 11.13. The gums can also be chemically classified into three groups: anionic seaweed polysaccharides, anionic exudate polysaccharides and nonionic seed polysaccharides (Table 11.14).

Plant hydrocolloids are used in various food and flavor systems. Frozen, easy-to-prepare baked goods have found a ready acceptance by consumers due to the ability of food processors to control those factors that lead to good flavor, color, texture, density, uniformity and shelf life. Natural plant hydrocolloids are used to obtain smooth, uniform body and texture, to give complete flavor release, to improve whipping, thickening power, gel, stability and emulsification.

The U.S. FDA has cleared these gums and they are listed as GRAS. However, they may not be used where precluded by standards of identity regulations.

TABLE 11.13 – Classification of Plant Hydrocolloids

Plant Exudates	
Arabic	*Acacia senegal*
Ghatti	*Anogeissus latifolia*
Karaya	*Sterculia or Cochlospermum*
Tragacanth	*Astragalus gummifer*
Seaweed Extracts	
Agar-Agar	*Gelidium gracilaria*
Irish Moss-Carrageenan	*Chondrus crispus*
	Gigartina mamillosa
Furcelleran	*Furcellaria fastigiata*
Alginates	*Phaeophycae*-Red seaweeds
Seed Gums	
Guar	*Cyamonsis tetragonoloba*
Locust Bean Gum	*Ceratonia siliqua*
Tamarind	*Tamarindus indica*

TABLE 11.14 – Chemical Groupings of Natural Plant Hydrocolloids

Anionic Seaweed Polysaccharides

- Agar – a linear polygalactose sulfuric acid ester.
- Alinates – linear polymers of mannuronic and guluronic acids.
- Carrageenan – a complex sulfate ester with high anhydrogalactose to galactose ratio, generally believed to be a combination of the kappa, lambda and iota fractions.

Anionic Exudate Polysaccharides

- Arabic – a complex of arabic acid, a highly branched polymer made up of galactose, rhamnose, arabinose and glucuronic acid.
- Ghatti – a complex of ghatti acid, composed of pentoses and hexuronic acids.
- Karaya – a complex polymer of galactose, rhamnose and glucuronic acid, partially acetylated.
- Tragacanth – a mixture of polysaccharides, tragacanthin and bassorin, polymers of fucose, xylose, arabinose and glucuronic acid.

Non-Ionic Seed Polysaccharides

- Guar – a straight chain mannan grouping with relatively regular branching on every second mannose by a single galactose unit.
- Locust Bean Gum – a straight chain mannan grouping with relatively regular branching on every fourth mannose group by single membered galactose units.
- Tamarind – a polysaccharide composed of galactose, xylose and glucose.

Agar

Red alga (class *Rhodohyceae*), and more particularly the agarophytes, such as *Gelidium cartilagineum* (Linn.) Gaillon (family *Gelidiaceae*), *Gracilaria confervoides* (Linn.) Greville (family *Sphaerococcaceae*), *Eucheuma isiforma* and their related species, are processed into agar. Production of agar reportedly dates back to the 17th century in Japan; the material as we know it today has been commercially available only since the late 1800's. Agar served as a food in the Orient for ages, probably in the form of flavored or sweetened gels. Agar forms a translucent, porous mass which can be reconstituted into a gel by boiling in water and then cooling. This observation formed the basis for the commercial production of agar by Japanese industry.

Agar is structurally a complex polysaccharide. Recent studies show agar to be composed of a mixture of at least two polysaccharides: agarose, the gelling agent, and a very viscous, weak-gelling component.

Agar is commercially available in bundles of thin, membranous, agglutinated strips or in cut, flaked, granulated, or powdered forms. Color varies from white to pale yellow to tan; it is either odorless or has a slight characteristic odor and a mucilaginous taste.

Agar has a wide variety of uses. It is employed in the bakery, confectionery, and dairy industries, in microbiological and culture media, in meat packing, and in other miscellaneous applications. In food products, agar is useful for its gelling and stabilizing properties. As a stabilizer it is utilized in pie fillings, piping gels, meringues, icings, cookies, cream shells, and similar products. In icings, a good use level ranges from 0.2-0.5%. Agar is often used in combination with gum guar and locust bean gum in doughnut glaze stabilizers; it is the preferred additive in jellied candies and in many specialty confectionery products, such as marshmallows and sugared fruit slices. It has been used as a filler in edible, rigid gels and as a thickening and gelling agent by poultry, fish and meat canners. Alone or in combination with gum guar, it also finds application in pet foods as well as meat pies.

Gum Arabic

Gum Arabic is the dried, gummy exudate obtained from *Acacia senegal* and various other Acacia species, family *Leguminosae*. Arabic was known over 4,000 years ago and is the most common and universally used of all natural gums. There are about 500 species of *Acacia*, but only a few are commercially important. The bulk of the available gum comes from the Sudan; however Senegalese and Nigerian gum have recently become more plentiful. African countries account for the balance of the crop. Sudanese gum or Kordofan products are considered best.

Arabic is available in various particle sizes ranging from coarse granules to fine powders, as well as in spray-dried form. Spray-dried Gum Arabic is a purified product with low microbial counts, widely used by both the food and pharmaceutical industries. Gum Arabic is white to yellowish white, practically tasteless and odorless. Gum Arabic is a neutral or slightly acidic salt of a complex polysaccharide containing calcium, magnesium and potassium ions.

Gum Arabic is the most widely used of all plant hydrocolloids. The uses of gum arabic depend upon its action as a protective colloid or stabilizer, the adhesiveness of its water solutions, and as a thickener. The food industries consume about 50% of the gum arabic imported into the United States. Gum Arabic is the preferred emulsifier in flavor emulsions; it is commonly employed at the level of 2 lb/gallon (0.24 kg/l) emulsion. It also serves to stabilize foams in the manufacture of soft drinks and beer and acts as an emulsifier in solution. Resultant emulsions can be spray-dried to encapsulate or fix flavor essential oils and oleoresins entrapped at levels of 20-25% to yield excellent spray-dried flavors. These are used in dry mixed desserts, soup bases, beverage and cake mixes.

Gum Arabic is also used in dairy products such as ices, sherbets and ice creams. Here it functions to retard both ice crystal formation and growth; a mixture of reacted arabic and carrageenan was patented as an ice cream stabilizer.

Gum Arabic is widely used in the candy industry. The gum is used to emulsify fats and retard sugar crystallization. It is used as a glaze on candy products and as a component of chewing gum, cough drops, and candy lozenges. In jujubes and pastilles, where sugar content is high and moisture content comparatively low, it prevents sugar crystallization and keeps fats uniformly distributed throughout the product preventing it from seeping to the surface and forming an easily oxidizable, greasy film. Here the gum is dissolved in water, the solution filtered, the sugar then added and boiled. The desired flavor should be added slowly without much stirring to minimize the formation of bubbles or opaque spots. Lozenges are also prepared from Gum Arabic by mixing finely ground or powdered sugar with a thick mucilage of Gum Arabic. Dietetic or sugarless candy drops and jujubes can be prepared from combinations of gum arabic, sorbitol and mannitol. Arabic at a level of 1-3% will give a hard candy, 5-35%, a medium center, and a soft drop can be obtained utilizing approximately 70% gum. The greater the percentage of arabic, the softer and more chewable the candy. An excellent glaze for marzipan and buns, Gum Arabic also acts as a protective coating in panned confectionery goods and may be used in coating nuts. It forms a thin, clear, transparent, adhesive film around nuts and seals in oils and flavor. Gum Arabic also improves the baking properties of rye and wheat flour at levels as low as 0.015%; the gum extends the shelf-life of bread by rendering it softer.

Gum Ghatti

Gum ghatti (Indian gum) is a complex water soluble polysaccharide. It is a plant exudate long in use whose name is derived from the word "ghats." which means passes, given to the gum because of its ancient mountain transportation routes. Gum ghatti is approved for food use and is in the GRAS list under the Federal Food, Drug and Cosmetic Act.

Gum ghatti is an amorphous exudate of the *Anogeissus latifolia* tree of the *Combretaceae* family. Ghatti has a bland taste and practically no odor; only about 90% of the gum disperses in water and this portion forms a colloidal dispersion.

Gum ghatti occurs as a calcium-magnesium salt; it forms viscous mixtures on dispersion in water up to 5% concentration or greater. These dispersions are non-Newtonian in behavior, as is true with most of the water soluble gums, and their viscosity increases geometrically with concentration while these dispersions are less viscous than those of gum arabic, gum ghatti is a good emulsifying agent, able to emulsify more difficult systems than gum arabic.

The adhesiveness of gum ghatti dispersions is similar to that of gum arabic. Because of its higher viscosity, it is not possible to prepare dispersions as concentrated as those with gum arabic. Gum ghatti does not form a true gel; films prepared from gum ghatti dispersions are relatively soluble and brittle. Gum ghatti has good emulsifying properties which serve as the basis for most of its applications. Gum ghatti is used in applications also served by gum arabic; it is often used in pharmaceutical preparations as an emulsifying agent. Gum ghatti is used in table syrup emulsions containing 2% butter to stabilize the emulsion; in such an application about 0.4% ghatti is used in combination with 0.08% lecithin. The refractive index of table syrup containing emulsified butter may be adjusted by additional quantities of ghatti to produce clarity.

Because of its high L-arabinose content, gum ghatti is hydrolyzed to prepare pure L-arabinose on a commercial scale; L-arabinose is used as a flavor adjunct in food products.

Gum Karaya

Gum Karaya was introduced as a substitute for gum tragacanth. It has many uses depending on its properties, as an adhesive, a binding agent, and its ability to absorb large amounts of water. It is the dried exudation of the tree *Sterculia urens*. Karaya is official in 'The National Formulary' (Am. Pharm. Assoc.); the commercially available gum comes from India. The gum is available in several grades, #1, #2, #3 and siftings; it is further processed by air separation and micro- pulverization. The best grades contain the lowest percentage of bark and other foreign organic matter. The color of a fine powder ranges from off white to pink to tan. Gum Karaya like tragacanth, does not form a true solution but absorbs water, swelling greatly; its solutions have a low pH.

Structurally, gum karaya is a complex molecule; in dilute solutions of gum, the viscosity increases linearly with concentration; higher concentrations of about 4% form rubbery paste-like gels. Gum solutions show increased viscosity and ropiness above pH 7; its excellent adhesive qualities become apparent when the gum is blended with an alkali, such as sodium borate or magnesium oxide. The gum absorbs water and swells to 70-100 times greater than its original volume. Gum karaya has the added advantage of not being metabolized or absorbed by the body.

The use of karaya in foods is limited. Since the gum prevents the bleeding of free water and retards ice crystal formation; it is used in sherbets, slush ices and ice pops at concentrations of 0.2-0.5%. The acidic nature of karaya allows for its use in cheese spreads; in this application it improves spreadability and prevents water separation. It is a binder in sausage casings and ground meats. Gum Karaya is used in French dressings and meringues as a stabilizer.

Furcellaran

Furcellaran (Danish agar) is an extract of the red alga *Furcellaria fastigiata* found along many coasts of the northern part of the Atlantic Ocean. It was developed as a substitute for Agar when normal supplies from East Asia were cut off during World War II. It is found extensively in inner Danish waters, but grows off Canada as well.

All commercial furcellaran is produced as the potassium salt; it is soluble in hot water and gels on cooling. It has a higher setting temperature than agar and is normally available in water gelling and milk gelling types.

Furcelleran is easily dispersed in cold water to a homogeneous suspension without lumps; furcellaran particles hydrate, swell and become more or less invisible, but do not dissolve. Dissolution requires heating of the suspension to 75–80°F (24–27°C) or at least heating to about the gel melting temperature. Hydration and dissolution are retarded by salts; furcellaran as the sodium salt is cold-water-soluble. Light boiling renders the product soluble in milk.

After cooling, aqueous solutions of furcellaran will set to form gels; furcellaran gels are thermoreversible and remelt when heated to a temperature of 15 to 20 degrees above their setting temperature. Furcelleran gels can incorporate many ingredients such as salts, acids, sugar and proteins; these all influence its gelling properties.

Gel strength is a function of concentration; the addition of potassium salts increases the gel strength. The elasticity of the gel can be improved by the admixture of locust bean gum or guar gum; furcellaran is compatible with most other gums as well.

Solutions of furcellaran can be autoclaved with minimum degradation or loss of gel strength if the pH is kept near neutral, but heating at pH's below 5 causes severe hydrolysis and degradation of gel strength.

Jams, jellies, and marmalades are easily made with this excellent gelling agent since boiling is not necessary; better retention of flavors also results. In the United States, food regulations required that pectin be used in jams and jellies; exceptions which can make use of furcellaran are imitation jams and jellies, diabetic or dietetic products, and baker's jellies. European meat and fish canners frequently use furcellaran as a gelling agent whereas, in the U.S., meat canners are often restricted by legislation to the use of gelatin. For gelling purposes, furcellaran is used in a concentration range of 0.5 to 3.0%.

When used in milk pudding preparations, furcellaran can be used either alone or in combination with starch. When used alone there is a tendency for milk gels to develop some syneresis, which can be eliminated by adding 0.6% to 1.0% starch. The level of furcellaran used is about 0.4% which gives gels having a smooth, glossy surface and a brittle, easily fractured texture. Gel powder mixes can also be made with nonfat milk solids and then prepared by heating with water.

In other water systems, furcellaran, at about 0.05%, is used to stabilize fruit pulp in fruit-pulp juices and soft drinks. It is used as a thickening or gelling component in a wide range of meat products such as meat pastes, meat pies, and minced-meat pie fillings. Limited applications have also been made in confectionery products field.

Guar Gum

Guar gum is derived from the seed of the guar plant, *Cyanaposis tetragonolobus*, family *Leguminosae*. This plant has been grown in India and Pakistan for centuries, where it is one of the most important crops, used as a food for both humans and animals.

The guar plant is a pod-bearing, nitrogen-fixing legume; seeds of the plant are composed of the hull (15%), germ (45%) and endosperm (40%). Guar gum is produced by milling the endosperm after removal of the hull and germ. A typical analysis of gum guar is: galactomannan 78–82%, moisture 10–15%, protein 4–5%, crude fiber 1.5–2.5% and ash 0.5–0.9%.

The chief property of guar gum is its ability to form viscous colloidal solutions when hydrated in cold water systems. These solutions show the typical variance of viscosity versus shear rate of non-Newtonian fluids. Viscosities of 0.3% solutions change only slightly with increasing shear rates, while solutions of 1% or greater show marked changes. Viscosity is dependent on time, temperature, concentration, pH, ionic strength and the type of agitation as well.

The hydration and water-binding properties of guar gum are responsible for its food stabilizing systems. Ice cream stabilizers, particularly high-temperature, short-time processes, use guar gum at a concentration of 0.3%; it improves body, texture, chewiness, and heat-shock resistance by binding free water present. These same properties render it useful in the stabilization of ice pops and sherbets. Guar is allowed at levels up to 3.0% in cold-pack cheese foods; the gum helps to eliminate syneresis and weeping. In soft cheeses, guar increases the yield of curd solids and gives curd a better texture; pasteurized process cheese spreads use a stabilizer consisting of guar, locust bean gum and emulsifier at 0.25–0.35% of total weight. Guar has been added to dough to retard dry-out; it is useful in cake and doughnut mixes at levels under 1%. In pie fillings, guar thickens and prevents shrinking and cracking of the filling. Used in icings to absorb free water, guar gum is mixed at a level of 1 part gum to 250 parts of sugar and 30 parts water; this prevents the icing from becoming sticky and adhering to the wrapper.

Gum guar has been used as a thickener in salad dressings and pickle and relish sauces at 0.2–0.8%;Tragacanth, however, is superior in these applications since gum guar will break down more readily at low pH levels. Gum guar, however, is used at a great advantage in meat sauces and gravies; this use allows a significant reduction in the solids content of the product. Gum guar alone or in combination with agar at levels of 0.5% is useful in processing canned meat products; it prevents fat migration during storage and stops syneresis and water accumulation and reduces the tendency for voids to be present in the can.

Gum guar has good mouth feel and adds body to improve thin or watery products. Thus, it can be used in dietetic beverages where sugar is absent. In addition, blends of guar gum and carrageenan are used in cocoa beverages as well as chocolate syrups. Guar gum is a versatile and effective suspending agent.

Locust Bean Gum

The carob pod or fruit is widely used as a foodstuff; it is very sweet and its flavor is further enhanced by roasting; it is commonly known as St. John's Bread. The gum is an off-white powder available in several particles sizes and viscosity grades.

Locust bean gum can influence the gelling of other polysaccharides. Gels can be made in a wide range of solids content and pH with carrageenan and potassium chloride. Gels of 85% agar and 15% carob gum are more elastic than those of agar alone.

Locust bean gum is widely used in many industries. It is an excellent ice cream stabilizer because of its ability to absorb water and its high swelling power. The gum imparts a smooth melt-down and excellent heat-shock resistance to ice cream. It is not affected by lactic acid or calcium salts. It is a low cost stabilizer and does not mask the flavor of the product. Carob bean gum acts as a binder and stabilizer in processed meats, salami, bologna, and pork sausages; it has a lubricating effect on the mix facilitating the extruding and stuffing operation; the gum yields a more homogenous product with better texture and also decreases weight loss during storage. In soft cheese manufacture, about 0.5% locust bean gum speeds up coagulation, increases the yield of curd solids by about 10%, and makes the curd easier to separate and remove; the resulting curd has good texture and the separated whey is limpid.

Locust bean gum is sometimes used to thicken soups at levels of 0.2–0.5%; it is also used as a thickener in pie fillings. The gum yields a clear, fruit-like filling when used at a level of 1.2% of the weight of the fruit juice and water. Locust bean gum is utilized as a stabilizer and binder in many prepared foods such as soup bases, sauces, and vegetable and fish dishes; it has been used to stabilize whipped cream, mayonnaise and tomato ketchup, as well as salad dressings.

Gum Tragacanth

Gum tragacanth is one of the most widely used natural emulsifiers and thickeners available to the food, drug and allied industries. The high viscosity imparted to water by the gum makes it useful for preparing aqueous suspensions of insoluble substances. Gum tragacanth is approved for food use and is on the GRAS list under the Federal Food, Drug and Cosmetic Act.

Gum tragacanth is the dried gummy exudation of several species of *Astragalus* (family *Leguminosae*).

When tragacanth is mixed with water, only the soluble fraction, called tragacanthin, dissolves to give a colloidal hydrosol whereas the insoluble fraction swells to a gel. Chemically, tragacanthin is a complex mixture of acidic polysaccharides. The Food Chemicals Codex has established standards for food grade gum tragacanth.

An important property of gum tragacanth is its ability to produce solutions with high viscosity. At 25°C (75°F), solution viscosity reaches a maximum is about 24 hours; a thick gel is produced at 2.4% concentration.

Gum tragacanth is widely used in many industries because of its stability to heat and acidity and because it is an effective emulsifying agent with an extremely long shelf-life. Gum tragacanth is widely used in the preparation of salad dressings, relishes, sauces, condiment bases, sweet pickle liquors, soft jellied products, such as gefilte fish, thick broths, beverage and bakery emulsions, ices and sherbets, bakery toppings and fillings, and confectionery cream centers. Because of its acid resistance and long shelf-life, gum tragacanth is useful in preparing stabilized French, Italian, Roquefort, and other creamy dressings, i.e. pourable types. A few, such as the French and Italian types, are covered by FDA standards of identity and must contain not less than 35% vegetable oil; the gum acts to thicken the water phase and prevents the oil phase from coalescing; generally 0.40–0.75% gum, based on the total weight of dressing, is used. The preferred procedure is to wet the gum with a small amount of oil to inhibit lumping and then disperse the mixture in water with rapid agitation. After all the ingredients have been added, the mixture is heated to approximately 72°C (160°F) for 39 min; it is then homogenized in a colloid mill or other type homogenizer.

Condiments and sauces are important product groups in which acid stability and long shelf-life are important. Vinegar is usually a primary ingredient and gum tragacanth acts as an emulsion stabilizer and thickener of the aqueous phase for such ingredients as spice flavorings and natural flavor extracts. Condiments are made by heating a smooth mixture of ingredients to boiling; the gum may be added to the condiment at the end of this boiling period, and the mixture may be cooled in a heat exchanger. Generally between 0.4 and 0.8% gum, based on total weight of sauce, barbecue sauce, or condiment, is used.

Gum tragacanth is used to stabilize bakery emulsions and fillings in which whole fruit is suspended in thick jelly giving clarity, brilliance, and improved texture. It is important to use a high grade gum for such an application to give the fruit a natural and rich appearance. Gum tragacanth is also used in frozen pie fillings.

Gum tragacanth has been used as a stabilizer in ice cream mixes at concentrations of 0.2–0.35% giving smooth body and texture. It is also used with frozen fruits that are to be suspended in the ice cream.

Xantham Gum

Xanthan gum is a relatively new hydrocolloid to the food industry, having been approved for use by the Food and Drug Administration in 1969. Since then, a number of food uses including canned products have been developed.

Xanthan gum is a high molecular weight polysaccharide is produced by the action of the microorganism *Xanthomonas campestris* on dextrose. The fermentation is carried out aerobically under stringent controls and the gum is recovered by precipitation with isopropyl alcohol. The resultant product produces high viscosity water solutions which are pseudoplastic, unusually stable to high temperatures and change viscosity very little with changes in temperature. Xanthan gum is compatible with a wide range of salts, acids and bases, with higher concentrations of these materials than most other thickeners. Xanthan gum forms thermoreversible gels when combined with locust bean gum.

Xanthan gum has been used widely in pourable salad dressing and as a necessary ingredient in the production of heat stable salad dressing. At a level of about 0.4%, xanthan gum produces a dressing that can be retorted at 240°F (116°C) for application in canned meat salads. It is also used to stabilize and improve the texture of canned puddings as well as low pH milk products such as sour cream, chip dips, cheese cake and yogurt. Canned sauces of all types are improved by the addition of small amounts of xanthan gum because of its resistance to thermal degradation and its excellent suspending properties.

Not yet fully examined, xanthan gum has shown promise as a process time reducing aid in starch-thickened sauces. Apparently, xanthan gum's high degree of pseudoplasticity results in an instantaneous reduction in viscosity, thus promoting better heat transfer. This is particularly evident in agitating retorts such as the FMC Orbitort.

Xanthan gum was approved as a general food additive without any quantity restrictions by the United States Food and Drug Administration on March 19, 1969 under CFR Title 21, Section 121.1224.

Alginates

Algin has been used by the canning industry for many years but only recently, has greater attention been paid to the unique functionality of this colloid and its derivatives for the development of new technology and products.

Alginates are high molecular weight polymers of the salts of D-mannuronic and L-guluronic acid. They are obtained by the alkaline extraction of a number of brown seaweeds, but principally *Macrocystis pyrifera* which grows off the West Coast of the United States. The propylene glycol ester is produced by the reaction of propylene oxide with alginic acid. The water soluble salts of alginic acid (sodium salt) form viscous solutions which increase in viscosity or gel in the presence of polyvalent metal ions such as calcium.

Sodium alginate has been used in can sealing compounds and as a stabilizer for canned chocolate milk. In the mid-1960s, propylene glycol alginate came into use as an emulsion stabilizer in canned vegetables such as corn containing butter sauce. The alginate, already well known as an excellent emulsion stabilizer for salad dressing, was used to stabilize a butter in water emulsion which also contained seasoning; the emulsion provided good dispersion of the butter throughout the product through retorting and when the product was served.

Probably the most unique application of algin in canning is a process in which a low viscosity sodium alginate is allowed to react under controlled conditions with a calcium salt. The results are a substantial reduction in process time and an improvement in product quality. This is accomplished by reformulating a starch thickened sauce by reducing the starch level to 1% from 4% or 5% and replacing the starch with 0.5–1% low viscosity sodium alginate; an insoluble calcium salt such as calcium carbonate or dicalcium phosphate dihydrate is added to the can just before closing in the form of a slurry for good dispersion. The resulting viscosity at the initial can temperature is only 10–50 centipoises rather than several hundred centipoises; a great improvement in heat transfer during come-up, processing and cooling is achieved. After processing, the algin reacts with calcium to cause a gradual thickening to the desired viscosity; this process may take several days.

Predictably this process works best in agitating retorts such as the FMC Sterilmatic or the Orbitort where forced convection heating shortens processing even more. In most products, such as stews, chow mein and vegetables and meat in various thickened sauces, process times have been shortened by fifty percent or more.

The sodium, potassium, ammonium and calcium salts of alginic acid were affirmed as GRAS (Generally Recognized As Safe) under Title 21 of the Code of Federal Regulations, Sections 184.1724 (Na), 184.1610 (K), 184.1133 (NH4), 184.1187 (Ca), respectively 1982.

Propylene glycol alginate is an approved food additive under CFR, Title 21, Section 172.858.

Carrageenan

Carrageenan consists of a group of galactan polysaccharides extracted from red seaweeds of the *Gigartinaceae*, *Solieriaceae* and *Phyllophoraceae* (*Solieriaceae*) families. The three principal types are referred to as kappa, iota, and lambda; they differ from one another principally in amount of ester sulfate, the position of the ester sulfate groups, and their 3,6 anhydro-D-galactose content.

Kappa-carrageenan is composed of alternating 1,3-linked galactose 4-sulfate and 1,4-linked 3,6 anhydro-D-galactose residues. It is most sensitive to K^+ ions, in the presence of which it can form rigid, thermally reversible aqueous gels.

Iota-carrageenan is composed of alternating 1,3-linked galactose 4-sulfate and 1,4-linked 3,6 anhydro-D-galactose-2-sulfate residues. It is most sensitive to Ca^{++} ions in the presence of which it forms elastic, thermally reversible aqueous gels.

Lambda-carrageenan is composed of alternating 1,3-linked galactose (about 70% contain 2-sulfate) and 1,4-linked galactose 6-sulfate residues. Lambda-carrageenan is nongelling, regardless of the cations with which it is associated.

Carrageenans are widely used in food applications for their suspending, stabilizing, thickening and gelling properties. Moreover, the unique ability of carrageenan to complex with milk protein has resulted in the development of numerous milk-based applications.

Carrageenan is a regulated food additive as given in CFR, Title 21, Section 172.620.

Uses in Canned Foods

For evaporated Milk, kappa-type carrageenans are effective in preventing fat separation at levels of from 0.005–0.01% by weight of the finished product while for infant formulas-Kappa- or iota-carrageenan stabilizes protein and prevents fat separation at levels of from 0.02–0.04%.

In canned products such as chocolate milk, eggnog, etc.–kappa- or iota-carrageenans are used at levels from 0.01–0.035% to maintain ingredients such as cocoa in suspension, prevent separation of fat and impart a rich mouthfeel.

Canned Meats–Kappa carrageenan with locust bean gum and/or iota carrageenan (0.8–1.4%) provides uniform distribution of cooked meats and associated fats in gelled broth systems. Ratios of kappa to locust bean gum or iota carrageenan may vary from 1:3 to 3:1 to provide texture variability.

Hams may be injected with a brine/curing solution containing kappa carrageenan at 0.4–0.8%; this aids in retention of the solution within the muscle tissue as well as preventing loss of soluble proteins during processing.

Canned Puddings–Iota-carrageenan, at a concentration of about 0.10%, is used as a partial replacement for starch to reduce cook viscosity, control syneresis and impart improved mouthfeel and flavor release characteristics.

Pet Foods–Kappa-carrageenan at 0.1–0.3% serves to prevent fat separation and thicken or lightly gel gravy.

Dessert Gels–A combination of kappa- and iota-carrageenan serves as a gelling agent at a combined total of about 0.75% for preparation of canned dessert gels that do not require refrigeration.

Fish Gels–Canned fish encased in a kappa/iota carrageenan gel of 0.5–0.75% concentration has improved flavor with condiments uniformly suspended.

Aerosol Products–Canned whipped toppings utilize kappa-or lambda-carrageenans to stabilize overrun and control syneresis at levels ranging from 0.03–0.10%.

Gelatin

Gelatin is a refined extract of collagenous tissue which forms clear, viscous solutions in water, or simply, a protein of high purity. It is one of the most versatile raw materials available today. This broad versatility can best be emphasized by pointing out its primary functions as a gel-former or as a protective colloid; it also can serve as a clarifier, binder, film-former, flocculator, thickener, moistener, texturizer, emulsifier, disperser, strengthener, air-entrainer, softener, tenderizer, foamer, tableter, imbibing agent, and protein source.

The most important property of gelatin is its function as a hydrocolloid. Gelatin is a superior protective colloid because of its particular chemical and physical structure; it is amphoteric; it forms a true sol in water and remains soluble through the entire range of pH, unless tanned. Its solutions form thermally reversible gels.

Gelatin is extracted from animal tissues which contain high proportions of the white connective tissue (collagen); tissues extracted commercially are skins, sinews, and bones. Gelatin may be extracted directly from these tissues by boiling water, but the rate of extraction and quality of gelatin are greatly improved by pretreating the collagenous tissue. The pretreatment (cure) may be a prolonged soak in saturated lime (calcium hydroxide) or an adjustment of pH by a soak in acid solution. Pretreatment also is used as the basis for classifying gelatin: "Type A" is gelatin derived from acid-cured tissue. while "Type B" is gelatin derived from lime-cured tissue.

Gelatin is extracted from cured tissue by three to five water extractions at progressively higher temperatures. The number of extractions varies from plant to plant. The first extraction contains the largest amount of gelatin, approximately 55-65%; this first extraction gelatin has a high bloom, ranging from 270 to 300. The remaining collagen protein, approximately 40%, is removed in successive extractions.

Each successive extraction yields gelatin of lower gel strength and viscosity. The dilute gelatin solution from hot water extraction is filtered, concentrated by vacuum evaporation and may be filtered again before drying. The gelatin

FIGURE 11.8 – The gelatin liquor is concentrated and chilled to form strands of gel which appear like spaghetti. (Courtesy Geo. A. Hormel Co., Industrial Products Div.)

solution is then chilled by either casting into ribbons or extruding as noodles, and the formed materials poured into a bed on an endless, open weave, stainless steel belt and passed through the dryer. The dryer is divided into zones in which the temperature and humidity of the drying air are controlled. The material leaves the dryer at approximately 10% moisture content; the bed is broken into pieces which are conveyed to the grinding equipment for reduction to the desired particle size. Each batch of material is tested for quality and grade according to the standard methods developed by the Gelatin Manufacturers Institute.

FIGURE 11.9 – The strands of gelatin gel are conveyed to drier belts and taken through a drier consisting of 10 heating zones. The gelatin drier, 140-ft. long, reduces the moisture level of the gelatin gel to 10%. (Courtesy Geo. A. Hormel Co., Industrial Products Div.)

Since a higher proportion of gelatin is extracted in the early extractions of acid cured skins, the proportion of high-test, "Type A" gelatin available to the customer is much greater then "Type B" gelatin. Demineralized bones and hide trimmings respond better to lime cure, while porkskins respond better to acid cure; most "Type A" gelatin is derived from porkskins.

Gelatin is nearly tasteless and odorless; it is a vitreous, brittle solid and is faintly yellow in color. Under ordinary conditions of temperature and humidity it contains between 9 and 13% moisture and has relative density of 1.3 to 1.4.

When gelatin granules are immersed in cold water, they hydrate into discrete, swollen particles; on being warmed, these swollen particles melt to form a solution, or more strictly speaking a dispersion. This method of preparing gelatin solutions is the easiest to follow, especially where high concentrations of solids are desired. The important properties of these solutions are functions of pH, ash content, method of manufacture, thermal history and concentration.

Dry gelatin stored in air-tight containers at room temperature remains unchanged for long periods of time.

Gelatin's most useful properties, gel strength and viscosity, are gradually weakened on prolonged heating in solution above about 40°C (104°F). Degradation may also be brought about by extremes of pH and by proteolytic enzymes including those which may result from the presence of microorganisms.

In some respects, collagen may be considered as an anhydride of gelatin, and the formation of soluble gelatin is thus regarded as hydrolysis of collagen into the characteristic, heterogeneous, molecular pattern of gelatin. Gelatin molecules represent various sized units, each a fragment of the collagenous chain from which it was derived. It other words, gelatin is not a single chemical entity; it is a generic term used to describe a mixture of fractions differing principally in molecular size. These fractions are composed entirely of amino acid radicals joined together by peptide linkages to form polymers varying in molecular weight between about 15,000 and 250,000.

Gelatin is not a complete protein for mammalian nutrition since it is lacking in the essential amino acid tryptophane and is deficient in sulfur-containing amino acids. Properly supplemented, its amino acid complement is available for supporting protein nutrition, as shown by experimental study.

Gel Strength

The formation of heat-reversible gels in water is one of gelatin's most important properties. The strength of the gels formed depends upon concentration and the intrinsic strength of the gelatin used which is a function both of structure and of molecular weight. Gel formation, although not fully understood, is believed to result from hydrogen bonding, with the gelatin molecules arranged in micelles forming a semi-solid gel and binding water. Since gelatin is used in many products for its gelforming quality, the quantitative measurement of this property is very important, not only as matter of control but also as an indication of the amount of gelatin required for a given purpose.

The determination of gel strength is performed on an instrument known as the Bloom gelometer, named for the originator of the apparatus and test method. Although full details of the method cannot be presented here, the procedure is essentially as follows: A water solution containing 6.67% gelatin is carefully prepared in a special, wide-mouth bottle, which is then placed in a chill bath maintained at (10.0 ± 0.1)°C for 17 hours. At the end of this time the firmness of the resulting gel is measured by the gelometer. The instrument delivers the amount of lead shot required to depress a standard plunger (12.7 mm diam). a distance of 4 mm into the surface of the gel. The shot is delivered at a controlled rate and the flow is cut off mechanically by an electromagnet. This weight of shot in grams is then known as the gel strength or Bloom rating of the gelatin. The greater the amount of shot required, the higher the strength of the gel. Commercial gelatins vary from 50 to 300 Bloom Grams.

Gelatin Desserts

Gelatin is particularly suited to gelatin desserts because it forms a sparkling clear jelly which does not synerize (bleed) and has a crisp, clean mouth feel that is not attained by any other vegetable hydrocolloid. Gelatins vary in their behavior in gelatin dessert formulas. A good gelatin for desserts should impart fast set to a firm jelly within two or three hours in the refrigerator, but should not be too firm in 24 hours, and should produce a clear, sparkling jelly at the pH of the dessert.

A gelatin dessert powder consists of a sweetener, gelatin, food acid, a buffer, salt, color, and a flavor. The amount of gelatin in the formula depends on the intended use and on the jelly strength of the gelatin, but generally falls in the range of 8 to 10% of total dry weight. Desserts for institutional use require a higher level of gelatin to maintain a firm jelly at room temperature, than do finished desserts held under refrigeration for long periods in display cabinets. Since gelatin desserts are adjusted to low pH to attain tartness, a gelatin which retains its jelly strength is very desirable.

Typical ingredients for a flavored gelatin dessert mix are:

TYPICAL GELATIN DESSERT FORMULA	
Gelatin	8-12%
Food Acid	2-3%
Buffer Salts	0.6-1%
Salt	0.3%
Flavor and Color as desired	
Sucrose[a] (table sugar) to	100%

[a]Sucrose may be partially or totally replaced by corn syrup or fructose syrup.

Three ounces (85 g) of the above mixture will gel one pint (473 ml) of liquid after setting two to three hours at refrigerator temperatures.

The gelatin is listed as a variable quantity, since gelatin dessert manufacturers use a variety of gel strengths. the lowest percentage requires gelatin of the highest gel strength. The gel strength of gelatin used in dessert blends varies from 175 to 300; the setting quality of the dessert is affected by the gel strength, concentration, viscosity, and pH of the gelatin. Either Type A or Type B gelatin, blended in the above mixture, produces excellent gelatin desserts.

A food acid, such as citric, is used to impart tartness to the finished dessert. Buffer salts, such as sodium citrate, are added to help maintain the desired level of acidity (pH). While some buffers may possibly accelerate setting time, an excess of acid may interfere with the setting and melting characteristics. Buffer salts permit the addition of enough acid to impart tartness without adversely affecting setting rate. Salt is added to help accentuate the flavor. Manufacturers are cautioned to seek the advice and guidance of reputable suppliers for their flavors and colors; an otherwise superior product can be ruined by the selection of an inadequate color as a deficient flavor.

Sugar in the formula need not be restricted to beet or cane sugar; in many blends, dextrose is also used. In dietetic or low calorie desserts, sugar is replaced in part, or completely by artificial sweeteners.

Fruits and vegetables can be suspended in the partially set dessert; fresh pineapple and papaya should be avoided since they contain enzymes which hydrolyze the gelatin and prevent gelling. In the preparation of the finished dessert, water added with the fruit, fresh or canned, or vegetables must be taken into consideration. Failure to compensate for this addition, usually results in a weak and flaccid dessert which requires a longer than usual gelling time. The dessert is readily dissolved in warm (150°F) (65°C) water during a few minutes stirring. When removed from the refrigerator, a gelatin dessert is sparkling, colorful and pleasing to the taste.

Jellied Meats

The purpose of gelatin in jellied meats is to gel the fluids around the meat and act as a binding agent.

Clarity is an important property in such products as headcheese and jellied tongue. The amount of gelatin to use in such products depends upon the original grade (Bloom strength) of the gelatin used and the amount of liquid used to surround the meat particles. With a high-test product, as little as 2.5% of the meat weight can be used. On the other hand, with a low-strength gelatin, as much as 4.5% may be needed. The amount of liquid or broth used to suspend the meat usually runs between half to three-quarters of the meat weight. The more broth used, the more gelatin is needed to maintain the desired strength of gel.

Gelatin is used in binding the juices which exude from the muscle tissues when canned hams are produced. Again, the amount of gelatin used to bind the liquid will depend upon its grade, or Bloom strength; it will also depend upon the heat processing given to the hams, since gelatin tends to lose strength under heat processing. Although the actual gel loss is greater with high-test material than with a lower grade, the proportion of loss is the same in both cases. Thus, the economies for proportion of one product to use in comparison to the other will be based upon the normal ratios of usage level. The usual level of gelatin to use for canned hams is between 0.5% and 1.0% of the meat weight.

Agar-agar may also be used as a stabilizer and/or thickener in canned, jellied meat products.

Gelatin for Fruit Juice, Wine and Beer Clarification

Gelatin is used extensively for clarification, or fining, of wine, beer, cider, and fruit juices. Among the products available for clarification, gelatin has the advantages of unlimited shelf life in the dry state, simple handling, rapid precipitation and brilliant clarification. Fining with gelatin, when done correctly at low doses and with minimum aeration does not modify the organoleptic qualities of the product. Gelatin reacts with tannins, pectins and similar materials, in the presence of a catalyst such as iron, to initiate flocculation and clarification. Degree of acidity of the product to be fined influences clarification. Clarification is generally completed by filtration and centrifugation.

Various grades of Type A or Type B gelatin are used depending on individual requirements. A; amounts used are commonly in the range of 0.002% to 0.015% based on the weight of material to be treated.

EMULSIFIERS (SURFACTANTS)

Emulsifiers are widely used in many foods, including canned items; they may be broadly classified by function. Typically they are used as solubilizers, emulsifiers and demulsifiers, detergents, crystallization modifiers, foaming and defoaming agents, wetting and lubricating agents, and complexing agents. In canned foods, as in others, many of these uses tend to overlap.

Emulsifiers usually act to alter the surface properties of materials they contact, hence the synonym "surfactants." An emulsifier or surfactant molecule is composed of a water-loving (hydrophilic) and a fat-loving (lipophilic) portion. When fat and water are mixed, the emulsifier orients across the interphase, i.e., lines up between the two liquids with its lipophilic portion in the fat and the hydrophilic portion in the water. By bridging the two immiscible liquids the emulsifier can maintain a stable dispersion of one liquid in the other. The size and strength of the hydrophilic and lipophilic components determines the HLB (Hydrophile-Lipophile Balance) value of the surfactant; lipophilic surfactants have low HLP values (2-9) while hydrophilic surfactants have high values (greater than 11).

The origin of a surfactant may be either synthetic or natural. Eggs, milk, meat, mustard, and soybeans are examples of natural foods which contain surface active materials. Synthetic emulsifiers are produced from a wide variety of edible materials. Use of both natural and synthetic emulsifiers is restricted to those materials which are "generally recognized as safe" (GRAS) by the U.S. Food and Drug Administration, or proved safe so that a petition for a specific application may be submitted to the FDA. Canned products containing meat or poultry, and packed under the supervision of the United States Department of Agriculture, may contain only those emulsifiers which have received USDA approval for the intended application.

Use of emulsifiers has shown a slow but steady increase as consumers and processors have developed an interest in more sophisticated canned foods. The addition of dill oil to processed pickles and pickle products requires an emulsifier to solubilize the oil in the brine. A hydrophilic emulsifier like polysorbate 80 is used at a level of about 2 parts to 80 per part of dill oil to provide a clear solubilization of the dill oil in the brine. Orange oil used to flavor canned orange drink and soda is similarly solubilized with a hydrophilic emulsifier.

Formation of a stable salad dressing emulsion can be accomplished using a combination of a hydrophilic emulsifier such as polysorbate 60, and a thickener. In pourable dressings a thickener such as xanthan gum is used at 0.4-0.6% while the emulsifier is used at 0.3% of the formula. Spoonable dressings such as imitation salad dressing and imitation mayonnaise can be formulated without egg using a thickener/emulsifier system. Elimination of egg minimizes cost variations, bacterial problems, and cholesterol content. Imitation salad dressing is prepared in the normal manner except that a moderate increase in starch is required and a small amount of emulsifier is used in place of the egg. The thickening property of egg is replaced in imitation mayonnaise by a stabilizer such as xanthan or low level of cooked starch. In both types of spoonables a hydrophilic emulsifier like polysorbate 60 is used for emulsification at 0.3% of the finished dressing; artificial color and flavor are used as desired.

Not all surfactant roles involve emulsification. For example, the amylose released from spaghetti during retorting may result in a slumped, gelled mass of partially disintegrated strands; monoglycerides can complex or tie up the amylose to minimize these defects. In canned bread the monoglyceride/amylose complex helps maintain a soft crumb structure during the long shelf life of this product; typical use levels for monoglycerides in these applications is 0.5-1.0% of the flour weight, added to the dough.

Another non-emulsifying role for surfactants is in stabilizing the oil in peanut butter. Peanut butter contains much free oil which tends to separate in a relatively short time; to overcome oil separation, 1-2.5% fully hydrogenated mono and diglycerides are added with the sweetener to crystallize a portion of the free oil, thereby preventing oil separation. In consumer shortenings 2.5–3% plastic mono and diglycerides and 0.5% hydrophilic emulsifier like polysorbate 60 may be included to give smooth, well aerated icings and light, tender cakes. Bottled salad oil containing 0.5% hydrophilic emulsifier, such as polysorbate 80, exhibits marked improvement in emulsion stability when used by the consumer for home-made salad dressings.

In canned products containing meat, a continuing problem is the accumulation of rendered fat at the top of the product. Because the fat is not freed until retorting takes place, prevention of the fat cap is difficult. The most effective technique for minimizing the problem with emulsifiers is to thoroughly blend the emulsifier as intimately as possible with the meat prior to retorting. Materials such as 0.1–0.2% sodium stearoyl-2-lactylate or 0.25–0.5% hard mono and diglycerides are recommended.

It is difficult to predict which surfactant will solve foaming and defoaming problems. In the formulation of liquid cocktail mixes or "frothers," hydrophilic emulsifiers such as polysorbate 60 act as a very effective foaming agent; the use level varies from as much as 3% in the concentrated "frother" to as little as 0.15% in a sour mix requiring only the addition of liquor.

Whereas the hydrophilic polysorbate esters are used as foaming agents, lipophilic-glycerol mono-oleate acts as a defoamer. In the production of jellies and jams, 20-50 ppm glycerol mono-oleate is added to break the foam which would ordinarily occur during boiling.

The common types of emulsifiers which are approved for food use are: glycerol esters, polyglycerol esters, propyleneglycol esters, glycerol-lacto esters, phosphated glycerol esters, sorbitan esters, polyoxyethylene sorbitan esters, lactic acid esters, and lecithin.

COLOR ADDITIVES

Color additives affect the aesthetic value of food products. The color of a food, and to a certain extent the texture, are the first impressions received by consumers and can be extremely important in determining selection among competitive products. Color differences from the norm are, in fact, often overweighed by the consumer in his evaluation of the quality of a product.

The 1960 Color Additives Amendment to the Food, Drug, and Cosmetic Act established two classifications: Certified and uncertified food color additives. The former are synthetic products which are manufactured by chemical processes, while the latter are primarily natural colors and their synthetic analogs. The Color Additives Amendment brought all color additives, not just synthetic products, under the jurisdiction of the law. Likewise, it required re-evaluation of all color additives, even those previously listed and certified as harmless. It also allowed FDA to set limits on the amounts of color additives used. The same law states that no color additive can be used if its use promotes deception of the consumer, that is, if it is used to cover a blemish, to conceal inferiority, or to mislead the consumer in any way. The spice saffron, for instance, cannot be used commercially as a coloring matter in a way that would lead purchasers to think they are buying an egg rich product.

Uniform compositional standards have also been established for color additives and there is provision for certification of manufacturer's individual batches of a color additive through chemical testing by the FDA, to insure purity and safety.

In addition, the Amendment established two lists of approved certified color additives: a permanent list, and a provisional list for color additives which have not been sufficiently investigated with regard to their safety for permanent listing. The Delaney cancer clause is also contained in the Amendment; this clause forbids the listing of any color additive which has been found to induce cancer in man or animals; it permits the appointment of a scientific advisory committee to make recommendations in cases involving the cancer clause.

If a food contains any color additive, the law deems the product misbranded unless its labeling states this fact. There are exceptions to the law, for example, which concern the labeling of butter and cheese; these exceptions apply solely to artificial coloring agents for these products.

A complete list of FDA-approved colors includes the following as of this writing:

TABLE 11.15 – Food Color Additives Exempted From Certification or Uncertified Food Color Additives

Color Additive	Restriction
Annatto Extract	None
Beta Carotene	None
Beet Powder or Dehydrated Beet	None
Beta-Apo-8'-Carotenal	15 mg/lb. or pt.
Canthaxanthin	30 mg/lb. or pt.
Caramel	None
Carmine	None
Corn Endosperm Oil	Chicken feed only
Carrot Oil	None
Cochineal Extract	None
Cottonseed Flour-toasted partially, defatted, cooked	None
Dried algae meal restriction	In chicken feed
Ferrous Gluconate	Coloring ripe olives

TABLE 11.15 – Food Color Additives Exempted From Certification or Uncertified Food Color Additives - Continued

Color Additive	Restriction
Fruit Juice & Vegetable Juice	None
Grape Skin Extract (Ecocianina)	Non-alcoholic beverages & beverages
Iron Oxide-synthetic	Dog & cat foods (max. 0.25%) bases
Paprika & Paprika Oleoresin	None
Riboflavin	None
Saffron	None
Tagetes Meal & Extract	In chicken feed
Titanium Dioxide	1% maximum
Turmeric & Turmeric Oleoresin	None
Ultramarine Blue	Coloring salt for animal feed - 0.5% maximum

These color additives cannot be used to color a standardized food unless the food standard so allows.

Annatto, beta-carotene and beta-apo-8'-carotenal are employed to color margarine, butter, ice cream, cheese and most other dairy type products. Caramel is extensively used to enrich the color of meat products and rye bread and to color root beer and cola type beverages. Titanium Dioxide is used in coloring some coffee whiteners, sandwich spreads and candies where whitening is required. Beet powder is used in instant gravy preparations along with caramel. Ferrous gluconate can only be used to color ripe olives.

Certified Color Additives

There are two main types of certified color additives-dyes and lakes. Dyes are materials which manifest their coloring power by being dissolved in a liquid or solvent. Lakes are pigments or insoluble forms of the dyes; the lakes show their coloring power in the dry state and color by dispersion. The FD&C lakes are merely alumina hydrate (aluminum hydroxide) on which dye has been absorbed.

COLOR ADDITIVES

The FD&C dyes are water soluble and are insoluble in nearly all organic solvents. Water solubility of most color additives is quite high and in most application methods solubility is usually no problem. FD&C Blue No. 2 (Indigotine) is an exception to this, and often it would be advantageous to have a greater solubility for FD&C Red No. 40.

For systems where anhydrous conditions are a consideration, glycerine and propylene glycol are used as solvents; in general, the color additives are more soluble in glycerine than in propylene glycol. Most are only very slightly soluble in ethyl alcohol, but use is often made of the reasonable solubility in alcohol of FD&C Red No. 3, FD&C Blue No. 1, and FD&C Green No. 3.

Good coloring technique recommends that the dyes be solubilized before addition to the colored product; however, it is often possible, where water is added in the process, to add the dry color additives to the batch and depend upon the added moisture and heat to dissolve the color in processing.

Dyes may be purchased as powder, granular, plating colors, wet-dry (blends), diluted (cut blends), liquid (aqueous), liquid (non-aqueous), and paste. The best form for any specific use will be dictated by the nature of the product, the process conditions employed and the amount of color additive used.

Classification of Certified Food Color Additives

Certified colors currently approved by U.S. Food and Drug Administration for use in foods are classified in two groups. These groups include (a) the permanently listed color additives and (b) the provisionally listed color additives. The two tables that follow present the color additives currently included in each list.

TABLE 11.16 – Current List of Certified Color Additives and Their Restrictions Permanently Listed Under 1960 Color Additives Amendment to FD&C Act

Color Additive	Restriction
FD&C Blue No. 1	For foods, ingested drugs and cosmetics.
FD&C Green No. 3	For foods, ingested drugs and cosmetics.
FD&C Red No. 3	For foods and ingested drugs.
FD&C Yellow No. 5	For foods and ingested drugs, (see Specific Labeling Requirements).
Citrus Red No. 2	For coloring skins of oranges (max. 2 ppm).
Orange B	On sausage casings (max. 150 ppm).
FD&C Red 40 & its Lake	For foods, ingested drugs and cosmetics.

TABLE 11.17 – Current List of Certified Color Additives and Their Closing Dates Permanently Listed Under 1960 Color Additives Amendment to FD&C Act

Color Additive	Closing Date for Food*, Drug & Cosmetic Use
FD&C Blue No. 2	Date of final decision on permanent listing.
FD&C Red No. 3	September 3, 1985
FD&C Yellow No. 5	September 3, 1985
FD&C Yellow No. 6	September 3, 1985
Lakes of these colors	September 3, 1985

*Applies to lakes only for FD&C Red No. 3 and FD&C Yellow No. 5 for food use. The straight color additives are already permanently listed for food and ingested drug use.

Problems with Food Color Additives

In using color additives many problems may be encountered such as those discussed below.

TABLE 11.18 – Problems with Food Color Additives and Their Probable Causes

Problem	Probable Cause(s)
Precipitation from color solution or colored liquid food	Color additives solubility limit exceeded. Not enough solvent used. Unexpected chemical reaction took place. Low temperatures employed, especially for concentrated color additive solution.
Dulling effects instead of bright, pleasing shades	Too much color additive used. Color additive exposed to high temperatures.
Specking and spotting during coloring of bakery and confectionery products	While making a solution, color additive not completely dissolved Liquid color additive containing sediment used. Attempted to disperse an aqueous color additive solution in products containing too much fat.
Fading due to light	Colored products not protected from sunlight.
Fading due to metals	Contact of color additive solutions or colored products with certain metals (zinc, tin, aluminum, etc.) not avoided during dissolving, handling or storing.
Fading due to microorganisms	Not thoroughly cleaned. Color-preparing facilities not clean enough to avoid contaminating reducing organisms.
Fading due to excessive heat	Excessive processing temperature used.
Fading due to oxidizing and reducing agents	Color reacted with oxidizers such as ozone or hypochlorites, or reducers such as SO_2 or ascorbic acid.
Fading due to strong acids or alkalis	Presence of such strong chemicals during coloring of certain foods encountered.
Fading due to retorting with protein material	Color used did not possess good stability under these conditions.
Poor shelf life with colored, canned, carbonated beverages	Excessive amount of certified azo-type dye used.

Use of Certified Color Additives in Processed Foods

As a general guideline, FD&C dyes and lakes may be used in any food product unless otherwise prohibited by special regulations such as standards of identity.

1. **Fruit Products**

The use of FD&C color additives in the coloring of Maraschino cherries is widely known and well documented. Usage levels range from 2–8 oz. (57–227 g) of certified color additive per 1,000 lbs. (454 kg) of cherries; it is suggested that the sulfur dioxide content not exceed 100 ppm.

The use of FD&C Red No. 3 in coloring cocktail cherries is well known to the trade. The advantage of this color additive is that it can be set (precipitated) by citric acid rendering the color additive non-bleeding in the cherries. While non-bleeding cherries of other shades are desired, the prospects are not bright for development of such non-bleeding color additives due to the nature of the remaining FD&C dyes.

Apple rings, crabapples, and flavored apple sauces are colored with combinations of FD&C water soluble dyes. Combinations of 50 parts FD&C Red No. 40 and 50 parts FD&C Yellow No. 6 are being used, and some FD&C Red No. 3 can be used for improved brightness. Four or 5 oz. (113–142 g) of color additive per 100 gallons (378 l) of syrup is a suggested color level. In flavored applesauces, 1–3 oz. (28–85 g) of color per 1,000 lbs. (454 kg) is used to suggest the flavor that is combined with the applesauce.

2. **Pickles and Relishes**

Because of its cost, variability, low flavor value, and lack of light stability, turmeric is being replaced in some pickles and relishes. Laboratory trials indicate that FD&C Yellow No. 5 can replace turmeric at the rate of 1 oz. (28 g) of certified color additive for 1 lb. (454 g) of turmeric. For those desiring certified color additives for relished, a combination of:

FD&C Yellow No. 5 – 2 parts, and

FD&C Blue No. 1 – 1 part,

used at the rate of 0.1 oz. to 1 oz. (3-28 g) per 100 gallons (378 l) of brine is particularly useful. If this blend is too bright or artificial looking, then the addition of a small amount of FD&C Red No. 40 is useful.

3. **Paprika and Other Colored Spiced Replacements**

Because of the cost and variability of oleoresin paprika, many food processors are replacing it in non-standardized food products; color additive manufacturers have a good deal of information available regarding the replacement of paprika in many products. The economics for replacements of oleoresin paprika are decidedly in favor of certified color additive; one part of certified color additive will replace 7 to 8 parts of oleoresin paprika in most wet products.

Food processors are encouraged to contact color additives suppliers who offer the technical service needed. Food manufacturers are also cautioned to check closely with color additive manufacturers to keep abreast of the regulatory developments.

Food packers and manufacturers should also keep in mind the FD&C Aluminum Lakes which are finding increasing uses in food products.

PRESERVATIVES

One of the most important functions of additives is in the preservation of foods. Chemical preservatives help distribute foods to the consumer with "fresh" flavor and appearance, and with increased resistance to the growth of microorganisms. It has been estimated that one-fifth of the world's food supply is lost by spoilage; thus, it is in this area of extending the shelf-life of foods that chemical additives have the most significance.

Preservatives may be classified into four types: antimicrobials and antibiotics, both of which control the growth of microorganisms, and antioxidants and sequestrants which help preserve flavor and color. It should be kept in mind that preservatives cannot improve poor quality foods; they only arrest the deterioration of good quality foods and are not a substitute for good sanitation and good manufacturing practices.

Mode of Action of Preservatives

The mechanisms whereby chemical preservatives inhibit the growth of microorganisms are not fully understood. Most studies in this field have been directed towards determining the efficiency of a particular preservative in a given type of food product against a known trial population of microorganisms. These studies reveal a number of factors that influence the activity of chemical preservatives but, in general, they were not designed to determine how the metabolism of the microorganism is affected. When this knowledge is obtained, it could lead to the use of more efficient techniques in chemical preservation. Studies on the major preservatives, benzoates, sulphur dioxide, and sorbates, have been inconclusive in elucidating the mode of action of these substances.

Experimental evidence indicates that preservatives interfere with many enzymatic processes, both aerobic and anaerobic, which affect the growth rate of both the aerobic and anaerobic microorganisms concerned. It is not known whether the molecules must actually pass into the microbial cells to produce the whole or part of their growth-inhibiting effect.

Empirical experiments have given valuable information on the factors that influence the efficiency of preservatives. The principal factors are: concentration of the preservative, composition of the food, and type of organism to be inhibited.

In general, the quantities of preservative permitted by regulations are inhibitory rather than lethal to contamination microorganisms. It is therefore essential that the microbiological population of the food to be treated is kept to a minimum by hygienic handling and processing. Permitted levels of preservative will preserve food with a normal microbial load for a useful peroid, but will be ineffective when incorporated into spoiling or grossly contaminated foodstuffs.

Composition of the food is important for two reasons: the pH of the product will determine the concentration of the acidic preservatives existing in the undissociated form, and the chemical constituents of the product will determine the proportion of the preservative that is rendered ineffective by chemical combination. This second point is particularly important when the use of sulphur dioxide is being considered.

It has been reported that the undissociated acid is the microbiologically active portion of the molecule of acidic preservatives; a high pH leads to a greater proportion of dissociated acid explaining the greater effectiveness of common preservatives at lower pH.

Antimicrobial Agents

Antimicrobials are added to prevent or retard the growth of yeasts, molds, and bacteria during storage, distribution, and use in the home. These organisms are a common source of food spoilage and some are a potential danger to health if they grow to large numbers in the food.

The mechanism of antimicrobial action is not completely understood, but it is thought that agents react with the cell to prevent its development and further reproduction.

Common antimicrobial agents used in foods are:

ANTIMICROBIAL AGENTS
Benzoic acid and sodium benzoate
Methyl and propyl p-hydroxbenzoates (Parabens)
Sorbates-Sorbic acid and potassium sorbate
Propionates-Sodium propionate and calcium propionate
Sulfites and sulfur dioxide
Nitrites

Benzoic acid and its salts are the most effective agents against yeast and bacteria in foods which are relatively acid in nature (2.5–4.0 pH). They are used in most carbonated beverages, fruit drinks, jams, jellies, and salted margarines at levels of 0.05–0.10%. A maximum level of 0.1% is allowed in the U.S., although levels up to 0.25% are allowed in some other countries.

The Parabens are esters of the benzoates and extend their activity into the neutral range of pH or higher. They are generally more active against molds and yeasts than bacteria and are often used in conjunction with sodium benzoate for similar applications but may be limited by taste and solubility constraints. A maximum level of 0.1% is allowed in the U.S.

The sorbates are generally most effective against yeasts and mold but are selectively active against bacteria as well. They are widely used to control microbial growth in cheeses, baked goods, dried fruits, wines, beverages, pickles, salad dressings, etc. Until recently sorbates were not used in yeast-raised baked goods, but it has been shown that with proper care, low levels can be used in the dough and combined with a surface application after baking. This surface application on yeast-raised and chemically-leavened products is commercially practiced on variety breads, English muffins and various types of rolls, buns and sweet goods. Typical use concentrations are in the range of 0.1–0.2% by weight.

Along with their broad microbial activity, sorbates are active over a wider pH range (up to 6.5) than benzoates and with less taste impact. Except in the case of specific standardized foods, U.S. regulations do not specify a maximum allowed level; typical use concentrations are summarized in Table 11.19.

Sorbates are often applied to cheese products by dipping them in a relatively concentrated solution (10–30% potassium sorbate) to obtain maximum protection at the surface against molds; with some cheese products sorbic acid is incorporated directly into the melt during processing.

The propionates are widely used in bakery products as a mold and rope (a bacteria) inhibitor at levels of around 0.32%. They are preferred to other agents in these products because they do not greatly inhibit the action of yeast during baking.

Sodium diacetate used in bread acting as an inhibitor against "rope" bacteria and mold but has been replaced by the propionates which are less expensive and which have similar activity.

TABLE 11.19 – Typical Sorbate Use Levels

Product	Use Levels (%)
Cheese & Cheese Products	0.2–0.3
Fruit Drinks	0.025–0.075
Beverage Syrups	0.1
Cider	0.05–0.1
Wine	0.02–0.04
Cakes & Icings	0.05–0.1
Buns, Breads, Muffins	0.1–0.2
Margarine (unsalted)	0.1
Vegetable Salads	0.05–0.1
Dried Fruits	0.02–0.05
Semi-moist Pet Foods	0.1–0.3
Salad Dressings (pour-type)	0.05–0.1

Sulfur dioxide and sulfites are generally employed in the production of wine and are the most effective inhibitors known for fruit juices and dried fruits. It allows the growth of yeast during fermentation and, at the same time, acts as a powerful fungistat and bacteriostat. Sulfur dioxide also acts as an antioxidant and prevents discoloration of fruits by inhibiting enzymatic browning. At present, sulfite is permitted as a preservative in all foods which are not an important source of vitamin B1.

Nitrites, used in the curing of meats and fish, are reported to have some bacteriostatic activity, but are not permitted for this purpose in other foods.

Antibiotics

The antibiotics are much more potent than the other chemical preservatives discussed so far and much interest and hope has been expressed in their utility in food preservation. They possess a much broader range of bactericidal and bacteriostatic properties and are not influenced by pH. Although they are used to some extent in other countries, there is concern that their wide use can create strains of resistant toxic organisms.

In the past, either oxytetracycline or chlorotetracycline has been used in this country to help preserve uncooked poultry and seafood to extend their marketing life by inhibiting bacterial decomposition. However, they are now prohibited by the FDA for the reason that they were being used as a substitute for good manufacturing practices. Another reason for the ban is that, although those antibiotics are heat labile, a residue may remain in treated foods after cooking.

Antioxidants

Antioxidants are employed as additives to prevent two other types of food spoilage—the development of off-flavors from the oxidation of fats, and the deterioration of flavor and color. They also prevent oxidative destruction of many of the vitamins and essential fatty acids in foods.

Since most foods, except for fruits and vegetables, contain large amounts of fats, antioxidants are extremely important to the food manufacturer for the purpose of extending the overall freshness and shelf life of many of his products. An important fact in the use of antioxidants is that they will not enhance the quality of a deteriorated product, but will only aid in retarding deterioration. Because of their function, antioxidants are always more effective if added before oxidative changes have had a chance to get started.

The antioxidants approved for food use are listed in the table that follows.

TABLE 11.20 – Antioxidants for Food Use

Butylated hydroxyanisole (BHA)	Tocopherols
Butylated hydroxytoluene (BHT)	Ascorbic acid
Propyl gallate (PG)	Sodium sulfite
Gum Guaiac	Erythorbic acid

The first three, BHA, BHT and PG, are the only ones in common use in fatty foods in this country. Tocopherols (Vitamin E) are not normally added to foods, but are important antioxidants which occur naturally in most vegetable oils. All these compounds are true antioxidants in that they retard auto-oxidation of materials such as polyunsaturated fats, essential oils, and Vitamin A, which contain unsaturated bonds.

Ascorbic acid, sodium sulfite and erythorbic acid are often classed as antioxidants but actually function as reducing agents; they react with oxygen to remove it temporarily from the food system. They are used primarily in fruit and vegetable products to prevent browning and color fading.

When oxidation of fat occurs, unsaturated bonds in the fat molecule are first activated to a free radical by the action of heat or light; metal ions such as copper and iron catalyze the formation of these free radicals. The free radical formed is highly reactive, and readily reacts with oxygen to produce hydroperoxides. These are very unstable compounds and easily break down to volatile aldehydes and ketones, which are responsible for off-flavors such as "rancid," "painty," and "grassy."

True antioxidants have the ability to reverse the initial formation of free radicals and return the fat to its original condition which is resistant to reacting directly with oxygen. Once oxidation gets underway, however, it continues like a chain reaction and increases at an ever increasing rate; this is why it is so important to have an antioxidant present at an early stage in processing.

When oxidation occurs with flavorings, it destroys their original character and they lose freshness. When coloring agents such as carotene are involved, the chemical structure responsible for color is destroyed and they fade or, at high levels of oxidation, actually bleach out.

The antioxidants BHA and BHT are widely used in fat containing foods other than meats. They are normally added as a combination at a total level of 0.02% based on fat content. As individual antioxidants, they can be used at levels of only 0.01%. They should be dissolved directly in the fat or oil portion of the food to be effective. Antioxidants are also employed in dry cereals and potato flakes and other dry mixes to prevent fat oxidation. They are almost universally found in beverages, candies and chewing gum to preserve flavor freshness. BHA and BHT are synergistic with citric acid.

Sequestering Agents

Antioxidants usually function best in the presence of sequestering or chelating agents which inactivate the metal ions which promote the initial stages of oxidation. Sequestrants act by complexing with the metal and forming a ring structure around the metal ion. The reactive sites of the ion are thus blocked, and it cannot enter into its usual reaction.

The common sequestrants used in food are given in the following table:

TABLE 11.21 – Sequestering Agents

Ethylene Diamine Tetra-acetic Acid (EDTA) and its Ca and Na salts
Lecithin
Citric acid and citrates
Phosphoric acid and phosphates
Tartaric acid

The ability of sequestering agents to inactivate trace metals has use in those cases where metals react directly with certain components in foods to produce off-colors. Examples include the graying of potatoes (iron), the greenish-gray discoloration in canned corn (copper, iron, and chromium), the surface darkening of yams and cauliflower (iron), and the pinking of canned pears (copper, iron, zinc). Sequestrants can retard all of these reactions;without sequestrants, kidney beans turn dark red during canned storage, but, the additive which will prevent the discoloration of canned green vegetables such as peas has not been found.

Another interesting application of sequestering agents is the use of EDTA or polyphosphates to prevent the formation of the glass-like struvite crystals in canned lobster, shrimp, and crabmeat by complexing out magnesium; the discoloration of fresh and canned shellfish can also be prevented with EDTA.

CHELATING (SEQUESTERING) AGENTS

Basic Concepts

Trace metals occur naturally in all food products and are present in varying amounts in processing water, depending on the source of supply. Chelating agents, also called sequestering agents, have the ability to bind unwanted trace metals in an extremely stable metal chelate structure. Certain problems, particularly discoloration and off flavors, caused by the presence of certain metal ions in trace quantities may be eliminated by addition of a chelating agent. Table 11.22 shows the basic chelation reaction.

TABLE 11.22 – Chelation is an Equilibrium Process

The extent to which complex formation occurs may be expressed by the equilibrium constant K for the reaction: $M + L = ML$

where $$K = \frac{[ML]}{[M]\,[L]}$$

M = metal ion

ML = metal-EDTA complex

Note: Expressions in brackets indicate molar concentrations.

The equilibrium constant K (also called stability constant) defines the ratio of chelated to unchelated metal in the system. Expressed in another way, it is an index of the affinity of EDTA for a specific metal ion. A high K value means a low value for metal ion concentration and vice versa. EDTA and its sodium and calcium salts are highly effective chelating agents.

Since K is almost always a large number, it is usually expressed as log K (to the base 10). Table 11.23 lists the log K values for the nine metallic ions most encountered in food products, and the amounts of Na_2EDTA and $CaNa_2EDTA$ required to chelate these materials.

Stability constants are of considerable practical importance in attacking chelation problems, for they indicate which metal ions will be chelated preferentially when EDTA is added to a solution of metal salts. Thus, in a system containing ferric, cupric and zinc ions, the iron, which has the highest stability constant (log K = 25.7), will be chelated first, then the copper (log K = 18.8), and finally, if there is enough EDTA, the zinc (log K = 16.5). The calcium in food grade $Na_2CaEDTA$ will be displaced in any system by all metal ions in Table 11.23, except magnesium. Food grade $Na_2CaEDTA$ should be used in systems to control calcium and magnesium.

There are many environmental factors affecting chelation, including pH, temperature, influence of other ions, and electrolyte content. From a practical standpoint, pH is the most important parameter to be considered. The most common interfering metal ions occurring in food products are iron and copper. Both forms of food grade EDTA effectively chelate copper and ferrous ions in the pH range of 2 to 12. The ferric complex of EDTA is extremely stable at pH's below 7, but above pH 8, the precipitation of ferric hydroxide begins to occur. Below pH 2, free EDTA is formed, leading to the breakdown of the metal complex.

TABLE 11.23 – Stability Constants of Metal-EDTA Complexes

Metal	Log K	g chelating agent per g metal ion Na_2EDTA[a]	$Na_2CaEDTA$[a]
Fe^{+++}	25.7	6.6	7.3
Cu^{++}	18.8	5.8	6.4
Ni^{++}	18.56	6.3	7.0
Zn^{++}	16.5	5.7	6.3
Co^{++}	16.21	6.3	7.0
Fe^{++}	14.3	6.6	7.3
Mn^{++}	13.56	6.8	7.5
Ca^{++}	10.70	9.3	–
Mg^{++}	8.69	15.3	–

[a]Food grade.

Regulatory Status

Regulations on a usage of calcium disodium EDTA and disodium EDTA are issued under conditions set forth in Section 409 of the 1958 Food Additives Amendment Act to the Food, Drug and Cosmetic Act. It should be noted that the tolerance levels for calcium disodium EDTA are based on anhydrous material hence tolerance levels for calcium disodium EDTA shown should be multiplied by a factor of 1.1 to determine the maximum amount of EDTA Na_2Ca Food Grade that can be used. Where both forms of EDTA are accepted, either product may be used separately or in combination with the other.

Applications

Food grade Na_2EDTA and $Na_2CaEDTA$ uses can be generally described as controls for two types of unwanted reactions in food and beverages:

(1) Control of reactions of trace metals with other organic and inorganic components in foods, which result in deterioration of color, texture, and development of precipitates. Examples of these types of reactions are the problems with end stem graying of potatoes during processing, the darkening of canned legumes during retorting and storage, and struvite formation in canned crab meat and shrimp. In wines and juices, cloudiness or haziness can occur which has been attributed to the reaction of trace amounts of copper and iron with organic substances such as tannins and pectins.

(2) Control of pro-oxidant effects of trace metals which cause the development of off-flavor and rancidity of oxidation-sensitive food. Fats and oils, milk products, salad dressings, etc., are particularly vulnerable to oxidative effects, and deterioration is accelerated by as little as 0.5–1.0 ppm copper or iron.

Food grade Na_2EDTA and $Na_2CaEDTA$ are accepted by the FDA for a number of canned legumes including chick, pinto and kidney beans, dry limas, and black-eye peas to promote color retention on processing and storage. Usually the additive is dissolved in water and added to the beans by way of the brine, but salt tablets containing pre-weighed amounts of Na_2EDTA or $CaNa_2EDTA$ are also available. EDTA can also be introduced when the dry beans are reconstituted; the additive level used in the soaking solution is usually 0.3–0.5%. EDTA should also be effective in promoting color retention of other legumes such as red beans, Great Northern, Michigan pea beans, etc. Canned, whole kernel and cream style corn are subject to a gray discoloration in the presence of trace amounts of copper and chromium; the addition of 100-200 ppm calcium disodium EDTA to the brine has been effective in minimizing this discoloration. The surface darkening of sweet potatoes, yams, eggplant, peas, cauliflower, asparagus and turnips is inhibited by EDTA. Fresh pineapple chunks treated with food grade $Na_2CaEDTA$ show improved retention of flavor.

Disodium EDTA, in conjunction with citric acid and antioxidants, has been found to preserve the color and flavor of fresh or frozen fruits during processing. Bananas, strawberries, cherries and cranberries are especially prone to discoloration. Food grade Na_2EDTA is FDA-accepted in strawberry pie filling and in freeze-dried bananas that are added to ready-to-cat cereals. Combinations of EDTA with antioxidants (e.g. BHA) are recommended for stabilizing oil of anise, bergamot, lemon, lavender, peppermint, and rosemary against oxidation. The discoloration of canned mushrooms can be minimized by the addition of $Na_2CaEDTA$ to the brine prior to retorting; levels up to 200 ppm of food grade $Na_2CaEDTA$ are available for this application. EDTA inhibits the storage discoloration (browning) of freeze-dried vegetables such as kohlrabi which is actually intensified by ascorbic acid.

Food grade $Na_2CaEDTA$ is accepted for use in both pickled cucumbers and cabbage to promote color, flavor, and texture retention. Trace amounts of copper and iron, which occur naturally in cucumbers and are present in brine, vinegar, etc., can adversely affect color and flavor during the long term fermentation and subsequent processing. Food grade $Na_2CaEDTA$ is favored for natural dills, sweet pickles, relishes, and other processed pickle products. The additive may be incorporated into the brine stock solution or later when packaged. Fresh packed pickles are also benefited by $CaNa_2EDTA$, particularly in flavor retention after the jars are opened and refrigerator stored.

EDTA has been found highly effective in preventing end-stem graying of white potatoes upon heat processing; addition of 0.1% food grade Na_2EDTA to the blanching bath will minimize the after-cooking gray discoloration of frozen french fries or sliced potatoes. For best results, it is suggested that the blanching bath be maintained at less than pH 5.5 with alum. The pick-up of disodium EDTA in the potato by this technique is less than 100 ppm, the maximum tolerance level permitted by the FDA. Food grade $Na_2CaEDTA$ is accepted for use in canned whole potatoes to minimize darkening during retorting; up to 110 ppm of the additive is permitted. The EDTA can be added in aqueous solution to the brine or it may be added by commercially available salt tablets containing preweighed amounts of the additive. Prepared raw potatoes, washed in bisulfite and packed in polyethylene bags, show a 20% increase in shelf life and resistance to mold attack when 1% disodium EDTA is added to the wash solution; treatment with EDTA does not alter the flavor or texture of potato products.

Greening of potato tubers under fluorescent lights is reduced by spraying with EDTA. Potato salads with improved keeping qualities are prepared with EDTA and sorbic acid or benzoic acid; the use of food grade $Na_2CaEDTA$ for this purpose is permitted.

ACIDULANTS

Acidulants are employed, both directly and indirectly, for more than two dozen separate purposes in food processing. One of their major functions as food additives is to enhance and to modify the flavor of the products. In this way, the food is rendered more palatable and attractive to consumers.

Equally important is the ability of food acids to aid in the preservation of foods and in simplifying certain processing operations. Besides this, acidulants serve other specific functions, such as gelling agents for pectin, as source of acidity in leavening and as catalysts for inducing inversion of sucrose.

Flavor Modifications

All acidulants when added to a food impart a degree of tartness, which if not excessive can add a subtle character to the overall flavor of the product. The amount of food acid added depends not only upon the type of food, but also upon the background and average preferences of the persons comprising a particular consumer market. Often a food is very popular in one area, but fails to be sold in another, due to the habits and certain differences between two groups of the population. It is one of the functions of a good processor to determine what differences exist in this respect and to modify his product in order to satisfy most population variations. This does not mean that new taste sensations and food combinations cannot be introduced into various areas, but that dominant flavor preferences should be carefully considered in creating additional markets and in selecting the proper areas for establishing new products.

Acidulants also have the ability to intensify the taste of certain flavoring agents which may be either present in a food or added to it. Some acidulants have blending properties which produce uniform taste effects from unrelated flavoring agents. The intensity and duration of the acid taste vary from one acidulant to another. Undesirable aftertastes can often be masked by adding an acid which prolongs the tartness sensation and extends other flavoring effects. Some acidulants appear to have actual flavor fixative properties and to enhance aroma. Some are used primarily for seasoning purposes as in salad dressings and sauces.

Many of the flavor properties of food acidulants are due to the hydrogen ions obtained upon dissociation in solution. Of equal importance is the extent of undissociation and the effect of the anions which contribute to modifying the flavor of the food and in their other uses. For this reason, many acidulants are equivalent in overall properties, but each may excel in some individual desired flavor characteristic.

Aiding Preservation

Shorter times can generally be employed for the sterilization of foods when acidulants are added, since the resistance of bacteria to heat is less the lower the pH. Organic acids show this effect at much higher pH than do inorganic acids, indicating that the undissociated acid as well as possibly the anions have an important role in killing organisms at elevated temperatures.

Several natural products such as tomatoes and various fruits normally contain large amounts of acids. Additional amounts of food acidulants may be required in canning for proper sterilization, especially if seasonal and weather conditions or the variety used leads to a lower-than-usual acid content. The addition of food acids, however, is only an aid to proper heat-processing. It does not overcome difficulties arising from improper washing of raw produce, poor sterilization or poor sanitary conditions.

Acidulants also act as synergists to the antioxidants added to foods to prevent rancidity and other deleterious reactions. As aids in the prevention of oxidation, acidulants serve several functions; many are capable of forming complexes with copper and iron salts, thereby often reducing the ability of these impurities to act as catalysts. The ability of acids to form chelates and to reduce oxidation has an effect on stabilizing color and reducing turbidity in clarified liquids such as fruit juices.

Food acidulants can have an inhibiting effect on enzymatic browning by reducing the pH below the range of maximum activity of specific enzymes.

Other Functions

Wide use is also made of acidulants for many special applications in addition to those previously described. Besides acting as gelling, leavening and inversion agents, food acids are capable of reacting with proteins in modifying the properties of baked goods and other products. They can be used as nutrients in certain fermentations such as the production of sourdough or be employed to eliminate this acid-producing step entirely.

When combined with mono- or polyhydric alcohols or monoglycerides they yield edible flavoring agents, antiheat-spattering agents and emulsifying agents. Certain of their salts are used as stabilizers and as materials for modifying the texture of foods like cheese and various spreads. Acid salts and some of the acids themselves serve as buffers in numerous food products. They also modify melt consistency in the manufacture of products like candy, lozenges and cheese; they are the source of the necessary acidity to maintain the pink color of meat and to yield benzoic acid, the active preservative, from benzoate of soda.

Malic Acid

Malic acid has a high solubility, smooth tart taste and unusual taste-blending and flavor-fixative qualities. Several of its physical properties closely resemble those of citric acid which might be expected from the similarity in chemical structures. Malic acid, however, differs from other food acids in its effect on taste sensations. It has a stronger apparent acidic taste than citric acid in water and in aqueous solutions containing other taste stimulating materials.

Malic acid does not show the same rapid build-up in acidic taste when taken into the mouth as do other acidulants; it has the advantage of eliminating the sensation of a sudden "burst" in flavor often encountered with other acids; it has excellent antibrowning properties towards fruits and other foods.

Both its powdered and granular forms are easy to handle; under most conditions, it remains free-flowing. Even when lumping occurs under extreme conditions, the agglomerates can be readily broken up due to their low cohesion.

Fumaric Acid

Fumaric acid is the most economical of the solid food acids both from the standpoint of cost and the quantities required. Its applications, however, are limited to some extent by its relatively low solubility in water at different temperatures.

It is one of the most acidic of the solid acids, both in the amount of hydrogen ions it gives to aqueous solutions and in the apparent acidic taste which it imparts. So as little as 60 per cent can be substituted for standard amounts of acidulants in common formulations, acid costs can be reduced as much as 50 per cent when its solubility permits such a substitution.

Fumaric acid increases the gel strength of gelatins and acts as a calcium ion liberator when incorporated in alginate preparations. It blends readily with other food acidulants and does not give a "burst" of acidic taste. Although fumaric acid does not have exceptional flavor-blending characteristics, it shows an affinity for certain flavoring agents like those in grapes by producing an aftertaste which serves to supplement the overall flavor.

Adipic Acid

This saturated dicarboxylic acid has found increasing use in foods. It gives excellent gelatin sets to food powders and is practically nonhygroscopic; its solubility is from four to five times that of fumaric acid at room temperatures.

Since it gives a smooth, mild tart taste without imparting an undesirable tang it is used in products having delicate flavors. With grape flavors, it yields a lingering supplementary flavor.

Its aqueous solutions have the lowest acidity of any of the common food acids. Since the pH of its solutions varies less than half a unit concentrations from 0.5 to 2.4 grams per 100 milliliters can be used as a buffering agent to maintain acidities within a pH range of 2.5 to 3.0. This is highly desirable in many food products. The pH of its solutions is low enough, however, to inhibit the browning of fruits and other foods.

Succinic Acid

Succinic acid is a nonhygroscopic acidulants of relatively low acid strength. Its apparent taste characteristics are very similar to the other acidulants of this type; there is some evidence that it has a rather slow taste build-up which is an advantage when it is used as an acidulant in certain foods. It gives a much greater latitude in the formulation of powdered foods and beverages, since it has a much greater solubility in water at room temperatures than the other nondeliquescent acids.

Succinic acid is one of the natural acids found in foods, such as broccoli, rhubarb, sugar beets, fresh meat extracts, various cheeses and sauerkraut. All of these products have very distinct and marked flavors which may be due in part to a flavor enhancement by the small amounts of succinic acid naturally present. This would suggest that succinic acid might have some interesting effects on various flavors which cannot be duplicated with other food acids.

Citric Acid

Citric acid occurs abundantly as a natural acid in citrus fruits, tomatoes, and in numerous other fruits and vegetables; it is widely used in processed foods. Its major advantages as an acidulant are its high solubility in water, the appealing effects on food flavor, and its potent metal-chelating action. Citric acid has been used in foods in the U.S. for over 100 years.

Both citric acid and its salts are allowed in various fruit juice drinks and diluted juice beverages. The acid may be employed in preparing mayonnaise and salad dressings. Citric acid and sodium citrate may be used in fruit butters, fruit jellies, and in preserves. The acid is used both to control the pH for optimum gel formation and as a flavoring agent.

Canned vegetables, with the exception of those specifically regulated, may contain citric acid as an acidulant; examples are artichoke hearts and tomatoes. The acid is also an optional ingredient in canning prune juice and figs.

Citric acid is extensively employed in the preparation of carbonated beverages to bring out flavor and impart a “tang” to many of the beverages; it chelates trace metals which may cause haze or deterioration of color or flavor. It is also employed to adjust the acidity of relishes, sauces, and other food products requiring flavor enhancement. In canned crab meat, lobster meat, scallops, and oysters, citric acid is used to inhibit discoloration and the development of off-flavors and odors.

Phosphoric Acid

Phosphoric acid is an inorganic acid and the strongest acid used as a food acidulant, giving the lowest pH. It is one of the most important acidulants and the least costly of all the acids used in food products. This combination of low cost, high water solubility, and pH reducing characteristics make phosphoric acid very attractive as a food acidulant in products where its use also offers flavor compatibility. While this acid is most extensively used in carbonated beverages, it is also used in cheeses and in brewing to adjust the pH, to neutralize caustic soda in peeling of fruit, and to a small extent in the manufacture of jams and jellies.

Phosphates, such as monocalcium and dicalcium phosphates and monosodium acid pyrophosphate are ingredients in baking powders. Calcium, magnesium, potassium, or sodium phosphates are employed as buffering agents. Monosodium, disodium, and trisodium phosphates are used in artificially sweetened fruit jellies. Various sodium phosphates increase the water-holding capacity of meat. Calcium and sodium hexametaphosphates, sodium pyrophosphate, and tetrasodium pyrophosphate are used as chelating agents.

FIRMING AGENTS

Firming agents are often employed in the processing of fruits and vegetables to improve texture. A small amount of a calcium salt helps retain the firm texture by preventing excessive softening during heating or canning. Some of the products in which firming agents are used are canned potatoes, tomatoes, apple slices, pickles and sweet peppers.

Except for a few aluminum sulfate salts used for pickles, most firming agents are calcium salts or mixtures of calcium salts. These agents function by forming an insoluble calcium gel of the pectin which holds the cell structure of the fruits and vegetables together; this prevents softening and solubilization of the pectin during heating.

A list of some approved firming agents is given below:

Firming Agents

Aluminum potassium sulfate
Aluminum sodium sulfate
Aluminum sulfate
Calcium carbonate
Calcium chloride
Calcium citrate
Calcium gluconate
Calcium hydroxide
Calcium phosphate

Some of these firming agents are also used as a jelling agent for fruit jellies and to aid in the coagulation of certain cheeses during processing.

ALTERNATIVE SWEETENERS AND FAT REPLACERS

Western eating habits have resulted in excessive caloric diets, which are high in fat and sugars, and are believed to be partially responsible for obesity and other health problems. The consumers' demand for low-fat, non-fat, reduced sugar and sugar free products has driven the food industry to develop ingredients that could replace fat and/or sugars in product formulations. Sugar substitutes are also important for diabetics and consumers concerned with tooth decay. Non-calorogenic foods have been introduced into the market to fill the latter need (Giese, 1993).

Alternative Sweeteners and Bulking Agents

Alternative sweeteners should meet five basic criteria in order to be considered as viable ingredients:

- Must be safe to use at the specified levels in products and approved by the regulatory agencies.
- Should be at least 30 times sweeter than sucrose with non or minimum off-flavors and aftertaste.
- Should be water soluble.
- Must be stable during the shelf life of a product.
- Should be cost effective compared to sucrose.

Alternative sweeteners may require the use of bulking agents to provide for the additional functional properties of sucrose.

In the U.S. three alternative sweeteners are presently approved: saccharin, acesulfame-K and aspartame.

Saccharin is an organic petroleum based compound, chemical name 1,2-benzisothiazolin-3-one -1,1- dioxide ($C_7H_5NO_3S$), 200 to 700 times sweeter than sucrose. It is commercially available as acid saccharin, sodium saccharin and calcium saccharin, in the form of white crystals or crystalline powder. It is a very cost-efficient sweetener but has a bitter metallic aftertaste that increases with higher concentrations. Saccharin has been declared safe by several expert international committees and is legally used in over 90 countries. The acceptable daily intake established by the Joint FAO/WHO Expert Committee on Food Additives is 2.5 mg/kg of body weight (Giese, 1993). In the U.S., FDA permits the use of saccharin, with restrictions on maximum levels and labeling requirements, in the following products: beverages, fruit juice drinks, bases or mixes, sugar substitute for cooking or table use, processed foods, chewing gum and flavor chips used in non-standardized bakery products (CFR, 1994).

Acesulfame-K or acesulfame potassium is the potassium salt of 6-methyl-1,2,3-oxathiazine-4(3H)-one-2,2-dioxide. It is 130 to 200 times sweeter than sucrose and manifests bitter and metallic flavors at high concentrations. It is particularly useful in mixtures with aspartame or sodium cyclamate due to a synergistic effect that enhances sweetness. More than 50 international studies have reported no toxic effects of acesulfame-K. FDA has established an acceptable daily intake of 15 mg/kg (Giese, 1993). The additive may be used in the following foods in the U.S.: dry, free-flowing sugar substitutes in packaged units; sugar substitute tables, chewing gum, dry bases for beverages, instant coffee and instant tea, dry bases for gelatins, puddings and pudding desserts, dry bases for dairy product analogs, confections, hard candy and soft candy (CFR, 1994).

Aspartame is a dipeptide of the methyl ester of L-phenylalanine linked to L-aspartic acid ($C_{14}H_{18}N_2O_5$).It is 180 times sweeter than sucrose, has a similar taste to sucrose with no bitter aftertaste, and acts as a taste intensifier and enhancer. It is also noncariogenic. Disadvantages are instability in acid environments and loss of sweetness during extended heating. FDA acceptable daily intake of aspartame is 50 mg/kg of body weight. Aspartame is approved for use in 75 countries with more than 500 product applications (Giese, 1993). In the U.S. it can be used as a sweetener in the following foods: dry, free-flowing sugar substitutes for table use (not to include use in cooking) in packaged units sugar substitute tablets for hot beverages, breakfast cereals, chewing gum, dry bases for beverages, instant coffee and tea beverages, gelatins, puddings and fillings, dairy product analog toppings, nonalcoholic flavored beverages, tea beverages, fruit juice based beverages and their concentrates or syrups, frozen stick-type confections and novelties, breath mints, hard and soft candy, refrigerated gelatins, puddings and fillings, fruit wine beverages; yogurt-type products; refrigerated flavored milk beverages, frozen desserts, frostings, toppings, fillings, glazes and icings for baked goods, frozen cheesecakes, fruit and fruit toppings, frozen dairy and nondairy frostings, toppings and fillings fruit spreads, fruit toppings and fruit syrups, malt beverages, baked goods and baking mixes (CFR, 1994).

There are other alternative sweeteners available in the market that are used in other countries or are used as flavors rather than sweeteners. The following is a list of some additional alternative sweeteners: cyclamates, peptide sweeteners such as Alitame, thaumatins, stevioside and rebaudiosides, glycyrrhizin, sucralose, dihydrochalcones, and L-sugars.

For some applications, simply replacing sucrose with an alternative sweetener is not adequate because sucrose also acts as a functional ingredient. In these cases, the use of bulking agents, i.e. ingredients that fill space and provide functional properties, is necessary to obtain an acceptable food product.

Examples of bulking agents include cellulose, polydextrose, maltodextrins, and polyols such as sorbitol, mannitol, xylitol, maltitol and hydrogenated starch hydrolysates (Giese, 1993).

Fat Replacers

Ingredients that can mimic fatty mouthfeel and perception are used as partial or complete fat replacers/substitutes. Ideally, they would provide the following attributes: viscosity (thickness, body, fullness), lubricity (creaminess, smoothness), absorption/ adsorption (physiological effect on tastebuds), and others (Glicksman, 1991). Most fat replacer ingredients available in the market can be classified into three categories: protein-based substitutes, synthetic compounds, and carbohydrate-based replacements. The choice depends on the food product, replacement level and initial fat content (Anonymous, 1990).

Protein-based substitutes are generally composed of egg and/or dairy proteins. They are prepared by a patented heating and blending process called microparticulation. The result is small spheroidal particles (0.1 to 2.0 μm) that the tongue perceives as fluid having the richness and creaminess associated with fat. Products such as Simplesse® (the NutraSweet Co., Ill.) can be used in frozen desserts, dairy products, salad dressing, mayonnaise, and margarine. They can not be used in products that will require frying or baking because the high temperature would coagulate the protein (Anonymous, 1990).

Synthetic compounds comprise fat-like substances that are resistant to the action of digestive enzymes and therefore do not provide calories. An example of this type of compounds is the sucrose polyester called Olestra® (Proctor & Gamble Co., Cincinnati, OH), which is a mixture of the hexato octaesters of sucrose with naturally occurring fatty acids. Possible applications include partial replacement of the fat in shortenings and cooking oils for domestic and industrial use. Some of these substances are used in low concentrations as emulsifiers in Japan, but they are not approved for food use in the United States at the present time (Glicksman, 1991).

Carbohydrate-based replacements have been widely used in the food industry to substitute fats and/or oils partially or completely in many different products. These materials are all long-chain polymers, mainly carbohydrate in structure, and are soluble or swellable in aqueous systems to provide the slippery, creamy and viscosity perception associated with fats. There are many brand name products in the market for specific uses. Some of these compounds may have applications in canned or aseptic products including gums (for formulated foods), polydextrose (for puddings, frostings and icings), corn starch maltodextrins, tapioca dextrins (for puddings, imitation sour cream, cheese sauces), potato starch maltodextrins (dips, frostings, mayonnaise-like products, meat products), modified potato starch (for imitation cream cheeses, soups), hemicelluloses and ß-glucans (Anonymous, 1990; Glicksman, 1991).

References

Giese, J. H. 1993. "Alternative sweeteners and bulking agents." *Food Technology* 47(1):114-126.

CFR. 1994. Food and Drugs. Code of federal regulations, Title 21 Parts 170 to 199, U.S. Government Printing Office, Washington, D.C.

Anonymous. 1990. "Fat substitute update." *Food Technology* 44(3):92-98.

Glicksman, M. 1991. "Hydrocolloids and the search for the 'oily grail.' " *Food Technology* 45(10):94, 96-102.

Appendix

APPENDIX TABLE 1 – Temperature Conversion

The numbers in bold face type refer to the temperature either in degrees Centigrade or Fahrenheit which it is desired to convert into the other scale. If converting from degrees Fahrenheit (°F) to degrees Centrigrade (°C) the equivalent temperature will be found in the left column, while if converting from degrees Centigrade to degrees Fahrenheit the answer will be found in the column on the right.

° C		° F
	-100 to 0	
-73.3	**-100**	-148
-67.8	**-90**	-130
-62.2	**-80**	-112
-56.7	**-70**	-94
-51.1	**-60**	-76
-45.6	**-50**	-58
-40.0	**-40**	-40
-34.4	**-30**	-22
-28.9	**-20**	-4
-23.3	**-10**	14
-17.8	**0**	32
	0 to 100	
-17.8	**0**	32
-17.2	**1**	33.8
-16.7	**2**	35.6
-16.1	**3**	37.4
-15.6	**4**	39.2
-15.0	**5**	41.0
-14.4	**6**	42.8
-13.9	**7**	44.6
-13.3	**8**	46.4
-12.8	**9**	48.2
-12.2	**10**	50.0
-11.7	**11**	51.8
-11.1	**12**	53.6
-10.6	**13**	55.4
-10.0	**14**	57.2
-9.44	**15**	59.0

° C		° F
-8.89	**16**	60.8
-8.33	**17**	62.6
-7.78	**18**	64.4
-7.22	**19**	66.2
-6.67	**20**	68.0
-6.11	**21**	69.8
-5.56	**22**	71.6
-5.00	**23**	73.4
-4.44	**24**	75.2
-3.89	**25**	77.0
-3.33	**26**	78.8
-2.78	**27**	80.6
-2.22	**28**	82.4
-1.67	**29**	84.2
-1.11	**30**	86.0
-0.56	**31**	87.8
0.00	**32**	89.6
0.56	**33**	91.4
1.11	**34**	93.2
1.67	**35**	95.0
2.22	**36**	96.8
2.78	**37**	98.6
3.33	**38**	100.4
3.89	**39**	102.2
4.44	**40**	104.0
5.00	**41**	105.8
5.56	**42**	107.6
6.11	**43**	109.4
6.67	**44**	111.2
7.22	**45**	113.0

° C		° F
7.78	**46**	114.8
8.33	**47**	116.6
8.89	**48**	118.4
9.44	**49**	120.2
10.00	**50**	122.0
10.6	**51**	123.8
11.1	**52**	125.6
11.7	**53**	127.4
12.2	**54**	129.2
12.8	**55**	131.0
13.3	**56**	132.8
13.9	**57**	134.6
14.4	**58**	136.4
15.0	**59**	138.2
15.6	**60**	140.0
16.1	**61**	141.8
16.7	**62**	143.6
17.2	**63**	145.4
17.8	**64**	147.2
18.3	**65**	149.0
18.9	**66**	150.8
19.4	**67**	152.6
20.0	**68**	154.4
20.6	**69**	156.2
21.1	**70**	158.0
21.7	**71**	159.8
22.2	**72**	161.6
22.8	**73**	163.4
23.3	**74**	165.2
23.9	**75**	167.0

APPENDIX TABLE 1 – Temperature Conversion - Continued

°C		°F	°C		°F	°C		°F
24.4	**76**	168.8	41.11	**106**	222.8	60.56	**141**	285.8
25.0	**77**	170.6	41.67	**107**	224.6	61.11	**142**	287.6
25.6	**78**	172.4	42.22	**108**	226.4	61.67	**143**	289.4
26.1	**79**	174.2	42.78	**109**	228.2	62.22	**144**	291.2
26.7	**80**	176.0	43.33	**110**	230.0	62.78	**145**	293.0
27.2	**81**	177.8	43.89	**111**	231.8	63.33	**146**	294.8
27.8	**82**	179.6	44.44	**112**	233.6	63.89	**147**	296.6
28.3	**83**	181.4	45.00	**113**	235.4	64.44	**148**	298.4
28.9	**84**	183.2	45.56	**114**	237.2	65.00	**149**	300.2
29.4	**85**	185.0	46.11	**115**	239.0	65.56	**150**	302.0
30.0	**86**	186.8	46.67	**116**	240.8	66.11	**151**	303.8
30.6	**87**	188.6	47.22	**117**	242.6	66.67	**152**	305.6
31.1	**88**	190.4	47.78	**118**	244.4	67.22	**153**	307.4
31.7	**89**	192.2	48.33	**119**	246.2	67.78	**154**	309.2
32.2	**90**	194.0	48.89	**120**	248.0	68.33	**155**	311.0
32.8	**91**	195.8	49.44	**121**	249.8	68.89	**156**	312.8
33.3	**92**	197.6	50.00	**122**	251.6	69.44	**157**	314.6
33.9	**93**	199.4	50.56	**123**	253.4	70.00	**158**	316.4
34.4	**94**	201.2	51.11	**124**	255.2	70.56	**159**	318.2
35.0	**95**	203.0	51.67	**125**	257.0	71.11	**160**	320.0
35.6	**96**	204.8	52.22	**126**	258.8	71.67	**161**	321.8
36.1	**97**	206.6	52.78	**127**	260.6	72.22	**162**	323.6
36.7	**98**	208.4	53.33	**128**	262.4	72.78	**163**	325.4
37.2	**99**	210.2	53.89	**129**	264.2	73.33	**164**	327.2
37.8	**100**	212.0	54.44	**130**	266.0	73.89	**165**	329.0
			55.00	**131**	267.8	74.44	**166**	330.8
			55.56	**132**	269.6	75.00	**167**	332.6
			56.11	**133**	271.4	75.56	**168**	334.4
	100 to 400		56.67	**134**	273.2	76.11	**169**	336.2
			57.22	**135**	275.0	76.67	**170**	338.0
37.78	**100**	212.0						
38.33	**101**	213.8	57.78	**136**	276.8	77.22	**171**	339.8
38.89	**102**	215.6	58.33	**137**	278.6	77.78	**172**	341.6
39.44	**103**	217.4	58.89	**138**	280.4	78.33	**173**	343.4
40.00	**104**	219.2	59.44	**139**	282.2	78.89	**174**	345.2
40.56	**105**	221.0	60.00	**140**	284.0	79.44	**175**	347.0

APPENDIX TABLE 1 – Temperature Conversion - Continued

°C		°F	°C		°F	°C		°F
80.00	**176**	348.8	99.44	**211**	411.8	133.33	**272**	521.6
80.56	**177**	350.6	100.00	**212**	413.6	134.44	**274**	525.2
81.11	**178**	352.4	100.56	**213**	415.4	135.56	**276**	528.8
81.67	**179**	354.2	101.11	**214**	417.2	136.67	**278**	532.4
82.22	**180**	356.0	101.67	**215**	419.0	137.78	**280**	536.0
82.78	**181**	357.8	102.22	**216**	420.8	138.89	**282**	539.6
83.33	**182**	359.6	102.78	**217**	422.6	140.00	**284**	543.2
83.89	**183**	361.4	103.33	**218**	424.4	141.11	**286**	546.8
84.44	**184**	363.2	103.89	**219**	426.2	142.22	**288**	550.4
85.00	**185**	365.0	104.44	**220**	428.0	143.33	**290**	554.0
85.56	**186**	366.8	105.56	**222**	431.6	144.44	**292**	557.6
86.11	**187**	368.6	106.67	**224**	435.2	145.56	**294**	561.2
86.67	**188**	370.4	107.78	**226**	438.8	146.67	**296**	564.8
87.22	**189**	372.2	108.89	**228**	442.4	147.78	**298**	568.4
87.78	**190**	374.0	110.00	**230**	446.0	148.89	**300**	572.0
88.33	**191**	375.8	111.11	**232**	449.6	150.00	**392**	575.6
88.89	**192**	377.6	112.22	**234**	453.2	151.11	**304**	579.2
89.44	**193**	379.4	113.33	**236**	456.8	152.22	**306**	582.8
90.00	**194**	381.2	114.44	**238**	460.4	153.33	**308**	586.4
90.56	**195**	383.0	115.56	**240**	464.0	154.44	**310**	590.0
91.11	**196**	384.8	116.67	**242**	467.6	155.56	**312**	593.6
91.67	**197**	386.6	117.78	**244**	471.2	156.67	**314**	597.2
92.22	**198**	388.4	118.89	**246**	474.8	157.78	**316**	600.8
92.78	**199**	390.2	120.00	**248**	478.4	158.89	**318**	604.4
93.33	**200**	392.0	121.11	**250**	482.0	160.00	**320**	608.0
93.89	**201**	393.8	122.22	**252**	485.6	161.11	**322**	611.6
94.44	**202**	395.6	123.33	**254**	489.2	162.22	**324**	615.2
95.00	**203**	397.4	124.44	**256**	492.8	163.33	**326**	618.8
95.56	**204**	399.2	125.56	**258**	496.4	164.44	**328**	622.4
96.11	**205**	401.1	126.67	**260**	500.0	165.56	**330**	626.0
96.67	**206**	402.8	127.78	**262**	503.6	166.67	**332**	629.6
97.22	**207**	404.6	128.89	**264**	507.2	167.78	**334**	633.2
97.78	**208**	406.4	130.00	**266**	510.8	168.89	**336**	636.8
98.33	**209**	408.2	131.11	**268**	514.4	170.00	**338**	640.4
98.89	**210**	410.0	132.22	**270**	518.0	171.11	**340**	644.0

APPENDIX TABLE 1 – Temperature Conversion - Continued

°C		°F	°C		°F	°C		°F
172.22	**342**	647.6	188.89	**372**	701.6		**400 to 500**	
173.33	**344**	651.2	190.00	**374**	705.2			
174.44	**346**	654.8	191.11	**376**	708.8	204	**400**	752
175.56	**348**	658.4	192.22	**378**	712.4	210	**410**	770
176.67	**350**	662.0	193.33	**380**	716.0	216	**420**	788
						221	**430**	806
177.78	**352**	665.6	194.44	**382**	719.6	227	**440**	824
178.89	**354**	669.2	195.56	**384**	723.2	232	**450**	842
180.00	**356**	672.8	196.67	**386**	726.8	238	**460**	860
181.11	**358**	676.4	197.78	**388**	730.4	243	**470**	878
182.22	**360**	680.0	198.89	**390**	734.0	249	**480**	896
						254	**490**	914
183.33	**362**	683.6	200.00	**392**	737.6	260	**500**	932
184.44	**364**	687.2	201.11	**394**	741.2			
185.56	**366**	690.8	202.22	**396**	744.8			
186.67	**368**	694.4	203.33	**398**	748.4			
187.78	**370**	698.0	204.44	**400**	752.0			

Interpolation Factors

°C		°F	°C		°F
0.56	**1**	1.8	3.33	**6**	10.8
1.11	**2**	3.6	3.89	**7**	12.6
1.67	**3**	5.4	4.44	**8**	14.4
2.22	**4**	7.2	5.0	**9**	16.2
2.78	**5**	9.0	5.56	**10**	18.0

APPENDIX TABLE 2 – Conversion Factors, English To Metric*

Mass

1 lb. (avoir)	= 453.6 gram (g)
	= 16 oz. (avoir)
	= 7000 grain
1 kilogram (kg)	= 1000 g
	= 1,000,000 milligram (mg)
	= 2.2 lb. (avoir)
1 ton (short)	= 2000 lb.
	= 907.2 kg
1 ton (long)	= 2240 lb.
	= 1016 kg

Length

1 ft.	= 30.48 centimeters (cm)
	= 0.3048 meters
1 in.	= 25.4 millimeters (mm)
	= 2.54 centimeters
	= 0.025 meters (m)
1 mm	= 0.0394 in.
1 cm	= 0.394 in.
	= 0.0328 ft.
1 meter	= 39.37 in.
	= 100 cm
	= 1000 mm

Viscosity

1 poise (absolute viscosity)	=100 centipoises
	=1.00 gram per (sec) (cm)
	=0.0672lb./(sec) (ft)
kinematic viscosity	=Viscosity in poises; Density in grams per cc

Volume

1 gal. (US)	= 128 fl. oz. (US)
	= 231 cu. in.
	= 3.785 liter (l)
	= 3785 milliliter (ml)
	= 0.833 gal. (Brit.)
1 cu. ft.	= 7.48 gal. (US)
	= 28.32 (l)
	= 0.0283 cu. meter
1 liter	= 0.264 gal. (US)
	= 1,000 ml
	= 33.8 oz. (US fl.)
1 fl. oz. (US)	= 29.57 ml
1 ml	= 1.000027 cu. centimeter (cc)

*Courtesy of Votator Division, Chemetron Corporation.

APPENDIX TABLE 2– Conversion Factors, English To Metric* - Cont.

Specific Gravity

Baume Hydrometers for liquids lighter than water...

$$\text{sp. gr.} = \frac{140}{130 + {}^\circ\text{Baume}}$$

$${}^\circ\text{Baume} = \frac{140}{\text{sp. gr.}} - 130$$

Baume Hydrometers for liquids heavier than water...

$$\text{sp. gr.} = \frac{145}{145 - {}^\circ\text{Baume}}$$

$${}^\circ\text{Baume} = 145 - \frac{145}{\text{sp. gr.}}$$

A.P.I. Hydrometers . . .

$$\text{sp. gr.} = \frac{141.5}{131.5 + {}^\circ\text{A.P.I.}}$$

$${}^\circ\text{A.P.I.} = \frac{141.5}{\text{sp. gr.}} - 131.5$$

Brix or Balling Hydrometers...

Scales read direct in percent (%) pure sucrose in water solutions, when measurement is taken at temperature indicated on hydrometer.

Salometer or Salimometer...

Salometer deg. = deg. Baume x 4.0

$$\text{sp. gr.} = \frac{\text{lbs./gal. at } 60^\circ\text{F}}{8.337}$$

$$= \frac{\text{lbs./cu. ft. at } 60^\circ\text{F}}{62.36}$$

Temperature

$${}^\circ\text{F} = ({}^\circ\text{C} \times {}^9/_5) + 32$$
$$= ({}^\circ\text{C} \times 1.8) + 32$$

$${}^\circ\text{C} = ({}^\circ\text{F} - 32) \times {}^5/_9$$
$$= \frac{{}^\circ\text{F} - 32}{1.8}$$

*Courtesy of Votator Division, Chemetron Corporation.

APPENDIX TABLE 2 – Conversion Factors, English To Metric* - Cont.

Liquid Weight

1 gal. (US)	= 8.34 lb. x sp. gr.
	= 3.78 kg x sp. gr.
1 cu. ft.	= 62.4 lb. x sp. gr.
	= 28.3 kg x sp. gr.
1 lb.	= 0.12 US gal. ÷ sp. gr.
	= 0.016 cu. ft. ÷ sp. gr.
	= 0.454 liter ÷ sp. gr.

Flow Rate

1 gpm	= 0.134 cu. ft./min.
	= 500 lbs./hr. x sp. gr.
500 lbs./hr.	= 1 gpm ÷ sp. gr.
1 cu. ft./min. (cfm)	= 448.8 gal./hr. (gph)
	= 472 cc/sec

Work

1 Btu (mean)*	= 251.9 g cal (mean)
	= 778 ft. lb.
	= 0.293 watt hr.
	= $^1/_{180}$ of heat required to change temp. of 1 lb. water from 32°F to 212°F
1 gram cal (mean)	= $^1/_{100}$ of heat required to change temp. of 1 gram water from 0°C to 100°C
1 hp-hr	= 2545 Btu (mean)
	= 0.746 kw hr
	= 641.3 kg cal (mean)
1 kw hr	= 3413 Btu (mean)
	= 860 kg cal (mean)
	= 1.34 hp-hr

*Courtesy of Votator Division, Chemetron Corporation.

APPENDIX TABLE 2 – Conversion Factors, English To Metric* - Cont.

Power		*Pressure*	
1 Btu/hr.	= 0.293 watt	1 lb./sq. in.	= 2.31 ft. water at 60°F
	= 12.96 ft. lb./min.		= 0.068 atmosphere
	= 0.252 kg cal/hr.		= 0.07 kg/sq. cm
	= 0.00039 hp		= 2.04 in. hg at 60°F
1 ton refrigeration (US)	= 288,000 Btu/24 hrs.	1 ft. water at 60°F	= 0.433 lbs./sq. in.
	= 12,000 Btu/hr.		= 0.884 in. hg at 60°F
	= 200 Btu/min.		= 0.0295 atmosphere
	= 3024 kg cal/hr.		= 0.03 kg/sq. cm
	= 83.33 lbs. ice melted/ hr. from & at 32°F	1 in. hg at 60°F	= 0.49 lbs./sq. in.
	= 2000 lbs. ice melted/ 24 hrs. from & at 32°F		= 1.13 ft. water at 60°F
			= 0.033 atmosphere
			= 0.034 kg/sq. cm
1 hp	= 550 ft. lb./sec.	1 atmosphere	= 14,696 lbs./sq. in. (or 14.7)
	= 746 watt		= 33.9 ft. water at 60°F
	= 2545 Btu/hr.		= 29.921 in. hg at 32°F
1 boiler hp	= 33,480 Btu/hr.		= 1.033 kg/sq. cm
	= 34.5 lbs. water evaporated /hr. from and at 212°F	lbs./sq. in. absolute (psia)	= lbs./sq. in. gauge (psig) + 14.7
	= 9.8 kw		
1 kw	= 3413 Btu/hr.		

*Courtesy of Votator Division, Chemetron Corporation.

APPENDIX TABLE 3 – Metric Conversion Table

Millimeters	x	.03937	=	Inches
Millimeters	=	25.400	x	Inches
Meters	x	3.2809	=	Feet
Meters	=	.3048	x	Feet
Kilometers	x	.621377	=	Miles
Kilometers	=	1.6093	x	Miles
Square Centimeters	x	.15500	=	Square Inches
Square Centimeters	=	6.4515	x	Square Inches
Square Meters	x	10.76410	=	Square Feet
Square Meters	=	.09290	x	Square Feet
Square Kilometers	x	247.1098	=	Acres
Square Kilometers	=	.00405	x	Acres
Hectares	x	2.471	=	Acres
Hectares	=	.4047	x	Acres
Cubic Centimeters	x	.061025	=	Cubic Inches
Cubic Centimeters	=	16.3866	x	Cubic Inches
Cubic Meters	x	35.3156	=	Cubic Feet
Cubic Meters	=	.02832	x	Cubic Feet
Cubic Meters	x	1.308	=	Cubic Yards
Cubic Meters	=	.765	x	Cubic Yards
Liters	x	61.023	=	Cubic Inches
Liters	=	.01639	x	Cubic Inches
Liters	x	.26418	=	US Gallons
Liters	=	3.7854	x	US Gallons
Grams	x	15.4324	=	Grains
Grams	=	.0648	x	Grains
Grams	x	.03527	=	Ounces, Avoirdupois
Grams	=	28.3495	x	Ounces, Avoirdupois
Kilograms	x	2.2046	=	Pounds
Kilograms	=	.4536	x	Pounds
Kilograms per square centimeter	x	14.2231	=	Pounds per sq. inch
Kilograms per square centimeter	=	.0703	x	Pounds per sq. inch
Kilograms per cubic meter	x	.06243	=	Pounds per cubic ft.
Kilograms per cubic meter	=	16.01890	x	Pounds per cubic ft.
Metric tons (1,000 Kilograms)	x	1.1023	=	Tons (2,000 pounds)
Metric tons (1,000 Kilograms)	=	.9072	x	Tons (2,000 pounds)
Kilowatts	x	.746	=	Horse-power
Kilowatts	=	1.3405	x	Horse-power
Calories	x	3.9683	=	British Thermal Units
Calories	=	.2520	x	British Thermal Units

APPENDIX TABLE 4 – Decimal Equivalents, Hundreths Of A Millimeter Into Inches

Millimeters	Inches	Millimeters	Inches	Millimeters	Inches
0.01	0.0004	0.34	0.0134	0.67	0.0264
0.02	0.0008	0.35	0.0138	0.68	0.0268
0.03	0.0012	0.36	0.0142	0.69	0.0272
0.04	0.0016	0.37	0.0146	0.70	0.0276
0.05	0.0020	0.38	0.0150	0.71	0.0280
0.06	0.0024	0.39	0.0154	0.72	0.0283
0.07	0.0028	0.40	0.0157	0.73	0.0287
0.08	0.0031	0.41	0.0161	0.74	0.0291
0.09	0.0035	0.42	0.0165	0.75	0.0295
0.10	0.0039	0.43	0.0169	0.76	0.0299
0.11	0.0043	0.44	0.0173	0.77	0.0303
0.12	0.0047	0.45	0.0177	0.78	0.0307
0.13	0.0051	0.46	0.0181	0.79	0.0311
0.14	0.0055	0.47	0.0185	0.80	0.0315
0.15	0.0059	0.48	0.0189	0.81	0.319
0.16	0.0063	0.49	0.0193	0.82	0.0323
0.17	0.0067	0.50	0.0197	0.83	0.0327
0.18	0.0071	0.51	0.0201	0.84	0.0331
0.19	0.0075	0.52	0.0205	0.85	0.0335
0.20	0.0079	0.53	0.0209	0.86	0.0339
0.21	0.0083	0.54	0.0213	0.87	0.0343
0.22	0.0087	0.55	0.0217	0.88	0.0346
0.23	0.0091	0.56	0.0220	0.89	0.0350
0.24	0.0094	0.57	0.0224	0.90	0.0354
0.25	0.0098	0.58	0.0228	0.91	0.0358
0.26	0.0102	0.59	0.0232	0.92	0.0362
0.27	0.0106	0.60	0.0236	0.93	0.0366
0.28	0.0110	0.61	0.0240	0.94	0.0370
0.29	0.0114	0.62	0.0244	0.95	0.0374
0.30	0.0118	0.63	0.0248	0.96	0.0378
0.31	0.0122	0.64	0.0252	0.97	0.0382
0.32	0.0126	0.65	0.0256	0.98	0.0386
0.33	0.0130	0.66	0.0260	0.99	0.0390
				1.00	0.0394

APPENDIX TABLE 5 – Decimal Equivalents
Inches To Millimeters

64ths	Decimals	Millimeters	64ths	Decimals	Millimeters
1/64	.0156	0.397	33/64	.5156	13.097
1/32	.0313	0.794	17/32	.5313	13.494
3/64	.0469	1.191	35/64	.5469	13.891
1/16	.0625	1.588	9/16	.5625	14.288
5/64	.0781	1.984	37/64	.5781	14.684
3/32	.0938	2.381	19/32	.5938	15.081
7/64	.1094	2.778	39/64	.6094	15.478
1/8	.1250	3.175	5/8	.6250	15.875
9/64	.1406	3.572	41/64	.6406	16.272
5/32	.1563	3.969	21/32	.6563	16.669
11/64	.1719	4.366	43/64	.6719	17.066
3/16	.1875	4.763	11/16	.6875	17.463
13/64	.2301	5.519	45/64	.7031	17.859
7/32	.2188	5.556	23/32	.7188	18.256
15/64	.2344	5.953	47/64	.7344	18.653
1/4	.2500	6.350	3/4	.7500	19.050
17/64	.2656	6.747	49/64	.7656	19.447
9/32	.2813	7.144	25/32	.7813	19.844
19/64	.2969	7.541	51/64	.7969	20.241
5/16	.3125	7.938	13/16	.8125	20.638
21/64	.3281	8.334	53/64	.8281	21.034
11/32	.3438	8.731	27/32	.8438	21.431
23/64	.3594	9.128	55/64	.8594	21.828
3/8	.3750	9.525	7/8	.8750	22.225
25/64	.3906	9.922	57/64	.8906	22.622
13/32	.4063	10.319	29/32	.9063	23.019
27/64	.4219	10.716	59/64	.9219	23.416
7/16	.4375	11.113	15/16	.9375	23.813
29/64	.4531	11.509	61/64	.9531	24.209
15/32	.4688	11.906	31/32	.9688	24.606
31/64	.4844	12.303	63/64	.9844	25.003
1/2	.5000	12.700	1	1.0000	25.400

APPENDIX TABLE 6 – Metric Weights and Measures

Linear Measure

10 millimeters (mm)	=	1 centimeter (cm)
10 centimeters	=	1 decimeter (dm) = 100 millimeters
10 decimeters	=	1 meter (m) = 1,000 millimeters
1,000 meters	=	1 kilometer (km)

Area Measure

100 square millimeters (mm^2)	=	1 square centimeter (cm^2)
10,000 square centimeters	=	1 sq. meter (m^2) = 1,000,000 square millimeters
10,000 square meters	=	1 hectar (ha)
1,000,000 square meters	=	1 square kilometer (km^2)

Volume Measure

1,000 millileters (ml)	=	1 liter (L)
1,000 liters (L)	=	1 cubic meter (m^3)

Weight

10 milligrams (mg)	=	1 centigram (cg)
10 centigrams	=	1 decigram (dg) = 100 milligrams
10 decigrams	=	1 gram (g) = 1,000 milligrams
1,000 grams	=	1 kilogram (kg)
1,000 kilograms	=	1 metric ton (t)

APPENDIX TABLE 7 – Tin Plate Basis Weights

The base box is the unit area of 112 sheets, 14 inches x 20 inches or 31.360 square inches (217.78 square feet). Basis weights, which determine the approximate thickness of the plates, are customarily expressed in pounds per base box.

Weight		Thickness
Lbs./Base Box (Basis Weight)	Lbs./Sq. Foot	(Inches)
45	0.2066	0.0050
50	0.2296	0.0055
55	0.2525	0.0061
60	0.2755	0.0066
65	0.2985	0.0072
70	0.3214	0.0077
75	0.3444	0.0083
80	0.3673	0.0088
85	0.3903	0.0094
90	0.4133	0.0099
95	0.4362	0.0105
100	0.4592	0.0110
107	0.4913	0.0118
112	0.5143	0.0123
118	0.5418	0.0130
128	0.5877	0.0141
135	0.6199	0.0149
139	0.6383	0.0153
148	0.6796	0.0163
155	0.7117	0.0171
168	0.7714	0.0185
175	0.8036	0.0193
180	0.8265	0.0198
188	0.8633	0.0207
195	0.8954	0.0215
208	0.9551	0.0229
210	0.9643	0.0231
215	0.9872	0.0237
228	1.0469	0.0251
210	1.0791	0.0259
240	1.1020	0.0264
248	1.1388	0.0273
255	1.1709	0.0281
268	1.2306	0.0295
270	1.2398	0.0297
275	1.2627	0.0303

Tin Plate is also produced for special uses in weights other than those shown in the above table.

APPENDIX TABLE 8 – Case Equivalents

The following table gives the equivalant in cases of 24/303's, 24/2's, 24/$2^1/_2$ and 6/10's of the more commonly used cans.

	Equivalent Cases			
Case of...	No. 303's	No. 2's	No. $2^1/_2$'s	No. 10's
48 6Z	0.7122	0.5854	0.4034	0.4386
72 8Z short	1.4064	1.1562	0.7965	0.8661
24 8Z tall	0.5134	0.4220	0.2908	0.3161
48 #1 flat	1.0552	0.8674	0.5976	0.6498
48 #1 picnic	1.2938	1.0634	0.7328	0.7967
24 #211 cyl	0.8042	0.6610	0.4555	0.4952
24 #2 vac (12Z)	0.8724	0.7171	0.4941	0.5372
24 #300	0.9021	0.7415	0.5109	0.5555
24 #1 tall	0.9852	0.8098	0.5580	0.6067
24 #303	1.0000	0.8220	0.5664	0.6158
24 #300 cyl	1.1513	0.9463	0.6521	0.7089
24 #2	1.2166	1.0000	0.6891	0.7492
24 #3 vac	1.4154	1.1634	0.8017	0.8716
24 #$2^1/_2$	1.7656	1.4512	1.0000	1.0873
12 #29Z	0.9644	0.7927	0.5462	0.5939
12 #32Z quart	1.0534	0.8659	0.5967	0.6487
12 #3 cyl	1.5341	1.2610	0.8689	0.9447
6 #5 squat	1.0111	0.8311	0.5727	0.6227
6 #10	1.6239	1.3348	0.9198	1.0000

The capacity of a 16 oz. and No. $2^1/_2$ glass jar is approximately the same as the No. 303 and No. $2^1/_2$ can, respectively.

[Source: *The ALMANAC of the Canning, Freezing and Preserving Industries*, E. E. Judge & Sons, Inc., Pub., Westminster, MD.]

APPENDIX TABLE 9 – Can Dimensions and Conversions, From U.S. System To Metric

Can sizes are given in the nomenclature usually employed in the industry, which avoids the confusion incident to conflicting local names of cans.

In this system the cans are identified by a statement of their dimensions (overall diameter and overall height). Each dimension is expressed as a number of three digits. The first digit gives the number of whole inches, while the next two digits give the additional fraction of the dimension expressed as sixteenths of an inch.

The first number given in the size of each can is the diameter, and the second number is the height. For example, a can designated as 303 x 406, is $3^3/_{16}$ inches in diameter and $4^6/_{16}$ inches high, within manufacturing tolerances.

The dimensions are "overall," the diameter being measured to the outside of the double seam, and the height including the entire seam at each end of the can.

The following table lists the dimensions of common can sizes used in the canning industry and their approximate metric equivalents. The metric equivalents were calculated on the basis of 1 inch = 25.40 millimeters.

Dimensions (diameter x height)			
Inches	Millimeters	Inches	Millimeters
202 x 204	54.0 x 57.2	307 x 113	87.3 x 46.0
202 x 214	54.0 x 73.0	307 x 200.25	87.3 x 51.2
211 x 109	68.3 x 39.7	307 x 306	87.3 x 85.7
211 x 212	68.3 x 69.9	307 x 400	87.3 x 101.6
211 x 304	68.3 x 82.6	307 x 409	87.3 x 115.9
211 x 400	68.3 x 101.6	307 x 510	87.3 x 142.9
300 x 109	76.2 x 39.7	307 x 512	87.3 x 146.1
300 x 400	76.2 x 101.6	401 x 411	103.2 x 119.1
300 x 407	76.2 x 112.7	404 x 307	108.0 x 87.3
301 x 106	77.8 x 34.9	404 x 700	108.0 x 177.8
301 x 408	77.8 x 114.3	603 x 405	157.2 x 109.5
303 x 406	81.0 x 111.1	603 x 408	157.2 x 114.3
303 x 509	81.0 x 141.3	603 x 700	157.2 x 177.8

{Source: National Food Processors Association Bulletin 26-L, 12th Ed., 1982.

APPENDIX TABLE 10 – Container Dimension Conversion Chart, From Metric (mm) To U.S. System (inches and sixteenths)

Example: A container dimension of 77 mm would convert to 0301 ($3^1/_{16}$ inches).

Dimension							
mm	Inches + 16ths of In.	mm	Inches + 16ths of In.	mm	Inches + 16ths of In.	mm	Inches + 16ths of In.
1	0001	41	0110	81	0303	121	0412
2	0001	42	0110	82	0304	122	0413
3	0002	43	0111	83	0304	123	0413
4	0003	44	0112	84	0305	124	0414
5	0003	45	0112	85	0306	125	0415
6	0004	46	0113	86	0306	126	0415
7	0004	47	0114	87	0307	127	0500
8	0005	48	0114	88	0307	128	0501
9	0006	49	0114	89	0308	129	0501
10	0006	50	0115	90	0309	130	0502
11	0007	51	0200	91	0309	131	0503
12	0008	52	0201	92	0310	132	0503
13	0008	53	0201	93	0311	133	0504
14	0009	54	0202	94	0311	134	0504
15	0009	55	0203	95	0312	135	0505
16	0010	56	0203	96	0312	136	0506
17	0010	57	0204	97	0313	137	0506
18	0011	58	0205	98	0314	138	0507
19	0012	59	0205	99	0314	139	0508
20	0013	60	0206	100	0315	140	0508
21	0013	61	0206	101	0400	141	0509
22	0014	62	0207	102	0400	142	0509
23	0014	63	0208	103	0401	143	0510
24	0015	64	0208	104	0402	144	0511
25	0100	65	0209	105	0402	145	0511
26	0100	66	0210	106	0403	146	0512
27	0101	67	0210	107	0403	147	0513
28	0102	68	0211	108	0404	148	0513
29	0102	69	0211	109	0405	149	0514
30	0103	70	0212	110	0405	150	0514
31	0104	71	0213	111	0406	151	0515
32	0104	72	0213	112	0407	152	0600
33	0105	73	0214	113	0407	153	0600
34	0105	74	0215	114	0408	154	0601
35	0106	75	0215	115	0408	155	0602
36	0107	76	0300	116	0409	156	0602
37	0107	77	0301	117	0410	157	0603
38	0108	78	0301	118	0410	158	0604
39	0109	79	0302	119	0411	159	0604
40	0109	80	0302	120	0412	160	0605

APPENDIX TABLE 10 – Container Dimension Conversion Chart,
From Metric (mm) To U.S. System (inches and sixteenths) - Continued

Example: A container dimension of 77 mm would convert to 0301 ($3^1/_{16}$ inches).

Dimension

mm	Inches + 16ths of In.	mm	Inches + 16ths of In.	mm	Inches + 16ths of In.	mm	Inches + 16ths of In.
161	0605	197	0712	233	0903	269	1009
162	0606	198	0713	234	0903	270	1010
163	0607	199	0713	235	0904	271	1011
164	0607	200	0714	236	0905	272	1011
165	0608	201	0715	237	0905	273	1012
166	0609	202	0715	238	0906	274	1013
167	0609	203	0800	239	0907	275	1013
168	0610	204	0801	240	0907	276	1014
169	0610	205	0801	241	0908	277	1014
170	0611	206	0802	242	0908	278	1015
171	0612	207	0802	243	0909	279	1100
172	0612	208	0803	244	0910	280	1100
173	0613	209	0804	245	0910	281	1101
174	0614	210	0804	246	0911	282	1102
175	0614	211	0805	247	0912	283	1102
176	0615	212	0806	248	0912	284	1103
177	0615	213	0806	249	0913	285	1104
178	0700	214	0807	250	0913	286	1104
179	0701	215	0807	251	0914	287	1105
180	0701	216	0808	252	0915	288	1105
181	0702	217	0809	253	0915	289	1106
182	0703	218	0809	254	1000	290	1107
183	0703	219	0810	255	1001	291	1107
184	0704	220	0811	256	1001	292	1108
185	0705	221	0811	257	1002	293	1109
186	0705	222	0812	258	1003	294	1109
187	0706	223	0812	259	1003	295	1110
188	0706	224	0813	260	1004	296	1110
189	0707	225	0814	261	1004	297	1111
190	0708	226	0814	262	1005	298	1112
191	0708	227	0815	263	1006	299	1112
192	0709	228	0900	264	1006	300	1113
193	0710	229	0900	265	1007	301	1114
194	0710	230	0901	266	1008	302	1114
195	0711	231	0902	267	1008	303	1115
196	0711	232	0902	268	1009	304	1200

APPENDIX TABLE 11 – Sodium Chloride Brine Tables for Brine at 60°F

Salometer Degrees	Specific Gravity	Baume Degrees	% Sodium Chloride By Wt.	Lbs. Per Gal. Brine NaCl	Lbs. Per Gal. Brine Water	Grams Per Liter Brine NaCl	Grams Per Liter Brine Water	Freezing Pt.°F*
0	1.000	0.0	.000	.000	8.328	.0	998.0	+32.0
2	1.004	0.6	.528	.044	8.318	5.28	996.5	+31.5
4	1.007	1.1	1.056	.089	8.297	10.61	994.0	+31.1
6	1.011	1.6	1.584	.133	8.287	15.97	992.8	+30.5
8	1.015	2.1	2.112	.178	8.275	21.38	991.3	+30.0
10	1.019	2.7	2.640	.224	8.262	26.84	989.9	+29.3
12	1.023	3.3	3.167	.270	8.250	32.35	988.3	+28.8
14	1.026	3.7	3.695	.316	8.229	37.86	985.9	+28.2
16	1.030	4.2	4.223	.362	8.216	43.43	984.5	+27.6
18	1.034	4.8	4.751	.409	8.202	49.03	982.7	+27.0
20	1.038	5.3	5.279	.456	8.188	54.65	981.0	+26.4
22	1.042	5.8	5.807	.503	8.175	60.32	979.4	+25.7
24	1.046	6.4	6.335	.552	8.159	66.13	977.4	+25.1
26	1.050	6.9	6.863	.600	8.144	71.88	975.7	+24.4
28	1.054	7.4	7.391	.649	8.129	77.27	973.9	+23.7
30	1.058	7.9	7.919	.698	8.113	83.56	971.8	+23.0
32	1.062	8.5	8.446	.747	8.097	89.49	969.9	+22.3
34	1.066	9.0	8.974	.797	8.081	95.42	968.0	+21.6
36	1.070	9.5	9.502	.847	8.064	101.4	965.8	+20.9
38	1.074	10.0	10.030	.897	8.047	107.5	963.8	+20.2
40	1.078	10.5	10.558	.948	8.030	113.5	961.8	+19.4
42	1.082	11.0	11.086	.999	8.012	119.6	959.6	+18.7
44	1.086	11.5	11.614	1.050	7.994	125.8	957.2	+17.9
46	1.090	12.0	12.142	1.102	7.976	132.0	955.3	+17.1
48	1.094	12.5	12.670	1.154	7.957	138.2	953.0	+16.2
50	1.098	12.9	13.198	1.207	7.937	144.5	950.6	+15.4
52	1.102	13.4	13.725	1.260	7.918	150.9	948.5	+14.5
54	1.106	13.9	14.253	1.313	7.898	157.2	946.2	+13.7
56	1.110	14.4	14.781	1.366	7.878	163.6	943.7	+12.8
58	1.114	14.8	15.309	1.420	7.858	170.1	941.3	+11.8

The above table applies to brine tested at the temperature of 60°F.

* Temperature at which freezing begins. Ice forms, brine concentrates, and the freezing point lowers to eutecic.

** Eutecic point. For brines stronger than eutecic, the temperatures shown are the saturation temperature for sodium chloride dihydrate. Brines stronger than eutecic deposit excess sodium chloride as dihydrate when cooled, and freeze at eutecic.

† Transition temperature from anhydrous salt to dihydrate.

† † Saturated brine at 60°F.

(Continued next page)

APPENDIX TABLE 11 – Sodium Chloride Brine Tables for Brine at 60°F - Continued

Salometer Degrees	Specific Gravity	Baume Degrees	% Sodium Chloride By Wt.	Lbs. Per Gal. Brine NaCl	Lbs. Per Gal. Brine Water	Grams Per Liter Brine NaCl	Grams Per Liter Brine Water	Freezing Pt.°F*
60	1.118	15.3	15.837	1.475	7.836	176.7	938.8	+10.9
62	1.122	15.8	16.365	1.529	7.815	183.2	936.2	+9.9
64	1.126	16.2	16.893	1.584	7.794	189.8	933.7	+8.9
66	1.130	16.7	17.421	1.639	7.772	196.5	931.2	+7.9
68	1.135	17.2	17.949	1.697	7.755	203.2	928.9	+6.8
70	1.139	17.7	18.477	1.753	7.733	209.9	926.3	+5.7
72	1.143	18.1	19.004	1.809	7.710	216.7	923.7	+4.6
74	1.147	18.6	19.532	1.866	7.686	223.5	921.0	+3.4
76	1.152	19.1	20.060	1.925	7.669	230.6	918.6	+2.2
78	1.156	19.6	20.588	1.982	7.645	237.4	915.9	+1.0
80	1.160	20.0	21.116	2.040	7.620	244.4	912.9	-.4
82	1.164	20.4	21.644	2.098	7.596	251.5	910.5	-1.6
84	1.169	21.0	22.172	2.158	7.577	258.5	907.7	-3.0
86	1.173	21.4	22.700	2.218	7.551	265.7	904.6	-4.4
88	1.178	21.9	23.228	2.279	7.531	272.9	902.1	-5.8
**88.3	1.179	22.0	23.310	2.288	7.528	274.1	901.6	-6.0**
90	1.182	22.3	23.755	2.338	7.506	280.1	899.1	-1.1
92	1.186	22.7	24.283	2.398	7.479	287.4	896.0	+4.8
94	1.191	23.3	24.811	2.459	7.460	294.7	893.5	+11.1
95	1.193	23.5	25.075	2.491	7.444	298.4	891.7	+14.4
96	1.195	23.7	25.339	2.522	7.430	302.1	890.1	+18.0
97	1.197	23.9	25.603	2.552	7.417	305.8	888.6	+21.6
98	1.200	24.2	25.867	2.585	7.409	309.6	887.4	+25.5
99	1.202	24.4	26.131	2.616	7.394	313.4	885.7	+29.8
99.6	1.203	24.5	26.285	2.634	7.386	315.4	884.8	+32.3†
100	1.204	24.6	26.395	2.647	7.380	317.1	884.2	+60.0††

The above table applies to brine tested at the temperature of 60°F.
* Temperature at which freezing begins. Ice forms, brine concentrates, and the freezing point lowers to eutecic.
** Eutecic point. For brines stronger than eutecic, the temperatures shown are the saturation temperature for sodium chloride dihydrate. Brines stronger than eutecic deposit excess sodium chloride as dihydrate when cooled, and freeze at eutecic.
† Transition temperature from anhydrous salt to dihydrate.
†† Saturated brine at 60°F.

SOURCE: Morton Salt Company.

APPENDIX TABLE 12 – Normal pH Ranges of Selected Commercially Canned Foods

Kind of Food	pH Range, approximate	Kind of Food	pH Range, approximate
Apples, whole	3.4-3.5	Grapefruit (cont.)	
Apple Juice	3.3-3.5	Pulp	3.4
Asparagus, green	5.0-5.8	Sections	3.0-3.5
Beans		Grapes	3.5-4.5
Baked	4.8-5.5	Ham, spiced	6.0-6.3
Green	4.9-5.5	Hominy, lye	6.9-7.9
Lima	5.4-6.3	Huckleberries	2.8-2.9
Beans, with pork	5.1-5.8	Jam, fruit	3.5-4.0
Beef, corned, hash	5.5-6.0	Jellies, fruit	3.0-3.5
Beets, whole	4.9-5.8	Lemons	2.2-2.4
Blackberries	3.0-4.2	Juice	2.2-2.6
Blueberries	3.2-3.6	Lime Juice	2.2-2.4
Boysenberries	3.0-3.3	Loganberries	2.7-3.5
Broccoli	5.2-6.0	Mackerel	5.9-6.2
Carrots, chopped	5.3-5.6	Molasses	5.0-5.4
Carrot Juice	5.2-5.8	Mushrooms	6.0-6.5
Cherry Juice	3.4-3.6	Olives, ripe	5.9-7.3
Chicken	6.2-6.4	Orange Juice	3.0-4.0
Chicken with noodles	6.2-6.7	Oysters	6.3-6.7
Chop Suey	5.4-5.6	Peaches	3.4-4.2
Cider	2.9-3.3	Pears (Bartlett)	3.8-4.6
Clams	5.9-7.1	Peas	5.6-6.5
Codfish	6.0-6.1	Pickles	
Corn		Dill	2.6-3.8
On-the-Cob	6.1-6.8	Sour	3.0-3.5
Cream-style	5.9-6.5	Sweet	2.5-3.0
Whole grain		Pimentos	4.3-4.9
Brine packed	5.8-6.5	Pineapple	
Vacuum packed	6.0-6.4	Crushed	3.2-4.0
Crab Apples, spiced	3.3-3.7	Sliced	3.5-4.1
Cranberry		Juice	3.4-3.7
Juice	2.5-2.7	Plums	2.8-3.0
Sauce	2.3	Potatoes	
Currant Juice	3.0	White	5.4-5.9
Fruit Cocktail	3.6-4.0	Mashed	5.1
Gooseberries	2.8-3.1	Potato Salad	3.9-4.6
Grapefruit		Prune Juice	3.7-4.3
Juice	2.9-3.4	Pumpkin	5.2-5.5

APPENDIX TABLE 12 – Normal pH Ranges of Selected Commercially Canned Foods - Continued

Kind of Food	pH Range, approximate	Kind of Food	pH Range, approximate
Raspberries	2.9-3.7	Soups (cont.)	
Rhubarb	2.9-3.3	Tomato	4.2-5.2
Salmon	6.1-6.5	Turtle	5.2_5.3
Sardines	5.7-6.6	Vegetable	4.7-5.6
Sauerkraut	3.1-3.7	Spinach	4.8-5.8
Juice	3.3-3.4	Squash	5.0-5.3
Shrimp	6.8-7.0	Strawberries	3.0-3.9
Soups		Sweet Potatoes	5.3-5.6
Bean	5.7-5.8	Tomatoes	4.1-4.4
Beef Broth	6.0-6.2	Juice	3.9-4.4
Chicken Noodle	5.5-6.5	Tuna	5.9-6.1
Clam Chowder	5.6-5.9	Turnip Greens	5.4-5.6
Duck	5.0-5.7	Vegetable	
Mushroom	6.3-6.7	Juice	3.9-4.3
Noodle	5.6-5.8	Mixed	5.4-5.6
Oyster	6.5-6.9	Vinegar	2.4-3.4
Pea	5.7-6.2	Youngberries	3.0-3.7

APPENDIX TABLE 13 – Calculated Sterilizing Values (F_0) For Some Current Commercial Processes

Product	Can Size	Approximate Calculated Sterlizing Value, F_0
Asparagus	All	2 to 4
Green beans, brine packed	# 2	3.5
Green Beans, brine packed	#10	6
Chicken Boned	All	6 to 8
Corn, whole kernel, brine packed	# 2	9
Corn, whole kernel, brine packed	# 10	15
Cream style corn	# 2	5 to 6
Cream style corn	# 10	2.3
Dog food	# 2	12
Dog food	# 10	6
Mackerel in brine	301 x 411	2.9 to 3.6
Meat loaf	# 2	6
Peas, brine packed	# 2	7
Peas, brine packed	# 10	11
Sausage, Vienna, in brine	Various	5
Chili con carne	Various	6

Courtesy of former American Can Co.

Glossary Of Terms

AAS. Atomic absorption spectrophotometry. Method used to quantitatively analyze for mineral elements, like sodium, phosphorus, chromium, cobalt.

ABSOLUTE HUMIDITY. Actual weight of water vapor contained in a unit volume or weight of air. See also RELATIVE HUMIDITY.

ABSORBENT. A substance having the ability to soak up or retain other substances, such as sugar or salt absorbing water when exposed to high relative humidity atmospheres.

ACID. A substance which increases the concentration of hydrogen ions (H+) in water, and reacts with a base to form a salt. See also Hydrogen Ion Concentration.

ACID FOODS. Any foods with a finished equilibrium pH value of 4.6 or smaller. Tomatoes, pears, pineapples, and the juices thereof, having a pH of less than 4.7, and figs having a pH of 4.9 or below are also classed as acid foods.

ACID NUMBER. Number or amount KOH required to neutralize the free fatty acids in 1 g of fat, wax, or resin.

ACIDIFIED FOOD. A low-acid food to which acid(s) or acid food(s) are added and which has a finished equilibrium pH of 4.6 or below and a water activity (a_w) greater than 0.85.

ACIDULANT. An acidifying agent, such as acetic acid or vinegar.

ACIDURIC. Microorganisms that can grow in high acid foods, i.e., with a pH value below 3.0. Generally are of low heat resistance.

ACTIVATED SLUDGE. Sludge floc produced in raw or settled waste-water by the growth of bacteria or other organisms in the presence of dissolved oxygen.

ACTIVATED SLUDGE PROCESS. A biological waste-water treatment process in which a mixture of wastewater and activated sludge is agitated and aerated.

ADDITIVE. Any substance, the intended use of which results or may reasonably be expected to result, directly or indirectly, in its becoming a component or otherwise affecting the characteristics of any food.

ADDITIVE, FOOD. See Food Additive.

ADSORBENT. Material on whose surface adsorption takes place.

ADSORPTION. Adhesion of a substance to the surface of a solid or liquid.

ADULTERANT (ADULTERATION). Foreign material in food, especially substances which are esthetically objectionable, hazardous to health, or which indicate that unsanitary handling or manufacturing practices have been employed.

AERATION. The bringing about of intimate contact between air and a liquid by bubbling air through the liquid or by agitation of the liquid to promote surface absorption of air.

AERATION TANK. A tank in which sludge, sewage, or other liquid waste is aerated.

AEROBES. Micro-organisms that need oxygen for growth. Obligate aerobes cannot survive in the absence of oxygen.

AEROBIC. Living or active only in the presence of free oxygen.

AERATOR. A device used to promote aeration.

AEROSOL. Colloidal suspension in which gas is the dispersant. Dispersion or suspension of extremely fine particles of liquid or solid in a gaseous medium.

AFDOUS. Association of Food and Drug Officials of the U.S.

AFLATOXINS. Highly toxic substances produced by certain molds on moist peanuts, corn, pecans and other foodstuffs during the growing and post-harvest period. The F.D.A. has set limits on the levels of aflatoxins produced in various food products. It is virtually impossible to produce agricultural commodities without low levels of aflatoxins.

AGAR. Dried, purified stems of a seaweed. Partly soluble and swells with water to form a gel. Used in soups, jellies, ice-cream, meat and fish pastes, in bacteriological media, as a stabilizer for emulsions. Also called agar-agar.

AGGLOMERATE. To gather, form or grow into a rounded mass, or to cluster densely.

AGING. See MATURATION.

AGING. Treatment of flour with oxidizing agents.

AID. Agency for International Development, U.S. Department of State.

AIR FLOTATION. Synonymous with flotation.

AJINOMOTO. See GLUTAMATE, SODIUM.

ALBEDO. The white inner layer of citrus fruit peel. Consists of sugars, cellulose and pectins; used as a source of pectin for commercial manufacture.

ALBUMEN. The white of an egg, composed principally of the protein albumin.

ALBUMIN. Any of a group of plant and animal proteins which are soluble in water, dilute salt solutions, and 50% saturated ammonium sulfate.

ALDEHYDES. A call of highly reactive organic chemical compounds obtained by oxidation of a primary alcohol.

ALGAE. Major group of lower plants, single and multi-celled, usually aquatic and capable of synthesizing their foodstuff by photosynthesis.

ALGINATES. Salts of alginic acid found in many seaweeds. Used as thickeners and stabilizers in ice-cream and synthetic cream, in artificial cherries, and as alginate sausage casings.

ALLERGEN. Any substance capable of producing allergy.

ALLERGY. A hypersensitivity to a specific substance or condition which in similar amounts is harmless to most people.

ALLSPICE (or Jamaica pepper). Dried fruits of the evergreen Pimenta officinalis, also known as pimento.

ALMOND, BITTER. Ripe seed of *Prunus amygdalus var. amars* (almond tree).

ALMOND, SWEET. Ripe seeds of *Prunus amygdalus var. dulcis.*

ALPHA-TOCOPHEROL. See Vitamin E.

ALUM (ALUMINUM AND POTASSIUM SULFATE). Used in foods as a buffer, a neutralizing agent, and as a firming agent, in baking powders to help generate carbon dioxide., and in water purification as a flucculating agent.

AMINO ACID. Proteins are composed of about 23 amino acids. Eight of them must be provided in the human diet, the essential amino acids. The remaining 15 can be synthesized in the body. Many amino acids are manufactured synthetically, and, lysine and methionine in particular, can be added to food and feeds to increase their nutritive value.

AMYLOPECTIN. A branched polysaccharide which together with amylose, makes up starch.

AMYLOSE. Straight chain polysaccharide which, together with amylopectin, makes up starch.

ANAEROBES. Micro-organisms that grow in the absence of oxygen. Obligate anaerobes cannot survive in the presence of oxygen. Facultative anaerobes normally grow in oxygen, but can also grow in its absence.

ANAEROBIC. Living or active in the absence of free oxygen.

ANALOGS. See Food Analogs.

ANHYDROGLUCOSE UNITS. The basic $C_6 H_{10} O_5$ unit that occurs repeatedly in all starch molecules.

ANION. Negatively charged ion such as hydroxide (OH–, carbonate (CO_3=), phosphate (PO_4=).

ANIONIC SURFACTANTS. Ionic surface-active agents in which the portion that associates with the internal phase is the anion; they include carboxylic acids, sulfuric acid esters, and sulfonic acids.

ANTHOCYANINS. Violet, red, and blue coloring matter of many fruits, flowers, and leaves. Depolarizers in electrochemical reactions; as such they cause trouble in canned foods by accelerating internal can corrosion.

ANTHOXANTHINS. Yellow to orange-red pigments present in plant materials.

ANTIBIOTIC. A substance that inhibits the growth of micro-organisms usually produced by other organisms such as penicillin.

ANTI-CAKING AGENT. Substance used in many salts and powders to keep them free-flowing. Anti-caking agents are used in such products as table salt, garlic and onion salts and powders, powdered sugar and malted milk powders.

ANTI-FOAMER. Liquid of low intrinsic surface tension that prevents formation of a foam.

ANTI-MICROBIAL. A compound which inhibits the growth of a microbe.

ANTI-MYCOTIC AGENT. A substance which destroys or inhibits the growth of molds and other fungi.

ANTIOXIDANTS. Substances that retard the oxidative rancidity of fats, or the oxidation of other substances.

ANTISEPTIC. A substance that prevents or inhibits the growth of micro-organisms on animate surfaces, such as skin.

AOAC. Association of Official Analytical Chemists.

AOM. Activated Oxygen Method.

APPARENT VISCOSITY. See VISCOSITY. Viscosity of a complex (non-Newtonian) fluid under given conditions.

AQUEOUS. Containing water.

ASCORBIC ACID. See Vitamin C.

ASEPSIS. Clean and free of micro-organisms.

ASEPTIC PROCESSING AND PACKAGING. The filling of a commercially sterilized cooled product into pre-sterilized containers, followed by aseptic hermetical sealing, with a pre-sterilized closure, in an atmosphere free of micro-organisms.

ASH. The residue of a substance which has been incinerated at about 525°C (975°F).

ATP (ADENOSINETRIPHOSPHATE). The prosthetic group of the enzyme hexokinase, which is involved in the fermentation of sugars such as glucose.

AUTOCLAVE. A vessel in which high temperatures can be reached by using high steam pressure. Bacteria are destroyed more readily at elevated temperatures, and autoclaves are used to sterilize food, for example in cans.

A_w. A symbol for "water activity". See "Water Activity".

B-CAROTENE. Pro-Vitamin A. A compound found naturally in many foods and also synthesized, which is converted by the human body into Vitamin A. See Vitamin A.

B VITAMINS. See Vitamin B Complex.

BACILLUS. A rod-shaped bacterium, varying in thickness from $^1/_{100,000}$th to $^1/_{10,000}$th of an inch, and in length from $^1/_{25,000}$th to $^1/_{1,000}$th on an inch. Some bacillus produce spores.

BACILLUS CEREUS. Spore-forming, rod-shaped bacterium, aerobic to facultative aerobic, proteolytic. It produces gastroenteritis caused by the release of an exoenterotoxin during lysis of *B. cereus* in the intestinal tract.

BACTERICIDE. Any substance that destroys bacteria, although not necessarily the spores of bacteria.

BACTERIOSTATIC. Preventing the growth of bacteria without killing them.

BAFFLE. Partition or plate that changes the direction or restricts the cross section of a fluid, thus increasing velocity or turbulence.

BAKING POWDER. Leavening agent which acts through the release of carbon dioxide (CO_2) during the baking process. Baking powder consists of sodium bicarbonate (baking soda), an acid or an acid salt which reacts with the bicarbonate prior to and during baking to release the carbon dioxide, and starch to absorb moisture during storage.

BAKING SODA (SODIUM BICARBONATE). Produces carbon dioxide when heated or when reacting with an acid.

BARRIER, GREASE-RESISTANT. A material that prevents or retards the transmission of grease or oils.

BARRIER, WATER-RESISTANT. A material that retards the transmission of water vapor.

BASE. Alkaline substances (pH greater than 7.0) which yield hydroxyl ions (OH-) in solution. See hydrogen-ion concentration.

BASE BOX. A unit of area of tin plate equivalent to 31,360 sq. in. The term "90# plate" means tin plate of such thickness that the above area weighs 90 lbs., considering commercial tolerances.

BASE PLATE PRESSURE. The force of the base plate holding the can body and end against the chuck during the seaming operation. In general, has the following effect on the seaming formation:

Low Pressure–short body hook

High Pressure–long body hook

BAUME. The name of one of the many hydrometer scales used for determining the relative density of liquids as compared to a standard liquid. There are two Baume scales. One for liquids lighter than water, the other for liquids heavier than water.

BEAD. A rounded depression around the surface of a container or end: used to stiffen or improve its appearance.

BEADED CAN. See also BEAD. A can reinforced by bead indentations in the body.

BENTONITE. A colloidal clay used as an absorbent. Also used in model systems for determining rate of heat penetration.

BERIBERI. A deficiency disease cause by the absence or insufficient levels of B-complex vitamins in the diet.

BHA. Butylated Hydroxyanisole. An antioxidant.

BHT. Butylated Hydroxytoluene. An antioxidant.

BIOASSAY. A test which used animals or micro-organisms for determining the biological activity of certain substances or the presence or concentration of nutrients in food.

BIODEGRADABILITY. Susceptibility of a chemical compound to depolymerization by the action of biological agents.

BIOLOGICAL OXIDATION. The process whereby, through the activity of living organisms in an aerobic environment, organic matter is converted to more biologically stable matter.

BIOLOGICAL OXYGEN DEMAND (BOD). Micro-organisms consume oxygen in their respiration. The BOD test determines uptake of oxygen by a contaminated material, e.g., sewage, water, etc., as a measure of microbial activity.

BLACK PLATE. Low carbon steel plate base for tin mill products, like tin plate.

BLANCHING. Heating by direct contact with hot water or live steam. It softens the tissues, eliminates air from the tissues, destroys enzymes, washes away raw flavors.

BLEACHING AGENTS. Used to whiten and "mature" flour and cheese in order to provide them with the characteristics necessary to produce an elastic, stable dough and neutralize colors which may be present in oils and fats.

BLEEDERS. Openings used to remove air that enters with steam, from retorts and steam chambers and to promote circulation of steam in such retorts and steam chambers. Bleeders may serve as a means of removing condensate.

BLOOM GELOMETER. An instrument to measure strength or firmness of gels.

BMR - BASAL METABOLIC RATE - The amount of energy utilized per unit time under conditions of basal as metabolism; expressed as calories per square meter of body surface or per kg of body weight per hour.

B.O.D. See BIOLOGICAL OXYGEN DEMAND.

BODY. Principal part of a container, usually the largest part in one piece containing the sides. May be round, or cylindrical, or other shape.

BODY HOOK. That flange portion of the can body that is turned back for the formation of the double seam.

BODY MAKER. A machine for automatic forming of a cylindrical metal can or drum body from a body blank. In the manufacture of tin cans, the body maker may also automatically weld the side seam.

BOILER SCALE. Deposit left inside boilers caused by evaporation of water and precipitation of water-soluble and insoluble substances.

BONDERIZED BLACK PLATE. Is also known as Chemically Treated Black Plate. This term is applied to can making quality black plate that is given a chemical treatment for the purpose of improving the adhesion of enamels and lacquers. The chemical treatment (chromate-phosphate wash) may also retard under film corrosion or, for short time, atmospheric corrosion.

BOTTOM SEAM. Also known as factory end seam. The double seam of the can end put on by the can manufacturer.

BOTULISM. A poisoning caused by substances formed by the bacterium *Clostridium Botulinum* under conditions of improper processing and storage of food. The spores of this bacterium are often found in soil and are likely to be present on soil-contaminated food.

BOUND WATER. Water chemically tied to food in the form of hydrates of inorganic salts or inorganic substances.

BRAN. Outer layers of the wheat kernel separated during milling.

BREAK-POINT CHLORINATION. Addition of chlorine to water beyond the point where chloramines are oxidized, and where further increases in the dosage of chlorine will result in a proportional increase of chlorine residual.

BRINE. Salt, sugar and water mixture in which most vegetables are canned. Water is not chlorinated.

BRINES. Salt solutions used in canning and pickling.

BRITISH THERMAL UNIT. BTU. The British engineering unit of heat quantity. It is approximately the quantity of heat which will raise the temperature of 1 lb. of water 1 degree F. BTU = 0.252 Cal. = 1054 joules.

BRIX. The measure of density of a solution, more particularly a solution containing sucrose, as determined by a hydrometer. Degrees Brix equal percent sucrose in water solution at 20°C (68°F).

BRIX/ACID RATIO. The ratio of the degrees Brix of a juice or syrup to the grams of a specified organic acid contained in the liquid, per hundred grams of the liquid.

BRIX HYDROMETER. Hydrometer graduated in percentage sugar 20°C (68°F).

BROASTING. A food service process involving pressure frying. It is more rapid than regular deep fat frying and results in less absorption of fat.

BROILING. To cook by subjecting to direct radiant heat.

BROMELIN. Protein digesting enzyme found in pineapple juice and stem tissues.

BROTH MEDIUM. A liquid medium for growth of microorganisms.

BROWNING REACTION. A reaction in foods, usually deteriorative, involving amino (e.g., from amino acids or proteins) and carbonyl (e.g., from glucose) groups; this reaction often leads to a brown discoloration and sometimes to off-flavors and changes in texture.

BTU. See BRITISH THERMAL UNIT.

BUCKLING (OF CANS). Cans becoming permanently distorted along the double seam; caused by excessive internal pressure.

BUFFER. Any substance in a fluid which tends to resist the change in pH (hydrogen-ion concentration) when acid or alkali is added.

BULK DENSITY. Weight per unit volume of a quantity of solid particles; depends on packing density.

BURSTING STRENGTH. The strength of material in pounds per square inch, measured by the Cady or Mullen tester.

"C" ENAMEL. Interior coating designed to prevent discoloration with foods containing sulphur. This enamel contains zinc compounds which react with liberated sulphur compounds to form white zinc sulphide, thus eliminating discoloration.

CAFFEINE. An alkaloid present in coffee, tea and cola. It is a stimulant to the heart and central nervous system.

CALCIFEROL. See Vitamin D.

CALCIUM. The most plentiful body mineral, important for structure and growth of bones and teeth. Assists in blood clotting. Important for proper functioning of nerves, muscles and heart. Good sources are milk and milk products, and leafy green vegetables.

CALCIUM PROPIONATE. A mold inhibitor.

CALCIUM STEARATE. An anti caking agent and emulsifier.

CALENDERING. Subjecting a material to pressure between two or more counter-rotating rollers.

CALIPER. Thickness, as related to paperboard, of a sheet measured under specified procedures expressed in thousandths of an inch. Thousandths of an inch are sometimes termed "points". The precision instrument used in the paperboard industry to measure thickness. To measure with a caliper.

CALORIE. A unit of heat; the amount of heat necessary to raise the temperature of a gram of water 1°C. Nutr itionists use the large Calorie or kilo-Calorie (spelled with capital C), which is 1,000 calories. One Calorie (kilo-Calorie) = 4184 joules or 3,968 BTU.

CAN, CYLINDER. A can whose height is relatively large compared to its diameter. Generally called a tall can.

CAN, FLAT. A can whose height is equal to or smaller than its diameter.

CAN, KEY OPENING. A can opened by tearing off a scored strip of metal around the body by means of a key, or any can opened by means of a key.

CAN, SANITARY. Full open top can with double seamed bottom. Cover double seamed on by packer. Ends are gasket or compound lined. Used for products which are process packed. Also known as a "Packer's Can".

CAP. See also CLOSURE. Any form or device used to seal off the opening of the container, so as to prevent loss of its contents.

CAP, LUG. A cap closure for glass containers in which impressions in the side of the cap engage appropriately formed members on the neck finish to provide a grip when the cap is given a quarter turn, as compared to the full turn necessary with a screw cap.

CAP, SCREW. A cylindrical closure having a thread on the internal surface of the cylinder capable of engaging a comparable external thread on the finish or neck of a container, such as glass bottle, collapsible tube, etc.

CAP, SNAP-ON. A type of closure for rigid containers. The sealing action of a snap-on cap is effected by a gasket in the top of the cap that is held to the neck of spout of the container by means of a friction fit on a circumferential bead. Material of construction is either metal or semi-rigid plastic.

CAP, TWO-PIECE VACUUM (TWO-PIECE VACUUM CAP). Standard C-T (continuous thread) or D-S (deep screw) caps, equipped with a separate disk or lid which is lined with sealing for vacuum-packing processes.

CARBOHYDRATES. Nutrients that supply energy. They help the body use fats efficiently and decrease the need for protein by furnishing energy so that protein is used for more important functions. Important sources are starches, cereal grains, rice, and vegetables such as potatoes, and sugars-honey, molasses, table sugar, syrups, candies.

CARCINOGEN. A cancer causing agent.

CAROTENOIDS. Red and orange pigments found in carrots and other vegetables. They are precursors of vitamin A.

CARRAGEENAN. A colloidal carbohydrate found in seaweeds (see Agar).

CASE. A non-specific term for a shipping container. In domestic commerce, "case" usually refers to a box made from corrugated or solid fiber board. In maritime or export usage, "case" refers to a wooden or metal box.

CATALASE. An enzyme which breaks down hydrogen peroxide into water and oxygen.

CATALYST. Substance that alters the rate of chemical change and remains unchanged at the end of a reaction.

CATEDRINES. Colorless flavonoids which change readily to brownish pigments.

CATION. Positively charged ion such as K^+, NH^{4+}.

CATONIC SURFACTANTS. Ionic surface active agents in which the portion that associates with the internal phase is the cation. They include simple amine salts, quaternary ammonium salts, amino imides and imidazolines. Cationic surfactants often have germicidal, anti-corrosive, and anti-static properties.

CELLOPHANE. A colorless, transparent flexible packaging material made of cellulose.

CELSIUS (°C). Temperature on a scale of 100° between the freezing point (0°) and the boiling point (100°) of water.

CENTIMETER (cm). One hundredth of a meter. Equivalent to 0.3937 inches. One inch equals 2.54 cm.

CENTIPOISE (cP). Unit of viscosity equal to 1/100 dyne/sec^2/cm^2.

CEPHALIN. A phospholipid whose composition is similar to that of lecithin; found in many living tissues, especially nervous tissue of the brain.

CERTIFIED COAL TAR COLORS. Synthetic food colors, each batch of which is certified as to its chemical nature and purity by the U.S. Food and Drug Administration.

CHALAZA. Membranous layer holding egg yolk to thick or thin albumen.

CHELATING AGENT. A substance which forms stable bonds with metal ions. See also EDTA and Sequestering Agents.

CHEMICAL OXYGEN DEMAND (COD). An indirect measure of the biochemical load exerted on the oxygen content of a body of water when organic wastes are introduced into the water. When the wastes contain only readily available organic bacterial food and no toxic matter, the COD values can be correlated with BOD values obtained from the same wastes.

CHILLING INJURY. Color or texture change on food surface resulting from over-exposure to low temperature.

CHLORINATION. Building up the chlorine content (as hypochlorous acid) to process or sanitize water supplies. See also IN-PLANT CHLORINATION and BREAK-POINT CHLORINATION.

CHOLESTEROL. Cholesterol is a lipid or fat-like substance. A form of cholesterol is converted by sunlight on the skin to form vitamin D. Cholesterol is found only in animal tissues and animal fats.

CHROMATOGRAPHY. A physical analytical method of separating components in a mixture.

CHUCK. Part of a closing machine which fits inside countersink and in chuck ring of can or lid or end during seaming operation.

CIGUATOXIN. Ciguatera toxin found in shellfish.

CINNAMON. Barks of various species of the genus Cinnamomum; split off shoots, cured and dried.

CIP. Clean in Place.

CLARIFYING AGENTS. Substances which aid in the removal of small particles of organic or inorganic matter from liquids. Vinegar often turns "Cloudy" without the use of clarifying agents.

CLIMACTERIC. A critical year or period, or one of marked change.

CLINCH. A very loose first operation seam designed to hold the can end in place, yet allow gas to escape during double seaming.

CLOSING MACHINE. Also known as a double seamer. Machine which double seams can end onto can bodies.

CLOSTRIDIA. Genus of spore forming bacteria. *Clostridium botulinum* is the most heat resistant of the food-poisoning organisms; its growth is inhibited at pH 4.6 and below, thus it is only a problem in low-acid foods. Produces an endotoxin, botulina, highly toxic in minute doses, but destroyed by heat. Destruction of this organism is generally accepted as the minimum standard of processing for low-acid and medium-acid canned food, although other Clostridia are more heat-resistant.

CLOSTRIDIUM PERFRINGENS-C. PERFRINGENS (welchii), type A is a Gram positive, anaerobe, spore-forming rod that causes a food infection, gastroenteritis, produces by the release of an enterotoxin. *C. perfringens* grows optimally at 43°C to 47°C (110°F to 117°F).

CLOSURE. The joint or seal which is made in attaching the cover to the glass container. Also, the type of closure, such as friction, lug, screw top, etc.

Cm. CENTIMETER. Equivalent to 0.394 in.

COAGULANT. A material, which, when added to liquid wastes or water, creates a reaction which forms insoluble floc particles that absorb and precipate colloidal and suspended solids.

COCCUS. Type of bacteria. Plural "*cocci*." A round cell, varying in diameter from 1/100,000th to 1/10,000th of an inch. There are various additions to this word, such as "*staphylococci*", meaning cocci occurring in groups, like bunches of grapes, and "*streptococci*" or *cocci* occurring in more or less long chains. *Cocci* do not produce spores. Certain *streptococci* and *staphylococci* cause food poisoning in fresh foods.

COCKED BASE PLATE. A base plate on a double seamer which is not parallel to seaming chuck. This results in a top double seam having a body hook uneven in length.

COCKED BODY. A can body which is not a perfect cylinder, i.e. open ends of cylinder not at right angles to body. This defect results in body hooks of uneven length at both ends. Where the body is long on one end, it will be short on the other end.

COD (CHEMICAL OXYGEN DEMAND). An indirect measure of the biochemical load exerted on the oxygen assets of a body of water when organic wastes are introduced into the water. It is determined by the amount of potassium dichromate consumed in a boiling mixture of chromic and sulfuric acids. The mount of oxidizable organic matter is proportional to the potassium dichromate consumed. Where the wastes contain only readily available organic bacterial food and no toxic matter, the COD values can be correlated with BOD values obtained from the same wastes.

CODE, CAN. Canner's identification stamped in relief on canner's end. Also, can maker's identification stamped in relief on manufacturer's end.

COEXTRUSION. A combination of two or more thermoplastics extruded as an entity by special dyes or made by combining extruded thermoplastics before they harden into films.

COKE TIN PLATE. See TIN PLATE, COKE.

COLD BREAK. Breaking food into pieces at ambient temperatures to allow enzyme activity for a short time, and then heating to halt enzyme activity.

COLD STERILIZATION. See Irradiation.

COLIFORM BACTERIA. Group of aerobic bacteria of which *Escherichia coli* is the most important member. Many coliforms are not harmful, but as they arise from feces they are useful as a test of contamination, particularly as a test for water pollution.

COLLAGEN. Connective tissue which holds muscle fibers together. (See also Elastin).

COLLOID. Fine particles (the disperse phase) suspended in a second medium (the dispersion medium; can be solid, liquid, or gas suspended in solid, liquid, or gas).

COLLOID MILL. Machine used to homogenize or emulsify foods.

COLLOIDAL SUSPENSION. Two-phase system having small dispersed particles suspended in a dispersant.

COLONY. A microscopically visible growth of microorganisms on a solid culture medium.

COME-UP-TIME. The time which elapses between the introduction of steam into the closed retort and the time when the retort reaches the required processing temperature.

COMMERCIAL STERILITY (OF FOOD). The condition achieved by application of heat which renders such food free of viable forms of microorganisms having public health significance, as well as any microorganisms of non-health significance capable of reproducing in the food under normal non-refrigerated conditions of storage and distribution. "Commercial sterility of equipment and containers used for aseptic processing and packaging of food means the condition achieved by application of heat, chemical sterilant(s), or other appropriate treatment which render such equipment and containers free of viable forms of microorganisms having public health significance, as well as any microorganisms of non-health significance capable of reproducing in the food under normal non-refrigerated conditions of storage and distribution.

COMPOUND (IN CANS). A sealing material consisting of a water or solvent emulsion or solution of rubber, either latex or synthetic rubber, placed in the curl of the can end. During seaming operation, the compound fills the spaces in the double seams, sealing them against leakage and thus effecting a hermetic seal.

CONGEAL. To change from a liquid to a semi-solid, non-fluid mass.

CONSISTENCY. Resistance of a fluid to deformation. For sample (Newtonian) fluids the consistency is identical with viscosity, for complex (non-Newtonian) fluids, identical with apparent viscosity.

CONSISTOMETER. One of the several types of instruments used to measure the consistency of foods.

CONTAMINATION. Entry of undesirable organisms into some material or container.

CONTINUOUS PHASE. External phase of an emulsion.

CONTINUOUS THREAD. An uninterrupted protruding helix on the neck of a container to hold screw-type closure.

CONTROLLED ATMOSPHERE (CA) STORAGE. Storage of foods in a hermetic warehouse where the concentrations of O_2, CO_2, and N_2 are controlled at specific levels.

CONVECTION. Natural or forced motion in a fluid induced by heat or the action of gravity.

CONVERT. To change to a lower molecular weight form, as by dextrinization, hydrolysis, etc.

COOLING. (a) In a freezing plant, the process of pre-cooling produce prior to placing it in quick-freezing chamber. (b) The process of cooling heated cans immediately after processing. Cans may be stationary or moving. In various methods, cans are immersed, partially covered or spray cooled.

COP. Clean-out-of-Place.

COUNTERSINK DEPTH. The measurement from the top edge of the double seam to the end panel adjacent to the chuck wall.

COVER. Can end placed on can by packer. Also known as top, lid, packer's end, canner's end.

CRITICAL FACTOR. Any property, characteristic, condition, aspect, or other parameter, variation of which may affect the scheduled process delivered and thus the commercial sterility of the product. This does not include factors which are controlled by the processor solely for purposes of product appearance, quality, and other reasons which are not of public health significance.

CROSS OVER. The portion of a double seam at the lap.

CROSS SECTION. Referring to a double seam. A section through the double seam.

CRUDE FIBER. The remaining substance measured by weight, after food materials are rigorously extracted with the hot acid and hot alkaline solvents. These remove food components from the original sample, leaving a residue which probably reflects the cellulose and lignin content of the food sample.

CRYOGENIC FREEZING. Very rapid freezing of food done by immersing or spraying with cold liquid, generally nitrogen at -320°F (–196°C).

CRYOGENIC LIQUIDS. Liquid nitrogen and liquid carbon dioxide.

CRYOVAC. A flexible, transparent, heat-shrinkable food packaging material used primarily for frozen poultry.

CRYPTOXANTHIN. One of the carotenoid plant pigments. Converted into Vitamin A in the animal body.

CRYSTAL SIZE. Grade designated for identifying the relative crystal size of non-ferrous metals. For tin plate corrosion purposes, the lower the numerical grade, the better the corrosion resistance.

C-T. Abbreviation for CONTINUOUS THREAD. Used in referring to the helical threaded neck-finish of glass containers or to closures designed for application to these finishes. C-T denotes continuity form of thread to differentiate it from the LUG, I-T, or other form of interrupted thread forms.

CULL. Product rejected because of inferior quality.

CULTURE. A population of microorganisms cultivated in a medium; *pure culture*-single kind of microorganism, *mixed culture*-two or more kinds of microorganisms growing together.

CULTURE MEDIUM. (pl.: MEDIA). Any substance or preparation suitable for and used for the growth and cultivation of microorganisms, *selective medium*-a medium composed of nutrients designed to allow only growth of a particular type of microorganism, *broth medium*-a liquid medium for growth microorganisms, *agar medium*-solid culture medium.

CURING. A food process used primarily for meat products such as ham consisting of the use of salts, sugar, and water to preserve food and provide certain quality attributes (desired texture, color, and flavor.)

CURING AGENTS. Salts and certain other compounds used to preserve meats such as ham, bacon, frankfurters, and bologna. Curing agents may modify the flavor and also stabilize the characteristic color of some meats.

CURL. The extreme edge of cover which is bent inward after end is formed. In double seaming, the curl forms the cover hook of the double seam.

CUT CODE. A break in the metal of a can end due to improper embossing marker equipment.

CUT-OVER. Sharp bend or break in the metal at the tip of the countersink. The cut-over occurs during seaming due to excess metal being forced over top of seaming chuck. Usually caused by heavy laps, i.e., laps containing excessive solder, but may be due to improper adjustment of the double seaming equipment.

CYANOCOBALAMIN (VITAMIN B-12). Important in the treatment of pernicious anemia.

"D" VALUE. Time in minutes at a specified temperature required to destroy 90% of the microorganisms in a population.

DEAERATION. Removal of oxygen from produce juices to prevent adverse effects on juice properties.

DEGRADATION. Deterioration, chemical breakdown.

DEHYDRATION. A food processing unit operation resulting in the removal of water from the food generally to the point where spoilage is prevented.

DELANEY CLAUSE. A section of the U.S. Food, Drug and Cosmetic Act, as amended, giving the U.S. Food and Drug Administration what has been interpreted as a clear mandate to forbid approval for inclusion in food products substances found to be cancer inducing in man or animals.

DENATURATION. To alter the original state of a food substance by physical or chemical means.

DENITRIFICATION. The process involving the facultative conversion by anaerobic bacteria of nitrates into nitrogen and nitrogen oxides.

DENSIMETER. Instrument for measuring the density or the specific gravity of liquids.

DES. Diethyl Stilbestrol. An estrogenic hormone. Controversial growth promoting in cattle.

DETERGENT. Surface-active material or combination of surfactants designed for removal of unwanted contamination from the surface of an article.

DETERIORATION. A non-biological, physical, or chemical change in food which adversely affects quality.

DEW POINT. The temperature at which air or other gases become saturated with vapor, causing the vapor to deposit as a liquid. The temperature at which 100% relative humidity is reached.

DEXTRINS. A polysaccharide, product of enzymatic or acid hydrolysis of starch. Used in preparing emulsions and thickening liquids and pastes.

DEXTROSE. A widely occurring crystallizable simple sugar which contains 6 carbon atoms in contrast to 12 found in sucrose.

DICER. Equipment which cuts fruit, vegetables and other foods into small cubes.

DIETARY FIBER. Refers to the combined, undigested carbohydrates in food and encompasses not only the cellulose and lignin found in crude fiber, but also hemicellulose, pectic substances, gums, and other carbohydrates not normally digested by man. Crude fiber as determined is more of a refined fiber, while dietary fiber is more closely related to a true crude fiber.

DIETETIC FOODS. Those foods which comprise a diet intended to prevent or cure certain physiological conditions. Examples are low-calorie or low-sodium diets.

DIFFUSION. Missing of molecules or atoms by random molecular or atomic motion.

DIGESTION. The biological decomposition of organic matter in sludge, resulting in partial gassification, liquefaction, and mineralization.

DIGLYCERIDES. See Glycerides.

DILL. Dried ripe fruit of *Anethum graveolens*. Used in pickles and soups.

DISINFECTANT. An agent that frees from infection by killing the vegetative cells of microorganisms.

DISODIUM GUANYLATE. A flavor enhancer.

DISODIUM INOSINATE. A flavor enhancer.

DISPERSION. Physical, usually temporary, mixture of two insoluble phases.

DISPOSAL. The discharge of waste water for its ultimate use.

DISSOLVING. Formation of a solution by dispersion of one material (solute) at a molecular (or less) level in another material (solvent).

DNA (DEOXYRIBONUCLEIC ACID). See Nucleic Acids.

DOMED. A curved profile container end used for strength or appearance.

DOUBLE SEAM. To attach an end to a can body by a method in which five (5) thicknesses of plate are interlocked or folded and pressed firmly together. A joint formed by interlocking the edges of both the end and body of a can.

DOUBLE SEAMED END. Part of a can which is attached to the body of a double seamed can to form the top or the bottom.

DRAINED WEIGHT, MAXIMUM. Weight of the solid portion of the product after draining the covering liquid for a specified time with the appropriate sieve.

DRIP. See thaw-exudate.

DROOP. Smooth projection of a double seam below bottom of normal seam. Usually occurs at the side seam lip.

DROP TEST. A test for measuring the properties of a container by subjecting the packaged product to a free fall from predetermined heights onto a surface with prescribed characteristics.

DRY ICE. Carbon dioxide in solid state.

EDTA. See Ethylenediamine tetra-acetic acid.

EFFLUENT. Waste water or other liquid, partially or completely treated or untreated, flowing out of a process operation, processing plant, or treatment plant.

ELASTIN. Connective tissues holding muscle fibers together. The principal component of elastic protein fiber (see Collagen).

ELECTROLYTIC. Denoting a coating of tin, electrodeposited upon the base metal. Electrolytic tin plate in use in the industry usually has coatings of approximately .25, .50, .75 and 1.25 lbs. per base box.

ELECTROPHORESIS. Migration of the electrically charged particles toward the oppositely charged electrode.

ELEMENTS, ESSENTIAL. See Essential Elements.

ELEMENDORF TEST. A test for measuring the tearing resistance of paper, paperboard, tape, and other sheet materials.

EMBOSS(-ED),(-ING). Raised design or lettering on the surface of an object.

EMULSIFIER (EMULSION). A compound or substance which promotes and stabilizes a finely divided dispersion of oil and water.

EMULSION. System consisting of two incompletely miscible liquids, one being dispersed as finite globules in the other. A small amount of a third substance may render the dispersion stable. The liquid broken up into globules is the dispersed (discontinuous) phase; the surrounding liquid is the external (continuous) phase.

ENAMEL. A vitreous or paint-like composition used as a protective coating usually baked onto the packaging material before fabrication into the finished container. On the inner surface of metal containers, its purpose is to protect either the contents or the container. On the outer surface, its purpose is to prevent corrosion or to decorate.

ENDOSPERM. Structural component of cereal grains made up mostly of starch and some protein.

ENDOTOXIN. A toxin produced with an organism liberated only when the organism disintegrates.

ENGINEERED FOODS. See Fabricated Foods.

ENRICHED. A term which refers to the addition of specific nutrients to a food as established in a standard of identity and/or quality.

ENTEROTOXIN. A toxin specific for cells of the intestine. Gives rise to symptoms of food poisoning.

ENZYMATIC BROWNING. The darkening of plant tissues or products produced by enzymatic reactions.

ENZYME. A compound of biological origin which accelerates a specific chemical reaction.

EPA. Environmental Protection Agency.

EQUILIBRIUM MOISTURE CONTENT. The moisture content of a substance at which it will neither gain or lose moisture in an atmosphere having given relative humidity.

EQUILIBRIUM pH. The pH of the macerated (thoroughly blended) contents of the product container. (See Maximum pH and Normal pH).

EQUILIBRIUM RELATIVE HUMIDITY. The relative humidity of the ambient atmosphere surrounding a substance when the substance neither gains nor loses moisture.

ERGOSTEROL. Provitamin D. Irradiated ergosterol has served as a vitamin D source for food enrichment.

ESCHERICHIA COLI. The strains of *E. coli* that produce an entero-pathogenic food poisoning syndrome.

ESSENTIAL ELEMENTS. Those elements necessary to maintain normal metabolic functions. Some are required in trace quantities (such as iron, copper, and zinc), while others are required in larger amounts (such as calcium and magnesium).

ESSENTIAL OILS. Flavor concentrates from spices or herbs which are generally produced by steam distillation and have no relatively high boiling constituents present.

ESTER. An organic compound formed by the reaction of an acid and an alcohol. Many flavoring agents are esters.

ETHYLENE OXIDE. A gas used to accelerate ripening of certain fruits. Also produced naturally by fruits during the ripening process.

ETHYLENEDIAMINE TETRA-ACETIC ACID, (EDTA). Forms stable complexes with metals hence called sequestering agent or chelating agent. Its calcium and sodium salts are used in foods to sequester traces of metallic impurities that cause food deterioration.

ETHYL VANILLIN. A flavoring agent.

EUTECTIC. A solution which has a melting point below that of any of the components taken separately.

EUTECTIC POINT. Temperature at which a substance exists simultaneously in the solid, liquid, and gaseous states.

EUTHROPHICATION. Applies to lake or pond becoming rich in dissolved nutrients, with seasonal oxygen deficiencies.

EXHAUST. Heating of food in cans prior to closing the cans to produce a partial vacuum in containers.

EXHAUSTER. Equipment to heat food in cans prior to closing the cans, so as to produce a partial vacuum in the containers.

EXOTOXIN. A toxin excreted by a microorganism into the surrounding medium.

EXTENDED AERATION. A modification of the activated sludge process that employs aeration periods of 24 hours or more, completely mixing, and high levels of mixed liquor solids.

EXTRUSION. The process of forcing a material in plastic condition through an orifice.

"F" VALUE. The number of minutes required to destroy a stated number of microorganisms at a defined temperature, usually 250°F (121°C), and when the "z" value is 18°F. "F" value is a common term employed in the canning industry to express the lethality or sterilizing value of a sterilization process. See also "z" value.

FABRICATED FOODS. Blend of food ingredients resulting in a product of special characteristics such as nutritive value or other quality attributes. Some are prepared to resemble well accepted animal or plant foods such as soybean burgers. Also called engineered foods.

FACTORY END. Bottom or can manufacturer's end.

FACULTATIVE BACTERIA. Bacteria which can exist and reproduce under either aerobic or anaerobic conditions.

FALSE SEAM. A small seam breakdown where the cover hook and body are not overlapped i.e., no hooking of body and cover hooks. See also KNOCKDOWN FLANGE.

FALSE SEAM. The cover hook and body hook are not tucked in.

FAO OF UN. Food and Agriculture Organization of the United Nations.

FATS. A nutrient providing the most concentrated source of energy, weight for weight supplying more than twice as much energy as carbohydrates or proteins. Fats are the molecular combination of glycerol and certain fatty acids.

FATTY ACIDS, ESSENTIAL. Name for two fatty acids, linoleic and arachidonic. They are dietary essentials.

FDA. U.S. Food and Drug Administration.

FEATHER. Beginning of a cut-over. At the top of the container's countersink, the metal is forced over the seaming chuck forming a sharp edge that may be detected with the fingernail. Commonly referred to as "Sharp Edge".

FERMENTATION. The action of microorganisms upon foods. Anaerobic respiration. Usually fermentation is undesirable, but sometimes it is produced intentionally, such as in the manufacture of vinegar from apple cider.

FIBER. See Dietary Fiber and Crude Fiber.

FICIN. A protein digesting enzyme found in figs.

FILL WEIGHT. The weight of the product particulates before processing. It does not include the weight of the container or covering liquid.

FINISH. The opening of a container shaped to accommodate a specific closure.

FIRMING AGENTS. Substances used to aid the coagulation of certain cheeses and to improve the texture of processed fruits and vegetables which might otherwise become soft.

FIRST OPERATION. The first operation in double seaming. In this operation the curl of the end is tucked under the flange of the can body which is bent down to form cover hook and body hook, respectively.

FISH FLOUR. See Fish Meal.

FISH MEAL. Ground up and dehydrated parts of fish not normally used for human food. Also made from whole fish of low market value. Not considered fit for human food in the U.S. Used as animal feed.

FLAME PEELING. Peeling of vegetables by charring the surface by exposing it to direct flame or hot gasses in rotary tube flame peelers.

FLANGE. To flare out the top of a can body to prepare it for double seaming to an end. Also the flaring projection around the end of a can body. The outermost projection of an end, cover, or cap.

FLANGE, DENTED. A flange damaged through abuse in handling, not in manufacture. May result in false seams, lips and breakdowns.

FLASH-PASTEURIZATION. Process in which the material is held at a much higher temperature than in normal pasteurization, but for a considerably shorter period.

FLATUS FACTORS. Substances contributing to the production of flatulence.

FLAT-SOURS. Thermophilic and thermoduric bacteria, facultative anaerobes, that attack carbohydrates with the production of acids, but without gas formation. Flat-sour spoiled canned foods therefore show no swelling of the ends.

FLAVEDO. The colored outer layer of citrus fruit peel. It contains the oil sacs and fruit pigments.

FLAVENOIDS. Pigments and color precursors commonly present in fruits and vegetables. They include the purple, blue, and red anthocyanins, the yellow anthoxanthins, and the colorless catechins and leucoanthocyanins.

FLAVOR. Attributes of food quality which the consumer evaluates with his senses of taste and smell.

FLAVORING AGENTS. Substances added to foods to enhance or change the taste of the food. This largest group of food additives includes spices, seeds, natural and synthetic flavor concentrates, and many others.

FLIPPER. A can having both ends flat, but with insufficient vacuum to hold the ends in place, thus a sharp blow will cause the end to become convex, but both ends may be pressed to their normal position.

FLOCCULATION. The process of forming larger masses from a large number of finer suspended particles.

FLOTATION. Removal of solids, oil, or fat from waste water by causing the material to float to the water surface with the aid of heat or entrained air.

FLOTATION GRADER. Equipment for grading peas and lima beans in a brine solution or water.

FLOUR, ALL-PURPOSE. Flour which can be used for making bread, cakes, or other baked "bread type" products.

FLUIDITY. Reciprocal of viscosity.

FLUMING. In-plant transportation of product or waste material through water conveyance.

FLUORIDATION. Process of adding traces of sodium flouride to drinking water to arrest or prevent dental decay.

FLUX. A chemical used to aid in soldering by removing the oxides.

FNB. Food and Nutrition Board. A branch of the National Academy of Sciences-National Research Council.

FOAM SEPARATION. Synonymous with flotation.

FOAMING AGENT. Surface-active material that is used specifically to form a dispersion of a gas in a liquid or solid medium.

FOOD ADDITIVE. Any substance intentionally or incidentally added to food to protect, modify or enhance some quality attribute, or preserve the freshness of the product.

FOOD ANALOGS. Fabricated foods resembling well accepted animal or plant foods.

FOOD CHEMICALS CODES. A set of standards for purity of food chemicals in terms of maximum allowable trace contaminants, and methods of analysis for the contaminants. Prepared by the Food Protection Committee of the National Academy of Sciences. National Research Council.

FOOD COLORS. Synthetic or natural substances added to foods to enhance the natural color of the food, or to give the food a color.

FOOD INFECTION. An illness caused by an infection produced by invasion, growth and damage to the tissue of the host due to the ingestion of viable pathogenic microorganisms associated with the food.

FOOD INTOXICATION. An illness resulting from the ingestion of bacterial toxin with or without viable cells. The illness does not require actual growth of cells in the intestinal tract.

FOOD POISONING. A general term applied to all stomach or intestinal disturbances due to food contaminated with certain micro-organisms or their toxins.

FOOD SCIENCE AND TECHNOLOGY. The field of study concerned with the application of science and technology to the processing, preservation, packaging, distribution, and utilization of foods and food products.

FOODSERVICE SYSTEM. A facility where large quantities of food intended for individual service and consumption are routinely provided, completely prepared. The term includes any such place regardless of whether consumption is on or off the premises and regardless of whether or not there is a charge for the food.

FOLIC ACID. The vitamin of the "B" group, essential in the synthesis of certain amino acids. Liver, yeast, and cheese are good sources.

FORTIFIED. Food to which specific nutrients have been added. Also "enriched".

FPC. Fish protein concentrate. A highly refined form of fish protein, white, colorless, flavorless powder. Contains approximately. 85% protein.

FREEZE DRYING. A process of dehydration in which the moisture is removed by the sublimation of ice from the frozen product.

FRUCTOSE. An alternate chemical name for levulose.

FUMIGANTS. Substances used to control growth of insects or microorganisms on foods.

FUNGICIDAL AGENT. Destroys existing fungal cells.

FUNGICIDE. Any substance that destroys fungi or inhibits the growth of spores or hypahe. Legally, sometimes the term is interpreted as also including yeasts and bacteria.

FUNGISTATIC AGENT. Prevents growth of fungi (molds) without necessarily killing the existing cells.

GAGE (GAUGE). Term used to designate the thickness of a plate.

GAS CHROMATOGRAPHY. A separation technique used in food analysis, involving passage of a gas through a column containing a fixed adsorbent phase. It is used principally as a quantitative analytical technique for volatile compounds.

GAS PACKING. Packaging in a gas-tight container in which any air has been replaced by a gas that contains practically no free oxygen, such as commercial carbon dioxide or nitrogen.

GASKET. In cans, a filler, usually of synthetic rubber, used in the seam for the purpose of making it hermetically tight.

G-CAP. A No. 70 (70 mm) cap with abnormally deep screw. Used primarily for mayonnaise and salad dressing.

GEL. Semisolid system that consists of a solid held in a liquid; a more solid form than a sol.

GELATINIZE. To cook starch in aqueous suspension to the point at which swelling of the granules takes place, forming a viscous sol.

GELATION. Solidifying, resulting in the formation of a gel.

GELOMETER. Instrument used to measure the time required for a fluid to gel. Also, instrument used to determine the firmness of a gel.

GERM. A microorganism; a microbe usually thought of as a pathogenic organism.

GERMICIDE. Substance that will kill all ordinary microorganisms that cause disease, but that is not necessarily capable of destroying bacterial spores.

GLUCOSE. An alternate chemical name for dextrose. A name given to corn syrups which are obtained by the action of acids and/or enzymes on corn starch.

GLUTAMATE SODIUM. Sodium salt of glutamic acid, an amino acid. Enhances the flavor of some foods. Frequently added to soup mixes, meat products, and certain other foods.

GLYCERIDES. Organic compounds resulting from the reaction of a fatty acid and glycerol. Mono and diglycerides are used as emulsifying agents. Among the triglycerides are the fats and oils.

GLYCOGEN. A sugar stored in the liver of animals.

GOITER. A condition produced by a shortage of iodine in the diet.

GOITROGENIC AGENTS. Any substance capable of initiating or promoting goiter.

GOSSYPOL. A toxic yellow pigment found in cottonseed.

GRADE. A level or rank of quality.

GRADING. The selection of produce for certain purposes. Produce is sorted for size, color, quality, ripeness, etc. May be done manually or mechanically on sizing belts, flotation graders, etc. Term also applied to finished products.

GRAIN. Measure of weight equivalent to 0.0648 grams.

GRAM (g). Metric unit of weight equal to 0.035 ounces. One Kilogram is equivalent to 1,000 grams, and one pound equals 453.6 grams.

GRAS. Generally Recognized as Safe.

GUAR GUM. A stabilizer, thickener, and emulsifier.

GUM. Class of colloidal substances that is exuded by plants.

GUM ARABIC (ACACIA). A stabilizer, thickener, and emulsifier.

HACCP SYSTEM (Hazard Analysis of Critical Control Points). An inspectional approach that determines what points in the process are critical for the safety of the product and how well the firm controls these points.

HALOPHILIC. Can grow or survive in a medium with a relatively high salt concentration.

HARD SWELL. Spoilage in which can ends are swelled too hard to be readily depressed by applying thumb pressure.

HEADSPACE, GROSS. The vertical distance between the level of the product (generally the liquid surface) and the inside surface of the lid in an upright rigid container (the top of the double seam of a can or the top edge of a glass jar).

HEADSPACE, NET. The vertical distance between the level of the product (generally the liquid surface) and the inside surface of the lid in an upright, rigid container having a double seam, such as a can.

HEAT EXCHANGER. Equipment for heating or cooling liquids rapidly by providing a large surface area and turbulence for the rapid and efficient transfer of heat.

HEAT, LATENT. Heat absorbed or liberated in a change of physical state such as evaporation, condensation, freezing or sublimation. Expressed as BTU per lb., kCal per kg or joules per kg.

HEAT, SENSIBLE. Heat that has gone into raising the temperature of steam without change of pressure or absolute humidity.

HEAVY LAP. A lap containing excess solder, also called a thick lap.

HEEL. The part of a container between the bottom bearing surface and the side wall.

HEPATITIS, INFECTIOUS. An infectious disease produced by a virus found in polluted waters and in shellfish growing in such waters. Also transmitted by unsanitary handling and preparation of other foods.

HERMETICALLY SEALED CONTAINER. A container which is designed and intended to be secure against the entry of microorganisms and to maintain the commercial sterility of its contents after processing.

HERRINGBONE SCORE. Weakening lines made in the body of a key opening can between and at an angle to the parallel scored lines. Designed to lead a tear back into the regular score line.

HISTIDINE. One of the essential amino acids.

HOMOGENIZATION. The process of making incompatible or immiscible components into a stabilized uniform suspension in a liquid medium.

HOMOGENIZER. Mixing machine used for the preparation of emulsions of fine particle size. The emulsion is forced at high pressure through the annular space between an adjustable valve and its seat.

HOOK, BODY. That portion of the edge of a can body which is turned back or the formation of a double seam.

HOOK COVER. That portion of an end which is turned back between the body and the body hook for the formation of an end seam.

HOOK EDGED, (SIDE SEAM). That portion of the edge of the body which is turned back for the formation of a locked side seam.

HOOK, UNEVEN. A body cover hook which is not uniform in length.

HORMONES. An internal secretion produced by the endocrine glands, secreted directly into the bloodstream to exercise a specific physiological action or other parts of the body. Many are made synthetically.

HOT DIP. Plate tinned by dipping into molten tin. Plate in use in the industry has coatings of 1.25, 2.50, etc., lbs. per base box.

HPLC. High Pressure Liquid Chromatography. An instrument for food chemical analysis.

HTST PROCESS. Pasteurization or sterilization process characterized by High Temperature applied for a Short Time.

HUMECTANT. A substance that is used to help maintain moisture in foods. Humectants are added to such foods as shredded coconuts and marshmallows.

HUSKER. Equipment for stripping husks off corn.

HYDROCOOLING. A process using cold water to cool foods immediately after harvest and prior to shipping to markets.

HYDROGENATED. Substances that have been reacted with hydrogen. Hydrogenation of fats results in a reduction of double bonds and consequently in a higher degree of saturation and in a higher melting point.

HYDROGEN-ION CONCENTRATION. Acidity or alkalinity of a solution measured by the concentration of hydrogen ions present. Also called pH.

HYDROGEN SWELL. Swell resulting from hydrogen generated in the can as a result of a reaction of the product with the metal of the can.

HYDROLYSIS. Process of splitting a molecule into smaller parts by chemical reaction with water.

HYDROMETER DENSIMETER. Device used for the measurement of specific gravity or density.

HYDROPHILIC. Attracted to water: water soluble.

HYGROSCOPIC. Absorbs water from water vapor in atmosphere.

HYPHAE. See Molds.

IFT. Institute of Food Technologists. The professional society of food scientists and technologists in the U.S.A.

IMPACT STRENGTH. The ability of a material to withstand mechanical shock.

INCUBATION. Holding cultures of microorganisms under conditions favorable to their growth. Also, the holding of a sample at a specified period of time before examination.

INCUBATION TIME. The time period during which microorganisms inoculated into a medium are allowed to grow.

INDICATOR. Usually refers to a pH indicator. Various dyes change color at specific degree of acidity or alkalinity and this color change is used as an indicator of pH.

INHIBITION. Prevention of growth or multiplication of microorganisms, or prevention of enzyme activity.

INITIAL TEMPERATURE (IT). The average temperature of the contents of the coldest container to be processed at the time the sterilizing cycle begins, as determined after thorough stirring or shaking of the filled and sealed container.

INOCULATE. The artificial introduction of microorganisms into a system.

INOCULATION. The artificial introduction of microorganisms into a growth medium. This can refer to the introduction of test organisms to food, to the accidental introduction of organisms to food, or to the start of yeasts or other desirable cultures such as yogurt. See Inoculum.

INOCULUM. The material containing microorganisms used for inoculation.

INOSITOL. A growth factor with properties similar to vitamins, generally listed with the vitamins of the B complex.

IN-PLANT CHLORINATION. Chlorination beyond the break-point of water used in a food plant, usually to a residual of 5 to 7 ppm.

INSECTICIDE. Substance used to kill or control insects. Many are of a long-lasting nature. Care is required in the use of insecticides.

INSPECTION BELT. Conveyor belt where materials are visually inspected.

INTERNATIONAL UNITS (I.U.) A quantity of a vitamin, hormone, antibiotic, or other substance that produces a specific internationally accepted biological effect.

INTOXICATION. The adverse physiological effects of an organism consuming a toxic material.

INVERT, OR INVERT SUGAR. The mixture of equal parts of dextrose and levulose produced by the action of acid or enzymes on solutions of sucrose.

INVERTASE. An enzyme that catalyses the breakdown of sucrose into glucose (dextrose) and fructose (levulose).

ION. Electrically charged portion of matter of atomic or molecular dimensions.

ION EXCHANGE. A reversible chemical reaction between a solid and a liquid by means of which ions may be interchanged between the two. It is in common use in water softening and water deionizing.

IRON. A mineral needed in small amounts. Iron is a vital part of hemoglobin, the red substance of blood which carries oxygen from the lungs to all body tissues, and assists the body cells in releasing energy from food. Important natural sources are liver, kidney, muscle meats, dry beans, whole grains, enriched breads and cereals, and dark green leafy vegetables.

IRON CHINK. Mechanical device used in salmon canning to automatically remove heads, tails, fins, and entrails.

ISO-Electric Point. The pH value at which precipitation of a certain protein occurs.

ISOLEUCINE. One of the amino acids that are essential for humans.

JAM. Product made by cooking to a suitable consistency properly prepared fruit with sugar, or sugar and dextrose, with or without water. No less than 45 lbs. fruit are used to each 55 lbs. of sugar or sugar and dextrose. Sometimes pectin and/or an acid are also added.

JELLY. Fruit jelly is the semisolid, gelatinous product made by concentrating to a suitable consistency the strained juice or the strained water extract from fruit, with sugar, or sugar and dextrose added. Sometimes pectin and/or an acid is also added. No less than 45 lbs. fruit are used to each 55 lbs. sugar or sugar and dextrose.

JOULE. Unit of energy. One joule is equivalent to 0.239 gram calories or 0.000,948 Btu.

JUMPED SEAM. Double seam which is not rolled tight enough adjacent to the lap, caused by jumping of the seaming rolls at the lap.

Kg. KILOGRAM or 1,000 grams, equivalent to 2.2046 lbs.

KILOCALORIE. See Calorie.

KILOGRAM (kg). A unit of weight in the metric system equivalent to 1,000 grams or 2.2046 lbs.

KILOPASCAL. Unit of pressure. One kilopascal equals 1,000 pascals. 1 atmosphere equals 1.01325×10^5 pascals. See Pascal.

KNOCKDOWN FLANGE. Body hook and cover hook in contact, but not tucked in.

KRAFT. A term derived from a German word meaning strength, applied to pulp, paper, or paperboard produced from virgin wood fibers by the sulphate process.

KWASHIORKOR. Term used to describe a syndrome which includes retarded growth and maturation, alterations in the skin and hair, and other changes caused by an extreme deficiency of protein intake. Occurs mostly in infants and young children.

L PLATE. A type of steel similar to MR but especially low in copper and phosphorus, normally used as base for 1.50# or heavier Hot Dip plate where exceptional corrosion resistance is needed.

L. ACIDOPHILUS. Bacteria used to produce buttermilk. One of the lactic acid producing bacteria.

LABEL. Any display of written, printed, or graphic matter on the container of any consumer commodity, affixed to any consumer commodity, or affixed to any package containing a consumer commodity.

LACQUER. See ENAMEL.

LACTOSE. A white, crystalline sugar found in milk. It is less sweet than sucrose.

LAGOON. A large pond used to hold wastewater for stabilization by natural processes.

LAP. Two thicknesses of material bonded together. Section at the end of side seam consisting of two layers of metal to allow for double seaming. As the term implies, the two portions of the side are seam lapped together rather than hooked as in the center of the side seam.

LATENT HEAT. The quantity of heat, measured in B.T.U.'s or calories, necessary to change the physical state of a substance without changing its temperature, such as in distillation. A definite quantity of heat, the latent heat, must be removed from water at 0°C (32°F) to change it to ice at 0°C.

LEACH. To subject to the action of percolating water on other liquid in order to separate soluble components.

LEAVENING. Yeasts or a blend of approved food additives used to raise dough in baking. See Baking Powder.

LECITHIN. A fatty substance (lipid) found in nerve tissue, blood, milk, egg yolk and some vegetables. Used as an emulsifier.

LETHAL. Capable of causing death.

LEUCINE. One of the amino acids that are essential for humans.

LEVULOSE. A highly soluble, simple sugar containing 6 carbon atoms. It crystallizes with great difficulty. It is sweeter than sucrose.

LID. Can end applied to open end of can in a cannery. Also known as top, cap or packer's end.

LIGNIN. A tough, fibrous material found in older plant cell walls.

LIME. Calcium oxide, a caustic white solid, which forms slaked lime (calcium hydroxide) when combined with water.

LINER. Generally, any linear material that separates a product within a container from the basic walls of the container.

LINOLEIC ACID. An unsaturated fatty acid occurring as a glyceride in vegetable oils. Essential in human nutrition.

LIP. Irregularity or defect in double seam occurring at the lap. Due to insufficient tucking or cover hook resulting in a short cover hook and characterized by a blowing or sharp "V" projection at the bottom of the double seam. Also known as a "Droop".

LIPID. Fats, phospholipids, waxes and other organic compounds often containing elements other than carbon, hydrogen, and oxygen, particularly phosphorus and nitrogen.

LIQUID SUGAR. A concentrated solution of refined sucrose or of a mixture of sucrose and invert sugar.

LOCK SEAM. A seam formed by the two edges of a can body which have previously been edged or bent into hooks. The final seam is composed of four thicknesses of plate.

LOW-ACID FOODS. Any foods, other than alcoholic beverages, with a finished equilibrium pH value greater than 4.6 and a water activity greater than 0.85 and also includes any normally low-acid fruits, vegetables, or vegetable products in which for the purpose of thermal processing the pH value is reduced by acidification. Tomatoes, pears, and pineapples, or the juices thereof, having a pH less than 4.7 and figs having a pH of 4.9 or below shall not be classed as low-acid foods.

LUG. A type of thread configuration; i.e., usually thread segments disposed equidistantly around a bottle neck (finish). The matching closure has matching portions that engage each of the thread segments.

LUG BOX. Large box used to haul fruit from fields to cannery.

LYCOPENE. A pigment contributing to the red of tomatoes, watermelons, and other foods.

LYE. A strong alkaline solution. Caustic soda (sodium hydroxide) is the most common lye.

LYE PEELING. Peeling a fruit or vegetable by soaking briefly in hot dilute sodium hydroxide, then scrubbing off the softened peel.

LYPASE. An enzyme which promotes the breakdown of fats.

LYSINE. One of the amino acids that are essential for humans.

MACRONUTRIENTS. Nutrients which are required in relatively large amounts by humans to maintain normal growth and other body functions.

MAILLARD REACTION. A group of organic reactions, especially between amino acids and reducing sugars, producing brown color and flavor changes in many foods materials. Also known as non-enzymatic browning.

MALIC ACID. A fruit acid found mostly in apples.

MALT. Sprouted, dried barley used in the brewing industry to help digest starches into sugars.

MAMMOTH GRADER. Large drum, perforated with graded holes, in which pears are graded progressively by size.

MARGARINE. A table spread made basically of an emulsion of water in oil with milk, common salt, coloring and flavoring substances, and betacarotene (pro-vitamin A).

MATURATION. The processing of developing quality in a product by aging under certain conditions.

MATURE. Fully grown and developed.

MATURING AGENTS. See Bleaching Agents.

MATURITY. The process of coming to full development.

MAYONNAISE. A food product made basically of an oil-in-water emulsion with egg yolk, vinegar, common salt, and flavoring and coloring ingredients.

MC STEEL. The type of steel similar to MR, but which has been rephosphorized to give it greater stiffness at the expense of some of its anti-corrosive properties.

MDR. See Minimum Daily Requirements.

MEAN. The average value of a number of observed data.

MEDIUM, SELECTIVE. A medium composed of nutrients designed to allow only growth of a particular type of microorganism.

MELTING. The change from the solid to the liquid state. Also the softening of harder compounds.

MESOPHYLLIC BACTERIA. Grow best at temperatures between 75° and 105°F; usually will not grow at temperatures below 50°F or above 110°F.

METER (m). Metric unit of length, equivalent to 39.37 in., or 3.28 ft.

METHIONINE. One of the amino acids that are essential for humans.

MEV. One million electron volts.

Mg/1. Milligrams per liter; approximately equals parts per million (ppm). A term used to indicate concentration of materials.

MICROAEROPHILES. Organisms which grow best in the presence of small amounts of atmospheric oxygen.

MICROENCAPSULATION. The process of forming a thin protective coating around a particle of a substance.

MICROGRAM. One-thousandth part of a milligram; symbol *µg*.

MICROLITER. One-thousandth of a milliliter.

MICRON. One-thousandth of a millimeter.

MICRONUTRIENT. Nutrients which are required by humans in relatively small or trace amounts to maintain normal growth and other body functions.

MICROWAVE COOKING. Use of radio-frequency energy for cooking.

MIL. A unit of linear measurement, equivalent to 0.001 inch.

MILLIGRAM (mg). One-thousandth of one gram.

MINERAL. In nutritional science, a term applied to chemical elements that act as body regulators through incorporation into hormones and enzymes. Some minerals (like calcium, phosphorus, and magnesium) are part of the body's structure.

MINIMUM DAILY REQUIREMENTS (MDR). The minimum quantities of specified vitamins and minerals deemed necessary to avoid dietary deficiencies as established by Food and Drug Administration labeling regulations in 1941 and later amendments. See UNITED STATES RECOMMENDED DAILY ALLOWANCES (U.S. RDA).

MIXTURE. Material composed of two or more substances, each of which retains its own characteristic properties.

mm. MILLIMETER. Equivalent to 0.001 meter, and to 0.0394 inch.

MOISTURE WATER VAPOR TRANSMISSION. The rate at which water vapor permeates through a plastic film or wall at a specified temperature and relative humidity.

MOLASSES. Syrup produced by washing raw sugar. It is boiled and as much sugar as possible crystallized out. The syrupy residue is molasses.

MOLDS. Microorganisms that belong to the fungi. The fungus body is usually composed of threads (hyphae, singular; hypha). These hyphae frequently branch in a more or less complex manner forming networks or webs, collectively called "mycelium". Hyphae may be one-celled or composed of many cells placed end to end. Fruiting bodies that grow from hyphae produce spores. Molds are much less heat resistant than bacteria.

MOLECULAR WEIGHT. Sum of the atomic weights of all the atoms in a molecule.

MOLECULE. The smallest theoretical quantity of a material that retains the properties exhibited by the material.

MONOGLYCERIDES. See Glycerides.

MONOSODIUM GLUTAMATE (MSG). See GLUTAMATE, SODIUM.

MR STEEL. The type of steel most often used in can making due to its good corrosion resistance and high ductility.

MRAD. Megarad or one million rads. (See Rads).

MULLEN TESTER. An instrument for testing the bursting strength of paper, paperboard, corrugated or solid fiberboard.

MYCELIA. See molds.

MYCOSTAT. See FUNGISTATIC AGENT.

MYCOTOXINS. Toxins produced by molds or fungi.

MYLAR. A synthetic polyester fiber or film.

MYOSIN. The protein of the muscle fiber.

"NATURAL FOODS". Term describing foods which are grown without chemical fertilizers or pesticides. Also foods in the preparation of which no synthetic preservatives are used.

NAS/NRC. National Academy of Sciences/ National Research Council.

NECK. The part of a container where the bottle cross-section decreases to form the finish.

NET WEIGHT, MINIMUM. The weight of all the product in the container, including brine or sauce, but not including the weight of the container.

NEUTRALIZE. To adjust the pH of a solution to 7.0 (neutral) by the addition of an acid or a base.

NEWTONIAN FLUIDS. Liquids which do not change in viscosity with a change in rate of shear.

NDGA. See NORDIHYDROGUAIARETIC ACID.

NIACIN. A water-soluble "B" group vitamin. Important natural sources are liver, meat, whole grain, and enriched bread and cereals.

NIH. National Institutes of Health.

NITRATE. A salt of nitric acid, usually sodium nitrate ($NaN0_3$), used to cure or preserve meats, especially hams. Saltpeter (potassium nitrate, KNO_3) has been used for many years as a curing ingredient. Nitrates occur naturally in leafy vegetables.

NITRIFICATION. The process of oxidizing ammonia by bacteria into nitrites and nitrates.

NITRITE. A salt of nitrous acid, usually sodium nitrite ($NaNO_2$), used in addition to sodium nitrate to cure ham or other meats. The use of nitrites allows much smaller quantities of nitrates to be used in the curing process with the same degree of protection from spoilage.

NITROSAMINES. Compounds which are formed from nitrates and other naturally present substances. They have been linked to cancer in laboratory test animals. Nitrosamines are also naturally occurring, normally in very small quantities. Concentration in food may increase during cooking.

NON-ENZYMATIC BROWNING. See MAILLARD REACTION.

NON-NEWTONIAN. Materials whose resistance to flow changes with a change in rate of shear.

NORDIHYDROGUAIARETIC ACID OR NDGA. Substance of plant origin used as an antioxidant for fats.

NOTCH. To cut away small portions of a blank usually at the corners to provide for features such as beading, double seaming, tongue profile, etc.

NUCLEIC ACIDS. Long-stranded molecules which play a primary role in the transmission of genetic traits, in the regulation of cellular functions, and in the formation of proteins.

NUTRIENTS. Compounds that promote biological growth.

NUTRITION INFORMATION PANEL. Appears on food labels to the right of the principal display panel. It provides information on the nutritional composition of the food.

NUTRITIONAL INHIBITOR. A natural component of food which adversely affects the utilization of a nutrient.

OLEORESINS. Flavor concentrates from spices or herbs prepared by extraction with volatile organic solvents.

OPEN LAP. A lap which failed due to various strains set up during manufacturing operations. Also caused by improper soldering.

OPEN TOP CAN. Another term for sanitary can.

"ORGANIC FOODS". See Natural Foods.

ORGANOLEPTIC. See SENSORY.

OSHA. Occupational Safety and Health Administration.

OSMOPHILIC. Can grow or survive in a medium very low in humidity or of low water activity.

OSMOSIS. Diffusion between two miscible fluids separated by a permeable wall.

OVERLAP. The distance the cover hook laps over the body hook in a can double seam.

O/W EMULSION. Oil-in-water emulsion; oil is the discontinuous or internal phase, water the continuous or external phase. An O/W emulsion is dispersible (dilutable) in water, but not in oil.

OXIDATION. The act of oxidizing which is brought about by increasing the number of positive charges on an atom or the loss of negative charges.

OXIDATION LAGOON. Synonymous with aerobic or aerated lagoon.

OXIDATION POND. Synonymous with aerobic lagoon.

OXIDATIVE RANCIDITY. The deterioration of fats and oils due to oxidation.

PACKAGE. Any container or wrapping in which a consumer commodity is enclosed for delivery or display to retail purchasers.

PACKER'S END. The can end put on by the packer or canner. Also known as lid, cover, top, or canner's end.

PACKING MEDIUM. The liquid or other medium in which the low-acid or acidified product is packed. For example, for "Peas in brine", the packing medium is brine.

PALATABILITY. Sensory attributes of foods, (e.g., aroma, flavor, texture, etc.) which affect their acceptability.

PALLET. A low, portable platform of wood, metal, fiberboard or combinations thereof, to facilitate handling, storage and transportation of materials as a unit.

PALLETIZED UNIT LOAD. A unitized load fixed to a pallet.

PALLETIZING. The forming of a pallet load.

PANELING. Distortion (side wall collapses) of a container caused by development of a reduced pressure (too high vacuum) inside the container.

PANTOTHENIC ACID. A "B" group vitamin, essential for the metabolism of fats and carbohydrates. Liver, yeast, kidney, and fresh vegetables are good natural sources.

PAPAIN. A protein digesting enzyme obtained from the juice of unripe papayas.

PAPER, WATER-RESISTANT. Paper that is treated by the addition of materials to provide a degree of resistance to damage or deterioration by water in liquid form.

PAPER, WET-STRENGTH. Paper that has been treated with chemical additives to aid in the retention of bursting, tearing or rupturing resistance when wet.

PASTEURIZATION. A heat treatment of food usually below 212°F, intended to destroy all organisms dangerous to health, or a heat treatment which destroys part but not all microorganisms that cause food spoilage or that interfere with a desirable fermentation.

PARENCHYMA CELL. The structural unit of the edible portion of most fruits and vegetables.

PASCAL. See Kilopascal.

PATHOGEN. Disease producing microorganism.

PATHOGENIC. Capable of producing disease.

PATULIN. A mycotoxin.

PBB or ppb. Parts per billion.

PCB'S. Polychlorinated bi-phenyls. A class of compounds known to cause cancer.

PECTIN. Plant tissues contain protopectins cementing the cell walls together. As fruit ripens, protopectin breaks down to pectin, and finally to pectic acid under the influence of enzymes. Thus over-ripe fruit loses its firmness and becomes soft as the adhesive between the cells breaks down. Pectin is the setting agent in jams and jellies. The albedo of oranges and lemons, and apple pomace are commercial sources of pectin. Used as a gelling agent and as an emulsifier and stabilizer.

PECTIN METHOXYLASE. Enzyme in tomato juice that splits methyl alcohol from pectin leaving pectic acid, which does not have the colloidal and thickening properties of pectin. Inactivated by pasteurization.

PELLAGRA. A nutritional deficiency disease produced by insufficient intake of niacin and/ or nicotinic acid in the diet. The disease is characterized by skin lesions, inflammation of the mouth, diarrhea, and central nervous system disorders.

PEMMICAN. Mixture of dried, powdered meat, and fat.

PENETROMETER. An instrument used to determine the firmness of a food.

PEPSIN. An enzyme found in gastric juice that promotes the digestion of proteins.

PER. See Protein Efficiency Ratio.

PERCOLATION. The movement of water through the soil profile.

PERICARP. The plant material surrounding the seed of fruits.

PERMEABILITY. The passage or diffusion of a gas, vapor, liquid, or solid, through a barrier without physically or chemically affecting it.

PESTICIDE. A chemical which kills plant or animal pests.

PESTICIDE RESIDUES. Small amounts of pesticides remaining in foodstuffs as a result of pest control operations.

PETRI DISH. A double glass or plastic dish used in cultivating microorganisms.

pH. The effective acidity or alkalinity of a solution; not to be confused with the total acidity or alkalinity, the pH scale is:

ACID SOLUTIONS	NEUTRAL	ALKALINE SOLUTIONS
0,1, 2, 3, 4, 5, 6	7	8, 9, 10, 11, 12, 13, 14

pH 7 is the neutral point (pure water). Decreasing values below 7 indicate increasing acidity, while increasing values above 7 indicate alkalinity. One pH unit corresponds to a tenfold difference in acidity or alkalinity, hence pH 4 is 10 times as acid as pH 5 and pH 3 is 10 times as acid as pH 4 and so forth. The same relationship holds on the alkaline side of neutrality, where pH 9 is 10 times as alkaline as pH 8, and so on. Most meat and fish products have pH values between 6 and 7, vegetables have pH values between 5 and 7, and fruits have pH values between 3 and 5.

pH, MAXIMUM. For acidified foods, the highest finished product equilibrium pH after processing. For acidified low-acid foods not controlled at pH 4.6 or below, this does not apply if the food receives a heat treatment which alone achieves commercial sterility.

pH, NORMAL. For low-acid canned foods, the pH of the product or primary ingredient (e.g., green beans) in its natural state before processing. For acidified foods, it is the pH of the primary ingredient (e.g., pimientos) in its natural state before acidification.

PHENYLALANINE. One of the amino acids that are essential for humans.

PHEOPHYTIN. A brown or olive-green plant pigment formed by the breakdown of chlorophyl.

PHOSPHOLIPIDS. Lipid compounds containing phosphoric acid and nitrogen. These compounds are important components of many cellular membranes.

PHYTATES. Salts of phytic acid, especially sodium phytate.

PHYTIC ACID. Chelating agent used for the removal of traces of metal ions. It is of nutritional interest because it interferes with the absorption of minerals from the intestinal tract, especially calcium and iron.

PICKING TABLE. The point where produce is manually inspected.

PICKLE LAG. The time required for hydrochloric acid to reach uniform rate of attack on tin plate. It is expressed in seconds.

PIN-HOLE. Synonym for perforation. Development of a small hole in the plate.

PLATE. Short name for tinplate, black plate, terne plate, aluminum plate, or any other basic rolled metal sheet.

PLATE, BLACK. See BLACK PLATE.

PLATE, COKE TIN. See TIN PLATE, COKE.

PLATE, COLD REDUCED. Plate produced by cold rolling of steel.

PLATE, DIFFERENTIAL. See TIN PLATE, DIFFERENTIAL.

PLATE, ELECTROLYTIC. See TIN PLATE, ELECTROLYTIC.

PLATE, TIN. See TIN PLATE.

POINT. Term used to describe the thickness of paperboard, a point being one thousandth of an inch.

POISONING, FOOD. See FOOD POISONING.

POLYMER. A very large, complex molecule formed by chemically binding together a large number of identical smaller units (or monomers).

POLYUNSATURATED. An unsaturated bond is a chemical structure into which additional hydrogen can be incorporated. Polyunsaturated fats contain fatty acids having more than one unsaturated bond. In general, polyunsaturated fats tend to be of plant origin and liquid.

POMACE. The crushed pulp of fruits pressed for juice.

POMES. Fruits, such as apples, quince, and pears.

POTABLE. Drinkable.

POTASSIUM NITRATE (SALTPETER). A preservative and a color fixative in meats and meat products.

POTASSIUM SORBATE. See SORBIC ACID.

POUCH. A small or moderate-sized bag, sack, or receptacle.

POURING AGENTS. See Anti-caking Agents.

PROPIONATES. Food additives having the property of inhibiting mold growth.

PPM. Parts per million. 1 ppm. = 0.000, 1 percent on weight basis. Also 1 mg/Kg = 1 ppm, and 0.032 oz./ton = 1 ppm.

PRESERVATION. Any physical or chemical process which prevents or delays decomposition of foods.

PRESERVATIVES. Any substance capable of retarding or arresting food spoilage or deterioration.

PRESSURE RIDGE. The pressure ridge is formed on the inside of the can body directly opposite the double seam, and is the result of the pressure applied by the seaming rolls during seam formation.

PRIMARY SPOILAGE. See also SECONDARY SPOILAGE. That spoilage due to bacterial or chemical action of product packed within the can.

PRIMARY WASTE TREATMENT. In-plant by-product recovery and wastewater treatment involving physical separation and recovery devices such as catch basins, screens, and dissolved air flotation.

PRINCIPAL DISPLAY PANEL. That part of a label on a food package that is most likely to be shown or examined under customary conditions of display for retail sale.

PROCESS AUTHORITY. The person or organization that scientifically establishes thermal processes for low-acid canned foods or processing requirements for acidified foods. The processes are based on scientifically obtained data relating to heat or acid resistance of public health and spoilage bacteria and/or upon data pertaining to heat penetration in canned foods. The process authority must have expert scientific knowledge of thermal and/or acidification processing requirements and have adequate experience and facilities for making such determinations.

PROCESS EFFLUENT. The volume of liquid discharged from a plant. It is composed of water with dissolved and suspended solids.

PROCESS, SCHEDULED. The process selected by the processor as adequate under the conditions of manufacture for a given product to achieve commercial sterility. This process is in excess of that necessary to ensure destruction of microorganisms of public health significance.

PROPIONATES. Food additives having the property of inhibiting mold growth.

PROPYL GALLATE. An antioxidant.

PROPYLENE GLYCOL. A solvent, wetting agent, and humectant.

PROTEIN. Large and extremely complex molecules consisting of from 50 to over 50,000 amino acids. Protein is the main nutrient responsible for building and maintaining body tissues. Sources of high quality protein are meat, poultry, fish and other seafoods, milk and milk products, and eggs. Sources of fairly good protein are legumes (dried beans, peas, soybeans), peanuts and other nuts.

PROTEIN CONCENTRATES. Food substances high in protein content obtained from natural protein-containing foods by partial elimination of non-protein food components.

PROTEIN EFFICIENCY RATIO (PER). A biological method for measuring the biological value of proteins.

PROTEIN ISOLATES. Protein concentrates containing over 90% protein.

PROXIMATE ANALYSIS. Determination of moisture (water), protein, fat, carbohydrates, ash, and crude fiber content of foods.

PSEUDOPLASTIC. Materials the viscosity of which decreases as the rate of shear to which the material is subjected increases. An example is tomato ketchup which decreases in consistency when agitated and can be poured more easily from a bottle. See Viscosity and Consistency.

PSIG. Pounds per square inch gauge pressure. For absolute pressure add 14.7 lbs. to psig pressure.

PSYCHROMETER. An instrument for measuring the humidity (water-vapor) content of air by means of two thermometers, one dry and one wet.

PSYCHROPHILIC BACTERIA. Have an optimum temperature for growth between 60° and 70°F. May grow at temperatures down to 32°F and up to 86°F.

PTOMAINE. Term that has been used to describe certain types of food poisoning known today to be caused by toxins produced by bacteria.

PUFA. Polyunsaturated Fatty Acids.

PULPING. Forcing soft food material through a screen resulting in a pureed food.

PUNCTURE TEST. A test to determine resistance of flexible packaging materials to puncturing.

PUREE. In food technology, a smooth, pulpy, thick fluid produced by very finely disintegrating a juicy food commodity such as a fruit or vegetable.

PUTREFACTION. Decomposition of proteins by microorganisms, producing disagreeable odors.

PYRIDOXINE. A "B" group vitamin (B_6). Meat, milk, fish, and yeast are the best sources.

QA. Quality Assurance.

QAC. Quaternary Ammonium Compounds (QUATS).

QUALITY CONTROL. A system for assuring that commercial products meet certain standards of identity, fill of container, and quality sanitation, and adequate plant procedures.

"R" ENAMEL. A protective lacquer (interior) used for acid products, fruits or colored vegetables. Used to prevent loss of color or discoloration of colored fruits and contact of product with tin.

RAD. A measure of energy absorbed. Equivalent to 100 ergs of energy absorbed per gram of material receiving ionizing radiation.

RADAPERTIZATION. Foods packed in hermetic containers and sterilized by irradiation (gamma rays).

RADICIDATION. Exposure of food to ionizing radiation at doses necessary to kill all non-spore forming pathogenic bacteria. Analogous to pasteurization.

RANCIDITY (RANCIDIFICATION). An oxidative deterioration in food fat whereby a typical off-odor and/or flavor is produced.

RAW WASTE. The wastewater effluent from the in-plant primary waste treatment system.

RECOMMENDED DIETARY ALLOWANCES (RDA). The RDA's are amounts of 15 vitamins and minerals plus protein and calories estimated to be needed for both sexes throughout the life cycle. The allowances will provide adequate amounts of nutrients to essentially all healthy persons in the United States under current living conditions. They are designed to afford a margin of safety above average physiological requirements to cover variations among individuals in the population. They were established by the Food & Nutrition Board of the National Academy of Sciences-National Research Council first in 1943 and revised several times since as new research data has become available. See United States RDA's.

RECYCLE. The return of a quantity of effluent from a specific unit or process to the feed stream of that same unit. This would also apply to return of treated plant wastewater for several plant uses.

REFRACTOMETER (ABBE REFRACTOMETER). Optical instrument that measures the percent of soluble solids in solution by the extent to which a beam of light is bent (refracted). Soluble solids scale is based on sugar concentration in a pure sucrose solution.

RELATIVE HUMIDITY. The ratio of actual humidity to the maximum humidity which air can retain without precipitation at a given temperature and pressure. Expressed as percent of saturation at a specified temperature. See also ABSOLUTE HUMIDITY.

RENDERING. Heating meat scraps to melt the fat which then rises to the surface, while water and remaining tissue settle below. The melted fat is then separated.

REP. Roentgen equivalent physical. A unit of measurement of ionizing radiation absorbed by materials. It has largely been replaced by the Rad (See Rad).

RETORT. Any closed vessel or other equipment used for the thermal sterilization of foods.

RETORT (RETORTABLE) POUCH. A flexible container in which food is placed to be heated to commercial sterility in a retort or other sterilization system. It is made of plastic films laminated to aluminum foil.

RETROGRADATION. Refers to reverting of starches from a soluble form to an insoluble form upon freezing or aging.

REVOLVING DRUM TEST. A test for measuring the protection to contents, or the retention properties of a container, or both, by subjecting the packaged products to rough handling in a standard revolving drum.

RHEOLOGY. Study of the deformation and flow of matter.

RHEOPECTIC (RHEOPEXY). Materials which increase in consistency with an increase in rate of shear.

RIBOFLAVIN (B_2). A water-soluble vitamin. Important sources are milk, liver, kidney, heart, meat, eggs, and dark leafy greens.

RICKETS. Bone defects caused by a shortage of Vitamin D in the diet.

RIPE. Fully developed, having mature seeds, and ready for use as a fresh food or for processing.

RIPENING. The sequence of changes in color, flavor, and texture which lead to the state at which the fruit or vegetable is acceptable to eat or to be processed.

ROD. See BACILLUS.

RODENTICIDE. Poisons designed to kill rodent pests such as mice and rats.

ROPE. A type of microbiological food spoilage characterized by bacterial colonies growing in long strands.

ROTARY WASHER. A common type of washer in which produce is tumbled and washed by sprays of water.

ROUGHAGE. See Dietary Fiber.

SACCHARIN. A non-nutritive sweetener, approximately 300 times as sweet as sucrose (common sugar).

SALMONELLA. A genus of bacteria that can cause infections in man that are characteristically gastrointestinal. A common source of these organisms is feces-soiled hands. Another is infected food that is allowed to stand in the proper growth conditions without sterilization. Destroyed by adequate heating as in the canning process.

SALMONELLOSIS. Infectious disease caused by bacteria of the genus Salmonella. See Salmonella.

SALT. A chemical compound derived from an acid by replacing the hydrogen atom with a metal or a positive ion. Salts may act as buffers in solution with acids or bases. Common or table salt (NaCl) is an example.

SANITARY CAN. See CAN, SANITARY.

SANITIZE. To reduce the microbial flora in or on articles such as food plant equipment or eating utensils to levels judged safe by public health authorities.

SANITIZER. A chemical agent that reduces the number of microbial contaminants on food contact surfaces to safe levels from the standpoint of public health requirements. Sanitizing can also be done by heating.

SAPONIFICATION. The process of hydrolysis of fats or oils of a fluid by an alkali to form soap.

SATURATED-UNSATURATED. Saturated fat contains fatty acids with only saturated molecular bonds. A saturated bond is a chemical structure which cannot accept additional hydrogen. Saturated fats tend to be of animal origin. Most vegetable oils contain a high proportion of unsaturated fats. Most unsaturated fats (such as peanut oil) are liquid at room temperature and most saturated fats (such as butter) are solid at room temperature. See Polyunsaturated.

SCHEDULED PROCESS. The ordinarily used filed scheduled process for a given product under normal conditions.

SCREENING. The removal of relatively course floating and suspended solids from wastewater by straining through screens.

SCURVY. A disease caused by a shortage of Vitamin C (ascorbic acid) in the diet.

SEALING SURFACE. The surface of the finish of the container on which the closure forms the seal.

SEAM COMPOUND. Rubber or other material applied inside can end curl to aid in forming a hermetic seal when end is double seamed.

SEAM, THICKNESS. The maximum dimension measured across or perpendicular to the layers of the seam.

SEAM, WIDTH. The maximum dimensions of a seam measured parallel to folds of the seam. Also referred to as the seam length or height.

SEAMER. Machine for double seaming can ends to the body of the can.

SECOND OPERATION. The finishing operation in double seaming. The hooks formed in the first operation are rolled tight against each other during the second operation.

SECONDARY SPOILAGE. Consists of those cans rusted or corroded as a result of bursting or leaking cans. May occur during warehousing.

SECONDARY TREATMENT. The waste treatment following primary in-plant treatment, typically involving biological waste reduction systems.

SEDIMENTATION. The falling or settling of solid particles in a liquid, as a sediment.

SENSIBLE HEAT. See HEAT, SENSIBLE.

SENSORY (SENSORY PROPERTIES). Pertaining to an impact of a food on the senses (e.g., vision, odor, taste, tactile senses).

SEQUESTERING AGENT. See ETHYLENEDIAMINE TETRA-ACETIC ACID.

SETTLING TANK. Synonymous with "Sedimentation Tank".

SEWAGE. Water after it has been fouled by various uses.

SHELF LIFE. The length of time that a container, or material in a container, will maintain market acceptability under specified conditions of storage. Also known as merchantable life.

SHORTENING. A mixture of partially hydrogenated fats, generally of plant origin, used for frying and for bakery products.

SIDE SEAM. The seam joining the two edges of a blank to form a can body.

SILICA GEL. A desiccant. A substance used for drying.

SILKER. Usually a reel-type washer for de-silking ears of corn.

SIZE GRADER. Belts or rotary drums with graduated holes through which produce can be sized mechanically.

SKIM MILK. Milk from which virtually all cream (fat) has been removed.

SLIPPER. A can having an incompletely finished double seam due to the can slipping on the base plate. In this defect, part of the seam will be incompletely rolled out. Term has same meaning as dead head when referring to seamers which revolve the can.

SLUDGE. The accumulated settled solids deposited from sewage or other wastes, raw or treated, in tanks or basins, and containing more or less water to form a semi-liquid mass.

SODIUM. Sodium is an essential element. It is naturally present in foods. Most of the sodium added to food is in the form of common salt.

SODIUM BICARBONATE. See Baking Soda.

SODIUM BISULFITE. A preservative.

SOFT SUGARS. Highly refined, dark colored, molasses-flavored sugars which are frequently called brown sugars. They have a relatively high content of mineral and other non-sucrose materials.

SOFT SWELL. Both ends of can swelled, but may be depressed fairly easily by thumb pressure.

SOLID FAT INDEX. A measure of the solidity of fats at various temperatures.

SOLUBLE SOLIDS (S.S.). Solids in solution largely made up of sucrose and other sugars, fruit acids, and mineral salts.

SOLVENTS. A substance which dissolves or holds another substance in solution such as common salt in water. Solvents are used in some foods as carriers for flavors, colors, stabilizers, emulsifiers, antioxidants, and other ingredients.

SORBIC ACID. Used to selectively inhibit growth of yeasts and molds.

SORBITOL. A humectant used to hold moisture in foods.

SOYBEAN MEAL. The residue remaining after solvent extraction of cracked soybeans.

SOYBEAN MILK. A product made from soybean protein, vegetable oils, and water.

SPC. Standard Plate Count. Method used to determine the number of specific microorganisms present in food, other substances, or surfaces.

SPICE. The bark, root, bud, flower, or fruit of plants used primarily to season foods. For example, pepper and cinnamon.

SPICE OILS. Extracts containing in concentrated form the substances responsible for the flavor and aroma of spices.

SPINNER. A container with a faulty double seam, caused by the container having been revolved by the seaming rolls, due to improper adjustments.

SPOILAGE. A process whereby food is rendered unacceptable through microbial or chemical action. See also PRIMARY SPOILAGE and SECONDARY SPOILAGE.

SPORES. Certain of the rod forms of bacteria produce spores. These are not reproductive bodies, as in the case of molds and yeasts, but are the resting stage of the organism. In the spore state, bacteria can survive extremes of cold, heat, drying, and other unfavorable conditions for long periods of time; and when the environment is again favorable, the spores germinate, and the organisms start another cycle of growth. Growing cells are called "vegetative" cells. Spore-forming bacteria which can grow in the presence or absence of air (facultative anaerobes) are classified in the genus *Bacillus*, while those which grow only in the absence of air are classified in the genus *Clostridium*.

SPRAY DRIER. Equipment in which material to be dried is sprayed as a fine mist into a hot-air chamber and falls to the bottom as dry powder. Period of heating is very brief. Dried powder consists of hollow particles of low density.

SPRINGER. Swelled can with only one end remaining out; on pressing this end it will return to normal, but the other end will bulge out.

STABILIZERS. Substances that stabilize emulsions.

STACK BURN. Condition resulting from placing cased cans in piles insufficiently cooled. Food may vary from over cooked to definitely burned flavor and color. Also, excessive corrosion of interior of container may result.

STALING. A physical-chemical process in cereal products, especially bread, whereby a characteristic "dry" texture develops.

STANDARD DEVIATION. Statistical measure of the scattering of data from the average; equal to the root mean square of the individual deviations from average.

STANDARD FOR GRADE. The formulated rules by which a product will be judged to fit one of the grade categories established for the class to which the product belongs.

STANDARD OF FILL OF CONTAINER, FDA. A statement which establishes the minimum weight or volume of a specific food which its container must hold, as determined by procedures specified in the standard, below which the food product is of substandard fill and must be clearly labeled "Below Standard of Fill".

STANDARD OF QUALITY, FDA. A statement which establishes a minimum quality for a specific food product below which it is of substandard quality and must be clearly labeled "Below Standard in Quality Good Food-Not High Grade".

STANDARDS OF IDENTITY, FDA. Regulations issued by the U.S. Food and Drug Administration to define the allowable ingredients, composition and other characteristics of food products.

STAPHYLOCOCCI. Spherical bacteria (*cocci*) occurring in irregular, grape-like clusters.

STAPHYLOCOCCUS AUREUS. Species of bacteria that are important as a cause of human infections and of food poisoning.

STARCH. White, odorless, and tasteless carbohydrates produced by plants as an energy store. Starches are primary foods for most animals and are broken down during digestion into sugars and thereby used for energy.

STARCH (HIGH AMYLOSE). A starch containing over 50% amylose (usually 55-70%).

STARTER CULTURE. A culture of micro-organism used to start a fermentation process.

STEAM-FLOW CLOSING MACHINE. Equipment to close containers while at the same time producing a vacuum in them by means of steam jets directed into and around the container.

STEAM TABLE. Stainless-steel trays used in foodservice for keeping prepared food warm, over live steam.

STEARIC ACID. A common saturated fatty acid with one of the longer lengths of carbon chain and highest number of hydrogen atoms.

STEARINE. The higher melting point glycerides that are separated from oils by winterization. Stearines are used in the manufacture of vegetable shortenings. (See Winterization).

STERILE. Free of living organisms. See also COMMERCIAL STERILITY.

STERILITY (OF FOOD), COMMERCIAL. See COMMERCIAL STERILITY.

STERILIZATION. Any process, chemical or physical, which will destroy all living organisms.

STERILIZATION PROCESS. The time-temperature treatment necessary to render canned foods commercially sterile.

STERILIZATION TIME. The time that lapses between the moment a retort reaches sterilization temperature, until steam is cut off.

STEROL. A complex and usually unsaturated solid alcohol compound commonly found in plant and animal lipids. Cholesterol is a sterol.

STILL RETORT. A retort for the sterilization of canned foods in batch amounts.

STORAGE LIFE. See SHELF LIFE.

STREPTOCOCCI. Cocci that divide in such a way that chains are formed.

SUBLIMATION. The physical process by which a substance passes directly from the solid state to the vapor or gas state, such as the evaporation of ice during freeze-drying.

SUCCULOMETER. An instrument used to measure the degree of maturity of corn.

SUCROSE. A sweet crystallizable, colorless sugar which constitutes the principal sugar of commerce. Refined cane and beet sugars are essentially 100% sucrose. Under certain conditions sucrose breaks down to dextrose and levulose.

SUGARS (SACCHARIDES). Sweet carbohydrates obtained directly from the juices of plants or indirectly from the hydrolysis of starches. Sugars constitute the primary energy source of both plants and animals.

SULPHIDE DISCOLORATION. The blackening of the interior of a can due to the liberation of sulphur compounds during sterilization of the food which react with the metal, forming tin sulphide.

SUPERCOOLING. Commonly referred to water freezing at a temperature several degrees below 32°F (0°C) bef ore some stimulus such as crystal nucleation or agitation initiates the freezing process.

SUPERHEATED STEAM. Saturated steam that has been heated at constant pressure above its saturation temperature.

SUPPLEMENTATION. See Enriching.

SURFACE-ACTIVE AGENT. Substance that affects the surface tension of a liquid. They include emulsifying agents, detergents, suspending agents, wetting agents, etc.

SURFACTANT. Surface-active agent.

SUSPENDED SOLIDS. The quantity of solids, both volatile and stable, in suspension which can be filtered out by a standard filter under a specified test procedure.

SUSPENSION. A homogenous mixture of an insoluble granular or powdered material with a fluid.

SWEATING. If very cold cans are placed in a warm, humid place, moisture will condense on their surface. This sweating may very easily contribute to rusting of the cans.

SWELL. (1) (Noun) A container with either one or both ends bulged by moderate or severe internal pressure. (2) (Verb) To bulge out by internal pressure, as by gases caused by biological or chemical action.

SWELL, HARD. A can of food which has spoiled to the point where both ends are bulged out and show no appreciable yield to thumb pressure. See SOFT SWELL, FLIPPER, SPRINGER, FLAT SOUR.

SWELL, HYDROGEN. See HYDROGEN SWELL.

SYNERESIS. Exuding of small amounts of liquids from gels.

SYNTHESIZE. To build up a compound by the union of simpler compounds or of its elements.

SYRUP. Water solution of sugar, usually sucrose.

TALLOW. Fat obtained from beef by the process of rendering.

TANNINS. Substances that posses astringency which influences flavor and contributes body to such beverages as coffee, tea, wine, and several fruit juices. Colorless tanning compounds, upon reaction with metal ions, form a range of dark colored complexes which may be red, brown, green, gray, or black.

TARTARIC ACID. An organic acid found in several fruits, particularly grapes.

TBHQ. Tertiary Butyl Hydroquinone. An antioxidant.

TEMPER. A measure of the ductility and hardness of steel plate.

TENDEROMETER. Instrument to measure the stage of maturity of peas to determine if they are ready for canning. Measures the force required to effect a shearing action.

TERATOGEN. An agent that causes physical defects in a developing embryo.

TERNE PLATE. Black plate coated on both sides by hot dipping in an alloy containing approximately 15% tin and 85% lead. Due to the lead content, terne plate is unsuitable for food products.

TERTIARY WASTE TREATMENT. Waste treatment systems used to treat secondary treatment effluent and typically using physical-chemical technologies to effect waste reduction.

TEXTURE. The food characteristics that deal with the sense of feel.

TEXTURIZER. A food additive which stabilizes, enhances or changes the texture of foods, such as puddings, ice cream, and many others.

THAW-EXUDATE (DRIP). Liquid which separates from frozen foods upon thawing consisting of water with small quantities of water soluble food components.

THERMAL PROCESS. The application of heat to food, either before or after sealing in a hermetically sealed container, for a period of time and at a temperature scientifically determined to achieve a condition of commercial sterility (i.e., the destruction of microorganisms of public health significance, as well as those capable of reproducing in the food under normal non-refrigerated conditions).

THERMOCOUPLE. A bi-metallic device to measure temperatures electrically.

THERMODURIC. Microorganisms that have the ability to withstand high temperatures, i.e., are highly heat resistant.

THERMOLABILE. Fairly easily destroyed by heat.

THERMOPHILES. Bacteria which grow optimally above 113°F.

THERMOPHILIC BACTERIA. Describes bacteria which require temperatures between 100–180°F for growth and grow optimally at 122–131°F.

THIAMINE. A water-soluble vitamin (B-1). Important sources are pork, heart, liver, kidney, dry beans and pears, whole grain and enriched bread and cereals.

THICKENING AGENT. A texturizer, such as starch and gelatin, which increases the consistency of a product. Gravies and soups are products that contain thickening agents.

THIXOTROPIC. Those food gels that break up (become more fluid) on being shaken, and reset on standing (become thick again).

THREONINE. One of the amino acids that are essential for humans.

THYXOTROPIC. Systems that show reversible alteration in their flow characteristics when work is performed on them, such as shaking.

TIN PLATE. Sheet steel, usually of special formula and temper, coated on both sides with a controlled thickness of pure tin.

TIN PLATE, CHARCOAL. A type of hot-dipped, tin-coated steel plate ranging from an average of 2.2 to 7 lbs. of tin per base box. For can manufacturing purposes in the U.S. this type of plate has been completely replaced by electrolytic plate.

TIN PLATE, COKE. A class of hot-dipped, tin-coated steel plate which carry tin in the range of 1.25 to 1.75 lbs. per base box. Now little used in the U.S.

TIN PLATE, DIFFERENTIAL. Electrolytic tin plate having different weights of tin coatings on opposite sides of the sheet.

TIN PLATE, ELECTROLYTIC. Black steel plate which has been coated on both sides by electro-deposition of commercially pure tin. Coating weights available are generally lower than on hot-dipped. Most frequently used weights are 0.25, 0.50, 0.75 and 1.00 lbs. of tin per base box (No. 25, No. 50, No. 75, and No. 100), the exact weight depending on the intended application.

TIN PLATE, HOT-DIPPED. Black plate which has been coated on both sides with commercially pure tin by a process wherein, after pickling, the sheets are passed successively through flux, molten tin and palm oil. The amount of coating can be varied to meet the requirements from a minimum of about 1.25 lb. per base box. Now little used in the U.S.

TIN PLATE, TYPE "L". Tin plate in which the base plate is low in copper and metalloids (S, As, P, etc.). Such plate has maximum corrosion resistance to highly corrosive foods.

TLC. Thin Layer Chromatography. An instrument for chemical analysis.

TOLERANCE. A specified allowance for deviations in weighing, measuring, etc., from the standard dimensions or weight.

TOMATO KETCHUP, CATSUP OR SAUCE. Product made of tomato puree, vinegar, sugar, salt, and spices.

TOP DOUBLE SEAM. The double seam formed by end attached by canner. Also known as packer's end seam.

TORR. A unit of atmospheric pressure equivalent to 1.0 mm of mercury.

TOTAL DISSOLVED SOLIDS (TDS). The solids content that is soluble and is measured as total solids content minus the suspended solids.

TOTAL SUSPENDED SOLIDS (TSS). Solids suspended in solution which, in most cases, can be removed by filtration.

TOXIN. An organic poison, a product of the growth of an organism. Some toxins are given off as waste products of a microorganism, and are called "exotoxins". Others are contained within the cells, and are liberated only when the cell dies and disintegrates. These are called "endotoxins". Toxins produced by *Clostridium botulinum* are thermolabile, that is, they are fairly easily destroyed by heat.

TOXICOLOGY. The science of poisons and their antidotes.

TRACE. A minute amount of a substance.

TRANSLUCENT. Descriptive of a material or substance capable of transmitting some light, but not clear enough to be seen through.

TRANSPARENT. Descriptive of a material or substance capable of a high degree of light transmission, (e.g., glass).

TRICHINOSIS. A muscle infection caused by a nematode. Humans develop trichinosis by consuming improperly cooked, infected pork meat, or by indirect contamination of other meats with the nematode.

TRIGLYCERIDES. See GLYCERIDES.

TRIM TABLES. Area where produce are hand cut and trimmed.

TRIMETHYLAMINE. A substance produced during the early stages of spoilage of fish. It gives fish its characteristic "fishy" odor. This odor does not necessarily indicate that the fish is inedible.

TRYPTOPHAN. One of the amino acids that are essential for humans.

TS. Total Solids.

UHT. Ultra High Temperature. Term used in reference to pasteurization of commercial sterilization of milk at a temperature of some 280°F for some 4 seconds.

ULTRA-VIOLET IRRADIATION. Lethal to many species of bacteria, but of poor penetrating power, thus only of value for surface sterilization or sterilizing the air.

UNITED STATES RECOMMENDED DAILY ALLOWANCE (U.S. RDA). Amounts of protein, 12 vitamins, and 7 minerals set by the Food and Drug Administration in 1973 as a revision of the MDR and utilizing the NAS/NRC Recommended Dietary Allowances as a base.

UPERIZATION. A method of sterilizing fluid foods by injecting steam under pressure to raise the temperature to 150°C (302°F). The added water is evaporated off.

USDA. United States Department of Agriculture.

VACUUM PACK (in canning). The term "vacuum pack" refers to products packed with little or no brine or water, which are sealed under a high mechanical vacuum, and which require maintenance of high vacuum to assure process adequacy.

VALINE. One of the amino acids that are essential for humans.

VEE (Vee Down). Is a "vee" shaped deformation in cover hook associated with drastically reduced cover hook dimension. In extreme cases can be detected by external examination of the seam.

VEGETATIVE CELLS. Stage of active growth of the microorganism, as opposed to the bacterial spore.

VENTING. Eliminating air from a retort prior to sterilizing canned foods.

VENTS. Openings controlled by gate, plug, cock, or other adequate valves used for the elimination of air during the venting period.

VIABLE. Living.

VINER. Equipment for removing peas, lima beans, and green beans from the vines on which they are harvested. In the case of peas and lima beans, viners also remove vegetable from the pod.

VINYL CHLORIDE. A synthetic plastic used in the manufacture of packaging materials.

VISCOMETER. An instrument to measure viscosity.

VISCOSITY. Internal friction or resistance to flow of a liquid. The constant ratio of shearing stress to rate of shear. In liquids for which this ratio is a function of stress, the term "apparent viscosity" is defined as this ratio.

VITAMIN. Vitamins are complex organic compounds, needed in small amounts, that are essential for certain metabolic functions in humans or other animals. Vitamins act as catalysts by helping other nutrients perform their functions. See CATALYST.

VITAMIN A. A fat-soluble vitamin, essential for vision in dim light. Most vitamin A is obtained from the body's conversion of carotene found in vegetables and fruits. Important sources are liver, dark green vegetables, and yellow fruit and vegetables, butter, and margarine.

VITAMIN B COMPLEX. Folic acid, niacin, pantothenic acid, pyridoxine, riboflavin, thiamine and biotin. The B vitamins are essential in human diets, and occur naturally in meats, wheat, etc.

VITAMIN B-6. See PYRIDOXIN.

VITAMIN B-12. See CYANOCOBALAMIN.

VITAMIN C. A water-soluble vitamin. Important sources are citrus fruits and juices, broccoli, Brussel sprouts, raw cabbage, collards, sweet and green peppers, potatoes and tomatoes. Also called ascorbic acid.

VITAMIN D. (Calciferol). A fat-soluble vitamin important in the prevention of rickets. Important sources are fish liver oil, fortified milk, and egg yolks.

VITAMIN E (a-Tocopherol). A fat-soluble vitamin important as a natural anti-oxidant. Vegetable oils, especially wheat-germ oils, are important sources.

VITAMIN K. Vitamin necessary for proper blood coagulation to prevent hemorrhages. Good sources are green leafy vegetables, porK liver, milk, and eggs.

VITELLINE MEMBRANE. The membrane enclosing the egg yolk.

VORTEX WASHER. Circular tank in which produce is washed by sprays which impart a swirling motion.

WASHERS. Equipment made in a variety of designs for washing produce prior to sizing, grading, trimming and blanching.

WATER ACTIVITY. A measure of water availability in food for microbial growth. The ratio of water vapor pressure of a food to the vapor pressure of pure water under identical conditions of temperature and pressure.

WATER BINDING. See BOUND WATER.

WAXY MAIZE. A variety of corn, the starch content of which consists solely of branched molecules.

WEAK LAP. The lap is soldered and both parts are together. However, strain on this lap, as twisting with the fingers, will cause the solder bond to break.

WHEY. The liquid and its dissolved lactose, minerals, and other minor constituents remaining after milk has been coagulated to separate the curd. Curd is made up of casein, most of the fat, and some lactose, water, and minerals from milk.

WHO of UN. World Health Organization of the United Nations.

WINTERIZATION. The process in vegetable oil refining by which the higher melting point glyceride (stearines) are removed from oils by chilling.

W/O EMULSION. Water-in-oils emulsion in which the water is the internal phase and the oil is the external or continuous phase. When diluted by the addition of an oil, W/O emulsions retain homogeneity.

WRINKLE, COVER HOOK. A degree of waviness occurring in the cover hook, acting as an indication of the tightness of the seam. Several numerical rating systems are used.

XANTHOPHYLLS. The yellow-orange pigments found in plant foods such as corn, peaches, and squash.

XEROPHILIC. Can grow or survive in a medium very low in humidity.

YEASTS. Spherical or more or less elongated cells, varying in normal width from $^{1}/_{10,000}$th to $^{1}/_{2,000}$th of an inch. Most yeasts break down sugars to carbon dioxide and alcohol. That process is called fermentation.

"Z" VALUE. The number of degrees Fahrenheit required for a specific bacterial thermal death time curve to pass through one log cycle.

SUBJECT INDEX

Figures Index

Tables Index

Forms Index

Appendix Index

NOTES

NOTES

NOTES